Beginning HTML, XHTML, CS[illegible] t®

Beginning
HTML, XHTML, CSS, and JavaScript®

Jon Duckett

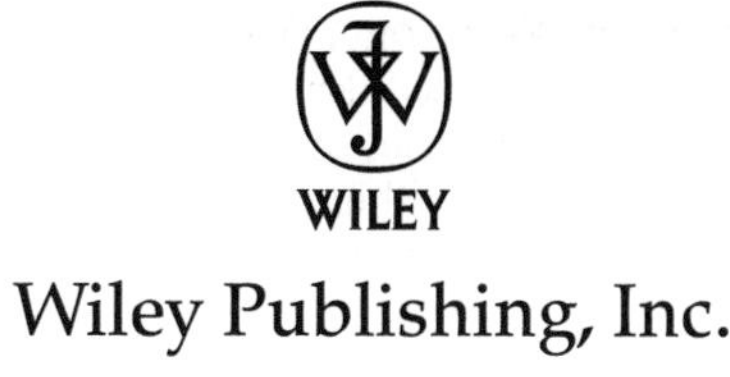

Wiley Publishing, Inc.

Beginning HTML, XHTML, CSS, and JavaScript®

Published by
Wiley Publishing, Inc.
10475 Crosspoint Boulevard
Indianapolis, IN 46256
www.wiley.com

Published simultaneously in Canada

ISBN: 978-0-470-54070-1

Manufactured in the United States of America

10 9 8 7 6 5 4 3 2 1

Library of Congress Control Number: 2009937840

About the Author

Jon Duckett has spent over a decade helping a wide range of companies implement innovative web strategies. Taking a hands-on approach, he designs many of the projects he works on and helps to code them. During this time, Jon has written several books covering web design, programming, accessibility, and usability.

About the Tech Editor

Chris Ullman is a freelance web developer and technical editor/author who has spent many years working in web technologies. Coming from a computer science background, he gravitated towards MS technologies during the summer of ASP (1997). He cut his teeth on Wrox Press ASP guides, and since then has edited or contributed to more than 30 books, most notably as lead author for Wrox's bestselling *Beginning ASP/ASP.NET 1.x/2* series. He lives in Cornwall and spends his non-computing time running, writing music, and attempting — with his wife, Kate — to curb the enthusiasm of three very boisterous young children.

Credits

Executive Editor
Carol Long

Project Editor
William Bridges

Technical Editor
Chris Ullman

Production Editor
Daniel Scribner

Copy Editor
Nancy Rapoport

Editorial Director
Robyn B. Siesky

Editorial Manager
Mary Beth Wakefield

Marketing Manager
David Mayhew

Production Manager
Tim Tate

Vice President and Executive Group Publisher
Richard Swadley

Vice President and Executive Publisher
Barry Pruett

Associate Publisher
Jim Minatel

Project Coordinator, Cover
Lynsey Stanford

Proofreader
Nancy Hanger

Indexer
Robert Swanson

Cover Designer
Michael E. Trent

Cover Image
© istockphoto.com/ Daft_Lion_Studio

Contents

Introduction

There are a lot of books about designing and building web pages, so thank you for picking up this one. During the relatively short life of the Web, many technologies have been introduced to help you create web pages, some of which have lasted, others of which have disappeared. Now the dust is beginning to settle, and commonly accepted best practices are emerging; so the aim of this book is to teach you how to create pages for the Web as it is *today* and will be for the next few years.

This book is different from many books because it teaches you more than just the code you need to learn to write web pages; I wanted to share some of the practical experience I have gained designing and building web sites over the past 12 years. Therefore, alongside the usual technical information, you will see advice on topics that range from how to approach the task of creating a new site to chapters that let you in on the techniques used by designers to make their pages more attractive. You will also find information about important topics such as accessibility and usability that any professional web programmer needs to understand. And, once you have worked through this book, it should continue to serve as a helpful reference text you can keep nearby and dip into as you need to.

As the title of this book suggests, you will be learning a few different languages in order to create effective and attractive web pages:

- HTML and XHTML are needed to explain the *structure* of any web pages. If you look at this page it is made up of a lot of words. On web pages it is the job of HTML and XHTML to explain the structure of the words — which words form a heading, where paragraphs start and end, and which text should have bullet points. These languages also specify links between different web pages and where images should appear.

  This book focuses mainly on teaching you XHTML, but you will be glad to know that by learning XHTML you will automatically be able to write HTML (because you can consider XHTML to be exactly the same as HTML, but with a few *extra* rules added — making it a little more strict). At the end of the book is a preview of HTML 5, the next version of HTML.
- CSS is used to control how your pages look. For example, you can use CSS to specify that a typeface should be a large, bold Arial typeface or that the background of a page should be a light green. You can also use CSS to control where different items appear on a page, such as placing three columns of text next to each other.
- JavaScript can add interactivity to your web pages. JavaScript is a huge topic in itself, so it is not covered in the same depth as XHTML and CSS, but I will teach you just enough JavaScript to write your own basic scripts and to enable you to incorporate many of the thousands of JavaScripts that are available for free on the Web.

About the Book

As you have already seen, you'll be learning how to control the structure of a web page using XHTML, how to style it using CSS, and how to add interactivity using JavaScript. Learning *how* this code works will give you a solid foundation for building web sites, and alongside this you will see plenty of practical advice that helps you learn about issues you are likely to meet when you start building sites.

While learning how to code, you will see lots of advice on *usability* — how to build web sites that are easy to use and enable visitors to achieve what they came for. In several parts of the book I also discuss issues regarding accessibility — making a site available to as many users as possible (in particular, people with disabilities, who may have impaired vision or difficulty using a mouse). In the same way that many countries have laws requiring architects to design buildings that are accessible, there are strict accessibility guidelines for building web sites to ensure they do not exclude visitors. A little careful thought before you build your web site means that people with vision impairments can either view your site with larger text or have it read to them by a piece of software called a *screen reader*. Whole books are dedicated to the topics of usability and accessibility and are aimed at web developers who need to learn how to make their code more accessible and usable. My aim is to teach you to code with these principles in mind from the start.

In addition to learning how to code usable and accessible web sites, I will also be sharing lots of tips and techniques that professional web designers use when creating new sites. These techniques make it easier for anyone to lay out pages in a more attractive way.

You will even learn about creating sites that work on devices such as mobile phones and game consoles, which are increasingly being used to access the Web. You will probably be relieved to know that many of the browsers on such devices employ the same languages that you will be learning in this book — and that by learning to use XHTML with CSS you will be able to create web sites that work on a variety of platforms, and will therefore last much longer than those written in older versions of HTML.

While it is important to learn the latest practices for creating web pages using these languages, if you intend to create web sites that anyone can access, you will also have to learn some older aspects of the languages you meet. This is important because not everyone has the latest web browser installed on his or her computer; as a result, the latest features may not work for everyone, and in such cases you need to learn techniques that will work in some older browsers that are still popular today. In order to make sure pages work in older browsers, you will see several occasions throughout the book where certain features of a language are marked as *deprecated*; this means that while this feature should still work in modern browsers, you are being warned that software might not support it much longer.

By the end of this book, you will be writing web pages that not only use the latest technologies, but also are still viewable by older browsers — pages that look great, and can also be accessed by those with visual and physical impairments. These are pages that not only address the needs of today's audiences but can also work on emerging technologies — and therefore the skills you will learn should be relevant longer.

Whom This Book Is For

This book is written for anyone who wants to learn how to create web pages, and for people who may have dabbled in writing web pages (perhaps using some kind of web-page authoring tool), but who want to really understand the languages of the Web, to give them more control over the pages they create.

More experienced web developers can also benefit from this book because it teaches some of the latest technologies and encourages you to embrace web standards that not only meet the needs of the new devices that access the Web, but also help make your sites available to more visitors.

You don't need any previous programming experience to work with this book. This is one of the first steps on the programming ladder. Whether you are just a hobbyist or want to make a career of web programming, this book will teach you the basics of programming for the Web. Sure, the term "programmer" might be associated with geeks, but as you will see by the end of the book, even if you would prefer to be known as a web designer, you need to know how to code in order to create great web sites.

What This Book Covers

By the end of this book, you will be able to create professional-looking and well-coded web pages.

Not only will you learn the code that makes up markup languages such as HTML and XHTML, but you will also see how to apply this code so you can create sophisticated layouts for your pages, positioning text and images where you would like them to appear and getting the colors and fonts you want. Along the way, you will see how to make your pages easy to use and available to the biggest audience possible. You will also learn practical techniques such as how to make your web site available on the Internet and how to get search engines to recognize your site.

The main technologies covered in this book are HTML, XHTML, and CSS. You will also learn the basics of JavaScript — enough to work on some examples that add interactivity to your pages and allow you to work with basic scripts. Along the way I introduce and point you to other technologies you might want to learn in the future.

The code I will encourage you to write is based on what are known as web standards; HTML, XHTML, and CSS are all created and maintained by the World Wide Web Consortium, or W3C (`http://www.w3.org/`), an organization dedicated to the development of the Web. You will also learn about some features that are not in these standards; it is helpful to know about some of these in case you come across such markup and need to know what it does. Where these are introduced, I make it clear they are not part of the standard.

What You Need to Use This Book

All you need to work through this book is a computer with a web browser (preferably Firefox 2 or higher, Safari 2 or higher, or Internet Explorer 6 or higher), and a simple text editor such as Notepad on Windows or TextEdit on Mac.

If you have a web-page editor program, such as Macromedia Dreamweaver or Microsoft FrontPage, you are welcome to use it. I will not be teaching you how to use these programs; rather, I will be teaching you how to write by hand the code that these programs produce. Even if you use one of these tools, when you understand the code it generates you can then go in and edit it, which means you have much greater control over how your sites look and the ability to make them more attractive.

How This Book Is Organized

The first chapter of this book will show you that the main task in creating a web site is *marking up* the text you want to appear on your site, using *elements* and *attributes*. As you will see, these elements and attributes describe the structure of a document (what is a heading, what is a paragraph of text, what is a link, and so on).

The first six chapters of the book describe the different elements and attributes that make up HTML and XHTML and how you can use them to write web pages. These chapters are organized into task-related areas, such as structuring a document into headings and paragraphs; creating links between pages; adding images, audio and video; and displaying tables. With each task or topic that is introduced, you will see an example first to give you an idea of what is possible; then you can look at the elements and attributes used in detail.

When you first read this book, you do not need to closely read the detailed explanations of every single element. As long as you understand the gist of the markup, feel free to move on, and then come back and look at the finer detail when you need it.

Each chapter ends with exercises designed to get you working with the concepts you've just learned. Don't worry if you have to go back and review the content of the chapter in order to complete the exercises: this book has been created with the intention that it should be a helpful reference for years to come, so don't feel that you need to learn everything by heart. Along the way, you'll see which browsers support each element and you'll learn plenty of handy tips, tricks, and techniques for creating professional web pages.

Once you have seen how to create and structure a document using HTML and XHTML, you will then learn how to make your pages look more attractive using CSS. For example, you'll learn how to change the typefaces and size of fonts, color of text backgrounds, and borders that go around items. In addition, you'll learn how to control where items appear on the page, which will allow you to create attractive layouts.

Having worked through the two chapters on CSS, and using the examples in the book, you should be able to write quite complex web pages. The chapters up to that point can then act as a helpful reference you can keep coming back to, and the examples will act as a toolkit for building your own sites.

Chapters 9 and 10 start to build on the theory you learned in the first half of the book, with practical advice on how to approach the creation of a new web site, determine who it is aimed at, and ensure that it meets the needs of its target audience.

These chapters also introduce many key issues regarding the design of web pages and how to make them more attractive. The design sections cover both the bigger picture — how to lay out your page — and also more detailed aspects, such as how to create effective navigation that allows users to find the pages they want on your site, and how to create effective forms to gather information from visitors.

Chapters 11 and 12 introduce you to JavaScript, a programming language that enables you to add interactivity to your pages. While the entire JavaScript language is too large to teach you in two chapters, you will learn how to create your own basic scripts and also how to integrate scripts other people have written into your pages. Thousands of free JavaScripts are already available on the Web, and having learned the basics of JavaScript, you'll see how easy it can be to add some very complex functionality to your site with just a few lines of code.

Chapter 13 prepares you to put your site on the Internet and covers web hosting, FTP, and validating your code. Finally, I will give you some ideas about where you can go next once you've worked through this book; there are lots of other things that you might want to add to your site or learn in order to advance your web skills, and this chapter gives you an idea of what else is possible.

The final chapter, Chapter 14, includes some checklists. These bring together some topics that are dotted throughout the book, such as accessibility and the differences between HTML and XHTML.

I have also included several helpful appendices, including a reference to XHTML elements and CSS properties. There is an appendix that explains how XHTML and CSS specify colors. Other appendices show you available character encodings, language codes, and escape characters that can be used with HTML, XHTML, CSS, and JavaScript. Finally, there is an appendix on old markup that should not really be used any longer — but that you might still come across when working on a site.

Conventions

To help you get the most from the text and keep track of what's happening, I've used a number of conventions throughout the book.

Try It Out

The *Try It Out* is an exercise you should work through, following the text in the book.

1. They usually consist of a set of steps.
2. Each step has a number.
3. Follow the steps through with your copy of the database.

Boxes like this one hold important, not-to-be forgotten information that is directly relevant to the surrounding text.

Notes, tips, hints, tricks, and asides to the current discussion are offset and placed in italics like this.

As for styles in the text:

- I *highlight* new terms and important words when we introduce them.
- I show keyboard strokes like this: Ctrl+A.
- I show file names, URLs, and code within the text like so: `persistence.properties`.
- Code appears like this:

```
In a monospaced font.
```

Source Code

As you work through the examples in this book, you may choose either to type in all the code manually or to use the source code files that accompany the book. All of the source code used in this book is available for download at `http://www.wrox.com`. Once at the site, simply locate the book's title (either by using the Search box or by using one of the title lists) and click the Download Code link on the book's detail page to obtain all the source code for the book.

Because many books have similar titles, you may find it easiest to search by ISBN; this book's ISBN is 978-0-470-54070-1.

Once you download the code, just decompress it with your favorite compression tool. Alternately, you can go to the main Wrox code download page at `http://www.wrox.com/dynamic/books/download.aspx` to see the code available for this book and all other Wrox books.

Errata

I've made every effort to ensure that there are no errors in the text or in the code. However, no one is perfect, and mistakes do occur. If you find an error in this book, such as a spelling mistake or faulty piece of code, I would be very grateful for your feedback. By sending in errata you may save another reader hours of frustration, and at the same time you will be helping to provide even higher quality information.

To find the errata page for this book, go to `www.wrox.com` and locate the title using the Search box or one of the title lists. Then, on the book details page, click the Book Errata link. On this page you can view all errata that has been submitted for this book and posted by Wrox editors.

A complete book list including links to errata is also available at `www.wrox.com/misc-pages/booklist.shtml`.

If you don't spot "your" error on the Errata page, click the Errata Form link and complete the form to send us the error you have found. We'll check the information and, if appropriate, post a message to the book's errata page and fix the problem in subsequent editions of the book.

p2p.wrox.com

For author and peer discussion, join the P2P forums at `p2p.wrox.com`. The forums are a Web-based system for you to post messages relating to Wrox books and related technologies and interact with other readers and technology users. The forums offer a subscription feature to e-mail you topics of interest of your choosing when new posts are made to the forums. Wrox authors, editors, other industry experts, and your fellow readers are present on these forums.

At `http://p2p.wrox.com` you will find a number of different forums that will help you not only as you read this book, but also as you develop your own applications. To join the forums, just follow these steps:

1. Go to `p2p.wrox.com` and click the Register link.
2. Read the terms of use and click Agree.
3. Complete the required information to join as well as any optional information you wish to provide and click Submit.
4. You will receive an e-mail with information describing how to verify your account and complete the joining process.

You can read messages in the forums without joining P2P but in order to post your own messages, you must join.

Once you join, you can post new messages and respond to messages other users post. You can read messages at any time on the Web. If you would like to have new messages from a particular forum e-mailed to you, click the Subscribe to this Forum icon by the forum name in the forum listing.

For more information about how to use the Wrox P2P, be sure to read the P2P FAQs for answers to questions about how the forum software works as well as many common questions specific to P2P and Wrox books. To read the FAQs, click the FAQ link on any P2P page.

Structuring Documents for the Web

In this chapter, you learn the key concept of creating any web page: how to give it *structure*. You need to add structure to a document so that web browsers can present the page to people who visit your site in a way they will understand. For example, imagine a news article that contains a headline (or title) and several paragraphs of text; if you wanted to put this article on the Web, you would need to add structure to the words in the document so that the browser knows which words are the headline, and where each paragraph starts and ends. To give a document structure, you'll need to learn how to create web pages using HTML. Or, to be a little more precise, this book focuses on a type of HTML known as XHTML.

In this chapter you will:

- Create several example web pages in XHTML.
- See how a web page describes its structure to a web browser.
- Discover the meaning of some key terms used by web designers, such as *elements*, *attributes*, *tags*, and *markup*.

By the end of the chapter, you will have learned the basic building blocks needed to build a web page, and will have put this into practice with several examples.

A Web of Structured Documents

Before we create our first web page, let's just take a moment to look at the printed information we see every day, and how it compares to what we see on the Web. Every day, you come across all kinds of printed documents — newspapers, train timetables, insurance forms. You can think of the Web as being a sea of documents that all link together, and bear a strong similarity to the printed documents that you meet in everyday life.

Every morning I used to read a newspaper. A newspaper is made up of several stories or articles (and probably a fair smattering of advertisements, too). Each story has a headline and then some paragraphs, perhaps a subheading, and then some more paragraphs; it may also include a picture or two.

I don't buy a daily paper anymore, as I tend to look at news online, but the structure of articles on news web sites is very similar to the structure of articles in newspapers. Each article is made up of headings, paragraphs of text, and some pictures (sometimes the pictures might be replaced by a video). The parallel is quite clear; the only real difference is that in a newspaper you may have several stories on a single page, whereas on the Web each story tends to get its own page. The news web sites also often use homepages that display the headline and a brief summary of the stories.

Consider another example: Say I'm catching a train to see a friend, so I check the schedule or timetable to see what time the trains go that way. The main part of the schedule is a *table* telling me what times trains arrive and when they depart from different stations. You can probably think of several types of documents that use tables. From the listings in the financial supplement of your paper to the TV schedule, you come across tables of information every day — and often when this information is put on the Web, these tables are recreated.

Another common type of printed document is a form. For example, on my desk at the moment, I have a form (which I really must mail) from an insurance company. This form contains fields for me to write my name, address, and the amount of coverage I want, along with checkboxes to indicate the number of rooms in the house and what type of lock I have on my front door. There are lots of forms on the Web, from simple search boxes that ask what you are looking for to the registration forms you are required to go through before you can place an online order for books or CDs.

As you can see, there are many parallels between the structure of printed documents you come across every day and pages you see on the Web. When it comes to writing web pages, it is the XHTML code you start learning in this chapter that tells the web browser how the information you want to display is structured — what text to put in a heading, or in a paragraph, or in a table, and so on — so that the browser can present it properly to the user.

Introducing HTML and XHTML

Even if you have never seen any HTML (Hypertext Markup Language) code, you may be familiar with the fact that it is used to create most web pages. There have been several versions of HTML since the Web began, and the development of the language is overseen by an organization called the W3C (World Wide Web Consortium).

The last major version of HTML was HTML 4.01 in December 1999. In January 2000, some stricter rules were added to HTML 4.01, creating what is known as XHTML (Extensible Hypertext Markup Language), and it is this version of the language that we will be focusing on throughout this book. Generally, you will see the term XHTML used in the rest of this book. Unless otherwise mentioned, the same rules apply to HTML.

I use this stricter XHTML syntax because it can be processed by more applications than HTML 4.01. If you are interested, there is a summary of the differences between HTML 4 and XHTML 1.0 in Chapter 14. There is also a brief look forward to what will be the next version of HTML, HTML 5, in another section of Chapter 14.

As its name suggests, XHTML is a *markup language*, which may sound complicated, until you realize that you come across markup every day. When creating a document in a word processor, you can add styles to the text to explain the document's structure. For example, you can distinguish headings from the main body of the text using a heading style (usually with a larger font). You can use the Return (or Enter) key to start a new paragraph. You can insert tables into your document to hold data, or create bulleted lists for a series of related points, and so on. While this does affect the presentation of the document, the key purpose of this kind of markup is to provide a structure that makes the document easier to understand.

When marking up documents for the Web, you are performing a very similar process, except you do it by adding things called *tags* to the text. With XHTML, the key thing to remember is that you are adding the tags to indicate the *structure* of the document (not how you want it to be presented); for example, which part of the document is a heading, which parts are paragraphs, what belongs in a table, and so on. Browsers such as Internet Explorer, Firefox, and Safari all use this markup to help present the text in a familiar fashion, similar to that of a word processor — main headings are bigger than the text in paragraphs, there is space above and below each paragraph, lists of bullet points have a circle in front of them. But the XHTML specification does not specify which font should be used or what size that font should be.

> *While earlier versions of HTML allowed you to control the presentation of a document — such as which typefaces and colors a document should use — XHTML markup is not supposed to be used to style the document; that is the job of CSS, which you meet in Chapter 7.*

Let's have a look at a very simple web page. As I mentioned in the Introduction, you don't need any special programs to write web pages — you can simply use a text editor such as Notepad on Windows or TextEdit on a Mac, and save your files with the .html file extension. You can download this example along with all the code for this book from the Wrox web site at `www.wrox.com`; the example is in the Chapter 1 folder (along with other examples from this chapter) and is called `ch01_eg01.html`.

```
<html>
  <head>
    <title>Popular Websites: Google</title>
  </head>
  <body>
    <h1>About Google</h1>
    <p>Google is best known for its search engine, although
       Google now offers a number of other services.</p>
    <p>Google's mission is to organize the world's
       information and make it universally accessible and
       useful.</p>
    <p>Its founders Larry Page and Sergey Brin started
       Google at Stanford University.</p>
  </body>
</html>
```

This may look a bit confusing at first, but it will all make sense soon. As you can see, there are several sets of angle brackets with words or letters between them, such as `<html>`, `<head>`, `</title>`, and `</body>`. These angle brackets and the words inside them are known as *tags*, and these are the markup I have been talking about. Figure 1-1 illustrates what this page would look like in a web browser.

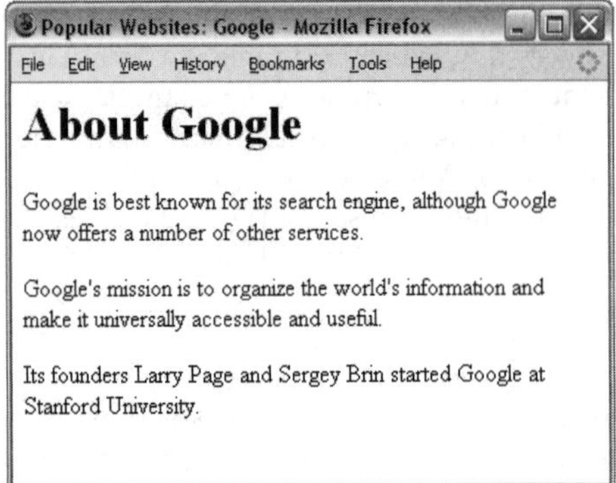

Figure 1-1

As you can see, this document contains the heading "About Google" and a paragraph of text to introduce the company. Note also that it says "Popular Websites: Google" in the very top-left of the browser window; this is known as the *title* of the page (to the right it says Mozilla Firefox, which is the browser this page was opened in).

To understand the markup in this first example, you need to look at what is written between the angle brackets and compare that with what you see in the figure, which is what you will do next.

Tags and Elements

If you look at the first and last lines of the code for the last example, you will see pairs of angle brackets containing the letters "html" Starting on the first line, the first angled bracket looks like a less-than sign, then there are the letters "html," followed by a second angled bracket, which looks like a greater-than sign. The two brackets and all of the characters between them are known as a *tag*.

In this example, there are lots of tags and they are all in pairs; there are *opening tags* and *closing tags*. The closing tag is always slightly different from the opening tag in that it has a forward slash after the first angled bracket: `</html>`.

A pair of tags and the content these include are known as an *element*. In Figure 1-2, you can see the heading for the page of the last example.

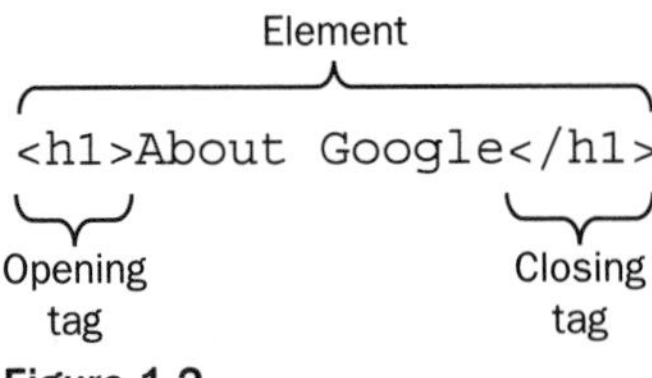

Figure 1-2

The opening tag says "This is the beginning of a heading" and the closing tag says "This is the end of a heading." Like most tags in XHTML, the text inside the angled brackets explains the purpose of the tag — here `h1` indicates that it is a level 1 heading (or top-level heading). As you will see shortly, there are also tags for subheadings (`<h2>`, `<h3>`, `<h4>`, `<h5>`, and `<h6>`). If we had not put tags around the words "About Google," it would just be another bit of text; it would not be clear that these words formed the heading.

Now look at the three paragraphs of text about the company; each one is placed between an opening `<p>` tag and a closing `</p>` tag. And, you guessed it, the `p` stands for paragraph.

> The basic distinction between tags and elements is very important to understand: a tag is made up of a left- and right-angle bracket and letters and numbers between those brackets, whereas elements are the opening and closing tags plus anything between the two tags.

As you can see, the tags throughout this example actually describe what you will find between them, creating the structure of the document. The text between the `<h1>` and `</h1>` tags is a heading, and between the opening `<p>` and closing `</p>` tags make up paragraphs. Indeed, the whole document is contained between opening `<html>` and closing `</html>` tags.

You will often find that terms from a family tree are used to describe the relationships between elements. For example, an element that contains another element is known as the *parent*, while the element that's between the parent element's opening and closing tags is called a *child* of that element. So, the `<title>` element is a child of the `<head>` element, the `<head>` element is the parent of the `<title>` element, and so on. Furthermore, the `<title>` element can be thought of as a grandchild of the `<html>` element.

It is worth noting that the tags in this example are all in lowercase characters; you will sometimes see web pages written in HTML where tags are uppercase (or a mix of uppercase and lowercase letters). When XHTML was introduced, with its stricter rules, it stated that all tags were written in lowercase.

> Just to emphasize, XHTML tags should always be written in lowercase letters.

Separating Heads from Bodies

Whenever you write a web page in XHTML, the whole of the page is contained between the opening `<html>` and closing `</html>` tags, just as it was in the last example. Inside the `<html>` element, there are two main parts to the page:

- **The <head> element:** Often referred to as the head of the page, this contains information *about* the page (this is not the main content of the page). For example, it might contain a title and a description of the page, or instructions on where a browser can find CSS rules that explain how the document should look. It consists of the opening <head> tag, the closing </head> tag, and everything in between.
- **The <body> element:** Often referred to as the body of the page, this contains the information you actually see in the main browser window. It consists of the opening <body> tag, closing </body> tag, and everything in between.

Together, the <html>, <head>, and <body> elements make up the skeleton of an XHTML document — they are the foundation upon which every web page is built.

Inside the <head> element of the first example page, you can see a <title> element:

```
<head>
  <title>Popular Websites: Google</title>
</head>
```

Between the opening <title> tag and the closing </title> tag are the words `Popular Websites: Google`, which is the title of this web page. When I introduced Figure 1-1, which showed the screenshot of this page, I called your attention to the words right at the top of the browser window. This is where browsers such as Internet Explorer, Firefox, and Safari display the title of a document; it is also the name they use when you save a page in your favorites, and it helps search engines understand what your page is about.

The real content of your page is held in the <body> element, which is what you want users to read, and this is shown in the main browser window.

> The <head> element contains information about the document, which is not displayed within the main page itself. The <body> element holds the actual content of the page that is viewed in your browser.

You may have noticed that the tags in this example appear in a symmetrical order. If you want to have one element inside another, then both the element's opening and closing tags must be inside the containing element. For example, the following is allowed:

```
<p> This paragraph contains some <em>emphasized text.</em></p>
```

whereas the following is wrong because the closing </em> tag is not inside the paragraph element:

```
<p> This paragraph contains some <em>emphasized text. </p></em>
```

In other words, if an element is to contain another element, it must wholly contain that element. This is referred to as *nesting* your elements correctly.

Attributes Tell Us About Elements

What really differentiates web documents from standard documents are the links (or hyperlinks) that take you from one web page to another. Let's take a look at a link by adding one to the example you just looked at. Links are created using an `<a>` element (the `a` stands for anchor).

Here we will add a link from this page to Google in a new paragraph at the end of the document. There is just one new line in this example (code sample `ch01_eg02.html`) and that line is highlighted:

```
<html>
  <head>
    <title>Popular Websites: Google</title>
  </head>
  <body>
    <h1>About Google</h1>
    <p>Google is best known for its search engine, although Google now offers a
       number of other services.</p>
    <p>Google's mission is to organize the world's information and make it
       universally accessible and useful.</p>
    <p>Its founders Larry Page and Sergey Brin started Google at Stanford
University.</p>
    <p><a href="http://www.Google.com/">Click here to visit Google's Web
    site.</a></p>
  </body>
</html>
```

Inside this new paragraph is the `<a>` element that creates the link. Between the opening `<a>` tag and the closing `</a>` tag is the text that you can click on, which says "Click here to visit Google's Web site." Figure 1-3 shows you what this page looks like in a browser.

Figure 1-3

If you look closely at the opening tag of the link, it carries something called an *attribute*. In this case, it's the `href` attribute; this is followed by an equal sign, and then a pair of quotation marks which contain the URL for Google's web site. In this case, the `href` attribute is telling you where the link should take you. You'll look at links in greater detail in the next chapter, but for the moment this illustrates the purpose of attributes.

Attributes are used to say something about the element that carries them, and they always appear on the opening tag of the element that carries them. All attributes are made up of two parts: a *name* and a *value*:

- The *name* is the property of the element that you want to set. In this example, the `<a>` element carries an attribute whose name is `href`, which you can use to indicate where the link should take you.
- The *value* is what you want the value of the property to be. In this example, the value was the URL of the site that the link should take you to, so the value of the `href` attribute is `http://www.Google.com`.

The value of the attribute should always be put in double quotation marks, and it is separated from the name by the equal sign. If you wanted the link to open in a new window, you could add a `target` attribute to the opening `<a>` tag as well, and give it a value of `_blank`:

```
<a href="http://www.Google.com" target="_blank">
```

This illustrates that elements can carry several attributes, although an element should never have two attributes of the same name.

> All attributes are made up of two parts, the attribute's name and its value, separated by an equal sign. Values should be held within double quotation marks. All XHTML attribute names should be written in lowercase letters.

Learning from Others by Viewing Their Source Code

When HTML first came out, a lot of people learned how to create pages by using a very handy feature that you'll find in most common browsers — the ability to look at the source code that made the page.

If you go to the View menu in your browser, and then look for an option that says View Source or Page Source, you should be able to see the code that created the page.

If you want to see how the author of a page achieved something on a page, this can be a very handy technique. Figure 1-4 shows how to look at the source of the Google homepage (the window on the right contains the source for the page).

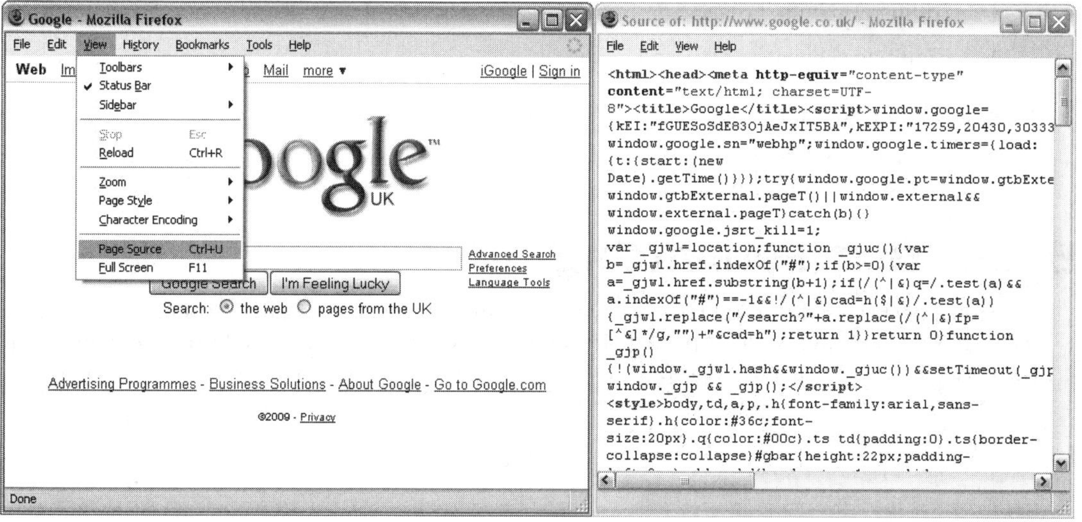

Figure 1-4

Elements for Marking Up Text

You now know that an XHTML page (also sometimes referred to as an XHTML document) is made up of elements that describe how its content is structured. Each element describes what you will find between its opening and closing tags. The opening tags can also carry attributes that tell you more about that particular element.

Equipped with this knowledge, you'll find that much of learning XHTML is a matter of learning what elements you can use, what each of these elements does, and what attributes each can carry.

You've already seen that every XHTML document starts off using the `<html>`, `<head>`, and `<body>` elements. You will come back to look at these elements in more detail near the end of the chapter, at which point you will also meet some attributes called *universal attributes* (so called because they can appear on every element). But I want to get you building pages as quickly as possible, so you're going to spend most of the remaining part of this chapter learning the different elements you can use to describe the structure of text:

- The six levels of headings: `<h1>`, `<h2>`, `<h3>`, `<h4>`, `<h5>`, and `<h6>`
- Paragraphs `<p>`, preformatted sections `<pre>`, line breaks `<br />`, and addresses `<address>`
- Presentational elements: `<b>`, `<i>`, `<u>`, `<s>`, `<tt>`, `<sup>`, `<sub>`, `<strike>`, `<big>`, `<small>`, and `<hr />`
- Phrase elements such as `<em>`, `<strong>`, `<abbr>`, `<acronym>`, `<dfn>`, `<blockquote>`, `<q>`, `<cite>`, `<code>`, `<kbd>`, `<var>`, `<samp>`, and `<address>`
- Lists such as unordered lists using `<ul>` and `<li>`, ordered lists using `<ol>` and `<li>`, and definition lists using `<dl>`, `<dt>`, and `<dd>`

- Editing elements such as <ins> and <del>
- Grouping elements: <div> and <span>

That may sound like a lot of elements, but I hope you'll be surprised at how quickly we can move through them.

Basic Text Formatting

Because almost every document you create will contain some form of text, the elements you are about to meet are likely to feature in most pages that you will build. In this section, you learn how to use what are known as *basic text formatting elements*:

- <h1>, <h2>, <h3>, <h4>, <h5>, <h6>
- <p>, <br />, <pre>

As you read through this section, it is worth being aware that, while one browser might display each of these elements in a certain way, another browser could display the same page in a slightly different way; for example, the typefaces used, the font sizes, and the spaces around these elements may differ between browsers (and therefore the amount of space a section of text takes up can vary, too).

Before you look at the elements themselves, it helps to know how text is displayed by default, without any elements. This will help demonstrate the importance of using markup to tell the browser if you want it to treat text differently.

White Space and Flow

Before you start to mark up your text, it's best to understand what XHTML does when it comes across spaces and how browsers treat long sentences and paragraphs of text.

You might think that if you put several consecutive spaces between two words, the spaces would appear between those words onscreen, but this is not the case; by default, only one space will be displayed. This is known as *white space collapsing*. Similarly, if you start a new line in your source document, or you have consecutive empty lines, these will be ignored and simply treated as one space, as will tab characters. For example, consider the following paragraph (taken from `ch01_eg03.html` in the code samples):

```
<p>This   paragraph shows how   multiple spaces     between     words are
treated as a single space. This is known as white space collapsing, and
the big spaces between    some of the    words will not appear   in the
browser.

It also demonstrates how the browser will treat multiple carriage returns
(new lines) as a single space, too.</p>
```

As you can see in Figure 1-5, the browser treats the multiple spaces and several carriage returns (where text appears on a new line) as if there were only one single space. It also allows the line to take up the full width of the browser window.

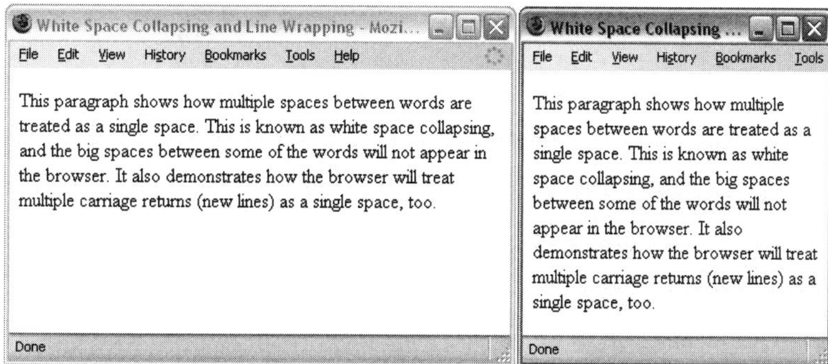

Figure 1-5

Now look at the code for this example again, and compare where each new line starts in the code with where each new line starts onscreen. As Figure 1-5 shows, unless told otherwise, when a browser displays text it will automatically take up the full width of the screen and *wrap* the text onto new lines when it runs out of space. You can see the effect of this even better if you open this example in a browser yourself and try resizing the browser window (making it smaller and larger) and notice how the text wraps at new places on the screen (this example is available with the rest of the download code for this book at `www.wrox.com`).

White space collapsing can be particularly helpful because it allows you to add extra spaces into your XHTML that will not show up when viewed in a browser. These spaces can be used to indent your code, which makes it easier to read. The first two examples in this chapter demonstrated indented code, where child elements are indented from the left to distinguish them from their parent elements. I do this throughout this book to make the code more readable. (If you want to preserve the spaces in a document, you need to use either the `<pre>` element, which you learn about later in the chapter, or an entity reference such as ` `, which you learn about in Appendix F.)

Now that you know how multiple spaces and line breaks are collapsed, you can see why it is important that you learn how to use the elements in the rest of this chapter to break up and control the presentation of your text.

Creating Headings Using <hn> Elements

No matter what sort of document you're creating, most documents have headings in one form or another. Newspapers use headlines, a heading on a form tells you the purpose of the form, the title of a table of sports results tells you the league or division the teams play in, and so on.

In longer pieces of text, headings can also help structure a document. If you look at the table of contents for this book, you can see how different levels of headings have been arranged to add structure to the book, with subheadings under the main headings.

XHTML offers six levels of headings, which use the elements `<h1>`, `<h2>`, `<h3>`, `<h4>`, `<h5>`, and `<h6>`. Browsers display the `<h1>` element as the largest of the six and `<h6>` as the smallest (although you will see in Chapter 7 that CSS can be used to override the size and style of any of the elements). The levels of heading would look something like those in Figure 1-6 (`ch01_eg04.html`).

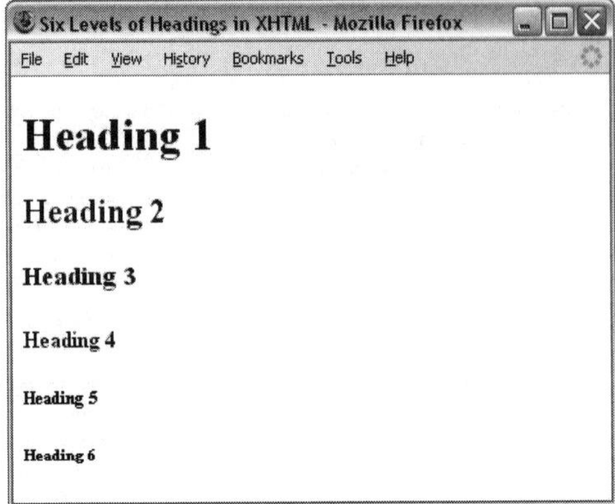

Figure 1-6

> Most browsers display the contents of the <h1>, <h2>, and <h3> elements larger than the default size of text in the document. The content of the <h4> element would be the same size as the default text, and the content of the <h5> and <h6> elements would be smaller unless you instruct them otherwise using CSS.

Here is another example of how you might use headings to structure a document (ch01_eg05.html), where the <h2> elements are subheadings of the <h1> element (this actually models the structure of this section of the chapter):

```
<h1>Basic Text Formatting</h1>
<p> This section is going to address the way in which you mark up text.
Almost every document you create will contain some form of text, so this
will be a very important section. </p>
<h2>Whitespace and Flow</h2>
<p> Before you start to mark up your text, it is best to understand what
XHTML does when it comes across spaces and how browsers treat long sentences
and paragraphs of text.</p>
<h2>Creating Headings Using hn Elements</h2>
<p> No matter what sort of document you are creating, most documents have
headings in some form or other...</p>
```

Figure 1-7 shows how this will look.

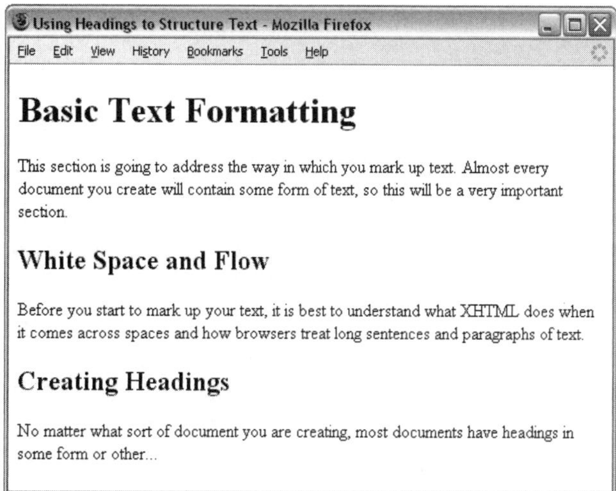

Figure 1-7

For each XHTML element, I will list the attributes it can carry, which will be helpful for future reference.

The six heading elements can all carry the universal attributes that you will meet at the end of the chapter as well as an attribute called `align`:

```
align class id style title dir lang xml:lang
```

The align Attribute (Deprecated)

The `align` attribute indicates whether the heading appears to the left, center, or right of the page (the default is the left). It can take the three values discussed in the table that follows.

You'll have noticed that the word "deprecated" appears in parentheses in the heading of this section. This indicates that the `align` attribute has been marked for removal from future versions of the HTML and XHTML specifications. You will see several elements and attributes in the book that have been deprecated, and it's best to avoid using them.

Despite being deprecated, I mention the `align` attribute here because you may still see it used on various elements. It has been marked as deprecated because it does not help describe the structure of the document — rather it is used to affect the presentation of the page. The `align` attribute has been replaced by two CSS properties: the `text-align` property to align text, and `float` to position larger items on a page (as you will see in Chapter 7).

Value	Meaning
`left`	The heading is displayed to the left of the browser window (or other containing element if it is nested within another element). This is the default value if the `align` attribute is not used.
`center`	The heading is displayed in the center of the browser window (or other containing element if it is nested within another element).
`right`	The heading is displayed to the right of the browser window (or other containing element if it is nested within another element).

Here is an example of using the deprecated `align` attribute (`ch01_eg06.html`):

```
<h1 align="left">Left-Aligned Heading</h1>
  <p>This heading uses the align attribute with a value of left.</p>
<h1 align="center">Centered Heading</h1>
  <p>This heading uses the align attribute with a value of center.</p>
<h1 align="right">Right-Aligned Heading</h1>
  <p>This heading uses the align attribute with a value of right.</p>
```

Figure 1-8 shows the effect of the `align` attribute in a browser.

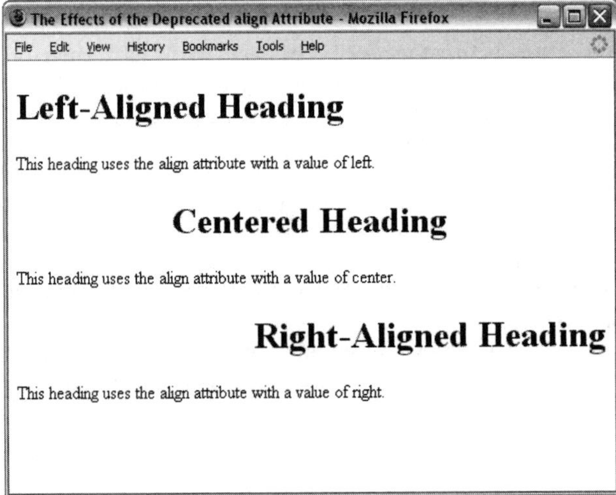

Figure 1-8

Creating Paragraphs Using the <p> Element

The <p> element offers another way to structure your text. Each paragraph of text should go in between an opening <p> and closing </p> tag, as in this example (ch01_eg07.html):

```
<p>Here is a paragraph of text.</p>
<p>Here is a second paragraph of text.</p>
<p>Here is a third paragraph of text.</p>
```

When a browser displays a paragraph, it usually inserts a new line before the next paragraph and adds a little bit of extra vertical space, as in Figure 1-9.

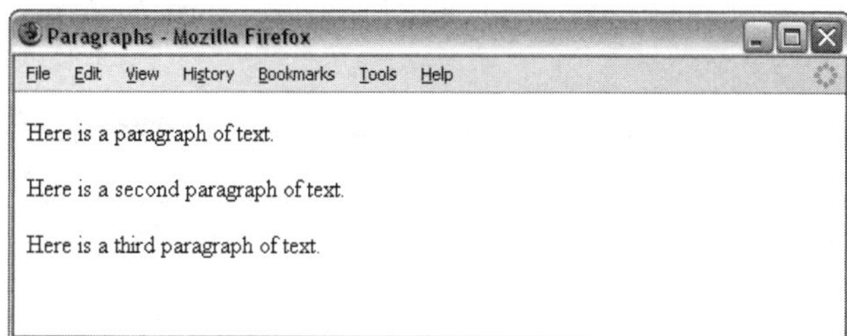

Figure 1-9

The <p> element can carry all the universal attributes and the deprecated align attribute:

```
align class id style title dir lang xml:lang
```

Creating Line Breaks Using the
 Element

Whenever you use the <br /> element, anything following it starts on the next line. The <br /> element is an example of an *empty element*; you don't need opening *and* closing tags, because there is nothing to go in between them.

Note that the
 element has a space between the characters br *and the forward slash.*

You will often see these written like so: <br>, which is the way it was written in earlier versions of HTML, but in XHTML the characters <br are followed by a space and a forward slash before the closing angled bracket.

You could use multiple <br /> elements to push text down several lines, and many designers use two line breaks between paragraphs of text rather than using the <p> element to structure text, as follows:

```
Paragraph one<br /><br />
Paragraph two<br /><br />
Paragraph three<br /><br />
```

While two `<br />` elements look very similar to using a `<p>` element, remember that XHTML markup is supposed to describe the structure of the content. So if you use two `<br />` elements between paragraphs, you are not describing the document structure.

Strictly speaking, `<br />` *elements should not be used to position text, and they should be used only within what is known as a block-level element. The* `<p>` *element is a block-level element; you will learn more about these near the end of this chapter.*

Here you can see an example of the `<br />` element in use within a paragraph (`ch01_eg08.html`):

```
<p>When you want to start a new line you can use the line break element.
So, the next<br />word will appear on a new line.</p>
```

Figure 1-10 shows you how the line breaks look after the words "next" and "do."

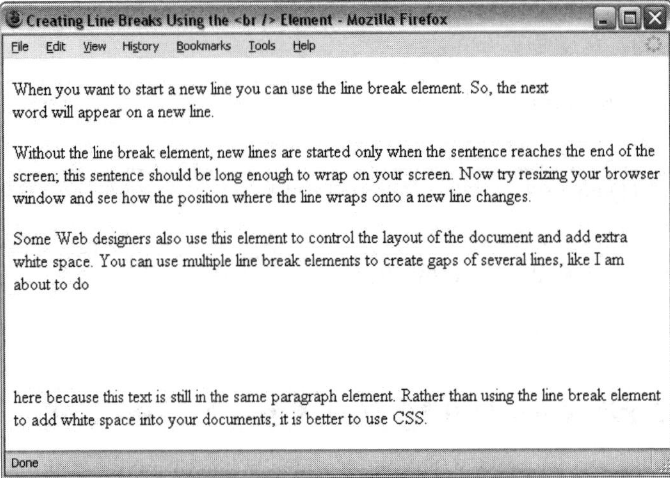

Figure 1-10

The `<br />` element can carry the following attributes (the `clear` attribute has been deprecated and is covered in Appendix I).

```
clear class id style title
```

Creating Preformatted Text Using the <pre> Element

Sometimes you want your text to follow the exact format of how it is written in the XHTML document — you don't want the text to wrap onto a new line when it reaches the edge of the browser; you don't want it to ignore multiple spaces; and you want the line breaks where you put them.

Any text between the opening <pre> tag and the closing </pre> tag will preserve the formatting of the source document. You should be aware, however, that most browsers would display this text in a monospaced font by default. (Courier is an example of a monospaced font, because each letter of the alphabet takes up the same width. In non-monospaced fonts, an *i* is usually narrower than an *m*.)

The most common uses of the <pre> element are to represent computer source code. For example, the following shows some JavaScript inside a <pre> element (ch01_eg09.html):

```
<pre>
function testFunction(strText){
   alert (strText)
}
</pre>
```

You can see in Figure 1-11 how the content of the <pre> element is displayed in the monospaced font; more important, you can see how it follows the formatting shown inside the <pre> element — the white space is preserved.

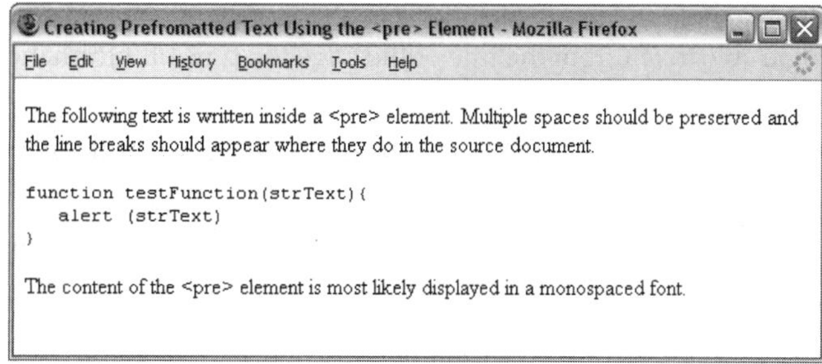

Figure 1-11

While tab characters can have an effect inside a <pre> element, and a tab is supposed to represent eight spaces, the implementation of tabs varies across browsers, so it is advisable to use spaces instead.

You will come across more elements that can be used to represent code later in this chapter in the section "Phrase Elements," which covers the <code>, <kbd>, and <var> elements.

Firefox, IE, and Safari support an extension to the XHTML recommendation that prevents line breaks: the <nobr> *element. (This retains the normal style of its containing element and does not result in the text being displayed in a monospaced font.) Because it is an extension, it is not part of the XHTML specification. The* <nobr> *element is covered in Appendix I.*

Try It Out Basic Text Formatting

Now that you've seen the basic elements that you will be using to format your text — headings and paragraphs — it's time to try putting that information to work.

In this example, you create a page for a fictional café called Example Café. We will be working on this example throughout the book to build up an entire site. This page is going to be the homepage for the site, introducing people to the cafe:

1. Add the skeleton of the document: the `<html>`, `<head>`, `<title>`, and `<body>` elements.

```
<html>
  <head>
    <title>Example Cafe - community cafe in Newquay, Cornwall, UK </title>
  </head>
  <body>
  </body>
</html>
```

The entire page is contained in the `<html>` element. The `<html>` element can contain only two child elements: the `<head>` element and `<body>` element. The `<head>` element contains the title for the page, and you should be able to tell from the title of the page the type of information the page will contain.

Meanwhile, the `<body>` element contains the main part of the web page — the part that viewers will actually see in the main part of the web browser.

2. Your page will have a main heading and some level 2 headings; these headings add structure to the information on the page:

```
<body>
  <h1>EXAMPLE CAFE</h1>
  <h2>A community cafe serving home cooked, locally sourced, organic food</h2>
  <h2>This weekend's special brunch</h2>
</body>
```

3. You can now fill out the page with some paragraphs that follow the headings:

```
 <body>
  <h1>EXAMPLE CAFE</h1>
    <p>Welcome to example cafe. We will be developing this site
throughout the book.</p>
  <h2>A community cafe serving home cooked, locally sourced, organic food</h2>
    <p>With stunning views of the ocean, Example Cafe offers the perfect
environment to unwind and recharge the batteries.</p>
    <p>Our menu offers a wide range of breakfasts, brunches and lunches,
including a range of vegetarian options.</p>
    <p>Whether you sip on a fresh, hot coffee or a cooling smoothie, you
never need to feel rushed - relax with friends or just watch
the world go by.</p>
    <h2>This weekend's special brunch</h2>
```

```
    <p>This weekend, our season of special brunches continues with scrambled egg
on an English muffin. Not for the faint-hearted, the secret to these eggs is
that they are made with half cream and cooked in butter, with no more than
four eggs in the pan at a time.</p>
</body>
</html>
```

4. Save the file as `index.html` and then open it in a web browser. The result should look something like Figure 1-12. The name `index.tml` is often given to the homepage of sites built in XHTML.

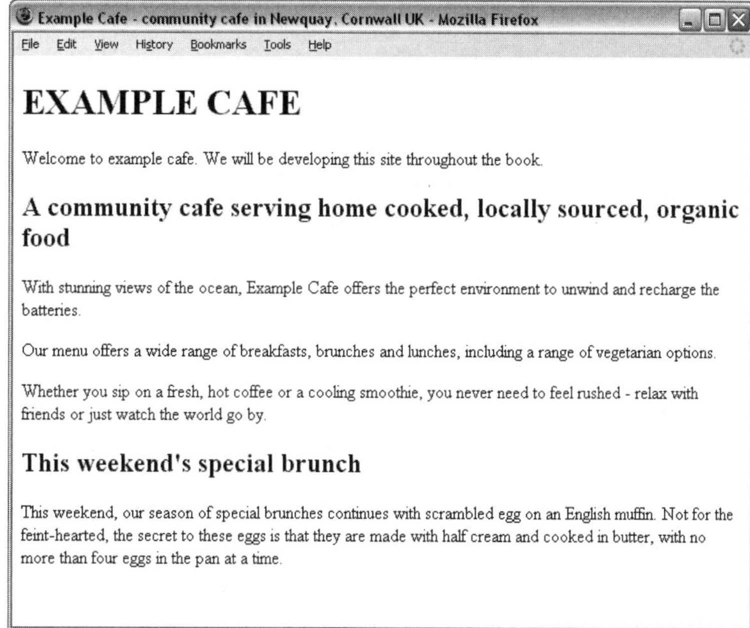

Figure 1-12

Presentational Elements

If you use a word processor, you will be familiar with the ability to make text bold, italic, or underlined; these are just three of the ten options available to indicate how text can appear in XHTML. The full list is bold, italic, monospaced, underlined, strikethrough, teletype, larger, smaller, superscripted, and subscripted text.

Technically speaking, these elements affect only the presentation of a document and the markup is of no other use. You can also achieve a similar appearance using CSS. However, they are still commonly used.

All the following presentational elements can carry the universal attributes and the UI event attributes that are covered at the end of the chapter.

Let's start by meeting the `<b>`, `<i>`, `<u>`, `<s>`, and `<tt>` elements. They are all demonstrated in `ch01_eg10.html` and you can see how they look in Figure 1-13.

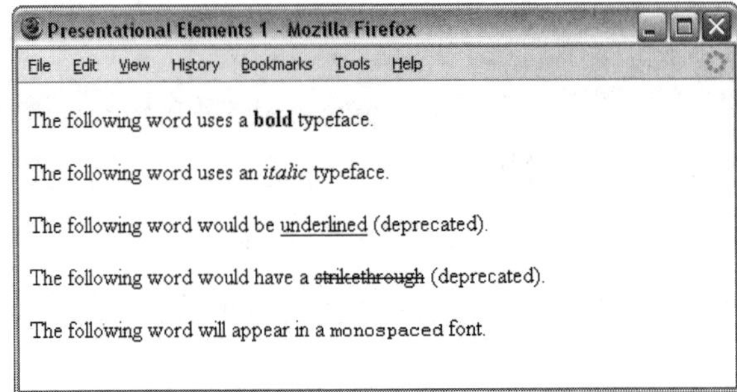

Figure 1-13

The <b> Element

Anything that appears in a `<b>` element is displayed in bold, like the word "bold" here:

```
The following word uses a <b>bold</b> typeface.
```

For those very interested in typography, it is worth noting that this does not necessarily mean the browser will use a boldface version of a font; some browsers use an algorithm to take a normal version of a font and make the lines thicker (giving it the appearance of being bold).

The contents of a `<b>` element will be displayed in the same way as the contents of the `<strong>` element. You will meet the `<strong>` element later; it is used to indicate that its contents have strong emphasis.

The <i> Element

The content of an `<i>` element is displayed in italicized text, like the word "italic" here:

```
The following word uses an <i>italic</i> typeface.
```

This does not necessarily mean the browser will look for an oblique or italicized version of the font. Most browsers use an algorithm to put the lines on a slant to simulate an italic font.

The contents of an `<i>` element will be displayed in the same way as the contents of the `<em>` element. You will meet the `<em>` element later; it is used to indicate that its contents have emphasis.

The <u> Element (Deprecated)

The content of a <u> element is underlined with a simple line:

```
The following word would be <u>underlined</u>
```

The <u> element is deprecated, although it is still supported by current browsers.

The <s> and <strike> Elements (Deprecated)

The content of an <s> or <strike> element is displayed with a strikethrough, which is a thin line through the text (<s> is just the abbreviated form of <strike>).

```
The following word would have a <s>strikethrough</s>.
```

Both the <s> and <strike> elements are deprecated, although they are still supported by current browsers.

The <tt> Element

The content of a <tt> element is written in monospaced font (like that of a teletype machine).

```
The following word will appear in a <tt>monospaced</tt> font.
```

Now let's take a look at the <sup>, <sub>, <big>, <small>, and <hr /> elements. They are all demonstrated in ch01_eg11.html and you can see what they look like in a browser in Figure 1-14.

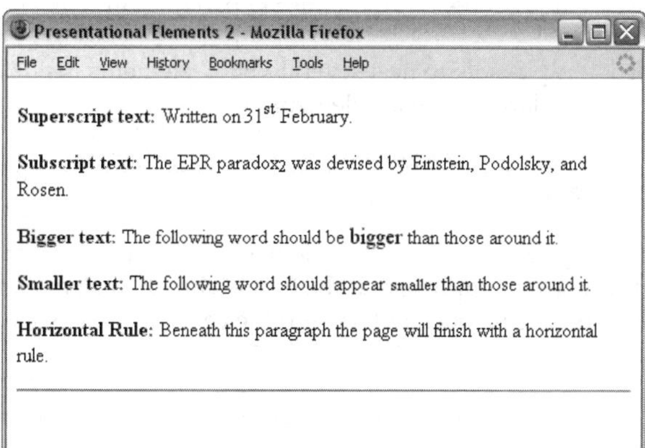

Figure 1-14

The <sup> Element

The content of a `<sup>` element is written in superscript; it is displayed half a character's height above the other characters and is also often slightly smaller than the text surrounding it.

```
Written on the 31<sup>st</sup> February.
```

The `<sup>` element is especially helpful in adding exponential values to equations, and adding the *st*, *nd*, *rd*, and *th* suffixes to numbers such as dates. However, in some browsers, you should be aware that it can create a taller gap between the line with the superscript text and the line above it.

The <sub> Element

The content of a `<sub>` element is written in subscript; it is displayed half a character's height beneath the other characters and is also often slightly smaller than the text surrounding it.

```
The EPR paradox<sub>2</sub> was devised by Einstein, Podolsky, and Rosen.
```

The `<sub>` element is particularly helpful to create footnotes.

The <big> Element

In early versions of HTML there were 7 standard sizes of text, and the `<big>` element was introduced to make the contents of this element one font size larger than the rest of the text surrounding it (up to the largest size — size 7). These days you should avoid using this element because it only has an effect on the look of the document; it does not help describe the document's structure or meaning. Instead you should use CSS to change the size of text.

```
The following word should be <big>bigger</big> than those around it.
```

When this element is used, it is possible to nest several `<big>` elements inside one another, and the content of each will get one size larger for each element.

The <small> Element

The `<small>` element is the opposite of the `<big>` element, and its contents are displayed one font size smaller than the rest of the text surrounding it. If the font is already the smallest, it has no effect. You can nest several `<small>` elements inside one another, and the content of each gets one size smaller for each element.

```
The following word should be <small>smaller</small> than those around it.
```

The use of this element is frowned upon, and you should aim to use CSS to change the size of text, rather than the `<small>` element.

The <hr /> Element

The `<hr />` element creates a horizontal rule across the page. It is an empty element, rather like the `<br />` element.

```
<hr />
```

This is frequently used to separate distinct sections of a page where a new heading is not appropriate.

Phrase Elements

Some of the elements in this section are displayed in a manner similar to the Presentational Elements `<b>`, `<i>`, `<pre>`, and `<tt>` that you have just read about, but the following elements are not just for presentational purposes; they also describe something about their content. For example, the words written in an `<em>` element will look just like the words in an `<i>` element, but the `<em>` element is supposed to indicate the addition of emphasis.

This section covers the following elements:

- `<em>` and `<strong>` for emphasis
- `<blockquote>`, `<cite>`, and `<q>` for quotations and citations
- `<abbr>`, `<acronym>`, and `<dfn>` for abbreviations, acronyms, and key terms
- `<code>`, `<kbd>`, `<var>`, and `<samp>` for computer code and information
- `<address>` for addresses

Several of these phrase elements were introduced after the presentational elements you just met. Some developers who learned HTML before these elements were introduced ignore them and just use the presentational elements because the results look the same. But you should be aware of them and preferably get into the habit of using these phrase elements where appropriate. For example, where you want to add emphasis to a word within a sentence you should use the `<em>` and `<strong>` elements rather than the presentational elements you just met; there are several good reasons for this, such as:

- Applications such as screen readers (which can read pages to web users with visual impairments) could add suitable intonation to the reading voice so that users with visual impairments could hear where the emphasis should be placed.
- Automated programs could be written to find the words with emphasis and pull them out as keywords within a document, or specifically index those words so that a user could find important terms in a document.

As you can see, appropriate use of these elements adds more information to a document (such as which words should have emphasis, which are parts of programming code, which parts are addresses, and so on) rather than just saying how it should be presented visually.

All the following phrase elements can carry the universal attributes and the UI event attributes covered at the end of the chapter.

The <em> Element Adds Emphasis

The content of an <em> element is intended to be a point of emphasis in your document, and it is usually displayed in italicized text. The kind of emphasis intended is on words such as "must" in the following sentence:

```
<p>You <em>must</em> remember to close elements in XHTML.</p>
```

You should use this element only when you are trying to add emphasis to a word, not just because you want to make the text appear italicized. If you just want italic text for stylistic reasons — without adding emphasis — you can use either the <i> element, or preferably use CSS.

The <strong> Element Adds Strong Emphasis

The <strong> element is intended to show strong emphasis for its content — stronger emphasis than the <em> element. As with the <em> element, the <strong> element should be used only when you want to add strong emphasis to part of a document. Most visual browsers display the strong emphasis in a bold font.

```
<p><em>Always</em> look at burning magnesium through protective colored
glass as it <strong>can cause blindness</strong>.</p>
```

Figure 1-15 shows how the <em> and <strong> elements are rendered in Firefox (ch01_eg12.html).

You need to remember that how the elements are presented (italics or bold) is largely irrelevant. You should use these elements to add emphasis to phrases, and therefore give your documents greater meaning, rather than to control how they appear visually. As you will see in Chapter 7, it is quite simple with CSS to change the visual presentation of these elements — for example, to highlight any words inside an <em> element with a yellow background and make them bold rather than italic.

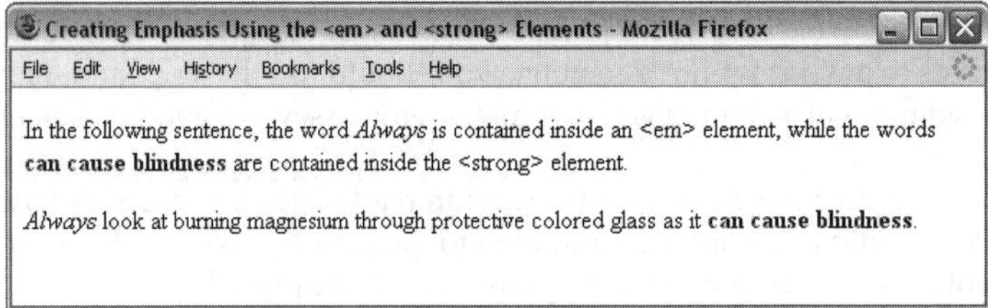

Figure 1-15

The <address> Element Is for Addresses

Many documents need to contain a snail-mail address, and there is a special <address> element that is used to contain addresses. For example, here is the address for Wrox, inside an <address> element (ch01_eg13.html):

```
<address>Wrox Press, 10475 Crosspoint Blvd, Indianapolis, IN 46256</address>
```

A browser can display the address differently than the surrounding document IE, Firefox, and Safari display it in italics, as you can see in Figure 1-16 (although you can override this with CSS).

Figure 1-16

The <abbr> Element Is for Abbreviations

You can indicate when you are using an abbreviated form by placing the abbreviation between opening `<abbr>` and closing `</abbr>` tags.

When possible, consider using a `title` attribute whose value is the full version of the abbreviations. For example, if you want to indicate that Bev is an abbreviation for Beverly, you can use the `<abbr>` element like so:

```
I have a friend called <abbr title="Beverly">Bev</abbr>.
```

If you are abbreviating a foreign word, you can also use the `xml:lang` attribute to indicate the language used.

The <acronym> Element Is for Acronym Use

The `<acronym>` element allows you to indicate that the text between opening `<acronym>` and closing `</acronym>` tags is an acronym.

When possible, use a `title` attribute on opening `<acronym>` tags whose value is the full version of the acronym. For example, if you want to indicate that XHTML was an acronym, you can use the `<acronym>` element like so (`ch01_eg14.html`):

```
This chapter covers marking up text in <acronym title="Extensible Hypertext
Markup Language">XHTML</acronym>.
```

As you can see from Figure 1-17, Firefox gives the `<abbr>` and `<acronym>` elements a dashed underline, and when you hover your cursor over the word, the value of the title attribute shows as a tooltip. Internet Explorer does not change the appearance of the element, although it does show the title as a tooltip.

If the acronym is in a different language, you can include an `xml:lang` attribute to indicate which language it is in.

The <dfn> Element Is for Special Terms

The `<dfn>` element allows you to specify that you are introducing a special term. Its use is similar to the italicized notes in this book used to introduce important new concepts.

Typically, you would use the `<dfn>` element the first time you introduce a key term and only in that instance. Most recent browsers render the content of a `<dfn>` element in an italic font.

For example, you can indicate that the term "XHTML" in the following sentence is important and should be marked as such:

```
This book teaches you how mark up your documents for the Web using
<dfn>XHTML</dfn>.
```

Figure 1-17 shows the use of the `<dfn>` element (`ch01_eg14.html`).

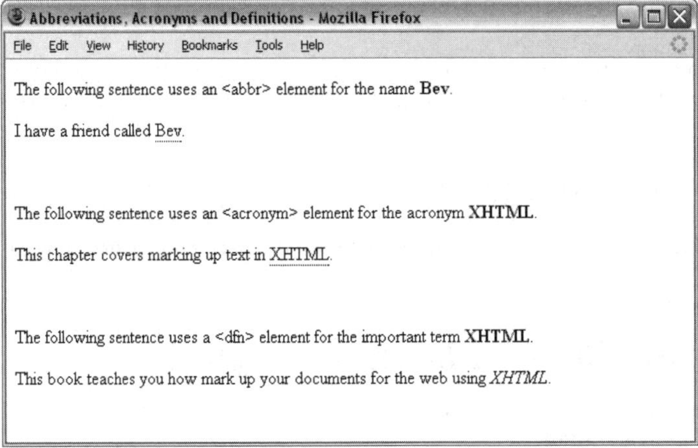

Figure 1-17

The <blockquote> Element Is for Quoting Text

When you want to quote a passage from another source, you should use the `<blockquote>` element. Note that there is a separate `<q>` element for use with smaller quotations, as discussed in the next section. Here's `ch01_eg15.html`:

```
<p>The following description of XHTML is taken from the W3C Web site:</p>
<blockquote>XHTML 1.0 is the W3C's first Recommendation for XHTML,
following on from earlier work on HTML 4.01, HTML 4.0, HTML 3.2 and HTML
2.0. </blockquote>
```

Text inside a `<blockquote>` element is usually indented from the left and right edges of the surrounding text, and some browsers uses an italicized font. (It should be used only for quotes — if you simply want an indented paragraph of text, you should use CSS. You can see what this looks like in Figure 1-18.

Using the cite Attribute with the <blockquote> Element

You can use the `cite` attribute on the `<blockquote>` element to indicate the source of the quote. The value of this attribute should be a URL pointing to an online document, if possible, the exact place in that document. Browsers do not currently do anything with this attribute, but it means the source of the quote is there should you need it in the future (`ch01_eg15.html`).

```
<blockquote cite="http://www.w3.org/markup/">XHTML 1.0 is the W3C's first
Recommendation for XHTML, following on from earlier work on HTML 4.01, HTML
4.0, HTML 3.2 and HTML 2.0.</blockquote>
```

The <q> Element Is for Short Quotations

The `<q>` element is intended to be used when you want to add a quote within a sentence, rather than as an indented block on its own (`ch01_eg15.html`):

```
<p>As Dylan Thomas said, <q>Somebody's boring me. I think it's me</q>.</p>
```

The XHTML recommendation says that the text enclosed in a `<q>` element should begin and end in double quotes. Firefox inserts these quotation marks for you, but IE8 was the first version of Internet Explorer to support the `<q>` element. So, if you want your quote to be surrounded by quotation marks, be warned that IE7 and earlier versions of IE will not display them.

The `<q>` element can also carry the `cite` attribute. The value should be a URL pointing to the source of the quote.

The <cite> Element Is for Citations

If you are quoting a text, you can indicate the source by placing it between an opening `<cite>` tag and closing `</cite>` tag. As you would expect in a print publication, the content of the `<cite>` element is rendered in italicized text by default (`ch01_eg15.html`).

```
This chapter is taken from <cite>Beginning Web Development</cite>.
```

If you are referencing an online resource, you should place your `<cite>` element inside an `<a>` element, which, as you'll see in Chapter 2, creates a link to the relevant document.

There are several applications that potentially could make use of the `<cite>` element. For example, a search application could use `<cite>` tags to find documents that reference certain works, or a browser could collect the contents of `<cite>` elements to generate a bibliography for any given document, although at the moment it is not widely enough used for either feature to exist.

You can see the `<blockquote>`, `<q>`, and `<cite>` elements in Figure 1-18.

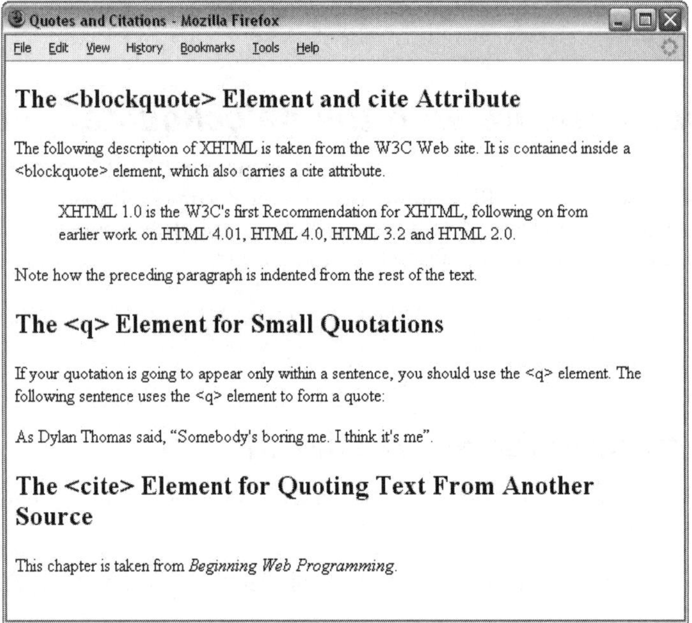

Figure 1-18

The <code> Element Is for Code

If your pages include any programming code (which is not uncommon on the Web), the following four elements will be of particular use to you. Any code to appear on a web page should be placed inside a `<code>` element. Usually the content of the `<code>` element is presented in a monospaced font, just like the code in most programming books (including this one).

> Note that when trying to display code on a web page (for example, if you were creating a page about web programming), and you wanted to include angled brackets, you cannot just use the opening and closing angle brackets inside these elements, because the browser could mistake these characters for actual markup. Instead you should use `<` instead of the left-angle bracket (<), and you should use `>` instead of the right-angle bracket (>). These replacement sets of characters are known as *escape codes* or *character entities*, and a full list of them appears in Appendix F.

Here you can see an example of using the <code> element to represent an <h1> element and its content in XHTML (ch01_eg16.html):

```
<p><code>&lt;h1&gt;This is a primary heading&lt;/h1&gt;</code></p>
```

Figure 1-19 shows you how this would look in a browser.

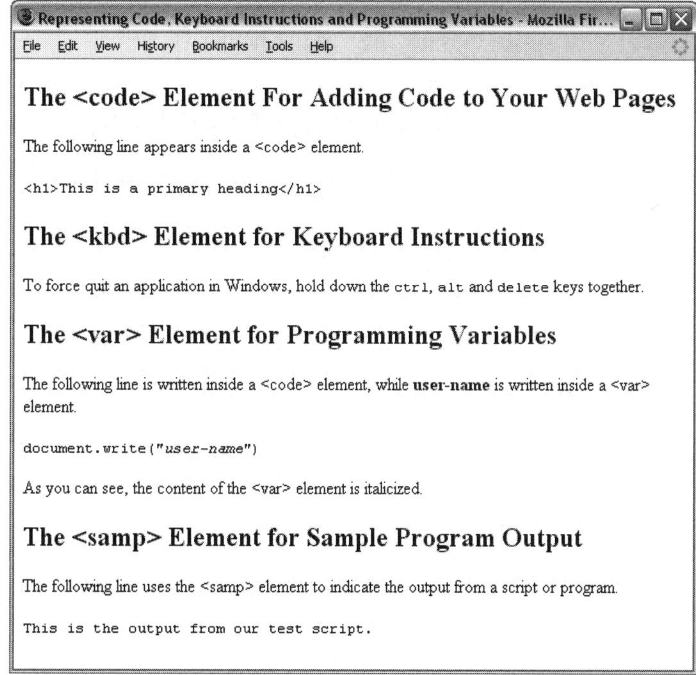

Figure 1-19

The <code> element is often used in conjunction with the <pre> element so that the formatting of the code is retained.

The <kbd> Element Is for Text Typed on a Keyboard

If, when talking about computers, you want to tell a reader to enter some text, you can use the <kbd> element to indicate what should be typed in, as in this example (ch01_eg16.html):

```
<p>To force quit an application in Windows, hold down the <kbd>ctrl</kbd>,
<kbd>alt</kbd> and <kbd>delete</kbd> keys together.</p>
```

The content of a <kbd> element is usually represented in a monospaced font, rather like the content of the <code> element. Figure 1-19 shows you what this would look like in a browser.

The <var> Element Is for Programming Variables

The `<var>` element is another of the elements added to help programmers. It is usually used in conjunction with the `<pre>` and `<code>` elements to indicate that the content of that element is a variable that can be supplied by a user (`ch01_eg16.html`).

```
<p><code>document.write("<var>user-name</var>")</code></p>
```

Typically, the content of a `<var>` element is italicized, as you can see in Figure 1-19. If you are not familiar with the concept of variables, they are covered in Chapter 11.

The <samp> Element Is for a Program Output

The `<samp>` element indicates sample output from a program, script, or the like. Again, it is mainly used when documenting programming concepts. For example (`ch01_eg16.html`):

```
<p>The following line uses the &lt;samp&gt; element to indicate the output
from a script or program.</p>
<p><samp>This is the output from our test script.</samp></p>
```

This tends to be displayed in a monospaced font, as you can see in Figure 1-19.

That brings you to the end of the phrase elements, but not quite the end of all the text elements.

Lists

There are many reasons you might want to add a list to your pages, from putting your five favorite albums on your homepage to including a numbered set of instructions for visitors to follow (like the steps you follow in the Try It Out examples in this book).

You can create three types of lists in XHTML:

- **Unordered lists**, which are like lists of bullet points
- **Ordered lists**, which use a sequence of numbers or letters instead of bullet points
- **Definition lists**, which allow you to specify a term and its definition

I'm sure you will think of more uses for the lists as you meet them and start using them.

Using the <ul> Element to Create Unordered Lists

If you want to make a list of bullet points, you write the list within the `<ul>` element (which stands for unordered list). Each bullet point or line you want to write should then be contained between opening `<li>` tags and closing `</li>` tags (the `li` stands for *list item*).

You should always close the `<li>` element. Even though you might see some HTML pages that leave off the closing tag, this is a bad habit you should avoid.

If you want to create a bulleted list, you can do so like this (`ch01_eg17.html`):

```
<ul>
  <li>Bullet point number one</li>
  <li>Bullet point number two</li>
  <li>Bullet point number three</li>
</ul>
```

In a browser, this list would look something like Figure 1-20.

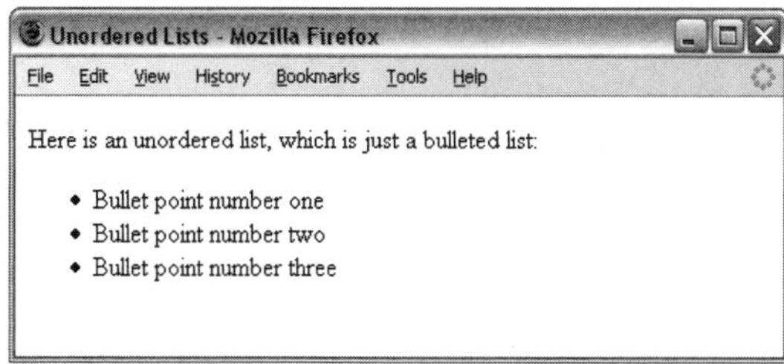

Figure 1-20

The `<ul>` and `<li>` elements can carry all the universal attributes and UI event attributes.

Ordered Lists

Sometimes, you want your lists to be ordered. In an ordered list, rather than prefixing each point with a bullet point, you can use either numbers (1, 2, 3), letters (A, B, C), or Roman numerals (i, ii, iii) to prefix the list item.

An ordered list is contained inside the `<ol>` element. Each item in the list should then be nested inside the `<ol>` element and contained between opening `<li>` and closing `</li>` tags (`ch01_eg18.html`).

```
<ol>
  <li>Point number one</li>
  <li>Point number two</li>
  <li>Point number three</li>
</ol>
```

The result should be similar to what you see in Figure 1-21.

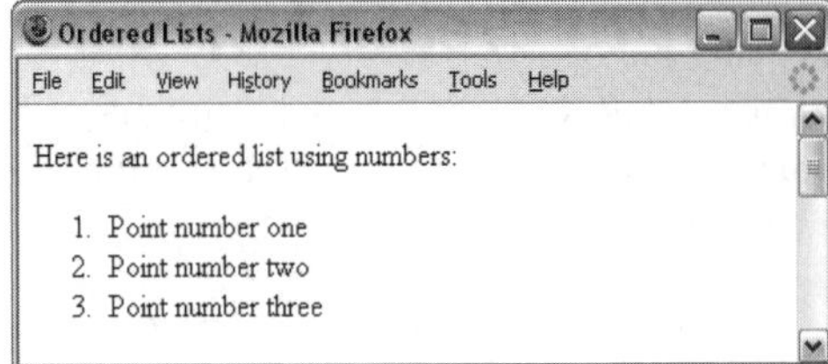

Figure 1-21

If you would rather have letters or Roman numerals than Arabic numbers, you can use the now-deprecated `type` attribute on the `<ol>` element.

Using the type Attribute to Select Numbers, Letters, or Roman Numerals in Ordered Lists (Deprecated)

The `type` attribute on the `<ol>` element enables you to change the ordering of list items from the default of numbers to the options listed in the table that follows, by giving the `type` attribute the corresponding character.

Value for type Attribute	Description	Examples
1	Arabic numerals (the default)	1, 2, 3, 4, 5
A	Capital letters	A, B, C, D, E
a	Small letters	a, b, c, d, e
I	Large Roman numerals	I, II, III, IV, V
i	Small Roman numerals	i, ii, iii, iv, v

For example, the following is an ordered list that uses small Roman numerals (`ch01_eg18.html`):

```
<ol type="i">
  <li>Point number one</li>
  <li>Point number two</li>
  <li>Point number three</li>
</ol>
```

You can see what this might look like in Figure 1-22.

The `type` attribute has been deprecated in favor of the CSS `list-style-type` property.

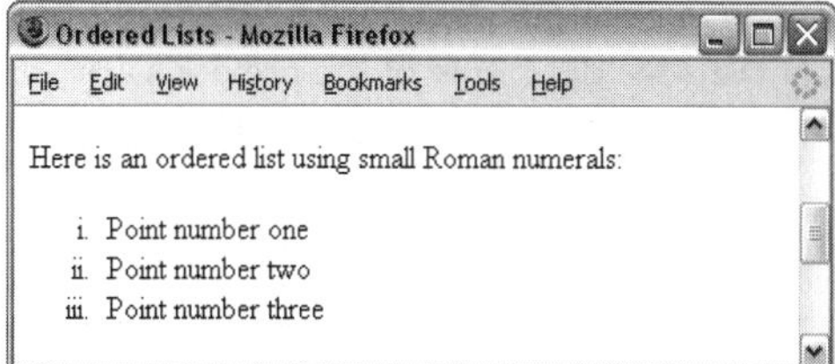

Figure 1-22

You also used to be able to use the type attribute on <li> elements, which would override the value in the <ol> element, but it has been deprecated and its use should be avoided. All the universal attributes and UI event attributes can be used with the <ol> elements, and also a special attribute start, to control the number at which a list starts.

Using the start Attribute to Change the Starting Number in Ordered Lists (Deprecated)

If you want to specify the number that a numbered list should start at, you can use the start attribute on the <ol> element. The value of this attribute should be the numeric representation of that point in the list, so a D in a list that is ordered with capital letters would be represented by the value 4 (ch01_eg18.html).

```
<ol type="A" start="4">
  <li>Point number one</li>
  <li>Point number two</li>
  <li>Point number three</li>
</ol>
```

You can see the result in Figure 1-23.

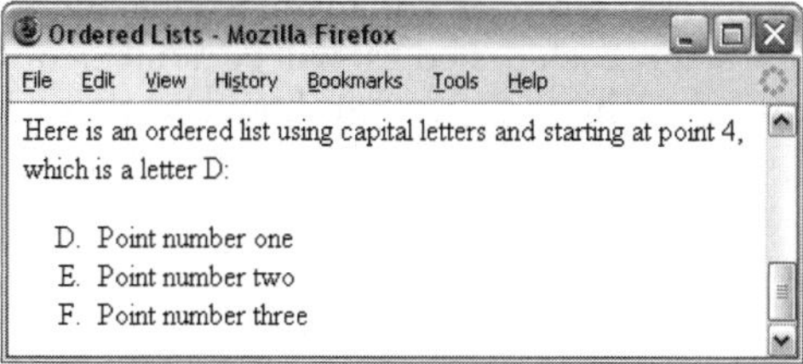

Figure 1-23

Definition Lists

The definition list is a special kind of list for providing terms followed by a short text definition or description for them. Definition lists are contained inside the <dl> element. The <dl> element then contains alternating <dt> and <dd> elements. The content of the <dt> element is the term you will be defining. The <dd> element contains the definition of the previous <dt> element. For example, here is a definition list that describes the different types of lists in XHTML (ch01_eg19.html):

```
<dl>
  <dt>Unordered List</dt>
  <dd>A list of bullet points.</dd>
  <dt>Ordered List</dt>
  <dd>An ordered list of points, such as a numbered set of steps.</dd>
  <dt>Definition List</dt>
  <dd>A list of terms and definitions.</dd>
</dl>
```

In a browser, this would look something like Figure 1-24 (ch01_eg19.html).

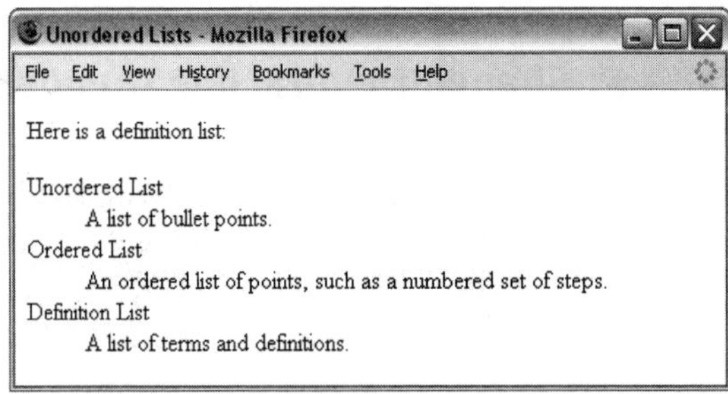

Figure 1-24

Each of these elements can carry the universal attributes and UI event attributes covered at the end of this chapter.

Nesting Lists

You can nest lists inside other lists. For example, you might want a numbered list with separate points corresponding to one of the list items. Each nested list will be numbered separately unless you specify otherwise using the start attribute. And each new list should be placed inside a <li> element (ch01_eg20.html):

```
<ol type="I">
  <li>Item one</li>
  <li>Item two</li>
  <li>Item three</li>
  <li>Item four
    <ol type="i">
      <li>Item 4.1</li>
      <li>Item 4.2</li>
      <li>Item 4.3</li>
    </ol>
  </li>
  <li>Item Five</li>
</ol>
```

In a browser, this will look something like Figure 1-25.

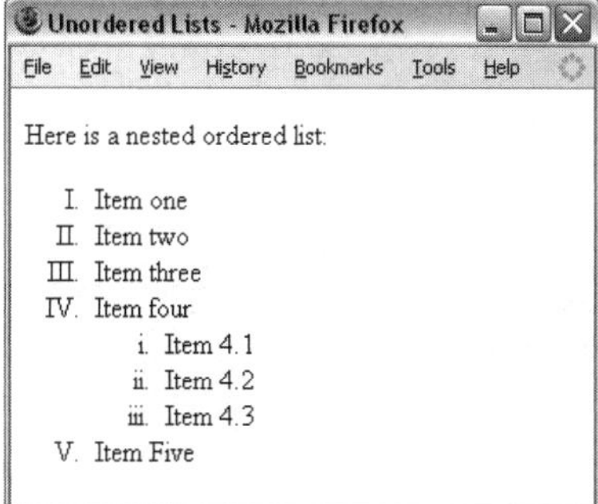

Figure 1-25

Try It Out Using Text Markup

Now that you've looked at the different elements and attributes you can use to mark up text, it is time to put them into practice. In this example, you use a selection of markup to create a page for our café site that displays a recipe for the world's best scrambled eggs. So open up your text editor or web page authoring tool and follow these steps:

1. Add the skeleton elements for the document: `<html>`, `<head>`, `<title>`, and `<body>`:

```
<html>
  <head>
    <title>Wrox Recipes - World's Best Scrambled Eggs</title>
  </head>
  <body>
  </body>
</html>
```

You have seen the skeleton several times now, so let's move on to add some content.

2. Add some appropriate heading elements into the body of the document; these help add structure to the page:

```
<body>
  <h1>Wrox Recipes - World's Best Scrambled Eggs</h1>
  <h2>Ingredients</h2>
  <h2>Instructions</h2>
</body>
```

3. After the `<h1>` element that tells you the recipe is for scrambled eggs, there will be a bit of an explanation about the recipe (and why it is the World's Best). You can see that several of the elements you have met so far are used in these two paragraphs.

```
<h1>Wrox Recipes - World's Best Scrambled Eggs</h1>
  <p>I adapted this recipe from a book called
    <cite cite="http://www.amazon.com/exec/obidos/tg/detail/-
    /0864119917/">Sydney Food</cite> by Bill Grainger. Ever since tasting
    these eggs on my 1<sup>st</sup> visit to Bill's restaurant in Kings
    Cross, Sydney, I have been after the recipe. I have since transformed
    it into what I really believe are the <em>best</em> scrambled eggs
    I have ever tasted.</p>
  <p>This recipe is what I call a <q>very special breakfast</q>; just look at
    the ingredients to see why. It has to be tasted to be believed.</p>
```

In the first sentence, the <cite> element has been used to indicate a reference to the book this recipe is adapted from. The next sentence makes use of the <sup> element so you can write "1st" and use superscript text — although you might like to note that this makes the gap between the first line and the second line of text larger than the gap between the second and third lines of text (as the superscript letters poke above the line). In the final sentence of the first paragraph there is emphasis on the word "best," as these really are the *best* scrambled eggs I have ever tasted.

In the second paragraph, another of the elements is at work; the <q> element is used for a quote.

4. After the first <h2> element, you will list the ingredients in an unordered list:

```
<h2>Ingredients</h2>
  <p>The following ingredients make one serving:</p>
    <ul>
      <li>2 eggs</li>
      <li>1 tablespoon of butter (10g)</li>
      <li>1/3 cup of cream <i>(2 3/4 fl ounces)</i></li>
      <li>A pinch of salt</li>
      <li>Freshly milled black pepper</li>
      <li>3 fresh chives (chopped)</li>
      </ul>
```

In the line that describes how much cream you need, there is an alternative measure provided in italics.

5. Add the instructions after the second <h2> element; these will go in a numbered list:

```
<h2>Instructions</h2>
    <ol>
      <li>Whisk eggs, cream, and salt in a bowl.</li>
      <li>Melt the butter in a non-stick pan over a high heat <i>(taking care
          not to burn the butter)</i></li>
      <li>Pour egg mixture into pan and wait until it starts setting around
          the  edge of the pan (around 20 seconds).</li>
      <li>Using a wooden spatula, bring the mixture into the center as if it
          were an omelet, and let it cook for another 20 seconds.</li>
```

```
        <li>Fold contents in again, leave for 20 seconds, and repeat until
          the eggs are only just done.</li>
        <li>Grind a light sprinkling of freshly milled pepper over the eggs
          and blend in some chopped fresh chives.</li>
  </ol>
  <p>You should only make a <strong>maximum</strong> of two servings per
    frying pan.</p>
```

You might note that the numbered list contains an italicized comment about not burning the butter, and the final paragraph contains a strong emphasis that you should cook no more than two batches of these eggs in a pan.

6. Save this example as `recipes.html`. When you open it in a browser you should see something like Figure 1-26.

Figure 1-26

I hope you will enjoy the eggs — go on, you know you want to try them now.

Editing Text

When working on a document with others, it helps if you can see changes that another person has made. Even when working on your own documents, it can be helpful to keep track of changes you make. There are two elements specifically designed for revising and editing text:

- The `<ins>` element for when you want to add text (usually shown underlined in a browser)
- The `<del>` element for when you want to delete some text (usually shown crossed out in a browser)

Here you can see some changes made to the following XHTML (`ch01_eg21.html`):

```
<h1>How to Spot a Wrox Book</h1>
<p>Wrox-spotting is a popular pastime in bookshops. Programmers like to find
the distinctive <del>blue</del><ins>red</ins> spines because they know that
Wrox books are written by <del>1000 monkeys</del><ins>Programmers</ins> for
Programmers.</p>
<ins><p>Both readers and authors, however, have reservations about the use
of photos on the covers.</p></ins>
```

This example would look something like Figure 1-27 in a browser.

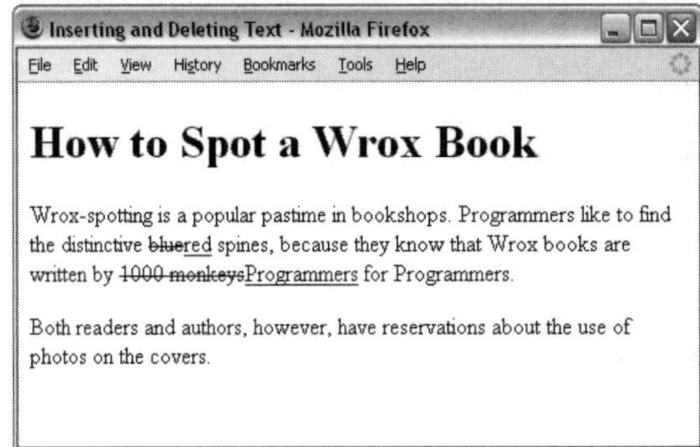

Figure 1-27

These features would also be particularly helpful as editing tools, to note changes and modifications made by different authors.

If you are familiar with Microsoft Word, the `<ins>` *and* `<del>` *elements are very similar to a feature called Track Changes (which you can find under the Tools menu). The track changes feature underlines new text additions and crosses through deleted text.*

You must be careful when using `<ins>` *and* `<del>` *to ensure that you do not end up with what is known as a block-level element (such as a* `<p>` *or an* `<h2>` *element) inside what is known as an inline element (such as a* `<b>` *or* `<i>` *element). You learn more about block-level elements and inline elements at the end of the chapter.*

You can use the `title` attribute to provide information as to who added the `<ins>` or `<del>` element and why it was added or deleted; this information is offered to users as a tooltip in the major browsers.

You might also use the `cite` attribute on the `<ins>` and `<del>` element to indicate the source or reason for a change, although this attribute is quite limiting, as the value must be a URI.

The `<ins>` and `<del>` elements can also carry a `datetime` attribute whose value is a date and time in the following format:

```
YYYY-MM-DDThh:mm:ssTZD
```

This formula breaks down as follows:

- `YYYY` represents the year.
- `MM` represents the month.
- `DD` represents the day of the month.
- `T` is just a separator between the date and time.
- `hh` is the hour.
- `mm` is the number of minutes.
- `ss` is the number of seconds.
- `TZD` is the time zone designator.

For example, `2009-04-16T20:30-05:00` represents 8:30 p.m. on April 16, 2009, according to U.S. Eastern Standard Time.

As you can see, the `datetime` *attribute is rather long to be entered by hand, and thus is more likely to be entered by a program that allows users to edit web pages.*

When you learn how to use CSS, you will see how it is possible to show and hide the inserted and deleted content as required.

Using Character Entities for Special Characters

You can use most alphanumeric characters in your document and they will be displayed without a problem. There are, however, some characters that have special meaning in XHTML, and for some characters there is not a keyboard equivalent you can enter. For example, you cannot use the angle brackets that start and end tags, as the browser can mistake them for markup. You can, however, use a set of different characters known as a *character entity* to represent these special characters. Sometimes you will also see character entities referred to as *escape characters*.

All special characters can be added into a document using the numeric entity for that character, and some also have named entities, as you can see in the table that follows.

Character	Numeric Entity	Named Entity
"	"	"
&	&	&
<	<	<
>	>	>

A full list of character entities (or special characters) appears in Appendix F.

Comments

You can put comments between any tags in your XHTML documents. Comments use the following syntax:

```
<!-- comment goes here -->
```

Anything after `<!--` until the closing `-->` will not be displayed. It can still be seen in the source code for the document, but it is not shown onscreen.

It is good practice to comment your code, especially in complex documents, to indicate sections of a document, and any other notes to anyone looking at the code.

You can even comment out whole sections of code. For example, in the following snippet of code you would not see the content of the `<h2>` element. You can also see there are comments indicating the section of the document, who added it, and when it was added.

```
<!-- Start of Footnotes Section added 04-24-04 by Bob Stewart -->
  <!-- <h2>Character Entities</h2> -->
  <p><strong>Character entities</strong> can be used to escape special
  characters that the browser might otherwise think have special meaning.</p>
<!-- End of Footnotes section -->
```

The <font> Element (Deprecated)

The `<font>` element allows you to control the presentation of text — its size, the typeface, and color. It has been deprecated, so its use should be avoided, but you are likely to come across it. If you want to read more about how to use the `<font>` element, it is covered in Appendix I. You might see the `<font>` element used like so:

```
<h3>Using the &lt;font&gt; element</h3>
<font face="arial, verdana, sans-serif" size="2" color="#666666">The
&lt;font&gt; element has been deprecated since HTML 4.0. You should now use
CSS to indicate how text should be styled. </font>
```

Understanding Block and Inline Elements

Now that you have seen many of the elements that can be used to mark up text, it is important to make an observation about all the elements that live inside the <body> element, because each one can fall into one of two categories:

- Block-level elements
- Inline elements

This is quite a conceptual distinction, but it will have important ramifications for other features of XHTML.

Block-level elements appear on the screen as if they have a carriage return or line break before and after them. For example, the <p>, <h1>, <h2>, <h3>, <h4>, <h5>, <h6>, <ul>, <ol>, <dl>, <pre>, <hr />, <blockquote>, and <address> elements are all block-level elements. They all start on their own new lines, and anything that follows them appears on its own new line, too.

Inline elements, on the other hand, can appear within sentences and do not have to appear on new lines of their own. The <b>, <i>, <u>, <em>, <strong>, <sup>, <sub>, <big>, <small>, <ins>, <del>, <code>, <cite>, <dfn>, <kbd>, and <var> elements are all inline elements.

For example, look at the following heading and paragraph; both of these elements start on new lines and anything that follows them goes on a new line, too. Meanwhile, the inline elements in the paragraph are not placed on their own new lines. Here is the code (ch02_eg22.html):

```
<h1>Block-Level Elements</h1>
  <p><strong>Block-level elements</strong> always start on a new line. The
  <code>&lt;h1&gt;</code> and <code>&lt;p&gt;</code> elements will not sit
  on the same line, whereas the inline elements flow with the rest of the
  text.</p>
```

You can see what this looks like in Figure 1-28.

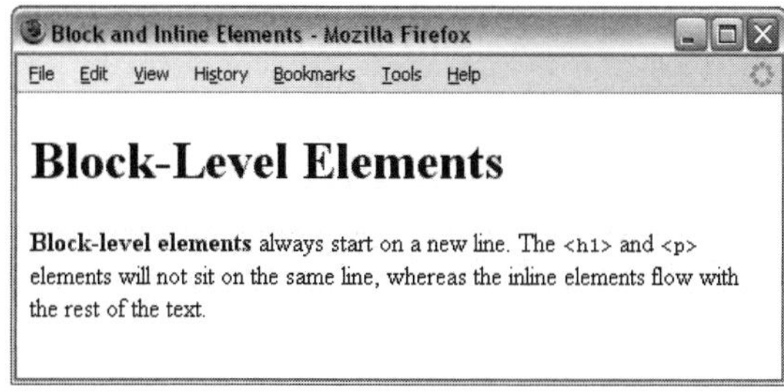

Figure 1-28

Strictly speaking, inline elements may not contain block-level elements, and can appear only within block-level elements (so you should not have a <b> element outside a block-level element). Block-level elements, meanwhile, can contain other block-level elements, and inline elements.

Grouping Elements with <div> and <span>

The <div> and <span> elements allow you to group several elements to create sections or subsections of a page. On their own, they will not affect the appearance of a page, but they are commonly used with CSS to allow you to attach a style to a section of a page (as you will see in Chapter 7). For example, you might want to put all the footnotes on a page within a <div> element to indicate that all the elements within that <div> element relate to the footnotes. You might then attach a style to this <div> element so that the footnotes appear using a special set of style rules.

The <div> element is used to group block-level elements:

```
<div class="footnotes">
  <h2>Footnotes</h2>
  <p><b>1</b> The World Wide Web was invented by Tim Berners-Lee</p>
  <p><b>2</b> The W3C is the World Wide Web Consortium which maintains many
Web standards</p>
</div>
```

It is considered good practice to use a `class` attribute whose value describes the contents of this group of elements when using a <div>. As you can see here, the value `footnotes` helps describe the contents of the <div>.

The <span> element, on the other hand, can be used to group inline elements only. So, if you had a part of a sentence or paragraph you wanted to group, you could use the <span> element. Here you can see that I have added a <span> element to indicate which content refers to an inventor. It contains both a bold element and some text:

```
<div class="footnotes">
  <h2>Footnotes</h2>
  <p><span class="inventor"><b>1</b> The World Wide Web was invented by Tim
     Berners-Lee</span></p>
  <p><b>2</b> The W3C is the World Wide Web Consortium which maintains many Web
     standards</p>
</div>
```

On its own, this would have no effect at all on how the document looks visually, but it does add extra meaning to the markup, which now groups the related elements, and it's particularly helpful to attach special styles to these elements using CSS rules.

The <div> and <span> elements can carry all the universal attributes and UI event attributes, as well as the deprecated `align` attribute.

The XML Declaration

At this point in the chapter, you have already learned a lot of markup that allows you to describe the structure of text in your pages, including headings and paragraphs, presentational and phrase elements, and lists. To wrap up this chapter, let's now spend a few pages looking at some aspects of XHTML which, to be completely honest, are both a little dull and have little effect upon how your pages will look. They are, however, very important in terms of writing pages according to the rules (especially if you want to create pages commercially), and there are some attributes that apply to most of the elements you have already met, and that you are likely to meet in the coming few chapters.

To start with, you'll sometimes see a line at the beginning of an XHTML document, a line known as the XML Declaration. The XHTML language was actually written using another language called Extensible Markup Language (XML). XML is used to create markup languages, and any XML document can begin with this optional XML declaration:

```
<?xml version="1.0" encoding="UTF-8" ?>
```

Because it is optional, some authors do not start their documents with it. If you include the XML declaration, it must be right at the beginning of the document; there must be nothing before it, not even a space. The `encoding` attribute indicates the encoding used in the document.

An encoding (short for character encoding*) attribute represents how a program or operating system stores characters that you might want to display. Because different languages have different characters, and indeed because some programs support more characters than others, there are several different encodings.*

Document Type Declaration

As mentioned, XHTML employs a *stricter syntax* than previous versions of HTML. For example, element and attribute names in XHTML must all be written in lowercase (whereas earlier versions of HTML were not case-sensitive), every element that has some content must have a corresponding closing element, and some of the elements and attributes may be marked as deprecated — meaning that they are likely to be phased out in future versions of HTML or XHTML.

While a web browser will usually display a page without a Document Type Declaration (indeed, none of the examples to date in this chapter included one), each XHTML page should really begin with a `DOCTYPE` declaration to indicate to a browser (or any other program) the version of HTML or XHTML that is being used in that page. We will therefore be including one in each example for the rest of the book.

While I have been talking about XHTML as one language, when it was created there were actually three versions or flavors of XHTML released — this was done to help existing web developers make the transition from HTML to XHTML:

- **Transitional XHTML 1.0**, which still allows developers to use the deprecated markup from HTML 4.1 (even though it is likely to be phased out). It does, however, require the author to use the new stricter syntax.
- **Strict XHTML 1.0**, which was to signal the path forward for XHTML, without the deprecated stylistic markup. It also obeys the new stricter syntax.
- **Frameset XHTML 1.0**, which is used to create web pages that use something called *frames* (you meet frames in Chapter 6).

If by now you are feeling a little overwhelmed by all the different versions of HTML and XHTML, don't be! Throughout this book, you will be primarily learning Transitional XHTML 1.0. In the process, you will learn which elements and attributes have been marked as deprecated and what the alternatives for are. If you avoid the deprecated elements and attributes, you will automatically be writing Strict XHTML 1.0.

The `DOCTYPE` declaration goes before the opening `<html>` tag in a document, and after the optional XML Declaration if you have used it.

If you are writing Transitional XHTML 1.0 (and include stylistic markup in your document), then your `DOCTYPE` declaration should look like this:

```
<!DOCTYPE html PUBLIC "-//W3C//DTD XHTML 1.0 Transitional//EN"
  "http://www.w3.org/TR/xhtml1/DTD/xhtml1-transitional.dtd">
```

If you are writing Strict XHTML 1.0, your `DOCTYPE` declaration will look like this:

```
<!DOCTYPE html PUBLIC "-//W3C//DTD XHTML 1.0 Strict//EN"
  "http://www.w3.org/TR/xhtml1/DTD/xhtml1-strict.dtd">
```

For frameset documents (discussed in Chapter 6), your `DOCTYPE` declaration would look like this:

```
<!DOCTYPE html PUBLIC "-//W3C//DTD XHTML 1.0 Frameset//EN"
  "http://www.w3.org/TR/xhtml1/DTD/xhtml1-frameset.dtd">
```

> A Strict XHTML document *must* contain the `DOCTYPE` declaration before the root element; however, you are not required to include the `DOCTYPE` declaration if you are creating a transitional or frameset document.

Having learned Transitional XHTML 1.0, you will be able to understand older versions of HTML and be safe in the knowledge that (unless specifically warned) your XHTML code will work in the majority of browsers used on the Web today.

Core Elements and Attributes

Now let's take a closer look at the four main elements that form the basic structure of every document: `<html>`, `<head>`, `<title>`, and `<body>`. These four elements should appear in every XHTML document that you write, and you will see them referred to throughout this book as the *skeleton* of the document.

The <html> Element

The `<html>` element is the containing element for the whole XHTML document. After the optional XML declaration and required `DOCTYPE` declaration, each XHTML document should have an opening `<html>` tag and each document should end with a closing `</html>` tag.

If you are writing Strict XHTML 1.0, the opening tag must also include something known as a *namespace identifier*. The concept of namespaces may seem a little odd at first, until you realize that anyone can create a markup language (for example, there are several industry-specific markup languages that allow different people in the industry to share data in a standard format). Since anyone can create a markup language, different markup languages end up using the same tag names, so namespaces help clarify which element belongs to which language. For example, you have seen the `<big>` and `<small>` XHTML elements already in this chapter; now imagine that a clothing company has a markup language for describing its products that includes the `<big>`, `<medium>`, and `<small>` elements for sizes. The purpose of a namespace is to specify which markup language the elements belong to.

The purpose of the namespace identifier for XHTML is to indicate that the markup in the document belongs to the XHTML 1.0 namespace. Therefore, the opening tag should look like this:

```
<html xmlns="http://www.w3.org/1999/xhtml">
```

While it is not strictly required in Transitional XHTML documents, it is a good practice to use it on all XHTML documents.

The `<html>` element can also carry the following attributes, which you will meet in the "Attribute Groups" section later in this chapter:

```
id dir lang xml:lang
```

> In earlier versions of HTML, a `version` attribute could be used to indicate which version of HTML the document is written in, although it is usually left off. XHTML documents should use the `DOCTYPE` declaration along with the `xmlns` attribute to indicate which version of XHTML they use.

The <head> Element

The `<head>` element is just a container for all other header elements. It is the first thing to appear after the opening `<html>` tag.

Each `<head>` element should contain a `<title>` element indicating the title of the document, although it may also contain any combination of the following elements, in any order:

- `<base>`, which you will meet in Chapter 2.
- `<object>`, which is designed to include images, JavaScript objects, Flash animations, MP3 files, QuickTime movies, and other types of files in a page. It is covered in Chapter 3.
- `<link>` to link to an external file, such as a style sheet or JavaScript file, as you will see in Chapter 7.
- `<style>` to include CSS rules inside the document; it is covered in Chapter 7.
- `<script>` for including script in the document, which you'll see in Chapter 11.
- `<meta>`, which includes information about the document such as keywords and a description, which are particularly helpful for search applications; this is covered in Chapter 13.

The opening `<head>` tag can carry the following attributes:

```
id dir lang xml:lang profile
```

The `profile` *attribute is not actually in use yet; the other attributes are covered in the "Attribute Groups" section later in this chapter.*

The <title> Element

You should specify a title for every page that you write using the `<title>` element (which, as you saw earlier in the chapter, is a child of the `<head>` element). It is presented and used in several ways:

- At the very top of a browser window (as you saw in the first example and Figure 1-1)
- As the default name for a bookmark in browsers such as IE, Firefox, and Safari
- By search engines that use its content to help index pages

Therefore, it is important to use a title that really describes the content of your site. For example, the homepage of this book should not just say "HomePage;" rather it should describe what your site is about. Rather than just saying Wrox Homepage, it is more helpful to write:

```
<title>Wrox: Programming Books, Learn XHTML, CSS, ASP.Net, PHP</title>
```

The test for a good title is whether visitors can tell what they will find on that page just by reading the title, without looking at the actual content of the page, and whether it uses words that people would use if they were going to search for this kind of information.

The `<title>` element should contain only the text for the title; it may not contain any other elements. The `<title>` element can carry the following attributes, which are covered in the following Attribute Groups section:

```
id dir lang xml:lang
```

The <body> Element

The `<body>` element appears after the `<head>` element and as you have already seen, it contains the part of the web page that you actually see in the main browser window, which is sometimes referred to as *body content*. The `<body>` element may carry all of the attributes from the *attribute groups* you are about to meet in the next section. You may also see the following deprecated attributes used on the `<body>` element in older HTML documents (they are covered in Appendix I):

```
background bgcolor alink link vlink text
```

You might also see several browser-specific attributes used on the `<body>` element; these are also covered in Appendix I:

```
language, topmargin, bottommargin, leftmargin, rightmargin, scroll,
bgproperties, marginheight, marginwidth
```

Attribute Groups

As you have seen, attributes live on the opening tag of an element and provide extra information about the element that carries them. All attributes consist of a *name* and a *value*; the name reflects a property of the element the attribute is describing, and the value is a value for that property. For example, the `xml:lang` attribute describes the language used within that element; a value such as `EN-US` would indicate that the language used inside the element is U.S. English. Many of the elements in XHTML can carry some or all of the attributes you will meet in this section; at first some of them may sound a little abstract, although they will make more sense as you see them used throughout the book. So don't worry if they do not make much sense at first.

There are three groups of attributes that many of the XHTML elements can carry:

- **Core attributes:** The `class`, `id`, and `title` attributes
- **Internationalization attributes:** The `dir`, `lang`, and `xml:lang` attributes
- **UI events:** Attributes associated with events such as `onclick`, `ondoubleclick`, `onmousedown`, `onmouseup`, `onmouseover`, `onmousemove`, `onmouseout`, `onkeypress`, `onkeydown`, and `onkeyup` (these are covered in more detail in Chapter 11)

> Together, the core attributes and the internationalization attributes are known as *universal attributes*.

Core Attributes

The four core attributes that can be used on the majority of XHTML elements (although not all) are:

```
id title class style
```

Throughout the rest of the book, where these attributes occasionally have special meaning for an element that differs from the description given here, I revisit them; otherwise their use can generally be described as you see in the subsections that follow.

The id Attribute

The `id` attribute can be used to uniquely identify any element within a page. You might want to uniquely identify an element so that you can link to that specific part in the document, or to specify that a CSS style or piece of JavaScript should apply to the content of just that one element within the document.

The syntax for the `id` attribute is as follows (where *string* is your chosen value for the attribute):

```
id="string"
```

For example, the `id` attribute could be used to distinguish between two paragraph elements, like so:

```
<p id="accounts">This paragraph explains the role of the accounts
department.</p>
<p id="sales">This paragraph explains the role of the sales department.</p>
```

Note that there are some special rules for the value of the `id` attribute. It must:

- Begin with a letter (A–Z or a–z) and can then be followed by any number of letters, digits (0–9), hyphens, underscores, colons, and periods (you may not start the value with a digit, hyphen, underscore, colon, or period).
- Remain unique within that document; no two `id` attributes may have the same value within one XHTML page.

Before the `id` attribute was introduced, the `name` attribute served a similar purpose in HTML documents, but its use was deprecated in HTML 4.01, and now you should generally use the `id` attribute in XHTML documents. If you need to use the `name` attribute, it is available in Transitional XHTML, but not Strict XHTML (unless specifically stated for a particular element).

The class Attribute

The `class` attribute is used to specify that an element belongs to a *class* of elements. For example, you might have a document that contains many paragraphs, and a few of those paragraphs might contain a summary of key points, in which case you could add a `class` attribute whose value is `summary` to the relevant `<p>` elements, to differentiate those paragraphs from the rest in the document.

```
<p class="summary">Summary goes here</p>
```

It is commonly used with CSS, so you will learn more about the use of the `class` attribute in Chapter 7, which introduces CSS. The syntax of the `class` attribute is as follows:

```
class="className"
```

The value of the attribute may also be a space-separated list of class names. For example:

```
class="className1 className2 className3"
```

The title Attribute

The `title` attribute gives a suggested title for the element. The syntax for the `title` attribute is as follows:

```
title="string"
```

The behavior of this attribute will depend upon the element that carries it, although it is often displayed as a tooltip or while the element is loading.

Not every element that *can* carry a `title` attribute really needs one, so when we meet an element that particularly benefits from use of this attribute, I will show you the behavior it has when used with that element.

The style Attribute (Deprecated)

The `style` attribute allows you to specify CSS rules within the element. You meet CSS in Chapter 7, but for now, here is an example of how it might be used:

```
<p style="font-family:arial; color:#FF0000;">Some text.</p>
```

As a general rule, however, it is best to avoid the use of this attribute. This attribute is marked as deprecated in XHTML 1.0 (which means it will be removed from future versions of HTML and XHTML). If you want to use CSS rules to govern how an element appears, it is better to use a separate style sheet instead. You will see each of these techniques in Chapter 7, which introduces CSS.

Internationalization

There are three internationalization attributes that help users write pages for different languages and character sets, and they are available to most (although not all) XHTML elements (which is important in multilingual documents).

```
dir lang xml:lang
```

We will look at each in turn next, but it is worth noting that even in current browsers, support for these attributes is still very patchy, therefore where possible you should specify a character set that will create text in the direction you require.

Here is the web address of a helpful W3C document that describes internationalization issues in greater detail, although we will briefly look at each of these attributes next:

```
http://www.w3.org/TR/i18n-html-tech-char/
```

The internationalization attributes are sometimes referred to as the i18n attributes, an odd name that comes from the draft-ietf-html-i18n specification in which they were first defined.

The dir Attribute

The `dir` attribute allows you to indicate to the browser the direction in which the text should flow; left to right or right to left. When you want to indicate the directionality of a whole document (or the majority of the document), it should be used with the `<html>` element rather than the `<body>` element for two reasons: Its use on the `<html>` element has better support in browsers, and it will apply to the header elements as well as those in the body. The `dir` attribute can also be used on elements within the body of the document if you want to change the direction of a small portion of the document.

The `dir` attribute can take one of two values, as you can see in the table that follows.

Value	Meaning
`ltr`	Left to right (the default value)
`rtl`	Right to left (for languages such as Hebrew or Arabic that are read right to left)

The lang Attribute

The `lang` attribute allows you to indicate the main language used in a document. It was kept in XHTML only for backwards compatibility with earlier versions of HTML, and has been replaced by the `xml:lang` attribute in new XHTML documents (which are covered in the next section). However, the XHTML recommendation suggests that you use both the `lang` and the `xml:lang` attributes on the `<html>` element in your XHTML 1.0 documents (to achieve maximum compatibility across different browsers).

The `lang` attribute was designed to offer language-specific display to users, although it has little effect in the main browsers. The real benefits of using the `lang` attribute are with search engines (which can tell the user which language the document is authored in), screen readers (which might need to pronounce different languages in different ways), and applications (which can alert users when they either do not support that language or it is a different language than their default language). When used with the `<html>` element the attribute applies to the whole document, although it can be used on other elements, in which case it just applies to the content of those elements.

The values of the `lang` attribute are ISO-639 standard two-character language codes. If you want to specify a dialect of the language, you can follow the language code with a dash and a subcode name. The table that follows offers some examples.

Value	Meaning
`ar`	Arabic
`en`	English
`en-us`	U. S. English
`zh`	Chinese

A list of language codes for most of the main languages in use today can be found in Appendix G.

The xml:lang Attribute

The `xml:lang` attribute is the XHTML replacement for the `lang` attribute. It is an attribute that is available in all languages that are written in XML (you may remember earlier in the chapter that I mentioned that XHTML was written in XML), which is why it is prefixed by the characters `xml:`. The value of the `xml:lang` attribute should be an ISO-639 country code like those listed in the previous section; a full list appears in Appendix G.

While it has no effect in the main browsers, other XML-aware applications and search engines may use this information, and it is good practice to include the `xml:lang` attribute in your documents. When used with the `<html>` element, it applies to the whole document, although it can be used on other elements, in which case it just applies to the content of those elements.

UI Events

The UI event attributes allow you to associate an *event*, such as a key press or the mouse being moved over an element, with a script (a portion of programming code that runs when the event occurs). For example, when someone moves a mouse over the content of a certain element you might use a script to make it change color.

You will meet the UI events in more detail in Chapter 12, although their names indicate quite clearly what event they are associated with; for example, `onclick` fires when a user clicks on that element's content, `onmousemove` fires when a mouse moves, and `onmouseout` fires when a user moves the mouse out of the content of a particular element.

There are ten events, known collectively as *common events*:

```
onclick ondoubleclick onmousedown onmouseup onmouseover onmousemove
onmouseout onkeypress onkeydown onkeyup
```

The `<body>` and `<frameset>` elements also have the following events for when a page opens or is closed:

```
onload onunload
```

Finally, there are a number of events that work with forms only (which are mentioned in Chapter 5 and again in Chapter 12):

```
onfocus onblur onsubmit onreset onselect onchange
```

Summary

In this chapter, you have seen how there are often similarities between web pages and print documents; for example, a news story in print or on the Web is made up of a headline, some paragraphs of text, maybe some subheadings, and one or more pictures. On the Web you need to explain the structure of these documents, and you do that using XHTML.

You have learned that the contents of a web page is marked up using elements that describe the structure of the document. These elements consist of an opening tag, a closing tag, and some content between the opening and closing tags. In order to alter some properties of elements, the opening tag may carry attributes, and attributes are always written as name value pairs. You know that XHTML can be thought of as the latest version of HTML, and that there are three different flavors of XHTML — in order to tell the browser which you are using, you can use a `DOCTYPE` declaration.

You also met a lot of new elements and learned the attributes they can carry. You've seen how every XHTML document should contain at least the `<html>`, `<head>`, `<title>`, and `<body>` elements, and how the `<html>` element should carry a namespace identifier.

The rest of this chapter dealt with elements that describe the structure of text:

- The six levels of headings: `<h1>`, `<h2>`, `<h3>`, `<h4>`, `<h5>`, and `<h6>`
- Paragraphs `<p>`, preformatted sections `<pre>`, line breaks `<br />`, and addresses `<address>`
- Presentational elements `<b>`, `<i>`, `<u>`, `<s>`, `<tt>`, `<sup>`, `<sub>`, `<strike>`, `<big>`, `<small>`, and `<hr />`
- Phrase elements such as `<em>`, `<strong>`, `<abbr>`, `<acronym>`, `<dfn>`, `<blockquote>`, `<q>`, `<cite>`, `<code>`, `<kbd>`, `<var>`, `<samp>`, and `<address>`
- Lists such as unordered lists using `<ul>` and `<li>`, ordered lists using `<ol>` and `<li>`, and definition lists using `<dl>`, `<dt>`, and `<dd>`
- Editing elements such as `<ins>` and `<del>`
- Grouping elements `<div>` and `<span>`

You will obviously use some of these elements more than others, but where an element fits the content you are trying to mark up, from paragraphs to addresses, you should try to use it, because structuring your text properly will help it last longer than if you just format it using line breaks and presentational elements.

Exercises

The answers to all of the exercises are in Appendix A.

1. Mark up the following sentence with the relevant presentational elements.

   The 1st time the **bold** man wrote in *italics*, he underlined several key words.

2. Mark up the following list, with inserted and deleted content:

   Ricotta pancake ingredients:

   - 1 ~~1/2~~ 3/4 cups ricotta
   - 3/4 cup milk
   - 4 eggs
   - 1 cup plain white flour

- ❑ 1 teaspoon baking powder
- ❑ ~~75g~~ 50g butter
- ❑ pinch of salt

3. You have already created the homepage for the Example Café site that we will be building throughout the book. You also created a recipes page. Now you need to create three more pages so that we can continue to build the site in coming chapters. Each page should start like the homepage, with a level 1 heading saying "Example Café," followed by the paragraph: "Welcome to Example Café. We will be developing this site throughout the book." After this:

    a. For a menu page, add a level 2 heading saying "Menu." This should be followed by a paragraph saying, "The menu will go here." Update the content of the <title> element to reflect that this page will feature the menus at the café. Save the file with the name menu.html.

    b. For an opening times page, add a level 2 heading saying "Opening hours." This should be followed by a paragraph saying "Details of opening hours and how to find us will go here." Update the <title> element to reflect that the page tells visitors opening hours and where to find the café. Save the file with the name opening.html.

    c. For the contact page, add a level 2 heading saying "Contact." This page should contain the address: 12 Sea View, Newquay, Cornwall, UK. Update the <title> element to reflect that the page tells visitors how to contact the cafe.

Links and Navigation

What really distinguishes the Web from other mediums is the way in which a web page can contain links (or *hyperlinks*) that you can click on to be taken from one page to another page. The link can be a word, phrase, or image.

When you link to another page in your own web site, the link is known as an *internal link*. When you link to a different site, it is known as an *external link*. In this chapter you will learn how to create both types of link. You will also see how you can link to a specific point within a page.

While you will learn the basics of linking from one Web page to another fairly quickly, it is also helpful to learn some other concepts, such as how to structure your site well by storing different files into separate folders or *directories*. Once you understand directory structure, you can link between pages of your own site using shorter links called *relative URLs*.

In this chapter, you learn the following:

- ❑ How to link between pages of your site
- ❑ How to link to other sites
- ❑ How to structure the folders on your web site
- ❑ How to link to specific parts of a page in your site

Basic Links

A link is specified using the `<a>` element. Anything between the opening `<a>` tag and the closing `</a>` tag becomes part of the link that users can click in a browser.

Linking to Other Web Pages

To link to another web page, the opening <a> tag must carry an attribute called href; the value of the href attribute is the name of the file you are linking to.

As an example, here is the <body> of the page ch02_eg01.html, which is in the code download for this chapter at www.wrox.com. This page contains a link to a second page called index.html:

```
<body>
   <p>Return to the <a href="index.html">home page</a>.</p>
</body>
```

As long as index.html is in the same folder as ch02_eg01.html, when you click the words "home page," the index.html page will be loaded into the same window, replacing the current ch02_eg01.html page. As you can see from Figure 2-1, the content of the <a> element forms the link.

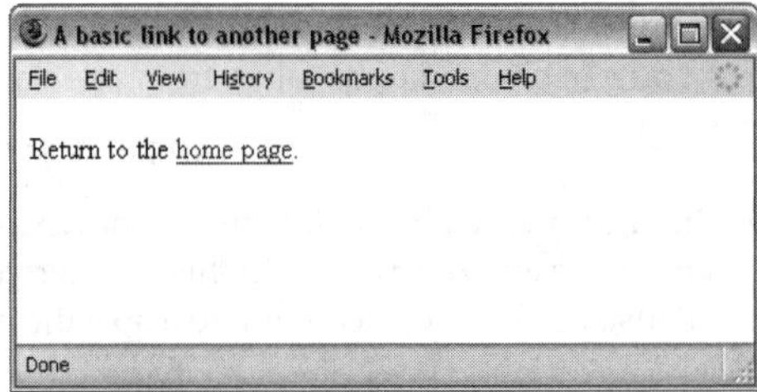

Figure 2-1

This is how the links for the download code for this chapter work. Remember that you can click the View menu in your browser and then select the View Source or Page Source option at any time to see what is going on in an XHTML page. Why not try it on the download code now?

If you want to link to a different site, you can use the <a> element again, but this time you specify the full web address for the page you want to link to rather than just the filename. Here is an example of a link that will take you to an external site, in this case the Wrox web site (ch02_eg02.html):

```
<body>
  <p>Why not visit the <a href="http://www.wrox.com/">Wrox web site</a>?</p>
</body>
```

As you can see, the value of the href attribute is what you would type into a browser if you wanted to visit the Wrox web site; the full web address is often referred to as a URL (Uniform Resource Locator).

When creating any link, you should try to make it concise and use words that let people know what they will see if they click on the link. One reason for this is that links are usually presented in a different color than the surrounding text, which makes them stick out more than the text around them. As a result, many people *scan* pages for links when they want to go to the next page without really reading the entire page. Therefore, people are more likely to keep exploring your web site if the links are easy to read and have a better explanation than just "click here."

Many web designers also use images inside the <a> element, which is something you will see in the next chapter. When you use an image, you should make sure that the image gives a clear indication of where the link will take you.

You can also use the `title` attribute on a link; the value of the `title` attribute should be a description of what the link will take you to, which will be displayed in a tooltip when you hover over the link. This can be especially helpful if you do use an image for a link.

The following is a link to the Google homepage (`ch02_eg03.html`):

```
<p><a href="http://www.Google.com/" title="Search the Web with
Google">Google</a>
is a very popular search engine.</p>
```

Figure 2-2 shows the `title` attribute, which gives further information about the link to the user, when the mouse is held over the link.

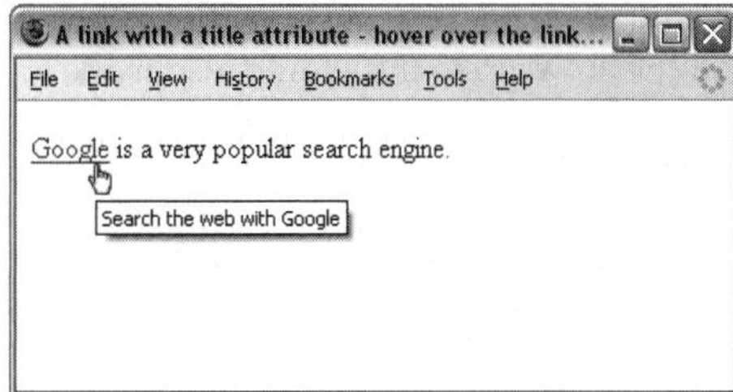

Figure 2-2

You should be aware that everything inside the <a> element gets rendered as a link, including white space around the text or images. Therefore it is best to avoid spaces directly after an opening <a> tag or before the closing </a> tag. For example, consider the following link with spaces just inside the <a> element (`ch02_eg04.html`):

```
Why not visit the<a href="http://www.wrox.com/"> Wrox Web site </a>?
```

As you can see in Figure 2-3, these spaces in the link will be underlined.

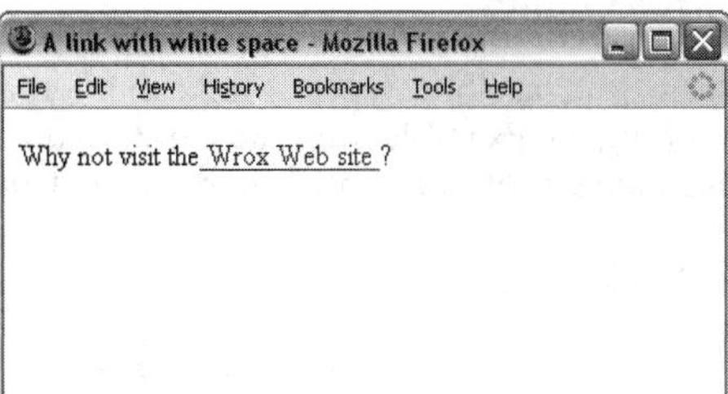

Figure 2-3

It is far better to use white space outside of these tags, like so:

```
Why not visit the <a href="http://www.wrox.com/">Wrox Web site</a>?
```

Of course, you should still have spaces between words inside the <a> element; it's just best if they are not inside the beginning or end of the link.

Linking to E-mail Addresses

You've probably seen a link that shows an e-mail address, which when clicked on opens a new e-mail in your e-mail program, ready for you to send an e-mail to that address.

To create a link to an e-mail address, you need to use the following syntax with the <a> element:

```
<a href="mailto:name@example.com">name@example.com</a>
```

Here, the value of the `href` attribute starts with the keyword `mailto`, followed by a colon, and then the e-mail address you want the mail sent to. As with any other link, the content of the <a> element is the visible part of the link shown in the browser, so this would also work:

```
<a href="mailto:name@example.com">E-mail us</a>.
```

There is one drawback to putting your e-mail address on a web page: some less scrupulous inhabitants of the Web use little programs to automatically search web sites for e-mail addresses. After they have found e-mail addresses on web sites, they will start sending spam to those addresses.

There are alternatives to creating a link to an e-mail address:

- Use an e-mail form that visitors fill out instead, because automated programs cannot use contact forms to collect e-mail addresses. The drawback is that an e-mail form requires a script to run on the web server (written in a language such as ASP.NET or PHP). Chapter 5 provides an example of an e-mail form.
- Write your e-mail address into the page using JavaScript (covered in Chapter 13). The idea behind this technique is that the programs that scour the Web for e-mail addresses cannot read the JavaScript version of an address.

Try It Out Creating Simple Links

Now it's your turn to create a page that has three types of link: an internal link, an external link, and an e-mail link. We will be developing the Example Café site we started in the last chapter, so open up the `contact.html` page that is in the sample application folder from Chapter 1:

1. Check that the page looks like this:

```
<?xml version="1.0" encoding="iso-8859-1"?>
<!DOCTYPE html PUBLIC "-//W3C//DTD XHTML 1.0 Transitional//EN"
"http://www.w3.org/TR/xhtml1/DTD/xhtml1-transitional.dtd">
<html xmlns="http://www.w3.org/1999/xhtml">
<head>
```

```
  <title>Example Cafe - community cafe in Newquay, Cornwal, UK</title>
  <meta http-equiv="Content-Type" content="text/html; charset=iso-8859-1" />
</head>

<body>

  <h1>EXAMPLE CAFE</h1>
  <p>Welcome to Example Cafe. We will be developing this site throughout
     the book.</p>

  <h2>Contact</h2>
  <p><address>12 Sea View, Newquay, Cornwall, UK</address></p>

</body>
</html>
```

2. We are going to start by adding navigation between the pages of the site. To start, replace the first paragraph (after the `<h1>` element) with links to the three other pages of the site. Each `<a>` element should contain the name of the page it links to, as shown here. We will group these links inside a `<div>` element:

```
<h1>EXAMPLE CAFE</h1>
  <div>
    <a href="">HOME</a>
    <a href="">MENU</a>
    <a href="">RECIPES</a>

  </div>
```

3. Add the name of the contact page, but do not make it a link (because this is the page that the user is already on, they do not need a link to it):

```
<h1>EXAMPLE CAFE</h1>
  <div>
    <a href="">HOME</a>
    <a href="">MENU</a>
    <a href="">RECIPES</a>
    CONTACT
  </div>
```

4. Add the filename of each of these pages as the value of the `href` attribute:

```
<h1>EXAMPLE CAFE</h1>
  <div>
    <a href="index.html">HOME</a>
    <a href="menu.html">MENU</a>
    <a href="recipes.html">RECIPES</a>
    CONTACT
</div>
```

Since these pages are all in the same folder, you only need to specify the file name; you do not need a full URL.

5. Under the address, add a link to the following page on Google Maps, like so: `info@examplecafe.com`:

```
<p><a href="http://maps.google.com/maps?q=newquay">Find us on Google
Maps</a></p>
```

This time the value of the `href` attribute is the web address you would type into your browser in order to find a map of Newquay in Google Maps.

6. Under the address, add a link to send an e-mail to `info@examplecafe.com`:

```
<p><a href="mailto:info@examplecafe.com">Mail Example Cafe</a></p>
```

This time the value of the `href` attribute begins with `mailto:` and this is followed by the e-mail address.

7. Save this file as `contact.html` in the same folder as the sample application for this chapter. Then open it up and take a look at it in your browser. You should end up with something that looks like Figure 2-4.

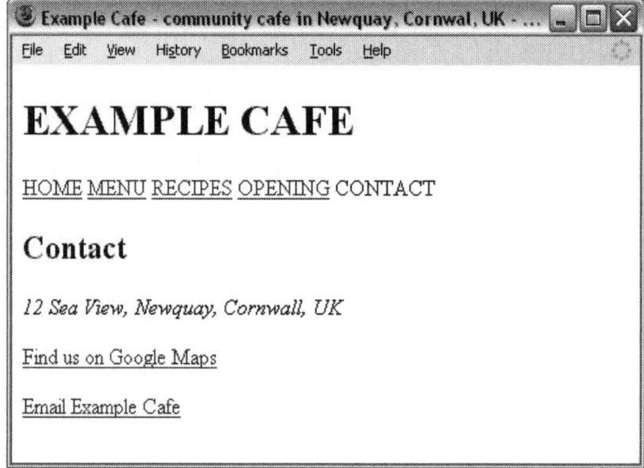

Figure 2-4

You have now seen how to create basic types of links, and you are ready to delve into the more in-depth topics. But first you need to read through a few pages that explain more about how you should organize the files in your web site into folders, and also understand the anatomy of a URL (the address that identifies pages and other resources on your web site).

Understanding Directories and Directory Structures

A *directory* is simply another name for a folder on a web site; in the same way that your hard drive contains different folders, a web site can be said to contain directories. Usually you will find that a web site contains several directories, and that each directory contains different parts of a web site. For example, a big site with several subsections will have a separate directory for each section of that site, and also different directories for different types of files (for example, images may live in one directory and style sheets in another).

In the same way that you probably organize the files on your hard drive into separate folders, it is important to organize the files on yourweb site into directories so that you can find what you are looking for more easily and keep control of all the files. As you can imagine, if all the files used in a web site resided in the same directory, that directory would quickly get very large and complicated.

Figure 2-5 shows an example directory structure for a news site, with separate folders for each section. Note also how the Music section has its own folders for subsections about Features, MP3s, and Reviews. In addition, the main folder has separate folders for different types of files used in the site: images, scripts, and style sheets.

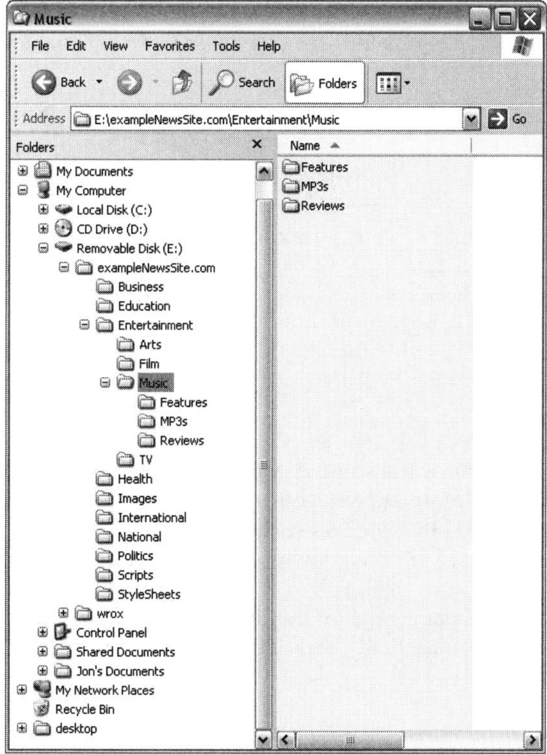

Figure 2-5

When you start to build any web site you should create a good directory structure that can withstand growth; it's surprising how a small web site can quickly grow and contain many more files than you initially imagined.

As you learn about linking, it's helpful to learn some of the terms that are used in describing directory structures and the relationships between directories, so look back at Figure 2-5 to see an example directory structure:

- The *root directory* (or root folder) is the main directory that holds the whole of you web site; in this case, it is called exampleNewsSite.com.
- A *subdirectory* is a directory that is within another directory. Here, Film is a subdirectory of Entertainment.
- A *parent directory* is a directory that contains another directory. Here, Entertainment is the parent directory of Arts, Film, Music, and TV.

Understanding URLs

A URL or *Uniform Resource Locator* specifies where you can find a resource on the web; you are probably most used to thinking of them as web addresses. As you move around the Web, you will see the URL of each web page in the address bar of your browser.

If you look at the example URL in Figure 2-6, there are three key parts to the URL: the scheme, the host address, and the filepath.

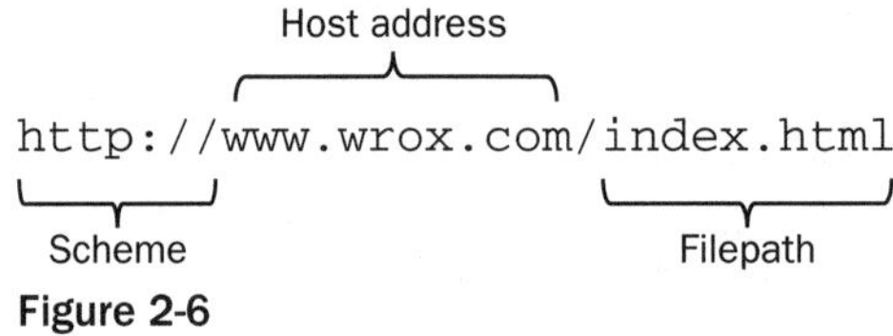

Figure 2-6

Let's look at each of these in turn.

The *scheme* identifies the way a file is transmitted. Most web pages use something called the *Hypertext Transfer Protocol* (HTTP) to pass information to you, which is why most web pages start with `http://`, although you might have noticed other prefixes such as `https://` when doing banking online (which is a more secure form of http) or `ftp://` when downloading large files.

The *host address* is usually the domain name for the site, e.g., `wrox.com`. Often you will see www before the domain name, although it is not actually part of the domain name itself. The host address can also be a number called an IP address.

All computers connected to the Internet can be found using an IP address. An IP address is a set of up to 12 digits separated by a period (full stop) symbol. When you enter a domain name into a browser, behind the scenes the name gets converted into the IP address for the computer(s) that stores the web site.

This is done by consulting a domain name server (DNS), which keeps a directory of domain names and the corresponding IP addresses.

The *filepath* always begins with a forward slash character, and may consist of one or more directory names (remember, a directory is just another name for a folder on the web server). The filepath may end with a filename at the end. Here, `BeginningXHTML.html` is the filename:

```
/books/BeginningXHTML.html
```

The filepath will usually correspond to the directory structure of the web site, so in this case the `BeginningXHTML.html` page would be found in a directory called `books`.

In fact it is not just web pages that have their own URLs; every file on the Web, including each image, has its own URL. So the filename could be an image rather than an XHTML page.

If a filename is not given, the web server will usually do one of three things (depending upon how it is configured):

- ❑ Look for a default file and return that. For web sites written in XHTML, the default file is usually `index.html`; if no filepath is specified, the server will look for a file called `index.html` in the root folder, or if a directory is specified it will look for an `index.html` file in that directory.
- ❑ Offer a list of files in that directory.
- ❑ Show a message saying that the page cannot be found or that you cannot browse the files in a folder.

When linking to pages on your own web site, you do not need to use all of three parts of the URL — you can just use the filepath and filename, as you will see in the next section.

Absolute and Relative URLs

An *absolute URL* contains everything you need to uniquely identify a particular file on the Internet. This is what you would type into the address bar of your browser in order to find a page. For example, to get the page about film on the fictional news site you met earlier in the chapter, you might type in the following URL (you may find it helpful to refer back to Figure 2-5 to see how the filepath corresponds to the directory structure):

```
http://www.exampleNewsSite.com/Entertainment/Film/index.html
```

As you can see, absolute URLs can quickly get quite long, and every page of a web site can contain many links. When linking to a page on your own site, however, you can use a shorthand form: relative URLs.

A *relative URL* indicates where the resource is in relation to the current page. The examples earlier in this chapter, which link to another page in the same directory, are examples of relative URLs. You can also use relative URLs to specify files in different directories. For example, imagine you are looking at the homepage for the entertainment section of the following fictional news site:

```
http://www.exampleNewsSite.com/Entertainment/index.html
```

You want to add a link to the index pages for each of the subsections: Film, TV, Arts, and Music. Rather than including the full URL for each page, you can use a relative URL. For example:

```
Film/index.html
TV/index.html
Arts/index.html
Music/index.html
```

As I am sure you agree, this is a lot quicker than having to write out the following:

```
http://www.exampleNewsSite.com/Entertainment/Film/index.html
http://www.exampleNewsSite.com/Entertainment/TV/index.html
http://www.exampleNewsSite.com/Entertainment/Arts/index.html
http://www.exampleNewsSite.com/Entertainment/Music/index.html
```

You might be interested to know that your web browser still requests the full URL, not the shortened relative URL, but it is the browser that is actually doing the work of turning the relative URLs into full absolute URLs.

Another benefit to using relative URLs within your site is that you can develop the site on your desktop or laptop without having bought a domain name. You can also change your domain name or copy a subsection of one site over to a new domain name without having to change all of the links, because each link is relative to other pages within the same site.

Relative URLs work only on links within the same web site; you cannot use them to link to pages on other domain names.

The subsections that follow provide a summary of the different types of relative URLs you can use.

Same Directory

When you want to link to, or include, a resource from the same directory, you can just use the name of that file. For example, to link from the homepage (`index.html`) to the "contact us" page (`contactUs.html`), you can use the following:

```
contactUs.html
```

Because the file lives in the same folder, you do not need to specify anything else.

Subdirectory

The Film, TV, Arts, and Music directories from Figure 2-5 were all subdirectories of the Entertainment directory. If you are writing a page in the Entertainment directory, you can create a link to the index page of the subdirectories like so:

```
Film/index.html
TV/index.html
Arts/index.html
Music/index.html
```

You must include the name of the subdirectory, followed by a forward slash character, and the name of the page you want to link to.

For each additional subdirectory, just add the name of the directory followed by a forward slash character. So, if you are creating a link from a page in the root folder of the site (such as the site's main homepage), use a relative URL such as the following to reach the same pages:

```
Entertainment/Film/index.html
Entertainment/TV/index.html
Entertainment/Arts/index.html
Entertainment/Music/index.html
```

Parent Directory

If you want to create a link from one directory to its parent directory (the directory that it is in), you use the `../` notation of two periods or dots followed by a forward slash character. For example, from a page in the Music directory to a page in the Entertainment directory, your relative URL looks like this:

```
../index.html
```

If you want to link from the Music directory to the root directory, you repeat the notation:

```
../../index.html
```

Each time you repeat the `../` notation, you go up another directory.

From the Root

It is also possible to indicate a file relative to the root folder of the site. So, if you wanted to link to the `contactUs.html` page from any page within the site, you use its path preceded by a forward slash. For example, if the Contact Us page is in the root folder, you just need to enter:

```
/contactUs.html
```

Alternatively, you can link to the Music section's index page from anywhere within that site using the following:

```
/Entertainment/Music/index.html
```

The forward slash at the start indicates the root directory, and then the path from there is specified.

The <base> Element

As I mentioned earlier, when a browser comes across a relative URL, it actually transforms the relative URL into a full absolute URL. The `<base>` element allows you to specify a base URL for a page that all relative URLs will be added to when the browser comes across a relative URL.

You specify the base URL as the value of the `href` attribute on the `<base>` element. For example, you might indicate a base URL for `http://www.exampleSite2.com/` as follows:

```
<base href="http://www.exampleSite2.com/" />
```

In this case, a relative URL like this one:

```
Entertainment/Arts/index.html
```

ends up with the browser requesting this page:

```
http://www.exampleSite2.com/Entertainment/Arts/index.html
```

Apart from the `href` attribute, the only other attribute a `<base>` element can carry is the `id` attribute.

Creating Links with the <a> Element

You have already seen examples of using the `<a>` element to create links. For the rest of the chapter we'll look more closely at the `<a>` element, and you'll see how it can be used to link to a specific part of a page.

As with all journeys, links have a starting point known as the *source*, and a finishing point known as the *destination*; in XHTML both points are called *anchors*. Each link that you see on a page that you can click is a *source anchor*, created using the `<a>` element. You can also use the `<a>` element to create markers in parts of your pages that allow you to link directly to that part of the page. These markers are called *destination anchors*.

Creating a Source Anchor with the href Attribute

The source anchor is what most people think of when talking about links on the Web — whether the link contains text or an image. It is something you can click expecting, to be taken somewhere else.

As you have already seen, any text contained between the opening `<a>` tag and closing `</a>` tag forms part of the link that a user can click on. The URL the user should be taken to is specified as the value of the `href` attribute.

For example, when you click the words `Wrox Web site` (which you can see are inside the `<a>` element) the link takes you to `http://www.wrox.com/`:

```
Why not visit the <a href="http://www.wrox.com/">Wrox Web site</a> to
find out about some of our other books?
```

If the following link were placed on the homepage of the fictional news site we have been looking at, it would take you to the main Film page of that site:

```
You can see more films in the <a href="Entertainment/Film/index.html">film
section</a>.
```

By default, the link looks something like the one shown in Figure 2-7, underlined and in blue text.

You need to specify a destination anchor only if you want to link to a specific part of a page, as described in the next section.

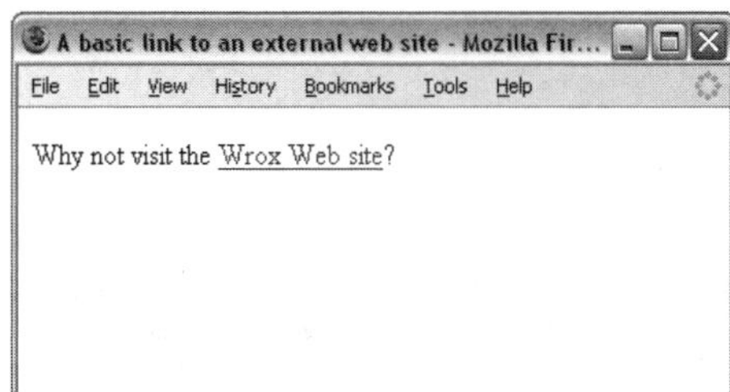

Figure 2-7

Creating a Destination Anchor Using the name and id Attributes (Linking to a Specific Part of a Page)

If you have a long web page, you might want to link to a specific part of that page in order to save the user from having to scroll up and down the page to find the relevant part. The *destination anchor* allows the page author to mark specific points in a page that a source anchor can point to.

Common examples of linking to a specific part of a page that you might have seen used on web pages include:

- "Back to top" links at the bottom of a long page
- A list of contents on a page that takes the user to the relevant section of that page
- Links within text to footnotes or definitions

You create a destination anchor using the <a> element again, but when it acts as a destination anchor rather than using an href attribute, you use the id attribute.

If you are looking at the source code of some older web pages, you may see a name attribute used as well, or even instead of the id attribute. You may remember from Chapter 1 that the name and id attributes were two of the universal attributes that most elements can carry. The id attribute is now the preferred way to create a destination anchor, but it was only introduced in version 4 of HTML, and the name attribute was used to perform the same function in previous versions.

By way of example, imagine that you have a long page with a main heading and several subheadings. The whole page does not fit on the screen at once, forcing the user to scroll, so you want to add links at the top of the page that take readers directly to each of the section headings on that page.

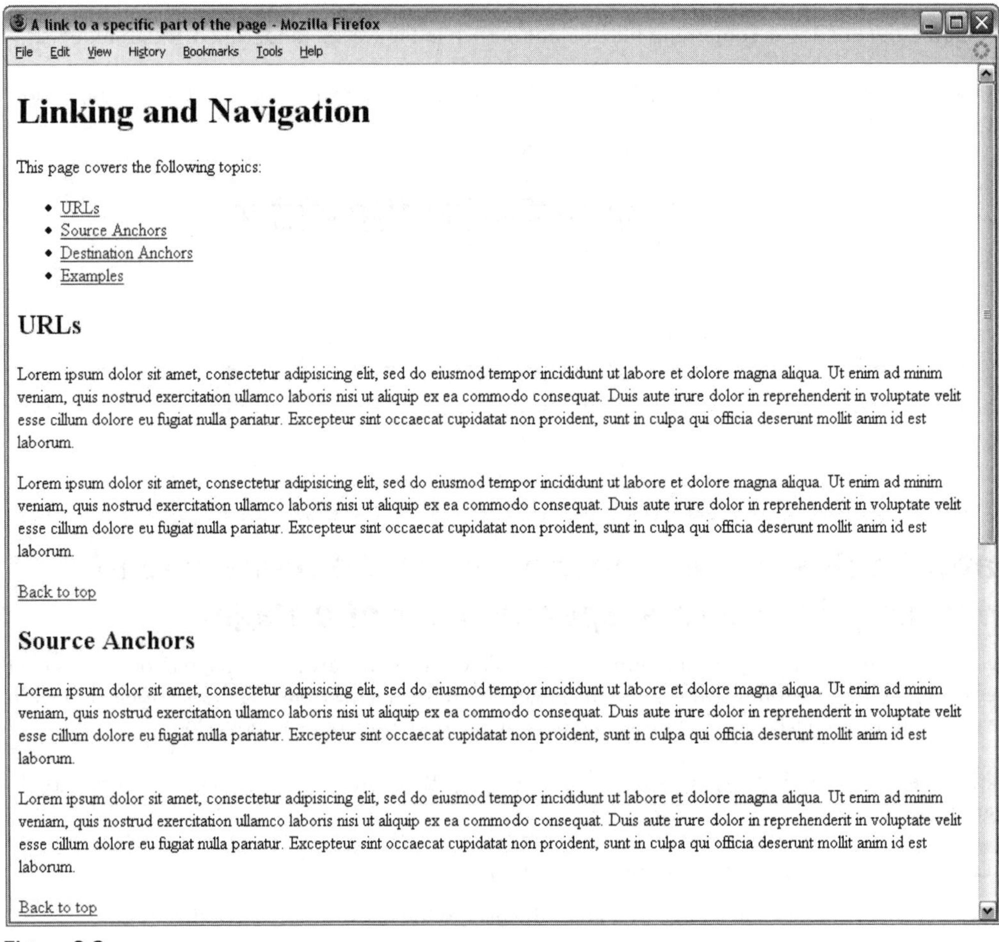

Figure 2-8

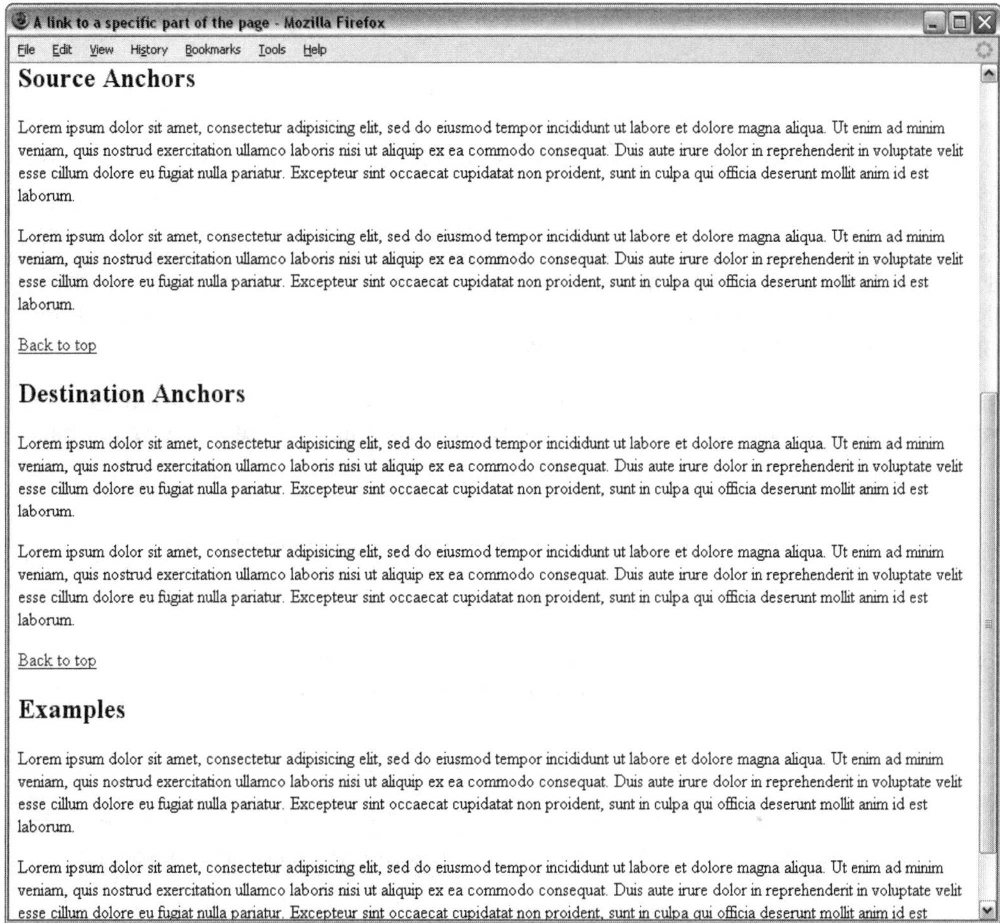

Figure 2-9

Before you can create links to each section of the page (using the source anchors), you have to add the destination anchors. Here you can see that inside the `<h2>` subheading elements, there is an `<a>` element with the `id` attribute whose value identifies each section (remember that a page should not contain two `id` attributes that have the same value):

```
<h1>Linking and Navigation</h1>
<h2><a id="URL">URLs</a></h2>
<h2><a id="SourceAnchors">Source Anchors</a></h2>
<h2><a id="DestinationAnchors">Destination Anchors</a></h2>
<h2><a id="Examples">Examples</a></h2>
```

With destination anchors in place, it's now possible to add source anchors to link to these sections. To link to a particular section, the value of the `href` attribute in the source anchor should be the same as the value of the `id` attribute on the corresponding destination element, preceded by a pound or hash sign (`#`).

```
<p>This page covers the following topics:
  <ul>
   <li><a href="#URL">URLs</a></li>
   <li><a href="#SourceAnchors">Source Anchors</a></li>
   <li><a href="#DestinationAnchors">Destination Anchors</a></li>
   <li><a href="#Examples">Examples</a></li>
  </ul>
</p>
```

If you take a look at Figure 2-8, you can see how the page has several links to the sections of the page; and in Figure 2-9, you can see what happens when the user clicks on the second link and is taken directly to that section of the page. You can see the full code for this example in the download code for this chapter, available from the Wrox web site; the file is `ch02_eg06.html`.

It is important for destination anchors to always have some content; otherwise some browsers will not find the destination. For example, you should not use the following to indicate the top of the page:

```
<a id="top"></a>
```

Rather, you should put this around the main heading or some other content, like so:

```
<h1><a id="top">Linking and Navigation</a></h1>
```

If someone wanted to link to a specific part of this web page from a different web site (such as the section on Source Anchors), he or she would add the full URL for the page, followed by the pound or hash sign and then the value of the `id` attribute, as follows:

```
http://www.example.com/HTML/links.html#SourceAnchors
```

> The value of a `name` or `id` attribute should be unique within the page, and source anchors should use the same combination of uppercase and lowercase characters as used in the destination anchors.

The <a> Element's Other Attributes

The `<a>` element can carry several attributes that we have not yet met. While these attributes are not used as much as those covered up to this point, for completeness it is worth quickly looking at them.

The `<a>` element supports all of the universal attributes, the UI event attributes, and the following attributes:

```
accesskey charset coords href hreflang rel rev shape style tabindex target
type
```

The accesskey Attribute

The `accesskey` attribute creates a keyboard shortcut that can be used to activate a link. For example, if you gave the `accesskey` attribute a value of `t`, when the user presses the T key along with either the Alt or Ctrl key (depending on the operating system), the link gets activated.

In some browsers, when a link is activated the browser immediately follows the link. In some other browsers, the link is just highlighted, and the user has to press the Enter (or Return) key for the link to be followed.

The `accesskey` attribute should be specified on the source anchor. For example, if you want to follow a link to the top of the page when the user presses the T key on his keyboard (with either Alt or Ctrl) you use the `accesskey` attribute like so:

```
<a id="bottom" accesskey="t">Back to top</a>
```

Note that the key is case-insensitive. You will see more about the `accesskey` attribute (and some examples) when you look at forms in Chapter 5.

The charset Attribute

The `charset` attribute indicates the character encoding of the document the URL points to. It is typically used only when you are linking to a page in a different language that uses a different character set.

The value must be a string that identifies the character set, such as UTF-8 or ISO-8859-1. (See Appendix E for the list of character sets.) This example links to a document in the Japanese character set:

```
<a href="http://www.amazon.co.jp/" charset="ISO-2022-JP">Amazon Japan</a>
```

This is particularly useful when linking to foreign language sites written in character encodings that some users might not be able to understand (or might not even be able to view — for example, not all American computers have the characters installed that are required in order to view Japanese text).

The coords Attribute

The `coords` attribute is designed for use on a source anchor when it contains an image. It allows you to create something known as an *image map*, which is where different parts of the same image link to different places. The value of the `coords` attribute will be a set of *x* and *y* coordinates that indicates which part of the image should follow the link. You will learn more about using images as links in Chapter 3.

The hreflang Attribute

The `hreflang` attribute indicates which language the page you are linking to is written in. It's designed to be used when linking to a page in a different language from the current document, and the value of this attribute is a two-letter *language code*. For example:

```
<a href="http://www.amazon.co.jp/" hreflang="JA">Amazon Japan</a>
```

Appendix G lists the language codes that are possible values for this attribute.

The rel Attribute

The `rel` attribute is used on the source anchor to indicate the relationship between the current document and the resource specified by the `href` attribute. The major browsers do not currently make any use of this attribute, although it is possible that automated applications could be written to use this information. For example, the following link uses the `rel` attribute to indicate that its destination is a glossary of terms used in the document:

```
For more information, please read the  <a href="#glossary"
rel="glossary">glossary</a>.
```

See the table that follows for possible values of the `rel` attribute.

Value	Description
`toc` (or `contents`)	A document that is a table of contents for the current document
`index`	A document that is an index for the current document
`glossary`	A document containing a glossary of terms that relate to the current document
`copyright`	A document containing the copyright statement for the current document
`start`	A document that is the first in a series of ordered documents, of which this is one document
`next`	A document that is the next in a series of ordered documents, of which this is one document
`prev` (or `previous`)	A document that is the previous in a series of ordered documents, of which this is one document
`help`	A document that helps users understand or navigate the page and/or site
`chapter`	A document that acts as a chapter within a collection of documents
`section`	A document that acts as a section in a collection of documents
`subsection`	A document that acts as a subsection in a collection of documents
`appendix`	A document that acts as an appendix in a collection of documents

The rev Attribute

The `rev` attribute provides the same role as the `rel` attribute but is used on the destination anchor to describe the relation between the destination and the source. It is currently not supported by major browsers.

The shape Attribute

If you want to create an image map, the `shape` attribute can be used to indicate the shape of an area that becomes a clickable *hotspot*. The `shape` attribute is covered in detail in Chapter 3, where you learn how to create image maps.

The tabindex Attribute

To understand the `tabindex` attribute, you need to know what it means for an element to gain *focus*. Any element that a user can interact with can gain focus. If the user clicks the Tab key on his or her keyboard when a page has loaded, the browser moves focus between the parts of the page that the user can interact with. The parts of the page that can gain focus include links and some parts of forms (such as the boxes that allow you to enter text). When a link receives focus, and the user presses Enter on the keyboard, the link is activated.

You can see focus working on the Google web site; if you repeatedly press the Tab key, you should see focus pass between links on the page. After it has passed across each link in turn, it goes onto the box where you enter search terms, across the site's buttons, and usually ends up back where you typed in the URL. Then it cycles around the same elements again as you keep pressing Tab.

The `tabindex` attribute allows you to specify the order in which, when the Tab key is pressed, the links (or form controls) obtain focus. So, when the user clicks the Tab key, you may want the focus to land on the key items on the page that the user might want to interact with (skipping some of the less-used features).

The value of the `tabindex` attribute is a number between 0 and 32767. A link whose `tabindex` attribute has a value of `1` receives focus before a link with a `tabindex` value of 20 (and if a value of `0` is used, the links appear in the order in which they appear in the document). Chapter 5 shows some examples of the `tabindex` being used with forms.

The target Attribute

By default, when you use the `<a>` element to create a link, the document you are linking to will open in the same browser window. If you want the link to open in a new browser window, you can use the `target` attribute with a value of `_blank`.

```
<a href="Page2.html" target="_blank">Page 2</a>
```

The title Attribute

As mentioned at the start of the chapter, it is good to use a `title` attribute on any links that contain images. It can also help provide additional information to visitors in the form of a visual text tooltip in most browsers or an auditory clue in voice browsers for the visually impaired. Figure 2-2 near the beginning of this chapter showed you what the `title` attribute looks like in Firefox when a user hovers over the link.

The type Attribute

The `type` attribute specifies the MIME type of the link. MIME types can be compared to file extensions, but are more universally accepted across different operating systems. For example, an HTML page would have the MIME type `text/html`, whereas a JPEG image would have the MIME type `img/jpeg`. (Appendix H includes a list of common MIME types.)

The following is an example of the type attribute being used to indicate that the document the link points to is an HTML document:

```
<a href="index.html" type="text/html">Index</a>
```

Theoretically, the browser could use the information in the type attribute to either display it differently or indicate to the user what the format of the destination is, although none use it at present.

Try It Out Creating Links Within Pages

Now it's your turn to try making a long page with links between different parts of the page. In this example, you are going to create the menu for our Example Café. So open the `menu.html` page from the sample application in your text editor or authoring tool:

1. The page should look like this when you begin:

```
<?xml version="1.0" ?>
<!DOCTYPE html PUBLIC "-//W3C//DTD XHTML 1.0 Strict//EN"
    "http://www.w3.org/TR/xhtml1/DTD/xhtml1-strict.dtd">
<html xmlns="http://www.w3.org/1999/xhtml" lang="en">

<head>
  <title>Example Cafe - community cafe in Newquay, Cornwal, UK</title>
</head>
<body>
  <h1>EXAMPLE CAFE</h1>
  <p>Welcome to Example cafe. We will be developing this site throughout
     the book.</p>

  <h2>Menu</h2>
  <p>The menu will go here.</p>
</body>
</html>
```

2. After the heading, replace the first paragraph with the links for the navigation, just like the ones you created in the last Try It Out for the `contact.html` page. The only difference this time is that the `CONTACT` option will be a link, but the `MENU` option will not be a link.

```
<a href="index.html">HOME</a>
MENU
<a href="recipes.html">RECIPES</a>
<a href="opening.html">OPENING</a>
<a href="contact.html">CONTACT</a>
```

3. Below this, add the headings for the different courses on offer. Each heading should have a destination anchor so that you can link directly to that part of the page, and the value of the `id` attribute will describe that section. The main heading also needs a destination anchor because it will be used for "Back to top" links. Remember that destination anchors require some content, so these anchors contain the text for the heading:

```
<h1><a id="top">Example Cafe Menu</a></h1>
<h2><a id="starters">Starters</a></h2>
<h2><a id="mains">Main Courses</a></h2>
<h2><a id="desserts">Desserts</a></h2>
```

4. Under the heading for the Example Café Menu, add links to the destination anchors for each course. These should go inside a <p> element:

```
<p><a href="#">Starters</a> |  <a href="#mains">Main Courses</a> | <a
href="#desserts">Desserts</a></p>
```

5. At the bottom of the page, you will have a note that states any items marked with a letter v are suitable for vegetarians. Links next to vegetarian items will point to this note, so it needs to have a destination anchor:

```
<p><a id="vege">Items marked with a (v) are suitable for vegetarians.</a></p>
```

6. You can just add in the items on the menu in a bulleted list. Note how the vegetarian items have a link down to the description of vegetarian dishes. Don't forget to add the "Back to top" links under each list.

```
<h2><a id="starters">Starters</a></h2>
<ul>
  <li>Chestnut and Mushroom Goujons (<a href="#vege">v</a>)</li>
  <li>Goat Cheese Salad  (<a href="#vege">v</a>)</li>
  <li>Honey Soy Chicken Kebabs</li>
  <li>Seafood Salad</li>
</ul>
<p><small><a href="#top">Back to top</a></small></p>

<h2><a id="mains">Main courses</a></h2>
<ul>
  <li>Spinach and Ricotta Roulade (<a href="#vege">v</a>)</li>
  <li>Beef Tournados with Mustard and Dill Sauce</li>
  <li>Roast Chicken Salad</li>
  <li>Icelandic Cod with Parsley Sauce</li>
  <li>Mushroom Wellington (<a href="#vege">v</a>)</li>
</ul>
<p><small><a href="#top">Back to top</a></small></p>

<h2><a id="desserts">Desserts</a></h2>
<ul>
  <li>Lemon Sorbet (<a href="#vege">v</a>)</li>
  <li>Chocolate Mud Pie (<a href="#vege">v</a>)</li>
  <li>Pecan Pie (<a href="#vege">v</a>)</li>
  <li>Selection of Fine Cheeses from Around the World</li>
</ul>
<p><small><a href="#top">Back to top</a></small></p>
```

7. Save your example as `menu.html` and take a look at it in your browser. You should end up with something that looks like Figure 2-10.

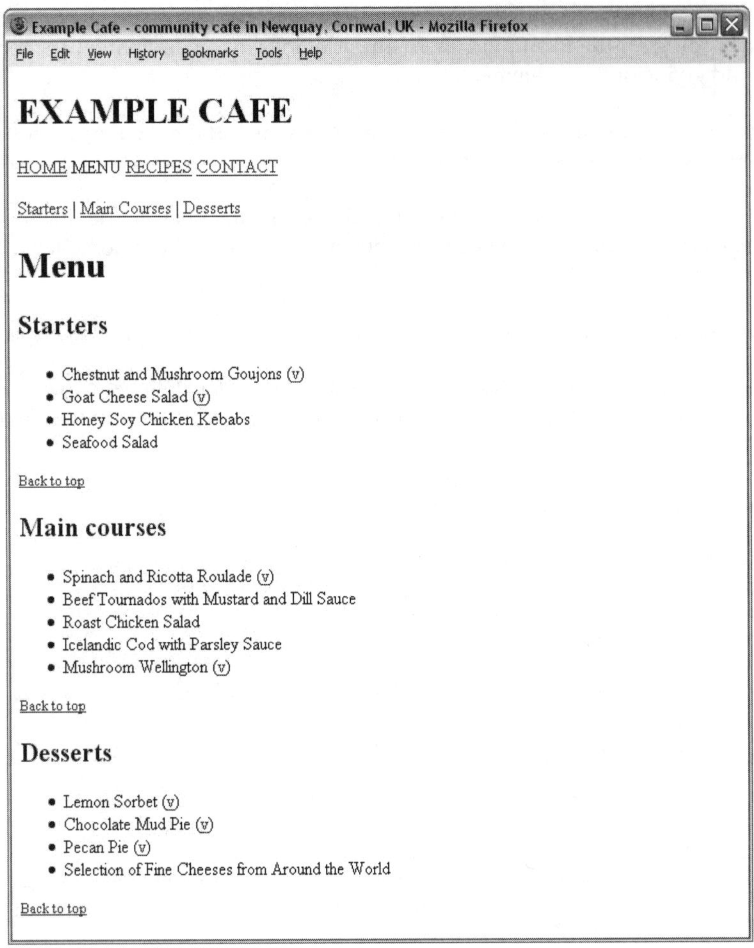

Figure 2-10

Advanced E-mail Links

As you saw at the beginning of the chapter, you can make a link open up the user's default e-mail editor, and automatically address an e-mail to you — or any other e-mail address you give. This is done like so:

```
<a href="mailto:info@example.org">info@example.org</a>
```

You can also specify some other parts of the message, such as the subject, body, and e-mail addresses that should be CC'd or BCC'd on the message.

To control other properties of the e-mail, you place a question mark after the e-mail address and then use name/value pairs to specify the additional properties. The name and the value are separated by an equal sign.

For example, to make the subject line of the e-mail *Inquiry*, you would add the `subject` property name followed by an equals sign, and then the term `Inquiry`, like so:

```
<a href="mailto:info@example.org?subject=Inquiry">
```

You can specify more than one property by separating the name/value pairs with an ampersand. Here you can see that the subject and a CC address have been added in:

```
<a href="mailto:info@example.org?subject=XHTML&cc=sales@example.org"></a>
```

The table that follows includes a full list of properties you can add.

Property	Purpose
`subject`	Adds a subject line to the e-mail; you can add this to encourage the user to use a subject line that makes it easier to recognize where the mail has come from.
`body`	Adds a message into the body of the e-mail, although you should be aware that users would be able to alter this message.
`cc`	Sends a carbon copy of the mail to the CC'd address; the value must be a valid e-mail address. If you want to provide multiple addresses you simply repeat the property, separating it from the previous one with an ampersand.
`bcc`	Secretly sends a carbon copy of the mail to the BCC'd address without any recipient seeing any other recipients; the value must be a valid e-mail address. If you want to provide multiple addresses, you simply repeat the property, separating it from the previous one with an ampersand.

If you want to add a space between any of the words in the subject line, you should add `%20` between the words instead of the space. If you want to create a line break in the body of the message, you should add `%0D%0A` (where 0 is a zero, not a capital O).

While an e-mail link can create an e-mail with all of these properties set, it does not stop the user from editing the values in their e-mail program.

It is common practice to add only the e-mail address in e-mail links. If you want to add subject lines or message bodies you may decide to use an e-mail form instead, like the one you will see in Chapter 5 (although these do require a script on the server that can process the form and send the e-mail).

Summary

In this chapter you learned about links. Links enable users to jump between pages and even between parts of an individual page (so that they don't have to scroll to find the place they need).

You have seen that you can use the `<a>` element to create source anchors, which are what most people think of when you mention links on the Web. The content of the source anchor is what users can click — and this should usually be an informative, concise description of what the user will see when they click on the link (rather than text such as "click here"), or it can be an image (as you will see in Chapter 3).

You can also use the `<a>` element to create destination anchors. Destination anchors are a little like index points or special markers, because they allow you to create links that take visitors directly to that part of the page. Destination anchors should always have some content.

Along the way, you learned more about URLs, in particular the difference between an absolute URL, as with those that appear in the address bar of your browser, and relative URLs, which describe where a resource is in relation to the document containing it. Learning the different ways in which relative URLs can be used will also be helpful as you head to the next chapter and learn about adding images and other objects into your documents.

Exercises

You can find the answers to all of the exercises in Appendix A.

1. Look back at the Try It Out example where you created a menu, and create a new page that links directly to each course on the menu. Then add a link to the main Wrox web site (`www.wrox.com`). The page should look something like Figure 2-11.

Figure 2-11

2. Go back to the pages in the sample application and make sure that you have updated the navigation for each page.

Images, Audio, and Video

In this chapter, you'll learn how to add images, animations, audio, and video to your site. This should start to breathe some life into the pages we've been creating so far.

You will start by learning how to add images to your documents using the `<img>` element. You also learn how to make an image a link, and even how to divide an image up into sections so that different parts of the image link to different pages — this is known as an *image map*.

Then we'll take a look at some of the main image formats that are used on the Web (JPEG, GIF, and PNG) and learn which image format to use for different types of images. This is very important because it can greatly affect the speed with which your web pages load (and as we all know, slow web sites frustrate users).

Once we have finished with images, we'll go on to look at how to add some more multimedia content to your site in the form of Flash, video, and audio. In doing so, we will meet the `<object>`, `<param>`, and `<embed>` elements. As you will see, Flash is used to embed more video and audio into web pages than any other technology.

By the end of the chapter, your pages should be looking a lot more exciting.

Adding Images Using the <img> Element

Images are added to a site using the `<img>` element, which has to carry at least two attributes: the `src` attribute, indicating the source of the image, and an `alt` attribute, which provides a description of the image.

For example, the following line would add the image called `logo.gif` into the page (in this case, the image lives in a directory called images). You can find this code at `ch03_eg01.html`.

```
<img src="logo.gif" alt="Wrox logo" />
```

Figure 3-1 shows you what this image looks like in a browser.

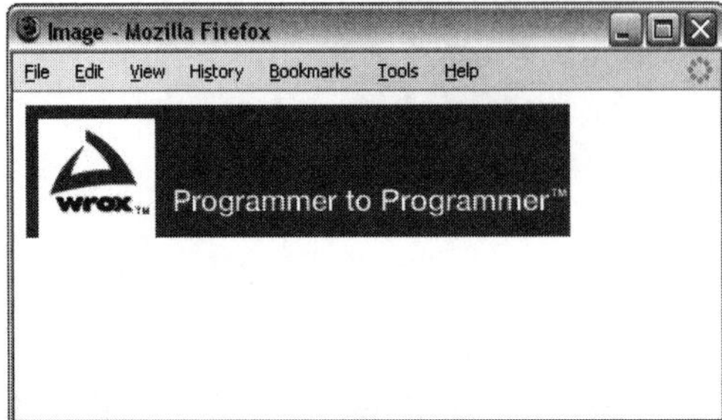

Figure 3-1

In addition to carrying all the universal attributes and the UI event attributes (which you met in Chapter 1), the `<img>` element can carry the following attributes:

```
src alt align border height width hspace vspace ismap usemap longdesc name
```

The src Attribute

The `src` attribute tells the browser where to find the image. The value is a URL and, just like the links you met in the last chapter, the URL can be an absolute URL or a relative URL.

```
<img src="logo.gif" />
```

Generally speaking, images for your site should always reside on your server. It is not good practice to link to images on other sites because if the owner of the other site decides to move that image, your users will no longer be able to see the image. Since the images are on your server, rather than being an absolute URL, the value is more likely to be a relative URL that uses the same shorthand notations you met in the last chapter when relative URLs were introduced.

Most web page authors create a separate directory (or folder) in the web site for images. If you have a very large site, you might even create different folders for different types of images. For example, you might keep any images that are used in the design of the interface (such as logos or buttons) separate from images that are used in the content of the site.

The alt Attribute

The `alt` attribute must appear on every `<img>` element and its value should be a text description of the image.

```
<img src="logo.gif" alt="Wrox logo" />
```

Often referred to as *alt text*, it is important that the value of this attribute really describe the image because:

- If the browser cannot display the image, this text alternative will be shown instead.
- Web users with visual impairments often use software called a screen reader to read a page to them, in which case the alt text describes the image they cannot see.
- While search engines are very clever, they cannot yet describe or index the contents of an image; therefore, providing a text alternative helps search engines index your pages and helps visitors find your site.

Sometimes images do not convey any information, and are only used to enhance the layout of the page. (For example, you might have an image that is just a decorative element but does not add any information to the page.) In such a case, the `alt` attribute should still be used but given no value, as follows:

```
<img src="stripy_page_divider.gif" alt="" />
```

The height and width Attributes

The `height` and `width` attributes specify the height and width of the image, and the values for these attributes are almost always shown in pixels (if you are not familiar with the concept of pixels, we will look at this in the section "Choosing the Right Image Format" later in the chapter).

```
<img src="logo.gif" alt="Wrox Logo" height="120" width="180" />
```

Technically, the values of these attributes can be a percentage of the browser screen. Or if the image is inside an element that takes up only part of the page, known as a *containing element*, then it would be a percentage of the containing element. If you do use a percentage, the number will be followed by a percent sign, but this is very rare, and showing an image at any size other than the size at which it was created can result in a distorted or fuzzy image.

Specifying the size of the image is considered good practice, so you should try to use these attributes on any image that you put on your pages. It also helps a page to load faster and more smoothly, because the browser knows how much space to allocate to the image and it can correctly render the rest of the page while the image is still loading.

While you can tell the browser to display images smaller or larger than they really are (by telling the browser that the width and height are different from what they really are), you should avoid doing this because your image will not be as clear. Rather, you should aim to create versions of images at the same size that you will use them on your web pages. Programs such as Photoshop, Photoshop Elements, Paint Shop Pro, or GIMP will help you do this.

It is also important not to use images that are bigger than they are shown on screen (for example, you should not use an image that is 800 pixels by 800 pixels if you will only be showing it at 100 pixels by 100 pixels on the screen), because the smaller an image, the smaller the size of the file (in terms of kilobytes). And the smaller the file size, the quicker the image loads in the browser. Also, when it comes to putting your site on the Web for others to see, it might save you money because you are often charged in relation to the total size of all the files you send to the people who visit your site.

Likewise, it is important not to show images larger than they really are. If you had a small image (say 100 pixels by 100 pixels) and tried to display it much larger (say 300 pixels by 300 pixels) it would appear grainy.

While it is not a good idea to do so, if you just specify the `height` or `width` attribute and leave out the other one, your browser will show the image to scale. Assume for a moment that you had an image that was 200 pixels wide by 100 pixels tall. If you just specified the width of the image as 200 pixels, it would try to show the image at its correct size: 200 pixels wide by 100 pixels tall. However, if you said that the image was 100 pixels wide and did not specify the height, the browser would try to make the image 50 pixels tall. Because it is 50 percent the width of the original image, it would display the image at 50 percent of its height. In other words, it maintains the *aspect ratio* of an image (its width divided by its height).

You could even distort images by providing a different width in relation to height.

Figure 3-2 shows an image at its actual size (top: 130 pixels by 130 pixels); the image magnified (middle: the `width` attribute is given a value of 160 pixels); and the image distorted (bottom: the `width` attribute is given a value of 80 pixels and the `height` attribute a value of 150 pixels).

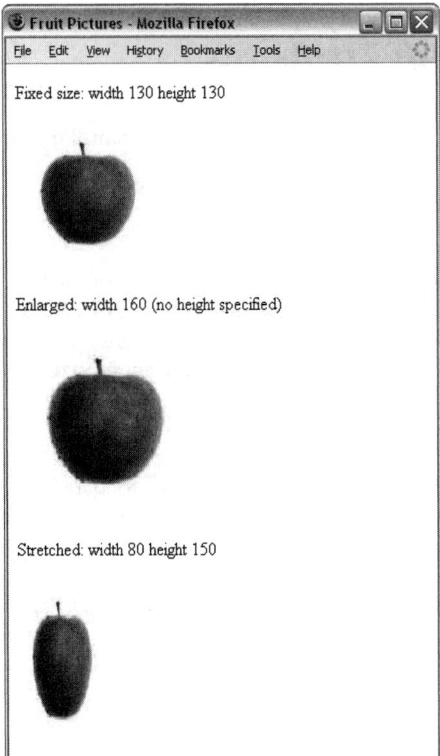

Figure 3-2

Here is the code for this example (`ch03_eg02.html`):

```
<p>Fixed size: width 130 height 130</p>
<img src="images/apple.jpg" alt="Photo of red apple" width="130"
    height="130" />
<p>Enlarged: width 160 (no height specified)</p>
<img src="images/apple.jpg" alt="Photo of red apple" width="160" />
```

```
<p>Stretched: width 80 height 150</p>
<img src="images/apple.jpg" alt="Photo of red apple" width="80" height="150" />
```

The rest of the attributes in this section are either deprecated (being phased out of use) or are rarely used, but they are mentioned here because you may come across them in older pages.

The align Attribute (Deprecated)

The `align` attribute was created to align an image within the page (or if the image is inside an element that is smaller than the full page, it aligns the image within that element).

```
<img src="images/cover.gif" alt="Book cover" align="left" />
```

The `align` attribute was particularly used by authors who wanted text to flow around an image; if you look at Figure 3-3 you can see three examples of text around the same image.

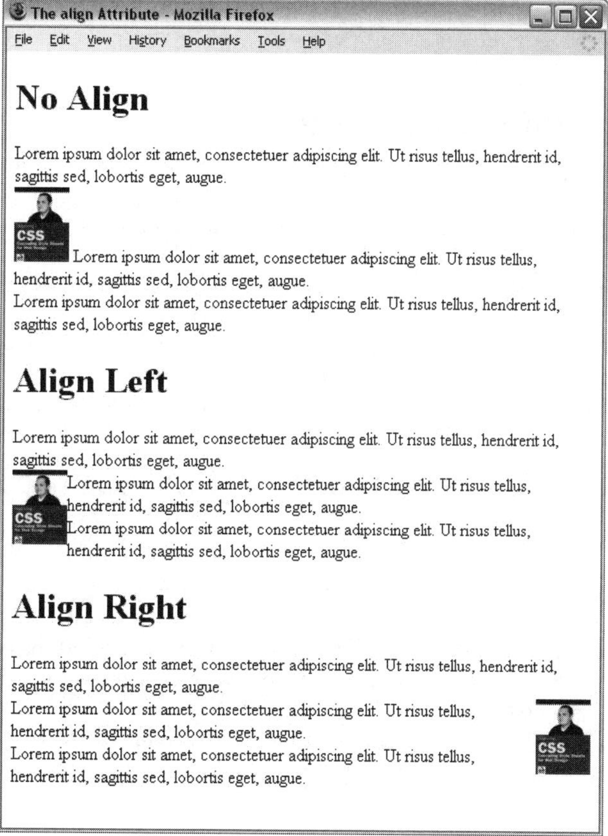

Figure 3-3

The `align` attribute can take one of the values in the table that follows. You may also come across the values `absbottom`, `texttop`, `absmiddle`, and `baseline`, which are not part of the XHTML specification; rather, they were added by the browser manufacturers and therefore can produce inconsistent results.

Value	Purpose
`top`	The top of the image is aligned with top of the current line of text.
`middle`	The middle of the image is aligned with the current text baseline.
`bottom`	The bottom of the image is aligned with the baseline of the current line of text (the default), which usually results in images rising above the text.
`left`	The image is aligned to the left side of the containing window or element and any text flows around it.
`right`	The image is aligned to the right side of the containing window or element and any text flows around it.

The border Attribute (Deprecated)

A border is a line that can appear around an image or other element. By default, images do not have borders, so you would only have used this attribute if you wanted to create a border around an image. The `border` attribute was created to specify the width of the border in pixels:

```
<img src="images/logo.gif" alt="Wrox Logo" border="2" />
```

Although images on their own do not have borders, you should be aware that Internet Explorer gives images a border when they are used as links; as a result, you commonly see code where `border="0"` is used on images that are used inside links. This attribute has been replaced by the CSS `border` property.

The hspace and vspace Attributes (Deprecated)

The `hspace` and `vspace` attributes can be used to control the amount of white space around an image.

```
<img src="images/logo.gif" alt="Wrox Logo" hspace="10" vspace="14" />
```

The value is the amount in pixels of white space that should be left around the edge of the image. It is similar to the image having a border around the image that is the same color as the background of the page. Before CSS, the `hspace` and `vspace` attributes were particularly helpful; they could create a gap between an image and text that flows around it. Without such a gap, the text becomes hard to read and doesn't look as professional. Figure 3-4 illustrates this idea (`ch03_eg04.html`).

Figure 3-4

These attributes have been deprecated, and you can achieve the same result by using the `border` or `margin` properties in CSS.

The ismap and usemap Attributes

The `ismap` and `usemap` attributes are used with image maps. Image maps are covered in the "Image Maps" section later in the chapter.

The longdesc Attribute

The `longdesc` attribute is used to indicate the URL of a document (or part of a document) containing a description for the image in more detail.

```
longdesc="../accessibility/profit_graphs.html"
```

Sometimes images can contain a lot of information — in particular graphs and charts. By providing a long description of the image, not only are you helping search engines understand information that they would not otherwise be able to process, but you are also helping those users who cannot see the image (because of visual impairment).

Unfortunately, the `longdesc` attribute is not supported by any of the major browsers, so in the meantime it is acceptable to place a link next to the image that takes you to a long description of the image. The link just has a letter `D` between the opening `<a>` tag and closing `</a>` tag (which stands for description). You can see an example of this in Figure 3-5 (`ch03_eg05.html`), where the link points to a description at the bottom of the same page. This is just like the internal links you met in the last chapter; if the entire page fits into the browser window you will not see anything happen, but if the page is longer than the browser window, when the user clicks on the link the browser will scroll to the bottom of the page.

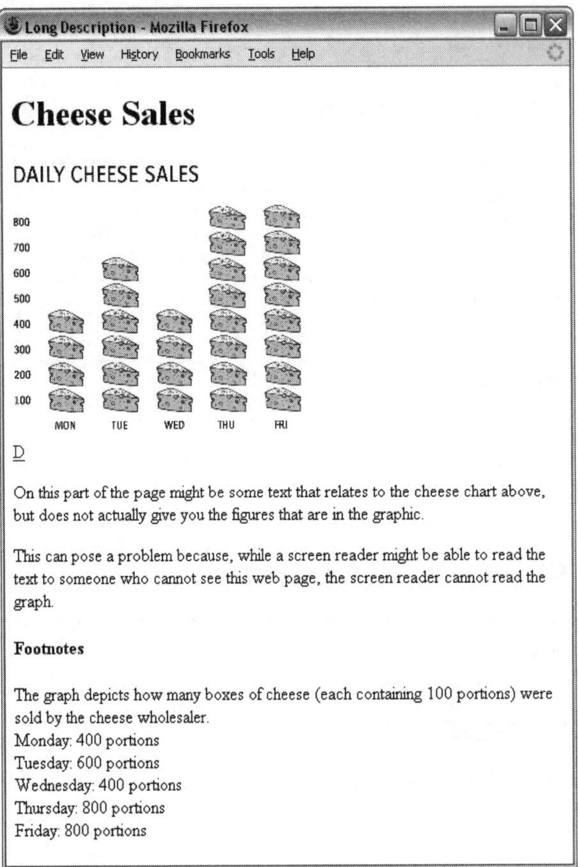

Figure 3-5

The name Attribute (Deprecated)

The `name` attribute allows you to specify a name for the image so that it can then be referenced from script code. It is the predecessor to, and has been replaced by, the `id` attribute.

```
name="image_name"
```

Try It Out Adding Images to a Document

In this example, you're going to add some images to our café example. We will add a logo for the café, and also a picture of the special brunch offer. So, open the homepage in a text editor or web-page authoring tool and follow these steps:

1. Replace the `<h1>` heading with the logo.gif that is in the images folder of the sample application.

```
<img src="images/logo.gif" alt="example cafe" width="194" height="80" />
```

The `src` attribute indicates the URL for the image. The URLs in this example are all relative URLs pointing to an `images` directory that is inside the folder that the example page is in.

The `alt` attribute should be used on every `<img>` element you write. The contents of the `alt` attribute will be shown if the browser cannot load the image and will describe the image to those who have vision impairments and cannot see it. It will also help search engines understand the content of your site.

2. Add the following after the navigation and before the `<h2>` element:

```
<img src="images/scrambled_eggs.jpg" width="622" height="370" alt="Photo of
   scrambled eggs on an English muffin" align="left" />
```

The `width` and `height` attributes tell the browser how big the image should be displayed. By including these attributes, the browser can lay out the page more smoothly, because it can continue to display other items on the page in the correct place without waiting for the image to download. While you can use these attributes to stretch or scale up an image, it is best to have the image the size you want to use it. If you want to make the image smaller, you should save a new version of it rather than just using these attributes. This will save your viewers' time and bandwidth.

3. Save the file and open it in your browser. You should end up with something that resembles Figure 3-6.

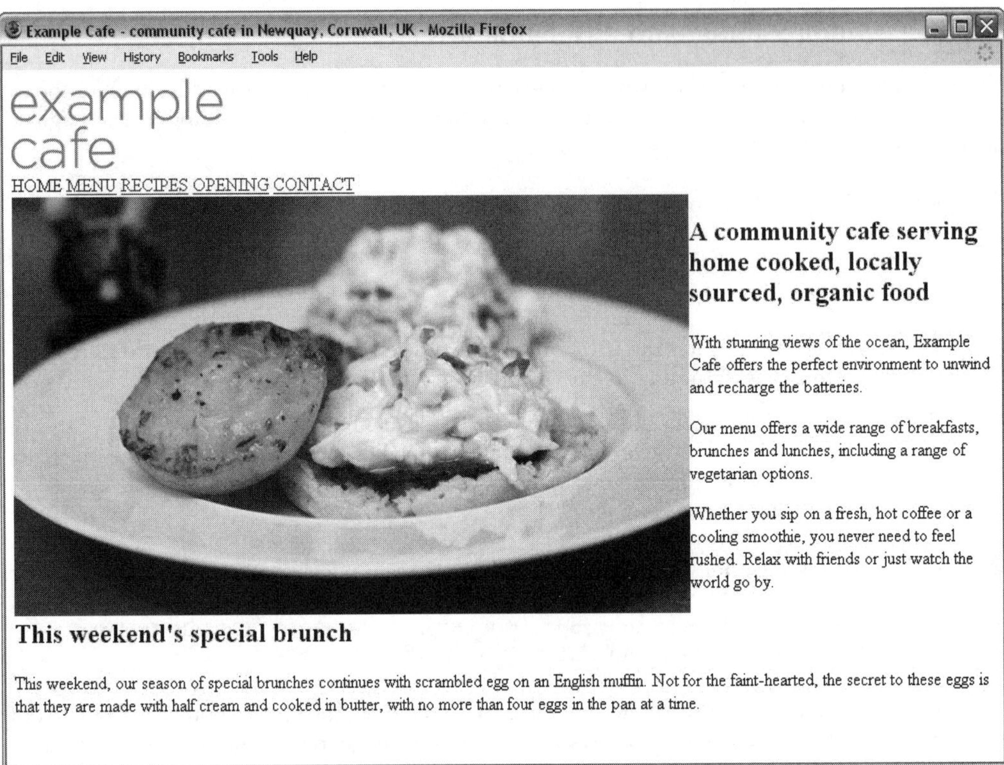

Figure 3-6

Using Images as Links

It's easy to turn an image into a link; rather than putting text between the opening <a> tag and the closing </a> tag (as you saw in the last chapter), you simply place an image inside these tags. Images are often used to create graphical buttons or links to other pages, as follows (ch03_eg06.html):

```
<a href="../index.html" title="Click here to return to the home page">
  <img src="images/logo.gif" width="338" height="79" alt="Wrox Logo" />
</a>
```

You can see what this looks like in Figure 3-7. This screenshot was purposely taken in IE to show you how IE draws a blue border around any image that is inside an <a> element. There is nothing in the XHTML specification that says a border should be drawn around images that are links, and none of the other browsers do this.

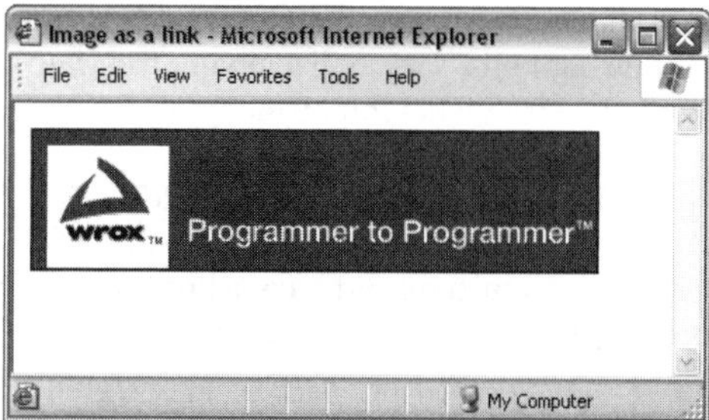

Figure 3-7

This border doesn't look very nice, so you could use the `border` attribute on the `<img>` element with a value of `0` pixels, or preferably use CSS to indicate that any `<img>` elements that are inside an `<a>` element should have no border (you learn how to do this in Chapter 7).

Image Maps

Image maps allow you to add multiple links to the same image, with each link pointing to a different page. They are particularly helpful when the image needs to be divided up in irregular shapes (such as maps). Each of these clickable areas is known as a *hotspot.*

In practice there are relatively few times when you will need to use an image map, but they are covered here because they are a type of image that can act as a link. Feel free to skim over this section to the discussion of file types and come back to the topic of image maps if you ever need to learn how to create one.

Figure 3-8 shows a GIF that you will see turned into an image map. When users click the circle, they see a page about the cafe; when they click the garden, they see a page about the sculpture garden, and when they click the studios, they see a page about the studios.

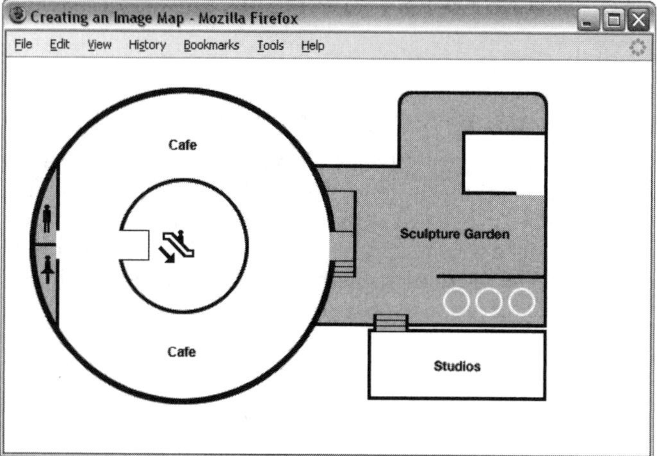

Figure 3-8

Obviously, you do not want to make hotspots too small; otherwise users would have difficulty in selecting the area they want. If this happens, they will soon get frustrated and leave your site. Image maps can also be difficult for people with visual impairments and motor control difficulties to navigate, so if the image map is an important tool for visitors to your site you should also offer text links as an option, too (and indicate the presence of these links in the `alt` text).

The way that image maps work is based upon x and y coordinates, measured from the top left-hand corner of the image. These coordinates are used in two ways:

- To specify where the hotspots are
- To work out where the user is clicking on the image.

By comparing the coordinates of the hotspots with the coordinates where the user clicks, the user can be sent to the link specified for that hotspot.

There are actually two types of image maps, both of which do the same job. The difference is how they work out which hotspot you clicked on.

- **Client-side image maps:** The web browser works out which part of the image the user has clicked on and takes the user to the appropriate page.
- **Server-side image maps:** The browser sends the server the coordinates, saying which part of the image the user clicked on, and these are processed by a script file on the server that determines which page the user should be sent to.

Client-Side Image Maps

Client-side image maps use XHTML code to tell the browser how the image will be divided up; then the browser can tell what part of the image someone clicks on and can send the user to the appropriate link. There are two methods to create a client-side image map:

- Using the `<map>` and `<area>` elements inside an `<img>` element
- Using the `<map>` element inside the `<object>` element

Let's look at each in turn.

Client-Side Image Maps Using <map> and <area>

This is the earlier of the two ways to create client-side image maps, and has been supported in browsers since Netscape 4 and IE4. The image that is going to form the map is inserted into the page using the `<img>` element just like any other image. An attribute called `usemap` is then added to the `<img>` element to indicate that this image needs to use the information held in the corresponding `<map>` element to turn the image into an image map. The `<map>` element then contains the information used to tell the browser how to split up the image so that it can send the user to the correct page.

The value of the usemap attribute begins with a pound or hash sign, followed by the value of the name attribute on the <map> element it uses.

The <map> element usually follows directly after the <img> element. It needs to carry only the name attribute to identify itself. The <map> element then contains two or more <area> elements, and it is these <area> elements that actually define the clickable hotspots.

The <area> element does this by specifying the shape and the coordinates that define the boundaries of each clickable hotspot. Here's an example from the image map that was used for the image in Figure 3-8 (the code for this example is in ch03_eg07.html).

```
<img src="cafe_map.gif" alt="Cafe Map" width="500" height="300"
  border="0" usemap="#cafe" />
<map name="gallery">
  <area shape="circle" coords="154,150,59" href="cafe.html" target="_self"
    alt="Cafe" >
  <area shape="poly" coords="272,79,351,79,351,15,486,15,486,218,272,218,292,
    166,292,136x,270,76" href="courtyard.html" target="_self"
    alt="Courtyard" />
  <area shape="rect" coords="325,224,488,286" href="kitchens.html"
    target="_self" alt="Kitchens" />
</map>
```

If you look at the <img> element, the value of the usemap attribute is #gallery; this corresponds to the value of the name attribute on the subsequent <map> element. Inside this, the <area> elements actually define the sections of the image that are clickable.

If you look at the <area> elements, the shape attribute indicates what kind of shape the hotspot will be, while the coords attribute specifies the position and size of the shape. For example, here the shape is a rectangle, and the coords attribute indicates the top-left and bottom-right corners of the rectangle:

```
<area shape="rect" coords="325,224,488,286" href="workshop.html"
    target="_self" alt="Artists workshops" />
```

The href and target attributes perform exactly the same function that they do when used on the <a> element. The attributes that the <area> element uses to create image maps are covered in the material that follows.

```
accesskey alt shape coords href nohref target tabindex taborder notab
```

The shape Attribute

The value of the shape attribute actually affects how the browser will use the coordinates specified in the coords attribute, and is therefore required. If you do not specify a shape attribute, the default value is a rectangle.

The table that follows shows the possible values of the `shape` attribute.

Value	Shape Created
`default`	The whole of the image not defined in an area (should be specified last)
`rectangle` or `rect`	Rectangle
`polygon` or `poly`	Polygon
`circle` or `circ`	Circle

You are better off using the abbreviated versions of the values, as they are better supported in older browsers. The value `default` should be used on the last `<area>` element if you want to indicate any sections of the image not otherwise indicated by an `<area>` element that has defined an area — it's like a catch-all for the rest of the image.

The coords Attribute

The `coords` attribute specifies the area that is the clickable hotspot. The number of coordinates you specify depends on the shape you are creating (and have specified in the `shape` attribute).

- A rectangle contains four coordinates. The first two coordinates represent the top left of the rectangle, and the second two the bottom right.
- A circle contains three coordinates; the first two are the center of the circle, while the third is the radius in pixels.
- A polygon contains two coordinates for each point of the polygon. So a triangle would contain six coordinates, a pentagon would contain ten, and so on. You do not need to specify the first coordinates again at the end because the shape is automatically closed.

Some web authoring and image-editing programs will help work out the coordinates of an image map for you; they provide a tool that allows you to select the areas you want to turn into a map and they use those shapes to create the coordinates for you. Figure 3-9 shows you Dreamweaver's Image Map tool — because each program is different, you should look in the help files for that program to see how yours creates an image map.

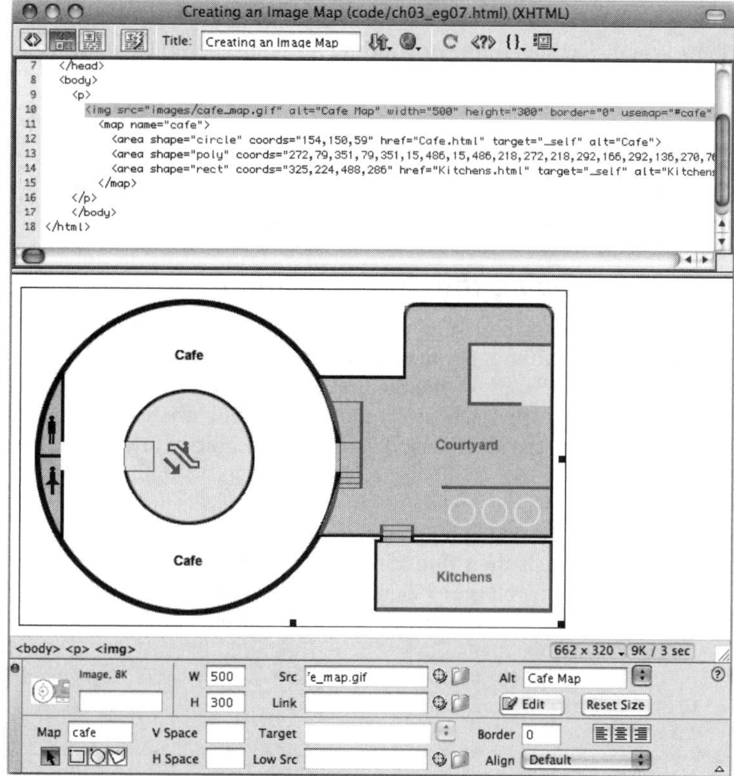

Figure 3-9

If you have two areas that overlap each other, the first one in the code will take precedence.

The href and nohref Attributes

The `href` attribute works just like the `href` attribute for an `<a>` element; its value is the URL of the page you want to load when the user clicks that part of the image.

If you do not want part of the image to link anyway, you should use the `nohref` attribute on that space to indicate that the area will not take you anywhere. If you use this attribute, you should give it a value of `nohref`. For example, if you wanted to make sure that the Kitchens area of the map did not link anywhere, the `<area>` element representing it should look like this:

```
<area shape="rect" coords="325,224,488,286" nohref="nohref" />
```

The alt Attribute

The `alt` attribute specifies a text alternative for that section of the image and works just like the `alt` attribute on the `<img>` element. It will actually override the `alt` text specified for the image when the user rolls over the area.

The target Attribute

The `target` attribute specifies which frame or window the page should be loaded into. Possible values are the same as for the `target` attribute of the `<a>` element.

The tabindex Attribute

The `tabindex` attribute allows you to specify the order in which users can tab through items on a page. The value is a number between 1 and 32,767. It is discussed in full in Chapter 5.

Client-Side Image Maps Using the <object> Element

HTML 4 started to promote the use of the `<object>` element rather than the `<img>` element for adding image maps to your documents (although you can still use the `<img>` element in Strict XHTML 1.0). Unfortunately, IE8, Firefox 3, and Safari 3 were the first versions of major browsers to support the creation of image maps using this approach, so for the moment you are better off sticking to the method described in the previous section, but I will describe the new technique anyway so that you know how it works.

The technique is very similar to the one you just met, but this time it is the `<object>` element that carries the `usemap` attribute (whose value is the value of the `name` attribute on the `<map>` element preceded by the pound or hash sign). Inside the `<object>` element, you use the familiar `<map>` element with the `name` attribute. Then inside the `<map>` element are standard `<a>` elements rather than `<area>` elements.

```
<object data="cafe_map.gif" type="image/gif" alt="Cafe Map" width="500"
   height="300" border="0" usemap="#cafe" />
<map name="cafe">
  <a shape="circle" coords="154,150,59" href="cafe.html" target="_self">Cafe</a>
  <a shape="poly"
coords="272,79,351,79,351,15,486,15,486,218,272,218,292,166,292,136,270,76"
    href="courtyard.html" target="_self">Courtyard</a>
  <a shape="rect" coords="325,224,488,286" href="kitchens.html" target="_
self">
    Kitchens</a>
</map>
```

Server-Side Image Maps

With server-side images, the `<img>` element sits inside an `<a>` element just like any image that is a link. But the `<img>` element carries a special `ismap` attribute, which tells the browser to send the server *x, y* coordinates representing what part of the image the user's mouse was on when he or she clicked the image map. Then a script on the server is used to determine which page the user should be sent to, based on the coordinates fed to it.

For example, look at the following link, where the `<img>` element carries the `ismap` attribute with a value of `ismap`:

```
<a href="../location/map.aspx"><img src="../images/states.gif" alt="map
of US States" border="0" ismap="ismap" /></a>
```

Now, if the user clicks the image 50 pixels to the right of the top-left corner of the image and 75 pixels down from that same corner, the browser will send this information with the URL like so:

```
http://www.example.org/location/map.aspx?50,75
```

You can see the coordinates appended at the end of the URL that is specified in the `<a>` element.

If you look at the code for other people's image maps, you may see some image maps whose `ismap` *attribute does not have a value. This is because in early versions of HTML, the attribute did not require a value. However, in XHTML every attribute requires a value, so the value of the* `ismap` *attribute became* `ismap`. *A server-side image map needs something on the server (a script, map file, or application) that can process the coordinates and determine which page the user should then be sent to. Because server-side image maps are processed on the server, the implementation of them is not covered by HTML or XHTML recommendations, and unfortunately there is not space to cover different possible implementations for each different platform here.*

Choosing the Right Image Format

Images and graphics can really bring your site to life, but it is important to learn how to prepare images for the Web. Otherwise, they can significantly increase the time it takes for a page to load.

When writing sites on your desktop or laptop computer, you may not realize how long a page will take to load; files that are sitting on your computer will load a lot faster than they would if they were on the Internet. Therefore, choosing the right image format and saving your images correctly will ensure that when you put your site on the Web for people to see, it will not be unnecessarily slow — and this should result in happier visitors. That is why we're going to round off this section on images by spending a few pages learning about image formats and how to pick the right one.

For practice purposes, you can download images from other sites by right-clicking the image (or Ctrl-clicking) and selecting either the `download image to disk` *or* `save image as` *options. Remember, however, that images are subject to copyright, and you could land yourself in legal trouble if you use other people's images on your site.*

Most static images on the Web are classified as *bitmapped images*. Bitmapped images divide a picture into a grid of *pixels* and specify the color of each pixel individually. If you look very closely at your computer screen you may be able to see the pixels that make up the screen. There are several different bitmap formats; common ones include JPEG, GIF, TIFF, PNG, and the rather confusingly named bitmap or BMP.

If you look at Figure 3-10, you can see an example of a bitmap image with one section that has been modified so that you can see how pixels make up the image.

Figure 3-10

The number of pixels in every square inch of the image is referred to as the *resolution* of the image. It is normal to save images that will be used on the Web at a resolution of 72 pixels per inch as this corresponds with the number of pixels in a square inch on your computer screen. By contrast, images used in print are usually supplied to printers at 300 dots per inch.

The more pixels or dots per inch an image contains, the larger the size (in KB) of the file, and the larger the file, the longer it takes to transfer over the Web. Therefore, any images that you use on the Web should be saved at a resolution of 72 dots per inch. If you saved them any larger, this would create unnecessarily large files that would take longer to download.

> *Note that while you can easily save an image that is 300 dots per inch at 72 pixels per inch for the Web, you cannot simply increase an image from 72 pixels per inch to 300 dots per inch, because you do not know what color the 228 pixels that are missing from every square inch should be. If you just try to increase the resolution of the image, it will often look grainy. Therefore, when you have a high-resolution 300-dots-per-inch picture, you should make a* copy *of it for use on the Web and keep the original version separately.*

Browsers tend to support three common bitmap graphics formats, and most graphics programs will save images in these formats:

- **GIF:** Graphics Interchange Format (pronounced either "gif" or "jif")
- **JPEG:** Joint Photographic Experts Group Format (pronounced "jay peg")
- **PNG:** Portable Network Graphics (pronounced "pee en gee" or "ping")

Let's take a quick look at each of these, because understanding how the format works helps you choose how to save an image.

GIF Images

GIF (or Graphics Interchange Format) images are created using a palette of up to 256 colors, and each pixel of the image is one of these 256 colors. Every different GIF image can have a different palette of 256 colors selected from a range of over 16 million colors. The program that saves the image also selects the palette that will best represent the images.

The GIF file stores the palette of colors in what is called a lookup table, and each pixel references the color information in the lookup table rather than each pixel having to specify its own color information. The advantage of this technique is that, if many pixels use the same colors, the image does not have to repeat the same color information and the result is a smaller file size. This makes GIF images more suited to graphics (where there are often areas of the same color — known as a *flat color*) and less suited to photographs (where there are often many more different colors).

This way of storing images is known as an *indexed color format*. Figure 3-11 shows a GIF file being created in Adobe Photoshop. You can see the color palette that is being used for this image represented in the set of squares halfway down the image on the right.

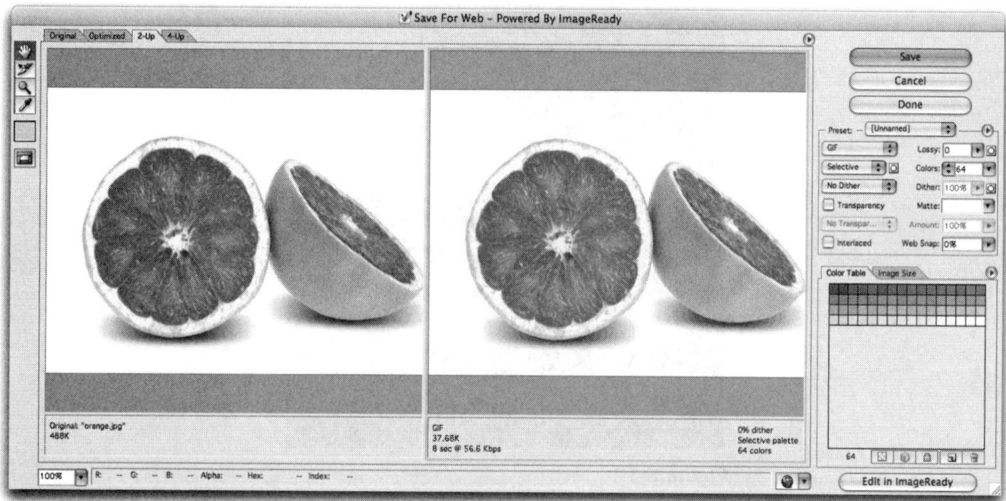

Figure 3-11

If a GIF contains fewer than 16 colors (in which case it can be referred to as a 4-bit GIF), the image will be less than half the file size of a GIF using 256 colors (known as an 8-bit GIF). Therefore, if you are creating an image that uses fewer than 16 colors, it is worth checking whether your program automatically saves your image as a 4-bit GIF, because this will result in a smaller file that's quicker to download than an 8-bit GIF.

Even if your image looks as though it just features two colors, say a black and white line drawing, it may use many more colors. For example, if you have a line drawing where the edges have been smoothed out by the graphics program (a process known as anti-aliasing), your image will contain more than two colors, because the edges use a variety of other colors to make them look smooth.

If the GIF needs to use more than 256 colors, then most graphics programs, when saving GIFs, will use a technique called *dithering* to better represent the extra colors. This means that they use two or more colors in adjacent pixels to create an effect of a third color. Dithering has the following two drawbacks:

- If you place a flat color next to a dithered color you will be able to see where the change occurs (because the dithered color is really made up of more than one color).
- It can result in some *banding* in colors. For example, when there is a smooth transition between one color and another color (referred to as a gradient), many more than 256 shades may be required to show the gradient; therefore, dithering would be used, but the result might be that the smooth gradient now looks like a series of stripes.

Figure 3-12 illustrates how even a simple gradient, when saved as a GIF, can result in banding because the image contains more than 256 colors. The bottom part of this image zooms into an area of the gradient where you can see that the gradient had vertical lines rather than a smooth transition from black to white.

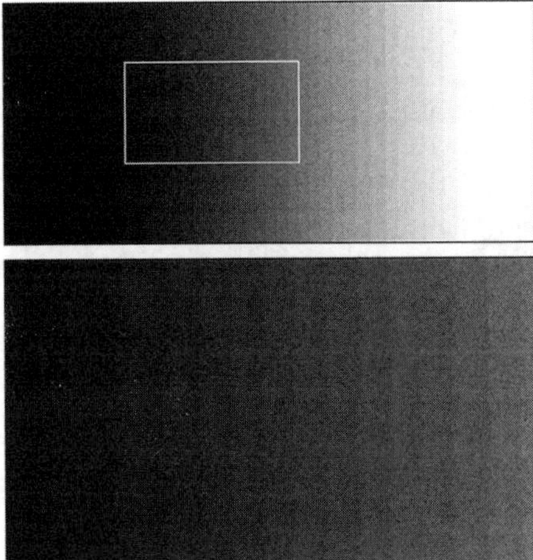

Figure 3-12

Because GIFs support only 256 colors and have to use dithering to achieve any further colors, they are not really suitable for detailed photographs, which tend to contain many more than 256 colors. If you have a photograph, gradient, or any image with similar shades of the same color next to each other, you are often better off using a JPEG, which can support unlimited colors, or sometimes a PNG — both of which you'll learn about shortly.

GIFs do have another handy feature: you can specify one or more colors in a GIF to represent a *transparent background* — in parts of the image that are the specified colors, the background will be allowed to show through.

This technique works best with images that have perfectly straight edges, because when you have a curved edge, an image editing program will often anti-alias the edge (use several shades) to make the image look smooth, as shown in Figure 3-13.

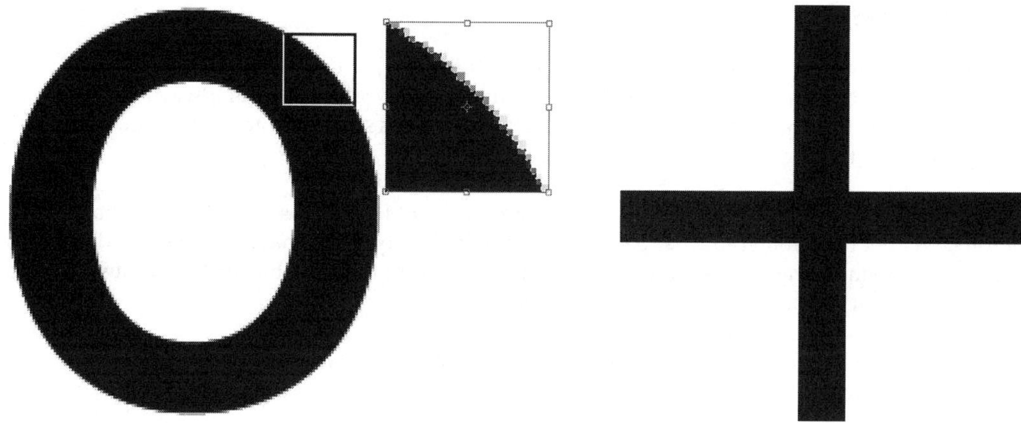

Figure 3-13

However, in a transparent GIF each pixel is either on or off, opaque or transparent — there are no degrees of transparency. As a result, if you try to use it with curved corners, the corners may appear pixelated. To help overcome this problem, you should try to make the transparency color as close to the background color as possible (or if you are using Photoshop, you can use the matte feature).

Figure 3-14 shows how a pixelated effect is created when a GIF is not created on a suitable background (notice the lighter pixels around the corners in particular).

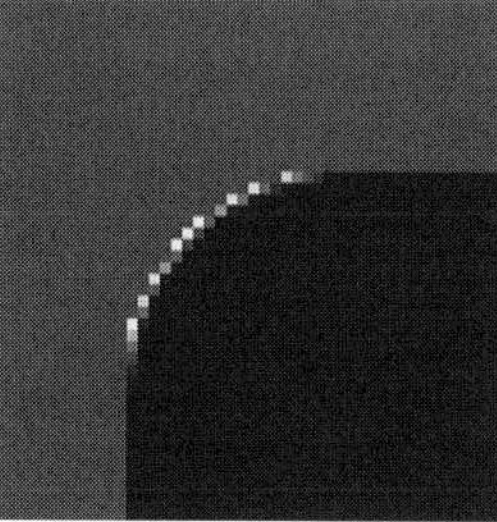

Figure 3-14

To make GIF files smaller, they are compressed using a technique called *LZW compression*, which scans rows of the image looking for consecutive pixels that share the same color. When it comes across pixels that are the same color it indicates that, from this point, *x* number of pixels should be written using the same color.

LZW compression is known as a *lossless compression* technique because no data is lost and therefore there is no loss of quality. This is contrasted with *lossy compression* techniques where some of the data is discarded during compression and therefore cannot be recovered from the compressed file.

Animated GIFs

GIF images can store more than one frame (or copy of the image) within a file, allowing the GIF to rotate between the versions/frames and create a simple animation. It works in a similar way to a flip-book animation, where the drawing on each page of the book changes slightly from the previous one, so that when a user flips the pages it looks as if the images are moving.

This works well if your animated image contains large areas of flat color, since when the image is compressed after the initial frame has been recorded only the pixels that have changed need to be stored with each subsequent frame. It is far less suitable, however, for photographic images because many more of the pixels change, resulting in a very large image.

It is also worth mentioning that attention-grabbing animated GIFs are often frowned upon by professional web designers, who tend to use them only sparingly.

Figure 3-15 shows you an animated GIF being created in Adobe Image Ready. The window on the right shows you that there are three dots on separate layers of the image. The window at the bottom shows you that in frame 1 of the animation, only the bottom dot shows, in frame two the bottom and middle dots show, and in the third frame all three dots show. Under each frame of the animation you can see how long each frame should appear (in each case it is 1 second).

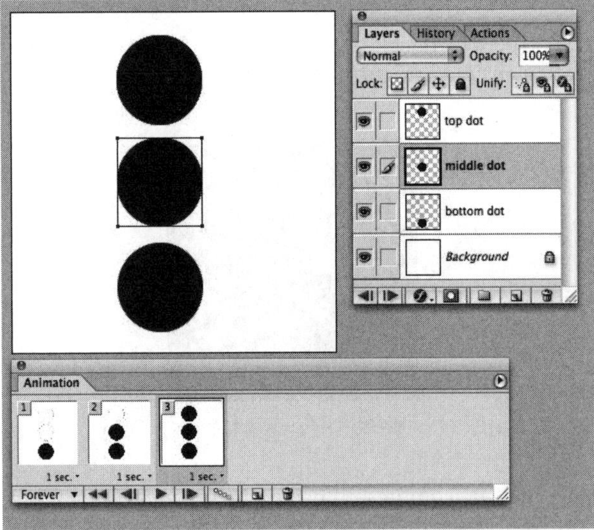

Figure 3-15

JPEG Images

The JPEG image format was developed as a standard for storing and compressing images such as photographs that use a wide range of colors. When you save a JPEG, you can usually specify by how much, if at all, you want to compress the image — which depends upon the image quality you want. The process of compressing a JPEG involves discarding color data that people would not normally perceive, such as small color changes. However, because the image format discards this data when the image is compressed, some of the data is lost and the original cannot be recreated from a compressed version — hence it is known as *lossy compression.*

The amount of compression you apply will change from image to image, and you can only judge how much to compress a JPEG by looking at it. Hence the size of the file varies depending upon how much you compress the image. When you are saving the image, you will often be asked for a percentage of quality to be used; 100 percent does not compress the picture at all, and for a photo you can often get down to around 60–70 percent (but not usually much lower). Some programs use words such as excellent, very good, good, and so on instead of percentages to describe the image quality.

A good image-editing program enables you to compare the original image side by side with the compressed version as you choose how much compression to add. Figure 3-16 shows you how Adobe Photoshop lets you compare two versions of the image next to each other as you prepare to save the JPEG for the Web. On the left, you have the original image, and on the right is the version that it is saving for use on the Web.

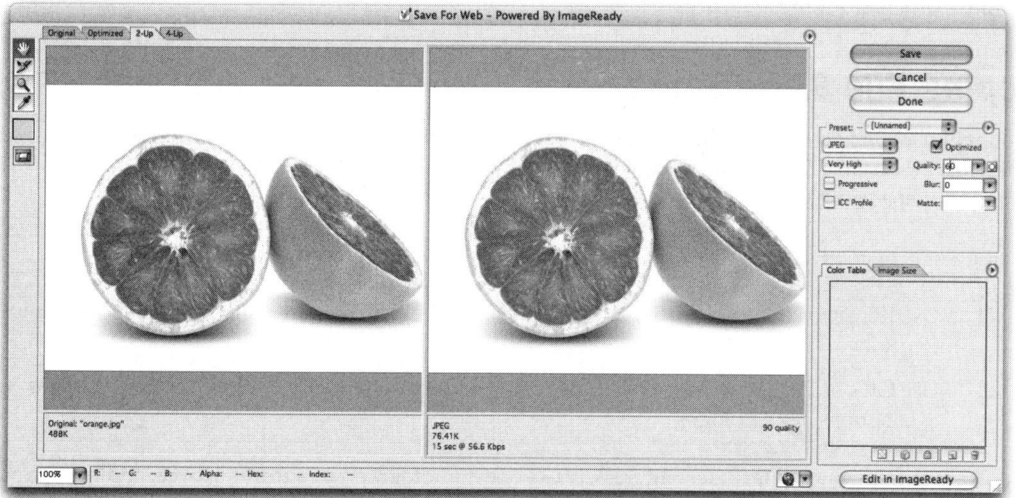

Figure 3-16

Because the JPEG format was designed to work with photo-realistic images, it does not work so well with images that have large amounts of flat color, or high-contrast hard edges (such as lettering and line drawings). As you increase compression in a JPEG you may also see banding start to show in colors that are very similar.

PNG Images

The Portable Network Graphics format is the most recent format on the block. It was developed in the late 1990s because the company that owns the patent for GIFs (Unisys) decided to charge companies that developed software for creating and viewing GIFs a license fee to use the technology. While web designers and web surfers are not directly affected by this charge, the companies that make the software they use are.

The PNG format was designed for the same uses as GIF images, but while it was being created the designers decided to solve what they thought were some of the disadvantages with the GIF format. The result is two types of PNG. The 8-bit PNG has the same limitations as an 8-bit GIF — only 256 colors, and when transparency is used each pixel is either on or off. Then there is the enhanced PNG-24, a 24-bit version, which has two major advantages:

- The number of colors available for use in an image is not restricted, so any color can be included without losing any data.
- A map (like the lookup table that indicates the color of each pixel in GIFs) is used to provide different levels of transparency for every pixel, which allows for softer, anti-aliased edges.

Furthermore, all PNGs tend to compress better than a GIF equivalent. The real drawback with the PNG format, however, is that some older browsers that are still in use today do not fully support the format. While basic support was offered in early versions of browsers, some of the more advanced features took longer to be implemented. For example, Internet Explorer was unable to deal with transparency correctly until version 7.

Keeping File Sizes Small

You will usually want to save the images for your site in the format that best compresses the image and therefore results in a smaller file size. Not only will your pages load faster, but you can save on the charges to host your site.

Usually one or another format will be the obvious choice for you. The rule of thumb is:

- Use JPEGs for photo-realistic pictures with a lot of detail, or subtle shade differences you want to preserve.
- Use GIFs or PNGs for images with flat color (rather than textured colors), and hard edges, such as diagrams, text, or logos.

Look at the following images (see Figure 3-17) — one a photograph of autumn leaves, and the second the logo of a fictional company called Wheels that uses only two colors.

Figure 3-17

The following table shows you the file size of each of these saved as a GIF and as a JPEG (where the JPEG is saved at 60 percent quality).

Image	JPEG	GIF
`Leaves`	54.81k	116.3k
`Wheels`	8.26k	6.063k

As you can see, the Wheels logo has areas of flat, plain color, whereas the photo of the forest uses lots of different shades. Therefore, the logo is better suited to the GIF or PNG formats, while the photo of the forest with all its shadows is suited better to the JPEG format.

Good image editing software is very helpful if you use a lot of images on your site. Adobe Photoshop is the most popular software used by professionals, although it is very expensive. There is, however, a limited functionality version called Photoshop Elements that includes many of the common features — including the Save for Web options. Two other popular image-editing programs are Paint Shop Pro (available from Corel at `www.corel.com`*) and a free image-editing program called Gimp (which you can download from* `www.gimp.org`).

If you have to include many large, complex photographic images on your site, it's good practice to offer users smaller versions of the images when the pages first load and then add a link to the larger version. These smaller images are often referred to as *thumbnails*, and you will usually see them in image galleries or on pages that contain summaries of information (such as the homepages of news sites and pages that list several products, from which you link to a page with more detail and larger images). Figure 3-18 shows you an example of using thumbnails in an image gallery (the small images at the bottom are smaller in physical size and file size than the counterparts that will show at the top).

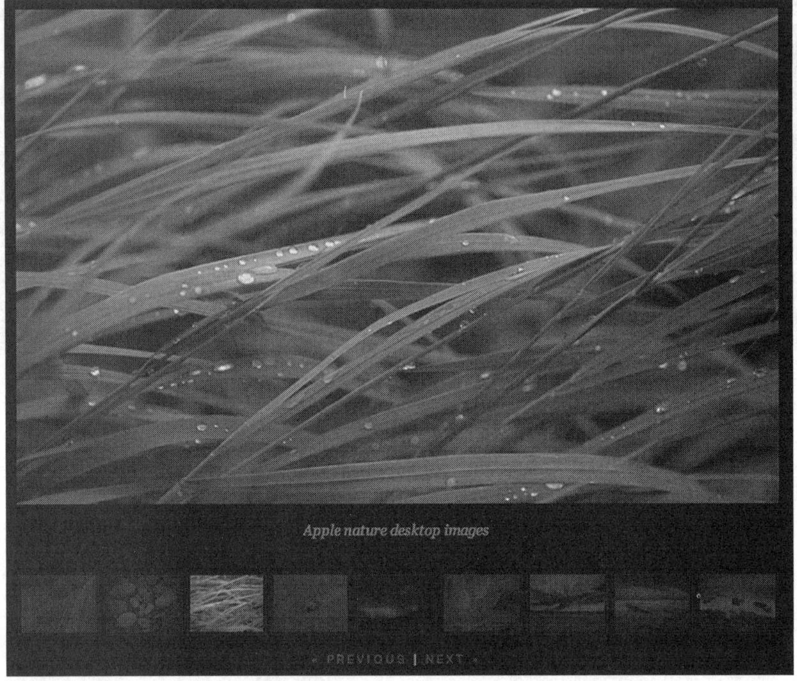

Figure 3-18

When creating the smaller version, scale the image down in an image-editing program. Do not simply alter the `width` and `height` attributes of the `<img>` or `<object>` elements, because users still have to download the full-sized image even though they are getting to see only a smaller version of it. (The full-sized image takes longer to download.) By creating a special thumbnail of any smaller images you use, your pages will load a lot quicker.

You may hear of a format called Vector format, which is more popular in illustration and animation software. Flash, SVG, and Silverlight all employ vector graphics. Vector formats store information in terms of coordinates, between which lines are drawn. Inside these lines a colored fill may be specified. Because they are based on coordinates, it is easy to increase the physical size of the image by increasing the gap between each point that the coordinates are plotted against. By default, browsers do not support Vector formats without the use of a plug-in. You learn more about plug-ins when we come to look at Flash later in the chapter.

Adding Flash, Video, and Audio to Your Web Pages

Having spent the first half of the chapter looking at adding images to your web pages, in the second half of the chapter we are going to look at adding Flash animations, video, and audio to your pages. Collectively, these are often referred to as *rich media*.

When it comes to showing Flash animations, video, and audio on your site, things get a little more complicated for two reasons:

- First, there are many different *formats* to learn about. Flash is fairly easy because there is just the one format for Flash animations, but there are many different formats for video, including AVI, Flash Video, MPEG, QuickTime, and Windows Media, and several formats for audio such as MP3 and WAV.
- Second, while browsers are built to display text and images, they do not automatically show the different formats of rich media. Instead browsers rely on additional programs known as *players* or *plug-ins*, and these players do not play every format (just as a DVD player would not be able to play a VHS video or a vinyl record). So, your choice of which format to use might be restricted by how many people have the player installed.

Some plug-ins are installed by default when you get a new computer, and when they are not installed users can download them (usually for free) from the web sites of the companies who make them. For example, the Flash plug-in is usually installed on new computers, but it can also be downloaded for free from the Adobe web site.

When considering which format to use for your rich media, you will want to consider the number of people who are likely to have the required plug-in installed on their computers. This is important because you cannot assume that people will download a plug-in just to access some content on your site.

In the next version of HTML (HTML 5) you are likely to see two new elements: `<audio>` *for adding audio files to web pages and* `<video>` *for adding video files. The* `<audio>` *element will be used to make it easier to add MP3 and WAVE files to pages; however, at the time of this writing the browser manufacturers were having trouble agreeing on the format of videos specified as using the* `<video>` *element. In either case, it is likely to take several years before either of these elements is widely used, because it will take a long time for web users to adopt the new browsers that will support these elements. (HTML 5 is discussed in more detail in Chapter 14.)*

In order to show rich media on your pages, you will need to learn a new element, the `<object>` element. We will have a detailed look at the `<object>` element at the end of the chapter when we have looked at how to use some of the different formats of rich media. But for now, you just need to know that the `<object>` element can tell the browser several things, including:

- The name of the file and where to find it
- The format of the file
- The type of plug-in used to play the file

Inside the `<object>` element, you can use the `<param>` element to pass extra information to the player (for example, you might want to tell a player to start playing automatically when the page loads, rather than waiting for the user to press a play button).

The `<param>` element is not the only markup you are likely to see inside the `<object>` element. But any other markup you see inside the `<object>` element is only likely to be shown if the browser cannot render the object (and the most common reason why it would not render the object would be because the required player is not installed). For example, you will commonly see the `<embed>` element used inside the `<object>` element.

Strictly speaking, the `<embed>` element was never part of the HTML or XHTML specifications, but years ago Microsoft used the `<object>` element for a technology called ActiveX (which only worked in IE), and as a result, other browser manufacturers used the `<embed>` element to embed items such as audio and video in a page instead. Therefore, you often find the `<embed>` element included inside the `<object>` element to ensure that if an older browser does not understand the `<object>` element it can try to display the content using the `<embed>` element.

When the `<embed>` element has to pass extra information to plug-ins, rather than using the `<param>` element it uses attributes; you will see examples of this shortly.

So for the remainder of this chapter we are going to look at:

- How to add Flash animations into your web pages
- How to display video in your web pages (and which format you should use)
- How to add audio to your pages (and which format you should use)
- The syntax of the `<object>` element.

When looking at video and audio, we will have a discussion about the different formats you can use, and the players that you need in order to play the different formats.

Adding Flash Movies to Your Site

Flash started off as a way to add animations into web pages, but quickly evolved to offer a high level of interactivity and the ability to deal with images, audio, and video. Now, not only is Flash widely used to add animation and interactivity to web pages, it is also the most popular way of displaying audio and video within web pages (for example, most of YouTube's and MySpace's video and audio is provided in Flash).

Most Flash files are created using the Flash authoring environment, which Adobe charges for, although there are a lot of sites that offer tools such as MP3 players, video players, slideshows, and more, all written in Flash, which you can use on your site without purchasing a copy of this program. While creating your own Flash files from scratch is beyond the scope of this book, I will show you how to include in your XHTML pages Flash files that have already been written.

If you do work on a project using the Flash authoring tool, your projects will be saved with the `.fla` file extension (and they are commonly referred to as FLA files). But before you can use such a file on the Web you will have to *export* it in the `.swf` format. When files have been exported into the `.swf` format, they go by one of two names, either SWF files or *Flash movies* (rather confusingly, they can be called Flash movies even if they do not contain any video).

The major browsers don't play SWF files by themselves; rather, they rely on a free plug-in called the *Flash Player*. The Flash Player is often pre-installed on computers, but it can also be downloaded from the `Adobe.com` web site. It is estimated that over 98 percent of web users have the Flash Player installed.

Let's briefly recap what you have learned about Flash, as there was quite a lot to take in there:

- You pay for the Flash authoring environment that allows you to create and edit FLA files. These files are saved with the `.fla` file extension.
- When you want to use Flash files on the Web, you export them to SWF files or Flash movies. These files have the `.swf` file extension.
- The free Flash Player plug-in needs to be installed in order for the browser to play the SWF files. It is estimated that over 98 percent of people have the Flash Player.

So let's look at the code used to add Flash to a page, by considering three different examples. We will start by looking at how to embed the YouTube player in a page you have written.

Adding the YouTube Flash Video Player to a Page

As I mentioned, the YouTube Player is written in Flash, and YouTube has made it very easy for users to embed the YouTube Player on their own pages. This is done simply by copying and pasting a line of code from the YouTube site into any web page; Figure 3-19 shows you where to find this line of code.

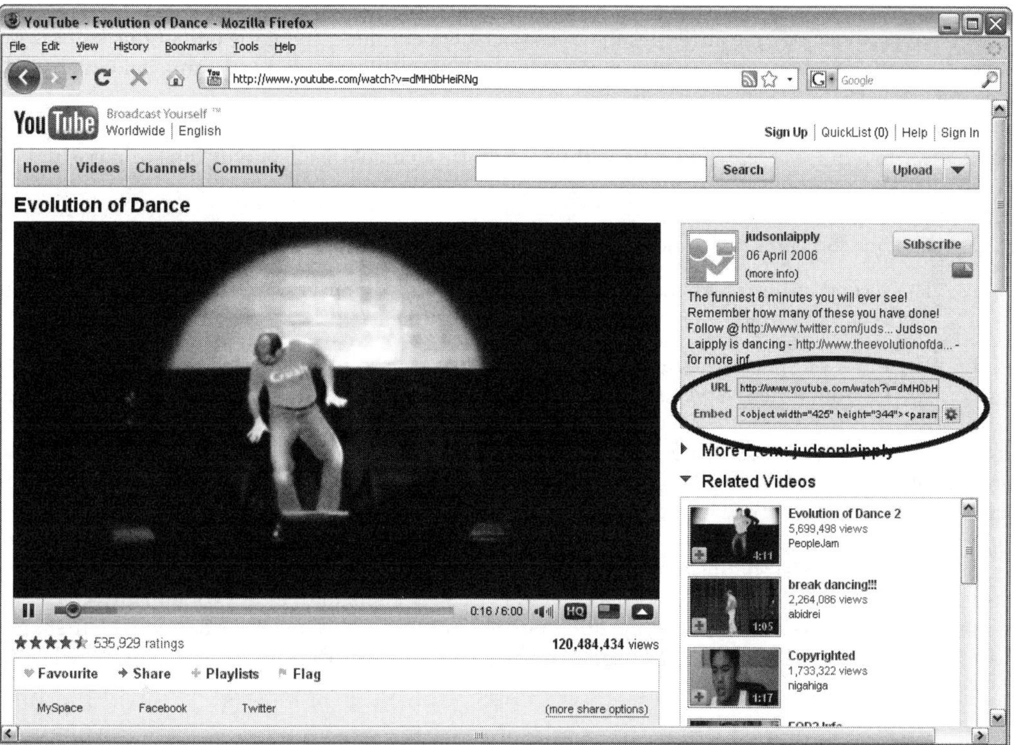

Figure 3-19

If you try this example on your desktop or laptop computer at home, you may get a warning message because the Flash Player is trying to communicate with a server on the Web (which can sometimes be considered a security risk). If you press "OK" the example may work; otherwise you may need to follow the instructions to alter your settings. If you ran this example on a server on the Web, you would not see this error message.

So let's look a little closer at the code YouTube offers to embed videos from YouTube (ch03_eg08.html):

```
<object width="425" height="344">
  <param name="movie"
    value="http://www.youtube.com/v/dMH0bHeiRNg&hl=en&fs=1"></param>
  <param name="allowFullScreen" value="true"></param>
  <param name="allowscriptaccess" value="always"></param>
    <embed src="http://www.youtube.com/v/dMH0bHeiRNg&hl=en&fs=1"
    type="application/x-shockwave-flash" allowscriptaccess="always"
    allowfullscreen="true" width="425" height="344"></embed>
</object>
```

On the opening <object> tag, you can see the width and height attributes specify the size of the Flash movie; these behave just like the width and height attributes on the <img> element, indicating how much space this item needs.

We will have a look at all the attributes the <object> element can carry at the end of this section, but it is worth mentioning here that YouTube's use of the <object> element is a little unusual because it does not carry a classid *or* a type attribute.

Inside the <object> element, you can see three <param> elements, each of which has a name and value attribute:

- The first indicates that a movie is to be loaded, along with the URL for the movie.
- The second indicates whether the player should allow the user to view the movie in full-screen mode.
- The third is a special property which, in this case, is used to ensure that the Flash movie can be played from different web sites (not just from the YouTube servers).

Note that these parameters are specific to this video player and do not necessarily apply to all Flash movies. Other parameters may be specific to a version of Flash; for example, the ability to show full-screen Flash movies was only introduced in Flash 9, which was released in 2006.

As mentioned at the start of this section, an <object> element often contains an <embed> element, and this is no exception. You may have noticed that the <embed> element does not contain any <param> elements; rather, it uses attributes on the opening tag to provide the same information. The first attribute is an src attribute — just like the one used on the <img> element indicating where to find the Flash file.

This is followed by a `type` attribute indicating that the file is a Flash movie. The next two attributes match the `<param>` elements you just met. The last two, `width` and `height`, specify the size of the Flash movie.

By adding this one line of code to your page, you will see the YouTube Player embedded on your page. The result should look like the screenshot in Figure 3-20.

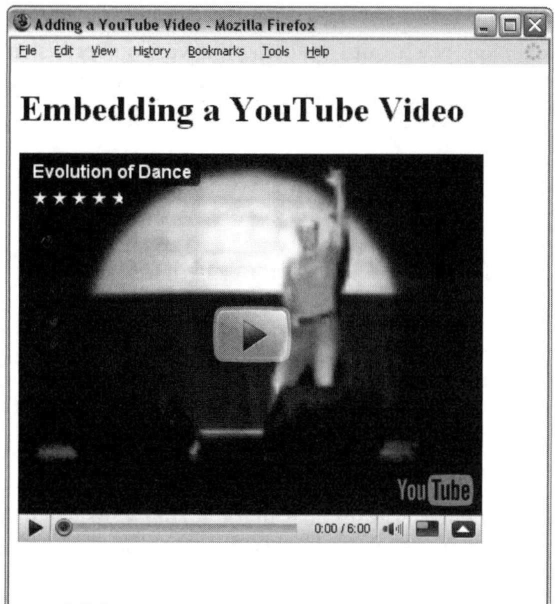

Figure 3-20

There are lots of sites that allow you to embed Flash tools in your own pages, for example:

- `ActiveDen.net` features the work of many Flash programmers, including music players, video players, image galleries, and other animations.
- `Flickr.com` and `Slide.com` both allow you to upload your own pictures to their site and then add Flash slideshows of these pictures to your own pages.
- `Last.fm` allows you to add music players to your page that feature songs it has uploaded to its servers.

All these sites provide you with the code that you need to add Flash movies into your pages, but to help you understand that code, I will show you how to add a basic Flash animation that I created to your page.

Adding Flash to a Page Using <object> and <embed> Elements

Copying the code from the YouTube web site is an easy way to add one of its videos to your site, but as I mentioned, the code that you see on the YouTube web site is slightly different from the code you might see used to add other Flash movies to your pages. Therefore, in this section you will see how to add a basic Flash animation to a web page using a slightly different technique. This simple animation was created using Flash 8, and when the FLA file was exported to create the SWF file, Flash also created the code to add the SWF file into a web page.

Flash 8 is not the latest version of Flash, but I am using this version because it demonstrates another way to add a Flash movie to a page using the `<object>` and `<embed>` elements, which you are likely to come across if you work with Flash (`ch03_eg09.html`):

```
<object classid="clsid:D27CDB6E-AE6D-11cf-96B8-444553540000"
    width="300" height="200"
    codebase="http://download.macromedia.com/pub/shockwave/cabs/flash/
    swflash.cab">
    <param name="movie" value="motion/flash_sample.swf" />
    <param name="play" value="true" />
    <param name="loop" value="false" />
    <embed src="motion/flash_sample.swf" width="300" height="200" play="true"
    loop="false" quality="best" type="application/x-shockwave-flash"
    pluginspage="http://www.macromedia.com/shockwave/download/index.cgi?
    P1_Prod_Version=ShockwaveFlash"></embed>
</object>
```

One interesting thing to note about this example is that the `<object>` element specifies `classid` and `codebase` attributes, both of which are commonly used on the `<object>` element (the YouTube example was an exception to this rule).

The `classid` attribute is there to specify which application should play the file (in this case the `classid` attribute identifies the Flash Player, but if you wanted to play a file using the Windows Media plug-in, you would use a different value of `6BF52A52- 394A-11D3-B153-00C04F79FAA6`).

The `codebase` attribute specifies where the plug-in or program required to play this file can be found if the user does not have it installed.

Inside are three `<param>` elements:

- The first specifies the Flash movie to play.
- The second specifies that the movie should play automatically.
- The third indicates that the movie should loop (when it comes to the end, it should start again).

The `<embed>` element provides similar information, but it does so using attributes:

- The `src` attribute indicates where the Flash movie can be found.
- The `width` and `height` attributes indicate how much space the player should take up.

- The `play` attribute indicates that the movie should start automatically when the page loads.
- The `loop` attribute indicates that when the movie has finished playing it should go back to the start and play again.
- The `quality` attribute indicates how high quality the Flash movie should be (this is not commonly used any more).
- The `pluginspage` attribute indicates where the Flash Player plug-in can be downloaded from if the user does not have it installed.

You can see what this looks like in Figure 3-21.

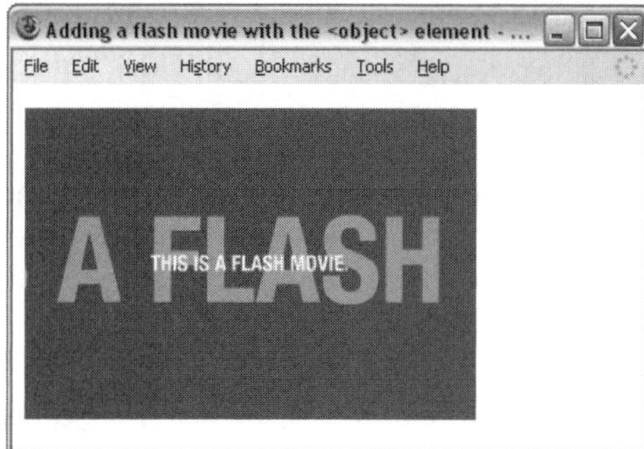

Figure 3-21

Adding Flash to a Page Using SWFObject

Recently, there has been a growing trend to use JavaScript to include Flash movies in pages, rather than the `<object>` and `<embed>` elements.

When adopting this technique, you create the page using a `<div>` element to hold the Flash movie and you should use CSS to make sure that the `<div>` element is the same width and height as the SWF file you want to include (you learn how to set the size of a `<div>` element in Chapter 7). This `<div>` element should also have an `id` attribute to uniquely identify that element.

Inside that `<div>` element you can use text and images that will be shown to users who do not have Flash installed.

A JavaScript is then added to the page; this script checks whether the browser has the Flash player installed. If it is installed, the JavaScript replaces the content of the specified element `<div>` with the SWF file.

In fact, the JavaScript not only checks that the user has the Flash player installed, but also that it is the required version. As you might have guessed, over the years there have been several versions of Flash, and the latest versions have new and improved features. But not everyone has the latest version of the plug-in, and if a browser does not have the minimum version required to play the SWF file, then the JavaScript will not attempt to load the Flash, leaving behind the content of the `<div>` element.

The most popular script for this is called SWFObject, and it can be downloaded from `http://code.google.com/p/swfobject/`. You do not really need any experience with JavaScript to use this technique. Let's look at an example; we will load exactly the same Flash movie that you saw in the last example, but this time we will use SWFObject (version 2.1) to include it in the page (`ch03_eg10.html`):

```
<?xml version="1.0" ?>
<!DOCTYPE html PUBLIC "-//W3C//DTD XHTML 1.0 Strict//EN"
    "http://www.w3.org/TR/xhtml1/DTD/xhtml1-strict.dtd">
  <html xmlns="http://www.w3.org/1999/xhtml" lang="en" xml:lang="en">
  <head>
    <title>Adding a flash movie with SWF Object</title>
    <script type="text/javascript" src="swfobject.js"></script>
    <script type="text/javascript">
        swfobject.embedSWF("flash/flash_sample.swf", "flash_movie", "300",
        "200", "8.0.0");
    </script>
</head>
<body>
    <div id="flash_movie">This element can contain content that search
      engines can index, and which is helpful to those who do not have Flash
      installed.</div>
  </body>
</html>
```

While the code is quite different, in the browser this example looks just like the last one; the only difference is the title of the page indicating that it has been written using SWFObject.

In this example, the `<div>` element carries an `id` attribute with a value of `"flash_movie"` (the `id` attribute is used to uniquely identify an element within a web page). It is this element that will be replaced with the Flash movie if the user has the appropriate version of Flash player installed.

At the top of the page, you can see two `<script>` elements. The first includes a separate JavaScript file whose location is specified using the `src` attribute (just as the `src` attribute on an image specifies where the image can be found):

```
<script type="text/javascript" src="swfobject.js"></script>
```

As you can see, it is loading a file called `swfobject.js`, and it is this file that does most of the work. You do not need to understand the content of this file or how it works, but if you are curious you can have a look at it in a text editor or any XHTML editing tool. The second `<script>` element calls the script that was included in the previous line and tells it four things so that it can do its job:

```
<script type="text/javascript">
    swfobject.embedSWF("flash/flash_sample.swf", "flash_movie",
      "300", "200", "8.0.0");
 </script>
```

The four parameters being passed in are shown in bold:

- `"flash/flash_sample.swf"` is the location of the Flash movie to be played.
- `"flash_movie"` is the value of the `id` attribute of the element that is to be replaced.

- `"300"` indicates the width of the movie in pixels.
- `"200"` indicates the height of the movie in pixels.
- `"8.0.0"` is the minimum version of Flash Player required to play the movie.

This approach has two additional advantages not mentioned yet:

- It is considered to be better for search engines. Because search engines cannot index Flash content well, they will see the XHTML content that would have been replaced.
- It is also considered good for accessibility purposes, because if users have disabled Flash there is alternative content for them.

As I already mentioned, there are several places where you can download Flash movies that you can use on your own sites (without necessarily using the Flash authoring tool). A good starting place is `http://ActiveDen.net/`, which features works by many authors.

You may have also heard of a technology called Silverlight, which has been developed by Microsoft. Silverlight is very similar to Flash; however, the first version was only released in 2006 and therefore far fewer people have the Silverlight plug-in installed compared with the number of people who have Flash Player installed. Until it has significantly more users, it is unlikely to challenge Flash on mainstream sites.

Now that you've seen how to include Flash movies in a web page, let's look at how to add films and audio into our pages. This starts to get a little more complicated, because while there is only one format for Flash movies (`.swf`) and one player (Adobe's Flash Player), there are several audio and video formats, many of which require different plug-ins.

Adding Videos to Your Site

One of the easiest ways to feature video on your site is to upload your video to a site such as YouTube, and then embed the YouTube player in your page using the code YouTube provides. However, you might decide that you don't want to have your video on YouTube or you might not want a YouTube-branded player on your site, so let's look at some alternatives.

When you want to play a video on the web there are two things you need to consider:

- **File format**: You need to choose the format of the video, and there are lots of different formats to choose from, including AVI, Flash Video, MPEG, QuickTime, and Windows Media. Which format you choose can influence the size of the file that users have to download and the quality of the picture they get to watch (because the formats use different compression techniques to create smaller files).
- **Plug-in needed to play that type of file**: Different formats require different plug-ins to play the movie. Some plug-ins are more popular than others (and are installed on a greater percentage of computers). Examples include Flash Player, QuickTime Player, RealPlayer, and Windows Media Player.

To tell a browser what kind of video you are going to play, you can use the `type` attribute on the `<object>` element. Its value is something known as a MIME type (for example, the MIME type of a QuickTime Movie is `video/x-mov`). You can think of MIME types as being a little like file extensions, in that they describe the format of the content. The browser can then check if it has a program needed to play that file format — and if so use that program to play the file.

To tell a browser what kind of plug-in to use, you can use the `classid` attribute. Its value is a rather long set of numbers/letters used to identify that plug-in. For example, the `classid` of the QuickTime Player plug-in is `02BF25D5-8C17-4B23-BC80-D3488ABDDC6B`.

The following table gives a rundown of the most common video formats on the Web, the file extensions they use, the MIME type, and default players on PC and Mac.

File format	File Extension	MIME Type	Default Player PC	Default Player Mac
Flash Video player	`.swf`	`application/x-shockwave-flash`	Flash Player (often pre-installed)	Flash Player (often pre-installed)
MPEG	`.mpg` or `.mpeg`	`video/mpeg`	(Usually) Windows Media Player	(Usually) Quick Time Player
Windows Media Video	`.wmv`	`video/x-ms-wmv`	Windows Media Player pre-installed	User must download Windows Media components
QuickTime Movie	`.mov`	`video/quicktime`	User must download plug-in	QuickTime Player pre-installed
AVI	`.avi`	`video/x-msvideo`	Windows Media Player pre-installed	User must download Windows Media components
Real Media	`.rm`	`application/vnd.rn-realmedia`	Real Player (often needs to be downloaded)	Real Player (needs to be downloaded)

When it comes to choosing which of these formats to show your video in, for most people the deciding factor is how many people will have the plug-in required to view that format (because you cannot expect people to download a plug-in just to watch a video on your site). For example, a Windows machine is likely to come with Windows Media Player already installed, but the latest versions of Windows Media Player are not being made for Mac. Likewise, Macs come with QuickTime installed, but you are likely to have to download a plug-in to play QuickTime files on a Windows machine. Here is a quick run-down of these formats (in estimated order of popularity).

- **FLV or Flash video** is by far the most popular format for showing videos on the Web, largely because the Flash Player plug-in is installed on more computers than any of the other plug-ins needed to show video. People familiar with the Flash authoring environment can easily create their own video players (which are in turn shown within the Flash Player plug-in), allowing them to control the look and feel of the player. The format also compresses well for use on the Web.
- **MPEG** is a format that takes its name from the group who developed it, the Motion Picture Experts Group. Most computers will have a player capable of playing MPEG movies because they can be played in Windows Media Player or QuickTime Player. The drawback of the MPEG format is that, even though it can be compressed in many ways, files often end up much larger than FLV formats (up to twice the size).
- **WMV** or Windows Media Video is part of the Microsoft Windows Media suite, and requires Windows Media to play it — which comes with new PCs but requires users on other platforms to download a plug-in.
- **MOV** files are based on QuickTime which was initially developed for Mac. It can be played on most other operating systems but again requires users to download a plug-in.
- **MP4** makes very small file sizes, but users need to install QuickTime to view it.
- **AVI** (audio/video interleaved) was originally developed as a rival to QuickTime for Windows. It is known as a container format because it contains a video compressed with another codec. This means that your computer may play some AVI files, and not others.
- **RealVideo** was one of the first formats used for showing video online. It requires a plug-in called RealPlayer to be installed on the computer. It is free but can be tricky to install. It is rapidly falling in popularity and is generally being replaced by FLV.

Since Flash Video is by far the dominant form of showing video on the web, that is the format we will focus on in this chapter.

Adding Videos Using Flash Video

There are several reasons why Flash Video is the most popular way to add video to a web site. These include:

- The Flash player is installed on more computers that are connected to the Web than players that show other video formats, which means that more people can view the FLV files.
- You can easily control the appearance of the player (the controls such as Play and Stop as well as the window around the video) using Flash, which means that people can create branded players.

- FLV files compress well, which means that the same piece of video in FLV format can be much smaller than in MPEG-1 format with minimal loss in quality. In turn this means that:
    - The videos are quicker to load and play.
    - It costs less to run a web site that uses FLV than one using larger formats, because when you have a web site you are usually charged for bandwidth (the amount of data you send from your site to people viewing it).

Another factor that has contributed to FLV being the most popular video format on the Web would be its use on sites like YouTube and MySpace, which show all their videos in Flash. When you upload a video to one of these sites you can do so in several formats (such as AVI, MPEG, and QuickTime), and the web sites will then convert the videos into the FLV format and play them in their own players.

If you would rather not upload your video to one of these sites, then you need to do two things:

- Convert the video from another format (such as AVI, MPEG, or QuickTime) and turn it into an FLV format.
- Write or download an FLV player. Remember that these are just Flash movies (like any other SWF file) that are written to play FLV files.

There are two common ways you can convert a video from other formats into FLV format:

- **Using Adobe software:** Since version 8 of Flash, Adobe, which makes the Flash authoring environment, has provided another piece of software specifically for converting video formats to FLV.
- **Third-party software:** There are several companies that have made software to convert different video formats into FLV files. One example is the Riva FLV encoder available from: `http://rivavx.de/?encoder`.

Rather than writing your own FLV player, you can download one. There are several players you can use even if you do not own the Flash authoring tool, such as:

- **OS FLV Player:** `www.osflv.com/`
- **JW FLV Player:** `www.longtailvideo.com/players/jw-flv-player/`
- **Flow Player:** `http://flowplayer.org`
- **SlideShowPro:** `http://slideshowpro.net/`

Each of these players has its own way of specifying where to find the FLV file (and some also allow you to have playlists of multiple videos), so it is important to check the documentation that comes with the player in order to see how to incorporate the FLV file. There is also a range of other video players, which you can purchase on `ActiveDen.net`.

Here you can see an example of an OS FLV player being embedded in a page using the SWF Object technique that you just met in the previous section (`ch03_eg11.html`).

```
<head>
  <script type="text/javascript" src="swfobject.js"></script>
  <script type="text/javascript">
    swfobject.embedSWF("flash/os_flv_player.swf?movie=video.flv",
    "flash_video", "400", "340", "8.0.0");
  </script>
</head>
<body>
  <div id="flash_video">The content of this element would be shown
    if the user does not have Flash installed. It should therefore be
    an image and short description of what the video is about.</div>
</body>
```

You can see what this looks like in Figure 3-22:

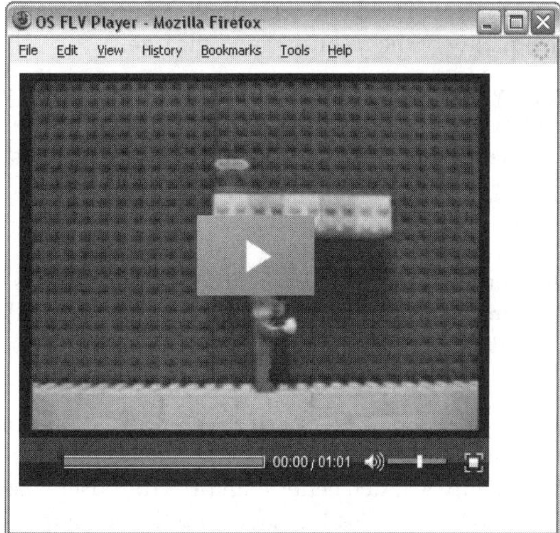

Figure 3-22

Video Size

When showing any video, you need to be aware of the physical size at which you are showing the video. It might be nice to show the video as large as possible, but the larger the video the larger the file size, and big files can be an issue for a couple of reasons:

- The smaller the file, the faster it downloads. Users are less likely to watch videos that take a long time to download, or keep pausing when the viewer is trying to watch them.
- The bigger the file, the more "bandwidth" you are using (bandwidth is the total size of files sent to visitors to your site). Because companies that host web sites often charge for bandwidth, you could end up with large bills if your video is popular. (This is a reason why many people will host their videos on sites such as YouTube — not only is it easy to upload video content and put it on your page, it is also cheaper.)

So there is always a balancing act between having a video big enough to show people what you want them to see, but not so big that it will not play smoothly on the average broadband connection.

It is also worth noting that version 9 of Flash introduced an option to make Flash movies play in a full-screen mode, which means that the player takes up the entire screen. In this mode, Flash Player can take a relatively small FLV video and use clever techniques to smooth the picture so that it can be watched at a much larger size. While the results can look a little grainy when sitting close to the computer monitor, the results can be more watchable from a distance. Most recent players have an option that allows users to watch videos in this full-screen mode.

If you have a long video, you might also want to consider splitting it into sections. By doing this you are less likely to pay for viewers to download an entire video that they may not watch to the end.

Adding Audio to Your Site

As with videos, when you want to add audio to your site you need to consider:

- **File format**: Different types of audio files are saved using different compression techniques, which can affect the quality of the recording and file size.
- **Plug-in needed to play that type of file**: As with video, visitors to your site need the right kind of player installed to play your chosen format. Luckily, there is a selection of file formats that you can play on most computers, so this is less of an issue than it is with video.

The most popular file types are:

- **MP3**: This is like the sound part of the MPEG video format. MP3 is one of the most popular formats for music recordings, and combines good compression with fairly good quality. Files are stored with the `.mp3` file extension and will play in most browsers. The MIME type for MP3s is `audio/mpeg`.
- **WAVE:** This format was developed by IBM and Microsoft, and again plays in most web browsers. WAVE files are stored with the `.wav` file extension. Typically, WAVE files are not compressed, so their quality is much better than MP3 (but users need good-quality speakers in order to hear the difference). The disadvantage with the uncompressed nature of the WAVE files is that the file sizes tend to be far larger than MP3s. The MIME type for WAVE files is `audio/x-wav`.

Three other formats that are used on the Web, all of which require their own plug-ins, are:

- **Windows Media Audio**, which requires the Windows Media plug-in
- **QuickTime**, which requires the QuickTime plug-in
- **Real Audio**, which requires the Real Media plug-in

In most cases you should use the MP3 format because it is most widely supported and has largely become the default standard for playing music on the Web, because MP3 files compress to relatively small file sizes while retaining a good sound quality. There are two main exceptions when you might like to look at a different format:

- If you need premium-quality audio, and you know that a lot of visitors to your site will have very good speakers attached to their computers (allowing them to benefit from the higher-quality audio), then you might want to consider WAVE files.
- If you need to control the number of times users can play the file, or prevent them from passing an audio file to another user, then you might need to consider audio formats that allow for Digital Rights Management or DRM (such as Windows Media Audio or Real Audio). DRM is a complex topic, which is beyond the scope of this book, but there is a lot of information about it online.

If the audio you want to play is not already in MP3 format, there are several tools that can help you create an MP3 from other audio formats. You can just search for "MP3 converter" in your favorite search engine.

You may also come across MIDI files. Rather than storing audio, MIDI files are a little more like a digital version of a score, and are used to tell your sound card (or other synthesizer) information about how to play a piece of music. It can indicate the different parts to be played on different instruments, give tempo information, and suggest how hard each instrument should play each note. The quality of sounds produced depends on the quality of the sound card.

Adding Audio Using Default Media Players

In some browsers, you do not need to download any extra plug-ins to play an MP3 or WAVE file. For example, you can just use the `<object>` element to include the audio file in the page, and the browser will automatically determine the type of plug-in needed to play your file by checking the value you have given for the `type` attribute (which is used to specify the MIME type of the file that you want to play).

Unfortunately, this technique is very unreliable because different versions of browsers expect slightly different usage of the `<object>` element, and there are also several preferences and settings that users can set on their computers that can affect whether a track will play. So even if you can get an `<object>` element to play an audio file on a page that is running on your computer, you cannot expect it to work the same on other machines.

Getting consistent results can be very problematic. To help reach a greater percentage of browsers, you may see the `<embed>` element used inside an `<object>` element. You may even come across examples where the `<embed>` element has been used without an `<object>` element, but this is also unlikely to work on as many browsers.

Here is an example of adding an MP3 to a web page; note how the `type` attribute on the `<object>` element has the value `audio/mpeg` (`ch03_eg12.html`):

```
<object width="300" height="42" type="audio/mpeg" data="audio/my_music.mp3">
  <param name="src" value="audio/my_music.mp3" />
  <param name="autoplay" value="true" />
  <param name="autostart" value="1" />
  <embed src="audio/my_music.mp3" width="300" height="42" ></embed>
</object>
```

As you can see from Figure 3-23, you get various results in different browsers. A player will be displayed in some browsers, but not in others, and when one does appear it can look different (and take up a different amount of space) than the next.

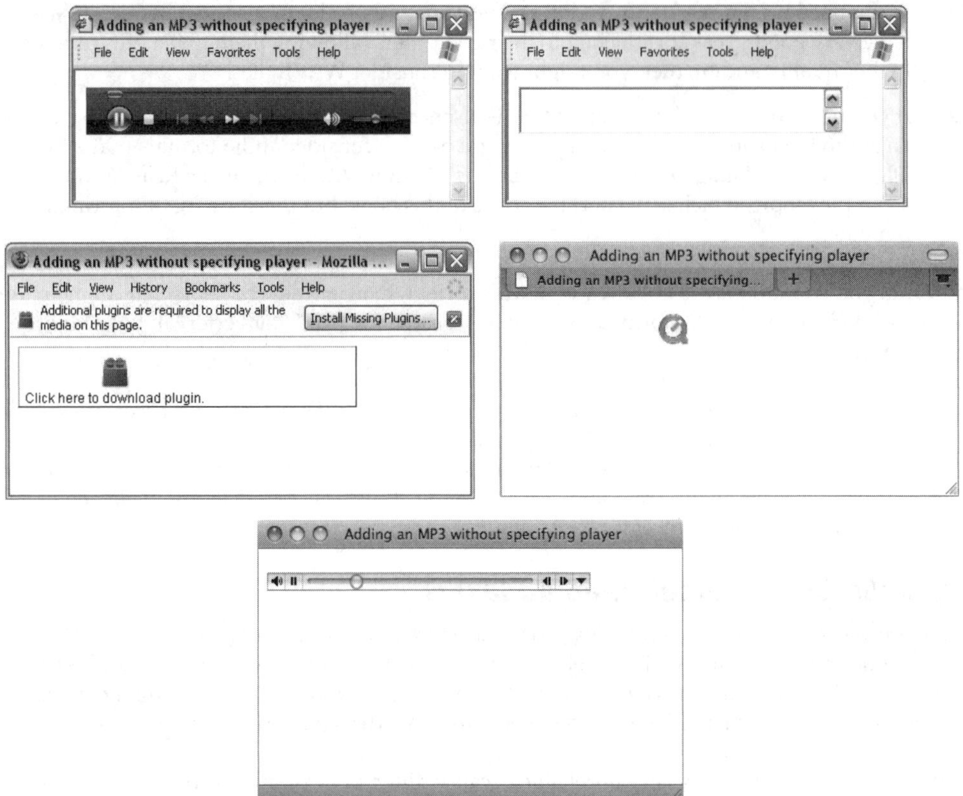

Figure 3-23

This example also shows that it is possible to control the size that the player appears using the `width` and `height` attributes, but it is important to bear in mind that the controls on different players may be of different sizes, so it is best not to make them too small. You may have also noticed the `<param>` elements that tell the player to automatically start playing when the audio file loads. The first, `autoplay`, is used by QuickTime Player, while `autoStart` is understood by Windows Media and RealPlayer. (The `<embed>` element uses the equivalent attributes.)

Some people try to resolve this problem by specifying which player to use by adding the `classid` attribute onto the `<object>` element. As you may remember, the value of this attribute is a long set of numbers/letters that identifies a particular player. However, if you specify a player, and users do not have that player installed, they will not be able to hear the audio without downloading the required plug-ins:

- `classid` for Windows Media 7+: `clsid:6BF52A52-394A-11D3-B153-00C04F79FAA6`
- `classid` for QuickTime: `clsid:02BF25D5-8C17-4B23-BC80-D3488ABDDC6B`
- `classid` for Real Player: `clsid:CFCDAA03-8BE4-11cf-B84B-0020AFBBCCFA`

While it is possible to hide the player (you can use CSS to hide the `<object>` *element, and the* `<embed>` *element can have a* `type` *attribute whose value is hidden), this is generally frowned upon because a user should be given the option to stop any audio that is played on a page.*

You may also have come across web sites that simply link to MP3 or WAV files. Some sites do this because it is more likely that the browser will be able to play the file if it links directly to it (rather than using the `<object>` and `<embed>` elements). When you click on the link, the browser plays the MP3 or WAVE files in the browser's default media player; for example, the following links would open up the files specified in the `href` attribute:

```
<a href="test.mp3">test mp3</a>
<a href="test.wav">test wav</a>
```

The drawback with both these techniques is that you have no control over the appearance of the player's interface. Therefore, a lot of people again turn to Flash when they want to create a player for audio files.

Adding MP3s to Your Pages Using Flash

In the same way that Flash has become the most popular way for showing videos on the Web (because more people have the Flash Player installed than any other media player), it has also become the most popular way to add an MP3 player to a web page. Not only do you have the advantage that it is far more likely to work in a visitor's browser, but you can also control the appearance of the interface for the player, and some Flash MP3 players allow you to create playlists that feature multiple tracks.

While you could write an MP3 player from scratch using the Flash authoring tool, several have already been written and are ready for use in your pages, such as:

- `http://musicplayer.sourceforge.net/`
- `http://www.wimpyplayer.com/`
- `http://code.google.com/p/mp3player/`
- `http://developer.yahoo.com/mediaplayer/`

There are also a variety of customizable players you can purchase from `ActiveDen.net`.

Here is an example of using the free Music Player from SourceForge.net (`ch03_eg13.html`):

```
<object type="application/x-shockwave-flash" width="400" height="170"
    data=" mp3_player.swf?playlist_url=playlist.xspf">
    <param name="movie" value="mp3_player.swf?playlist_url=playlist.xspf" />
</object>
```

In this example, you can see that the `<object>` element carries four attributes:

- A `type` attribute, indicating that the player is a Flash movie.
- The `height` and `width` attributes, indicating how much space this player will take up.
- A `data` attribute, which tells the browser where to find the Flash movie that plays the MP3 files (`mp3_player.swf`). It also tells the Flash movie where to find a playlist of the MP3s that it should play called `playlist.xspf` (you can find out more about the playlist format if you download the player from SourceForge).

Inside the `<object>` element is a `<param>` element. This `<param>` element again passes the location of the Flash movie and the playlist. Figure 3-24 shows you what this would look like in a browser.

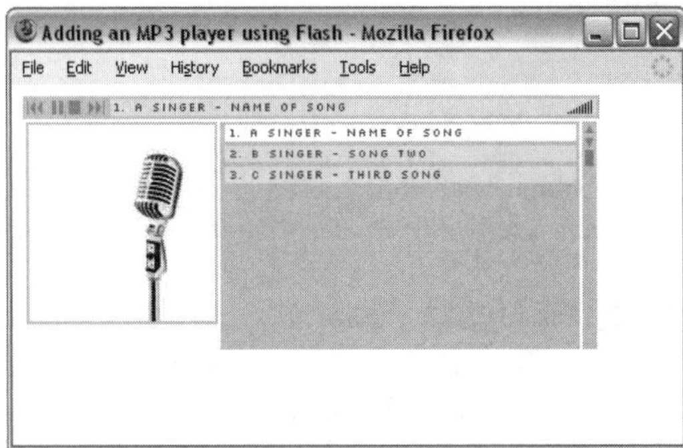

Figure 3-24

When you download a Flash MP3 player, it is likely to come with the code that the authors of the player recommend you use to embed the player in your page. The various players often require that you set different parameters to control the appearance and settings of the player, so it is best to check the instructions for using the player on the web site you download the player from. For example, some Flash MP3 players allow you to control such things as:

- The colors of the player
- Setting a list of tracks to play (rather than just one track)
- Whether to automatically start the MP3 playing when the page is loaded

When picking a player it is worth looking at the features offered by different players to see which one suits you best.

If your chosen player does not come with instructions for using the player with SWF Object, and you want to use this technique for including Flash in your pages, you can usually adapt the code to work with SWF Object. For example, here is an example of how to include the same Flash MP3 player you just met in your page using SWF Object (`ch03_eg14.html`):

```
<head>
  <title>Adding an MP3 player using Flash</title>
  <script type="text/javascript" src="swfobject.js"></script>
  <script type="text/javascript">

swfobject.embedSWF("flash/xspf_player.swf?playlist_url=flash/playlist.xspf",
   "flash_mp3_player", "400", "170", "8.0.0");
  </script>
</head>
<body>
  <div id="flash_mp3_player">Here is where the Flash MP3 Player goes.</div>
</body>
```

Automatically Playing Audio and Video When a Page Loads

Having seen several techniques that allow you to add audio and video to your page, it is important to consider the issue of whether the audio or video should play automatically when the page loads.

- More people are likely to watch or listen to a file if it starts up automatically than if they are forced to interact with a player. However, some visitors to your site might leave the page very quickly if the browser starts to play audio when they were not expecting it to (particularly if they are browsing your site at work). If a visitor has anticipated hearing audio on your site, this is less likely to be an issue. (A site owned by a record label or video production company is far more likely to have audio than a site owned by an accountant or a builder.) So when deciding whether to play audio or video when a page loads, consider what your users would expect to see.
- If you do automatically play audio or video when a page loads, always offer a clear pause or mute button that allows the user to turn off the sound.
- People can tire of hearing the same track repeatedly, so if you expect people to regularly visit your site or spend a long time on it, try to avoid repetitious use of the same tracks, and offer clear options for the user to turn off the music.
- If the audio and video files are hosted on your server, you will be paying for the bandwidth of the files being played. Therefore, if the file starts automatically when the page loads, you might be paying for people to watch and listen to files that they aren't interested in.

Because the `<embed>` element is deprecated, it is covered in Appendix I.

A Closer Look at the <object> and <param> Elements

Now that you have seen several examples of how to add rich media to your web pages, we'll finish off the chapter with a closer look at the `<object>` and `<param>` elements in the same way that we have covered the syntax of other elements in previous chapters. Because the `<embed>` element is deprecated, it is covered in Appendix I.

The <object> element can carry all the universal attributes, the UI event attributes, and the following attributes:

```
archive border classid codebase codetype data declare height width hspace
vspace name standby tabindex usemap
```

We'll take a look at each of these here, although the ones you will most commonly use are the classid attribute, the type attribute, and the id attributes (discussed in Chapter 1).

The archive Attribute

The archive attribute is of particular use with Java-based applications. The value should be a space-separated list of URLs to the resources the object needs in order to run (such as Java classes).

The border Attribute (Deprecated)

The border attribute specifies the width of the border to appear around the object; the value is specified in pixels. However, it is deprecated and you should use the border property in CSS instead.

The classid Attribute

The classid attribute is designed to specify the type of application that is required (such as the type of media player) in order for the browser to process a file.

For example, when you want to include a Flash movie the classid attribute would use a special value that indicates the object loaded should be the Flash Player. If you wanted to play a QuickTime movie you may indicate that the QuickTime plug-in should be loaded. When you are working with Java, the value of this attribute is likely to be the Java class you want to include.

The following is an example of a classid to embed a player to show a QuickTime movie:

```
classid="clsid:02BF25D5-8C17-4B23-BC80-D3488ABDDC6B"
```

The codebase Attribute

If the browser does not have the required plug-in (or other code) required to display the file specified in the <object> element, then the codebase attribute specifies the base URL where a plug-in can be downloaded. The idea is that if the browser cannot display the file it will offer the user the option to download the necessary files. For example, if you were working with Java, it might look like this:

```
codebase="http://www.example.org/javaclasses/"
```

The codetype Attribute

The codetype attribute specifies the MIME type of the application or code required to play the file (not to be confused with the MIME type of the file itself). For example, if you wanted to embed an Excel spreadsheet into a web page, you would have a codetype attribute like this:

```
<object data="sales.xls" codetype="application/vnd.ms-excel">
```

Browsers can use the codetype attribute to skip over unsupported media types without having to download unnecessary objects. Appendix H covers MIME types.

The declare Attribute

The `declare` attribute is used to declare an object without instantiating it. It saves you from having to download an object until it is actually required.

It is a Boolean attribute, and while it does not need a value in HTML, all attributes in XHTML require a value, so you would use the following:

```
declare="declare"
```

The data Attribute

If the object has a file to process or play, then the `data` attribute specifies the URL for that file. For example, here is a URL to an MP3:

```
data="http://www.example.com/mp3s/newsong.mp3"
```

This is similar to the `src` attribute that is used on the `<img>` element, and the value can be a relative URL.

The height and width Attributes

The `height` and `width` attributes specify the height and width of an object. The values should be in pixels or a percentage of the containing element. They are treated just like `height` and `width` attributes of the `<img>` element. The use of these attributes should make the page load faster because the browser can lay out the rest of the page without completely loading the object.

The hspace and vspace attributes (Deprecated)

The `hspace` and `vspace` attributes specify the amount of white space that should appear around an object, just as when they are used with the `<img>` element. They have been replaced by the `margin` and `border` properties of CSS.

The name Attribute (Deprecated)

The `name` attribute provides a name that can be used to refer to the object, in particular for use in scripts. It has been replaced by the `id` attribute in XHTML.

The standby Attribute

The `standby` attribute specifies a text string that will be used when the object is loading:

```
standby="Trailer for Harry Potter 27 is loading"
```

The value should be a meaningful description of the object that is loading.

The tabindex Attribute

The `tabindex` attribute indicates the tab index of the object within a page. Tabbing order is discussed in Chapter 5.

The usemap Attribute

The `usemap` attribute indicates that the object is an image map containing defined areas that are hyperlinks. Its value is the map file used with the object. It can be a complete URL to an external file or a reference to the value of an inline `<map>` element's `name` attribute. See the "Image Maps" section earlier in this chapter.

The <param> Element

The `<param>` element is used to pass parameters to an object. The kinds of parameters an object requires depend upon what the object does; for example, if an object has to load a Flash MP3 player into the page, you will probably need to specify where the MP3 file can be found. Alternatively, if you are adding a video to a page, your object might allow you to tell it whether to automatically play the video when the page loads, or whether to wait for the user to press a play button in order for it to start.

In addition to the universal attributes and basic events, the `<param>` element can carry the following attributes:

```
name type value valuetype
```

The name and value Attributes

The `name` and `value` attributes act as a name/value pair (rather like attributes themselves). The `name` attribute provides a name for the parameter you are passing to the application, while the `value` gives the value of the parameter.

Here are a couple of examples, taken from a QuickTime movie. The first parameter indicates the source of the file being loaded to play, while the second indicates that the movie should start playing automatically as it is loading (without the user having to start it):

```
<param name="src" value="movieTrailer.mov" />
<param name="autoplay" value="true" />
```

If you were working with a Java applet, you could use the `name` and `value` attribute to pass values into a method.

The valuetype Attribute

If your object accepts parameters, then the `valuetype` attribute indicates whether the parameter will be a file, URL, or indeed another object. The table that follows shows the possible values.

Value	Purpose
`data`	The parameter value is a simple string — this is the default value.
`ref`	The parameter value is a URL.
`object`	The parameter value is another object.

The type Attribute

This specifies the MIME type of the content being used in the object. For example, you might want to specify that you were passing an MP3 file, in which case you would use the `value` attribute like so:

```
value="audio/mpeg"
```

Summary

In this chapter, you have learned how to make your pages look a lot more exciting by adding images and other multimedia objects.

Images can really add life to a page, but they can also increase the time it takes to load a page. Therefore it pays to save any images you want to show on the Web in either JPEG, GIF, or PNG formats, which compress well (creating smaller files) while retaining quality.

The GIF and PNG formats are the formats of choice for images with flat colors, while JPEGs are better for photographic images and graphics with gradients of the same color.

When looking at images, you also learned how to make image links, and how to create an image map, which divides an image into separate parts that you can click on.

Moving on, you saw how to add Flash movies, video, and audio to your site. You learned that there are two important factors in adding video and audio to your site; first, the format you are going to add the content in (the file type), and second, the kind of technology you would use to play the files.

For adding videos to web pages, you found that FLV is the most popular format, and that FLVs are played in a Flash Movie (which in turn requires the Flash Player plug-in to be installed on your machine).

For audio, MP3 is the most common format, and many web programmers prefer to use Flash to play their MP3 files because it has more consistent results in different browsers, and also allows them to control the appearance of the interface for the player.

Now you should be well-equipped to add images and rich media to your pages, which should make them look more appealing and attract more visitors.

Exercises

The answers to all the exercises are in Appendix A.

1. Add the images of icons that represent a diary, a camera, and a newspaper to the following example. All of the images are provided in the `images` folder in the download code for Chapter 3.

```
<h1>Icons</h1>
<p>Here is an icon used to represent a diary.</p>
<img src="images/diary.gif" alt="Diary" width="150" height="120" /><br />

<p>Here is an icon used to represent a picture.</p>
Camera image goes here<br />

<p>Here is an icon used to represent a news item.</p>
Newspaper image goes here<br />
```

Your finished page should resemble Figure 3-25.

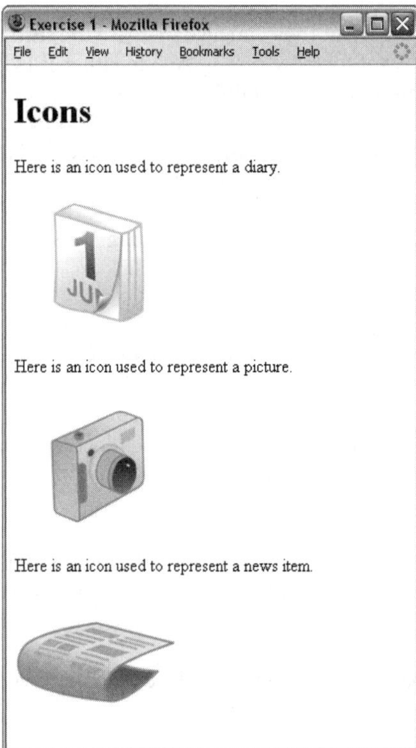

Figure 3-25

2. Look at the images shown in Figures 3-26 and 3-27 and decide whether you are more likely to get smaller file sizes and better quality images if you save them as GIFs or JPEGs.

Figure 3-26

Figure 3-27

3. Go through the files for the sample application and replace the main heading with the logo on each page. On every page except for the homepage, make sure that the image links back to the `index.html` page.

Tables

Tables display information in rows and columns; they are commonly used to display all manner of data that fits in a grid such as train schedules, television listings, financial reports, and sports results. In this chapter, you learn when to use tables, and the markup that you need to create them.

To begin this chapter, we'll look at some examples of tables, then quickly move onto the basic elements that are used to create them. Having learned the basics, you can then go on to learn some of the more advanced features of tables such as adding captions and headings, and how to achieve more complicated table layouts. Along the way, you will also learn some deprecated markup that was designed to control the appearance of tables because, even though it is preferable to use CSS to control the way a page looks, you may sometimes come across pages that use the older markup.

The chapter ends with a discussion of accessibility issues that relate to tables, because it is important to understand how a screen reader would read the contents of a table to users with visual impairments.

Introducing Tables

In order to work with tables, you need to start thinking in *grids*, so let's start off by looking at some examples of how popular web sites use tables.

In Figure 4-1 you can see the NFL web site. This page shows the standings for each team in a table. You can see a list of teams down the left, and for each team there are columns providing different stats, including number of games won, lost, or tied.

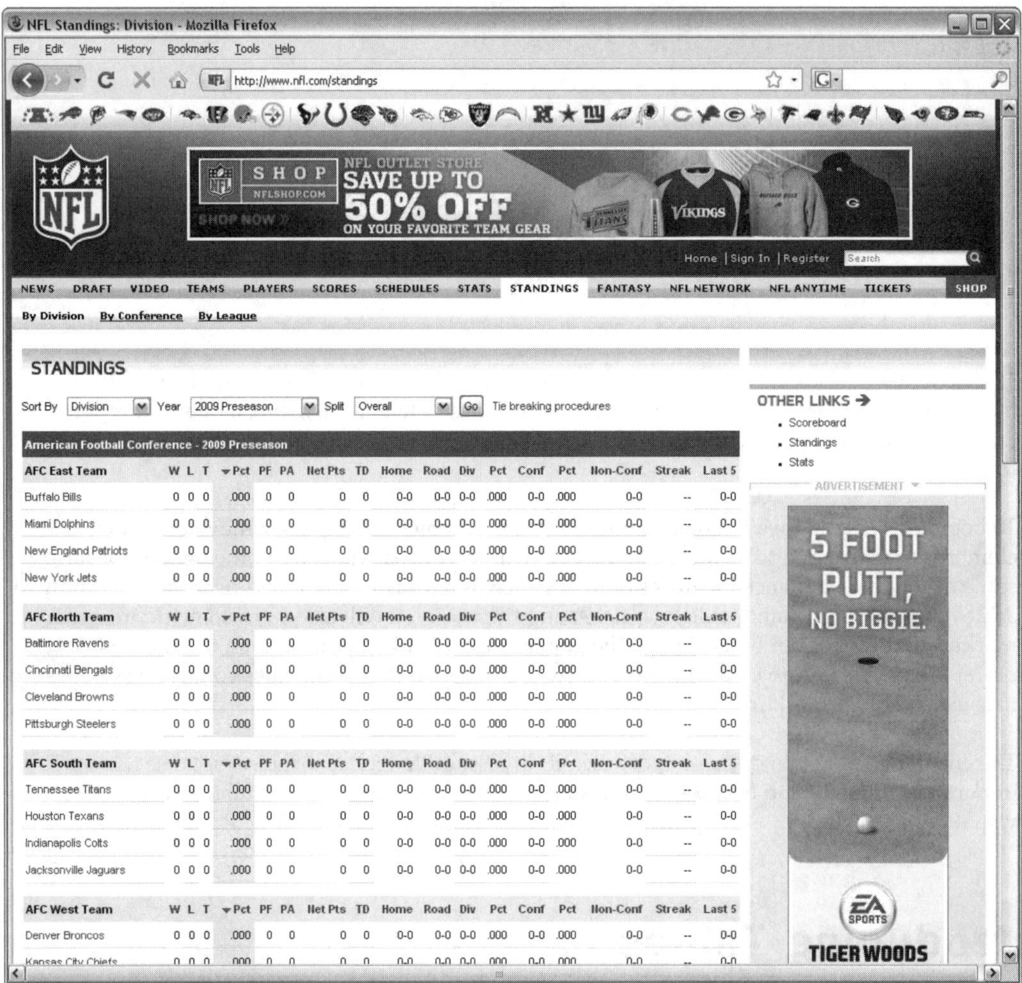

Figure 4-1

Figure 4-2 shows the Bloomberg web site. This page shows major stock markets. In this case, there are tables for different regions around the world (in this screenshot, you can see North and Latin America as

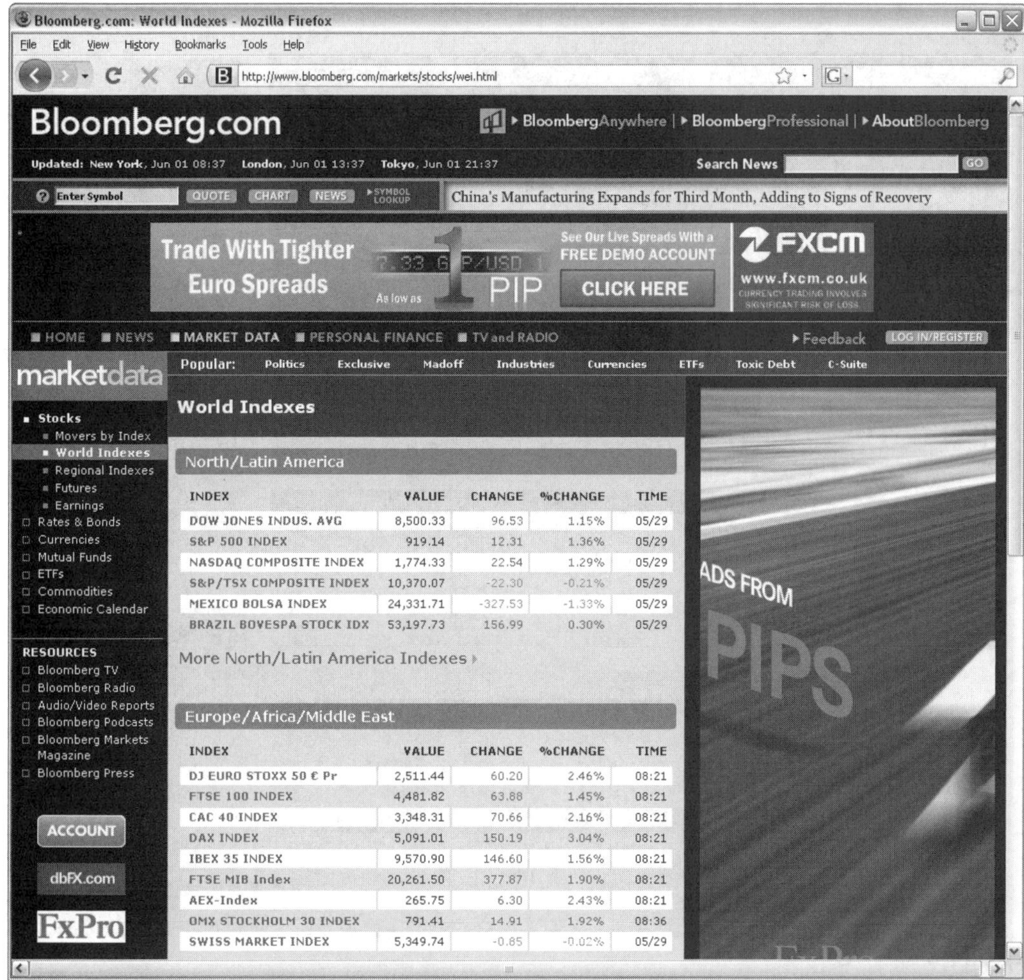

Figure 4-2

the first region, followed by Europe, Africa, and the Middle East). Each table contains the major indexes trading in that region down the left-hand side, followed by columns that show the current value, fluctuations in values, and date/time of the stats.

In Figure 4-3 you can see the web site for the Heathrow Express, a train between Central London and London's Heathrow Airport. The tables on this page show the times that the trains run.

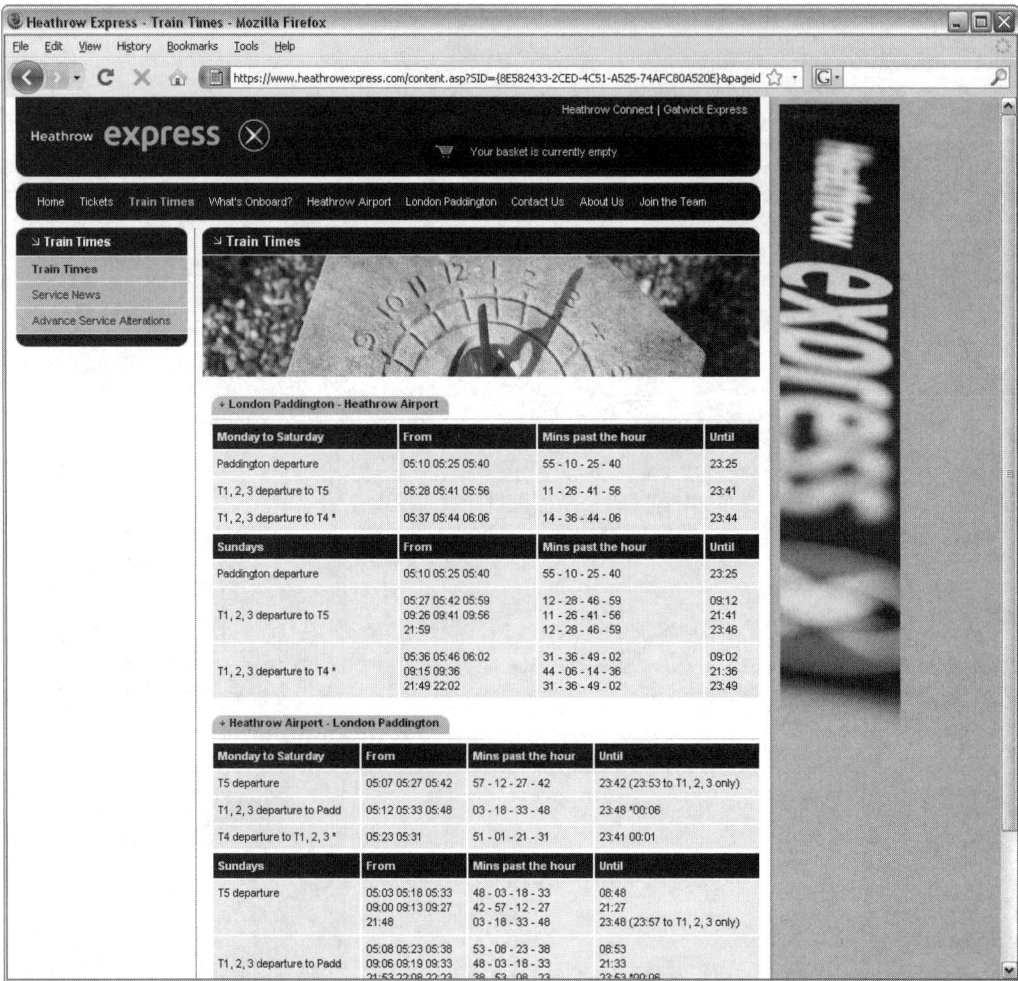

Figure 4-3

In Figure 4-4, you can see the *New York Times* web site. On this page, the tables provide television listings.

Figure 4-4

I hope these examples give you a better idea of what a table is and when you might want to use one. I am not suggesting that every web site that displays stock market data or television listings should use a table — rather that you should consider using a table when you need to display information that sits well in a grid of rows and columns. If you are looking at a web page and want to know whether that page is using a table to control how the data is laid out, you can always look at the source for that page and look for the elements you are about to read about in this chapter.

You can think of a table as being very similar to a spreadsheet because it is made up of rows and columns, as shown in Figure 4-5.

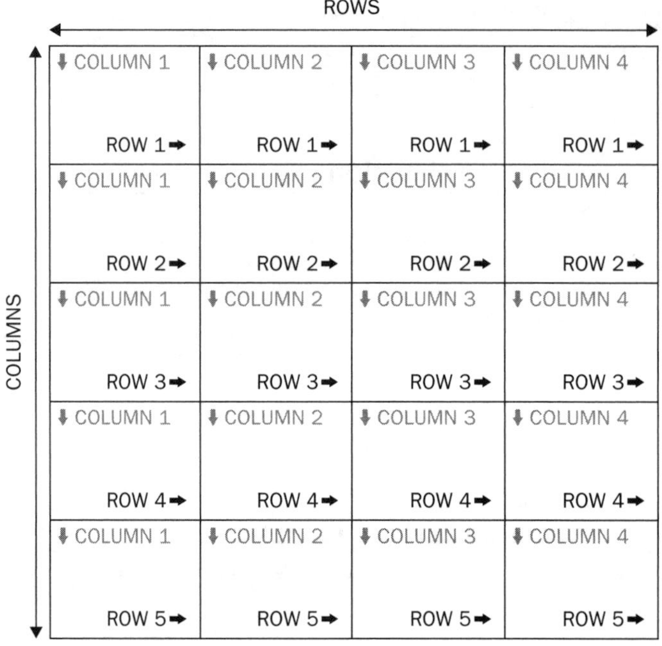

Figure 4-5

Here you can see a grid of rectangles. Each rectangle is known as a *cell*. A *row* is made up of a set of cells on the same line from left to right, and a *column* is made up of a line of cells going from top to bottom.

Let's look at an example of a very basic XHTML table so that you can see how they are created (see Figure 4-6).

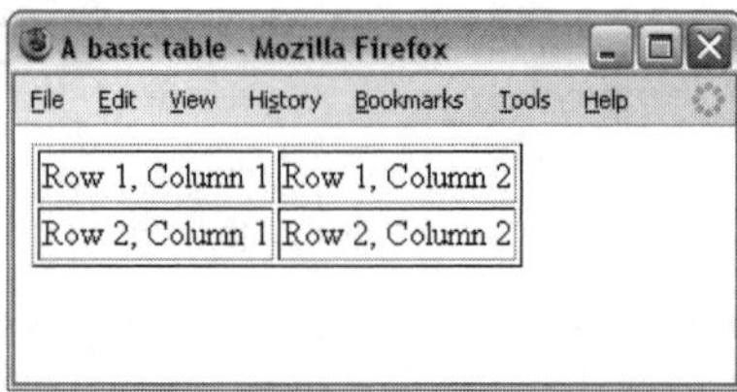

Figure 4-6

You create a table in XHTML using the `<table>` element. Inside the `<table>` element, the table is written out row by row. A row is contained inside a `<tr>` element — which stands for *table row*. Each cell is then written inside the row element using a `<td>` element — which stands for *table data*.

Here is the code that was used to create this basic table (ch04_eg01.html):

```
<table border="1">
  <tr>
    <td>Row 1, Column 1</td>
    <td>Row 1, Column 2</td>
  </tr>
  <tr>
    <td>Row 2, Column 1</td>
    <td>Row 2, Column 2</td>
  </tr>
</table>
```

When writing code for a table in a text editor, I'm always extra careful to start each row and cell on a new line and to indent table cells inside table rows as shown. If you are using a web page authoring tool such as Dreamweaver, it will probably automatically indent the code for you.

Many web page authors find it particularly helpful to indent the code for a table because leaving off just one tag in a table can prevent the entire table from being displayed properly. Indenting the code makes it easier to keep track of the opening and closing of each element.

Take a look at the same code again. This time, it has not been split onto separate lines or indented, and I'm sure you will agree it's much harder to read.

```
<table border="1"><tr><td>Row 1, Column 1</td><td>Row 1, Column 2</td></tr><tr>
<td>Row 2, Column 1</td><td>Row 2, Column 2</td></tr></table>
```

All tables will follow this basic structure, although there are additional elements and attributes that allow you to control the presentation of tables. If a row or column should contain a heading, a <th> element should be used in place of the <td> element for the cells that contain a heading. By default, most browsers render the content of a <th> element in bold text.

> **Each cell must be represented by either a <td> or a <th> element in order for the table to display correctly, even if there is no data in that cell.**

Let's take a look at a slightly more complicated table (see Figure 4-7). This time the table includes headings. In this example, the table shows a financial summary for a small company.

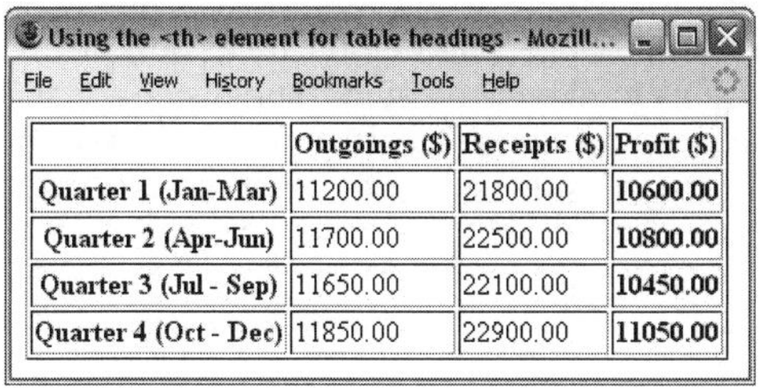

Using the <th> element for table headings - Mozill...

File Edit View History Bookmarks Tools Help

	Outgoings ($)	**Receipts ($)**	**Profit ($)**
Quarter 1 (Jan-Mar)	11200.00	21800.00	**10600.00**
Quarter 2 (Apr-Jun)	11700.00	22500.00	**10800.00**
Quarter 3 (Jul - Sep)	11650.00	22100.00	**10450.00**
Quarter 4 (Oct - Dec)	11850.00	22900.00	**11050.00**

Figure 4-7

Here is the code that was used to create this table (ch04_eg02.html):

```
<table border="1">
  <tr>
    <td></td>
    <th>Outgoings ($)</th>
   <th>Receipts ($)</th>
    <th>Profit ($)</th>
  </tr>
  <tr>
    <th>Quarter 1 (Jan-Mar)</th>
    <td>11200.00</td>
    <td>21800.00</td>
    <td><b>10600.00</b></td>
  </tr>
  <tr>
    <th>Quarter 2 (Apr-Jun)</th>
    <td>11700.00</td>
    <td>22500.00</td>
    <td><b>10800.00</b></td>
  </tr>
  <tr>
    <th>Quarter 3 (Jul - Sep)</th>
    <td>11650.00</td>
    <td>22100.00</td>
    <td><b>10450.00</b></td>
  </tr>
  <tr>
    <th>Quarter 4 (Oct - Dec)</th>
    <td>11850.00</td>
    <td>22900.00</td>
    <td><b>11050.00</b></td>
  </tr>
</table>
```

The first row is made entirely of headings for outgoings, receipts, and profit. Note how the top-left cell in Figure 4-7 is empty; in the code for the table, we still need an empty `<td>` element to tell the browser that this cell is empty (otherwise it has no way of knowing that there is an empty cell here).

In each row, the first cell is also a table heading cell (indicated using a `<th>`), which states which quarter the results are for. Then the remaining three cells of each row contain table data and are contained inside the `<td>` elements.

The figures showing the profit (in the right-hand column) are contained within a `<b>` element, which shows the profit figures in a bold typeface. This demonstrates how any cell can, in fact, contain all manner of markup. The only constraint on placing markup inside a table is that it must nest within the table cell element (be that a `<td>` or a `<th>` element). You cannot have an opening tag for an element inside a table cell and a closing tag outside that cell — or vice versa.

When creating tables, many people do not actually bother with the <th> element and instead use the <td> element for every cell — including headers. You should, however, aim to use the <th> element whenever you have a table heading.

As you can see from the examples so far in this chapter, tables can take up a lot of space and make a document longer, but clear formatting of tables makes it much easier to see what is going on in your code. No matter how familiar the code looks when you write it, you will be glad that you made good use of structure if you have to come back to it a year later.

Basic Table Elements and Attributes

Now that you've seen how basic tables work, this section describes the elements in a little more detail, introducing the attributes they can carry. Some of the attributes allow you to create more sophisticated table layouts. Feel free to skim through this section fairly quickly; once you know what is possible to do with the markup, you can always come back again and study the markup more closely in order to see how to achieve what you want.

The <table> Element Creates a Table

The <table> element is the containing element for all tables. It can carry the following attributes:

- All the universal attributes
- Basic event attributes for scripting

The <table> element can carry the following deprecated attributes. Even though they are deprecated, you will still see many of them in use today:

```
align bgcolor border cellpadding cellspacing dir frame rules summary width
```

The align Attribute (Deprecated)

Although it is deprecated, the `align` attribute is still frequently used with tables. When used with the <table> element, it indicates whether the table should be aligned to the `left` (the default), `right`, or `center` of the page. (When used with cells, as you will see shortly, it aligns the content of that cell.) You use the attribute like so:

```
<table align="center">
```

You can put a whole table inside a single cell of another table (or inside other block-level elements), and if a table is contained within another element, the `align` attribute will indicate whether the table should be aligned to the left, right, or center of that element.

When the `align` attribute is used on a table, text should flow around it (rather like it can flow around an image). For example, here is a left-aligned table that is followed by some text (`ch04_eg03.html`):

```
<table border="1" align="left">
  <tr>
    <td>Row 1, Column 1</td>
    <td>Row 1, Column 2</td>
  </tr>
  <tr>
    <td>Row 2, Column 1</td>
    <td>Row 2, Column 2</td>
  </tr>
</table>
Lorem ipsum dolor sit amet, consectetuer adipiscing elit...
```

The text should flow around the table, as shown in the first table in Figure 4-8.

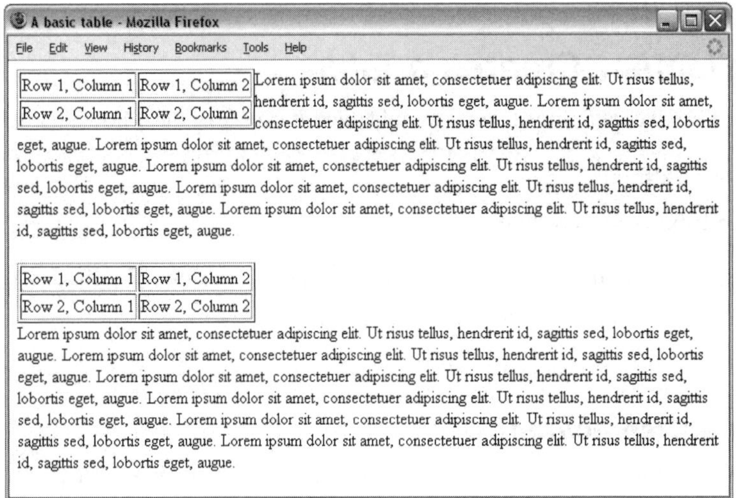

Figure 4-8

If you do not want the text to flow around the table, you can use the CSS `clear` property on the element after it (you will learn about this in Chapter 8). Alternatively, you *could* place a line break after the table and add the `clear` attribute, which is also deprecated `<br clear="left" />` (although the CSS `clear` property would be the preferred method). This is demonstrated in the second table of Figure 4-8.

```
</table>
<br clear="left" />
Lorem ipsum dolor sit amet, consectetuer adipiscing elit...
```

The `clear` attribute indicates how the browser should display the next line after the line break. With the value of `left`, the text can begin only when there is nothing positioned on the left margin of the browser window (or containing element). The `clear` attribute is covered in more detail in Appendix I.

The bgcolor Attribute (Deprecated)

The `bgcolor` attribute sets the background color for the table. The value of this attribute should either be a color name or a six-digit code known as a *hex code*. The way in which colors are specified in XHTML and CSS is covered in Appendix D. (The `bgcolor` attribute has been replaced by the `background-color` property in CSS.)

The syntax is as follows:

```
bgcolor="red"
```

The border Attribute (Deprecated)

If you use the `border` attribute, a border will be created around both the table and each individual cell. The value for this attribute is the width you want the outside border of the table to be, in pixels. If you give this attribute a value of `0`, or if you do not use this attribute, then you should not get any borders on either the table or any cells. (This has been replaced by the `border` property in CSS.)

```
border="0"
```

While this attribute is deprecated, it has been used in several of the examples in this chapter so that you can clearly see where the edge of each table cell is.

The cellpadding Attribute (Deprecated)

The `cellpadding` attribute is used to create a gap between the edges of a cell and its contents. The value for this attribute determines the amount of space or padding inside each wall of the cell, specified either in pixels or as a percentage value (where the percentage is a percentage of the width of each cell).

`cellpadding="5"` or `cellpadding="2%"`

As you can imagine, if two table cells sat next to each other and both contained writing, there could be a problem. If there were not a gap between the edge of the cells and the writing, the words would butt up against each other, making them hard to read. Similarly, if there were a border around each cell and the text touched the border, it could be hard to read. Therefore, adding padding to cells makes their contents easier to read.

This attribute has been replaced by the `padding` property in CSS.

The cellspacing Attribute (Deprecated)

The `cellspacing` attribute is used to create a space between the borders of each cell. The value for this attribute can be either the amount of space you want to create between the cells, in pixels, or a percentage value.

```
cellspacing="6" or cellspacing="2%"
```

This attribute has been replaced by the `margin` property in CSS.

The dir Attribute

The `dir` attribute is supposed to indicate the direction of text that is used in the table. Possible values are `ltr` for left to right text and `rtl` for right to left (for languages such as Hebrew and Arabic):

```
dir="rtl"
```

If you use the `dir` attribute with a value of `rtl` on the `<table>` element, then the cells appear from the right first, and each consecutive cell is placed to the left of that one.

The frame Attribute (Deprecated)

The `frame` attribute is supposed to control the appearance of the outermost border of the whole table, referred to here as its *frame*, with greater control than the `border` attribute. If both the `frame` and `border` attributes are used, the `frame` attribute takes precedence. The syntax is:

```
frame="frameType"
```

The following table shows the possible values for the `frame` attribute.

Value	Purpose
`void`	No outer border (the default)
`above`	A border on the top only
`below`	A border on the bottom only
`hsides`	A border on the top and bottom
`lhs`	A border on the left side of table
`rhs`	A border on the right side of table
`vsides`	A border on the left and right sides of table
`box`	A border on all sides
`border`	A border on all sides

Support for the `frame` attribute is not perfect across browsers, and its role has been replaced by the CSS `border` property, which can give better results.

The rules Attribute (Deprecated)

The `rules` attribute is used to indicate which inner borders of the table should be displayed. For example, you can just specify that the rows *or* columns should have lines between each of them. Here is the syntax; the default value is `none`.

```
rules="ruleType"
```

The following table shows the possible values for the `rules` attribute:

Value	Purpose
`none`	No inner borders (the default)
`groups`	Displays inner borders between all table groups (groups are created by the `<thead>`, `<tbody>`, `<tfoot>`, and `<colgroup>` elements)
`rows`	Displays horizontal borders between each row
`cols`	Displays vertical borders between each column
`all`	Displays horizontal and vertical borders between each row and column

Again, support for this attribute is not perfect, and it has been deprecated in favor of the CSS `border` property, which achieves better results.

The summary Attribute

The `summary` attribute is supposed to provide a summary of the table's purpose and structure for non-visual browsers such as speech browsers or Braille browsers. The value of this attribute is not rendered in IE or Firefox, but if the text before the table doesn't clearly explain what will be found in the table, you should aim to use it in your pages:

```
summary="Table shows the operating profit for the last four quarters. The
first column indicates the quarter, the second indicates outgoings, the
third indicates receipts, and the fourth indicates profit."
```

The width Attribute (Deprecated)

The `width` attribute is used to specify the width of the table, and usually its value is given in pixels.

```
width="500"
```

It is also possible to use a percentage of the available space, the available space generally being the width of the browser, unless the table sits inside another element within the body of the page, in which case it is a percentage of the size of the containing element.

```
width="90%"
```

The <tr> Element Contains Table Rows

The `<tr>` element is used to contain each row in a table. Anything appearing within a `<tr>` element should appear on the same row. It can carry five attributes, three of which have been deprecated in favor of using CSS.

```
align bgcolor char charoff valign
```

The align Attribute (Deprecated)

The `align` attribute specifies the position of the content of all of the cells in the row.

```
align="alignment"
```

The table that follows lists the possible values for the `align` attribute:

Value	Purpose
`left`	Content is left-aligned.
`right`	Content is right-aligned.
`center`	Content is centered horizontally within the cell.
`justify`	Text within the cell is justified to fill the cell.
`char`	Cell contents are aligned horizontally around the first instance of a specific character (for example, numbers could be aligned around the first instance of a decimal point).

By default, any `<td>` cells are usually left-aligned, whereas any `<th>` cells are usually centered. While Firefox 2+ supports justified text, IE does not, and neither IE nor Firefox support the value `char`.

The bgcolor Attribute (Deprecated)

The `bgcolor` attribute sets the background color for the row. The value of this attribute should be either a color name or a hex code or color value, as discussed in Appendix D.

```
bgcolor="red"
```

The `bgcolor` attribute is commonly used on the `<tr>` element to shade alternate rows of a table with different colors, thus making it easier to read across each row.

The char Attribute

If the `align` attribute has been given a value of `char`, then the `char` attribute is used to specify that the contents of each cell within the row will be aligned around the first instance of a particular character known as an *axis character*. The default character for this attribute is the decimal place, and the idea is that decimal figures would be aligned by the decimal point like so:

```
13412.22
  232.147
 2449.6331
    2.12
```

The syntax is as follows:

```
char="."
```

Unfortunately, this potentially very helpful attribute is not supported at the time of this writing, and there is no requirement for browsers to support it.

The charoff Attribute

The `charoff` attribute is used in association with the `char` attribute, and indicates an offset for the `char` attribute. For example, if it is given a value of `2`, then the elements are aligned with the character that is two characters along from the one specified by the `char` attribute. It can also take a negative value.

If this attribute is omitted, the default behavior is to make the offset the equivalent of the longest amount of text content that appeared before the character specified in the `char` attribute.

```
charoff="2"
```

Unfortunately, this attribute is not supported at the time of this writing, and there is no requirement for browsers to support it.

The valign Attribute (Deprecated)

The `valign` attribute specifies the vertical alignment of the contents of each cell in the row. The syntax is as follows:

```
valign="verticalPosition"
```

The table that follows shows the possible values of the `valign` attribute:

Value	Purpose
`top`	Aligns content with the top of the cell
`middle`	(Vertically) aligns content in the center of a cell
`bottom`	Aligns content with the bottom of the cell
`baseline`	Aligns content so that the first line of text in each cell starts on the same horizontal line

The <td> and <th> Elements Represent Table Cells

Every cell in a table will be represented by either a `<td>` element for cells containing table data or a `<th>` element for cells containing table headings.

By default, the contents of a `<th>` element are usually displayed in a bold font, horizontally aligned in the center of the cell. The content of a `<td>` element, meanwhile, will usually be displayed left-aligned and not in bold (unless otherwise indicated by CSS or another element).

The `<td>` and `<th>` elements can both carry the same set of attributes, and the attribute only applies to that one cell carrying it. Any effect these attributes have will override settings for the table as a whole or any containing element (such as a row).

In addition to the universal attributes and the basic event attributes, the `<td>` and `<th>` elements can also carry the following attributes:

```
abbr align axis bgcolor char charoff colspan headers
height nowrap rowspan scope valign width
```

The abbr Attribute

The `abbr` attribute is used to provide an abbreviated version of the cell's content.

```
abbr="description of services"
```

While the major browsers do not currently support this attribute, it's possible that it will be used by some of the increasing number of devices with small screens accessing the Internet. For example, if a browser with a small screen is being used to view the page, the content of this attribute could be displayed instead of the full content of the cell.

The align Attribute (Deprecated)

The `align` attribute sets the horizontal alignment for the content of the cell.

```
align="alignment"
```

The possible values for the `align` attribute are `left`, `right`, `center`, `justify`, and `char`, each of which was described earlier in "The < tr > Element Contains Table Rows" section.

The axis Attribute

The `axis` attribute allows you to add conceptual categories to cells and therefore represent *n*-dimensional data. The value of this attribute would be a comma-separated list of names for each category the cell belonged to.

```
axis="heavy, old, valuable"
```

Rather than having a visual formatting effect, this attribute allows you to preserve data, which then may be used programmatically, such as querying for all cells belonging to a certain category.

The bgcolor Attribute (Deprecated)

The `bgcolor` attribute sets the background color for the cell. The value of this attribute should be either a color name or a hex code — both are covered in Appendix D.

```
bgcolor="red"
```

It has been replaced by the `background-color` property in CSS.

The char Attribute

The `char` attribute specifies a character, the first instance of which should be used to horizontally align the contents of a cell. (See the full description in the "The `char` Attribute" subsection within the "The <tr> Element Contains Table Rows" section earlier in the chapter.)

The charoff Attribute

The `charoff` attribute specifies the number of offset characters that can be displayed before the character specified as the value of the `char` attribute. (See the full description in the "The `charoff` Attribute" subsection within the "The `<tr>` Element Contains Table Rows" section earlier in the chapter.)

The colspan Attribute

The `colspan` attribute is used when a cell should span across more than one column. The value of the attribute specifies how many columns of the table a cell will span across. (See the section "Spanning Columns Using the `colspan` Attribute" later in this chapter.)

```
colspan="2"
```

The headers Attribute

The `headers` attribute is used to indicate which headers correspond to that cell. The value of the attribute is a space-separated list of the header cells' `id` attribute values:

```
headers="income q1"
```

The main purpose of this attribute is to support voice browsers. When a table is being read to you, it can be hard to keep track of which row and column you are on; therefore, the `header` attribute is used to remind users which row and column the current cell's data belongs to.

The height Attribute (Deprecated)

The `height` attribute allows you to specify the height of a cell in pixels, or as a percentage of the available space:

`height="20"` or `height="10%"`

It has been replaced by the CSS `height` property.

The nowrap Attribute (Deprecated)

The `nowrap` attribute is used to stop text from wrapping onto a new line within a cell. You would use `nowrap` only when the text really would not make sense if it were allowed to wrap onto the next line (for example, a line of code that would not work if it were spread across two lines). When it was initially introduced in HTML, it was used without an attribute value, but that would not be allowed in XHTML. Rather, you would have to use the following:

```
nowrap="nowrap"
```

The rowspan Attribute

The `rowspan` attribute specifies the number of rows of the table a cell will span across, the value of the attribute being the number of rows the cell stretches across. (See the example in the section "Spanning Rows Using the `rowspan` Attribute" later in this chapter.)

```
rowspan="2"
```

The scope Attribute

The `scope` attribute can be used to indicate which cells the current header provides a label or header information for. It can be used instead of the `headers` attribute in basic tables, but does not have much support.

```
scope="range"
```

The table that follows shows the possible values of the attribute:

Value	Purpose
`row`	Cell contains header information for that row.
`col`	Cell contains header information for that column.
`rowgroup`	Cell contains header information for that rowgroup (a group of cells in a row created using the `<thead>`, `<tbody>`, or `<tfoot>` elements).
`colgroup`	Cell contains header information for that colgroup (a group of columns created using the `<col>` or `<colgroup>` element, both of which are discussed later in the chapter).

The valign Attribute (Deprecated)

The `valign` attribute allows you to specify the vertical alignment for the content of the cell. Possible values are `top`, `middle`, `bottom`, and `baseline`, each of which was discussed earlier in the chapter in the subsection entitled "The `valign` Attribute" within the section "The `<tr>` Element Contains Table Rows."

The width Attribute (Deprecated)

The `width` attribute allows you to specify the width of a cell in pixels, or as a percentage of the table:

```
width="150" or width="30%"
```

You only need to specify the `width` attribute for the cells in the first row of a table, and the rest of the rows will follow the first row's cell widths.

If you had already specified a `width` attribute for the `<table>` element, and the widths of individual cells add up to more than that width, most browsers will squash those cells to fit them into the width of the table.

You can also add a special value of `*`, which means that this cell will take up the remaining space available in the table. So if you have a table that is 300 pixels wide and the first two cells in a row are specified as being 50 pixels wide, if the third cell has a value of `*`, it will take up 200 pixels — the remaining width of the table. If the width of the table had not been specified, then the third column would take up the remaining width of the browser window.

It is worth noting that you cannot specify different widths for different `<td>` elements that belong in the same column. So, if the first row of a table had three `<td>` elements whose widths were 100 pixels, the second row could not have one `<td>` element whose width was 200 pixels and two that were 50 pixels.

Try It Out — An Opening Hours Table

In this example, you will create a table that shows the opening hours of the Example Café web site we have been working on throughout the book. The table will look like the one shown in Figure 4-9.

Figure 4-9

1. Start off by opening the `contact.html` file in your text or XHTML editor; we will be adding a table to show serving hours beneath the e-mail link.

2. The table is contained within the `<table>` element and its content is then written out a row at a time. The table has three rows and eight columns.

Starting with the top row, you have eight table heading elements. The first `<th>` element is empty because the top-left corner cell of the table is empty. The next seven elements contain the days of the week.

In the second row of the table, the first cell acts as a heading for that row, indicating the meal (breakfast). The remaining cells show what times these meals are served. The third row follows the same format as the second row but shows times for lunch.

```
<table>
  <tr>
    <th></th>
    <th>Monday</th>
    <th>Tuesday</th>
    <th>Wednesday</th>
    <th>Thursday</th>
    <th>Friday</th>
    <th>Saturday</th>
    <th>Sunday</th>
  </tr>
  <tr>
    <th>Breakfast</th>
    <td>7:00am - 10:00am</td>
    <td>7:00am - 10:00am</td>
    <td>7:00am - 10:00am</td>
    <td>7:00am - 10:00am</td>
    <td>7:00am - 11:00am</td>
    <td>8:00am - 11:30pm</td>
    <td>8:00am - 11:30pm</td>
  </tr>
  <tr>
    <th>Lunch</th>
    <td>11:30am - 2:30pm</td>
    <td>11:30am - 2:30pm</td>
    <td>11:30am - 2:30pm</td>
    <td>11:30am - 2:30pm</td>
    <td>11:30am - 2:30pm</td>
    <td>11:30am - 3:30pm</td>
    <td>11:30am - 3:30pm</td>
  </tr>
</table>
</body>
```

As long as you accept that each row is written out in turn, you will have no problem creating quite complex tables.

3. Save your file as `contact.html`.

Adding a <caption> to a Table

Whether your table shows results for a scientific experiment, values of stocks in a particular market, or what is on television tonight, each table should have a caption so that visitors to your site know what the table is for.

Even if the surrounding text describes the content of the table, it is good practice to give the table a formal caption using the `<caption>` element. By default, most browsers will display the contents of this element centered above the table, as shown in Figure 4-10 in the next section.

The `<caption>` element appears directly after the opening `<table>` tag; it should come before the first row:

```
<table>
  <caption> Opening hours for the Example Cafe</caption>
  <tr>
```

By using a `<caption>` element, rather than just describing the purpose of the table in a previous or subsequent paragraph, you are directly associating the content of the table with this description — and this association can be used by screen readers and by applications that process web pages (such as search engines).

Grouping Sections of a Table

In this section, you are going to look at some techniques that allow you to group together cells, rows, and columns of a table, and learn the advantages that doing this can bring. In particular, you will see how to do the following:

- Use the `rowspan` and `colspan` attributes to make cells stretch over more than one row or column
- Split a table into three sections: a head, body, and foot
- Group columns using the `<colgroup>` element
- Share attributes between unrelated columns using the `<col>` element

Spanning Columns Using the colspan Attribute

As you saw when looking at the `<td>` and `<th>` elements, both can carry an attribute called `colspan` that allows the table cell to span (or stretch) across more than one column.

If you look at Figure 4-10, you can see a table that has three rows; the cells of the table are shaded to illustrate the `colspan` attribute in action:

- The first row has three columns of equal width, and there is one cell for each column.
- In the second row, the first cell is the width of one column, but the second cell spans the width of two columns.
- The third row has just one cell that spans all three columns.

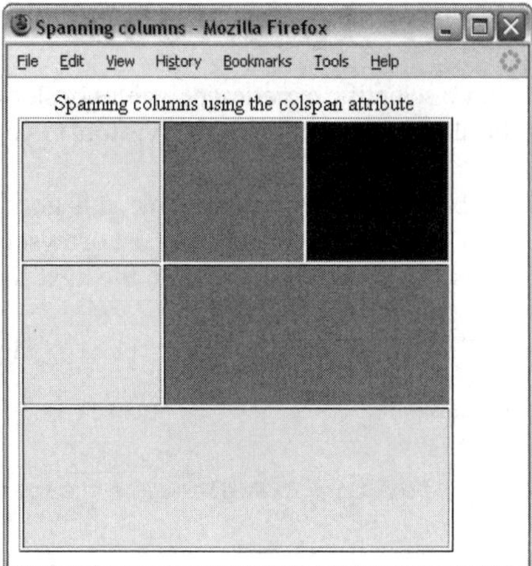

Figure 4-10

Let's take a look at the code for this example to see how the colspan attribute is used. This example also uses the deprecated border, width, height, and bgcolor attributes in order to illustrate a point visually (ch04_eg04.html):

```
<table border="1">
  <caption>Spanning columns using the colspan attribute</caption>
  <tr>
    <td bgcolor="#efefef" width="100" height="100"> </td>
    <td bgcolor="#999999" width="100" height="100"> </td>
    <td bgcolor="#000000" width="100" height="100"> </td>
  </tr>
  <tr>
    <td bgcolor="#efefef" width="100" height="100"> </td>
    <td colspan="2" bgcolor="#999999"> </td>
  </tr>
  <tr>
    <td colspan="3" bgcolor="#efefef" height="100"> </td>
  </tr>
</table>
```

In the first row, you can see that there are three <td> elements, one for each cell.

In the second row, there are only two <td> elements, and the second of these elements carries a colspan attribute. The value of the colspan attribute indicates how many columns the cell should stretch across. In this case, the second cell spans two columns; therefore, it has a value of 2.

In the final row, there is just one <td> element, and this time the colspan attribute has a value of 3, which indicates that it should take up three columns.

As I mentioned at the start of this chapter, when dealing with tables you have to think in terms of grids. This grid is three cells wide and three rows tall, so the middle row could not have two equal-sized cells (because they would not fit in the grid — you cannot have a cell spanning 1.5 columns).

An example of where the `colspan` attribute might be useful is in creating a timetable or schedule where the day is divided into hours — some slots lasting one hour, others lasting two to three hours.

You might also have noticed the use of the non-breaking space character (` `) in the cells, which is included so that the cell has some content; without content for a table cell, some browsers will not display the background color (whether that color is specified using CSS or the deprecated `bgcolor` attribute).

Spanning Rows Using the rowspan Attribute

The `rowspan` attribute does much the same thing as the `colspan` attribute, but it works in the opposite direction: it allows cells to stretch vertically across cells. You can see the effect of the `rowspan` attribute in Figure 4-11.

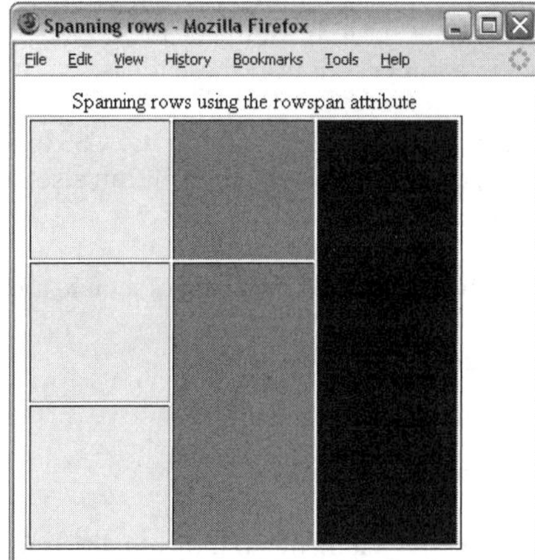

Figure 4-11

When you use a `rowspan` attribute, the corresponding cell in the row beneath it must be left out (`ch04_eg05.html`):

```
<table border="1">
  <caption>Spanning rows using the colspan attribute</caption>
  <tr>
    <td bgcolor="#efefef" width="100" height="100"> </td>
    <td bgcolor="#999999" width="100" height="100"> </td>
    <td rowspan="3" bgcolor="#000000" width="100" height="100"> </td>
  </tr>
  <tr>
    <td bgcolor="#efefef" height="100"> </td>
    <td rowspan="2" bgcolor="#999999"> </td>
```

```
    </tr>
    <tr>
      <td bgcolor="#efefef" height="100"> </td>
    </tr>
  </table>
```

The `rowspan` *and* `colspan` *attributes were popular with designers who used tables to control the layout pages, but tables are rarely used to lay out pages these days, and this technique has largely been replaced by the use of CSS to control layouts.*

Splitting Up Tables Using a Head, Body, and Foot

There are occasions when you may wish to distinguish between the body of a table (where most of the data is held) and the headings or maybe even the footers. For example, think of a bank statement: you may have a table where the header contains column headings, the body contains a list of transactions, and the footer contains the balance in the account.

If the table is too long to show on a screen, then the header and footer might remain in view all the time, while the body of the table gains a scrollbar. Similarly, when printing a long table that spreads over more than one page, you might want the browser to print the head and foot of a table on each page. Unfortunately, the main browsers do not yet support these ideas.

However, if you add these elements to your tables, you can use CSS to attach different styles to the contents of the `<thead>`, `<tbody>`, and `<tfoot>` elements. It can also help those who use aural browsers, which read pages to users.

The three elements for separating the head, body, and foot of a table are:

- `<thead>` to create a separate table header
- `<tbody>` to indicate the main body of the table
- `<tfoot>` to create a separate table footer

A table may also contain several `<tbody>` elements to indicate different "pages," or groups of data.

> **Note that the `<tfoot>` element must appear before the `<tbody>` element in the source document.**

Here you can see an example of a table that makes use of these elements (`ch04_eg06.html`):

```
<table>
  <thead>
    <tr>
      <th>Transaction date</th>
      <th>Payment type and details</th>
      <th>Paid out</th>
```

```
      <th>Paid in</th>
      <th>Balance</th>
    </tr>
  </thead>
  <tfoot>
    <tr>
      <td></td>
      <td></td>
      <td>$1970.27</td>
      <td>$2450.00</td>
      <td>$8940.88</td>
    </tr>
  </tfoot>
  <tbody>
    <tr>
      <td>12 Jun 09</td>
      <td>Amazon.com</td>
      <td>$49.99</td>
      <td></td>
      <td>$8411.16</td>
    </tr>
    <tr>
      <td>13 Jun 09</td>
      <td>Total</td>
      <td>$60.00</td>
      <td></td>
      <td>$8351.16</td>
    </tr>
    <tr>
      <td>14 Jun 09</td>
      <td>Whole Foods</td>
      <td>$75.28</td>
      <td></td>
      <td>$8275.88</td>
    </tr>
    <tr>
      <td>14 Jun 09</td>
      <td>Visa Payment</td>
      <td>$350.00</td>
      <td></td>
      <td>$7925.88</td>
    </tr>
    <tr>
      <td>15 Jun 09</td>
      <td>Cheque 122501</td>
      <td></td>
      <td>$1450.00</td>
      <td>$9375.88</td>
    </tr>
  </tbody>
  <tbody>
    <tr>
```

```
        <td>17 Jun 09</td>
        <td>Murco</td>
        <td>$60.00</td>
        <td></td>
        <td>$9315.88</td>
      </tr>
      <tr>
        <td>18 Jun 09</td>
        <td>Wrox Press</td>
        <td></td>
        <td>$1000.00</td>
        <td>$10315.88</td>
      </tr>
      <tr>
        <td>18 Jun 09</td>
        <td>McLellans Bakery</td>
        <td>$25.00</td>
        <td></td>
        <td>$10290.88</td>
      </tr>
      <tr>
        <td>18 Jun 09</td>
        <td>Apple Store</td>
        <td>$1350.00</td>
        <td></td>
        <td>$8940.88</td>
      </tr>
    </tbody>
  </table>
```

Figure 4-12 shows what this example looks like in Firefox, which supports the `thead`, `tbody`, and `tfoot` elements. Note that this example uses CSS to give the header and footer of the table a background shade.

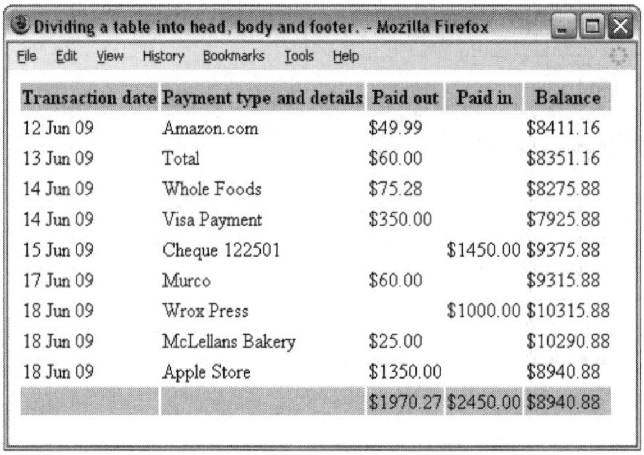

Dividing a table into head, body and footer. - Mozilla Firefox

File Edit View History Bookmarks Tools Help

Transaction date	Payment type and details	Paid out	Paid in	Balance
12 Jun 09	Amazon.com	$49.99		$8411.16
13 Jun 09	Total	$60.00		$8351.16
14 Jun 09	Whole Foods	$75.28		$8275.88
14 Jun 09	Visa Payment	$350.00		$7925.88
15 Jun 09	Cheque 122501		$1450.00	$9375.88
17 Jun 09	Murco	$60.00		$9315.88
18 Jun 09	Wrox Press		$1000.00	$10315.88
18 Jun 09	McLellans Bakery	$25.00		$10290.88
18 Jun 09	Apple Store	$1350.00		$8940.88
		$1970.27	$2450.00	$8940.88

Figure 4-12

All three elements carry the same attributes. In addition to the universal attributes, they can carry the following attributes (each of which was covered in the earlier section "Basic Table Elements and Attributes"):

```
align char charoff valign
```

Grouping Columns Using the <colgroup> Element

If two or more columns are related, you can use the `<colgroup>` element to explain that those columns are grouped together.

For example, in the following table, there would be six columns. The first four columns are in the first column group, and the next two columns are in the second column group (`ch04_eg07.html`):

```
<table>
  <colgroup span="4" class="mainColumns" />
  <colgroup span="2" class="subTotalColumns" />
  <tr>
    <td>1</td>
    <td>2</td>
    <td>3</td>
    <td>4</td>
    <td>5</td>
    <td>6</td>
  </tr>
</table>
```

When the `<colgroup>` element is used, it comes directly after the opening `<table>` tag and carries a `span` attribute, which is used to indicate how many columns the group contains.

In this example, the `class` attribute is used to attach CSS rules that tell the browser the width of each column in the group and the background color for each cell. You will learn more about CSS in Chapter 7, but it is worth noting that some browsers support only a subset of the CSS rules for this element.

You can see what this example looks like in Figure 4-13.

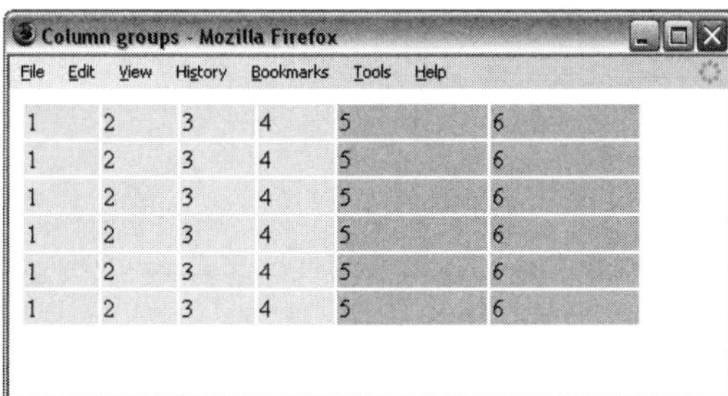

Figure 4-13

In addition to the universal attributes, the `<colgroup>` element can carry the following attributes:

```
align char charoff span valign width
```

Columns Sharing Styles Using the <col> Element

The `<col>` element was introduced to specify attributes of the columns in a `<colgroup>` (such as width or alignment of cells within that column). Unlike the `<colgroup>` element, the `<col>` element does not imply structural grouping and is therefore more commonly used for presentational purposes.

The `<col>` elements are always empty elements, which means they do not have any content, although they do carry attributes.

For example, the following table would have six columns, and the first five, while not a group in their own right, could be formatted differently than the last column because it belongs to a separate set (`ch04_eg08.html`):

```
<table>
  <colgroup span="6">
    <col span="5" class="mainColumns" />
    <col span="1" class="totalColumn" />
  </colgroup>
  <tr>
    <td></td>
    ...
    <td></td>
  </tr>
</table>
```

You can see what this looks like in Figure 4-14.

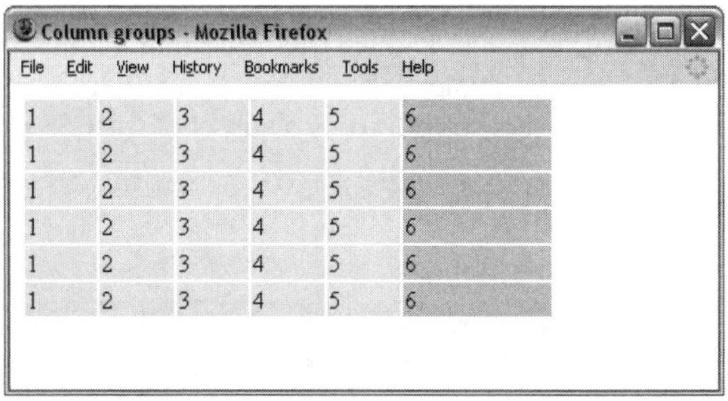

Column groups - Mozilla Firefox

File Edit View History Bookmarks Tools Help

1	2	3	4	5	6
1	2	3	4	5	6
1	2	3	4	5	6
1	2	3	4	5	6
1	2	3	4	5	6
1	2	3	4	5	6

Figure 4-14

The attributes that the `<col>` element can carry are the same as for the `<colgroup>` element.

Nested Tables

As mentioned earlier in the chapter, you can include markup inside a table cell, as long as the whole element is contained within that cell. This means you can even place another entire table inside a table cell, creating what's called a *nested table*. Figure 4-15 shows you an example of a table that shows a schedule for a weekend of activities.

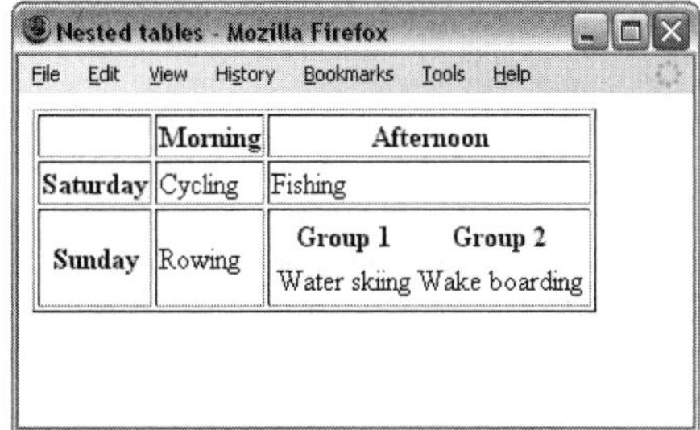

Figure 4-15

In the bottom-right cell of this table is a second table that divides up the attendees into two groups. (`ch04_eg09.html`):

```
<table>
  <tr>
    <th></th>
    <th>Morning</th>
    <th>Afternoon</th>
  </tr>
  <tr>
    <th>Saturday</th>
    <td>Cycling</td>
    <td>Fishing</td>
  </tr>
  <tr>
    <th>Sunday</th>
    <td>Rowing</td>
    <td>
          <table>
            <tr>
                 <th>Group 1</th>
                 <th>Group 2</th>
                </tr>
               <tr>
                <td>Water ski-ing</td>
                <td>Wake boarding</td>
               </tr>
         </table>
        </td>
  </tr>
</table>
```

Now that you've seen how to create a nested table, it is worth noting that they should be used very sparingly, because they are quite hard for those who rely upon screen readers to follow. You are about to see this in the next section.

Accessible Tables

By their nature, tables can contain a lot of data and they provide a very helpful visual representation of this information. When looking at a table, it is easy to scan across rows and up and down columns to find a particular value or compare a range of values. If you think back to the examples you saw at the very start of the chapter (the NFL sports results or the train timetable), you would not need to read all the content of the table just to find out how your team is doing this season or when a train is leaving.

However, for those who listen to pages on a voice browser or a screen reader, tables can be much harder to understand. For example, if you imagine having a table read to you, it would be much more difficult to compare entries across a row or column because you have to remember what you have heard so far (it is not as easy to scan back and forth).

Yet with a little thought or planning, you can make tables a lot easier for all to understand. Here are some things you can do to ensure your tables are easy to understand:

- Add captions to your tables. The `<caption>` element clearly associates a caption with a table, and the screen reader will read the caption to the user before they see the table so that they know what to expect. If the listener knows what to expect, it will be easier to understand the information.
- Always try to use the `<th>` element to indicate a table heading.
- Always put headings in the first row and the first column.
- Avoid using nested tables (like the one you saw in the previous section), as this will make it harder for the user of a screen reader to follow.
- Avoid using `rowspan` and `colspan` attributes, which again make it harder for the user with a screen reader to follow. If you do use them, make sure that you use the `scope` and `headers` attributes, which are discussed shortly.
- Learn how a voice browser or screen reader would read a table, and the order in which the cells are read out; this will help you to understand how to structure your tables for maximum ease of use (we will see examples of this in the following section).
- If you use the `scope` and `headers` attributes to clearly indicate which headings apply to which rows and columns, then screen readers can help users retrieve headings for a particular cell. If you imagine someone having a table read to him or her, the screen reader will often give the user an option to hear the headers that are relevant to that cell again (without having to go up to the first row or back to the first cell in the column to hear the heading that corresponds with that cell).

You already saw how to add a caption to a table, so let's move on and see how tables are read to a user, or how they are *linearized*.

How to Linearize Tables

When a screen reader is being used to read a table, it will tend to perform what is known as *linearization*, which means that the reader starts at the first row and reads the cells in that row from left to right, one by one, before moving on to the next row, and so on until the reader has read each row in the table. Consider the following simple table (`ch04_eg10.html`):

```
<table border="1">
  <tr>
    <td>Column 1, Row 1</td>
    <td>Column 2 Row 1</td>
  </tr>
  <tr>
    <td>Column 1, Row 2</td>
    <td>Column 2, Row 2</td>
  </tr>
</table>
```

Figure 4-16 shows what this simple table would look like in a browser.

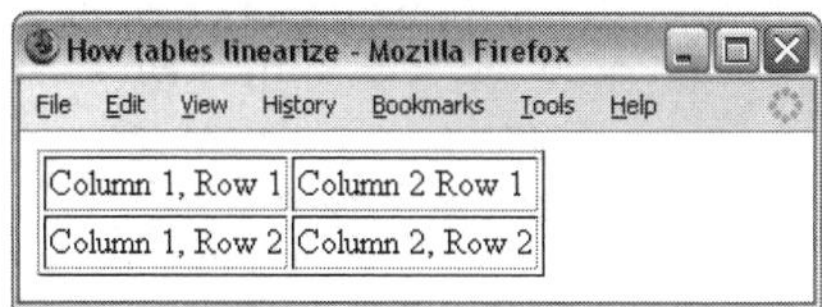

Figure 4-16

The order in which the cells in Figure 4-16 would be read is therefore:

- Column 1 Row 1
- Column 2 Row 1
- Column 1 Row 2
- Column 2 Row 2

This small example is fairly easy to follow. But imagine a larger table: the headings will be read first, followed by a row of data. If the table had several more columns, it would be very hard to remember which column you were in. (Even worse, if you use nested tables, it becomes far harder for users to follow where they are, because one table cell can contain an entirely new table that often has different numbers of rows or columns.)

Luckily, most screen readers are able to remind the user of the column and row they are currently in, but this works far better when the table uses `<th>` elements for headers. And if you are building a complex table, you can also enhance this information using the `id`, `scope`, and `headers` attributes, covered in the following section.

Using the id, scope, and headers Attributes

The `id`, `scope`, and `headers` attributes have already been mentioned in this chapter, when we looked at the attributes that the `<td>` and `<th>` elements can carry. Here we will take a look at how they can be used to record the structure of a table better and make it more accessible.

When you make a cell a heading, adding the `scope` attribute to the `<th>` element, helps you indicate which cells that element is the heading for. If you give it a value of `row`, you are indicating that this element is the header for that row; given the value of `column`, it indicates that it is the header for that column. You can also have values for a `rowgroup` or `columngroup`.

Value	Purpose
`row`	Cell contains header information for that row.
`col`	Cell contains header information for that column.
`rowgroup`	Cell contains header information for that rowgroup — a group of cells in a row created using the `<thead>`, `<tbody>`, or `<tfoot>` elements. (There is no corresponding element for columns like the `<colgroup>` element.)
`colgroup`	Cell contains header information for that colgroup (a group of columns created using the `<col>` or `<colgroup>` element, both of which are discussed later in the chapter).

The `headers` attribute performs the opposite role to the `scope` attribute, because it is used on `<td>` elements to indicate which headers correspond to that cell. The value of the attribute is a space-separated list of the header cells' `id` attribute values, so here you can tell that the headers for this cell would have `id` attributes whose values are `income` and `q1`.

```
headers="income q1"
```

The main purpose of this attribute is to support voice browsers. When a table is being read to you, it can be hard to keep track of which row and column you are on; therefore, the `header` attribute is used to remind users which row and column the current cell's data belongs to.

Try It Out — An Accessible Timetable

In this Try It Out, you are going to create a new page for the Example Café web site featuring a timetable for a weekend cookery course, with morning and afternoon sessions over two days. It should look like the screenshot in Figure 4-17.

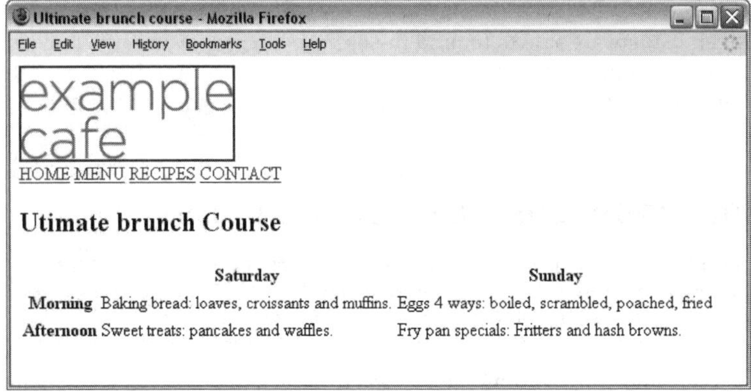

Figure 4-17

While you cannot see it from this screenshot, the table is specifically designed to be accessible for those with visual impairments.

1. Because this example contains deprecated attributes, you need to set up the skeleton of this page to handle a Transitional XHTML 1.0 document:

```
<?xml version="1.0" encoding="UTF-8"?>
<!DOCTYPE html PUBLIC "-//W3C//DTD XHTML 1.0 Transitional//EN"
    "http://www.w3.org/TR/xhtml1/DTD/xhtml1-transitional.dtd">
<html xmlns="http://www.w3.org/1999/xhtml" lang="en">
<head>
  <title>Ultimate brunch course</title>
</head>
<body>
</body>
</html>
```

2. The table has three rows and three columns; the first row and the left column contain headings and therefore use `<th>` elements. The remaining table cells use a `<td>` element. While you are adding these elements, you'll add in some content for the table, too:

```
<body>
<table>
  <tr>
    <th></th>
    <th>Tuesday</th>
    <th>Wednesday</th>
  </tr>
  <tr>
    <th>Morning</th>
    <td>Baking bread: loaves, croissants and muffins.</td>
    <td>Sweet treats: pancakes and waffles.</td>
  </tr>
  <tr>
    <th>Afternoon</th>
    <td>Eggs 4 ways: boiled, scrambled, poached, fried.</td>
    <td>Fry pan specials: Fritters and hash browns.</td>
  </tr>
</table>
</body>
```

3. The next stage is to add `id` attributes to the `<th>` elements that have content, and header attributes to the `<td>` elements to indicate which headers apply to those elements; this approach improves accessibility for visitors who use screen readers. The value of the `header` attributes should correspond to the values of the `id` attributes indicating which headings correspond to each cell:

```
<table>
  <tr>
    <th></th>
    <th id="Saturday">Saturday</th>
    <th id="Sunday">Sunday</th>
```

```
  </tr>
  <tr>
    <th id="Morning">Morning</th>
    <td headers="Saturday Morning" abbr="Bread">Baking bread: loaves,
croissants and muffins.</td>
    <td headers="Sunday Morning" abbr="Eggs">Eggs 4 ways: boiled,
scrambled, poached, fried </td>
  </tr>
  <tr>
    <th id="Afternoon">Afternoon</th>
    <td headers="Saturday Afternoon" abbr="Sweet breakfasts">Sweet treats:
pancakes and waffles.</td>
    <td headers="Sunday Afternoon" abbr="Fried foods">Fry pan specials:
Fritters and hash browns.</td>
  </tr>
</table>
```

4. Save your file as `course.html`. To be honest, this example is quite a bit more complex than most tables you will come across. Not many people have gotten into the practice of using the `id` and `header` attributes on `<table>` elements, but it makes tables a lot easier to use for those with visual impairments, in particular on larger tables that have a lot of columns and rows. Neither will you often see the `abbr` attribute used on table cells. In fact, if you look at the code for other people's web sites, you are still more likely to come across the use of lots of deprecated attributes rather than these attributes.

Including attributes like these will help set you apart from other coders who have not yet learned to make their tables more accessible. Furthermore, awareness of accessibility issues is required in an increasing number of jobs, so you should learn how to use such attributes.

Summary

In this chapter, you have seen how tables can be a powerful tool when creating pages. You have seen how all tables are based on a grid pattern and use the four basic elements: `<table>`, which contains each table; `<tr>`, which contains the rows of a table; `<td>`, which contains a cell of table data; and `<th>`, which represents a cell that contains a heading.

You have also seen how you can add headers, footers, and captions to tables. It is particularly helpful to add a `<thead>` and `<tfoot>` element to any table that may be longer than a browser window or sheet of printed paper, as these could help a reader relate between the content and the information in headers or footers.

You can now make cells span both columns and rows, although you should avoid doing this in tables that contain data, as it makes them harder for aural browsers to read to a user. You have also seen how to group columns so that you can preserve structure, and so they can share styles and attributes.

Finally, you saw some of the accessibility issues regarding use of tables. It is important to be aware of the process of linearization, which a screen reader performs before reading a table to a user, so that your sites are accessible to users with visual impairments. You also need to know how you can provide extra information that indicates the headers for each cell.

In the next chapter, you learn about using forms to collect information from visitors.

Exercises

The answers to all of the exercises are in Appendix A.

1. Where should the `<caption>` element for a table be placed in the document and, by default, where is it displayed?
2. In what order would the cells in Figure 4-18 be read out by a screen reader?

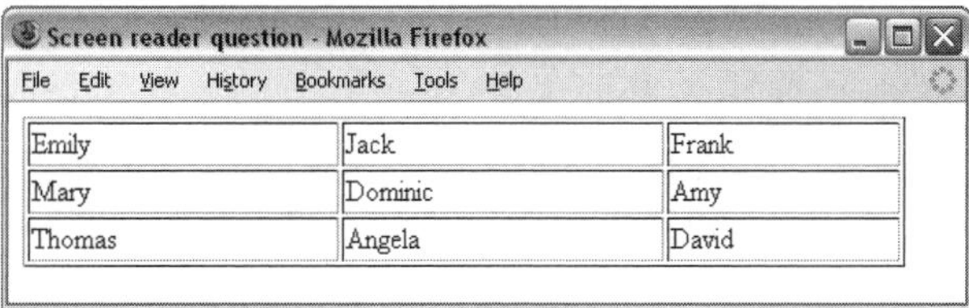

Figure 4-18

3. Create a table to hold the data shown in Figure 4-19. To give you a couple of clues, the document must be Transitional XHTML 1.0 because the `width` attribute is used on the cells of the first row of the table. You have also seen examples of how the border is generated in this chapter, using another deprecated attribute, but on the `<table>` element rather than the cells.

Figure 4-19

Forms

Almost every time you want to collect information from a visitor to your site, you need to use a *form*. Some forms are quite complex, such as those that allow you to book plane tickets or purchase insurance online. Others are quite simple, such as the search box on the homepage of Google.

Many of the forms you will fill out online bear a strong resemblance to paper forms you have to fill out. On paper, forms are made up of areas to enter text, boxes to check (or tick), options to choose from, and so on. Similarly, on the Web you can create a form by combining what are known as *form controls*, such as textboxes (to enter text into), checkboxes (to place a cross in), select boxes and radio buttons (to choose from different options), and so on. In this chapter, you learn how each of these different types of controls can be combined into a form.

In this chapter then, you'll learn the following:

- How to create a form using the `<form>` element
- The different types of form controls you can use to make a form — such as text input boxes, radio buttons, select boxes, and submit buttons
- What happens to the data a user enters
- How to make your forms accessible
- How to structure the content of your forms

By the end of the chapter, you will be able to create all kinds of forms to collect information from visitors to your site.

XHTML is used only to present the form to the user; it does not allow you to say what happens with that data once it has been collected. To get a better idea of what happens to the data once it has been collected from a form, you will need to look at a book on a server-side language, such as ASP.NET or PHP (you can see a range of books on these topics at `www.wrox.com`*).*

Introducing Forms

Let's start by looking at a couple of examples of forms. First, Figure 5-1 shows you the Google homepage. This contains two kinds of form controls:

- A **text input**, which is where you enter your search term.
- **Submit buttons**, which are used to send the form to the server. There are two on this form: you can see the words "Google Search" written on the first one and "I'm Feeling Lucky" on the second.

Figure 5-1

Now let's look at a more complicated example. Figure 5-2 shows part of an insurance form, which actually spreads over several pages. It shows many more types of form controls:

- **Select boxes**, sometimes referred to as drop-down lists, such as the one in the top left of Figure 5-2 to say how long you have been driving.
- **Radio buttons**, such as the ones in the top-right corner with Yes or No options. When you have a group of radio buttons, you can only pick one response.
- **Checkboxes**, such as the ones at the bottom of the screenshot indicating how you can be contacted (by e-mail, post, or phone). When you have a group of checkboxes, you can pick more than one response.
- **Text inputs**, to enter a date of birth and registration number.

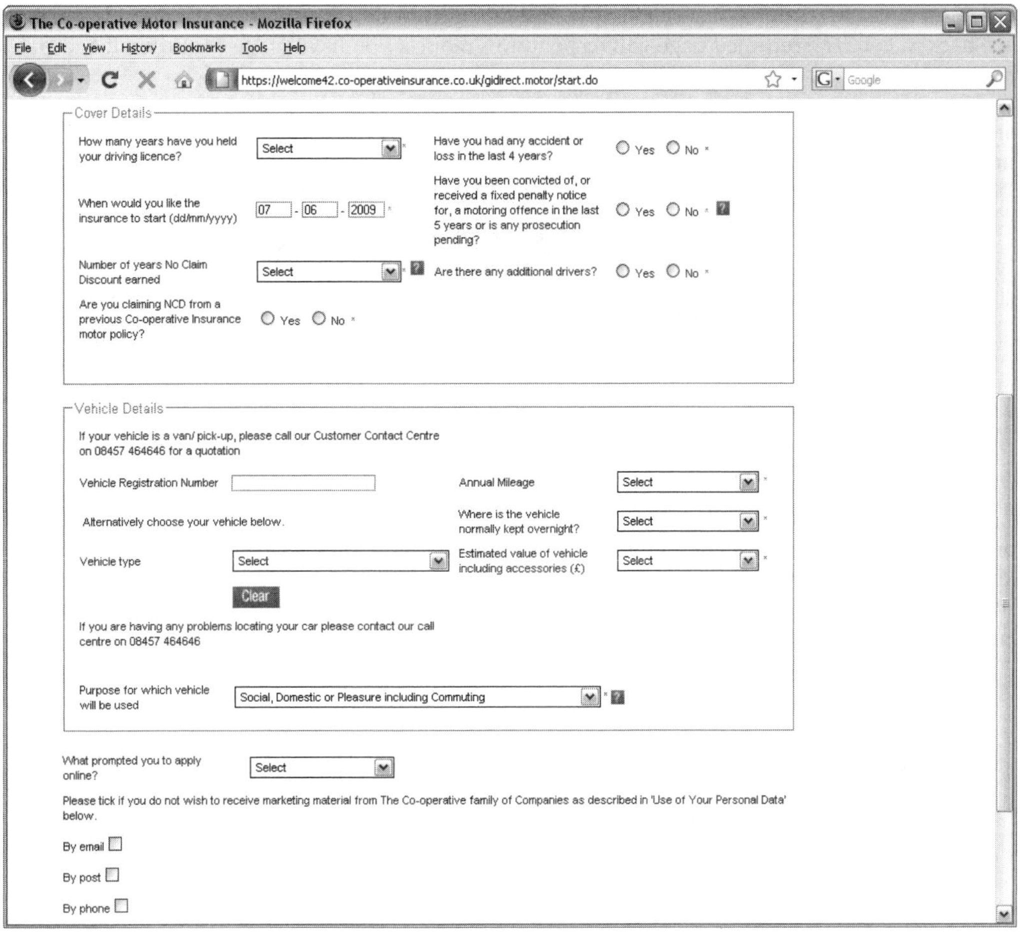

Figure 5-2

There are two additional types of form controls not shown in these examples: a text area (which is a multi-line text input), and file select boxes (which allow you to upload files), both of which you will meet later in the chapter.

Any form that you create will live inside an element called `<form>`, and the form controls (the text input boxes, drop-down boxes, checkboxes, a submit button, and so on) live between the opening `<form>` and closing `</form>` tags. A `<form>` element can also contain other XHTML markup as you would find in the rest of a page.

Once users have entered information into a form, they usually have to click what is known as a *submit button* (although the actual text on the button may say something different such as Search, Send, or Proceed — and often pressing the Return key on the keyboard has the same effect as clicking this button). This indicates that the user has filled out the form, and this usually sends the form data to a web server.

Once form data arrives at the server, a script or other program processes the data and sends a new web page back to you. The returned page will respond to a request you have made or acknowledge an action you have taken.

For example, you might want to add the search form shown in Figure 5-3 to your page (ch05_eg01.html).

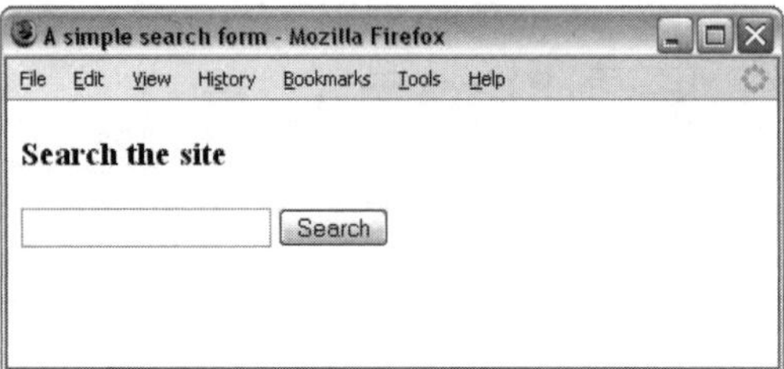

Figure 5-3

You can see that this form contains a textbox for the user to enter the keywords of what he or she is searching for, and a submit button, which has been set to have the word "Search" on it. When the user clicks the Search button, the information is sent to the server. The server then processes the data and generates a new page for that user telling what pages meet the search criteria (Figure 5-4).

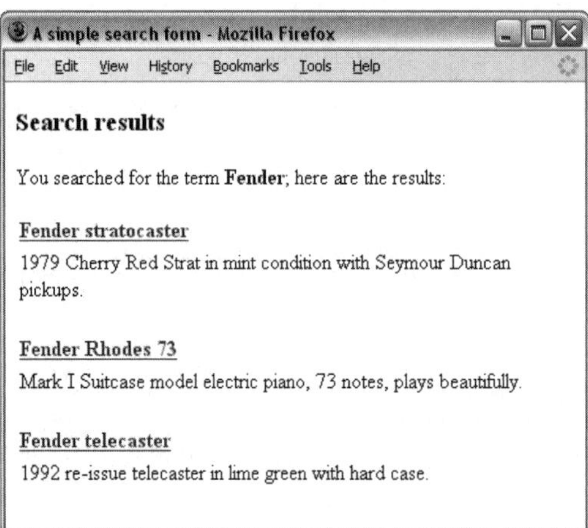

Figure 5-4

When a browser sends data to the server, it is transmitted in *name/value* pairs. The *name* corresponds to the name of the form control, and the *value* is what the user has entered (if the user can type an answer) or the value of the option selected (if there is a list of options to choose from).

Each item needs both a name and a value because, if you have five textboxes on a form, you need to know which data corresponds to which textbox. The processing application can then process the information from each form control individually.

Here is the code for the simple search form shown in Figure 5-3:

```
<form action="http://www.example.org/search.aspx" method="get">
   <h3>Search the site</h3>
   <input type="text" name="txtSearchItem" />
   <input type="submit" value="Search" />
</form>
```

The `<form>` element carries an attribute called `action` whose value is the URL of the page on the web server that handles search requests. Meanwhile, the `method` attribute indicates which of two HTTP methods will be used in getting the form data to the server. (You learn the difference between the `get` and `post` methods later in the chapter.)

In order to start creating forms, you first need to look at the `<form>` element in a little more detail, and then go through each of the different types of form controls and see how they sit inside the `<form>` element.

Creating a Form with the <form> Element

As you have already seen, forms live inside an element called `<form>`. The `<form>` element can also contain other markup, such as paragraphs, headings, and so on, although it may not contain another `<form>` element.

Providing you keep your `<form>` elements separate from each other (and no `<form>` element contains another `<form>` element), your page may contain as many forms as you like. For example, you might have a login form, a search form, and a form to subscribe to a newsletter, all on the same page. If you do have more than one form on a page, users will be able to send the data from only one form at a time to the server.

Every `<form>` element should carry at least two attributes:

```
action method
```

A `<form>` element may also carry all of the universal attributes, the UI event attributes, and the following attributes:

```
enctype accept accept-charset onsubmit onreset
```

The action Attribute

The `action` attribute indicates what happens to the data when the form is submitted. Usually, the value of the `action` attribute is a page or program on a web server that will receive the information.

For example, if you had a login form consisting of a username and password, the details the user enters may get passed to a page written in ASP.NET on the web server called `login.aspx`, in which case the `action` attribute could read as follows:

```
<form action="http://www.example.org/membership/login.aspx">
```

The method Attribute

Form data can be sent to the server in two ways, each corresponding to an *HTTP method*:

- The `get` method, which sends data as part of the URL
- The `post` method, which hides data in something known as the HTTP headers

You learn more about these two methods later in the chapter, where you will learn what they mean and when you should use each one.

The id Attribute

The `id` attribute allows you to uniquely identify the `<form>` element within a page, just as you can use it to uniquely identify any element on a page.

It is good practice to give every `<form>` element an `id` attribute, because many forms make use of style sheets and scripts, which may require the use of the `id` attribute to identify the form.

The value of the `id` attribute should be unique within the document, and it should also follow the other rules for values of the `id` attribute mentioned in Chapter 1. Some people start the value of `id` and `name` attributes for forms with the characters `frm` and then use the rest of the value to describe the kind of data the form collects — for example, `frmLogin` or `frmSearch`.

The name Attribute (Deprecated)

As you have already seen through its use on other elements, the `name` attribute is the predecessor to the `id` attribute, and as with the `id` attribute, the value should be unique to the document.

Generally, you will not need to use this attribute, but when you do use it you can give it the same value as the `id` attribute. You will often see the value of this attribute begin with the characters `frm` followed by the purpose of the form (such as `frmLogin` or `frmSearch`).

The onsubmit Attribute

At some point, you have probably filled in a form on a web site, and then, as soon as you have clicked the button to send the form data (even before the page is sent to the server), been shown a message telling you that you have missed entering some data, or entered the wrong data. When this happens, the chances are you have come across a form that uses the `onsubmit` attribute to run a script in the browser that checks the data you entered before the form is sent to the server.

When a user clicks a submit button, something called an *event* fires. It is rather like the browser raising its hand and saying, "Hey, I am sending this form data to the server." The idea behind these events is that a script (usually written in JavaScript) can be run before the data is sent to the server to check that users have filled in the necessary parts of the form in a format the server expects. The value of the `onsubmit` attribute should be a script function that would be used when this event fires.

So, an `onsubmit` attribute on the `<form>` element might look like this:

```
onsubmit="validateFormDetails();"
```

We will look at scripts in Chapters 11 and 12, but for the moment all you need to know is that, in the line of code above, the `onsubmit` attribute tells the browser that when the user presses the submit button, the browser should run the script called `validateFormDetails()`, and that this script is probably in the `<head>` element.

There are two key advantages to making some checks on the form before it is sent to the server:

- If users have missed information, they do not have to wait the extra time it would take for the page to be sent to the server and then returned with details of their errors. It is far quicker if it is checked in the browser first.
- The server does not have to receive as many forms with errors, because the browser will have already made some checks before it receives the data (therefore, saving the load on the server).

The onreset Attribute

Some forms contain a `reset` button that empties the form of all details, although the button might say something like `clear form` instead; when this button is pressed, an `onreset` event fires and a script can be run.

When the `onreset` attribute is used, its value is a script (as with the `onsubmit` attribute) that is executed when the user clicks the button that calls it.

The `onreset` *event and attribute are used a lot less than* `onsubmit`*. If you offer a Clear Form button, however, it is good to confirm with users that they did intend to clear the form before performing the action (in case they have pressed it by accident).*

The enctype Attribute

If you use the HTTP `post` method to send data to the server, you can use the `enctype` attribute to specify how the browser encodes the data before it sends it to the server. Browsers tend to support two types of encoding:

- `application/x-www-form-urlencoded`, which is the standard method most forms use. Browsers use this because some characters, such as spaces, the plus sign, and some other non-alphanumeric characters cannot be sent to the web server. Instead, they are replaced by other characters which are used to represent them.
- `multipart/form-data`, which allows the data to be sent in parts, where each consecutive part corresponds to a form control, in the order it appears in the form. It is commonly used when visitors have to upload files (such as photos) to a server. Each part can have an optional content-type header of its own indicating the type of data for that form control.

If this attribute is not used, browsers use the first value. As a result, you are likely to use this attribute only if your form allows users to upload a file (such as an image) to the server, or if they are going to use non-ASCII characters, in which case the `enctype` attribute should be given the second value:

```
enctype="multipart/form-data"
```

The accept-charset Attribute

Different languages are written in different *character sets* or groups of characters. However, when creating web sites, developers do not always build them to understand all different languages. The idea behind the `accept-charset` attribute is that it specifies a list of character encodings that a user may enter and that the server can then process. Values should be a space-separated or comma-delimited list of character sets (as shown in Appendix E).

For example, the following indicates that a server accepts UTF-8 encodings:

```
accept-charset="utf-8"
```

The accept Attribute

The `accept` attribute is similar to the `accept-charset` attribute except it takes a comma-separated list of content types (or file types) that the server processing the form can handle. Unfortunately, none of the main browsers supports this feature.

The idea is that a user would not be able to upload a file of a different content type other than those listed. Here, you can see that the only types intended to be uploaded are images that are GIFs or JPEGs:

```
accept="image/gif, image/jpg"
```

Since the main browsers currently ignore this attribute, if you were to use it visitors would still be able to upload any file. A list of MIME types appears in Appendix H.

The target Attribute

The `target` attribute is usually used with the `<a>` element to indicate which frame or browser window the link should be loaded into. It can also be used with a form to indicate which frame or window the form results open in when the user has submitted a form (frames are covered in the next chapter).

White Space and the <form> Element

You should also be aware that when a browser comes across a `<form>` element it often creates extra white space around that element. This can particularly affect your design if you want a form to fit in a small area, such as putting a search form in a menu bar. If CSS will not cure this problem in the browsers you are targeting, the only way to avoid the problem is through careful placement of the `<form>` element.

To avoid the extra space created, you can try either placing the `<form>` element near the start or end of the document, or, if you are using tables for layout purposes in a Transitional XHTML 1.0 document, between the `<table>` and `<tr>` elements. (You should be aware that this latter approach is a cheat, and therefore it might cause an error if you tried to validate the page. However, most browsers will still display the table and form as you intended.)

Form Controls

You've met the `<form>` element, so this section goes on to cover the different types of form controls that live inside the `<form>` element to collect data from a visitor to your site. You will see:

- Text input controls
- Buttons
- Checkboxes and radio buttons
- Select boxes (sometimes referred to as drop-down menus and list boxes)
- File select boxes
- Hidden controls

Text Inputs

Text input boxes are used on many web pages. Possibly the most famous text input box is the one right in the middle of the Google homepage that allows you to enter what you are searching for.

On a printed form, the equivalent of a text input is a box or line in or on which you write a response.

There are actually three types of text input used on forms:

- **Single-line text input controls:** Used for items that require only one line of user input, such as search boxes or e-mail addresses. They are created using the `<input>` element and sometimes referred to simply as "textboxes."
- **Password input controls:** These are just like the single-line text input, except they mask the characters a user enters so that the characters cannot be seen on the screen. They tend to either show an asterisk or a dot instead of each character the user types, so that someone cannot simply look at the screen to see what a user types in. Password input controls are mainly used for entering passwords on login forms or sensitive details such as credit card numbers. They are also created using the `<input>` element.
- **Multi-line text input controls:** Used when the user is required to give details that may be longer than a single sentence. Multi-line input controls are created with the `<textarea>` element.

Let's take a look at each of these types of text input in turn.

Single-Line Text Input Controls

Single-line text input controls are created using an `<input>` element whose `type` attribute has a value of `text`. Here is a basic example of a single-line text input used for a search box (`ch05_eg02.html`):

```
<form action="http://www.example.com/search.aspx" method="get"
  name="frmSearch">
  Search:
  <input type="text" name="txtSearch" value="Search for" size="20"
         maxlength="64" />
  <input type="submit" value="Submit" />
</form>
```

Figure 5-5 shows what this form looks like in a browser.

Figure 5-5

Just as some people try to start form names with the characters `frm`, it is also common to start text input names with the characters `txt` to indicate that the form control is a textbox. This can be particularly handy when working with the data on the server, to remind you what sort of form control sent that data. However, some programmers prefer not to use this notation, so if you are working with someone else on a project, it is worth discussing that person's preference at the start of the work.

The table that follows lists the attributes the `<input>` element can carry when creating a text input control. Note how the purpose of the `name` attribute is quite specific on this element, and different from its use on other elements you have met already.

Attribute	Purpose
`type`	This attribute is required, and indicates the type of input control you want to create. The value for this attribute should be `text` when you want to create a single-line text input control. The attribute is required because the `<input>` element is also used to create other form controls such as radio buttons and checkboxes.
`name`	This attribute is also required, and is used to give the name part of the name/value pair that is sent to the server (remember, each control on a form is represented as a name/value pair where the name identifies the form control and the value is what the user entered).

Attribute	Purpose
value	Provides an initial value for the text input control that the user will see when the form loads. You would only use this attribute if you want something to be written in the text input when the page loads (such as a cue to tell the user what he or she should be entering).
size	Allows you to specify the width of the text input control in terms of characters; the search box in the earlier example is 20 characters wide. The size property does not affect how many characters users can enter (in this case they could enter 40 characters even when the size property has a value of 20); it just indicates how many characters wide the input will be. If users enter more characters than the size of the input, they can scroll right and left to see what they have entered using the arrow keys.
maxlength	Allows you to specify the maximum number of characters a user can enter into the text box. Usually after the maximum number of characters has been entered, even if the user keeps pressing more keys, no new characters will be added.

When an `<input>` element's `type` attribute has a value of `text`, it can also carry the following attributes:

- All of the universal attributes
- `disabled`, `readonly`, `tabindex`, and `accesskey`, which are covered later in the chapter

Password Input Controls

If you want to collect sensitive data such as passwords and credit card information, you can use the password input. The password input masks the characters the user types on the screen by replacing them with either a dot or asterisk, so that they would not be visible to someone looking over the user's shoulder.

Password input controls are created almost identically to the single-line text input controls, except that the `type` attribute on the `<input>` element is given a value of `password`.

Here you can see an example of a login form that combines a single-line text input control and a password input control (`ch05_eg03.html`):

```
<form action="http://www.example.com/login.aspx" method="post">
  Username:
  <input type="text" name="txtUsername" value="" size="20" maxlength="20" />
  <br />
  Password:
  <input type="password" name="pwdPassword" value="" size="20"
  maxlength="20" />
  <input type="submit" value="Submit" />
</form>
```

As you can see, it is common to start the name of any password with the characters `pwd` *so that when you come to deal with the data on the server, you know the associated value came from a password input box.*

Figure 5-6 shows you how this login form might look in a browser when the user starts entering details.

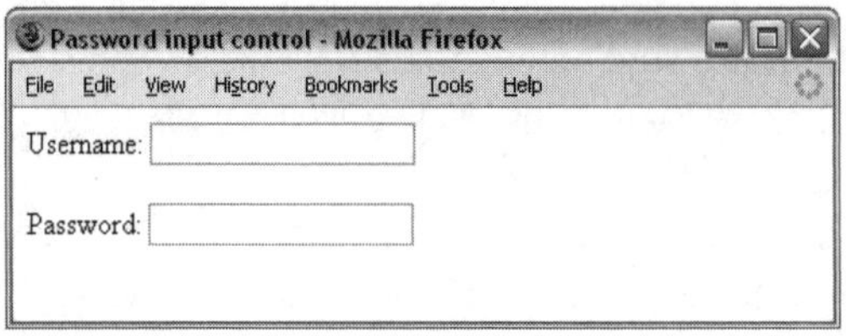

Figure 5-6

While passwords are hidden on the screen, they are still sent across the Internet as clear text, which is not considered very secure. In order to make them secure you should use an SSL connection between the client and server and encrypt any sensitive data (such as passwords and credit card details). SSL connections and encryption should be covered in a book about server-side languages such as ASP.NET and PHP.

Multiple-Line Text Input Controls

If you want to allow a visitor to your site to enter more than one line of text, you should create a multiple-line text input control using the `<textarea>` element.

Here is an example of a multiple-line text input used to collect feedback from visitors to a site (`ch05_eg04.html`):

```
<form action="http://www.example.org/feedback.aspx" method="post">
 Please tell us what you think of the site and then click submit:<br />
  <textarea name="txtFeedback" rows="20" cols="50">
Enter your feedback here.
  </textarea>
 <br />
 <input type="submit" value="Submit" />
</form>
```

Note that the text inside the `<textarea>` element is not indented (in the same way that other code in this book is indented). Anything written between the opening and closing `<textarea>` tags is treated as if it were written inside a `<pre>` element, and formatting of the source document is preserved. If the words "Enter your feedback here" were indented in the code, they would also be indented in the resulting multi-line text input on the browser.

Figure 5-7 shows what this form might look like.

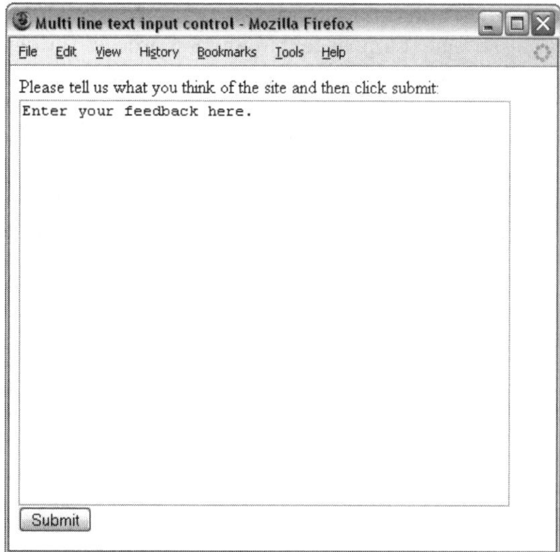

Figure 5-7

In the figure, you can see the writing between the opening `<textarea>` and closing `</textarea>` tags, which is shown in the text area when the page loads. Users can delete this text before adding their own text, and if they do not delete the text from the textbox it will be sent to the server when the form is submitted. Users often just type after any text written in a `<textarea>` element, so you may choose to avoid adding anything in between the elements, but you should still use both opening and closing `<textarea>` tags; otherwise, older browsers may not render the element correctly.

The `<textarea>` element can take the attributes shown in the table that follows.

Attribute	Purpose
`name`	The name of the control. This is used in the name/value pair that is sent to the server.
`rows`	Used to specify the size of a `<textarea>`; it indicates the number of rows of text a `<textarea>` element should have and therefore corresponds to the height of the text area.
`cols`	Used to specify the size of a `<textarea>`; it specifies the number of columns of text and therefore corresponds to the width of the box. One column is the average width of a character.

The `<textarea>` element can also take the following attributes:

- All of the universal attributes
- `disabled`, `readonly`, `tabindex`, and `accesskey`, which are covered later in the chapter
- The UI event attributes

By default, when a user runs out of columns in a <textarea>, the text is wrapped onto the next line (which means it just flows onto the next line as text in a word processor does), but the server will receive it as if it were all on one line. Because some users expect the sentences to break where they see them break on the screen, the major browsers also support an extra attribute called `wrap` that allows you to indicate how the text should be wrapped. Possible values are as follows:

- `off` (the default), which means scrollbars are added to the box if the user's words take up more space than the allowed width, and users have to scroll to see what they have entered
- `virtual`, which means that wherever the text wraps, users see it on the new line but it is transmitted to the server as if it were all on the same line unless the user has pressed the Enter key, in which case it is treated as a line break
- `physical`, which means that wherever the user sees the text start on a new line, so will the server

The `wrap` attribute is not, however, part of the XHTML specification.

Buttons

Buttons are most commonly used to submit a form, although they are sometimes used to clear or reset a form and even to trigger client-side scripts. (For example, on a basic loan calculator form within the page, a button might be used to trigger the script that calculates repayments without sending the data to the server.) You can create a button in three ways:

- Using an <input> element with a `type` attribute whose value is `submit`, `reset`, or `button`
- Using an <input> element with a `type` attribute whose value is `image`
- Using a <button> element

With each different method, the button will appear slightly different.

Creating Buttons Using the <input> Element

When you use the <input> element to create a button, the type of button you create is specified using the `type` attribute. The `type` attribute can take the following values to create a button:

- `submit`, which creates a button that submits a form when pressed
- `reset`, which creates a button that automatically resets form controls to their initial values as they were when the page loaded
- `button`, which creates a button that is used to trigger a client-side script when the user clicks that button

Here you can see examples of all three types of button (`ch05_eg05.html`)

```
<input type="submit" name="btnVoteRed" value="Vote for reds" />
<input type="submit" name="btnVoteBlue" value="Vote for blues" />
<br /><br />
<input type="reset" value="Clear form" /> <br /><br />
<input type="button" value="calculate" onclick="calculate()" />
```

Figure 5-8 shows what these buttons might look like in Firefox on a PC (a Mac displays them in the standard Mac style for buttons).

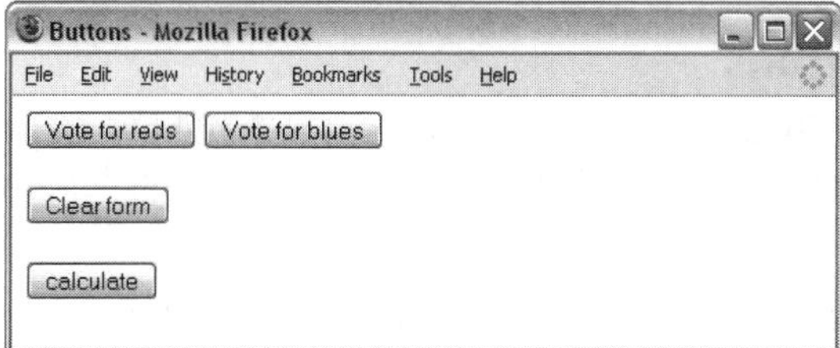

Figure 5-8

The table that follows shows the attributes used by the buttons.

Attribute	Purpose
`type`	Specifies the type of button you want and takes one of the following values: `submit`, `reset`, or `button`.
`name`	Provides a name for the button. You need to add only a `name` attribute to a button if there is more than one button on the same form (in which case it helps to indicate which of the buttons was clicked). It is considered good practice, however, to give the button a name anyway to provide an indication of what the button does.
`value`	Enables you to specify what the text on the button should read. If a `name` attribute is given, the value of the `value` attribute is sent to the server as part of the name/value pair for this form control. If no value is given, then no name/value pair is sent for this button.
`onclick`	Used to trigger a script when the user clicks the button; the value of this attribute is the script that should be run.

In the same way that you can trigger a script when the user clicks a button, you can also trigger a script when the button gains or loses focus with the `onfocus` and `onblur` event attributes.

When an `<input>` element has a `type` attribute whose value is `submit`, `reset`, or `button`, it can also take the following attributes:

- All the universal attributes
- `disabled`, `readonly`, `tabindex`, and `accesskey`, which are discussed later in the chapter
- The UI event attributes

If you do not use the `value` attribute on the submit button, you may find that a browser displays text that is inappropriate to the purpose of the form — for example, IE displays the text `Send Query`, which is not ideal for a login button form.

Using Images for Buttons

You can use an image for a button rather than using the standard button that a browser renders for you. Creating an image button is very similar to creating any other button, but the `type` attribute has a value of `image`:

```
<input type="image" src="submit.jpg" alt="Submit" name="btnImage" />
```

Note how you can start the value of a `name` *attribute for a button with the characters* `btn`, *in keeping with the naming convention that I mentioned earlier. (When you refer to the name of the form control in other code, the use of this prefix will help remind you what type of form control the information came from.)*

Because you are creating a button that has an image, you need to have two additional attributes, which are listed in the table that follows.

Attribute	Purpose
`src`	Specifies the source of the image file.
`alt`	Provides alternative text for the image. This will be displayed when the image cannot be found and also read to people using voice browsers. (It was first supported only in IE5 and Netscape 6.)

If the image button has a `name` attribute, when you click it, the browser sends a name/value pair to the server. The name will be what you provide for the `name` attribute and the value will be a pair of x and y coordinates for where on the button the user clicked (just as you saw when dealing with server-side image maps in Chapter 3).

In Figure 5-9, you can see a graphical submit button. Both Firefox and IE change the cursor when the user hovers over one of these buttons to help users know that they can click on it.

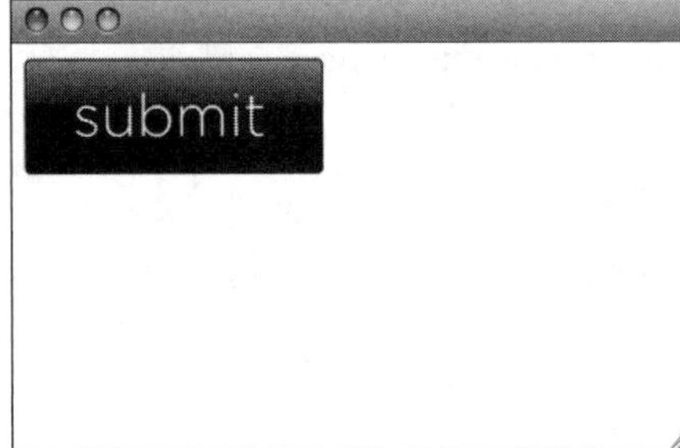

Figure 5-9

Creating Buttons Using the <button> Element

The `<button>` element is a more recent introduction that allows you to specify what appears on a button between an opening `<button>` tag and a closing `</button>` tag. So you can include textual markup or image elements between these tags.

This element was first supported in IE4 and Netscape 6, but the browsers that do support this element also offer a relief (or 3D) effect on the button, which resembles an up or down motion when the button is clicked.

Here are some examples of using the `<button>` element (`ch06_eg06.html`):

```
<button type="submit">Submit</button>
<br /><br />
<button type="reset"><b>Clear this form,</b> I want to start again</button>
<br /><br />
<button type="button"><img src="submit.gif" alt="submit" /></button>
```

As you can see, the first submit button just contains text, the second reset button contains text and other markup (in the form of the `<b>` element), and the third submit button contains an `<img>` element.

Figure 5-10 shows what these buttons would look like.

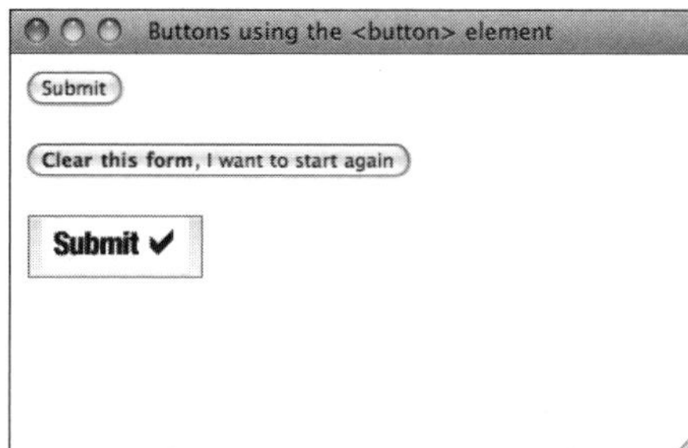

Figure 5-10

Checkboxes

Checkboxes are just like the little boxes on paper forms in which you can place a cross or tick. As with light switches, they can be either on or off. When they are checked they are on — the user can simply toggle between on and off positions by clicking the checkbox.

Checkboxes can appear individually, with each having its own name, or they can appear as a group of checkboxes that share a control name and allow users to select several values for the same property.

Checkboxes are ideal form controls when you need to allow a user to:

- ❑ Provide a simple yes or no response with one control (such as accepting terms and conditions)
- ❑ Select several items from a list of possible options (such as when you want a user to indicate all the skills they have from a given list)

A checkbox is created using the `<input>` element whose `type` attribute has a value of `checkbox`. Following is an example of some checkboxes that use the same control name (`ch05_eg07.html`):

```
<form action="http://www.example.com/cv.aspx" method="get" name="frmCV">
Which of the following skills do you possess? Select all that apply.
   <input type="checkbox" name="chkSkills" value="xhtml" />XHTML <br />
   <input type="checkbox" name="chkSkills" value="CSS" />CSS<br />
   <input type="checkbox" name="chkSkills" value="JavaScript" />JavaScript<br />
   <input type="checkbox" name="chkSkills" value="aspnet" />ASP.Net<br />
   <input type="checkbox" name="chkSkills" value="php" />PHP
</form>
```

For consistency with the naming convention we have used for form elements throughout the chapter, you can start the name of checkboxes with the letters `chk`.

Figure 5-11 shows how this form might look in a browser. Note how there is a line break after each checkbox, so that it clearly appears on each line (if you have checkboxes side by side, users are likely to get confused about which label applies to which checkbox).

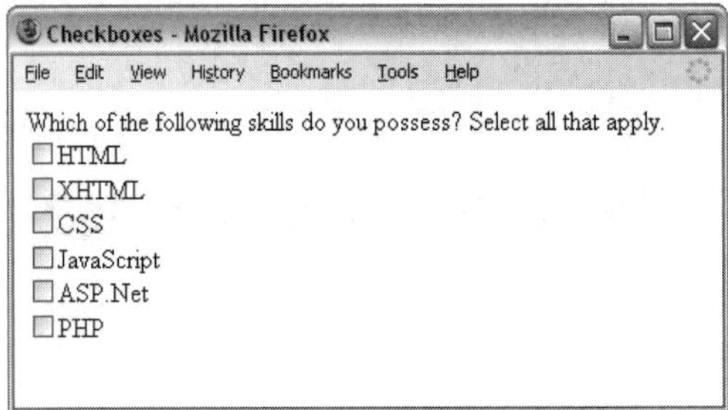

Figure 5-11

Because all the selected skills will be sent to the processing application in the form of name/value pairs, if someone selects more than one skill there will be several name/value pairs sent to the server that all share the same name.

In contrast, here is a single checkbox, acting like a simple yes or no option:

```
<form action="http://www.example.org/accept.aspx" name="frmTandC"
method="get">
  <input type="checkbox" name="chkAcceptTerms" checked="checked" />
   I accept the <a href="terms.htm">terms and conditions</a>.<br />
  <input type="submit" />
</form>
```

Note how the `<input>` element that creates this checkbox does not carry a `value` attribute. In the absence of a `value` attribute, the value is `on`. In this example, you can also see an attribute called `checked`, with a value of `checked`, which indicates that when the page loads the checkbox is selected.

The table that follows shows the attributes that an `<input>` element whose `type` attribute has a value of `checkbox` can carry.

Attribute	Purpose
`type`	Indicates that you want to create a checkbox.
`name`	Gives the name of the control. Several checkboxes may share the same name, but this should happen only if you want users to have the option of selecting several items from the same list — in which case, they should be placed next to each other on the form.
`value`	The value that will be sent to the server if the checkbox is selected.
`checked`	Indicates that when the page loads the checkbox should be selected.

Checkboxes can also carry the following attributes:

- All universal attributes
- `disabled`, `readonly`, `tabindex`, and `accesskey` which are discussed later in the chapter
- UI event attributes

Radio Buttons

Radio buttons are similar to checkboxes in that they can be either on or off, but there are two key differences:

- When you have a group of radio buttons that share the same name, only one of them can be selected. Once one radio button has been selected, if the user clicks another option, the new option is selected and the old one deselected.
- You should not use radio buttons for a single form control where the control indicates on or off, because once a lone radio button has been selected it cannot be deselected again (without writing a script to do that).

Therefore, a group of radio buttons are ideal if you want to provide users with a number of options from which they must pick only one. In such situations, an alternative is to use a drop-down select box that allows users to select only one option from several. Your decision between whether to use a select box or a group of radio buttons depends on three things:

- **User expectations:** If your form models a paper form where users would be presented with several checkboxes, from which they can pick only one, then you should use a group of radio buttons.
- **Seeing all the options:** If users would benefit from having all the options in front of them before they pick one, you should use a group of radio buttons.
- **Space:** If you are concerned about space, a drop-down select box will take up far less space than a set of radio buttons.

The term "radio buttons" comes from old radios. On some old radios, you could press only one button at a time to select the radio station you wanted to listen to from the ones that had been set. You could not press two of these buttons at the same time on your radio, and pressing one would pop the other out.

The `<input>` element is again called upon to create radio buttons, and this time the `type` attribute should be given a value of `radio`. For example, here radio buttons are used to allow users to select which class of travel they want to take (`ch05_eg08.html`):

```
<form action="http://www.example.com/flights.aspx" name="frmFlightBooking"
      method="get">
   Please select which class of travel you wish to fly: <br />
  <input type="radio" name="radClass" value="First" />First class <br />
  <input type="radio" name="radClass" value="Business" />Business class <br />
  <input type="radio" name="radClass" value="Economy" />Economy class <br />
</form>
```

As you can see, the user should be allowed to select only one of the three options, so radio buttons are ideal. You can also start the name of a radio button with the letters `rad`. Figure 5-12 shows you what this might look like in a browser.

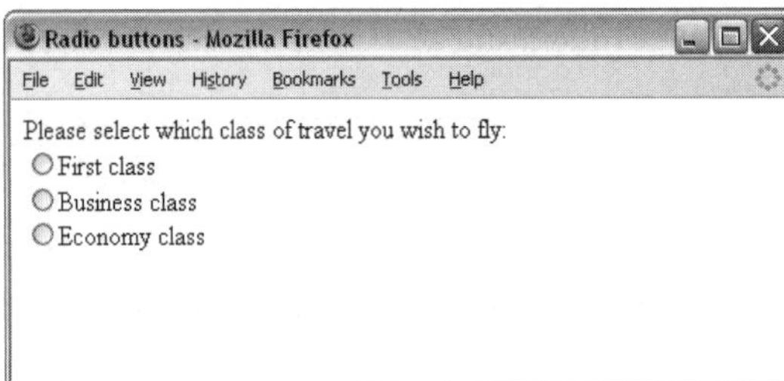

Figure 5-12

The table that follows lists the attributes for an `<input>` element whose `type` attribute has a value of `radio`.

Attribute	Purpose
`type`	To indicate that you want a radio button form control.
`name`	The name of the form control.
`value`	Used to indicate the value that will be sent to the server if this option is selected.
`checked`	Indicates that this option should be selected by default when the page loads. Remember that there is no point using this with a single radio button as a user can't deselect the option. If you use this attribute, the value should also be checked in order for the attribute to be XHTML-compliant.
`size`	This attribute indicates the size of the radio button in pixels, but this attribute does not work in IE8 or Firefox 3.

Radio buttons can also take the following attributes:

- All the universal attributes
- All the UI event attributes
- `disabled`, `tabindex`, and `accesskey`, which are covered later in the chapter

When you have a group of radio buttons that share the same name, some browsers will automatically select the first option as the page loads, even though they are not required to do so in the HTML specification. Therefore, if your radio buttons represent a set of values — say for a voting application — you might want to set a medium option to be selected by default so that, should some users forget to select one of the options, the results are not overly biased by the browser's selection. To do this, you should use the checked attribute.

Select Boxes

A drop-down select box allows users to select one item from a drop-down menu. Drop-down select boxes can take up far less space than a group of radio buttons.

Drop-down select boxes can also provide an alternative to single-line text input controls where you want to limit the options that a user can enter. For example, imagine that you were asking which country someone was from. If you had a textbox, visitors from the United States could enter different options such as U.S.A., U.S., United States, America, or North America, whereas with a select box you could control the options they could enter.

A drop-down select box is contained by a `<select>` element, while each individual option within that list is contained within an `<option>` element. For example, the following form creates a drop-down select box for the user to select a color (`ch05_eg09.html`):

```
<select name="selColor">
   <option selected="selected" value="">Select color</option>
   <option value="red">Red</option>
   <option value="green">Green</option>
   <option value="blue">Blue</option>
</select>
```

As you can see here, the text between the opening `<option>` tags and the closing `</option>` tags is used to display options to the user, while the value that would be sent to the server if that option were selected is given in the `value` attribute. You can also see that the first `<option>` element does not have a value and that its content is `Select color`; this is to indicate to the user that he or she must pick one of the color choices. Finally, notice again the use of the letters `sel` at the start of the name of a select box.

Figure 5-13 shows what this would look like in a browser.

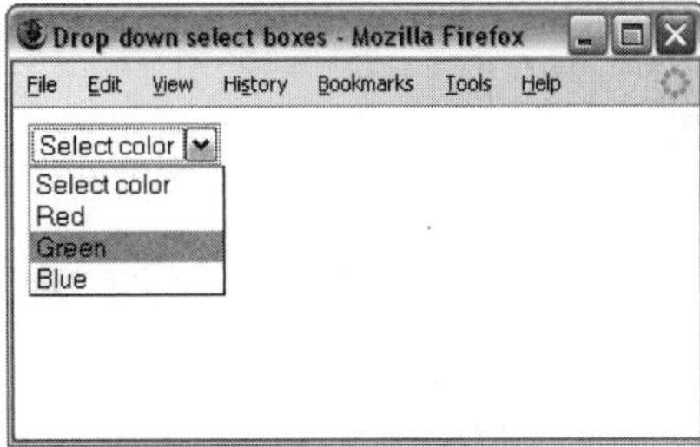

Figure 5-13

Note that the width of the select box will be the width of the longest option displayed to the user; in this case, it will be the width of the text `Select color`.

The <select> Element

The `<select>` element is the containing element for a drop-down list box; it can take the attributes shown in the table that follows:

Attribute	Purpose
`name`	The name for the control.
`size`	Can be used to present a scrolling list box, as you will see shortly. Its value would be the number of rows in the list that should be visible at the same time.
`multiple`	Allows a user to select multiple items from the menu. If the attribute is not present, the user may select only one item. In earlier versions of HTML, this attribute did not have a value. However, to be valid XHTML it should be given the value of `multiple` (i.e., `<select multiple="multiple">`). Note that the use of this attribute will change the presentation of the select box, as you will see in the section "Selecting Multiple Options with the multiple Attribute" later in this chapter.

According to the XHTML specification, a `<select>` element *must* contain at least one `<option>` element, although in practice it should contain more than one `<option>` element. After all, a drop-down list box with just one option might confuse a user.

The <option> Element

Inside any `<select>` element, you will find at least one `<option>` element. The text between the opening `<option>` and closing `</option>` tags is displayed to the user as the label for that option. The `<option>` element can take the attributes shown in the table that follows.

Attribute	Purpose
value	The value that is sent to the server if this option is selected.
selected	Specifies that this option should be the initially selected value when the page loads. This attribute may be used on several <option> elements even if the <select> element does not carry the multiple attribute. Although earlier versions of XHTML did not require a value for this attribute, in order to be valid XHTML you should give this attribute a value of selected.
label	An alternative way of labeling options, which uses an attribute rather than element content. This attribute is particularly useful when using the <optgroup> element, which is covered a bit later in this chapter.

Creating Scrolling Select Boxes

As I mentioned earlier, it's possible to create scrolling menus where users can see a few of the options in a select box at a time. In order to do this, you just add the size attribute to the <select> element. The value of the size attribute is the number of options you want to be visible at any one time.

While scrolling select box menus are rarely used, they can give users an indication that several possible options are open to them and allow them to see a few of the options at the same time. For example, the following is the code for a scrolling select box that allows the user to select a day of the week (ch05_eg10.html):

```
<form action="http://www.example.org/days.aspx" name="frmDays" method="get">
  <select size="4" name="selDay">
    <option value="Mon">Monday</option>
    <option value="Tue">Tuesday</option>
    <option value="Wed">Wednesday</option>
    <option value="Thu">Thursday</option>
    <option value="Fri">Friday</option>
    <option value="Sat">Saturday</option>
    <option value="Sun">Sunday</option>
  </select>
<br /><br /><input type="submit" value="Submit" />
</form>
```

As Figure 5-14 shows, the user can clearly see that he or she has several options; to save space only a few of the available options are shown.

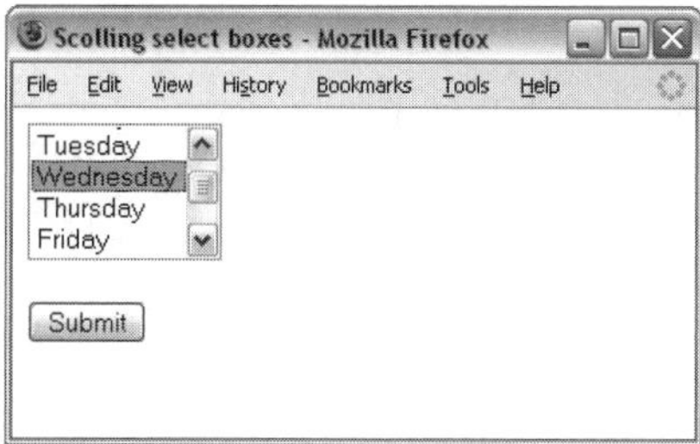

Figure 5-14

Note that the `multiple` attribute, which you meet in the next section is not used on this element.

Selecting Multiple Options with the multiple Attribute

The `multiple` attribute allows users to select more than one item from a select box. The value of the `multiple` attribute should be the word `multiple` in order for it to be valid XHTML (although earlier versions of HTML allowed this attribute to appear without a value). When you use this attribute it is always a good idea to tell people how to select multiple items: by holding down the control key and clicking on the items they want to select.

The addition of this attribute automatically makes the select box look like a scrolling select box. Here you can see an example of a multiple-item select box that allows users to select more than one day of the week (`ch05_eg11.html`):

```
<form action="http://www.example.org/days.aspx" method="get" name="frmDays">
  Please select more than one day of the week (to select multiple days
    hold down the control key and click on your chosen days):<br />
  <select name="selDays" multiple="multiple">
    <option value="Mon">Monday</option>
    <option value="Tue">Tuesday</option>
    <option value="Wed">Wednesday</option>
    <option value="Thu">Thursday</option>
    <option value="Fri">Friday</option>
    <option value="Sat">Saturday</option>
    <option value="Sun">Sunday</option>
  </select>
<br /><br /><input type="submit" value="Submit">
</form>
```

The result is shown in Figure 5-15, where you can see that even without the addition of the `size` attribute, the select box is still represented in the same way as a scrolling one.

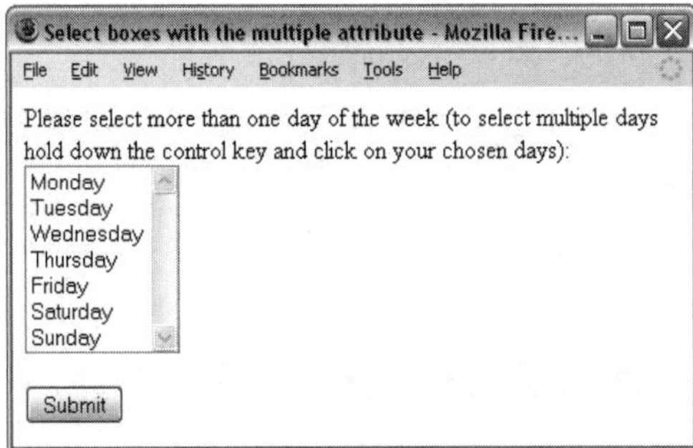

Figure 5-15

Grouping Options with the <optgroup> Element

If you have a very long list of items in a select box, you can group them together using the `<optgroup>` element, which acts just like a container element for all the elements you want within a group.

The `<optgroup>` element can carry a `label` attribute whose value is a label for that group of options. In the following example, you can see how the options are grouped in terms of type of equipment (`ch05_eg12.html`):

```
<form action="http://www.example.org/info.aspx" method="get" name="frmInfo">
  Please select the product you are interested in:<br />
  <select name="selInformation">
    <optgroup label="Hardware">
      <option value="Desktop">Desktop computers</option>
      <option value="Laptop">Laptop computers</option>
    </optgroup>
    <optgroup label="Software">
      <option value="OfficeSoftware">Office software</option>
      <option value="Games">Games</option>
    </optgroup>
    <optgroup label="Peripherals">
      <option value="Monitors">Monitors</option>
      <option value="InputDevices">Input Devices</option>
      <option value="Storage">Storage</option>
   </optgroup>
</select>
<br /><br /><input type="submit" value="Submit" />
</form>
```

You will find that different browsers display `<optgroup>` elements in different ways. Figure 5-16 shows you how Safari on a Mac displays options held by `<optgroup>` elements, whereas Figure 5-17 shows you the result in Firefox on a PC.

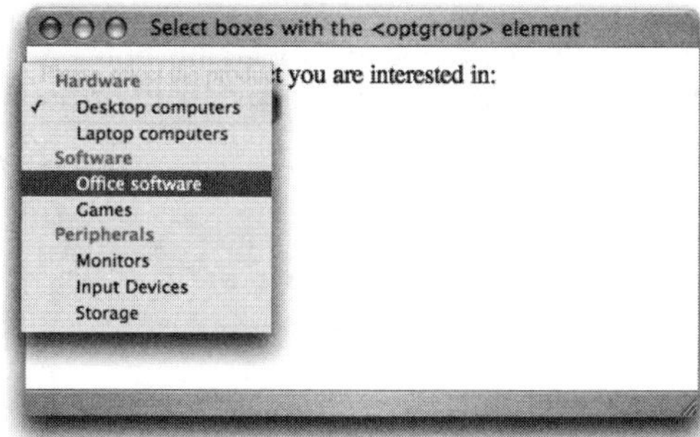

Figure 5-16

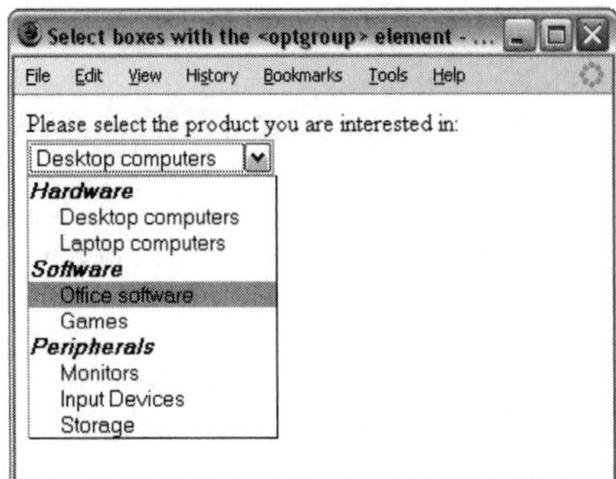

Figure 5-17

An alternative option for grouping elements is to add an `<option>` element that carries the `disabled` attribute, which you will learn about shortly (`ch05_eg13.html`):

```
<form action="http://www.example.org/info.aspx" method="get" name="frmInfo">
  Please select the product you are interested in:<br />
  <select name="selInformation">
    <option disabled="disabled" value=""> — Hardware — </option>
      <option value="Desktop">Desktop computers</option>
      <option value="Laptop">Laptop computers</option>
    <option disabled="disabled" value=""> — Software — </option>
      <option value="OfficeSoftware">Office software</option>
      <option value="Games">Games</option>
    <option disabled="disabled" value=""> — Peripherals — </option>
      <option value="Monitors">Monitors</option>
      <option value="InputDevices">Input Devices</option>
      <option value="Storage">Storage</option>
  </select>
<br /><br /><input type="submit" value="Submit" />
</form>
```

As you will see later in the chapter, the use of the `disabled` attribute prevents a user from selecting the option that carries it. With the careful use of a couple of dashes, the groups of options become more clearly defined, as you can see in Figure 5-18.

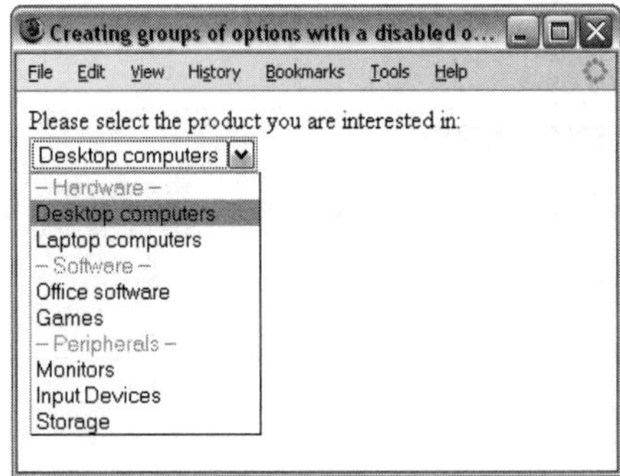

Figure 5-18

You may occasionally see drop-down list boxes used for navigation, and sometimes they use JavaScript to take you directly to that page. The use of JavaScript to take you to a page without pressing a submit button is considered bad usability. One of the main reasons for this is that users can select the wrong section by accident; for example, if a user tries to select options using his or her up and down arrow keys, the script may fire as soon as he or she comes across the first option.

Attributes for Select Boxes

For completeness, the following is the full list of attributes that the `<select>` element can carry:

- `name`, `size`, and `multiple`, all of which you have met
- `disabled` and `tabindex`, which are covered later in the chapter
- All universal attributes
- UI event attributes

Meanwhile, the `<option>` element can carry the following attributes:

- `label`, which you have already seen
- `disabled`, which you learn more about later in the chapter
- All universal attributes
- UI event attributes

File Select Boxes

If you want to allow a user to upload a file to your web site from his or her computer, you will need to use a *file upload box*, also known as a *file select box*. This is created using the `<input>` element (again), but this time you give the `type` attribute a value of `file` (`ch05_eg14.html`):

```
<form action="http://www.example.com/imageUpload.aspx" method="post"
      name="fromImageUpload" enctype="multipart/form-data">
  <input type="file" name="fileUpload" accept="image/*" />
<br /><br /><input type="submit" value="Submit" />
</form>
```

When you are using a file upload box, the `method` *attribute of the* `<form>` *element must be* `post`.

There are some attributes in this example that you learned about at the beginning of the chapter.

- The `enctype` attribute has been added to the `<form>` element with a value of `multipart/form-data` so that each form control is sent separately to the server. This is required on a form that uses a file upload box.
- The `accept` attribute has been added to the `<input>` element to indicate the MIME types of the files that can be selected for upload. In this example, the `accept` attribute is indicating that any image format can be uploaded, as the wildcard character (the asterisk) has been used after the `image/` portion of the MIME type. Unfortunately, this is not supported by Firefox 3 or IE8, which means that any file at all (not just images) could be uploaded.

In Figure 5-19 you can see that when you click the Browse button in Firefox, a file dialog box opens up enabling you to browse to a file and select which one you want to upload. It is worth noting that different browsers sometimes show this control in slightly different ways (for example, Safari has a button saying Choose File instead of Browse).

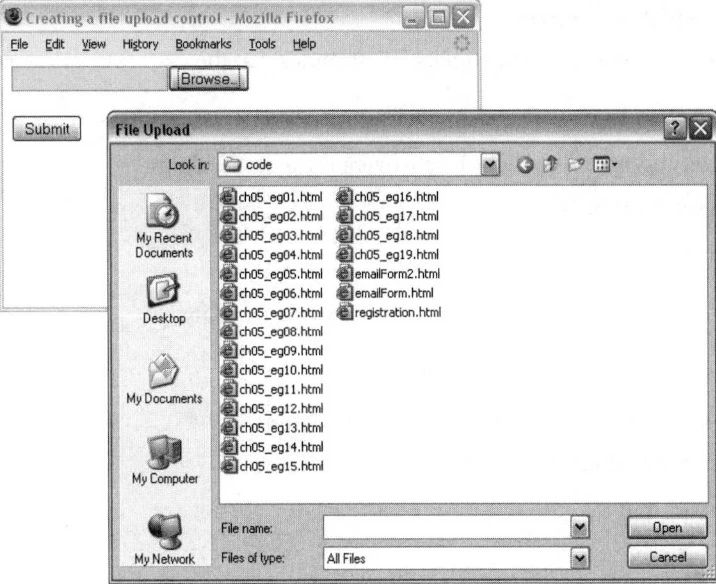

Figure 5-19

An `<input>` element whose `type` attribute has a value of `file` can take the following attributes:

- `name`, `value`, and `accept`, which you have already seen
- `tabindex`, `accesskey`, `disabled`, and `readonly`, which are covered later in the chapter
- All universal attributes
- UI event attributes

Hidden Controls

Sometimes you will want to pass information between pages without the user seeing it; to do this, you can use hidden form controls. It is important to note, however, that while users cannot see them in the web page, if they were to look at the source code for the page they would be able to see the values in the code. Therefore, hidden controls should not be used for any sensitive information that you do not want the user to see.

You may have come across forms on the Web that span more than one page. Long forms can be confusing and splitting them up can help a user. In such cases, it will often be necessary to pass values that a user has entered into the first form (on one page) onto the form in the second page, and then onto another page. Hidden elements are one way in which programmers can pass values between pages.

You create a hidden control using the `<input>` element whose `type` attribute has a value of `hidden`. For example, the following form contains a hidden form control indicating which section of the site the user was on when he or she filled in the form (`ch05_eg15.html`):

```
<form action="http://www.example.com/vote.aspx" method="get" name="fromVote">
  <input type="hidden" name="hidPageSentFrom" value="home page" />
  <input type="submit" value="Click if this is your favorite page of our
  site." />
</form>
```

Hidden form controls need both the `name` and `value` attributes in order to be sent with the rest of a form.

Figure 5-20 shows that the hidden form control is not shown on the page, but it is available in the source for the page.

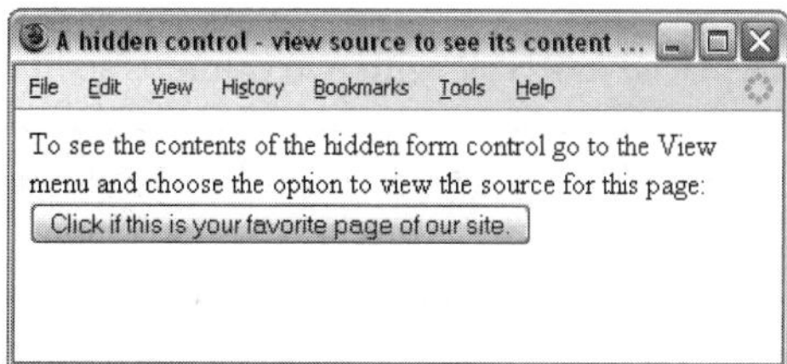

Figure 5-20

As you will see in Chapter 8, you can also hide form controls using the CSS `display` *and* `visibility` *properties.*

Object Controls

The HTML 4.0 specification introduced the capability to use objects — embedded in an `<object>` element — inside the `<form>` element. For example, you may want to use an object that enables some kind of graphical interaction, and then store its value with the name of the object. However, this feature is not implemented in the main browsers at the time of this writing.

Try It Out   Creating a Contact Form

In this example, you are going to combine several of the form controls to make up a contact form for our Example Café.

1. Create a new Transitional XHTML 1.0 document, with the skeleton in place. Then add a heading:

```
<?xml version="1.0" ?>
<!DOCTYPE html PUBLIC "-//W3C//DTD XHTML 1.0 Transitional//EN"
"http://www.w3.org/TR/xhtml1/DTD/xhtml1-transitional.dtd">
<html xmlns="http://www.w3.org/1999/xhtml" lang="en" xml:lang="en">
<head>
  <title>Contact Us</title>
</head>
<body>

<h1>Contact Us</h1>
<p>Use the following form to send a message to Example Cafe</p>

</body>
</html>
```

2. The form is going to be placed in a table with two columns so that the instructions are in the left column, and the form controls are aligned in the right column. (Without this, the form controls would look uneven across the page.) This is quite a common technique in writing forms.

   In the first two rows you can add a text input for the visitor's e-mail address using an `<input>` element whose `type` attribute has a value of `text`. You can also set the size of the form control and the maximum number of characters a user can enter.

   Add the following table under the paragraph that tells people to use the form to send a message:

```
<table>
      <tr>
        <td>Your email</td>
        <td><input type="text" name="txtFrom" id="emailFrom"
          size="20" maxlength="250" /></td>
      </tr>
```

3. This first row of the table is followed by a second row containing a text area for their message. The size of the text area is specified using the `rows` and `cols` attributes:

```
<tr>
  <td>Message</td>
  <td><textarea name="txtBody" id="emailBody" cols="50"
  rows="10"></textarea></td>
</tr>
```

4. In the next row, you can add a select box so that the user can tell you how they heard of the café:

```
<tr>
  <td>How did you hear of us?</td>
  <td>
    <select name="selReferrer">
      <option value="google">Google</option>
      <option value="ad">Local newspaper ad</option>
      <option value="friend">Friend</option>
      <option value="other">Other</option>
     </select>
  </td>
</tr>
```

5. In the final row, add a checkbox to indicate whether the visitor wants to sign up for e-mail updates. This is created with the `<input>` element, whose `type` attribute has a value of `checkbox`. The checkbox should be selected by default, and this is indicated using the `checked` attribute:

```
<tr>
  <td>Newsletter</td>
  <td><input type="checkbox" name="chkBody" id="newsletterSignup"
    checked="checked" />
    Ensure this box is checked if you would like to
    receive email updates</td>
</tr>
</table>
```

6. Finally, you need to add a submit button, again using the `<input>` element so that the visitor can send the message to the café:

```
<input type="submit" value="Send message" />
```

7. Save the file as `emailForm.html` and open it in your browser; it should look something like Figure 5-21.

Figure 5-21

Now that you've seen the basics of forms, it is time to look at more advanced features that you can use to enhance your forms.

Creating Labels for Controls and the <label> Element

Forms can be confusing enough at the best of times. I've received many insurance and tax forms that have left me scratching my head, and I'm sure I'm not the only one.

If you are creating a form for your site, it is worth spending time to provide good labeling so that the user knows what data he or she should be entering where. If visitors have difficulty understanding your form, they will be less likely to complete the form (in particular if they are purchasing something), or they are more likely to make a mistake when filling it in.

Some form controls, such as buttons, already have labels. For the majority of form controls, however, you will have to provide the label yourself.

For controls that do not have a label, you should use the `<label>` element. This element does not affect the form in any way other than telling users what information they should be entering (`ch05_eg16.html`).

```
<form action="http://www.example.org/login.aspx" method="post"
name="frmLogin">
  <table>
    <tr>
      <td><label for="Uname">User name</label></td>
      <td><input type="text" id="Uname" name="txtUserName" /></td>
    </tr>
    <tr>
      <td><label for="Pwd">Password</label></td>
      <td><input type="password" id="Pwd" name="pwdPassword" /></td>
    </tr>
  </table>
</form>
```

You can see that this form has been placed inside a table; this ensures that even if the labels are of different lengths, the text inputs are aligned in their own column. If a list of text inputs is not aligned, it can be harder to use.

As you can see here, the `<label>` element carries an attribute called `for`, which indicates the form control associated with the label. The value of the `for` attribute should be the same as the value of the `id` attribute on the corresponding form control. For example, the textbox form control, where a user enters his or her username, has an `id` attribute whose value is `Uname`, and the label for this textbox has a `for` attribute whose value is also `Uname`.

Figure 5-22 shows you what this login screen looks like.

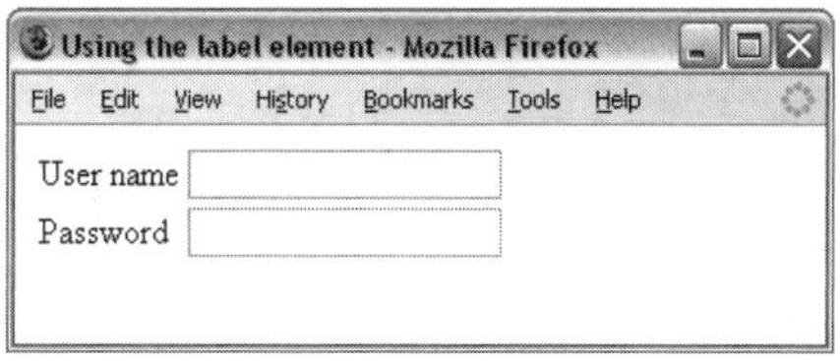

Figure 5-22

The label may be positioned before or after the control. For textboxes and drop-down select boxes, it is generally good practice to have the label on the left or above the form control, whereas for checkboxes and radio buttons it is often easier to associate the label with the correct form control if they are on the right.

You should have a new `<label>` element for each form control.

Another way to use the `<label>` element is as a containing element. When you use the `<label>` element this way, you do not need to use the `for` attribute because it applies to the form element that is inside it. This kind of label is sometimes known as an *implicit label*. For example:

```
<form action="http://www.example.org/login.aspx" method="post"
name="frmLogin">
  <label>Username <input type="text" id="Uname" name="txtUserName" /></label>
  <label>Password <input type="password" id="Pwd" name="pwdPassword" />
  </label>
</form>
```

The drawback to this approach is that you cannot control where the label appears in relation to the form control, and you certainly cannot have the label in a different table cell from the form control, as the markup would not nest correctly.

Structuring Your Forms with <fieldset> and <legend> Elements

Large forms can be confusing for users, so it's good practice to group together related form controls. The `<fieldset>` and `<legend>` elements do exactly this — help you group controls.

- The `<fieldset>` element creates a border around the group of form controls to show that they are related.
- The `<legend>` element allows you to specify a caption for the `<fieldset>` element, which acts as a title for the group of form controls. When used, the `<legend>` element should always be the first child of the `<fieldset>` element.

Figure 5-23 shows these elements in action. You can see that the form has been divided into four sections: Contact Information, Competition Question, Tiebreaker Question, and Enter Competition.

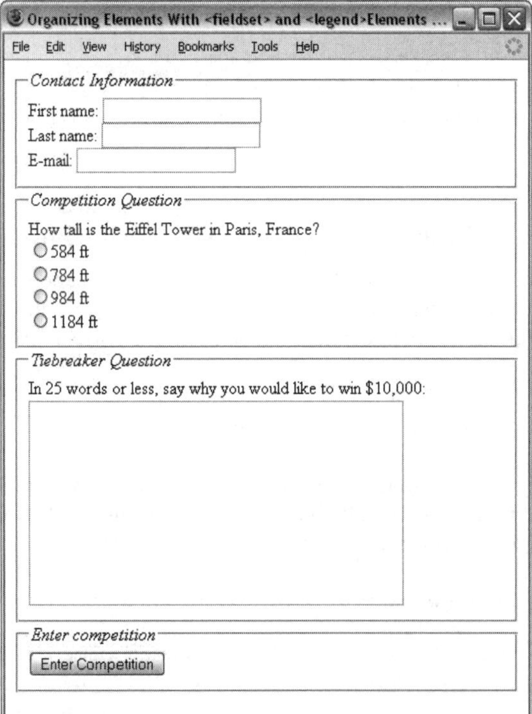

Figure 5-23

Let's take a look at the code for this example. You can see how the <fieldset> elements create borders around the groups of form controls, and how the <legend> elements are used to title the groups of controls. Remember, when you use the <legend> element, it must be the first child of the <fieldset> element (ch05_eg17.html).

```
<form action="http://www.example.org/competition.aspx" method="post"
name="frmComp">
 <fieldset>
  <legend><em>Contact Information</em></legend>
   <label>First name: <input type="text" name="txtFName" size="20" />
   </label><br />
   <label>Last name: <input type="text" name="txtLName" size="20" /></label>
   <br />
   <label>E-mail: <input type="text" name="txtEmail" size="20" /></label>
   <br />
  </fieldset>
  <fieldset>
  <legend><em>Competition Question</em></legend>
   How tall is the Eiffel Tower in Paris, France? <br />
   <label><input type="radio" name="radAnswer" value="584" />
      584ft</label><br />
   <label><input type="radio" name="radAnswer" value="784" />
      784ft</label><br />
   <label><input type="radio" name="radAnswer" value="984" />
      984ft</label><br />
   <label><input type="radio" name="radAnswer" value="1184" />
       1184ft</label><br />
  </fieldset>
  <fieldset>
    <legend><em>Tiebreaker Question</em></legend>
      <label>In 25 words or less, say why you would like to win $10,000:
        <textarea name="txtTiebreaker" rows="10" cols="40"></textarea>
      </label>
  </fieldset>
  <fieldset>
    <legend><em>Enter competition</em></legend>
       <input type="submit" value="Enter Competition" />
  </fieldset>
</form>
```

The <fieldset> element can take the following attributes:

- All the universal attributes
- The basic event attributes

If you use a table to format your form, the entire `<table>` element must appear inside the `<fieldset>` element. If a `<fieldset>` resides within a table that is used to format the page, then the entire fieldset must reside within the same cell.

The `<legend>` element can take the following attributes:

- `accesskey`, which you will learn about in the next section.
- `align`, which you have seen already, and is deprecated — you should use CSS positioning instead.
- All the universal attributes.
- UI event attributes.

Focus

When a web page featuring several links or several form controls loads, you may have noticed that you are able to use your Tab key to move between those elements (or Shift+Tab to move backward through elements). As you move between them, the web browser tends to add some type of border or highlighting to that element (be it a link or a form control). This is known as *focus*.

Only elements that a user can interact with, such as links and form controls, can receive focus. Indeed, if a user is expected to interact with an element, that element *must* be able to receive focus.

An element can gain focus in three ways:

- An element can be selected using a pointing device such as a mouse or trackball.
- Elements that can gain focus can be navigated between using the keyboard — often using the Tab key (or Shift+Tab to move backward through elements). As you are about to see, the elements in some documents can be given a fixed *tabbing order*, indicating the order in which elements gain focus when the user pressed the tab key.
- A web-page author can indicate that an element should receive focus when a user presses a keyboard shortcut known as an *access key*. For example, if the page author set the access key on a search box to be the key for the letter *s*, on a PC you would likely press the Alt key plus the access key (Alt+S), whereas on a Mac you would press the Control key with an access key (Control+S), and the corresponding form control would gain focus.

Tabbing Order

If you want to control the order in which elements can gain focus, you can use the `tabindex` attribute to give that element a number between 0 and 32767, which becomes part of the tabbing order. Every time the user presses the Tab key, the focus moves to the element with the next highest tabbing order (and again, Shift+Tab moves focus in reverse order).

The following elements can carry a `tabindex` attribute:

```
<a> <area> <button> <input> <object> <select> <textarea>
```

After a user has tabbed through all elements in a document that can gain focus, then focus may be given to other browser features (most commonly the address bar).

To demonstrate how tabbing order works, the following example gives focus to the checkboxes in a different order than you might expect (`ch05_eg18.html`):

```
<form action="http://www.example.com/tabbing.aspx" method="get"
  name="frmTabExample">
  <input type="checkbox" name="chkNumber" value="1" tabindex="3" /> One<br/>
  <input type="checkbox" name="chkNumber" value="2" tabindex="7" /> Two<br/>
  <input type="checkbox" name="chkNumber" value="3" tabindex="4" /> Three<br />
  <input type="checkbox" name="chkNumber" value="4" tabindex="1" /> Four<br/>
  <input type="checkbox" name="chkNumber" value="5" tabindex="9" /> Five<br/>
  <input type="checkbox" name="chkNumber" value="6" tabindex="6" /> Six<br/>
  <input type="checkbox" name="chkNumber" value="7" tabindex="10" />Seven<br />
  <input type="checkbox" name="chkNumber" value="8" tabindex="2" />Eight<br />
  <input type="checkbox" name="chkNumber" value="9" tabindex="8" /> Nine<br/>
  <input type="checkbox" name="chkNumber" value="10" tabindex="5" /> Ten<br/>
<input type="submit" value="Submit" />
</form>
```

In this example, the checkboxes receive focus in the following order:

```
4, 8, 1, 3, 10, 6, 2, 9, 5, 7
```

Figure 5-24 shows how Firefox 2 for PC will, by default, give a yellow outline to form elements as they gain focus (other browsers give different outlines — Internet Explorer uses blue lines). I have zoomed in on the item in focus so you can see it in closer detail.

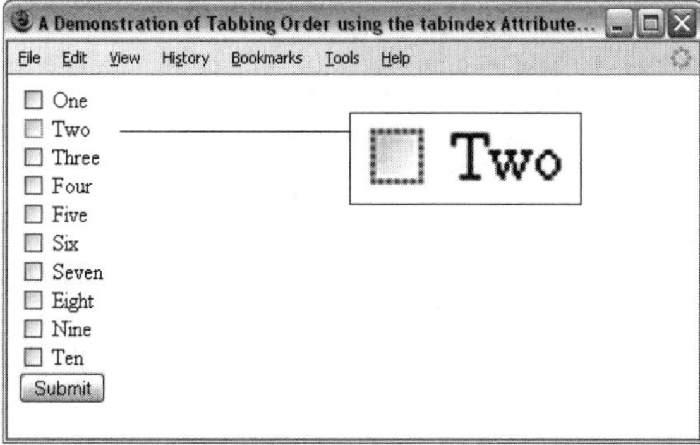

Figure 5-24

Elements that could gain focus but do not have a `tabindex` attribute are automatically given a value of `0`; therefore, when you specify a `tabindex` value, it should be `1` or higher, rather than `0`.

If two elements have the same value for a `tabindex` attribute, they will be navigated in the order in which they appear in the document. So, once the elements that have a `tabindex` of `1` or more have been cycled through, the browser will cycle through the remaining elements (which have a value of `0`) in the order in which they appear in the page.

> *Note that if an element is disabled, it cannot gain focus and does not participate in the tabbing order. Also, if you use a Mac you may need to check your Keyboard Shortcuts settings in system preferences; at the bottom of the window where it says "Full Keyboard Access," this needs to have the "All Controls" option selected.*

Access Keys

Access keys act just like keyboard shortcuts. The access key is a single character from the document's character set that is expected to appear on the user's keyboard. When this key is used in conjunction with another key or keys (such as Alt with IE on Windows, Alt and Shift with Firefox on Windows, and Control on an Apple), the browser automatically goes to that section. (Exactly which key must be used in conjunction with the access key depends upon the operating system and browser.)

The access key is defined using the `accesskey` attribute. The value of this attribute is the character (and key on the keyboard) you want the user to be able to press (in conjunction with the other key/keys that are dependent upon the operating system and browser).

The following elements can carry an access key attribute:

```
<a> <area> <button> <input> <label> <legend> <textarea>
```

To see how access keys work, you can revisit the example of a competition form (`ch05_eg17.html`), which was covered in the section "Structuring Your Forms with <fieldset> and <legend> Elements" earlier in this chapter. Now the `accesskey` attributes can be added to the `<legend>` elements:

```
<legend accesskey="c"><u>C</u>ontact Information</legend>
<legend>Competition Question</legend>
<legend accesskey="t"><u>T</u>iebreaker Question</legend>
<legend>Enter competition</legend>
```

The new version of this file is `ch05_eg19.html` in the download code. (Extra `<br />` elements have been added to show how the screen scrolls to the appropriate section when an access key is used.) As a hint to users that they can use the access keys as shortcuts, information has also been added to the information in the `<legend>` element by underlining the access key. Figure 5-25 shows how this updated example looks in a browser.

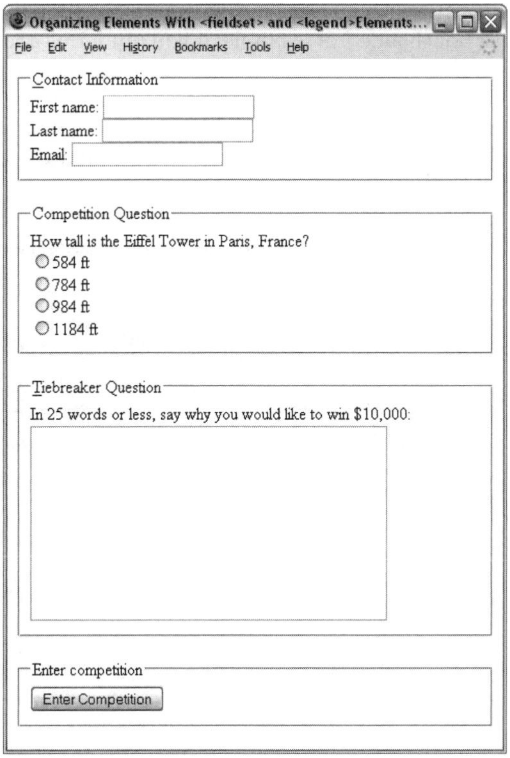

Figure 5-25

The effect of an access key being used depends upon the element that it is used with. With <legend> elements, such as those shown previously, the browser scrolls to that part of the page automatically and gives focus to the first form control in the section. When used with form controls, those elements gain focus. As soon as the element gains focus, the user should be able to interact with it (either by typing in text controls or pressing the Enter or Return key with other form controls).

When using letters a–z, it does not matter whether you specify an uppercase or lowercase access key, although, strictly speaking, it should be lowercase.

Disabled and Read-Only Controls

Throughout the chapter, you have seen that several of the elements can carry attributes called `disabled` and `readonly`:

- The `readonly` attribute prevents users from changing the value of the form controls themselves, although it may be modified by a script. The name and value of any `readonly` control *will* be sent to the server. The value of this attribute should be `readonly`.
- The `disabled` attribute disables the form control so that users cannot alter it. A script can be used to re-enable the control, but unless a control is re-enabled, the name and value will not be sent to the server. The value of this attribute should be `disabled`.

A `readonly` control is particularly helpful when you want to stop visitors from changing a part of the form, perhaps because it must not change (for example, if you put terms and conditions inside a text area).

The `disabled` attribute is particularly helpful when preventing users from interacting with a control until they have done something else. For example, you might use a script to disable a submit button until all of the form fields contain a value.

The following table indicates which form controls work with the `readonly` and `disabled` attributes.

Element	readonly	disabled
`<textarea>`	Yes	Yes
`<input type="text" />`	Yes	Yes
`<input type="checkbox" />`	No	Yes
`<input type="radio" />`	No	Yes
`<input type="submit" />`	No	Yes
`<input type="reset" />`	No	Yes
`<input type="button" />`	No	Yes
`<select>`	No	Yes
`<option>`	No	Yes
`<button>`	No	Yes

The following table indicates the main differences between the `readonly` and `disabled` attributes.

Attribute	readonly	disabled
Can be modified	Yes by script, not by user	Not while disabled
Will be sent to server	Yes	Not while disabled
Will receive focus	Yes	No
Included in tabbing order	Yes	No

Sending Form Data to the Server

When your browser requests a web page and when the server sends a page back to the browser, you use the Hypertext Transfer Protocol (HTTP).

There are two methods that a browser can use to send form data to the server — HTTP `get` and HTTP `post` — and you specify which should be used by adding the `method` attribute on the `<form>` element.

If the `<form>` element does not carry a `method` attribute, then by default the `get` method will be used. If you are using a file upload form control, you must choose the `post` method (and you must set the `enctype` attribute to have a value of `multipart/form-data`). Let's take a closer look at each of these methods.

HTTP get

When you send form data to the server using the HTTP `get` method, the form data is appended to the URL that is specified in the `action` attribute of the `<form>` element.

The form data is separated from the URL using a question mark. Following the question mark, you get the name/value pairs for each form control. Each name/value pair is separated by an ampersand (`&`).

For example, take the following login form, which you saw when the password form control was introduced:

```
<form action="http://www.example.com/login.aspx" method="get">
 Username:
 <input type="text" name="txtUsername" value="" size="20" maxlength="20"><br />
 Password:
 <input type="password" name="pwdPassword" value="" size="20" maxlength="20">
 <input type="submit" />
</form>
```

When you click the submit button, your username and password are appended to the URL `http://www.example.com/login.aspx` in what is known as the *query string*. It should look like this:

```
http://www.example.com/login.aspx?txtUsername=Bob&pwdPassword=LetMeIn
```

Note that when a browser requests a URL with any spaces or unsafe characters such as /, \ , =, &, and + (which have special meanings in URLs), they are replaced with a hex code to represent that character. This is done automatically by the browser, and is known as *URL encoding*. When the data reaches the server, the server will usually un-encode the special characters automatically.

One of the advantages of passing form data in a URL is that it can be bookmarked. If you look at searches performed on major search engines such as Google, they tend to use the `get` method so that the page can be bookmarked.

The `get` method, however, has some disadvantages. Indeed, when sending sensitive data such as the password shown here, or credit card details, you should not use the `get` method because the sensitive data becomes part of the URL and is in full view to everyone (and could be bookmarked).

You should not use the HTTP get method when:

- You are dealing with sensitive information, such as passwords or credit card details (because the sensitive form data would be visible as part of a URL).
- You are updating a data source such as a database or spreadsheet (because someone could make up URLs that would alter your data source).
- Your form contains a file upload control (because uploaded files cannot be passed in the URL).
- Your users might enter non-ASCII characters such as Hebrew or Cyrillic characters.

In these circumstances, you should use the HTTP post method.

HTTP post

When you send data from a form to the server using the HTTP post method, the form data is sent transparently in what is known as the *HTTP headers*. While you do not see these headers, they are not, strictly speaking, secure on their own. If you are sending sensitive information such as credit card details, the data should be sent under a *Secure Sockets Layer*, or *SSL*, and they should be in encrypted.

If the login form you just saw was sent using the post method, it could be represented like this in the HTTP headers:

```
User-agent: MSIE 7
Content-Type: application/x-www-form-urlencoded
Content-length: 35
...other headers go here...
txtUserName=Bob&pwdPassword=LetMeIn
```

Note that the last line is the form data, and that it is in exactly the same format as the data after the question mark in the get method — it would also be URL-encoded so any spaces or unsafe characters such as /, \ , =, &, and + (which have special meanings in URLs) are replaced with a hex code to represent that character as they were in HTTP get requests.

There is nothing to stop you from using the post method to send form data to a page that also contains a query string. For example, you might have one page to handle users who want to subscribe to or unsubscribe from a newsletter, and you might choose to indicate whether a user wanted to subscribe or unsubscribe in the query string. Meanwhile, you might want to send their actual contact details in a form that uses the post method because you are updating a data source. In this case, you could use the following <form> element:

```
<form action="http://www.example.com/newsletter.asp?action=subscribe"
      method="post">
```

The only issue with using the HTTP post method is that the information the user entered on the form cannot be bookmarked in the same way it can when it is contained in the URL. So you cannot use it to retrieve a page that was generated using specific form data as you can when you bookmark a page generated by most search engines, but it is good for security reasons.

Try It Out Contact Form Revisited

It is time to revisit the contact form from the earlier Try It Out section in this chapter. This time, you will use techniques learned in the later part of the chapter to add a new field and to make it more usable.

1. Open the file `emailForm.html` that you made earlier in the chapter and save it as `emailForm2.html` so that you have a different copy to work with.

2. You should place `<label>` elements around the instructions that described the purpose of the form control. This `<label>` element should carry the `for` attribute, whose value is the value of the `id` attribute on the corresponding form control, like this one:

```
<tr>
  <td><label for="emailFrom">Your email</label></td>
  <td><input type="text" name="txtFrom" id="emailFrom"
    size="20" tabindex="1" maxlength="250" /></td>
</tr>
```

3. Add in a new single-line text input to the beginning of the form, indicating to whom the message is being sent. This input should be read-only:

```
<tr>
  <td><label for="emailTo">To</label></td>
  <td><input type="text" name="txtTo" readonly="readonly"
    id="emailTo" size="20" value="Example Cafe" /></td>
</tr>
```

4. Set the tab index so that the input that allows visitors to enter their e-mail addresses receives focus first, followed by the text area where the visitors enter their messages:

```
<tr>
  <td><label for="emailFrom">Your email</label></td>
  <td><input type="text" name="txtFrom" id="emailFrom" size="20"
    tabindex="1" maxlength="250" /></td>
</tr>

<tr>
  <td><label for="emailBody">Message</label></td>
  <td><textarea name="txtBody" id="emailBody" cols="50" rows="10"
tabindex="2"></textarea></td>
</tr>
```

5. Now it is time to split the form into two sections using the `<fieldset>` element. In order to make sure that the elements nest correctly, each fieldset will need its own table. The first section will indicate that it is for information about the visitor's message.

```
<fieldset>
    <legend>Your message:</legend>
    <table>
      <tr>
        <td><label for="emailTo">To</label></td>
        <td><input type="text" name="txtTo" readonly="readonly" id="emailTo"
          size="20" value="Example Cafe" /></td>
      </tr>

      <tr>
        <td><label for="emailFrom">Your email</label></td>
        <td><input type="text" name="txtFrom" id="emailFrom" size="20"
          tabindex="1" maxlength="250" /></td>
      </tr>

      <tr>
        <td><label for="emailBody">Message</label></td>
        <td><textarea name="txtBody" id="emailBody" cols="50" rows="10"
          tabindex="2"></textarea></td>
      </tr>

    </table>
  </fieldset>
```

The second section is for information about the company (how the user found the site and if the user wants to be on the mailing list):

```
<fieldset>
    <legend>How you found us:</legend>
    <table>
      <tr>
        <td><label for="emailBody">How did you hear of us</label></td>
        <td>
        <select name="selReferrer">
              <option value="google">Google</option>
           <option value="ad">Local newspaper ad</option>
           <option value="friend">Friend</option>
           <option value="other">Other</option>
        </select>
          </td>
      </tr>

      <tr>
        <td><label for="newsletterSignup">Newsletter</label></td>
        <td><input type="checkbox" name="chkBody" id="newsletterSignup"

       checked="checked" /> Ensure this box is checked if you would like
        to receive email updates</td>
      </tr>
    </table>
  </fieldset>
```

This extended registration form is now a lot more usable. If you save the file again and open it in your browser, you should find something that resembles Figure 5-26.

Figure 5-26

Summary

This chapter has introduced you to the world of creating online forms, which are a vital part of many sites. In most cases, when you want or need to directly collect information from a visitor to your site you will use a form, and you have seen several different examples of forms in this chapter.

You have learned how a form lives inside a `<form>` element and that inside a form there are one or more form controls. You have seen how the `<input>` element can be used to create several kinds of form controls, namely single-line text input controls, checkboxes, radio buttons, file upload boxes, buttons, and hidden form controls. There are also the `<textarea>` elements for creating multiple line text inputs and the `<select>` and `<option>` elements for creating select boxes.

Once you have created a form with its form controls, you need to ensure that each element is labeled properly so that users know what information they should enter or which selection they will be making. You can also organize larger forms using the `<fieldset>` and `<label>` elements and aid navigation with `tabindex` and `accesskey` attributes.

Finally, you learned when you should use the HTTP `get` or `post` methods to send form data to the server.

Next, it is time to look at the last of our core XHTML chapters, which covers framesets. You will see more about form design in Chapter 12, which covers some design issues that will make your forms easier to understand.

Exercises

The answers to all the exercises are in Appendix A.

1. Create an e-mail feedback form that looks like the one shown in Figure 5-27.

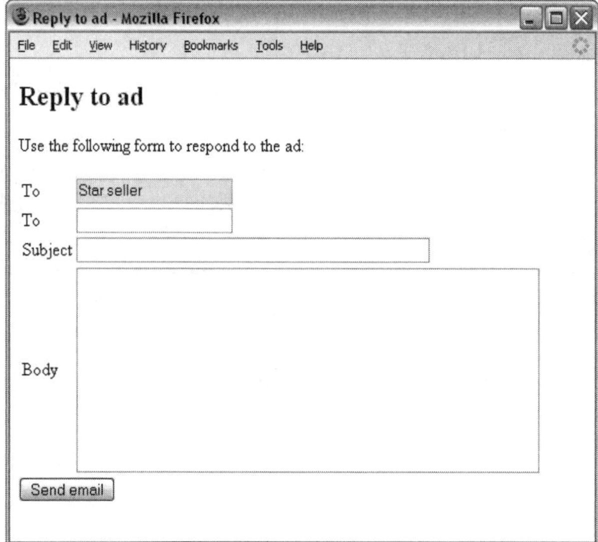

Figure 5-27

Note that the first textbox is a `readonly` textbox so that the user cannot alter the name of the person the mail is being sent to.

2. Create a voting or ranking form that looks like the one shown in Figure 5-28.

Figure 5-28

Note that the following <style> element was added to the <head> of the document to make each column of the table the same fixed width, with text aligned in the center (you'll see more about this in Chapter 7).

```
<head>
  <title>Voting</title>
  <style type="text/css">td {width:100; text-align:center;}</style>
</head>
```

Frames

Frames divide a browser window into two or more separate pieces or panes, with each pane containing a separate web page. One of the key advantages that frames offer is that you can load and reload single panes without having to reload the entire contents of the browser window. A collection of frames in the browser window is known as a *frameset*.

A frameset divides the window into rows and columns (rather like a table). The simplest of framesets might just divide the screen into two rows, whereas a complex frameset could use several rows and columns.

There is also a special kind of frame called an *iframe* which is a single window that can sit anywhere inside a page.

In this chapter you learn the following:

- How to create a frameset document with multiple frames
- How to create inline frames (or iframes), which are single windows that sit within another page
- How to deal with users whose browsers cannot use frames

I should warn you early on that there are actually very few cases in which most developers consider using frames. I will explain the main reasons why in the second section of this chapter, after showing a simple example that helps you understand what frames are. You are more likely to use iframes, which are covered near the end of the chapter.

Introducing the Frameset

To help you understand frames, let's look at an example. Figure 6-1 shows you a frameset document in a browser. This frameset divides the page into three parts, and each separate part of the page is a separate XHTML document.

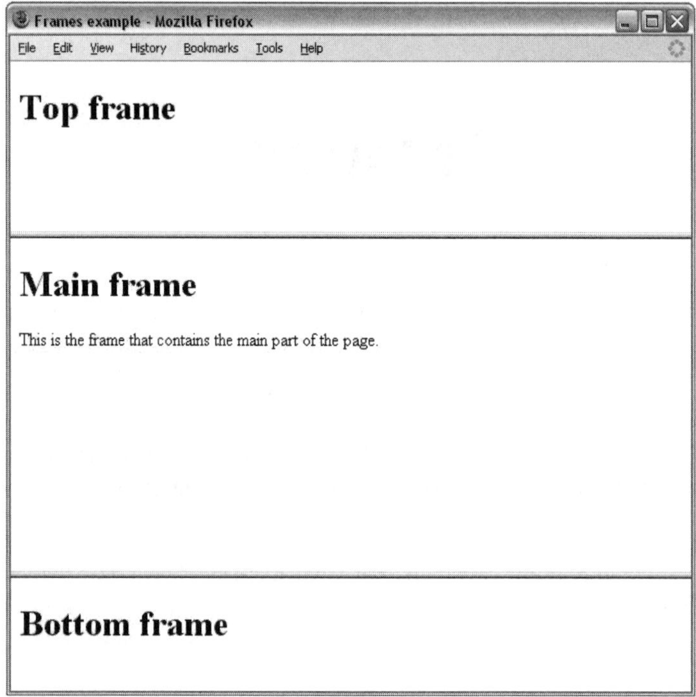

Figure 6-1

You may remember from Chapter 1 that you can start an XHTML page with a `DOCTYPE` declaration to explain which version of XHTML you are using: transitional, strict, or frameset. When creating a page that uses frames, you should use the frameset `DOCTYPE` declaration because you will be using a few elements in different ways than other XHTML documents.

First, you use the `<frameset>` element instead of the `<body>` element, as this defines the rows and columns your page is divided into. Each frame is then represented by a `<frame>` element.

You also need to learn the `<noframes>` element, which provides a message for users whose browsers do not support frames.

To get a better idea of how frames work, here is the code for the frameset shown previously in Figure 6-1 (`ch06_eg01.html`):

```
<?xml version="1.0" encoding="iso-8859-1"?>
<!DOCTYPE html PUBLIC "-//W3C//DTD XHTML 1.0 Frameset//EN"
  "http://www.w3.org/TR/xhtml1/DTD/xhtml1-frameset.dtd">
<html>
<head>
  <title>Frames example</title>
</head>
<frameset rows="150, *, 100">
    <frame src="top_frame.html" />
    <frame src="main_frame.html" />
    <frame src="bottom_frame.html" />
    <noframes><body>
      This site uses a technology called frames. Unfortunately, your
      browser does not support this technology. Please upgrade
      your browser and visit us again!
    </body></noframes>
</frameset>
</html>
```

If you look at the start of the code, you can see the frameset `DOCTYPE` declaration is used, which allows you to use these frame-related elements in the rest of the page. The `<body>` element has been replaced with the `<frameset>` element; also, there should be no markup between the closing `</head>` tag and the opening `<frameset>` tag, other than a comment if you want to include one.

As you will see shortly, the `<frameset>` element must carry the two attributes `rows` and `cols`, which specify the number of rows and columns that make up the frameset. In our example there are just three rows, the first being 150 pixels high, the third just 100 pixels high, and the second taking up the rest of the page (the asterisk is used to indicate that the remaining part of the page should be used in this place).

```
<frameset rows="150, *, 100">
```

Inside the `<frameset>` element are the empty `<frame>` elements. The `<frame>` elements indicate a URL of the document that will be loaded into that frame; the URL is specified using the `src` attribute (this is very similar to the way an image file is specified in an `<img>` element). There is also a `<noframes>` element whose contents will be displayed if the user's browser does not support frames.

In this example, the pages that are loaded into the top frame, middle frame, and bottom frame are:

- `top_frame.html`
- `main_frame.html`
- `bottom_frame.html`

To see a slightly more complicated example, take a look at Figure 6-2, which uses another frameset in the middle frame containing vertical frames.

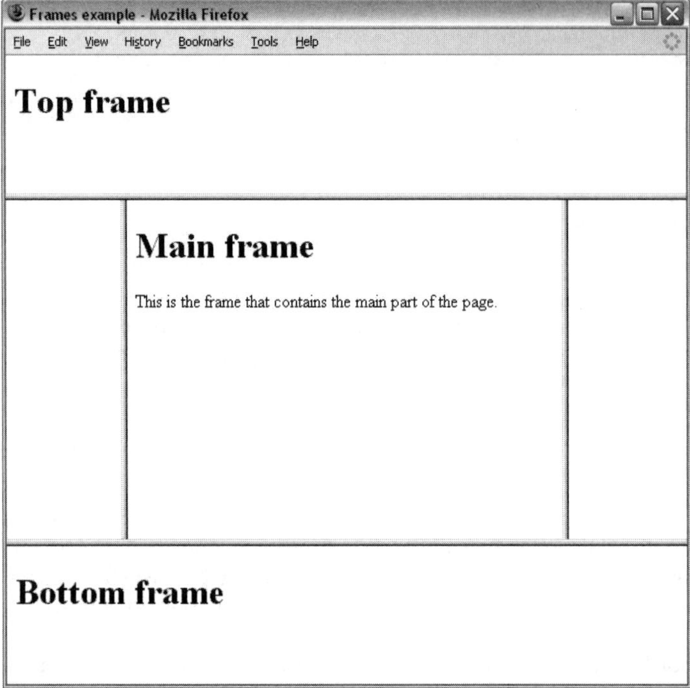

Figure 6-2

Before you take a closer look at the syntax, let's just have a look at when you might want to use frames.

When To Use Frames

It is quite rare to see frames in use these days. Personally, there are very few (if any) circumstances in which I would suggest that you use frames in a page. Here are some of the drawbacks you should be aware of when it comes to using frames:

- One of the fundamental concepts when the Web was created was that every page should correspond to a single URL — with a frameset you have a single page made up of several URLs.
- Search engines can have difficulty indexing the content of individual frames; some just index the frameset document. This means that the only content that they see is the contents of the `<noframes>` element, so you should include any content or keywords that you want indexed within the `<noframes>` element (not just a message that warns users that the site uses frames).
- Imagine you put your logo and links between pages of the site in one frame, and the content of the site in a second frame; these are just two normal web pages. Should a search engine find the URL for one of these pages (perhaps someone else links directly to one of these pages), the search engine would show only the content of the individual frame — not the frameset document — so the user might see only the navigation or only the content.

- The browser's Back button might not work as users expect (taking them to something else).
- Some smaller devices cannot cope with frames.
- If you have a frame that contains navigation, then it's hard to indicate which page is "on" (because content could load in one frame without telling the navigation frame which page it is showing).
- You need to have a separate web page for each frame in the browser window, which means your site will be made up of more pages, making maintenance more difficult.
- It's much harder for users with screen readers to navigate pages that use frames.

The cases in which you are most likely to want to consider using frames include:

- If you want to display a lot of content in one single page and you cannot split the document into separate pages, then a frame might be useful to create a navigation bar that links to the subsections of the long document.
- When you have a lot of data in one part of the page that you do not want the user to have to reload while another part of the page changes. Examples might include a photography site where you have lots of thumbnails in one frame, and the main picture in another. Rather than reloading the thumbnails each time a visitor wants to look at a new main picture, the browser can just reload the main picture.

In both cases, you can achieve the same results using JavaScript.

While you know my opinion on frames, you may have a project that requires them, so let's take a look at the syntax for using frames in a little more detail.

The <frameset> Element

The `<frameset>` element replaces the `<body>` element in frameset documents. It is the attributes of the `<frameset>` element that specify how the browser window will be divided up into rows and columns. These attributes are as follows:

- `cols` specifies how many columns are in the frameset.
- `rows` specifies how many rows are in the frameset.

The `<frameset>` element contains a `<frame>` element for each frame of the document (each cell of the grid constructed by the `<frameset>` element) and a `<noframes>` element to indicate what should be displayed if the user's browser does not load frames.

In addition to the `rows` and `cols` attributes, the frameset element can also take the following attributes:

```
class id onload onunload rows style title
```

Most browsers also support the following attributes (which are covered here because of their popularity), even though they are not part of the XHTML specification.

```
onblur onfocus border bordercolor frameborder framespacing
```

The cols Attribute

The `cols` attribute specifies both the number of columns in the frameset and the width of each column. Because you have to specify the width of each of the columns (separated by a comma), the number of values you provide automatically tells the browser how many columns there are in the frameset. For example, here are three values indicating that there are also three columns:

```
cols="20%, 60%, 20%"
```

Here, the first column takes up 20 percent of the width of the browser window, the second takes up 60 percent, and the third takes the last 20 percent.

You can specify the width of a column in four ways:

- Pixels, which specify a fixed size for each column
- A percentage of the browser window
- Relative widths, which are an alternative way to express percentages of the browser window
- A wildcard symbol, which is used to represent the remaining part of the page not specified using one of the other methods

You can mix and match these different ways of specifying column widths, but if you do mix them you should be aware of the precedence they take (discussed after the four methods).

If you do not specify a `cols` attribute, the default value is 100 percent, so if you do not add the cols attribute, then there will be one column that takes up 100 percent of the width of the browser.

Absolute Values in Pixels

To specify the width of a column in pixels, you just use a number. (You do not need to use `px` or any other characters after the number.) For example, here are three columns: the first is 100 pixels, the second is 500 pixels, and the third takes up the remainder of the page (using the wildcard symbol `*`).

```
cols="100, 500, *"
```

If you just use pixels for each of the columns, and the width of the window is less or more than the specified values, then the browser will adjust the width of each column in proportion to the width of the browser window. So, if you want three columns of 100 pixels, you might try to specify it like this:

```
cols="100, 100, 100"
```

However, if the browser window were 600 pixels wide, you would end up with three columns of 200 pixels. Therefore, if you really want to specify fixed widths that won't grow, use a wildcard character after the third column and either make the content of the fourth frame blank (or do not include a `<frame>` element for it):

```
cols="100, 100, 100, *"
```

Interestingly, if you have four columns 200 pixels wide, and the browser window is only 600 pixels wide, your columns would all be squashed proportionately to 150 pixels wide; the window will not use scrollbars to make the page 800 pixels wide.

A Percentage of the Browser Window or Parent Frame

To specify the width of a column as a percentage of a window you use a number followed by the percent sign. For example, the following attribute value specifies two columns, one of 40 percent and another of 60 percent of the browser window:

```
cols="40%, 60%"
```

If you specify widths as percentages, and they add up to more or less than 100 percent, the browser will adjust widths proportionately.

Relative Widths Between Columns

As an alternative to percentages, you can use relative widths of the browser window, which are best illustrated with an example. Here, the window is divided into sixths: the first column takes up half of the window, the second takes one-third, and the third takes one-sixth:

```
cols="3*, 2*, 1*"
```

You can tell that the window is divided up into sixths by adding up the values of the relative widths.

The Wildcard Symbol

The asterisk, or wildcard symbol, indicates the "rest of the window." Here, the first column is 400 pixels wide and the second frame takes up the remainder of the browser window:

```
cols="400, *"
```

If two rows or columns are given the wildcard symbol, then the remaining width is divided by these two columns.

Mixing Measurements and Resizing Windows

If you mix measurements, you should be aware that widths specified in pixels always take priority over percentages, relative widths, and the wildcard symbol. Consider the following example with three columns:

```
cols="250, *, 250"
```

If the browser window is only 510 pixels wide, then the center frame will be only 10 pixels wide. This demonstrates that you have to be careful when designing framesets, otherwise there might not be enough space for users to see what you want them to see.

Furthermore, if the user resizes his or her window to less than 500 pixels wide, the browser will try to show as much of the columns defined using absolute widths as possible, ignoring any columns defined using relative widths.

Whenever a user resizes his or her window, percentages and relative widths are recalculated, but absolute widths remain the same.

Remember that each column should have a corresponding <frame> element. If you specify too many columns and not enough frame `<frame>` elements, the rightmost columns end up being a blank space; whereas if you specify too many `<frame>` elements the extra ones will be ignored.

The rows Attribute

The `rows` attribute works just like the `cols` attribute and can take the same values, but it is used to specify the rows in the frameset. For example, the following `rows` attribute will specify three rows: the top row should be 100 pixels tall, the second should be 80 percent of the screen, and the bottom row should take up the screen that is left (if anything):

```
rows="100, 80%, *"
```

The default value for the `rows` attribute is 100 percent, so if you do not specify a `rows` attribute, one row will take up 100 percent of the height of the browser.

Browser-Specific Extensions to the <frameset> Element

Most common browsers (such as IE, Firefox, and Safari) support some very important extensions to the `<frameset>` element that really deserve mention here. As you may have noticed in the first example, by default, a frame creates a border and you will likely want to control the appearance of this border. While you can now use CSS to control these properties, you may come across some of these attributes if you look at older code that uses frames.

The border Attribute

The `border` attribute specifies the width of the border of each frame in pixels.

```
border="10"
```

Figure 6-3 shows you what the first example looks like with a border of 10 pixels. If you compare this with Figure 6-2, you will be able to see a taller gray line between each of the frames (`ch06_eg02.html`):

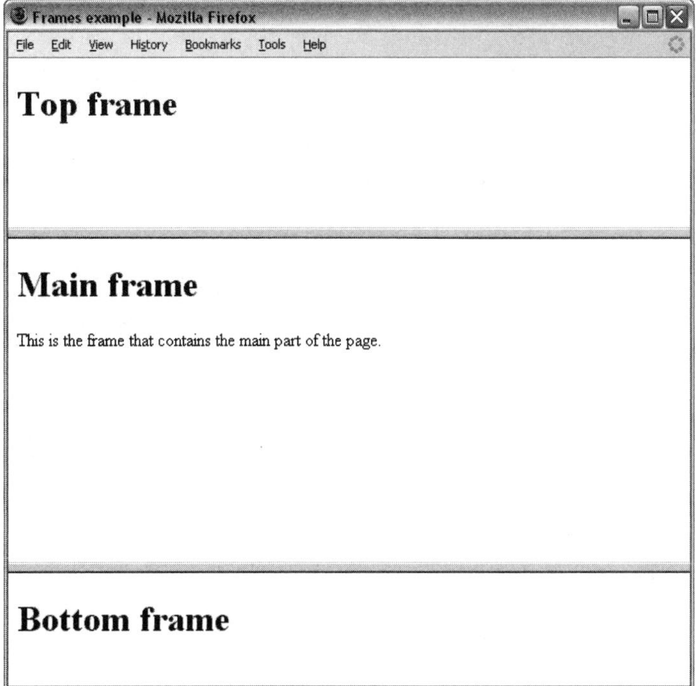

Figure 6-3

If you do not want a border, you can give this attribute a value of `0`.

When you are first creating a frameset document, it can be a good idea to set this attribute to have a value of 1, even if you do not want borders, as it makes it easier to see where the frames are; you can easily remove them by altering this one attribute on the `<frameset>` element.

The frameborder Attribute

The `frameborder` attribute specifies whether a border should be displayed between frames. The following indicates that there should not be any borders (which is the same as if the `border` attribute is given a value of `0`):

```
frameborder="0"
```

The table that follows shows possible values for the `frameborder` attribute.

Value	Purpose
`1` or `yes`	Indicates borders should be shown, the default value (`yes` is not part of HTML 4 but is still supported by common browsers)
`0` or `no`	Indicates borders should not be shown (`no` is not part of HTML 4 but is still supported by common browsers)

Figure 6-4 shows what the frames would look like without a border — you cannot see where one frame ends and another begins unless you have different background colors or background images for the pages in the frames (`ch06_eg04.html`).

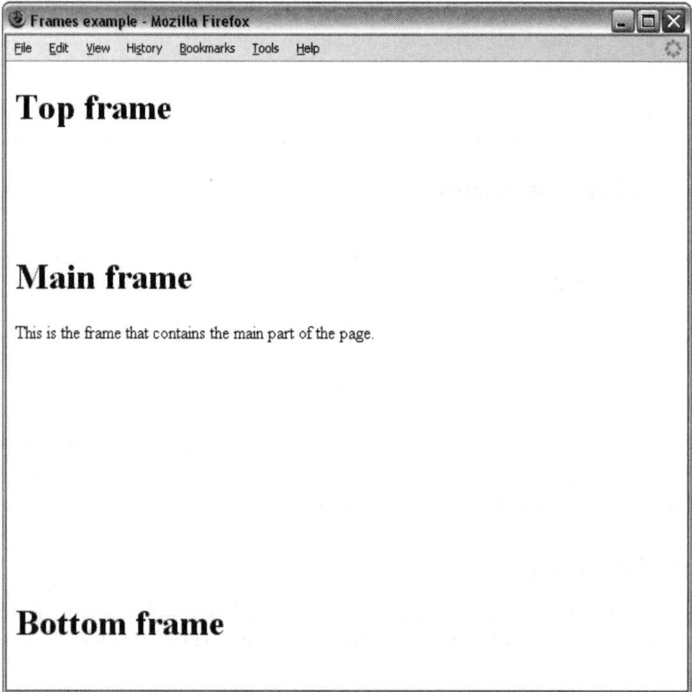

Figure 6-4

The framespacing Attribute

The `framespacing` attribute only works in Internet Explorer; it specifies the amount of space between frames in a frameset. The value should be given in pixels and the default value is 2 if not otherwise specified.

```
framespacing="25"
```

Figure 6-5 shows what the first example from this chapter (shown in Figure 6-1) would look like with a `framespacing` attribute indicating a 25-pixel gap between frames (`ch06_eg05.html`).

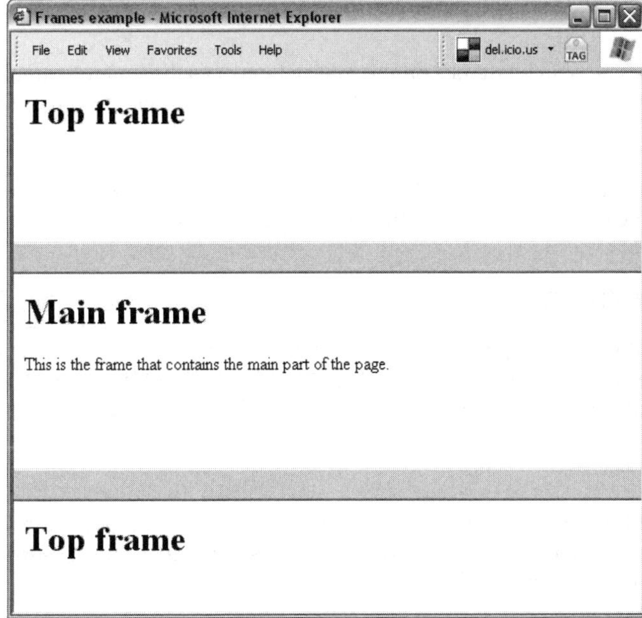

Figure 6-5

Several other browser-specific attributes are covered in Appendix I.

The <frame> Element

The `<frame>` element indicates what goes in each frame of the frameset. It is always an empty element, and therefore should not have any content, although each `<frame>` element should always carry one attribute, `src`, to indicate the page that should represent that frame.

The `<frame>` element can carry any of the universal attributes and the following attributes:

```
frameborder marginwidth marginheight noresize scrolling longdesc src name
```

There are no CSS styles related to the `<frame>` element.

The src Attribute

The `src` attribute indicates the file that should be used in the frame.

```
src="main_frame.html"
```

The value for the `src` attribute is a normal web page, so you must have a corresponding page for each `<frame>` element.

While the value of this attribute will generally be a file on your server, its value can be any URL, so you can use the `src` attribute to specify another site.

You might find that some search engines on the Internet (such as the image search on Google) will create a frameset whereby the top of the page remains the search site and the bottom of the page is the page of the site that features the image.

If you use a frame like this, it is good practice to offer a link that will close the top frame and allow the viewer to view just the content of the main frame (as Google does).

The name Attribute

The `name` attribute allows you to give a name to a frame. The name is used when you create links in one frame that load pages into a second frame, in which case the second frame needs a name to identify itself as the *target* of the link. You will see more about making links between frames later in the chapter.

```
name="main_frame"
```

You should note that the `name` attribute has not been replaced by the `id` attribute (as opposed to the way that the `name` attribute on some other HTML elements was replaced by the `id` attribute when XHTML was introduced as the successor to HTML).

The frameborder Attribute

The `frameborder` attribute specifies whether or not the borders of that frame are shown; it overrides the value given in the `frameborder` attribute on the `<frameset>` element if one is given, and the possible values are the same. The table that follows shows the possible values of the `frameborder` attribute.

Value	Purpose
`1` or `yes`	Indicates borders should be shown, the default value. (`yes` is not part of HTML 4 but is still supported by IE and Netscape.)
`0` or `no`	Indicates borders should not be shown. (`no` is not part of HTML 4 but is still supported by IE and Netscape.)

The marginwidth and marginheight Attributes

The margin is the space between the three-dimensional border of a frame and its contents.

The `marginwidth` attribute enables you to specify the width of the space between the left and right of the frame's borders and the frame's content. The value is given in pixels.

The `marginheight` attribute enables you to specify the height of the space between the top and bottom of the frame's borders and its contents. The value is given in pixels.

```
marginheight="10" marginwidth="10"
```

The noresize Attribute

By clicking and dragging on the borders of a frame, you are usually able to resize that frame. This is helpful if users cannot read everything in a frame, but it does make it harder for the designer to control the layout of the page.

The `noresize` attribute prevents a user from resizing the frame. It should take a value of `noresize`:

```
noresize="noresize"
```

Bear in mind that if you use the `noresize` *attribute, users who cannot see the entire content of a frame can't resize the frames to view the missing material.*

The scrolling Attribute

If the content of a frame does not fit in the space it has been allocated, the browser will likely provide users with scrollbars so they can read the rest of the content for that frame.

You can control the appearance of the scrollbars that appear on the frame using the `scrollbar` attribute:

```
scrolling="yes"
```

This attribute can take one of three possible values, as listed in the table that follows.

Value	Purpose
`yes`	Indicates that the frame must always contain a set of scrollbars whether or not they are required, although IE just shows a vertical scrollbar and Firefox acts as if it were just set to `auto`.
`no`	Indicates that the frame must not contain a set of scrollbars even if the content does not fit into the frame.
`auto`	Indicates that the browser should include scrollbars when the content does not fit in the frame, but otherwise should not show them.

The longdesc Attribute

The `longdesc` attribute enables you to provide a link to another page containing a long description of the contents of the frame. The value of this attribute should be the URL pointing to where that description will be found.

```
longdesc="framedescription.html"
```

The W3C indicates that the value of this URL must not be an anchor within the same page.

The <noframes> Element

If a user's browser does not support frames (which is very rare these days), the contents of the `<noframes>` element should be displayed to the user.

You should place a `<body>` element inside the `<noframes>` element because if a browser does not understand the `<frameset>` element, it should ignore the `<frameset>` element and the `<noframes>` element, then display what is inside the `<body>` element contained in the `<noframes>` element.

You should think very carefully about how you phrase the contents of this element. You should *not* just write something like this element:

```
<noframes><body>This site requires frames.</body></noframes>
```

First, this will make little sense to average users as it is unlikely that they have studied XHTML and know what frames are. Rather, you should offer a more descriptive example content, along these lines:

```
<noframes><body>This site makes uses of a technology called frames.
Unfortunately, the browser you are using does not support this technology.
We recommend that you update your browser. We apologize for any
inconvenience this causes.</body></noframes>
```

Second, because search engines have difficulty indexing the content of the individual frames, you can add information that they will understand inside the `<noframes>` element to help them to record what your site is about.

You can use other XHTML markup within the `<body>` element if you want to present your message nicely.

In an ideal world, if you used frames you would have a non-frames version of the site as well. Realistically, this requires a lot of work, so a helpful alternative is to provide links to the pages that make up the frames so that the user can still see the content of the site.

Creating Links Between Frames

One of the most popular uses of frames is to place navigation bars in one frame and then load the pages with the content into a separate frame. This is particularly helpful in three situations:

- When your main document is very long and the navigation bar provides shortcuts to parts of the main document (acting like a table of contents that is always in view).
- When your navigation bar contains files that take a while to load (such as thumbnails of photographs in a gallery). By using frames, the user does not need to reload the navigation bar each time he or she views a new page.
- When you do *not* want to reload the whole page.

As you have already seen, each `<frame>` element can carry the `name` attribute to give each frame a name. This name is used in the links to indicate which frame the new page should load into. Consider this very simple example:

```
<frameset cols="200, *">
  <frame src="frames/linksNav.html" />
  <frame src="frames/linksMain.html" name="main_page" />
</frameset>
```

There are two columns in this example, and only one row. The left-hand frame containing the navigation bar is 200 pixels wide. The right-hand frame where the content goes takes up the remaining part of the page. When you click on the links in the left-hand frame, the content opens up in the right-hand frame as you can see in Figure 6-6:

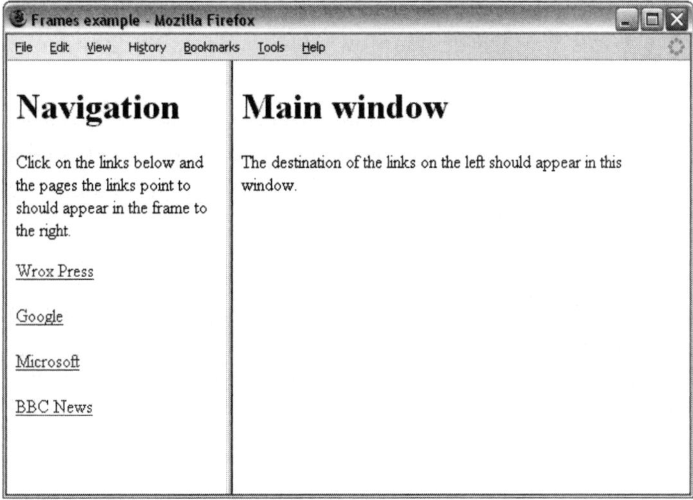

Figure 6-6

In order to specify that links should open up in the right-hand frame, the second `<frame>` element (which creates the right-hand frame) carries a `name` attribute whose value is `main_page`. The links in the navigation carry the `target` attribute whose value is set to `main_page` to indicate that the links should open in the `<frame>` element whose `name` attribute has a value of `main_page`. Here are the links in the `linksNav.html` file:

```
<a href="http://www.wrox.com" target="main_page">Wrox Press</a><br /><br />
<a href="http://www.google.com" target="main_page">Google</a><br /><br />
<a href="http://www.microsoft.com" target="main_page">Microsoft</a><br /><br />
<a href="http://news.bbc.co.uk/" target="main_page">BBC News</a><br /><br />
```

The `target` attribute can also take the attribute values listed in the table that follows.

Value	Purpose
`_self`	Loads the page into the current frame.
`_blank`	Loads a page into a new browser window, opening a new window (same as using a target that doesn't exist).
`_parent`	Loads the page into the parent window, which in the case of a single frameset is the main browser window (the page will replace all the frames), or in nested frames it replaces the frame that the frameset lives inside.
`_top`	Loads the page into the browser window, replacing any current frames.

If you are creating links to external pages, you should usually use the `_top` value for the `target` attribute so that the external site replaces your whole site; after all, your users probably don't want to view other web sites in frames of your site. Or, if you do not want the user to leave your site, you should open external sites in new windows.

Forgetting to add the `name` attribute to the `<frame>` element or the `target` attribute to the `<a>` element are the most common reasons why beginners have problems creating web sites that use frames. If either is missing, the browser just loads the link in that frame.

Setting a Default Target Frame Using the <base> Element

You can set a default target frame using the `<base>` element in any page that contains links that should open in another frame (the `<base>` element lives inside the `<head>` element). The `<base>` element should carry an attribute called `target`, whose value is the name for the frame you want the content to be loaded into. So you could add the following to `linksNav.html` to specify a default frame target:

```
<head>
  <base target="main_page" />
</head>
```

Nested Framesets

You have seen that a single frameset gives you a fixed grid-like structure of rows and columns rather like a table. If you want to create a more complex design, you might choose to use a nested frameset.

You create a nested frameset by using a second `<frameset>` element in the place of one of the `<frame>` elements. Take a look at the following example (`ch06_eg07.html`):

```
<frameset rows="*, 300, *">
  <frame src="frames/top_frame.html" />
  <frameset cols="*, 400, *">
    <frame src="frames/blank.html" />
    <frame src="frames/main_frame.html" />
    <frame src="frames/blank.html" />
  </frameset>
  <frame src="frames/bottom_frame.html" />
</frameset>
```

This example creates a set of three rows. In the middle row is a nested frameset with three columns. You can see that the two side columns actually share the same file. Figure 6-7 shows what this example looks like in a browser.

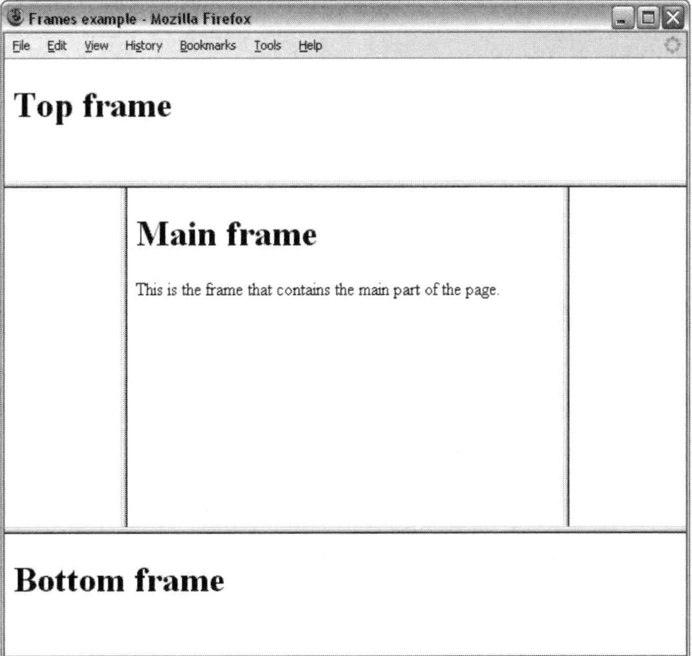

Figure 6-7

Try It Out A Frame-Based Play Viewer

We don't have a need for frames on our café site, so in this Try It Out you're going to create a frame-based viewer for finding the different acts of Shakespeare's *A Comedy of Errors*.

The idea behind the viewer is that you have one long page that contains the entire play, and then there is a frame on the right that allows you to navigate between the scenes of the play.

Before you start to build the example, it would help to have a look at what you are going to create. You can see the page in Figure 6-8.

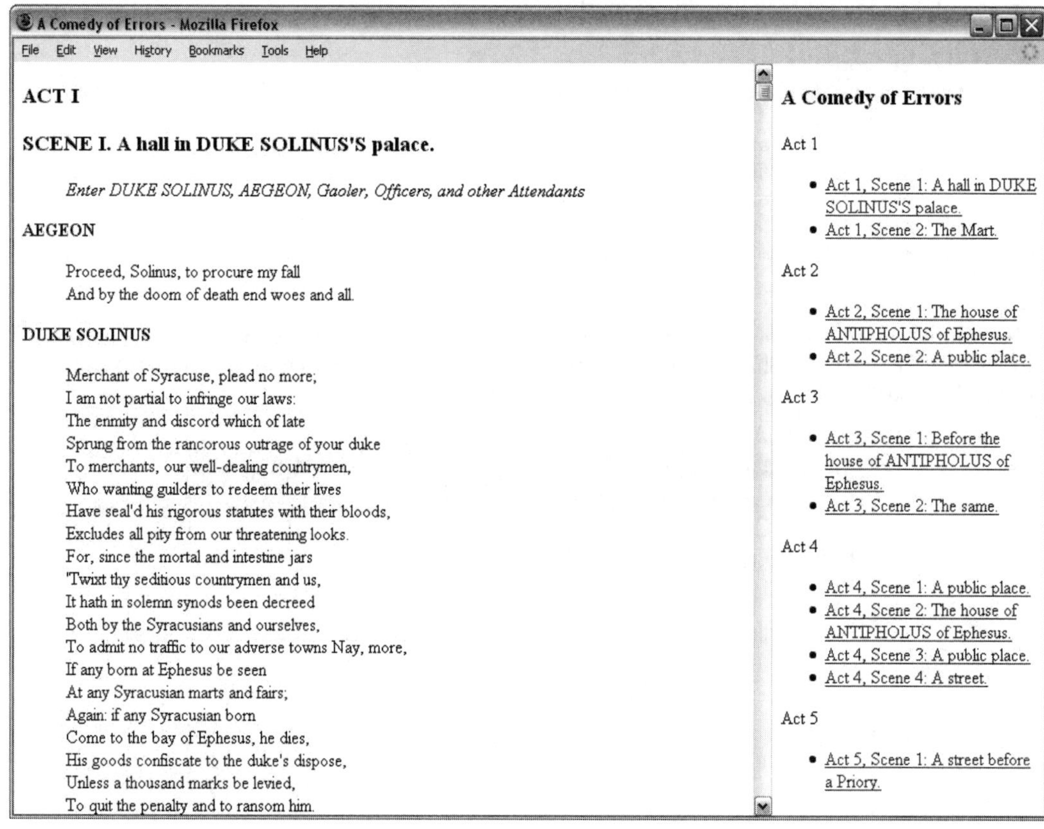

Figure 6-8

Three files actually make up this example:

- `viewer.html`, which contains the frameset for play and navigation
- `navigation.html`, which is the right-hand frame
- `comedyoferrors.html`, which is the page with the play

You will work through these pages in this order:

1. Start your text editor or web page editor and create a skeleton of a frameset document, remembering that this will be slightly different from the documents you have been creating so far. The following code is for `viewer.html`:

```
?xml version="1.0" encoding="iso-8859-1"?>
<!DOCTYPE html PUBLIC "-//W3C//DTD XHTML 1.0 Frameset//EN"
"http://www.w3.org/TR/xhtml1/DTD/xhtml1-frameset.dtd">
<html xmlns="http://www.w3.org/1999/xhtml">
  <head>
    <title>A Comedy of Errors</title>
  </head>
</html>
```

2. Divide the page up into two frames. The one on the right is fixed at 200 pixels wide, while the one on the left takes up the remaining part of the screen.

   As you can see, this requires the use of a `<frameset>` element instead of a `<body>` element, which divides the page into the two columns.

   The `<frameset>` element holds two `<frame>` elements, one for each column.

```
<frameset cols="*,250">
  <frame src="comedyoferrors.html" name="main_page" />
  <frame src="navigation.html" scrolling="no" />
</frameset>
<noframes><body>
      This site uses a technology called frames. Unfortunately, your
      browser does not support this technology. Please upgrade your
      browser and visit us again! <a href="comedyoferrors.html">Click
      here to view A Comedy of Errors without links to scenes.</a>
<body></noframes>
```

3. The *A Comedy of Errors* file is created for you (you probably don't have time to type it all out), but it is worth noting that it contains `id` attributes that indicate the start of each section. The next step is to create a new file called `navigation.html` to form the content of the navigation frame in the right pane.

   This is just a normal XHTML document, so start the skeleton as you usually would.

```
<?xml version="1.0" encoding="iso-8859-1"?>
<!DOCTYPE html PUBLIC "-//W3C//DTD XHTML 1.0 Transitional//EN"
"http://www.w3.org/TR/xhtml1/DTD/xhtml1-transitional.dtd">
<html xmlns="http://www.w3.org/1999/xhtml">
<head>
  <title>Navigation</title>
</head>
<body>
</body>
</html>
```

4. In the `navigation.html` page, there are links to each scene in each act of the play. Note how the `target` attribute has a value of `main_frame` to ensure that the link opens in the left-hand pane:

```
Act 1
<ul>
  <li><a href="comedyoferrors.html#act1_scene1" target="main_frame">Act 1,
    Scene 1: A hall in DUKE SOLINUS'S palace.</a></li>
  <li><a href="comedyoferrors.html#act1_scene2" target="main_frame">Act 1,
    Scene 2: The Mart.</a></li>
</ul>
```

Try the file by opening `viewer.html`; the result should look like the screen shot you saw at the beginning of the chapter.

Inline or Floating Frames with <iframe>

There is another kind of frame known as an *iframe* (sometimes referred to as an *inline frame* or *floating frame*), which can appear anywhere within a standard XHTML page; it does not need to appear either in a `<frameset>` element or even in a document that uses the frameset document type declaration.

An iframe acts like a window cut into an XHTML page through which you can see another web page. You can specify the URL of the page to appear in the window, the width and height of the window, and whether or not it should have borders. Any text that surrounds the frame would flow around it in the same way text can flow around an image. You create an iframe with the `<iframe>` element, and you specify the URL of the page to appear in the iframe using the `src` attribute (just as you would with an image).

The following is a simple example of a floating frame. If you look at the `src` attribute you can tell that the iframe embeds a Google map into the page, while the `width` and `height` attributes indicate the size of the iframe (`ch06_eg08.html`):

```
<body>
<h1>Floating frame</h1>
<p>Here you can see a map.
  <iframe src="http://maps.google.co.uk/maps?q=Newquay,+Cornwall,+United+
Kingdom&
    output=embed"
    width="425" height="350">
    Cannot see the map?
    <a href=" http://maps.google.co.uk/maps?q=Newquay,+Cornwall,+United+
Kingdom">
    Click here to view our location on Google Maps</a>.
  </iframe>
It should show you where to find us.</p>
</body>
```

When creating an iframe, you should use both an opening `<iframe>` tag and a closing `</iframe>` (it should not be an empty element). Anything between these is shown only to those whose browsers do not support iframes (in this example you can see that a link to the map has been offered to users that do not see the iframe). If your iframe contained information that you would want a search engine to index, you could include the text that you want it to index in here.

You can see what this page looks like in Figure 6-9.

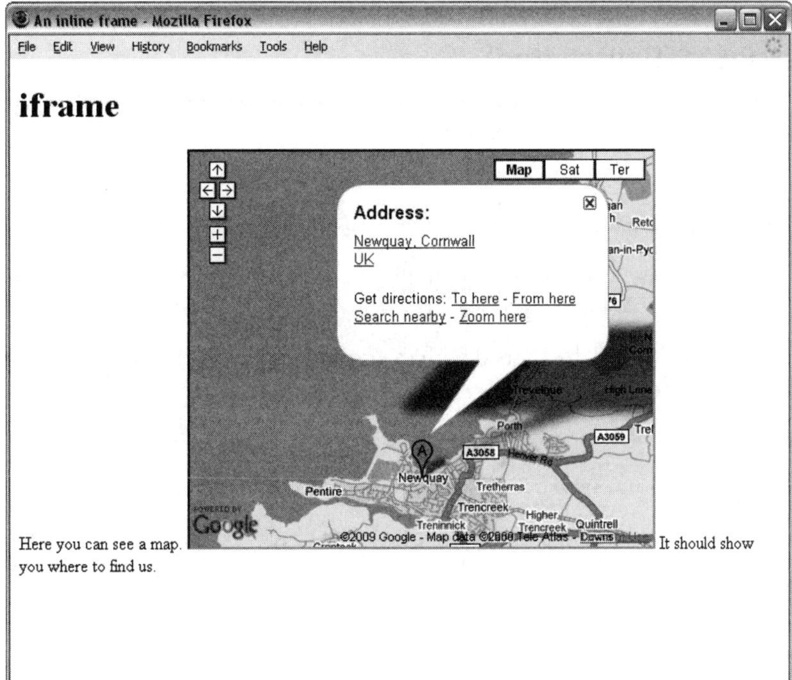

Figure 6-9

Let's take a closer look at the syntax for the `<iframe>` element.

The <iframe> Element

The `<iframe>` element sits in the middle of a normal XHTML page to create an inline frame. The only attribute it must carry is the `src` attribute, whose value is the URL of the page to be included (wherever the `<iframe>` element is in the document), although it is also good to add the `height` and `width` attributes to control its size. Remember that this element does not have to be part of the frameset document type.

In addition to the universal attributes, the `<iframe>` element can carry these attributes:

```
align height width frameborder longdesc marginwidth marginheight name
scrolling src
```

There are no events or CSS styles that are particular to the `<iframe>` element.

The src Attribute

The `src` attribute is required on the `<iframe>` element as it indicates where the browser can find the page to show in the iframe, just as it does on the `<frame>` element.

The align Attribute (Deprecated)

The `align` attribute indicates how the text that is outside of the floating frame will appear. It can take one of the values listed in the table that follows.

Value	Purpose
`left`	The frame will be aligned with the left margin of the page, allowing the text to flow around it to the right.
`right`	The frame will be aligned with the right margin of the page, allowing the text to flow around it to the left.
`top`	The top of the frame will be inline with the text around it.
`middle`	The middle of the frame will be inline with the text around it.
`bottom`	The bottom of the frame will be inline with the text around it (the default setting as you can see from Figure 6-9).

The height and width Attributes

The `height` and `width` attributes enable you to specify the height and width of a frame just as you would with an image.

```
height="250" width="500"
```

The value of the `height` and `width` attributes can be given in pixels (as in the preceding line of code) or in percentages of the browser or parent element if it is contained by another element (as in the line of code that follows).

```
height="20%" width="40%"
```

Keep in mind, however, that users with different screen resolutions will see different amounts of the screen. If you do not specify a height or width, the browser works out a size based on the full size of the screen.

The frameborder Attribute

The `frameborder` attribute specifies whether the borders of the frame are shown; the value should be the number of pixels the border should be. A value of `0` means that there would be no border.

```
frameborder="0"
```

The longdesc Attribute

The `longdesc` attribute allows you to specify a link to another page where there is a description in text of what would otherwise be in the frame. This is particularly helpful if you are putting images, charts, or graphs in the frame, as they make your site accessible to those with visual impairments. It can also be used if the user is having trouble loading the frame.

```
longdesc="../textDescriptions/iframe1.html"
```

The marginheight and marginwidth Attributes

The `marginheight` and `marginwidth` attributes allow you to specify the distance in pixels between the border of the frame and the content of the frame.

```
marginewidth="8" marginheight="8"
```

The `marginwidth` attribute allows you to specify the distance between left and right borders and the content, while the `marginheight` attribute specifies the distance between top and bottom borders and the content.

The scrolling Attribute

If the iframe is not big enough to show all of the content, then the `scrolling` attribute specifies whether the frame should have scrollbars (just as it does for the `<frame>` element).

Try It Out — Adding a Map to the Café

In this example you will use an iframe to add a Google map to the contact page of the Example Café.

1. Open the contact page for the Example Café. The map will go just before the link to the Google Maps web site:

```
<h2>Contact</h2>
  <p><address>12 Sea View, Newquay, Cornwall, UK</address></p>
  <p><a href="http://maps.google.com/maps?q=newquay">Find us on Google
    Maps</a></p>
  <p><a href="mailto:info@examplecafe.com">Email Example Cafe</a></p>
```

2. Go to `maps.google.com` and enter a location for your café. When you have a map loaded, click the link that says "link" just above the top right-hand corner of the map. You should see a textbox containing an iframe, as in Figure 6-10.

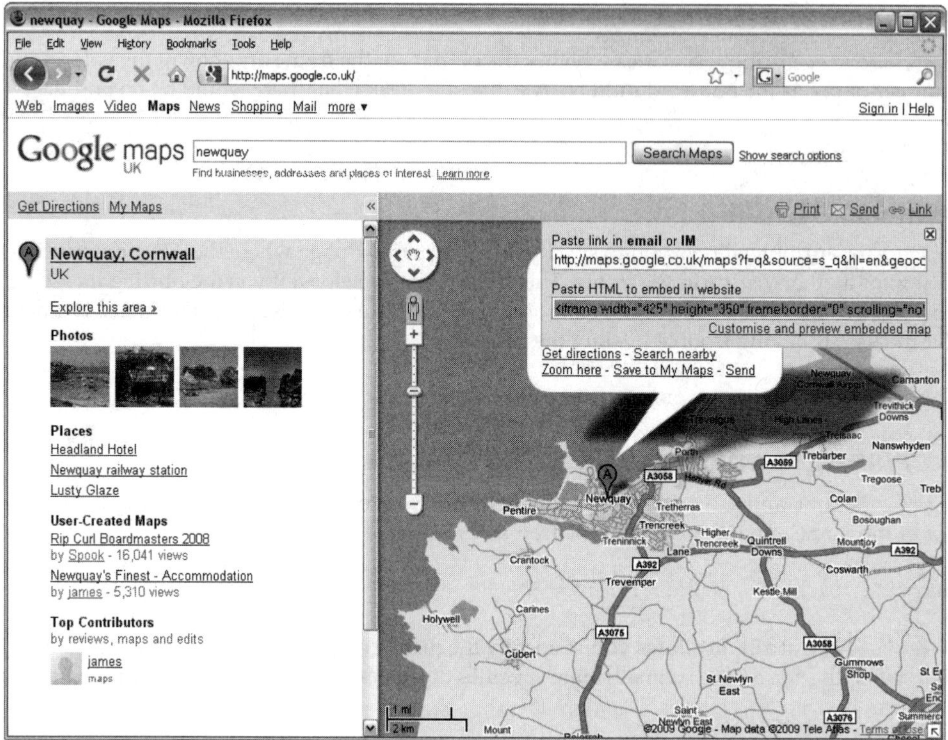

Figure 6-10

3. After the first paragraph, paste the code from the Google Maps site. You may find that there is a lot more code than we used in the version earlier in the chapter.

```
<iframe width="425" height="350" frameborder="0" scrolling="no" marginheight="0"
    marginwidth="0" src="http://maps.google.co.uk/maps?source=ig&amp;hl=en&amp;
    q=Newquay,+Cornwall,+United+Kingdom&amp;ie=UTF8&amp;cd=1&amp;
    geocode=FShAAQMdHG-y_w&amp;split=0&amp;sll=53.800651,-4.064941&amp;
    sspn=6.881357,14.941406&amp;ll=50.420058,-5.079117&amp;
    spn=0.018513,0.038624&amp;t=h&amp;z=14&amp;iwloc=A&amp;output=embed">
</iframe><br />
<small>
    <a href="http://maps.google.co.uk/maps?source=embed&amp;hl=en&amp;
        q=Newquay,+Cornwall,+United+Kingdom&amp;ie=UTF8&amp;cd=1&amp;
        geocode=FShAAQMdHG-y_w&amp;split=0&amp;sll=53.800651,-4.064941&amp;
        sspn=6.881357,14.941406&amp;ll=50.420058,-5.079117&amp;spn=0.018513,
        0.038624&amp;t=h&amp;z=14&amp; iwloc=A" style="color:#0000FF;
        text- align:left">
        View Larger Map</a></small>
```

4. Note how this code uses the attributes we have met:

- `width` and `height` specify the size of the frame.
- The `frameborder` attribute has a value of `0` so that the iframe does not have the default border.
- The scrolling attribute is set to `no` because the map is larger than the size of the window and you do not want scrollbars on this frame.
- `marginheight` and `marginwidth` have a value of `0` to prevent gaps inside the frame.
- This is followed by a long URL that contains a lot of information about the location even though the following would be enough: `http://maps.google.co.uk/maps?q=newquay,+Cornwall,+United+Kingdom&output=embed`

Your new contact page should look like Figure 6-11.

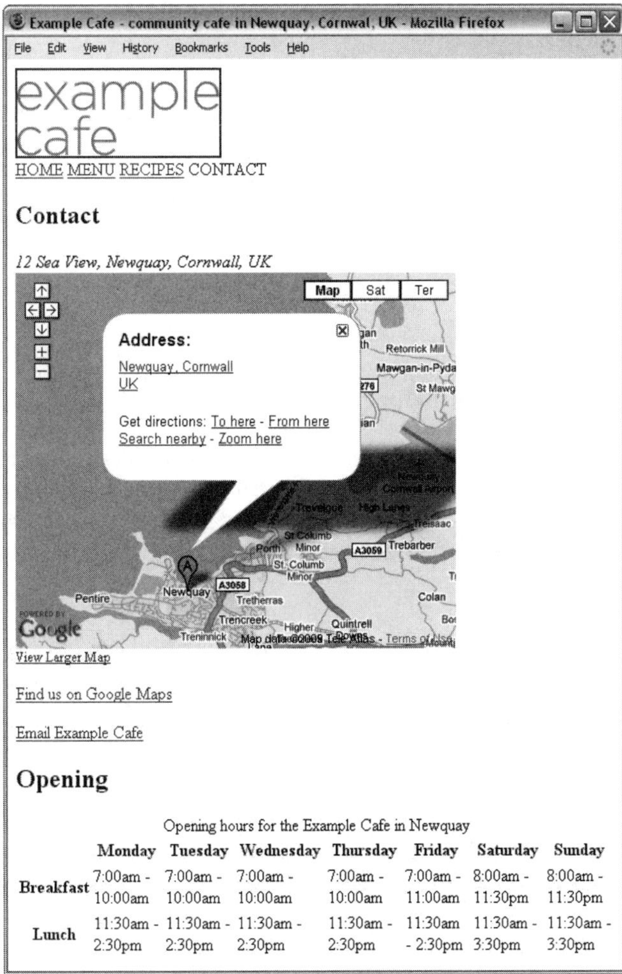

Figure 6-11

Summary

In this chapter, you learned about frames, which allow you to divide a browser window into separate panes. Each of these panes contains a discrete XHTML document that can be loaded and reloaded separately from the other frames.

Frames are particularly helpful if part of your page's content remains the same while the main body changes; for example, when either the main body is long (and you want the navigation to remain in view) or the navigation takes a long time to load (and you do not want to reload it for each page).

The chapter covered two types of frames:

- The more traditional frameset document, which uses the `<frameset>` element to divide the screen into rows and columns. The `<frameset>` element then contains a `<frame>` element corresponding to each part of the window. These frames belong to the frameset document type and require a different `DOCTYPE` declaration than other XHTML documents because the `<frameset>` element replaces the `<body>` element.
- The more recent inline or floating frame, which lives in a normal XHTML page, and allows only the content of the frame to be reloaded. Inline frames can appear anywhere within the document.

As I have already mentioned, frames are often replaced by the use of JavaScript (or AJAX) to reload parts of pages.

Exercises

The answers to all of the exercises are in Appendix A.

1. Create a frameset like the one shown in Figure 6-12, where clicking a fruit loads a new page in the main window. When the page loads in the main window, it will carry the details for the appropriate fruit (to save time, you can use the images and fruit description pages in the code download, but try to create the frameset and navigation on your own).

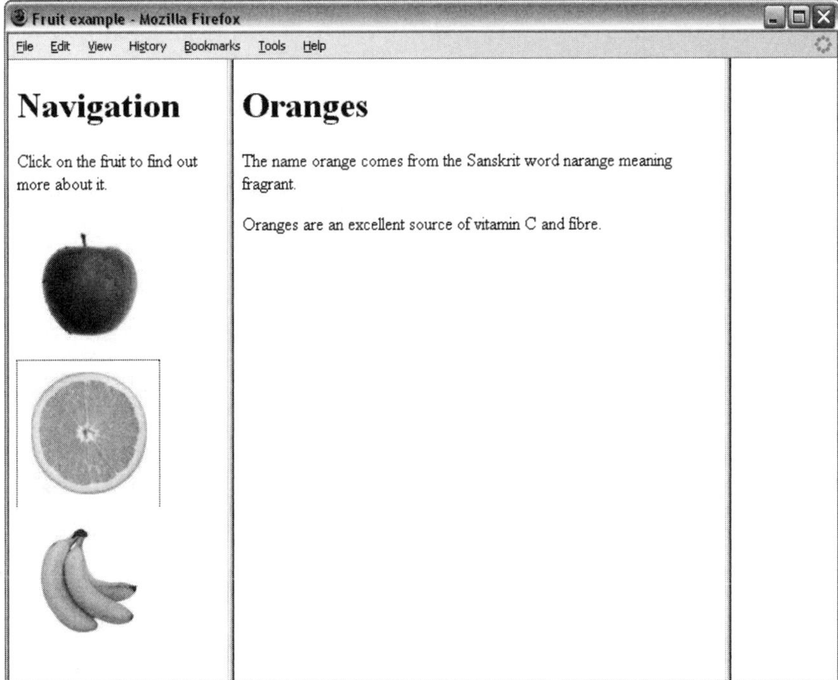

Figure 6-12

2. Create an `<iframe>` like the one shown in Figure 6-12, where you can load two different documents inside the iframe window in the current page.

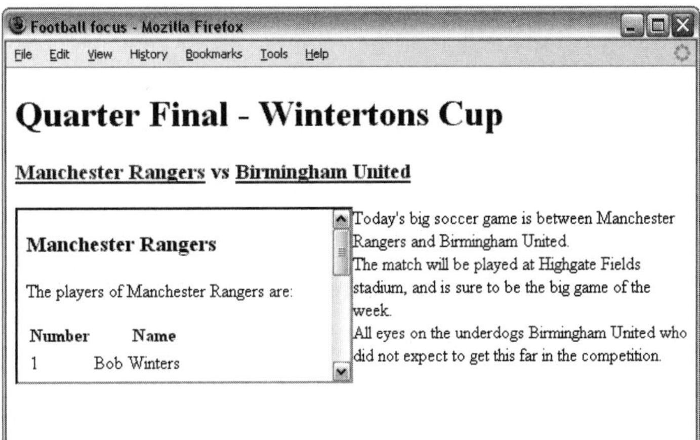

Figure 6-13

Cascading Style Sheets

Having learned how to structure the content of your documents using XHTML's wide variety of elements and attributes, you're now going to start making your pages look a lot more exciting.

You're going to learn how to use *cascading style sheets* (or CSS for short) to take control of the style of your pages, including the colors and size of fonts, the width and colors of lines, and the amount of space between items on the page. The cascading style sheets specification works by allowing you to specify *rules* that say how the content of elements within your document should appear. For example, you can specify that the background of the page is a cream color, the contents of all `<p>` elements should be displayed in gray using the Arial typeface, and that all `<h1>` elements should be in red using the Times New Roman typeface.

In this chapter you learn the following:

- What makes up a CSS rule
- How to place CSS rules within your document and how to link to an external CSS document
- How properties and values control presentation of different elements within your document
- How to control the presentation of text using CSS
- How CSS is based on a box model, and how you set different properties for these boxes (such as width and styles of borders)

By the end of the chapter, you should be confidently writing CSS style sheets and should have learned many of the properties you can use to affect the presentation of any document using CSS.

In the next chapter, you will continue to learn more CSS properties, as well as how CSS can be used to position the content of elements within a page.

Introducing CSS

CSS works by allowing you to associate *rules* with the elements that appear in a web page. These rules govern how the content of those elements should be rendered. Figure 7-1 shows you an example of a CSS rule, which is made up of two parts:

- The *selector*, which indicates which element or elements the declaration applies to (if it applies to more than one element, you can have a comma-separated list of several elements)
- The *declaration*, which sets out how the elements referred to in the selector should be styled

Figure 7-1

The rule in Figure 7-1 applies to all `<td>` elements and indicates that they should be 36 pixels wide.

The declaration is also split into two parts, separated by a colon:

- A *property*, which is the property of the selected element(s) that you want to affect, in this case the `width` property.
- A *value*, which is a specification for this property; in this case it is that the table cells should be 36 pixels wide.

This is very similar to the way that HTML/XHTML elements can carry attributes and how the attribute controls a property of the element; the attributes' value would be the setting for that property. For example, a `<td>` element could have a `width` attribute whose value is the width you want the table to be:

```
<td width="36"></td>
```

With CSS, however, rather than your having to specify the attribute on each instance of the `<td>` element, the selector indicates that this one rule applies to all `<td>` elements in the document.

Here is an example of a CSS rule that applies to several different elements (in this example, the `<h1>`, `<h2>`, and `<h3>` elements). A comma separates the name of each element that this rule will apply to. The rule also specifies several properties for these elements with each property-value pair separated by a semicolon. Note how all the properties are kept inside the curly braces:

```
h1, h2, h3 {
  font-weight:bold;
  font-family:arial;
  color:#000000;
  background-color:#FFFFFF;}
```

Even if you have never seen a CSS rule before, you should now have a good idea of what this rule is doing. There are three heading elements named in the selector (`<h1>`, `<h2>`, and `<h3>`), and this rule says that where these headings are used they will be written in a bold Arial font in black with a white background.

If there is only one property-value pair in the declaration, you do not need to end it with a semicolon. However, because a declaration can consist of several property-value pairs, and each property-value pair within a rule must be separated by a semicolon, it is good practice to start adding semicolons every time you write a rule in case you want to add another rule later. If you forget to add the semicolon, any further property-value pairs will be ignored.

A Basic Example

Let's have a look at an example that shows how a set of CSS rules can transform the look of an XHTML page. CSS rules can live inside the XHTML document, although for this example we will be making a separate file to hold the CSS rules, and the XHTML page will contain a link to this file, which is known as a *style sheet*.

Before we meet the CSS style sheet, take a look at Figure 7-2, which shows the XHTML page we will be styling on its own before the CSS rules have been attached.

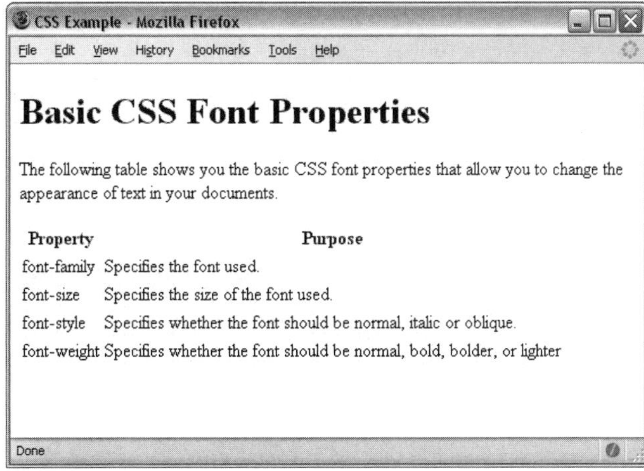

Figure 7-2

Here is the code for the page you saw in Figure 7-2 (`ch07_eg01.html`). It contains a heading, a paragraph, and a table. Inside the `<head>` element is a `<link>` element that tells the browser where to find the style sheet that will style this page; the location of the style sheet is given as the value of the `href` attribute. Also look at how some of the `<td>` elements carry a `class` attribute whose value is `code`; this is used to distinguish the table cells that contain code from other `<td>` elements in the document.

```
<?xml version="1.0" encoding="iso-8859-1"?>
<!DOCTYPE html PUBLIC "-//W3C//DTD XHTML 1.0 Strict//EN"
    "http://www.w3.org/TR/xhtml1/DTD/xhtml1-strict.dtd">
<html xmlns="http://www.w3.org/1999/xhtml" lang="en">
<head>
  <title>CSS Example</title>
  <link rel="stylesheet" type="text/css" href="ch07_eg01.css" />
</head>
<body>
<h1>Basic CSS Font Properties</h1>
<p>The following table shows you the basic CSS font properties that allow
you to change the appearance of text in your documents.</p>
<table>
  <tr>
    <th>Property</th>
    <th>Purpose</th>
  </tr>
  <tr>
    <td class="code">font-family</td>
    <td>Specifies the font used.</td>
  </tr>
  <tr>
    <td class="code">font-size</td>
    <td>Specifies the size of the font used.</td>
  </tr>
  <tr>
    <td class="code">font-style</td>
    <td>Specifies whether the font should be normal, italic or oblique.</td>
  </tr>
  <tr>
    <td class="code">font-weight</td>
    <td>Specifies whether the font should be normal, bold, bolder,
    or lighter</td>
  </tr>
  </table>
</body>
</html>
```

Now let's take a look at how to style this page. Figure 7-3 shows how the page will look with the style sheet attached.

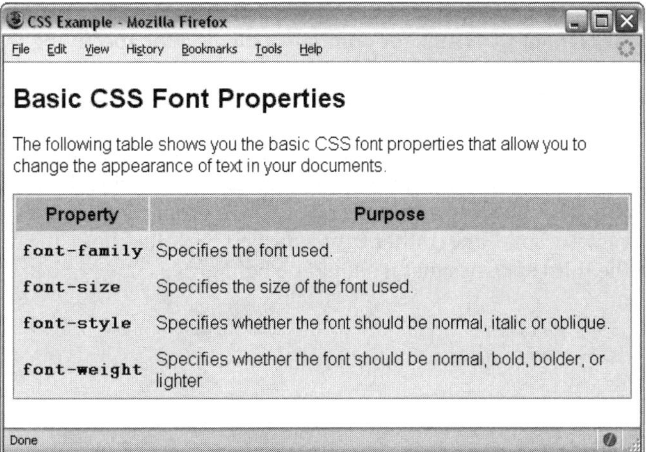

Figure 7-3

You can create a CSS style sheet in the same editor you are using to create your XHTML pages; once you have created a CSS file it is saved with the file extension .css.

The style sheet for this example, `ch07_eg01.css`, uses several CSS rules; we will go through them one at a time so that you can see what each one does.

Before the first rule, however, there is a comment to tell us which file this style sheet was written for. Anything between the opening `/*` and closing `*/` will be ignored by the browser and therefore will not have an effect on the appearance of the page:

```
/* Style sheet for ch07_eg01.html */
```

After the comment, the first rule applies to the `<body>` element. It specifies that the default color of any text and lines used on the page will be black and that the background of the page should be in white. The colors here are represented using a hex code (the different ways to specify colors are covered in detail in Appendix D). It also states that typeface used throughout the document should be Arial. If Arial is not available, Verdana will be used instead; failing that, it will use its default font group that corresponds to that generic font group.

```
body {
   color: #000000;
   background-color:#ffffff;
   font-family:arial, verdana, sans-serif; }
```

I always specify a `background-color` *property for the body of a document because some people change the default background color of the windows on their computers (so that it is not a glaring white); if you do not set this property, the background color of those users' browsers will be whatever color they have selected.*

The next two rules simply specify the size of the contents of the `<h1>` and `<p>` elements, respectively (as you will see later in the chapter `pt` stands for points — a method for specifying the sizes of fonts):

```
h1 {font-size:18pt;}
p {font-size:12pt;}
```

Next, it is time to add a few settings to control the appearance of the table. First we give it a light gray background. Then, we draw a border around the edge. Three properties are used to describe the border — the first says it is a solid line (rather than a dashed or dotted line), the second says it should be 1 pixel thick, and the third specifies that it should be light gray:

```
table {
   background-color:#efefef;
   border-style:solid;
   border-width:1px;
   border-color:#999999;}
```

Within the table, the table headings should have a medium gray background color (slightly darker than the main body of the table), the text should appear in a bold font, and between the edge of the cell and the text there should be 5 pixels of padding. (As you will see in more detail later in the chapter, *padding* is the term used for space between the edge of a box and the content inside it.)

```
th {
   background-color:#cccccc;
   font-weight:bold;
   padding:5px;}
```

The individual table data cells also have 5 pixels of padding (like the headings). Adding this space makes the text much easier to read, and without it the text in one column might run up right next to the text in the neighboring column:

```
td {padding:5px;}
```

Finally, you may have noticed in Figure 7-3 that the cells of the table that contained the names of CSS properties were in a Courier font. If you look at the corresponding table cells in the XHTML document, they carried a `class` attribute whose value was `code`. On its own, the `class` attribute does not change the display of the document (as you can see from Figure 7-2), but the `class` attribute does allow you to associate CSS rules with elements whose `class` attribute has a specific value. Therefore, the following rule applies only to `<td>` elements that carry a `class` attribute whose value is `code`, not to all `<td>` elements:

```
td.code {
   font-family:courier, courier-new, serif;
   font-weight:bold;}
```

When you want to specify an element whose `class` attribute has a specific value, you put the value of that `class` attribute preceded by a period (or full stop) symbol.

There you have the first example; you can find the code for this example with the download code for the rest of the book. This example provides you with an overview of how CSS works. Therefore, for the rest of this chapter, and the following chapter we need to look at:

- The properties you can use to control the appearance of various elements, and the values they can take. The different properties are grouped throughout this chapter and the next. For example, the properties that affect the appearance of fonts are together, and those that affect borders are together and so on.
- Different selectors that allow you to specify which elements these properties apply to; the basic example featured just a few of the many methods you can use to indicate which elements are controlled by which style rules.
- How CSS treats each element in a web page as if it were in its own box and how this affects the way in which you lay out web pages.

Along the way you will also see where you can use CSS rules in your documents, the units of measurements used in CSS (such as pixels, and percentages), and a very powerful concept called inheritance.

If you have used the View Source option in your browser to see how other people have built their web pages, you will probably be glad to hear that you can also look at other people's style sheets. To do this, you need to look at the source code for a web page and find the URL for the style sheet (note that it may be a relative URL); you can then enter the full URL for the stylesheet into the address bar of your browser and the rules will either appear in the window or your browser will ask if you want to download the style sheet.

Inheritance

One of the powerful features of CSS is that, when a property has been applied to one element, it will often be *inherited* by child elements (elements contained within the element that the rules were declared upon). For example, once the `font-family` property had been declared for the `<body>` element in the previous example, it applied to all of the elements inside the `<body>` element. This saves you from having to repeat the same rules for every single element that makes up a web page.

If another rule is more specific about which elements it applies to, then it will override any properties associated with the `<body>` element or any other containing element. In the preceding example, most of the text was in an Arial typeface, as specified in the rule associated with the `<body>` element, although there were a few table cells that used a Courier typeface. The table cells that were different had a `class` attribute whose value was `code`:

```
<td class="code">font-size</td>
```

Here you can see the rule associated with these elements:

```
td.code {
   font-family:courier, courier-new, serif;
   font-weight:bold;}
```

This rule takes precedence over the one associated with the `<body>` element because the selector is more specific about which element it applies to.

The way in which some properties inherit saves you from having to write out rules and all the property-value pairs for each element and makes for a more compact style sheet. Appendix C contains a handy reference to CSS properties and tells you which ones do and do not inherit.

Where You Can Add CSS Rules

The example that you saw at the beginning of the chapter placed the CSS rules in a separate file known as an *external style sheet*. CSS rules can also appear in two places inside the XHTML document:

- Inside a `<style>` element, which sits inside the `<head>` element of a document
- As a value of a `style` attribute on any element that can carry the `style` attribute

When the style sheet rules are held inside a `<style>` element in the head of the document, they are referred to as an *internal style sheet.*

```
<head>
  <title>Internal Style sheet</title>
  <style type="text/css">
  body {
    color:#000000;
    background-color:#ffffff;
    font-family:arial, verdana, sans-serif; }
  h1 {font-size:18pt;}
  p {font-size:12pt;}
</style>
</head>
```

When `style` attributes are used on XHTML elements, they are known as *inline style rules*. For example:

```
<td style="font-family:courier; padding:5px; border-style:solid;
border-width:1px; border-color:#000000;">
```

Here you can see that the properties are added as the value of the `style` attribute. You still need to separate each property from its value with a colon and each of the property-value pairs from each other with a semicolon. However, there is no need for a selector here (because the style is automatically applied to the element that carries the `style` attribute), and there are no curly braces.

The `style` attribute was deprecated in Transitional XHTML and is not allowed in Strict XHTML 1.0 because it introduces stylistic markup to the web page, when it should only contain markup that explains semantics and structure of the document.

The <link> Element

The `<link>` element is used in web pages to describe the relationship between two documents; for example, it can be used in an XHTML page to specify a style sheet that should be used to style a page. You may also see the `<link>` element used in XHTML pages for other purposes, for example to specify an RSS feed that corresponds with a page.

It is a very different kind of link than the `<a>` element because the two documents are automatically associated — the user does not have to click anything to activate the link.

The `<link>` element is always an empty element, and when used with style sheets it must carry three attributes: `type`, `rel`, and `href`. Here is an example of the `<link>` element used in an XHTML page indicating that it should be styled by a CSS file called `interface.css`, which lives in a subdirectory called `CSS`:

```
<link rel="stylesheet" type="text/css" href="../CSS/interface.css" />
```

In addition to the core attributes, the `<link>` element can also take the following attributes:

```
charset dir href hreflang media rel rev style target type
```

You have met many of these already, so the more important ones are discussed in the following sections along with some of the less common ones.

The rel Attribute

The `rel` attribute is required and specifies the relationship between the document containing the link and the document being linked to. The key value for working with style sheets is `stylesheet`.

```
rel="stylesheet"
```

The other possible values for this element are discussed in Chapter 1.

The type Attribute

The `type` attribute specifies the MIME type of the document being linked to; in this case, we are dealing with a CSS style sheet, so the MIME type is `text/css`:

```
type="text/css"
```

The other MIME types are listed in Appendix H.

The href Attribute

The `href` attribute specifies the URL for the document being linked to.

```
href="../stylesheets/interface.css"
```

The value of this attribute can be an absolute or relative URL (which were covered in Chapter 2), but it is usually a relative URL because the style sheet is part of the site.

The hreflang Attribute

The `hreflang` attribute specifies the language that the resource specified is written in. When used, its value should be one of the language codes specified in Appendix G.

```
hreflang="en-US"
```

The media Attribute

The `media` attribute specifies the output device that is intended for use with the document:

```
media="screen"
```

While this attribute is not always used, it is becoming increasingly important as people access the Internet in different ways using different devices. See the following table for the possible values.

Value	Uses
`screen`	Non-paged computer screens (such as desktop computers and laptops)
`tty`	Media with a fixed-pitch character grid, such as teletypes, terminals, or portable devices with limited display capabilities
`tv`	TV devices with low-resolution, color screens, and limited ability to scroll down pages
`print`	Printed documents, which are sometimes referred to as *paged media* (and documents shown onscreen in print preview mode)
`projection`	Projectors
`handheld`	Handheld devices, which often have small screens, rely upon bitmapped graphics, and have limited bandwidth
`braille`	Braille tactile feedback devices
`embossed`	Braille paged printers
`aural`	Speech synthesizers
`all`	Suitable for all devices

The <style> Element

The `<style>` element is used inside the `<head>` element to contain style sheet rules within a web page, rather than linking to an external document. It is also sometimes used when a single page needs to contain just a few extra rules that do not apply to the other pages of the site which all share the same style sheet.

For example, here is a style sheet attached to the XHTML document using the `<link>` element you just learned about, as well as a `<style>` element containing an additional rule for `<h1>` elements:

```
<head>
  <title>
  <link rel="stylesheet" type="text/css" href="../styles/mySite.css" />
  <style type="text/css">
    h1 {color:#FF0000;}
  </style>
</head>
```

When you use the `<style>` element it should always carry the `type` attribute. Here is a full list of the attributes it can carry:

```
dir lang media title type
```

Some browsers also support the `id` and `src` attributes although they are not part of any W3C recommendation.

Advantages of External CSS Style Sheets

If two or more documents are going to use a style sheet, you should use an external style sheet. There are several reasons for this, including:

- It saves you repeating the same style rules in each page.
- You can change the appearance of several pages by altering just the style sheet rather than each individual page. This means it is easier to update your site if you want to, for example, change the style of font used in all headings or alter the color of all links.
- Once a visitor to your site has downloaded the CSS style with the first page of your site that uses it, subsequent pages will be quicker to load (because the browser retains a copy of the CSS style sheet and the rules do not have to be downloaded for every page). This also puts less strain on the server (the computer that sends the web pages to the people viewing the site) because the pages it sends out are smaller.
- The style sheet can act as a style template to help different authors achieve the same style of document without learning all of the individual style settings.
- Because the web pages do not contain the style rules, different style sheets can be attached to the same document. So you can use the same XHTML document with one style sheet when the viewer is on a desktop computer, another style sheet when the user has a handheld device, another style sheet when the page is being printed, another style sheet when the page is being viewed on a TV, and so on. You can reuse the same document with different style sheets for different visitors' needs.
- A style sheet can import and use styles from other style sheets, allowing for modular development and good reuse. (For example, I have a style sheet that I import into other style sheets whenever I want to include examples of programming code in a web page—I do not need to write the style rules again and again.)
- If you remove the style sheet, you can make the site more accessible for those with visual impairments, because you are no longer controlling the fonts and color schemes.

It is fair to say, therefore, that whenever you are writing a whole site, you should be using an external style sheet to control the presentation of it (rather than putting CSS rules in the individual web pages), although as you will see in the next chapter you might use several external style sheets for different aspects of the site.

CSS Properties

You now know that styling a web page using CSS involves creating rules, and that these rules contain two parts: firstly, a selector to indicate which elements the rule applies to, and secondly, one or more properties which control the presentation of these elements.

So, if there is a part of the page that you want to make a certain color or size, then you need to find the corresponding property to control those elements.

The properties are grouped together into related functionality; for example, there are properties that allow you to control the presentation of tables, lists, and backgrounds. The following table shows the main properties available to you, all of which you meet in this chapter or Chapter 8.

FONT	**BACKGROUND**	border-right-color
font	background	border-right-style
font-family	background-attachment	border-right-width
font-size	background-color	border-top
font-size-adjust	background-image	border-top-color
font-stretch	background-position	border-top-style
font-style	background-repeat	border-top-width
font-variant	**BORDER**	**MARGIN**
font-weight	border	margin
TEXT	border-color	margin-bottom
color	border-style	margin-left
direction	border-width	margin-right
letter-spacing	border-bottom	margin-top
text-align	border-bottom-color	**PADDING**
text-decoration	border-bottom-style	padding
text-indent	border-bottom-width	padding-bottom
text-shadow	border-left	padding-left
text-transform	border-left-color	padding-right
unicode-bidi	border-left-style	padding-top
white-space	border-left-width	
word-spacing	border-right	

DIMENSIONS	z-index	list-style-type
height	**OUTLINES**	marker-offset
line-height	outline	**GENERATED CONTENT**
max-height	outline-color	content
max-width	outline-style	counter-increment
min-height	outline-width	counter-reset
min-width	**TABLE**	quotes
width	border-collapse	**CLASSIFICATION**
POSITIONING	border-spacing	clear
bottom	caption-side	cursor
clip	empty-cells	display
left	table-layout	float
overflow	**LIST and MARKER**	position
right	list-style	visibility
top	list-style-image	
vertical-align	list-style-position	

There are some properties that I will not be covering in this book either because they are very rarely used or because there is little support for them. (For example, I avoid covering aural style sheets because there are not many aural browsers that support them.) You can find out more about these properties on the following web sites or you can pick up a book dedicated to CSS:

- www.w3.org/style/css/
- www.devguru.com/Technologies/css/quickref/css_index.html
- www.w3schools.com/css/css_reference.asp

Controlling Text

Several properties allow you to control the appearance of text in your documents. These can be split into two groups:

- Those that directly affect the *font* and its appearance (including the typeface used, whether it is regular, bold or italic, and the size of the text)
- Those that would have the same effect on the text irrespective of the font used (these include color of the text and the spacing between words or letters)

The following table lists the properties that directly affect the font (the first of these two groups):

Property	Purpose
`font`	Allows you to combine several of the following properties into one
`font-family`	Specifies the typeface or family of font that should be used
`font-size`	Specifies the size of a font
`font-weight`	Specifies whether the font should be normal or bold
`font-style`	Specifies whether the font should be normal, italic, or oblique
`font-stretch`	Allows you to control the width of the actual characters in a font
`font-variant`	Specifies whether the font should be normal or small caps
`font-size-adjust`	Allows you to alter the aspect ratio of the size of the font's characters

Before looking at these properties in detail, it helps to understand some key terms used in typography. Perhaps most importantly, a font is not the same thing as a typeface:

- A *typeface* is a family of fonts, such as the Arial family.
- A *font* is a specific member of that family, such as Arial 12-point bold.

You will often see the terms used interchangeably, but it is helpful to be aware of the distinction.

Typefaces tend to belong to one of two groups: serif and sans-serif fonts. Serif fonts have extra curls on letters. For example, if you look at Figure 7-4, the first l contains a *serif* on the top of the letter and at the bottom of the letter, whereas sans-serif fonts have straight ends to the letters, such as in the second example. The third common style of a typeface is a monospaced serif font. Every letter in a monospaced font is the same width, whereas non-monospaced fonts have different widths for different letters. (For example, in serif and sans-serif fonts, the *l* tends to be narrower than the *m*.)

lm lm lm

serif font sans-serif font monospace font

Figure 7-4

Serif fonts are generally assumed to be easier to read for long periods of printed text. But on the Internet many people find serif fonts harder to read for long stretches, largely because the resolution of a computer screen is not as good as printed documents, which makes the less detailed sans-serif fonts easier to read.

So that we can study the properties that affect fonts, most of the examples in the following section will use a similar structure; paragraphs of text will be repeated, and each `<p>` element will carry a `class` attribute with a different value—for example:

```
<p class="one">Here is some text in a sans-serif font.</p>
<p class="two">Here is some text in a serif font.</p>
<p class="three">Here is some text in a monospaced font.</p>
```

You can then see how different properties affect each `<p>` element by writing a separate rule for each paragraph. You can use the value of the `class` attributes in the CSS selectors to create rules that apply just to one `<p>` element at a time.

The font-family Property

The `font-family` property allows you to specify the typeface that should be used for any text inside the element(s) that a CSS rule applies to.

When choosing typefaces it is important to know that browsers can only display XHTML text in the font you have specified if that typeface is installed on that computer. So, if you specified a font such as Futura or Garamond, and I do not have them on my computer, I would see the text in a different font—not the one you specified.

This is why, if you look at a selection of web sites, you will notice that most rely heavily on a very small selection of typefaces installed on most computers that access the Web, in particular Arial, Courier/Courier New, Georgia, Times/Times New Roman, and Verdana. (From this list, Arial and Verdana are particularly popular because they are considered easy to read online.)

To help matters, you can specify a list of typefaces so that, if the user does not have your first choice of typeface installed on their computer, the browser can try to show the text in your second or third choice. Each typeface in the list is separated by a comma, and if the name contains spaces (such as `times new roman` or `courier new`) you should place the name of the typeface in double quotation marks (`ch07_eg02.css`), like so:

```
p.one {font-family:arial, verdana, sans-serif;}
p.two {font-family:times, "times new roman", serif;}
p.three {font-family:courier, "courier new", monospace;}
```

Figure 7-5 shows what this example would look like in a browser; you can see the different types of fonts used for each paragraph (`ch07_eg02.html`).

Figure 7-5

You may notice that each list of typefaces in the previous example ends with so-called *generic font* names (sans-serif, serif, and monospace). The idea behind these is that each computer will have a font that corresponds to one of five generic font groups (sans-serif, serif, monospace, cursive, and fantasy), and if it cannot find the typefaces you have specified, it can use its choice of font that corresponds to that generic font group:

Generic font name	Type of font	Example
`serif`	Fonts with serifs	Times
`sans-serif`	Fonts without serifs	Arial
`monospace`	Fixed-width fonts	Courier
`cursive`	Fonts that emulate handwriting	Comic Sans
`fantasy`	Decorative fonts for titles and so on	**Impact**

One thing to keep in mind when choosing a list of fonts is that each font can be of different heights or widths, so you will probably want to choose a list of fonts that are of a similar size (otherwise the layout could look very different to what you would expect). For example, Courier New is quite short and wide, so if this was your first choice it would not be good to have Impact as a second choice because Impact is quite tall and narrow.

When designers want to use a specific typeface that is not likely to be on the majority of users' computers, they often use a GIF image for that text. It is generally frowned upon to use images for large sections of text, but for logos or headings and other small amounts of text, this is a good solution. If you do this, remember that you must provide the text that would be seen in the image as the value of the `alt` attribute.

There are several efforts to allow web designers to use fonts that the public are not likely to have on their computers. Apart from using images, two you might like to consider are: SIFR, which uses a combination of Flash and JavaScript (`http://novemberborn.net/sifr`*), and Typekit (*`http://typekit.com/`*).*

The font-size Property

The `font-size` property enables you to specify a size for the font. You will often see the value for this property specified in pixels, like so:

```
p.twelve {font-size:12px;}
```

However, there are many other ways you can provide a value:

- Length (along with pixels, there are several other units of length which you will learn about in the section "Lengths" later in this chapter)

```
px em ex pt in cm pc mm
```

- Absolute size (each of these values corresponds to a fixed size)

```
xx-small x-small small medium large x-large xx-large
```

- Relative size (this value is relative to the surrounding text)

```
smaller larger
```

- Percentage (a percentage is calculated as a proportion of the element that contains the text)

```
2% 10% 25% 50% 100%
```

The use of percentages rather than pixels is becoming increasingly widespread because it allows users to increase and decrease the sizes of fonts if they are having trouble reading them.

Here is an example of each of these ways to specify a value for the `font-size` property:

```
p.one {font-size:xx-small;}
p.twelve {font-size:12px;}
p.thirteen {font-size:3pc;}
p.fourteen {font-size:10%;}
```

Figure 7-6 shows you how a selection of these font sizes work in the browser. (`ch07_eg03.html` and `ch07_eg03.css` contain several examples of different ways of specifying size and compare how they look.)

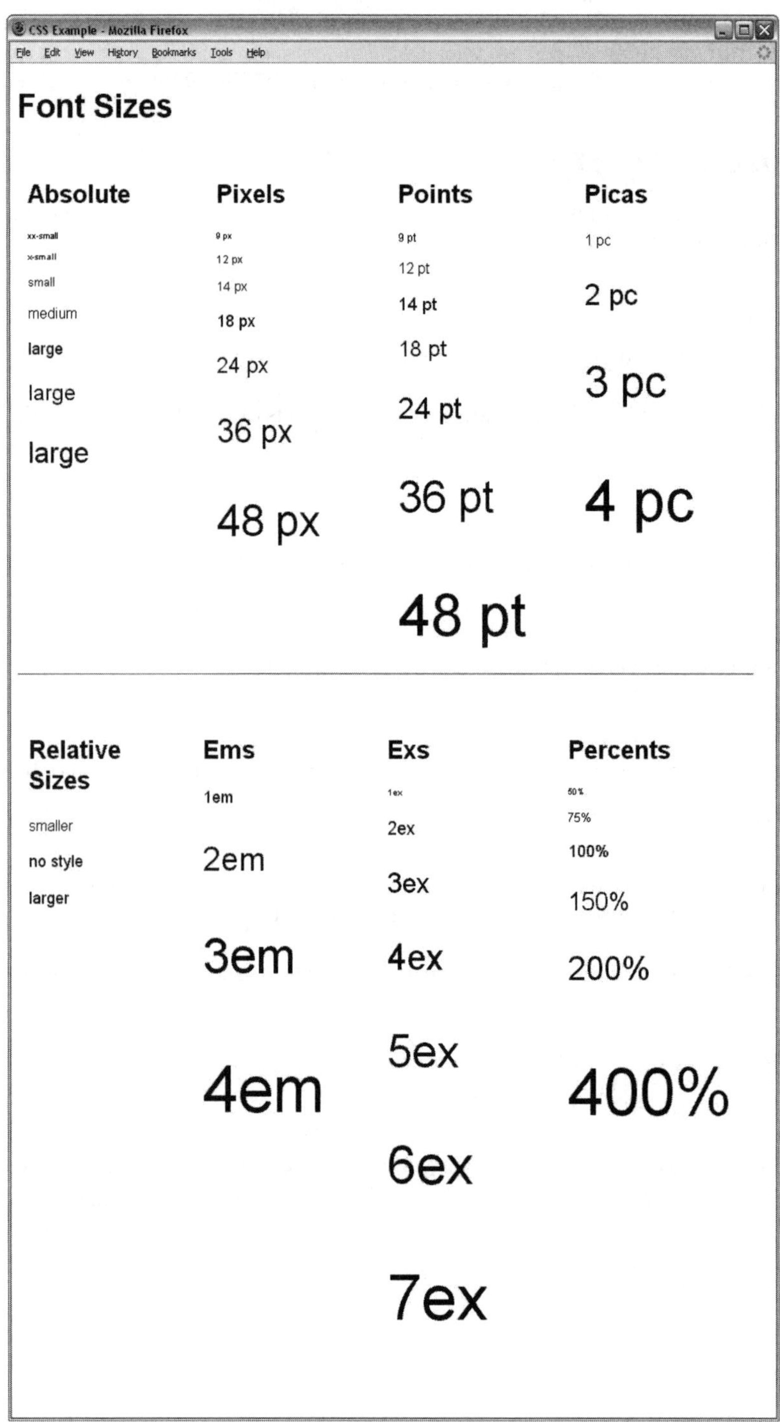
CSS Example - Mozilla Firefox
File Edit View History Bookmarks Tools Help
Font Sizes
Absolute
xx-small
x-small
small
medium
large
large
large
Pixels
9 px
12 px
14 px
18 px
24 px
36 px
48 px
Points
9 pt
12 pt
14 pt
18 pt
24 pt
36 pt
48 pt
Picas
1 pc
2 pc
3 pc
4 pc
Relative Sizes
smaller
no style
larger
Ems
1em
2em
3em
4em
Exs
1ex
2ex
3ex
4ex
5ex
6ex
7ex
Percents
50%
75%
100%
150%
200%
400%

Figure 7-6

The font-weight Property

Most fonts have different variations, such as bold and italic. When typographers create a new font, it is not unusual for them to individually craft a separate, thicker version of each character for the bold variation.

Despite all this careful work, rather than finding the bold version of a typeface, browsers tend to use an algorithm that takes the normal version of the font and makes it thicker. Because it uses an algorithm, it means you can also create a lighter version of fonts, too. This is what the `font-weight` property is for.

The possible values for `font-weight` are:

```
normal bold bolder lighter 100 200 300 400 500 600 700 800 900
```

The following example uses several of these values (`ch07_eg04.css`):

```
p.one {font-weight:normal;}
p.two {font-weight:bold;}
p.three {font-weight:normal;}
p.three span {font-weight:bolder;}
p.four {font-weight:bold;}
p.four span {font-weight:lighter;}
p.five {font-weight:100;}
p.six {font-weight:200;}
```

Figure 7-7 shows you how these values appear in the browser (`ch07_eg04.html`).

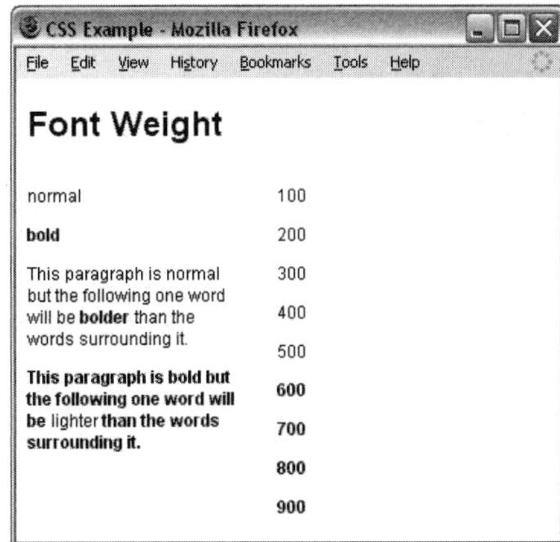

Figure 7-7

Of these values, `bold` is most commonly used, although you might also come across the use of `normal` (especially if a large section of text is already bold and an exception has to be created where just a few words are not in bold).

The font-style Property

The `font-style` property allows you to specify that a font should be `normal`, `italic`, or `oblique`, and these are the values of the `font-style` property; for example:

```
p.one {font-style:normal;}
p.two {font-style:italic;}
p.three {font-style:oblique;}
```

Figure 7-8 shows you how these values appear in the browser (from `ch07_eg05.css`).

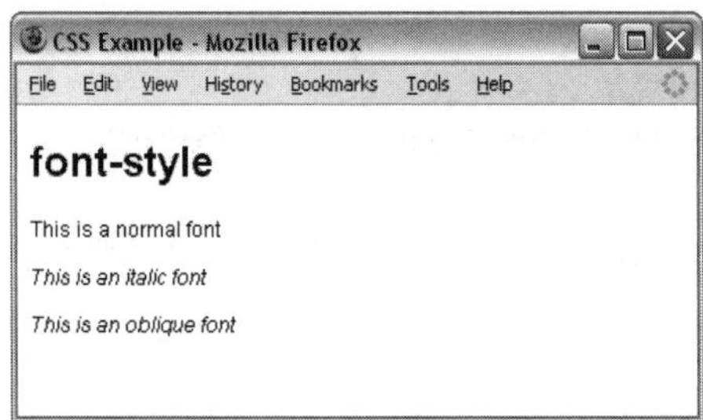

Figure 7-8

In typography, an italic version of a font would normally be a specifically stylized version of the font based on calligraphy, whereas an oblique version of font would take the normal version of the font and place it at an angle. In CSS, when you specify a `font-style` property should be `italic`, browsers will usually take the normal version of the font and simply render it at an angle (as you would expect with an oblique version of a font).

The font-variant Property

There are two possible values for the `font-variant` property: `normal` and `small-caps`. A small caps font looks like a smaller version of the uppercase letterset.

For example, look at the following paragraph, which contains a `<span>` with a `class` attribute (`ch07_eg06.html`):

```
<p>This is a normal font, but then <span class="smallcaps">there
are some small caps</span> in the middle.</p>
```

Now look at the style sheet (`ch07_eg06.css`):

```
p {font-variant:normal;}
span.smallcaps {font-variant:small-caps;}
```

As you can see from Figure 7-9, the rule associated with the `<span>` element indicates that its content should be shown in small caps.

Figure 7-9

The font-stretch Property

At the time of this writing, there was no support for this property in the main browsers (IE8 and Firefox 3), but I shall mention it for those interested in type. In the same way that some typefaces have condensed and extended versions with thinner or thicker characters, the `font-stretch` property sets the width of the characters in a font. It can take the following fixed values:

```
ultra-condensed extra-condensed condensed semi-condensed semi-expanded
expanded extra-expanded ultra-expanded
```

Or it can take relative values, where the value is in relation to that of the containing element:

```
normal wider narrower
```

For example, if it were supported, you would be able to make a condensed Arial font using the following syntax:

```
p {font-family:arial; font-stretch:condensed;}
```

The font-size-adjust Property

At the time of this writing, the `font-size-adjust` property does not have any support in the main browsers (IE8 and Firefox 3), but its purpose is to allow you to change a font's *aspect value,* which is the ratio between the height of a lowercase letter *x* in the font and the height of the font.

For example, Verdana has an aspect value of 0.58 (which means that when the font's size is 100 px, its x-height is 58 pixels). Times New Roman has an aspect value of 0.46 (which means that when the font's size is 100 px, its x-height is 46 pixels). This makes Verdana easier to read at smaller sizes than Times New Roman. By altering a font's aspect value you can, therefore, change its height.

Text Formatting

In addition to the properties that affect the font, there are several properties to affect the appearance or formatting of your text (independently from the font it is shown in). They are listed in the table that follows.

Property	Purpose
`color`	Specifies the color of the text
`text-align`	Specifies the horizontal alignment of the text within its containing element
`vertical-align`	Specifies the vertical alignment of text within containing element
`text-decoration`	Specifies whether the text should be underlined, overlined, strikethrough, or blinking text
`text-indent`	Specifies an indent from the left border for the text
`text-transform`	Specifies that the content of the element should all be uppercase, lowercase, or capitalized
`text-shadow`	Specifies that the text should have a drop shadow
`letter-spacing`	Controls the width between letters (known to print designers as *tracking*)
`word-spacing`	Controls the amount of space between each word
`white-space`	Specifies whether the white space should be collapsed, preserved, or prevented from wrapping
`direction`	Specifies the direction of text (similar to the `dir` attribute)

The color Property

The `color` property allows you to specify the color of the text. The value of this property can either be a hex code for a color or a color name. (The way in which colors are specified for the Web is discussed further in Appendix D.)

For example, the following rule would make the content of paragraph elements red (`ch07_eg07.html`):

```
p {color:#ff0000;}
```

The text-align Property

The `text-align` property works like the deprecated `align` attribute would with text. It aligns the text within its containing element or the browser window. The table that follows displays possible values.

Value	Purpose
`left`	Aligns the text with the left border of the containing element
`right`	Aligns the text with the right border of the containing element
`center`	Centers the content in the middle of the containing element
`justify`	Spreads the width across the whole width of the containing element

Figure 7-10 shows you how these would work in a table that is 500 pixels wide.

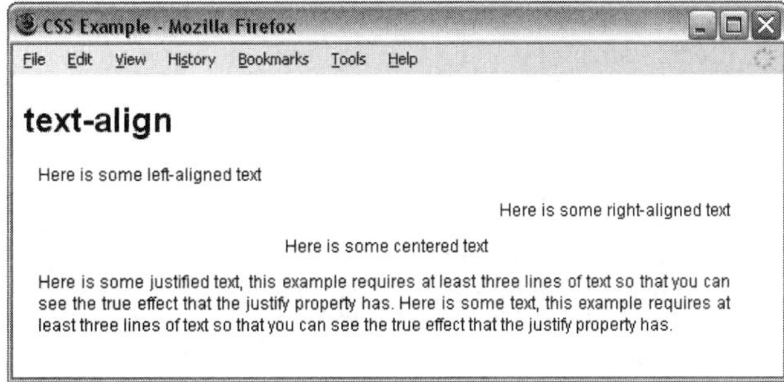

Figure 7-10

Here are the rules for each row of this example (`ch07_eg08.css`):

```
.leftAlign {text-align:left;}
.rightAlign {text-align:right;}
.center {text-align:center;}
.justify {text-align:justify;}
```

The vertical-align Property

The `vertical-align` property is useful when working with inline elements, in particular images and portions of text. It allows you to control their vertical positioning within the containing element, for example:

```
span.footnote {vertical-align:sub;}
```

It can take several values, as you can see in the table that follows.

Value	Purpose
`baseline`	Everything should be aligned on the baseline of the parent element (this is the default setting).
`sub`	Makes the element subscript. With images, the top of the image should be on the baseline. With text, the top of the font body should be on the baseline.
`super`	Makes the element superscript. With images, the bottom of the image should be level with the top of the font. With text, the bottom of the descender (the parts of letters such as *g* and *p* that go beneath the line of text) should align with the top of the font body.
`top`	The top of the text and the top of the image should align with the top of the tallest element on the line.
`text-top`	The top of the text and the top of the image should align with the top of the tallest text on the line.
`middle`	The vertical midpoint of the element should be aligned with the vertical midpoint of the parent.
`bottom`	The bottom of the text and the bottom of the image should align with the bottom of the lowest element on the line.
`text-bottom`	The bottom of the text and the bottom of the image should align with the bottom of the lowest text on the line.

This property may also accept a length and a percentage value.

You can try out all of these in your browser using `ch07_eg09.html`.

Figure 7-11 shows you some of these values.

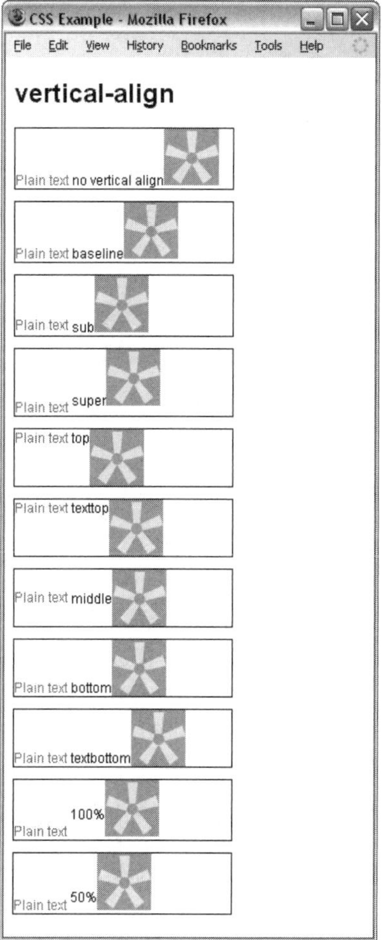

Figure 7-11

The text-decoration Property

The `text-decoration` property allows you to specify the values shown in the following table.

Value	Purpose
`underline`	Adds a line under the content.
`overline`	Adds a line over the top of the content.
`line-through`	Adds a line through the middle of the content, such as strikethrough text. In general, this should be used only to indicate text that is marked for deletion.
`blink`	Creates blinking text (which is generally frowned upon and considered annoying).

Here are these properties used on separate paragraphs (`ch07_eg10.css`):

```
p.underline {text-decoration:underline;}
p.overline {text-decoration:overline;}
p.line-through {text-decoration:line-through;}
p.blink {text-decoration:blink;}
```

Figure 7-12 shows you what they look like in Firefox. Note that the `blink` property works in Firefox but not in Internet Explorer.

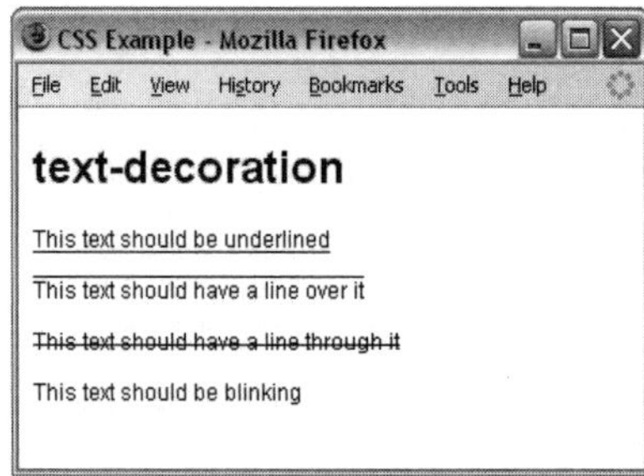

Figure 7-12

The text-indent Property

The `text-indent` property allows you to indent the first line of text within an element. In the following example it has been applied to the second paragraph:

```
<p>This paragraph should be aligned with the left-hand side of the browser. </p>
<p class="indent">Just the first line of this paragraph should be indented by
3 em, this should not apply to any subsequent lines in the same paragraph. </p>
```

Now, here is the rule that indents the second paragraph (`ch08_eg11.css`):

```
.indent {text-indent:3em;}
```

You can see what this looks like in Figure 7-13.

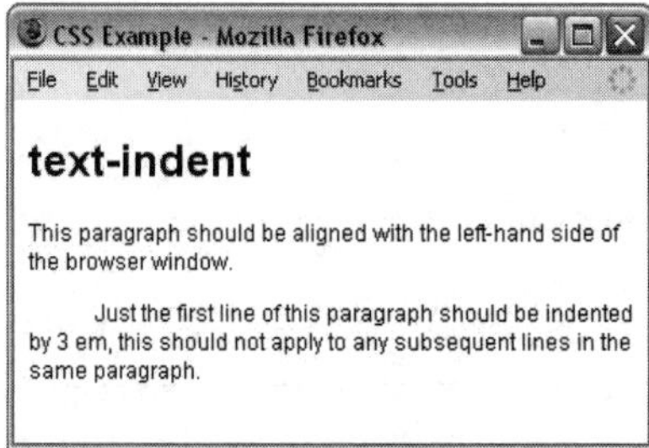

Figure 7-13

The text-shadow Property

The `text-shadow` property is supposed to create a *drop shadow*, which is a dark version of the word just behind it and slightly offset. This has often been used in print media, and its popularity has meant that is has gained its own CSS property. The value for this property is quite complicated because it can take a color followed by three lengths:

```
.dropShadow {text-shadow: #999999 10px 10px 3px;}
```

After the color has been specified, the first two lengths specify how far from the original text the drop shadow should fall (using X and Y coordinates), while the third specifies how blurred the drop shadow should be.

At the time of this writing, this property does not work in IE8 or Firefox 3 (although support is likely to be added in future versions). The property does work in recent versions of Safari (on Mac), Opera, and Konqueror. Figure 7-14 shows what this example (`ch07_eg12.css`) looks like in Safari on a Mac.

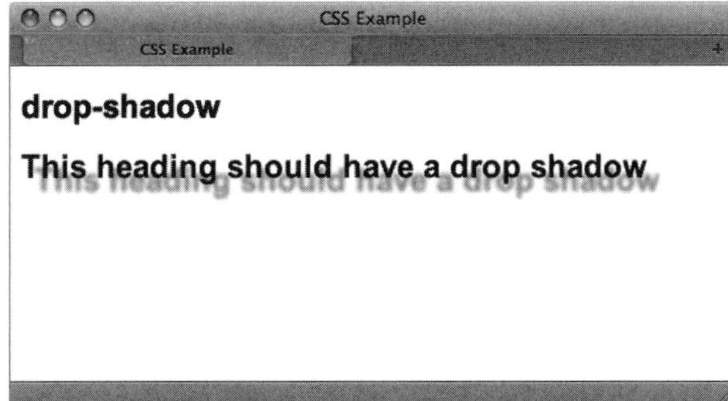

Figure 7-14

The text-transform Property

The `text-transform` property allows you to specify the case for the content of an element. The possible values are shown in the table that follows.

Value	Purpose
`none`	No change should take place.
`capitalize`	The first letter of every word should be capitalized.
`uppercase`	The entire content of the element should be uppercase.
`lowercase`	The entire content of the element should be lowercase.

To demonstrate this property, in the following example there are four paragraphs:

```
<p class="none">This text has not been transformed</p>
<p class="capitalize">The first letter of each word will be capiltalized</p>
<p class="uppercase">All of this text will be uppercase</p>
<p class="lowercase">ALL OF THIS TEXT WILL BE LOWERCASE</p>
```

Here you can see the four different values for the `text-transform` property in use (`ch07_eg13.css`):

```
p.none {text-transform:none;}
p.capitalize {text-transform:capitalize;}
p.uppercase {text-transform:uppercase;}
p.lowercase {text-transform:lowercase;}
```

Figure 7-15 shows you how the paragraphs would appear in a browser with these styles applied.

Figure 7-15

The letter-spacing Property

The `letter-spacing` property controls something that print designers refer to as *tracking*: the gap between letters. Loose tracking indicates that there is a lot of space between letters, whereas tight tracking refers to letters being squeezed together. No tracking refers to the normal gap between letters for that font.

If you want to increase or decrease the spacing between letters, you are most likely to specify this in pixels or something known as an em (although it can be any unit of length that CSS supports—and we will be looking at the CSS units of length later in the chapter).

If you have a section of text where letter spacing has been altered, then you can specify that an element should have no tracking using the keyword `normal`.

The first paragraph of the following example shows normal tracking. The second paragraph shows a gap of 3 pixels being used between each letter. The third paragraphs shows a gap between each letter of 0.5 em. The final paragraph shows spacing cut by 1 pixel from what it would have been in normal tracking (`ch07_eg14.css`):

```
.two {letter-spacing:3px;}
.three {letter-spacing:0.5em;}
.four {letter-spacing:-1px;}
```

Figure 7-16 gives you an indication of what this looks like in a browser.

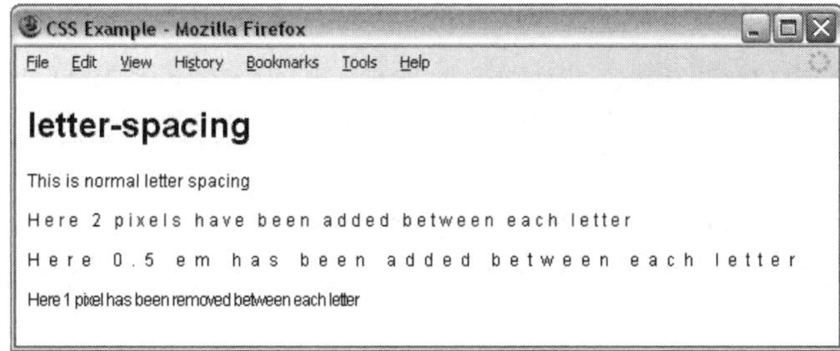

Figure 7-16

The word-spacing Property

The `word-spacing` property sets the gap between words, and its value should be a unit of length. In the example that follows (`ch07_eg15.css`), in the first paragraph there is a standard gap between each of the words. In the second paragraph the gap is 10 pixels between each of the words. In the final paragraph the gap has been cut to 1 pixel less than normal spacing:

```
.two {word-spacing:20px;}
.three {word-spacing:-1px;}
```

Figure 7-17 gives you an indication of what this looks like.

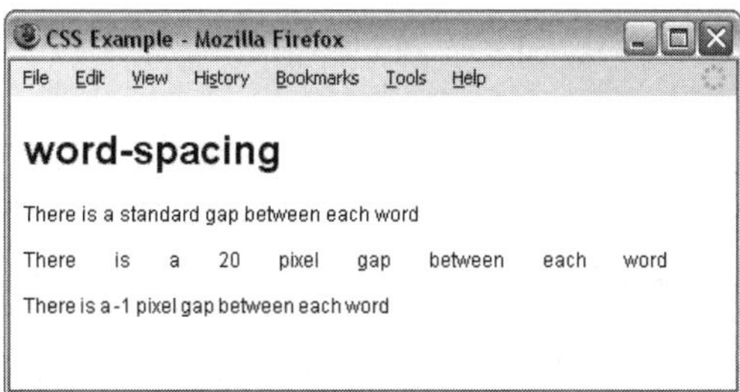

Figure 7-17

The white-space Property

As you saw in Chapter 1, browsers change any two or more spaces next to each other into a single space and make any carriage returns a single space, too. The `white-space` property controls whether or not white space is preserved, offering the same results as the XHTML `<pre>` element where white space is preserved and the `nowrap` attribute where text is only broken onto a new line if explicitly told to. See the table that follows for the possible values for this property.

Value	Meaning
normal	Normal white space collapsing rules are followed.
pre	White space is preserved just as in the <pre> element of XHTML, but the formatting is whatever is indicated for that element (it is not a monospaced font by default like the <pre> element).
nowrap	Text is broken onto a new line only if explicitly told to with a element; otherwise text does not wrap.

For example, you can use the white-space property like so (ch07_eg16.css):

```
.pre {white-space:pre;}
.nowrap {white-space:nowrap;}
```

You can see both of these properties working in Figure 7-18.

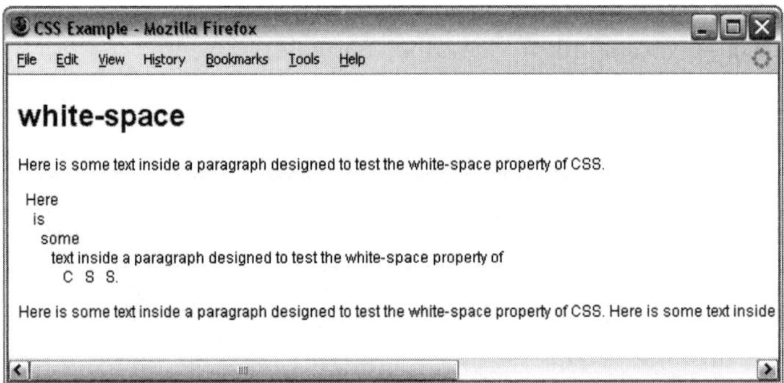

Figure 7-18

The direction Property

The direction property is rather like the dir attribute and specifies the direction in which the text should flow. The following table shows the possible values.

Value	Meaning
ltr	The text flows from left to right.
rtl	The text flows from right to left.
inherit	The text flows in the same direction as its parent element.

For example, here are rules for two paragraphs indicating different directions for the text (`ch07_eg17.css` used with `ch07_eg17.html`):

```
p.ltr {direction:ltr;}
p.rtl {direction:rtl;}
```

In practice, both IE and Firefox use this property much as the `align` attribute is used. The value `rtl` will simply right-align text, as you can see in Figure 7-19. Note, however, that the period (or full stop) is to the left of the sentence in the paragraph that is supposed to be running right to left.

Figure 7-19

Text Pseudo-Classes

While you are learning about text, there are two pseudo-classes that can help you work with text. These pseudo-classes allow you to render either the first letter or the first line of an element in a different way than the rest of that element.

The first-letter Pseudo-Class

The `first-letter` pseudo-class allows you to specify a rule just for the first letter of an element. This is most commonly used on the first character of a new page, either in some magazine articles or in books.

Here is an example of the `first-letter` pseudo-class applied to a `<p>` element that has a `class` attribute whose value is `introduction`. Note how the selector for the element and the `first-letter` pseudo-class are separated by a colon (`ch07_eg18.css` used with `ch07_eg18.html`):

```
p.introduction:first-letter {font-size:42px;}
```

You can see the effect of this `first-letter` pseudo-class in Figure 7-20 (which also shows the next pseudo-class we will be looking at).

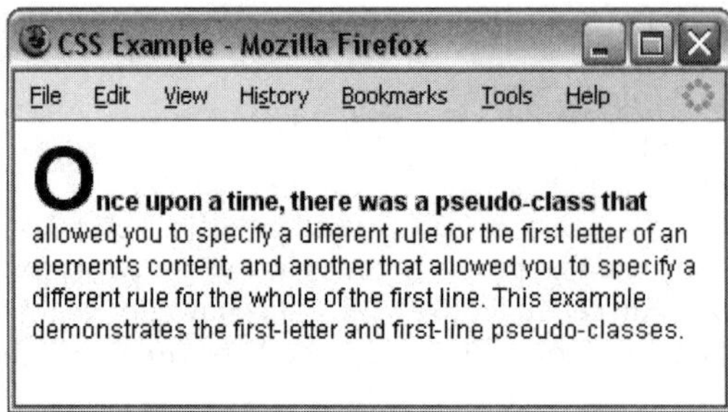

Figure 7-20

The first-line Pseudo-Class

The `first-line` pseudo-class should allow you to render the first line of any paragraph differently from the rest of the paragraph. Commonly this might be in a bold font so that the reader can clearly see an introduction (for articles) or the first line (for poems).

The name of the pseudo-class is separated from the selector for the element by a colon:

```
p.introduction:first-line {font-weight:bold;}
```

It is worth trying this example out in a browser, because if you resize the window so that there is less text on the first line, you will see how only the first line of text in the browser will be given this new style. You can see the `first-line` pseudo-class in action in Figure 7-20, which also demonstrates the `first-letter` pseudo-class.

Try It Out Styling the Example Café Text

Now that you've learned about using CSS to format text, it is time to try putting what you have learned into practice by starting to add styles to the Example Café web site.

1. We will be creating an external style sheet, so start your text editor and create a file called `interface.css`, and save it in a folder called `css` along with the rest of the Example Café files. At the beginning of the style sheet add a comment to explain what the style sheet is for:

```
/* style sheet for Example Cafe */
```

2. We want the default font family to be Arial. If the user does not have Arial installed, then we can suggest Verdana, failing which the computer's default sans-serif font.

```
body {font-family:arial, verdana, sans-serif;}
```

3. It would be nice to have the headings stand out in a different font, so we will have Georgia as the first choice for headings, and then Times, and finally the default Serif font. I would also like them to appear in gray rather than black, so we can specify a color for the headings using

the `color` property (which is discussed in more detail in the following chapter). Because we are making all headings the same, we should specify the styles in a single rule like so:

```
h2 {georgia, times, serif;
    color:#666666;}
```

4. The paragraphs of text might look a little better slightly smaller than the default size of text, let's make them 90% of the default size. We will also make the text dark gray rather than black.

```
p {font-size:90%;
   color:#333333;}
```

5. Now let's look at the navigation. In particular, we want to control the appearance of the links in the navigation. In order to do this, we are going to have to open the XHTML pages and add an `id` attribute to the `<div>` element that contains the navigation.

```
<div id="navigation">
  HOME
  <a href="menu.html">MENU</a>
  <a href="recipes.html">RECIPES</a>
  <a href="opening.html">OPENING</a>
  <a href="contact.html">CONTACT</a>
</div>
```

6. Now we need to add a selector, which will specify that we only want to select `<a>` elements that live inside an element that has an `id` attribute whose value is `navigation`; we do this using the hash or pound symbol followed by the value of the `id` attribute. We will specify that these links should be a light blue to match the logo:

```
#navigation a {color:#3399cc;}
```

7. By default, links appear with underlines; we can remove these by using the `text-decoration` property with a value of `none`:

```
#navigation a {color:#3399cc;
    text-decoration:none;}
```

8. Finally, in the XHTML pages we need to add the `<link>` element, which will associate the style sheet with the pages; this should be added to every page:

```
<link rel="stylesheet" type="text/css" href="css/interface.css" />
```

Now all of the pages in the example should be using this same style sheet and your homepage should look a little more like the example in Figure 7-21.

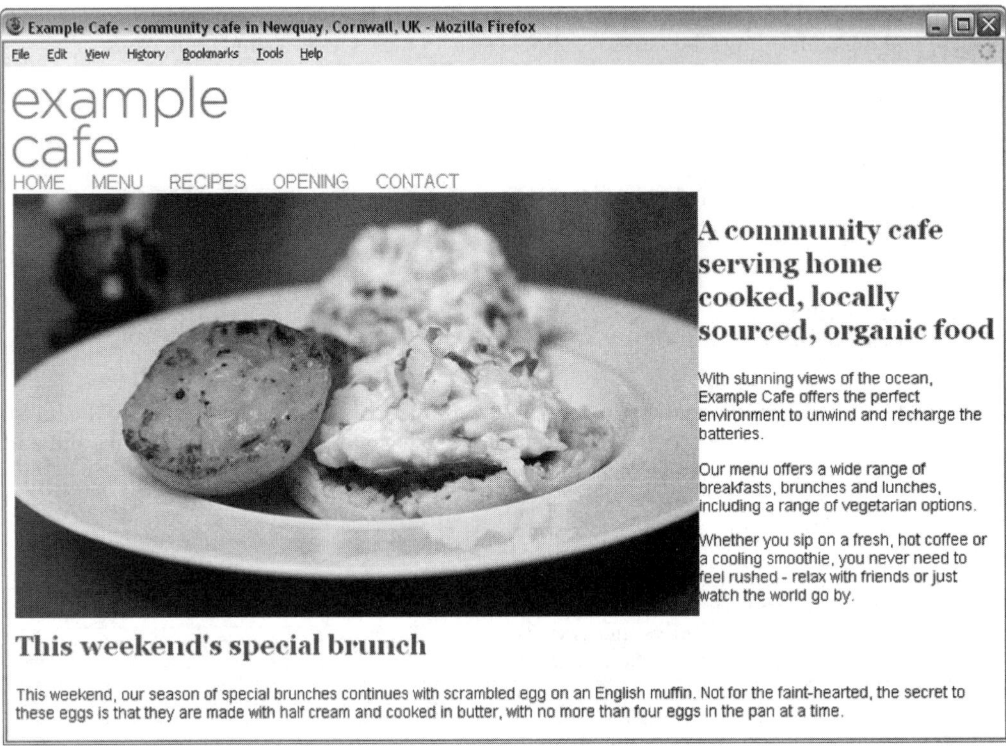

Figure 7-21

Selectors

So far, you have seen lots of examples of properties that affect the presentation of text, and you have seen how these properties are applied to elements using style rules. Before we continue to look at more properties, we need to look at some more fundamental issues. We will start by looking at how you can use different types of *selector* to specify which elements a style sheet rule will apply to before going on to look at the different units of measurements used in CSS.

You can specify which elements a style sheet rule applies to in several ways, not just by using the names of the elements as you have seen so far in this chapter (which is, incidentally, known as a *simple selector*), or using the value of the `class` attribute or `id` attribute. Let's take a look at the different types of selector that are available to specify which element(s) a CSS rule applies to.

Universal Selector

The *universal selector* is an asterisk; it is like a wildcard and matches all element types in the document.

```
*{}
```

If you want a rule to apply to all elements, you can use this selector. Sometimes it is used for default values that will apply to the whole of the document (such as a `font-family` and `font-size`) unless another more specific selector indicates that an element should use different values for these same properties.

It is slightly different from applying default styles to the `<body>` element, as the universal selector applies to every element and does not rely on the property being inherited from the rules that apply to the `<body>` element.

The Type Selector

The *type selector* matches all of the elements specified in the comma-delimited list. It allows you to apply the same rules to several elements. For example, if you wanted to apply the same rules to different sized heading elements, the following would match all `h1`, `h2`, and `h3` elements:

```
h1, h2, h3 {}
```

The Class Selector

The *class selector* allows you to match a rule with an element (or elements) carrying a `class` attribute whose value matches the one you specify in the class selector. For example, imagine you had a `<p>` element with a `class` attribute whose value was `BackgroundNote`, like so:

```
<p class="BackgroundNote">This paragraph contains an aside.</p>
```

You can use a class selector in one of two ways here. One way is to simply assign a rule that applies to any element that has a `class` attribute whose value is `BackgroundNote`, like so, preceding the value of the `class` attribute with a period or full stop:

```
.BackgroundNote {}
```

Or you can create a selector that selects only the `<p>` elements that carry a `class` attribute with a value of `BackgroundNote` (not other elements) like so:

```
p.BackgroundNote {}
```

If you have several elements that can all carry a `class` attribute with the same value (for example a `<p>` element and a `<div>` element could both use the `class` attribute with the same value) *and* you want the content of these elements to be displayed in the same manner, you will want to use the former notation. If the styles you are defining are specific to just the `<p>` element whose `class` attribute has a value of `BackgroundNote`, then you should use the latter notation.

A `class` attribute can also contain several values separated by a space — for example:

```
<p class="important code">
```

You can use the following syntax to indicate an element that has a `class` attribute whose value contains both `important` *and* `code` (although IE7 was the first version of Internet Explorer to support this syntax).

```
p.important.code {}
```

The ID Selector

The *id selector* works just like a class selector, but works on the value of `id` attributes. Rather than using a period or full stop before the value of the `id` attribute, you use a hash or pound sign (`#`). So an element with an `id` attribute whose value is `abstract` can be identified with this selector.

```
#abstract
```

Because the value of an `id` attribute should be unique within a document, this selector should apply only to the content of one element (and you should not have to specify the element name).

The Child Selector

The *child selector* matches an element that is a direct child of another. In this case it matches any `<b>`elements that are direct children of `<td>` elements. The names of the two elements are separated by a greater-than symbol to indicate that `b` is a child of `td` (>) which is referred to as a *combinator*:

```
td>b {}
```

This would enable you to specify a different style for `<b>`elements that are direct children of the `<td>` element compared with `<b>`elements that appear elsewhere in the document.

As a direct child of the `<td>` element, no other tags would sit between the opening `<td>` tag and the `<b>`element. For example, the following selector does not make sense because the `<b>`element should not be a direct child of a `<table>` element (instead, a `<tr>` element is more likely to be the direct child of a `<table>` element):

```
table>b {}
```

IE7 was the first version of Internet Explorer to support the child selector.

The Descendant Selector

The *descendant selector* matches an element type that is a descendant of another specified element (or nested inside another specified element), not just a direct child. While the greater-than symbol is the combinator for the child selector, for the descendent selector the combinator is the space. Take a look at this example:

```
table b {}
```

In this case, the selector matches any `<b>`element that is a child of the `<table>` element, which means it would apply to `<b>`elements both in `<td>` and `<th>` elements.

This is a contrast to the child selector because it applies to all of the children of the `<table>` element, rather than just the direct children.

The Adjacent Sibling Selector

An *adjacent sibling selector* matches an element type that is the next sibling of another. For example, if you want to make the first paragraph after any level 1 heading a different style from other `<p>` elements you can use the adjacent sibling selector like so to specify rules for just the first `<p>` element to come after any `<h1>` element:

```
h1+p {}
```

IE7 was the first version of Internet Explorer to support the adjacent sibling selector.

The General Sibling Selector

The *general sibling selector* matches an element type that is a sibling of another, although it does not have to be the directly preceding element. So, if you had two `<p>` elements that are siblings of an `<h1>` element, they would both use the rules of this selector.

```
h1~p {}
```

The general sibling selector is part of CSS3; IE7 was the first version of Internet Explorer to support the general sibling selector and Firefox 2 was the first version of Firefox to support it.

Using Child and Sibling Selectors To Reduce Dependence on Classes in Markup

The child and adjacent sibling selectors are both very important because they can reduce the number of `class` attributes you need to add into an XHTML document.

It is very easy to add classes for all kinds of eventualities. For example, if you wanted the first paragraph after an `<h1>` element to be shown in bold, you might have been tempted to add a `class` attribute to the first `<p>` element after every `<h1>` element. While this would work, your markup can be littered with all kinds of classes that are only there to make it easier to control the presentation of the pages.

If you then decided you wanted the first two `<p>` elements after every `<h1>` element to be bold, you might have to go back and add in new class attributes for the second `<p>` elements after every `<h1>` element. So the child and adjacent sibling selectors add a lot of flexibility to how you style documents and can make for much cleaner markup.

Take a look at the following XHTML content (`ch07_eg19.html`):

```
<p>Paragraph One: not inside a div element.</p>
<div>
  <p>Paragraph One: inside a div element</p>
  <p>Paragraph Two: inside a div element </p>
  <p>Paragraph Three: inside a div element </p>
  <p>Paragraph Four: inside a div element </p>
  <p>Paragraph Five: inside a div element </p>
</div>
```

Using the adjacent and adjacent sibling and child selectors only, you are going to create a page that looks like the one shown in Figure 7-22.

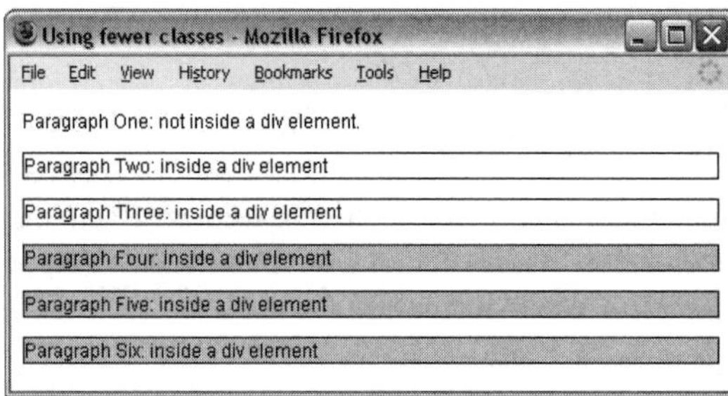

Figure 7-22

The three different paragraph styles are as follows:

- The first paragraph has no border or background color.
- The paragraphs inside the <div> element all have borders.
- The last three paragraphs have a gray background as well as their border.

I have not used three different classes to specify different paragraph styles; rather, I have one rule that controls the font used for all paragraphs:

```
p {font-family:arial, verdana, sans-serif;}
```

The following is the second rule for any paragraph that is a child of a <div> element. (Because the first paragraph is not inside a <div> element, the rule does not apply to the first paragraph.)

```
div>p {border:1px solid #000000;}
```

The third rule matches any paragraph that is also a third consecutive <p> element. (Because the fourth and fifth <p> elements have two previous <p> elements, this rule applies to them, as well as the third <p> element inside the <div>.)

```
p+p+p {background-color:#999999;}
```

Remember that this example will not work in IE6 or earlier versions of Internet Explorer, as these selectors were first introduced in IE7.

Attribute Selectors

Attribute selectors enable you to use the attributes that an element carries, and their values, in the selector. There are several types of attribute selector and they allow far more complex ways of selecting elements in a document.

The use of attribute selectors is fairly limited because they have only been supported in the latest versions of browsers. Some of the attribute selectors in the following table are from CSS3, which has not yet been completed.

Name	Example	Matches
Existence selector	`p[id]`	Any <p> element carrying an attribute called `id`.
Equality selector	`p[id="summary"]`	Any <p> element carrying an attribute called `id` whose value is `summary`.
Space selector	`p[class~="XHTML"]`	Any <p> element carrying an attribute called `class`, whose value is a list of space-separated words, one of which is exactly the same as `XHTML`.
Hyphen selector	`p[language|="en"]`	Any <p> element carrying an attribute called `language` whose value begins with `en` and is followed with a hyphen (this particular selector is designed for use with language attributes).
Prefix selector (CSS3)	`p[attr^"b"]`	Any <p> element carrying any attribute whose value begins with `b`. (CSS3)
Substring selector (CSS3)	`p[attr*"on"]`	Any <p> element carrying any attribute whose value contains the letters `on`. (CSS3)
Suffix selector (CSS3)	`p[attr$"x"]`	Any <p> element carrying any attribute whose value contains the ends in the letter `x`. (CSS3)

Internet Explorer implemented these attribute selectors in IE7, and in order for them to work, the XHTML document must have the strict `!DOCTYPE` declaration. Firefox started to support them in Firefox 2.

Let's have a look at an example of using these attribute selectors; here are seven different paragraph elements, each carrying different attributes/attribute values (`ch07_eg20.html`):

```
<p id="introduction">Here's paragraph one; each paragraph has different
attributes.</p>
<p id="summary">Here's paragraph two; each paragraph has different
attributes.</p>
<p class="important XHTML">Here's paragraph three; each paragraph has
different attributes.</p>
<p language="en-us">Here's paragraph four; each paragraph has different
attributes.</p>
<p class="begins">Here's paragraph five; each paragraph has different
attributes.</p>
<p class="contains">Here's paragraph six; each paragraph has different
attributes.</p>
<p class="suffix">Here's paragraph seven; each paragraph has different
attributes.</p>
```

Now let's look at a CSS style sheet that uses attribute selectors to associate different style rules with each of these elements (`ch07_eg20.css`):

```
p[id] {border:1px solid #000000;}
p[id="summary"] {background-color:#999999;}
p[class~="XHTML"] {border:3px solid #000000;}
p[language|="en"] {color:#ffffff; background-color:#000000;}
p[class^="b"]{border:3px solid #333333;}
p[class*="on"] {color:#ffffff; background-color:#333333;}
p[class$="x"] {border:1px solid #333333;}
```

You can see the result in Firefox 3.0 in Figure 7-23.

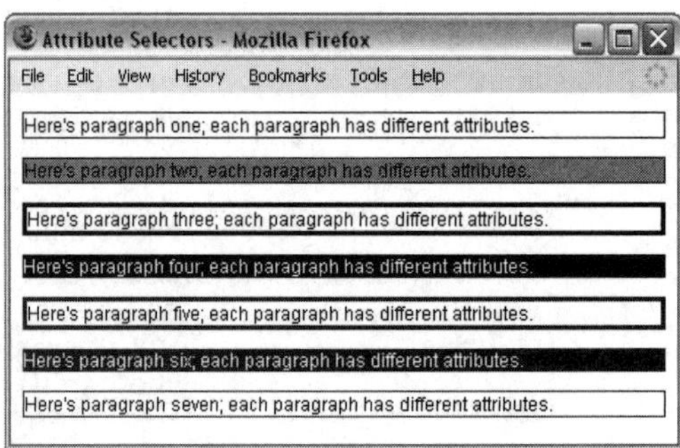

Figure 7-23

Because XHTML is case-sensitive, all selectors should match the case of the element name that they are supposed to match.

Lengths

You have already seen that the values of some CSS properties are given as *lengths* (such as the size of fonts, height of lines of text, and gaps between words and letters), and you will come across more properties whose values are expressed as lengths later in the chapter. So, let's take a moment to look at the three ways lengths can be specified in CSS:

- ❑ Relative units
- ❑ Absolute units
- ❑ Percentages

Relative Units

There are three types of relative units: pixels, which relate to the resolution of the screen, and em's and ex's both of which relate to the size of fonts.

px

The *pixel*, referred to in code as `px`, is by far the most commonly used unit of length in CSS. A pixel is the smallest unit of resolution on a screen and if you look very closely at your screen you might just be able to see the square dots that are the pixels.

Technically, the size of a layout that uses pixels as a unit of measurement *can* depend upon the viewing medium (keep reading to see why I say "can"), which is why it is counted as a relative unit.

Most computer screens have a resolution of 72 dots per inch (dpi), but you will find that laser and bubble jet printers are usually set with a higher resolution—my current printer runs at 300 dpi. In contrast, mobile devices can have a lower resolution than computer screens or (in the case of some smart phones such as the iPhone) a higher resolution.

So, a table that is 500 pixels wide could be 9.9444 inches wide on a 72 dpi screen, 1.666 inches wide at 300 dpi, or 13.888 inches wide on a 32 dpi screen (and a screen that is only 32 dpi is unlikely to be that much over 13 inches wide).

In reality, when you print a web page from your browser, it will adjust the pixels to present a readable version of the document. In fact, CSS recommends that in such cases user agents rescale pixel units so that reading at arm's length 1 pixel would correspond to about 0.28 mm or $\frac{1}{90}$ of an inch.

em

An *em* is equivalent to the height of the current font, and because the size of fonts can vary throughout a document, the height of the em unit can be different in different parts of the document. Furthermore, because users can change the size of text in their browser, the em unit is capable of varying in relation to the size of the text that the user has selected.

This means that the em unit is most commonly used for measurements of elements that contain text and for controlling spacing between text (for example it can be used in the `line-height` property to set the gaps between lines of text in relation to their height).

While the em unit is equivalent to the height of a font, it is often thought to have derived from the width of a lowercase *m*; you may also hear the term *en*, which equates to half an *em*.

ex

The *ex* should be the height of a lowercase *x*. Because different fonts have different proportions, the ex is related to the font size and the type of font. In Figure 7-24, you can see the *x* in the Courier typeface is smaller than the *x* in the Impact typeface.

Figure 7-24

Absolute Units

Generally speaking, absolute units are used far less than relative units (and you will rarely come across designs that use these units of measurement). The following table shows the *absolute units* that are used in some CSS properties.

Unit	Full Name
`pt`	A point
`pc`	A pica
`in`	An inch
`cm`	A centimeter
`mm`	A millimeter

I shouldn't really need to clarify inches, millimeters, or centimeters, but the other two are more interesting. A point is $\frac{1}{72}$ of an inch (the same as a pixel in most computer screen resolutions), and a pica is $\frac{1}{12}$ of an inch (12 points). Typographers tend to use points to measure font sizes and leading (the gaps between lines), while picas are used to measure line lengths.

Percentages

Percentages give a value in relation to another value. For example, if your page only contained two paragraphs, and you wanted each to take up half of the width of the browser, then the paragraphs might be given a `width` property with a value of `50%`. However, if the `<p>` element were inside another element that you knew was 500 pixels wide, they would take up 50 percent of the width of that containing element (or 250 pixels) each.

Introducing the Box Model

The *box model* is a very important concept in CSS because it determines how elements are positioned within the browser window. It gets its name because CSS treats every element as if it were in a *box*.

As you can see in the table that follows, every box has three properties you must be aware of.

Property	Description
`border`	Even if you cannot see it, every box has a border. This separates the edge of one box from other surrounding boxes.
`margin`	The margin is the distance between the border of a box and the box next to it.
`padding`	This padding is the space between the content of the box and its border.

You can get a better idea of these properties in Figure 7-25, which shows the various parts of the box (the black line is the border).

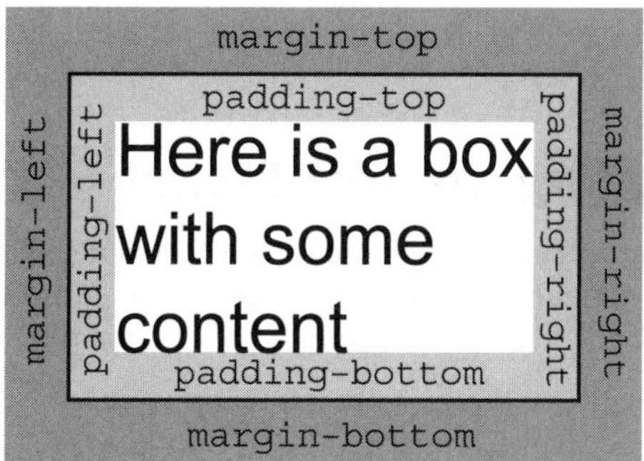

Figure 7-25

You can use CSS to individually control the border, margin, and padding on each side of a box; you can specify a different width, line-style and color for each side of the boxes' border.

The `padding` and `margin` properties are especially important in creating what designers refer to as *white space*; this is the space between the various parts of the page. For example, if you have a box with a black border and the box contains black text, you would not want the text to touch the border because it would make the text harder to read. Giving the box padding helps separate the text from the line around the edge.

Meanwhile, suppose you have two boxes next to each other, both with borders. If there is not a margin between them the boxes will run into each other, and the line where the boxes meet could look thicker than the other lines.

There is, however, an interesting issue with margins: when a bottom margin of one element meets the top margin of another, only the larger of the two will show. (If they are the same size, then the margin will be equivalent to the size of just one of the margins.) Figure 7-26 shows the vertical margins of two adjacent boxes collapsing (note that this only applies to vertical margins; the same is not true for left and right margins).

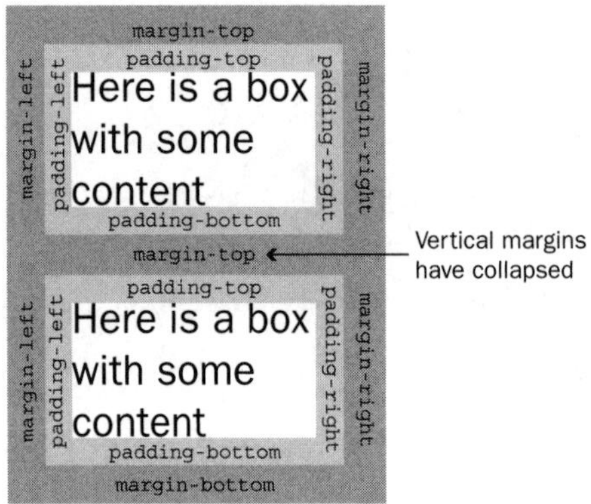

Figure 7-26

To really understand how the box model works with elements, take a look at the example in the next section.

An Example Illustrating the Box Model

To illustrate the box model we will add a border to each of the elements in a web page. The <body> element creates one box that contains the whole page, and inside that box each heading, paragraph, image, or link creates another box. First, here is the XHTML for the page (ch09_eg21.html):

```
<?xml version="1.0" ?>
<!DOCTYPE html PUBLIC "-//W3C//DTD XHTML 1.0 Transitional//EN"
    "http://www.w3.org/TR/xhtml1/DTD/xhtml1-transitional.dtd">
<html xmlns="http://www.w3.org/1999/xhtml" lang="en" xml:lang="en">
<head>
  <title>Understanding the Box Model</title>
  <link rel="stylesheet" type="text/css" href="ch07_eg19.css" />
</head>
<body>
  <h1>Thinking Inside the Box</h1>
  <p class="description">When you are styling a web page with CSS you
  must start to think in terms of <b>boxes</b>.</p>
  <p>Each element is treated as if it generates a new box. Each box can have
  new rules associated with it.</p>
  <img src="images/boxmodel.gif" alt="How CSS treats a box" />
  <p>As you can see from the diagram above, each box has a <b>border</b>.
  Between the content and the border you can have <b>padding</b>, and
  outside of the border you can have a <b>margin</b> to separate this box
  from any neighboring boxes.</p>
</body>
</html>
```

Using just one CSS rule you can see how each element involved with the body of the document — `<body>`, `<h2>`, `<p>`, `<img>`, and `<b>` — gets treated as if it were in a separate box. You can do this by adding a CSS rule that will add a border around each of these elements, you will learn more about these properties shortly (`ch07_eg21.css`).

```
body, h1, p, img, b {
   border-style:solid;
   border-width:2px;
   border-color:#000000;
   padding:2px;}
```

Each box can be presented differently, for example we can give the `<h1>` and `<bold>` elements a gray background to help distinguish them from other elements.

```
h1, b {background-color:#cccccc;}
```

Figure 7-27 shows you what this page looks like in a browser. While it is not too attractive, the lines show you the borders of the boxes (and demonstrate how boxes are created for each element).

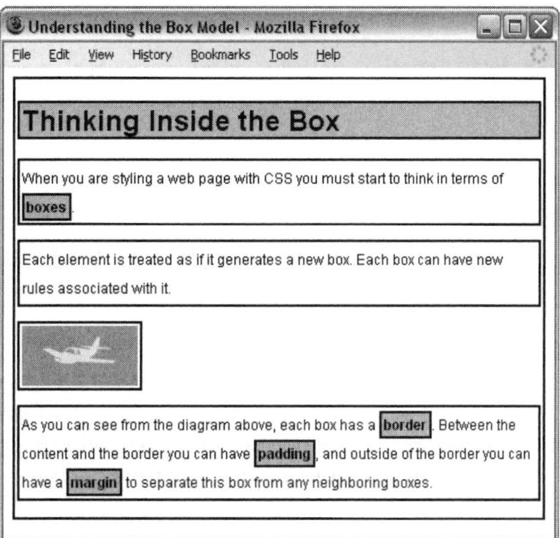

Figure 7-27

You may remember from Chapter 1 that there is a difference between *block level elements* and *inline elements*; the difference becomes quite important when working with CSS because it determines how each box is displayed.

- The `<h1>` and `<p>` elements are examples of block-level elements. Each block level element starts on a new line, and the box around a block level element takes up the full width of the browser (or the full width of the element it sits inside).
- The `<b>`element is an example of an inline element. Its box sits in the middle of the paragraph and it does not take up the width of a whole line (it *flows* within its containing element).

The `<img />` element may look like it is a block-level element because it starts on its own line, but it is actually an inline element. You can tell this because the border around it takes up only the width of the image; if it were a block-level element, the border would reach across the full width of the browser. The image is on its own line only because the elements on either side of it *are* block-level elements (and therefore the surrounding elements appear on their own lines).

In Strict XHTML, this image element should be placed inside a block-level element, as you are only supposed to have block-level elements as children of the `<body>` element. While it does not matter in Transitional XHTML, you could simply fix this issue by putting the element inside a `<div>` element (which you might remember is a block-level grouping element).

Now that you know how each element is treated as if it were in its own box, let's take a look at the properties that control the borders, margins, and padding for each box.

The Border Properties

The `border` properties allow you to specify how the border of the box representing an element should look. There are three properties of a border you can change:

- `border-color` to indicate the color a border should be
- `border-style` to indicate whether a border should be a solid, dashed, or double line, or one of the other possible values
- `border-width` to indicate the width a border should be

The border-color Property

The `border-color` property allows you to change the color of the border surrounding a box. For example:

```
p {border-color:#ff0000;}
```

The value can be a color name or a hex code for the color (colors are discussed in greater detail in Appendix D). It can also be expressed as values for red, green, and blue; between 0 and 255; or percentages of red, green, and blue. See the table that follows for examples.

Color Name	hex	RGB Values	RGB Percentages
`red`	`#ff0000`	`rgb(255,0,0)`	`rgb(100%,0,0)`
`green`	`#00ff00`	`rgb(0,255,0)`	`rgb(0,100%,0)`
`blue`	`#0000ff`	`rgb(0,0,255)`	`rgb(0,0,100%)`

You can individually change the color of the bottom, left, top, and right sides of a box's border using the following properties:

- `border-bottom-color`
- `border-right-color`
- `border-top-color`
- `border-left-color`

The border-style Property

The `border-style` property allows you to specify the line style of the border:

```
p {border-style:solid;}
```

The default value for this property is `none`, so no border would be shown automatically. The table that follows shows the possible values.

Value	Description
`none`	No border. (Equivalent of `border-width:0;`)
`solid`	Border is a single solid line.
`dotted`	Border is a series of dots.
`dashed`	Border is a series of short lines.
`double`	Border is two solid lines; the value of the `border-width` property creates the sum of the two lines and the space between them.
`groove`	Border looks as though it is carved into the page.
`ridge`	Border looks the opposite of `groove`.
`inset`	Border makes the box look like it is embedded in the page.
`outset`	Border makes the box look like it is coming out of the canvas.
`hidden`	Same as `none`, except in terms of border-conflict resolution for table elements.

Figure 7-28 shows an example of what each of these would look like (taken from `ch07_eg22.html`). Note that even though the last four examples in Figure 7-27 look very similar, they are different, and you can try them for yourself with the download code for this example.

You can individually change the style of the bottom, left, top, and right borders of a box using the following properties:

- `border-bottom-style`
- `border-right-style`
- `border-top-style`
- `border-left-style`

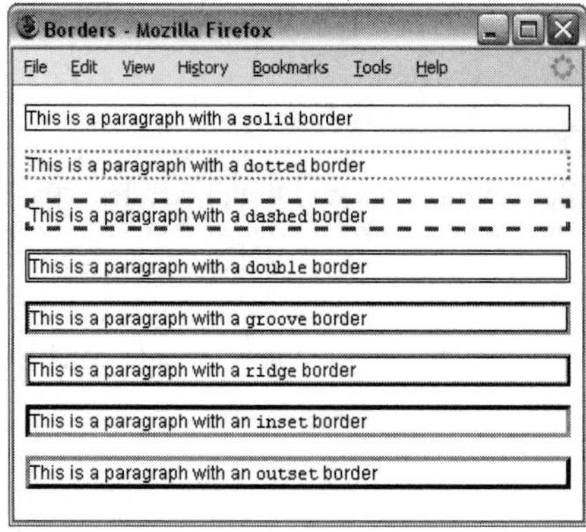

Figure 7-28

The border-width Property

The `border-width` property allows you to set the width of your borders; usually the width is specified in pixels.

```
p {border-style:solid;}
   border-width:4px;}
```

The value of the `border-width` property cannot be given as a percentage, although you could use any absolute unit or relative unit, or one of the following values:

- `thin`
- `medium`
- `thick`

The actual width of the `thin`, `medium`, and `thick` values are not specified in the CSS recommendation in terms of pixels; so the actual width that corresponds to these keywords is dependent on the browser.

You can individually change the width of the bottom, top, left, and right borders of a box using the following properties:

- `border-bottom-width`
- `border-right-width`
- `border-top-width`
- `border-left-width`

Expressing Border Properties Using Shorthand

The `border` property allows you to specify color, style, and width of lines in one property:

```
p {border: 4px solid red;}
```

If you use this shorthand, the values should not have anything (other than a space) between them. You can also specify the color, style, and width of lines individually for each side of the box in the same way using these properties:

- `border-bottom`
- `border-top`
- `border-left`
- `border-right`

The padding Property

The `padding` property allows you to specify how much space should appear between the content of an element and its border:

```
td {padding:5px;}
```

The value of this property is most often specified in pixels, although it can use any of the units of length we met earlier, a percentage, or the word `inherit`.

The padding of an element will not inherit by default, so if the `<body>` element has a padding property with a value of 50 pixels, this will not automatically apply to all other elements inside it. If the value `inherit` is applied to any elements, only then will they have the same padding as their parent elements.

If a percentage is used, the percentage is of the containing box, and if the value of 10 percent is specified, there would be 5 percent of each side of the box as padding.

You can specify different amounts of padding inside each side of a box using the following properties:

- `padding-bottom`
- `padding-top`
- `padding-left`
- `padding-right`

The `padding` attribute is especially helpful in creating white space between the content of an element and any border it has. Take a look at the following two paragraphs in Figure 7-29.

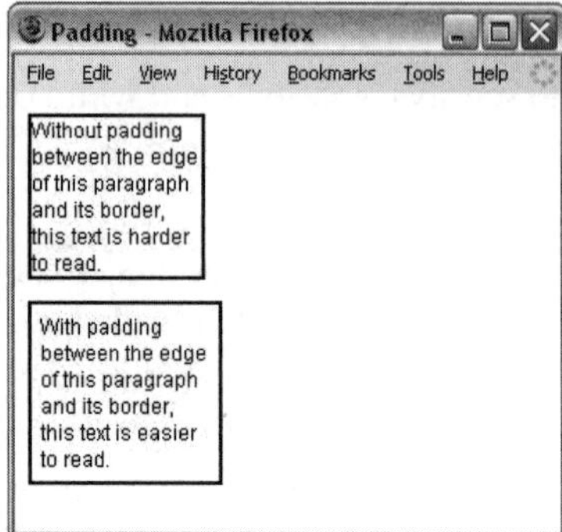

Figure 7-29

If you look at the CSS rules for these two paragraph elements, you can see that by default the first paragraph has no padding; it must be specified if you want a gap like the one shown in the second paragraph (`ch07_eg23.css`).

```
.a, .b {border-style:solid;
  border-color:#000000;
  border-width:2px;
  width:100px;}
.b {padding:5px;}
```

Sometimes an element may not have a visible border, but it will have a background color or pattern; in such cases giving the box some padding will help make your design more attractive.

The margin Property

The `margin` property controls the gap between boxes, and its value is either a length, a percentage, or `inherit`, each of which has exactly the same meaning as it did for the `padding` property you just saw.

```
p {margin:20px;}
```

As with the `padding` property, the values of the `margin` property are not inherited by child elements unless you use the value `inherit`.

Also, remember that when one box sits on top of another box, only the larger of the two margins will show (or if both are equal the size of one margin).

You can also set different values for the margin on each side of the box using the following properties:

- `margin-bottom`
- `margin-top`
- `margin-left`
- `margin-right`

If you look at the following example (see Figure 7-30, which shows `ch07_eg24.html`), you can see three paragraphs, which look as if they are spaced equally. However, they have taller margins on the top than the bottom, and therefore where two boxes meet, the bottom margin is ignored: the margins are *collapsed* (note that this only happens to the vertical margins, not the left and right margins).

The example also shows how to set the left and right margins on the side of inline elements—where you see the highlighted words. Again, this is not the most attractive example, but it illustrates how both block and inline boxes use margins.

The words in the paragraphs that are emphasized using the `<em>` element have `margin-left` and `margin-right` properties set. Because these `<em>` elements also have a background color set, you can really see (in Figure 7-30) how the margins to the left and the right separate the words from the surrounding words.

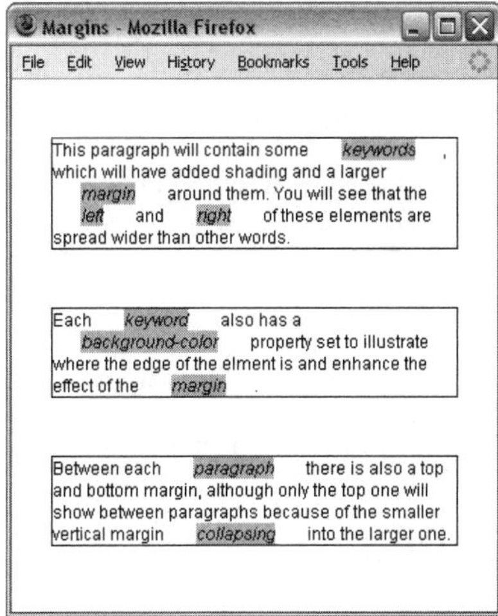

Figure 7-30

Here are the rules from `ch07_eg24.css`:

```
body {
   color:#000000;
   background-color:#ffffff;
   font-family:arial, verdana, sans-serif;
   font-size:12px;}
p {
   margin-top:40px;
   margin-bottom:30px;
   margin-left:20px;
   margin-right:20px;
   border-style:solid;
```

```
    border-width:1px;
    border-color:#000000;}
em {
    background-color:#cccccc;
    margin-left:20px;
    margin-right:20px;}
```

Dimensions of a Box

Now that you've seen the border that surrounds every box, the padding that can appear inside the border of each box, and the margin that can go outside the border, it is time to look at the properties that allow you to control the dimensions of boxes.

Property	Purpose
`height`	Sets the height of a box
`width`	Sets the width of a box
`line-height`	Sets the height of a line of text (like leading in a layout program)
`max-height`	Sets the maximum height for a box
`min-height`	Sets the minimum height for a box
`max-width`	Sets the maximum width for a box
`min-width`	Sets the minimum width for a box

The height and width Properties

The `height` and `width` properties allow you to set the height and width for boxes. They can take values of a length, a percentage, or the keyword `auto` (the default value being `auto`, which means the box is just large enough to house its contents).

Here you can see the CSS rules for two paragraph elements, the first with a `class` attribute whose value is `one` and the second whose `class` attribute has a value of `two` (`ch07_eg25.css`):

```
p.one {
  width:200px; height:100px;
  padding:5px; margin:10px;
  border-style:solid; border-color:#000000; border-width:2px;}
p.two {
  width:300px; height:100px;
  padding:5px; margin:10px;
  border-style:solid; border-color:#000000; border-width:2px;}
```

As you can see in Figure 7-31, the first paragraph will be 200 pixels wide and 100 pixels high, while the second paragraph will be 300 pixels wide and 100 pixels high.

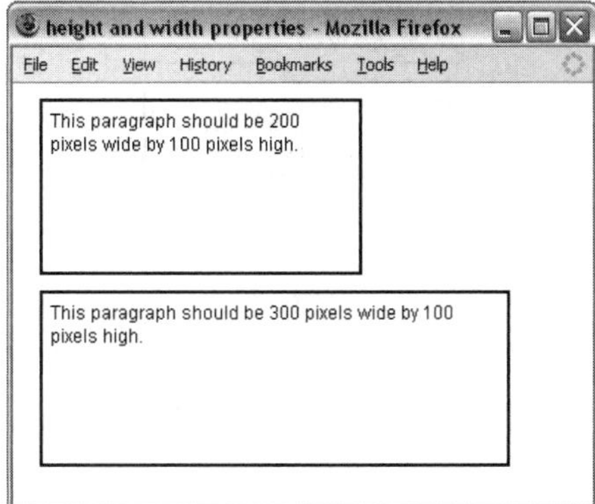

Figure 7-31

The most common unit of measurement for boxes is pixels, although percentages and ems are often used in layouts that stretch and contract to fit the size of the browser window.

The line-height Property

The `line-height` property is one of the most important properties when laying out text. It allows you to increase the space between lines of text (known to print designers as *leading*).

The value of the `line-height` property can be a length or a percentage. It is a good idea to specify this property in the same measurement in which you specify the size of your text.

Here you can see two rules setting different `line-height` properties (`ch07_eg26.css`):

```
p.two {
  line-height:16px;}
p.three {
  line-height:28px;}
```

As you can see in Figure 7-32, the first paragraph does not have a `line-height` attribute, whereas the second and third paragraphs correspond to the preceding rules. Adding some extra height between each line of text can often make it more readable, especially in longer articles.

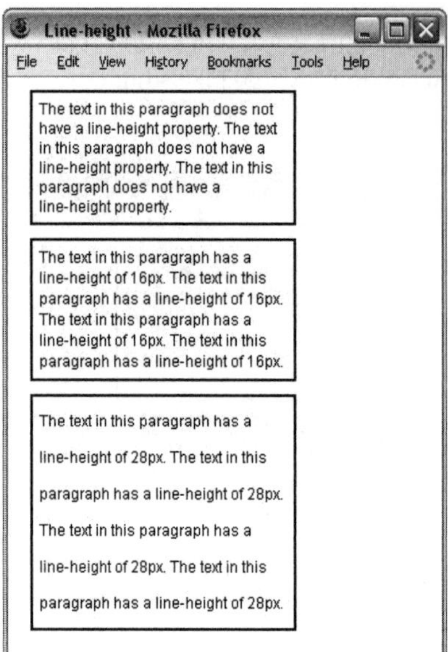

Figure 7-32

In long paragraphs I try to use leading of around 1.5 times the height of the font. This property can also be helpful when you need to add spacing around single lines of text.

The max-width and min-width Properties

The `max-width` and `min-width` properties allow you to specify a maximum and a minimum width for a box. This should be particularly useful if you want to create parts of pages that stretch and shrink to fit the size of users' screens. The `max-width` property will stop a box from being so wide that it is hard to read (lines that are too long are harder to read on screens), and `min-width` will help prevent boxes from being so narrow that they are unreadable. It is important to note, however, that IE7 and FF2 were the first of the major browsers to support these properties.

The value of these properties can be a number, a length, or a percentage, and negative values are not allowed. For example, take a look at the following rule, which specifies that a `<div>` element may not be less than 200 pixels wide and no wider than 500 pixels wide (`ch07_eg27.css`):

```
div {min-width:200px;
   max-width:500px;
   padding:5px;
   border:1px solid #000000;}
```

You can see what this looks like in Figure 7-33, which shows two browser windows, and you can try it for yourself using `ch07_eg27.html` in the code download. The first window is opened to over 500 pixels wide, and the box does not stretch wider than 500 pixels; the second window is closed to less than 200 pixels, at which point the browser starts to show a horizontal scrollbar because you cannot see the full width of the box.

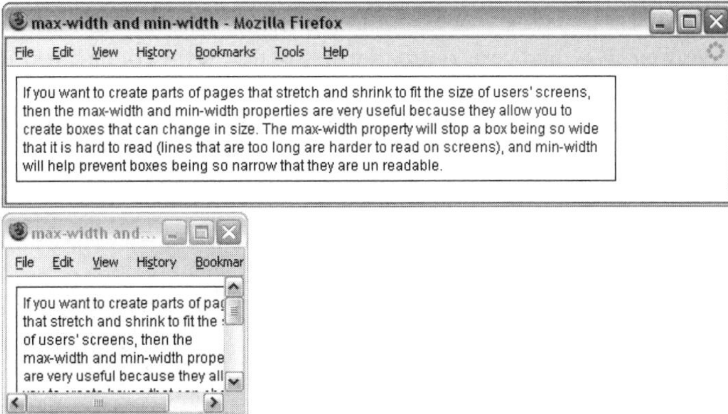

Figure 7-33

The min-height and max-height Properties

The `min-height` and `max-height` properties correspond with the `min-width` and `max-width` properties, but specify a minimum height and maximum height for the box. Again, it is important to note that IE7 and Firefox 2 were the first major browsers to support these properties.

The value of these properties can be a number, a length, or a percentage, and negative values are not allowed. Take a look at the following example (`ch07_eg28.css`):

```
div {min-height:50px;
   max-height:200px;
   padding:5px;
   border:1px solid #000000;}
```

Again, these properties are very useful in creating layouts that can be resized depending upon the size of the user's browser window. However, you can see an interesting phenomenon in Figure 7-34: If the content of the box takes up more space than the box is allowed because of these rules, the content can overflow out of the box (you will learn how to deal with this in the next section).

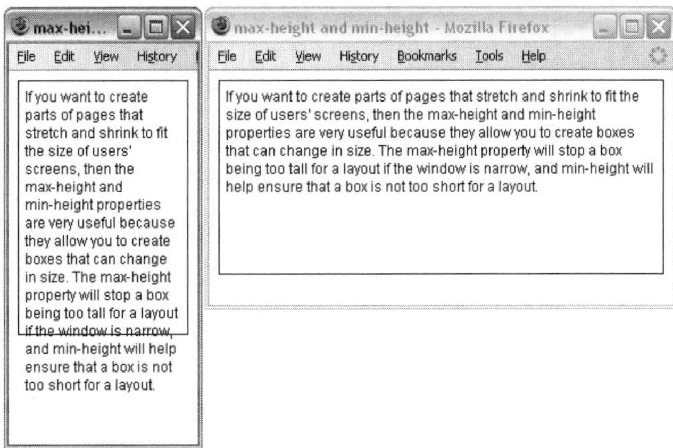

Figure 7-34

The overflow Property

As you just saw in Figure 7-34, when you control the size of a box, the content you want to fit in the box might require more space than you have allowed for it. This not only happens with the `min-height` and `max-height` or `min-width` and `max-width` properties, but also for a number of other reasons.

The `overflow` property was designed to deal with these situations and can take one of the values shown in the table that follows.

Value	Purpose
`hidden`	The overflowing content is hidden.
`scroll`	The box is given scrollbars to allow users to scroll to see the content.

Take a look at the following example, where the width of two `<div>` elements has been controlled by the `max-height` and `max-width` properties so that the content of the `<div>` elements does not fit in the box. For the first element, I have set the `overflow` property to have a value of `hidden` and the second to have a value of `scroll` (`ch07_eg29.css`).

```
div {max-height:75px;
   max-width:250px;
   padding:5px;
   margin:10px;
   border:1px solid #000000;}
div.one {overflow:hidden;}
div.two {overflow:scroll;}
```

Now take a look at Figure 7-35, which shows `ch07_eg29.html`. You can see the effect of these two properties — in the first box the text is simply cut off when it runs out of space, and in the second box a scrollbar is created allowing users to scroll to the appropriate content.

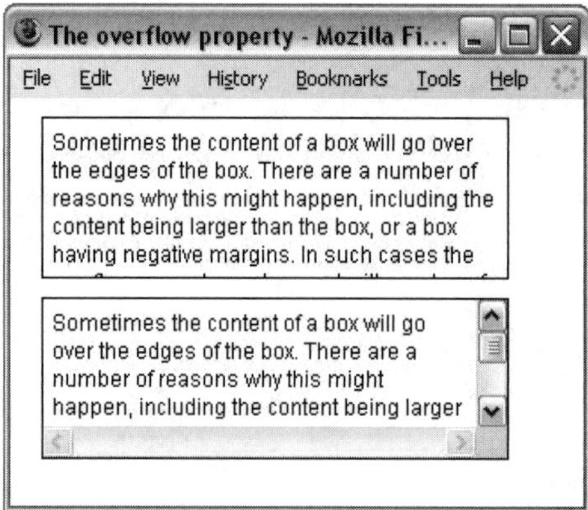

Figure 7-35

Internet Explorer Box Model Bug

When you come to build sites using CSS you will probably come across a well-documented bug in the Internet Explorer Box Model that affects the width of boxes.

IE treated the width of a box as though it included the width of any border it had been given *and* the width of the padding in the size of the box. However, the CSS specification says that the width of a box should only be the width of the content (not including the border or padding). You can see this in Figure 7-36:

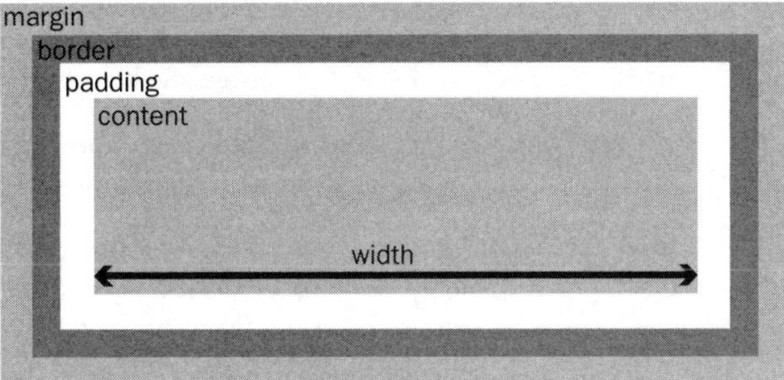

IE Box Model

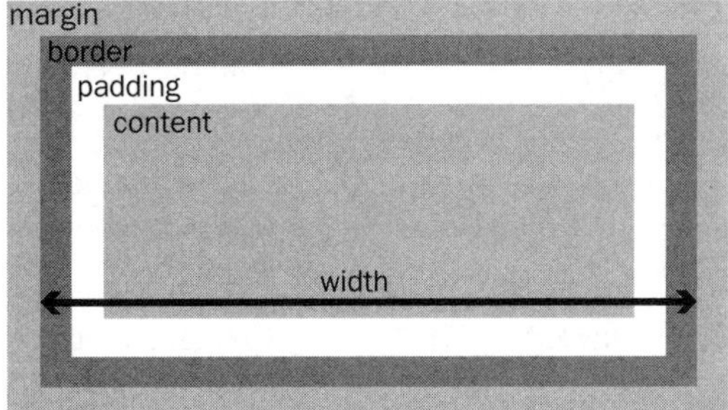

Figure 7-36

IE6 resolved this problem because it was able to run in two "modes":

- Standards-compliant mode follows the CSS specification. You can make sure IE6 or above is running in standards-compliant mode by including one of the `!DOCTYPE` declarations that you met in Chapter 1.
- Quirks mode retains the bug, and IE6 or above will run in Quirks mode when there is no `!DOCTYPE` declaration.

Try It Out A Style Sheet for Code

I often find the need to display code online. So I wrote the following style sheet to enable me to define styles very similar to those you see in this book, for showing code on the Web. As you will see in the next chapter, this code can then be included in other style sheets when needed, which means it is a reusable style sheet.

The style sheet features several styles for block and inline elements. The table that follows shows the styles you will be creating.

Style Name	Inline or Block	Use
`codeInText`	Inline	For a bit of code written in the middle of a sentence, shown in a monospace font
`codeForeground`	Block	Highlighted code in a monospace font for showing examples
`codeBackground`	Block	Like `codeForeground`, but not highlighted because it has been seen before, or is not the key point of the example
`keystroke`	Inline	Keys a user should enter on the keyboard, distinguishable because it is italic
`importantWords`	Inline	The first use of a key term; helps users scan the document because it appears in a bold font
`boxText`	Block	Creates a block of important or key notes that is in a box and has background shading
`background`	Block	Creates a block of italic text that has an aside or interesting note

1. The first thing to do is create class selectors for each of these styles. Element names are not used for several of the styles here because the styles could apply to different elements (for example, box text could be in a `<p>` element or a `<div>` grouping other elements). The selectors that do use elements are the ones representing code.

```
code.codeInText{}
code.codeForeground {}
code.codeBackground {}
.keystroke {}
.importantWords {}
.boxText {}
.background {}
```

2. Now it's time to start adding declarations to each selector inside the curly brackets. First is the `codeInText` style for words that appear in the middle of a sentence or paragraph that represent code. In the same tradition as most written matter on programming, the code will be displayed in a monospaced font. The first choice of typeface — specified using the `font-family` property — is Courier, failing which the browser should try to find Courier New, and if it cannot find that typeface, it will use its default monospaced font (although most computers do have Courier or Courier New installed).

   To make the code easier to read, this font will appear in bold text, as indicated using the `font-weight` property.

```
.codeInText {font-family:courier, "courier new", monospace;
  font-weight:bold;}
```

3. The second style is the `codeForeground` style. This style uses the same type of font as the `codeInText` style.

   Here are a few things to take note of:

   - The `codeForeground` style should always be displayed as a block-level element, but just in case the class is incorrectly used with an inline element, the `display` property is used with a value of `block` to ensure that it is displayed as a block (you will see more of this property in Chapter 8).
   - You will also see that the `letter-spacing` property has been used with a negative value because monospace fonts tend to take up quite a bit of width on the page. So, to help get as many characters as possible on the same line, it is given a value of –0.1 of an em (or 10 percent of a font's height).
   - All lengths in the style sheet are specified in ems so that they relate to the default size of the text in the document. If some of these elements were given in absolute sizes, they might have suddenly appeared a lot smaller or larger than the surrounding text.
   - The background color of the `codeForeground` style is gray. This helps the code stand out and makes it more readable. A one and a half em-sized padding has been added inside the box so that the text does not go right to the edge of the background color — this also makes the code easier to read.
   - The margin ensures that the box does not touch any other boxes or paragraphs. It has a smaller margin on the bottom than the top, as do all of the styles in this style sheet that use the margin property.

```
.codeForeground {
  font-family:courier, "courier new", monosapce; font-weight:bold;
  letter-spacing:-0.1em;
  display:block;
  background-color:#cccccc;
  padding:0.5em;
  margin-bottom:1em; margin-top:1.5em;}
```

4. The `codeBackground` style is identical to the `codeForeground` style except that the `background-color` is white.

```
.codeBackground {
  font-family:courier, "courier new", monosapce; font-weight:bold;
  letter-spacing:-0.1em;
  display:block;
  background-color:#ffffff;
  padding:0.5em;
  margin-bottom:1em; margin-top:1em;}
```

5. The `keystroke` style is in a Times typeface, or Times New Roman if Times is not available; otherwise, the default serif typeface for the browser is used. The `keystroke` style should also be italicized as follows:

```
.keyStroke {
  font-family:times, "Times New Roman", serif;
  font-style:italic;}
```

6. The `importantWords` style is simply bold:

```
.importantWords {font-weight:bold; }
```

7. The `boxText` style has a bold font with a very light gray background; what really differentiates it is that it has a border. As with the `codeForeground` style, `boxText` has some padding so that the text does not reach the border — making it easier to read — and it has a margin to inset it from the left and right as well as vertically to separate it from other elements. Note that the bottom margin is slightly smaller than the top margin.

```
.boxText {
  font-weight:bold;
  background-color:#efefef;
  width:90%;
  padding:1em;
  margin-left:3em; margin-right:3em; margin-bottom:1em; margin-top:1.5em;
  border-style:solid; border-width:1px; border-color:#000000;}
```

8. The final style is the `background` style. This style is italic and has the same amount of padding and margins as the `boxText` style.

```
.background {
  font-style:italic;
  width:90%;
  padding:1em;
  margin-left:3em; margin-right:3em; margin-bottom:1em; margin-top:1em;}
```

9. For this example, I also included a rule for the `<p>` element and a rule for the `<body>` element (although they are not part of the standard CSS I use for code styles):

```
body {
   color:#000000;
   background-color:#ffffff;
   font-family:arial, verdana, sans-serif;
   font-size:12px;}
p {margin-bottom:1em; margin-top:1.5em;}
```

10. Save this file as `codeStyles.css`. Then take a look at the following XHTML file, which makes use of this style sheet. As you can see, the `<link />` element indicates that this is the style sheet to be used for this example. You can then see the elements with the `class` attributes that relate to these styles:

```
<?xml version="1.0" ?>
<!DOCTYPE html PUBLIC "-//W3C//DTD XHTML 1.0 Transitional//EN"
    "http://www.w3.org/TR/xhtml1/DTD/xhtml1-transitional.dtd">
<html xmlns="http://www.w3.org/1999/xhtml" lang="en">
<head>
  <title>CSS Example</title>
  <link rel="stylesheet" type="text/css" href="codeStyles.css" />
</head>
<body>
<p>You are about to see some <code class="codeInText">codeInText</code>
followed by some <span class="importantWords">importantWords</span>, and the
font for a <span class="keystroke">keystroke</span>.</p>
<p>Next you will see some foreground code:</p>
<code class="codeForeground">p {font-family:arial, sans-serif;
font-weight:bold;}</code>
<p>Next you will see some background code:</p>
<code class="codeBackground">p {font-family:arial, sans-serif;
font-weight:bold;}</code>
<p class="boxText">This is some boxed text for important statements.</p>
<p class="background">Here is a background comment or aside.</p>
</body>
</html>
```

If you look at this example in the browser, it should look like the screenshot in Figure 7-37.

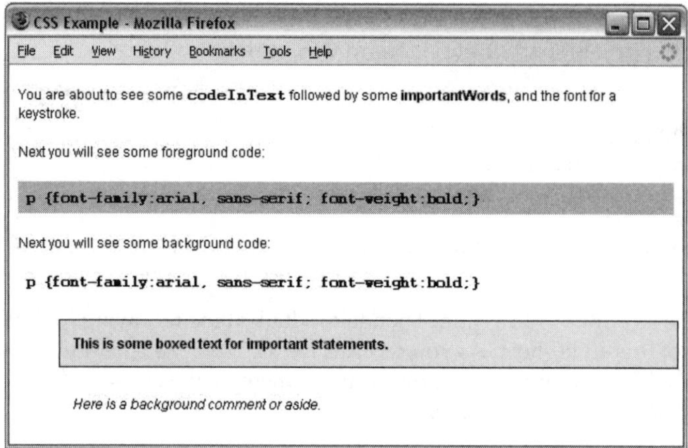

Figure 7-37

Summary

In this chapter, you learned how to write a CSS style sheet. You have seen that a CSS style sheet is made up of rules that first select the element or elements to which the rules will apply and then contain property-value pairs that specify how the element's content should appear.

You have learned how you can change the appearance of fonts and text.

You now know that CSS manages to render a document by treating each element as if it were a separate box and then using the properties to control how each box should appear, and you have learned how to set the dimensions and borders, padding, and margins for each box.

In the next chapter, you not only learn some more properties, you also see how you can use CSS to position elements on a page, which will enable you to create attractive layouts for pages. You even see how you can insert content from a style sheet into a document, deal with bulleted lists, create counters, and more.

Exercises

1. In the exercises for this chapter, you are going to continue to work on the Example Café web site:

   a. First, open the index.html page and add a `<div>` element just inside the opening `<body>` tag and the closing `</body>` tag, and give the element an `id` attribute whose value is `page`. Repeat this for each page of the site.

   b. Now, in the style sheet add a rule that gives this element a margin, border, and padding so that it looks like the border in Figure 7-38.

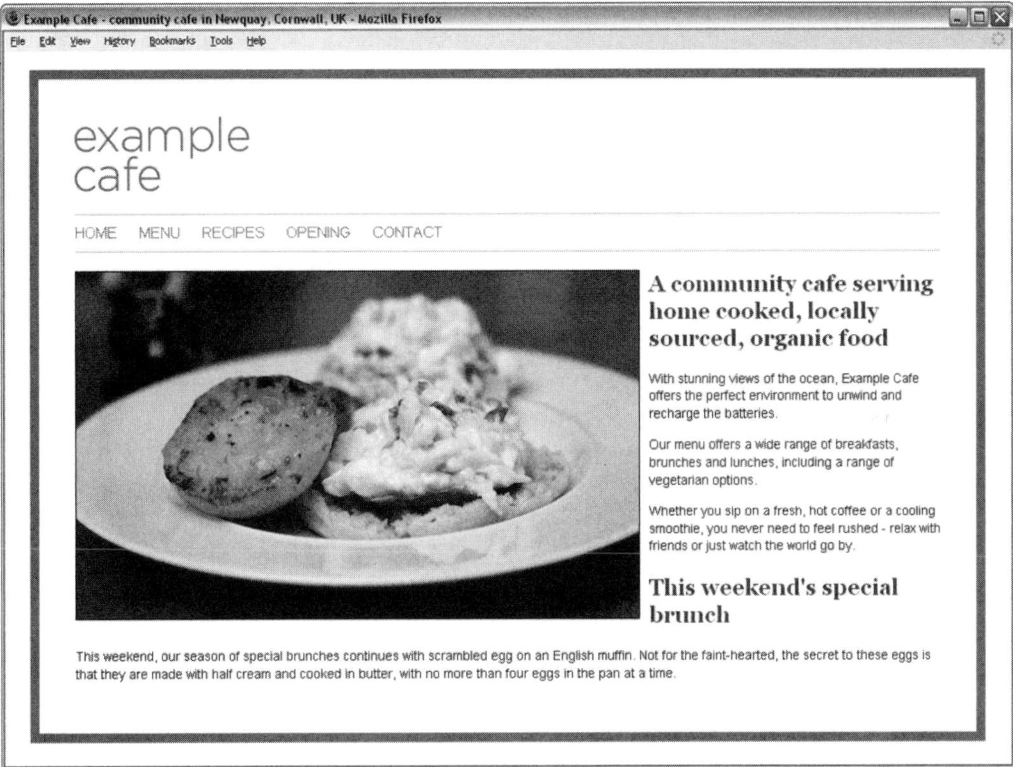

Figure 7-38

2. Create a CSS rule that will make the following changes to the navigation:
    a. Add a single pixel gray border on the top and bottom.
    b. Give it 20 pixels of margin above and below the gray lines.
    c. Give it 10 pixels of padding on the top and bottom in the box.
    d. Add a margin to the right of each link in the navigation.
3. Give the main image on the homepage a `class` attribute whose value is `main_image`, then create a rule that gives the image a single-pixel black border, and also give the image a 10-pixel margin on the right and bottom sides of the image.
4. Increase the gaps between each line of text to 1.3 em.

5. Take a look at the following XHTML page:

```
<?xml version="1.0" encoding="iso-8859-1"?>
<!DOCTYPE html PUBLIC "-//W3C//DTD XHTML 1.0 Transitional//EN"
    "http://www.w3.org/TR/xhtml1/DTD/xhtml1-transitional.dtd">
<html xmlns="http://www.w3.org/1999/xhtml" lang="en">
<head>
  <title>Font test</title>
  <link rel="stylesheet" type="text/css" href="tableStyles.css" />
</head>
<body>
<table>
  <tr>
    <th>Quantity</th>
    <th>Ingredient</th>
  </tr>
  <tr class="odd">
    <td>3</td>
    <td>Eggs</td>
  </tr>
  <tr>
    <td>100ml</td>
    <td>Milk</td>
  </tr>
  <tr class="odd">
    <td>200g</td>
    <td>Spinach</td>
   </tr>
   <tr>
     <td>1 pinch</td>
     <td>Cinnamon</td>
   </tr>
 </table>
</body>
</html>
```

Now create the `tableStyles.css` style sheet, which makes this example look like it does in Figure 7-39.

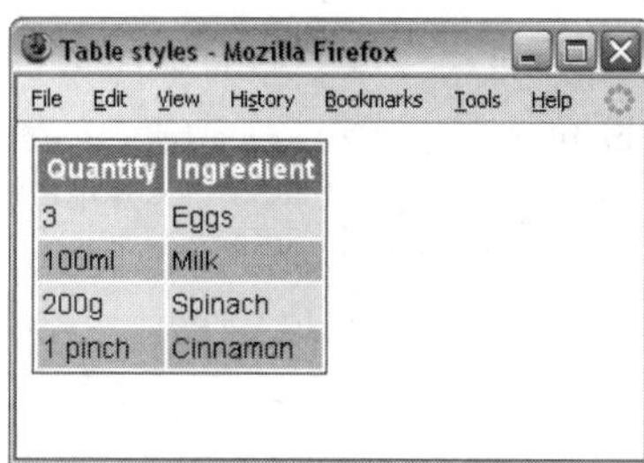

Figure 7-39

Don't worry about getting the sizes exactly the same as the screenshot, but do make sure you have padding in the cells and a border around the outside. The white border is created by default in IE; you will find out how to remove this in Chapter 8.

More Cascading Style Sheets

In this chapter, you will continue to learn how to use CSS to control presentation of XHTML web pages, starting with CSS properties that enable you to control presentation of links, backgrounds, list styles, table styles, and outlines around boxes. You will then learn a technique to add content to a page (even if it was not in the XHTML document) using the `:before` and `:after` pseudo-classes. Finally, you will see how CSS can be used to position boxes on the page, which will allow you to create attractive layouts for your pages.

By the end of the chapter, you will know how to use CSS to control the following:

- Presentation of links
- Backgrounds of document
- Styles of bullet points and numbered lists
- Appearance of tables
- Outlines around boxes
- Elements that can gain focus or are active
- Addition of content to the XHTML document before or after an element
- The three positioning schemes that allow you to determine where on a page a box will appear — something that prepares you to use CSS to create layouts

Occasionally in this chapter, you will come across a feature that is not yet implemented by the main browsers, but it is worth learning these now as they are likely to be used as standard in the near future.

Links

Most browsers show links in blue with an underline and change the color of links you have already visited, unless you tell them to do otherwise. The following are properties often used with links:

- `color`: Changes the colors of the links
- `background-color`: Highlights the link, as if it had been highlighted with a highlighter pen
- `text-decoration`: Commonly used to control whether the link is underlined or not, although it can also specify that text should have a strikethrough, blink, or be overlined

While you can just create rules that apply to the `<a>` element to set properties such as `color` and `text-decoration`, there are also four *pseudo-classes* that can give greater control over presentation of links.

Pseudo-class	Purpose
`link`	Styles for links in general
`visited`	Styles for links that have already been visited
`hover`	Styles for when someone is hovering over a link
`active`	Styles for links that are currently active (being clicked)

Using these pseudo-classes allows you to change properties of links when the user hovers over them (making them a slightly different color, maybe adding a highlight and underlining them), and also the properties of links that have been visited (for example, making them a slightly different color — which helps users know where they have been).

When used, these properties should be specified in the order listed in the table above. Here is an example that will change the styles of links as users interact with them (`ch08_eg01.css`):

```
body {background-color:#ffffff;}
a {
  font-family: arial, verdana, sans-serif;
  font-size:12px;
  font-weight:bold;}
a:link {
  color:#0000ff;
  text-decoration:none;}
a:visited {
  color:#333399;
  text-decoration:none;}
a:link:hover {
  background-color:#e9e9e9;
  text-decoration:underline;}
a:active {
  color:#0033ff;
  text-decoration:underline;}
```

Figure 8-1 gives you an idea of how links will look with this style sheet (`ch08_eg01.html`), although it is rather hard to see the full effect of this in print, with the links changing as the user rolls the mouse over links and visits the sites, so try the example out with the downloaded code for this chapter.

Figure 8-1

Backgrounds

As you saw in the last chapter, CSS treats each element as if it were its own box. You can control the background of these boxes using the following properties (when used on the `<body>` element they affect the entire browser window).

Property	Purpose
`background-color`	Specifies a background color
`background-image`	Specifies an image to use as the background
`background-repeat`	Indicates whether the background image should be repeated
`background-attachment`	Indicates a background image should be fixed in one position on the page, and whether it should stay in that position when the user scrolls down the page
`background-position`	Indicates where an image should be positioned
`background`	A shorthand form that allows you to specify all of these properties

The background-color Property

The `background-color` property allows you to specify a single solid color for the background of any element.

When the `background-color` property is set for the `<body>` element, it affects the whole document, and when it is used on any other element it will use the specified color inside the border of the box created for that element.

The value of this property can be a color name, a hex code, or an RGB value (colors are covered in greater depth in Appendix D). For example (`ch08_eg02.css`):

```
body {background-color:#cccccc; color:#000000;}
b {background-color:#FF0000; color:#FFFFFF;}
p {background-color: rgb(255,255,255);}
```

Figure 8-2 `ch08_eg02.html` used with the styles above from `ch08_eg02.css`:

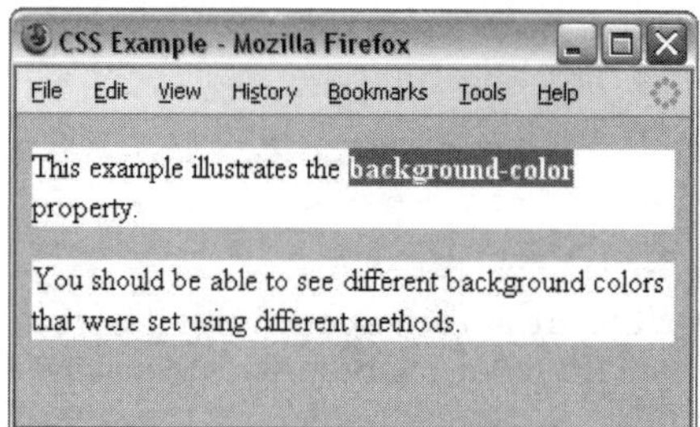

Figure 8-2

I add a rule for the `<body>` element to set the `background-color` property for every style sheet I write because some people set their computers to have a background other than plain white (often because it causes less strain on their eyes). When the background color of an operating system is changed, browsers usually use that color, too (along with applications such as word processors). If you do not specify this property, you cannot guarantee that the visitors to the site have the same background color as you want them to have.

The background-image Property

As its name suggests, the `background-image` property enables you to add an image to the background of any box in CSS. This can be very useful in many situations, from adding a subtle texture or shading to adding a distinctive design to the back of elements or entire pages.

The value for this property should start with the letters `url`, followed by the URL for the image in brackets and quotes like so:

```
body {background-image: url("images/background.gif");}
```

If both a `background-image` property and the `background-color` property are used, then the `background-image` property takes precedence. It is good practice to supply a `background-color` property with a background image and give it a value similar to the main color in the background image because the page will use this color while the background image is loading or if it cannot display the image for any reason.

Here is an example of using a single background image, which is 200 pixels wide and 150 pixels high. By default, this image is repeated all across the page (`ch08_eg03.css`). The `background-color` property is set to be the same color as the background of the image (just in case the image cannot be loaded):

```
body {
  background-image: url("images/background.gif");
  background-color: #cccccc;}
```

Figure 8-3 shows what this looks like in a browser (`ch08_eg03.html`).

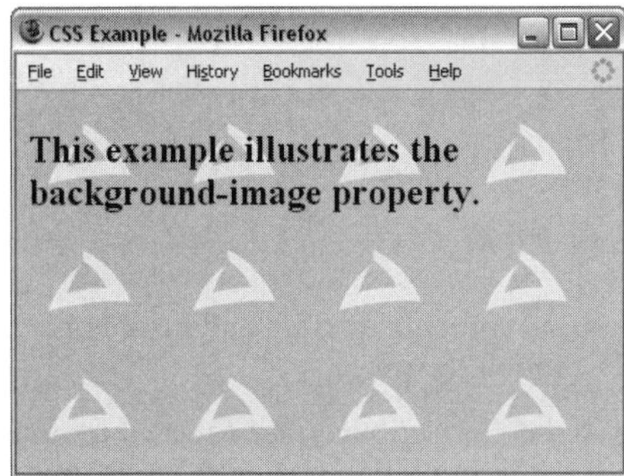

Figure 8-3

This is not a great example of how to use a background image because there is not enough contrast between the colors used in the background image and the text that appears on top of it, which makes the text harder to read. But it does illustrate the point that you must make sure that there is sufficient contrast between any background image and the writing that appears on top of it; otherwise, users will have trouble reading the text.

If you do use an image behind text, it is worth remembering that low-contrast images (images that are made up of similar colors) often make better backgrounds because it is harder to find a color that will be readable on top of a high-contrast image.

Figure 8-4 shows an improved example of the background image, where the text is on a solid color, which makes it easier to read. This time I have also used a larger image (`ch08_eg04.html`).

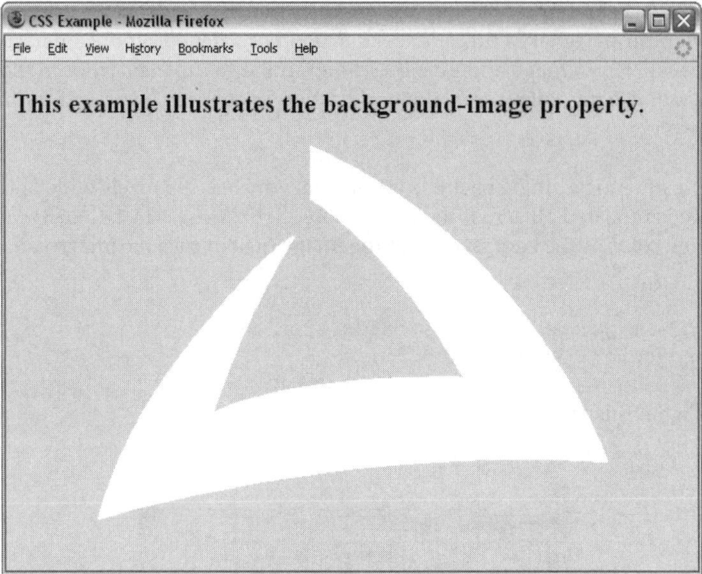

Figure 8-4

There are a few points to note about how background images work:

- There is no way to express the intended width and height of a background image, so you need to save it at the size you want it to appear.
- There is no equivalent to the `alt` attribute (alternate text for those not able to see the image for any reason); therefore, a background image should not be used to convey any important information that is not described on the page in text as well.
- Background images are often shown on the page after other items have been rendered, so it can look as if they take a long time to load.
- The `background-image` property works well with most block-level elements, although some older browsers can have problems showing background images in tables.

The background-repeat Property

When you specify a `background-image`, and the box is bigger than the image, then the image is repeated to fill up the whole box, creating what is affectionately known as *wallpaper*.

If you do not want your image to repeat all over the background of the box, you should use the `background-repeat` property, which has four helpful values, as you can see in the table that follows:

Value	Purpose
`repeat`	This causes the image to repeat to cover the whole page (it is the default therefore rarely used).
`repeat-x`	The image will be repeated horizontally across the page (not down the whole page vertically).
`repeat-y`	The image will be repeated vertically down the page (not across horizontally).
`no-repeat`	The image is displayed only once.

These different properties can have interesting effects. It is worth looking at each in turn. You have already seen the effect of the `repeat` value (as this is the default behavior when the property is not used. The value `repeat-x` creates a horizontal bar following the browser's x-axis (`ch08_eg05.css`):

```
body {
  background-image: url("images/background_small.gif");
  background-repeat: repeat-x; }
```

You can see the result of using this property in Figure 8-5.

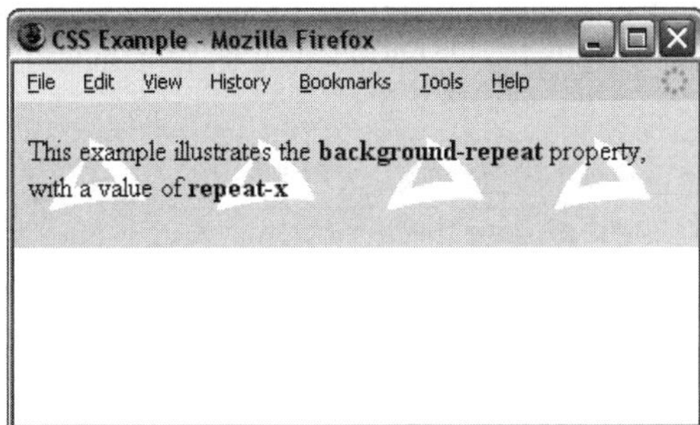

Figure 8-5

The `repeat-y` value works just like `repeat-x` but in the other direction, vertically following the browser's y-axis (`ch08_eg06.css`):

```
body {
  background-image: url("images/background_small.gif");
  background-repeat: repeat-y; }
```

In Figure 8-6, you can see the result with the sidebar coming down the left.

Figure 8-6

The final value was `no-repeat`, leaving one instance of the image that by default will be in the top-left corner of the browser window (`ch08_eg07.css`):

```
body {
  background-image: url("images/background_small.gif");
  background-repeat: no-repeat;
  background-color: #eaeaea;}
```

You can see the result in Figure 8-7; note how the background color of the page has been set to the same color as the image we have been using — this makes the image blend in with the page better.

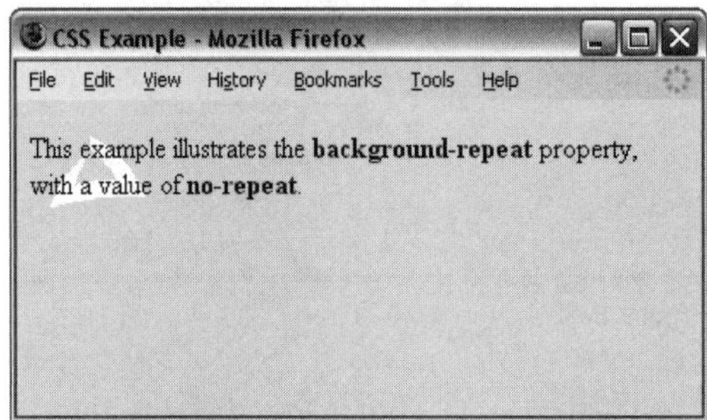

Figure 8-7

The background-position Property (for Fixing Position of Backgrounds)

You may want to alter the position of this image, and you can do this using the `background-position` property, which takes the values shown in the table that follows:

Value	Meaning
`x% y%`	Percentages along the *x* (horizontal) and *y* (vertical) axis
`x y`	Absolute lengths along the *x* (horizontal) and *y* (vertical) axis in pixels
`left`	Shown to the left of the page or containing element
`center`	Shown to the center of the page or containing element
`right`	Shown to the right of the page or containing element
`top`	Shown at the top of the page or containing element
`center`	Shown at the center of the page or containing element
`bottom`	Shown at the bottom of the page or containing element

Here is an example of fixing the position of the image as shown in Figure 8-8 (`ch08_eg08.css`):

```
body {
  background-image: url("images/background_small.gif");
  background-position: 50% 20%;
  background-repeat: no-repeat;
  background-color: #eaeaea; }
```

This image will be horizontally centered (because it should be 50 percent of the screen's width from the left-hand side of the page) and a fifth of the way down from the top of the screen (because it is positioned 20 percent of the window height from the top of the screen). It is worth trying this example in the code download and changing the size of the browser window to see how the background image will remain in the center of the browser window horizontally and a fifth of the way down the window vertically when you change the size of the window.

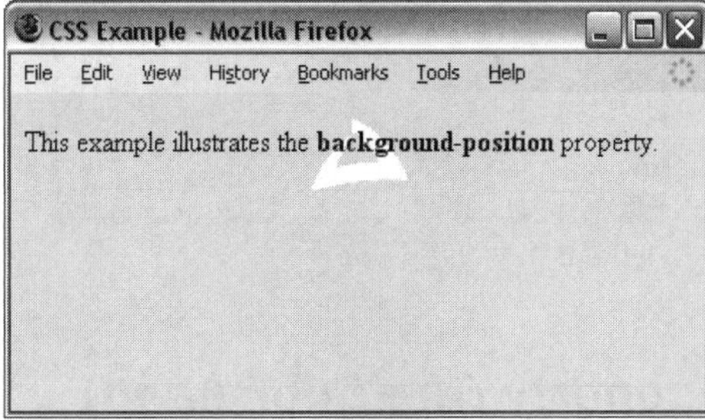

Figure 8-8

The background-attachment Property (for Watermarks)

When you specify a background image you can use the `background-attachment` property to specify whether the image is fixed in its position, or whether it moves as the user scrolls up and down the page.

Value	Purpose
`fixed`	The image will not move if the user scrolls up and down the page.
`scroll`	The image stays in the same place on the background of the page. If the user scrolls up or down the page, the image moves, too.

Here is an example where the image will stay in the middle of the page even when the user scrolls further down (`ch08_eg09.css`):

```
body {
  background-image: url("images/background_small.gif");
  background-attachment: fixed;
  background-position: center;
  background-repeat: no-repeat;
  background-color: #eaeaea; }
```

Figure 8-9 shows that the user has scrolled halfway down the page and the image is in the center of the browser window (the background looks exactly the same as it would have when the user was at the top of the page).

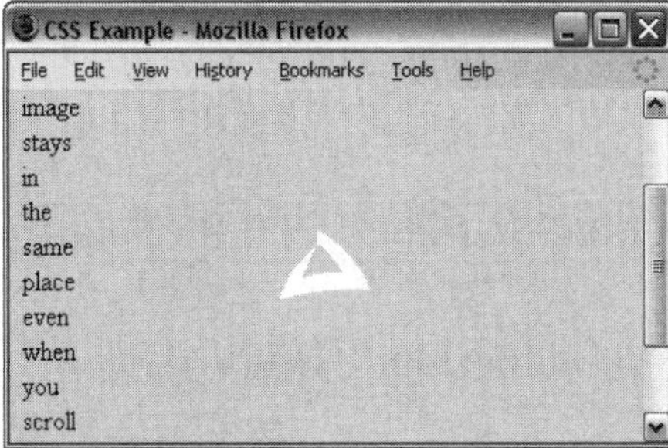

Figure 8-9

The background Property (the Shorthand)

The `background` property allows you to specify several of the background properties at once. The values can be given in any order, and if you do not supply one of the values, the default value will be used.

- `background-color`
- `background-image`

- background-repeat
- background-attachment
- background-position

For example, you can just write:

```
body {background: #cc66ff; url("images/background_small.gif") fixed
no-repeat center;}
```

This creates exactly the same effect as the example shown in Figure 8-9.

Lists

Back in Chapter 1, you learned how to use the `<ul>` and `<li>` elements to create lists with bullet points (also known as unordered lists) and the `<ol>` and `<li>` elements to create numbered (or ordered) lists. In this section you will learn about the CSS properties you can use to control lists.

Property	Purpose
`list-style-type`	Allows you to control the shape or appearance of the marker (the marker is another name for the bullet point or number).
`list-style-position`	When a list item takes up more than one line, this property specifies where the marker should appear in relation to the text.
`list-style-image`	Specifies an image for the marker rather than a bullet point or number.
`list-style`	Serves as shorthand for the preceding properties.
`marker-offset`	Specifies the distance between a marker and the text in the list.

The list-style-type Property

The `list-style-type` property allows you to control the shape or style of bullet point (also known as a *marker*) in the case of unordered lists and the style of numbering characters in ordered lists.

The table that follows shows the standard styles for an unordered list.

Value	Marker
`none`	None
`disc (default)`	A filled-in circle
`circle`	An empty circle
`square`	A filled-in square

The table that follows shows values for ordered lists that are supported in most browsers.

Value	Meaning	Example
`decimal`	Number	1, 2, 3, 4, 5
`decimal-leading-zero`	0 before the number	01, 02, 03, 04, 05
`lower-alpha`	Lowercase alphanumeric characters	a, b, c, d, e
`upper-alpha`	Uppercase alphanumeric characters	A, B, C, D, E
`lower-roman`	Lowercase Roman numerals	i, ii, iii, iv, v
`upper-roman`	Uppercase Roman numerals	I, II, III, IV, V

The `list-style-type` property can either be used on the `<ul>` and `<ol>` elements (in which case it applies to the entire list) or on the individual `<li>` elements. The following example demonstrates all these styles (`ch08_eg10.html`):

```
li.a {list-style-type:none;}
li.b {list-style-type:disc;}
li.c {list-style-type:circle;}
li.d {list-style-type:square;}
li.e {list-style-type:decimal;}
li.f {list-style-type:lower-alpha;}
li.g {list-style-type:upper-alpha;}
li.h {list-style-type:lower-roman;}
li.i {list-style-type:upper-roman;}
```

You can see the result with examples of each kind of bullet in Figure 8-10.

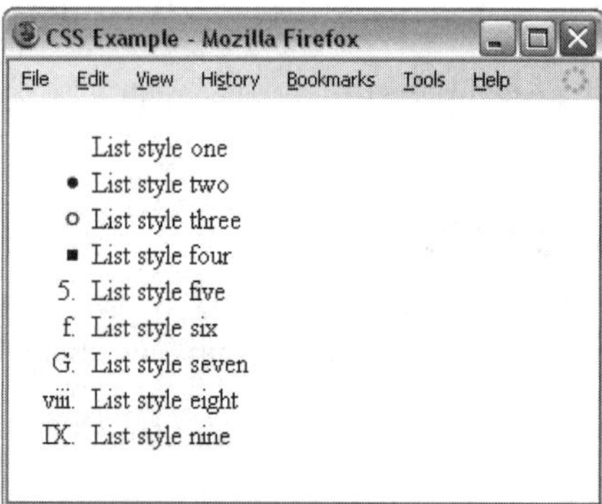

Figure 8-10

The list-style-position Property

Lists are indented into the page, and the `list-style-position` property indicates whether the marker should appear inside or outside of the box containing the main points. There are two values for this property, as you can see in the table that follows:

Value	Purpose
inside	The marker is inside the block of text (which is indented).
outside	The marker sits to the left of the block of text (this is the default value if this is not specified).

Here you can see how this property is written; in this case it is given on the <ul> or <ol> elements (ch08_eg11.css):

```
ul {list-style-position:outside;}
ol {list-style-position:inside;}
```

Figure 8-11 shows you what this would look like in a browser.

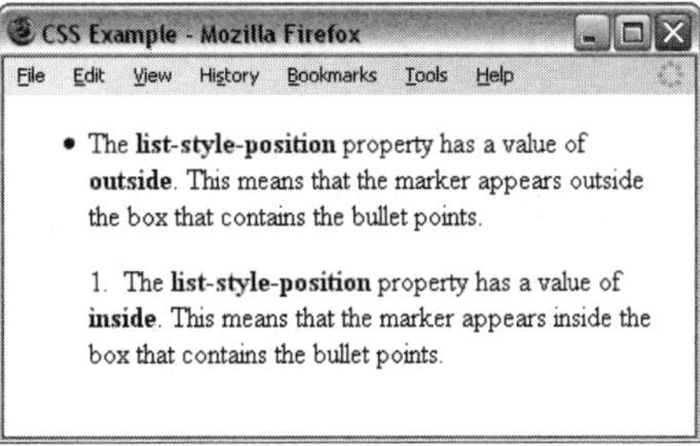

Figure 8-11

As you can see, the text is indented in both cases, and the value of this property indicates whether the marker is inside this box or outside of the box.

The list-style-image Property

The list-style-image property allows you to specify an image so that you can use your own bullet style. The syntax is similar to the background-image property; the value starts with the letters url and is followed by the URL for the image in brackets and quotation marks (ch08_eg12.css):

```
li {list-style-image: url("images/bulletpoint.gif");}
```

You can see an example of some triangular bullet points in Figure 8-12.

Figure 8-12

If the image cannot be displayed, the browser should just display a dot rather than a broken image symbol.

> *If you are using nested lists, this value will inherit from its parent element. To prevent this from happening, you can use the* `list-style-image` *property on the nested list and give it a value of* `none`.

The list-style Property (the Shorthand)

The `list-style` property is a way of expressing more than one of these properties at once. They can appear in any order. For example:

```
ul {list-style: inside circle;}
```

Remember that you can also set the `border`, `padding`, and `margin` properties for `<ul>`, `<ol>`, `<li>`, `<dl>`, `<dt>`, and `<dd>` elements, as each element has its own box in CSS.

Tables

In the last chapter, you saw a couple of examples that use CSS with tables. Properties that are commonly used with the `<table>`, `<td>`, and `<th>` elements include the following:

- `border` to set the properties of the border of a table.
- `padding` to set the amount of space between the border of a table cell and its content — this property is very important to make tables easier to read.
- Properties to change text and fonts.
- `text-align` to align writing to the left, right, or center of a cell.
- `vertical-align` to align writing to the top, middle, or bottom of a cell.
- `width` to set the width of a table or cell.
- `height` to set the height of a cell (often used on a row as well).
- `background-color` to change the background color of a table or cell.
- `background-image` to add an image to the background of a table or cell.

You should be aware that, apart from the `background-color` and `height` properties, it is best to avoid using these properties with `<tr>` elements, as browser support for these properties on rows is not as good as it is for individual cells.

To demonstrate how some of these properties are used with a table, take a look at the one shown in Figure 8-13; it might look familiar because you saw it at the beginning of the last chapter, but this time it has an added `<caption>` element (`ch08_13.html`).

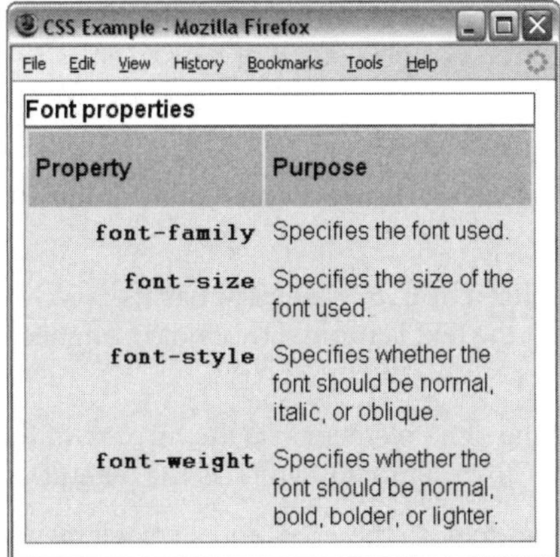

Figure 8-13

Now take a look at the style sheet for this table (ch08_eg13.css):

```
body {color:#000000; background-color:#ffffff;}
h1 {font-size:18pt;}
p {font-size:12pt;}
table {
   background-color:#efefef;
   width:350px;
   border-style:solid;
   border-width:1px;
   border-color:#999999;
   font-family:arial, verdana, sans-serif;}
caption {
  font-weight:bold;
  text-align:left;
  border-style:solid; border-width:1px; border-color:#666666;
  color:#666666;}
th {
  height:50px;
  font-weight:bold;
  text-align:left;
  background-color:#cccccc;}
td, th {padding:5px;}
td.code {
   width:150px;
   font-family:courier, courier-new, serif;
   font-weight:bold;
   text-align:right;
   vertical-align:top;}
```

Here are some key points to note about this example. You will be altering settings of some of these properties using new properties that you will meet throughout this section.

- The rule for the `<table>` element uses a `width` property to fix the width of the table to 350 pixels; otherwise, it would take up as much of the screen as needed to show as much text as possible on one line.
- The rule for the `<table>` element also has a `border` property set, which creates a single-pixel border all around the table. Note, however, that none of the other cells in the table inherits this property.
- The rule that applies to the `<caption>` element has its `font-weight`, `border`, and `text-align` properties set. By default the text is normal (not bold), aligned in the center, and without a border.
- The rule that applies to the `<th>` element sets the `height` of the headings to 50 pixels, and the text is aligned left (rather than centered, which is the default).
- There is a rule that applies to both the `<th>` and `<td>` elements, and this indicates that both should have a padding property set to `5px` so that the content of the cells does not touch the border of those cells. Creating space around the cells is very important and makes the table more readable.
- The final rule states that the `<td>` elements whose `class` attribute has a value of `code` are given a `width` property whose value is `150px` (150 pixels). This ensures that the content of this whole column remains on one line. Unfortunately, there is no way to assign a style to a column, but in the case of the `width` property, once it has been set on one element it does not need to be set on all the others in the column.

You may also have noticed in Figure 8-13 that there is a white line around the two columns (which is particularly noticeable around table header cells). Browsers automatically add this to separate each cell from its neighbor. You can, however, remove this gap using a property called `border-spacing`, which you'll learn about in the next section.

Table-Specific Properties

In the following section you will meet five properties that can only be used with tables, and also some values for the `border-style` property that only apply to tables. Most of these properties were first supported in IE7 and FF2.

Property	Purpose
`border-collapse`	Where the borders of two table cells touch, this property indicates whether *both* borders should be visible, or whether the browser should pick just one of the borders to show.
`border-spacing`	Specifies the width of the space that should appear between table cells.
`caption-side`	Specifies which side of a table the caption should appear on.
`empty-cells`	Specifies whether the border should be shown if a cell is empty.
`table-layout`	If the space you have allocated for a table is not enough to fit the contents, browsers will often increase the size of the table to fit the content in — this property can force a table to use the dimensions you specify.

The border-collapse Property

Where two table cells meet, you can tell the browser to show just one of the borders (rather than both — which is the default behavior). You can do this using the `border-collapse` property, which can take two values:

Value	Purpose
`collapse`	Horizontal borders will be collapsed and vertical borders will abut one another.
`separate`	Separate rules are observed. This value opens up additional properties to give you further control.

If two adjacent table cells have different border styles, and you have specified that borders should be collapsed, there is a complex set of rules to specify which border should be shown — rather than try to learn these rules it is quicker to simply try your table out in a browser.

To illustrate how the `border-collapse` property works, the following style rules apply to two tables: the first has a `border-collapse` property with a value of `collapse`, the second has a value of `separate`, and both tables contain adjacent cells with dotted and solid lines (`ch08_eg14.css`):

```
table.one {border-collapse:collapse;}
table.two {border-collapse:separate;}
td.a {border-style:dotted; border-width:3px; border-color:#000000;
  padding:10px;}
td.b {border-style:solid; border-width:3px; border-color:#333333;
  padding:10px;}
```

Figure 8-14 shows you how, with a value of `collapse`, the browser collapses borders into each other so that the solid border takes precedence over the dotted border. This wouldn't look as odd if the borders were both solid, but it does illustrate the point well.

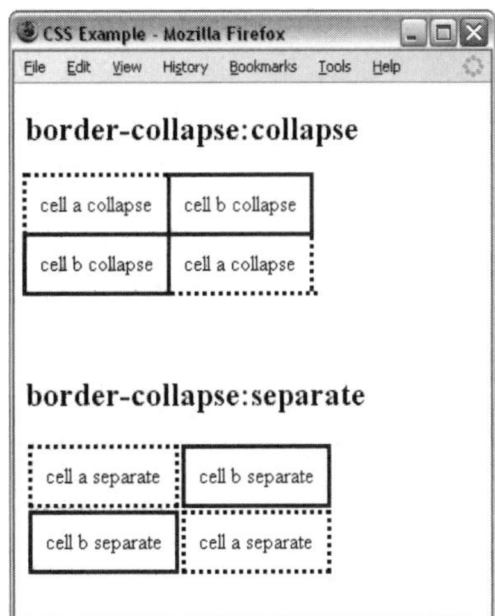

Figure 8-14

If you do not specify that the borders should be collapsed, then two further properties control border presentation:

- `border-spacing`
- `empty-cells`

The following sections discuss these properties.

The border-spacing Property

The `border-spacing` property specifies the distance that separates adjacent cells' borders. If you provide one value, it will apply to both vertical and horizontal borders:

```
table.one {border-spacing:15px;}
```

Or you can specify two values, in which case the first refers to the horizontal spacing and the second to the vertical spacing:

```
table.two {border-spacing:2px 4px;}
```

You can see what this looks like in Figure 8-15 (`ch08_eg15.html` styled with `ch08_eg15.css`):

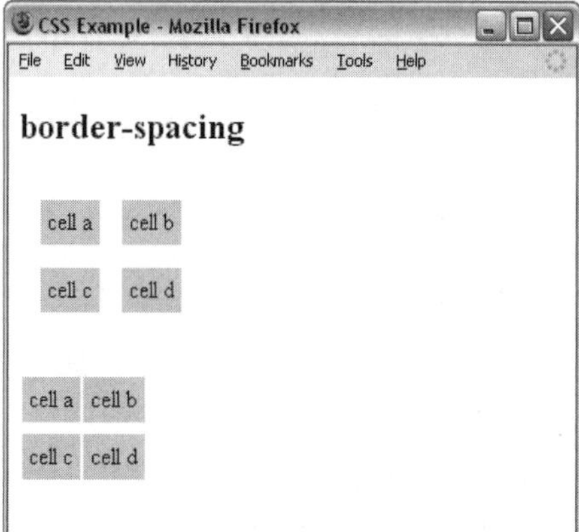

Figure 8-15

The empty-cells Property

The `empty-cells` property indicates whether a cell without any content should have a border displayed. It can take one of three values, as you can see in the table that follows.

Value	Purpose
show	Borders will be shown even if the cell is empty (this is the default value).
hide	Borders will be hidden if cell is empty.
inherit	Borders will obey the rules of the containing table (only of use in nested tables).

If you want to explicitly hide or show borders of empty cells, you should use this property because some versions of IE and Firefox treat empty cells differently.

Here you can see a table with two empty cells: an empty `<th>` element and an empty `<td>` element (`ch08_eg16.html`):

```
<table>
  <tr>
    <th></th>
    <th>Title one</th>
    <th>Title two</th>
  </tr>
  <tr>
    <th>Row Title</th>
    <td>value</td>
    <td>value</td>
  </tr>
  <tr>
    <th>Row Title</th>
    <td>value</td>
    <td></td>
  </tr>
</table>
```

The following code shows the `empty-cells` property used to hide borders of empty cells in the `<table>` element (`ch08_eg16.css`):

```
table {
   width:350px;
   border-collapse:separate;
   empty-cells:hide;}
td {padding:5px;
   border-style:solid;
   border-width:1px;
   border-color:#999999;}
```

Figure 8-16 shows what the table looks like without borders for empty cells.

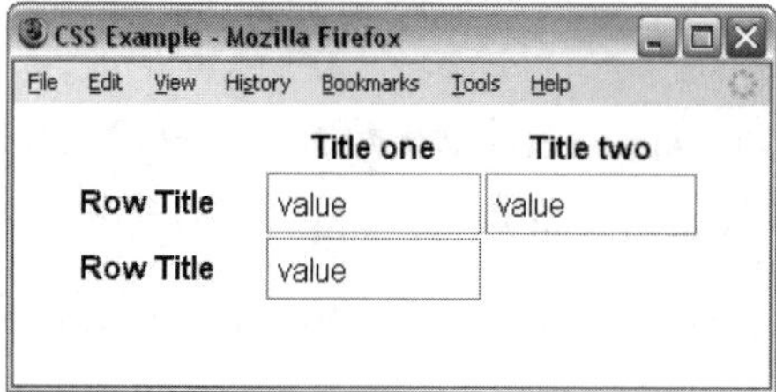

Figure 8-16

The caption-side Property

The `caption-side` property is for use with the `<caption>` element to indicate on which side of the table the caption should go. The following table lists the possible values.

Value	Purpose
`top`	The caption will appear above the table (the default).
`right`	The caption will appear to the right of the table.
`bottom`	The caption will appear below the table.
`left`	The caption will appear on the left side of the table.

For example, here you can see the caption being set to the bottom of the table (`ch08_eg17.css`):

```
caption {caption-side:bottom}
```

Figure 8-17 shows you the `caption-side` property at work; you can see that the caption for this table has moved to the bottom of the table (rather than the top).

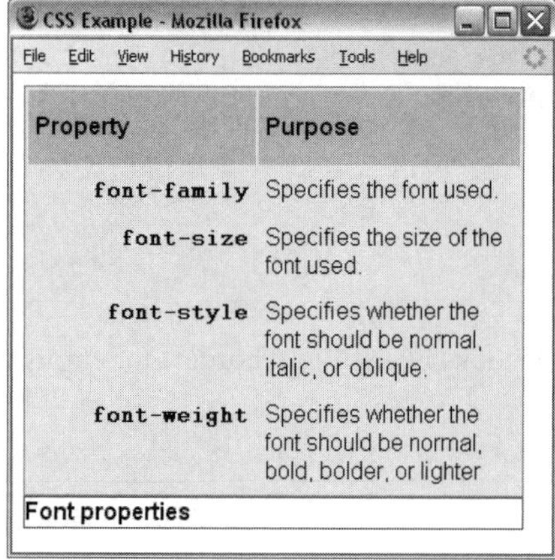

Figure 8-17

The table-layout Property

When you specify a width for a table or table cell, but the content does not fit into the space you have allowed, a browser can give the table more space to fit the content. The `table-layout` property allows you to force the browser to stick to the widths you specify, even if this makes the content unreadable.

See the table that follows for the three possible values this property can take.

Value	Purpose
`auto`	The browser looks through the entire table for the widest unbreakable content in the cells. This is slower at rendering, but more useful if you do not know the exact size of each column. This is the default value.
`fixed`	The width of a table cell only depends on the widths you specified for the table and its cells. This speeds up rendering.
`inherit`	Will obey the rules of the containing table (only of use in nested tables).

In the following example there are two tables, each with just one cell. The cells contain the letters of the alphabet, and there is a space before the last three letters. Normally, each table cell will be as wide as the longest unbroken set of characters in a cell — in this case, the letters A through W (`ch08_eg18.html`).

```
<table class="one">
  <tr>
    <td>ABCDEFGHIJKLMNOPQRSTUVW XYZ</td>
  </tr>
</table>

<table class="two">
  <tr>
    <td>ABCDEFGHIJKLMNOPQRSTUVW XYZ</td>
  </tr>
</table>
```

Now, if you look at the CSS for this example, you can see that the width of the table is set to 75 pixels — not enough for the letters A through W. One table has the `table-layout` property set to `auto`, the other to `fixed` (`ch08_eg18.css`).

```
table {width:75px;}
table.one {table-layout:auto;}
table.two {table-layout:fixed;}

td {
   padding:5px;
   border-style:solid;
   border-width:1px;
   border-color:#999999;}
```

You can see the results of this example in Figure 8-18; by default the table will make enough space for the letters A through W. However, when the second table is forced to stick to the width specified in the CSS, the letters spill out over the edge of the table.

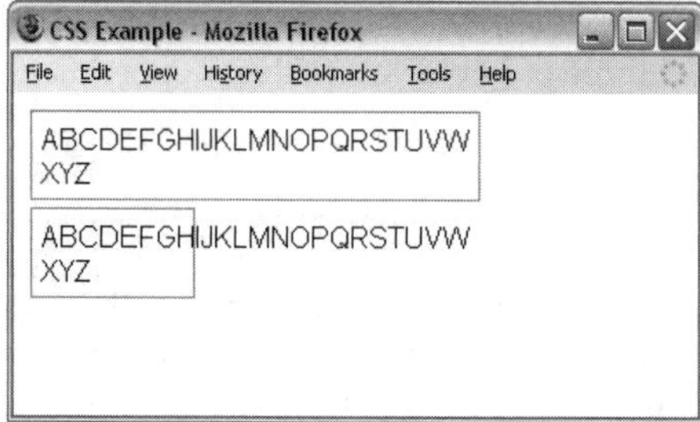

Figure 8-18

To prevent the letters spilling out over the edge you could use the `overflow` property, which you will meet later in the chapter.

There are several other CSS properties that allow you to control groups of cells in one rule. They are not covered in this book because support for them is still patchy. Should you want to look them up on the Web, they are as follows:

- IE 5 and later supports `table-header-group` and `table-footer-group`.
- Firefox supports `inline-table`, `table-row`, `table-column-group`, `table-column`, `table-row`, and `table-cell`.

Outlines

Outlines are similar to the borders that you met in the last chapter, but there are two crucial differences:

- An outline does not take up space.
- Outlines do not have to be rectangular.

The idea behind the outline properties is that you might want to highlight some aspect of a page for the user; this property will allow you to do that without affecting the flow of the page (where elements are positioned) in the way that a physical border would take up space. It's almost as if the outline style sits on top of the page.

Unfortunately, the outline properties are not supported by Internet Explorer 8 (or earlier versions). They do work in other major browsers (although there can be some slight variations in appearance in different browsers).

The table that follows lists the four outline properties.

Property	Purpose
outline-width	Specifies the width of the outline
outline-style	Specifies the line style for the outline
outline-color	Specifies the color of the outline
outline	Shorthand for above properties

Note that the outline is always the same on all sides; you cannot specify different values for different sides of the element.

The outline-width Property

The `outline-width` property specifies the width of the outline to be added to the box. Its value should be a length or one of the values `thin`, `medium`, or `thick` — just like the `border-width` attribute.

```
input {border-width:2px;}
```

The outline-style Property

The `outline-style` property specifies the style for the line (`solid`, `dotted`, or `dashed`) that goes around the box. Its value should be one of the values used with the `border-style` property you learned about in Chapter 7. For example:

```
input {outline-style:solid;}
```

The outline-color Property

The `outline-color` property allows you to specify the color of the outline. Its value should either be a color name, a hex color, or an RGB value, as with the `color` and `border-color` properties you learned about in Chapter 7. For example:

```
input {outline-color:#ffoooo;}
```

The outline Property (the Shorthand)

The `outline` property is the shorthand that allows you to specify values for any of the three properties discussed previously in any order you like. The following example features a paragraph of text:

```
<p>Inside this paragraph the word in <b>bold</b> is going to have an
outline.</p>
```

There is a rule that says the contents of the `<b>` element should have an 8-pixel dashed red border around the edge (`ch08_eg19.css`):

```
b {outline: #ff0000 8px dashed;}
```

Figure 8-19 shows you what this example looks like, although the border is in black here, not red. Note how the outline does not affect the position of other items on the page (in the same way that the border properties would); it just sits on top of the rest of the page.

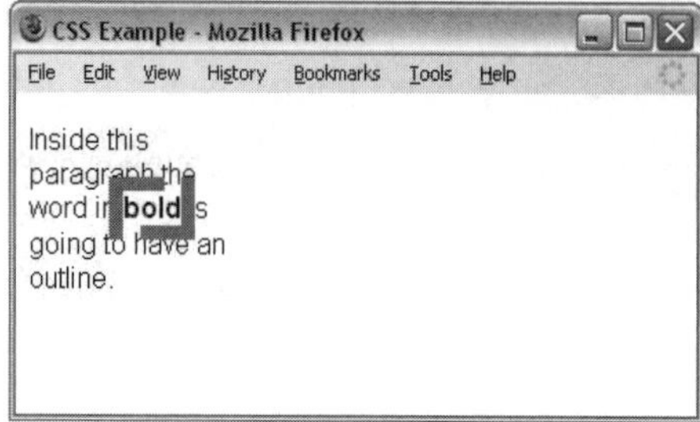

Figure 8-19

The :focus and :active Pseudo-Classes

You may remember that in Chapter 5 the topic of focus came up. An element needs to be able to gain focus if a user is going to interact with it; for example, focus can be given to links and form controls.

When an element gains focus, browsers tend to give it a slightly different appearance. The `:focus` pseudo-class allows you to associate extra rules with an element when it gains focus to make it more pronounced. Meanwhile the `:active` pseudo-class allows you to associate further styles with elements when they are activated — such as when a user clicks a link.

Here is an example of a rule that will change the `background-color` property of an `<input>` element when it gains focus (`ch08_eg20.css`):

```
input {
       border:none;
       background-color:#dddddd;}
input:focus {background-color:#c4c4c4;}
```

As you can probably imagine, this could offer users help in knowing which item they should currently be filling in as they work their way through a form; in Figure 8-20 you can see that the form input that has focus has a darker background than other input elements.

IE8 was the first version of IE to support the `:focus` pseudo-class.

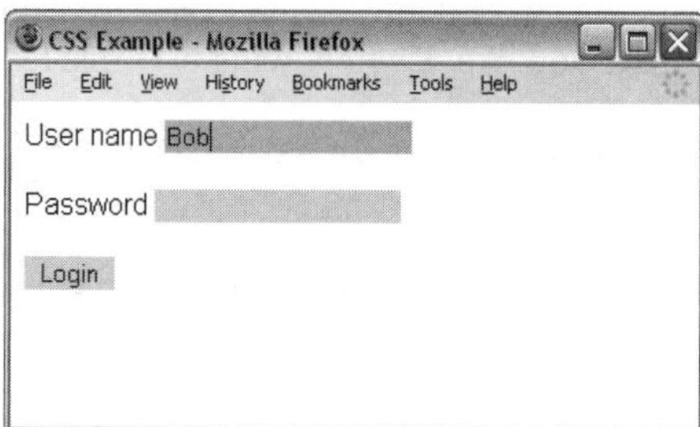

Figure 8-20

Generated Content

CSS2 introduced a powerful way to add content before or after a specified element, even if it was not in the XHTML document. To do this, the `:before` and `:after` pseudo-elements are added to the selector and then the `content` property is used to specify what should be inserted into the document.

The `:before` and `:after` pseudo-elements work to a limited degree in IE7 or higher and have good support in Firefox.

The :before and :after Pseudo-Elements

The `:before` and `:after` pseudo-elements enable you to add text before or after each instance of an element defined in a selector. For example, the following CSS rule adds the words "You need to register to read the full article" after each instance of a <p> element that carries the `class` attribute whose value is `abstract` (`ch08_eg21.css`):

```
p.abstract:after {content: "You need to register to read the full
  article.";
  color:#ff0000;}
```

Here you can see that the pseudo-element `:after` is used at the end of the selector. Then, inside the declaration, you can see the `content` property; the text in quotes will be added to the end of the element. The `content` property can add a number of types of content to the document, not just text, and you will see these in the next section.

The default styles for the parent element will be adopted if no other declarations are added to the rule, although in this example a property was added to indicate that the content should be written in red. You can see this pseudo-element in use in Figure 8-21.

Figure 8-21

By default, the element created using these pseudo-classes will be inline unless you use the `display` *property with a value of* `block`*. If the element identified in the selector is an inline element you should not use the* `display` *property to turn it into a block-level element.*

The content Property

The `content` property is used with the `:before` and `:after` pseudo-elements to indicate what content should be added to the document. The table that follows lists the values it can take; each value inserts different types of content into the XHTML document it is supposed to be styling.

Value	Purpose
A string	Inserts plain text. (The term "string" is a programming term for a set of alphanumeric characters, not a CSS property.) The text may not include quotes (which in turn means that it cannot include XHTML markup that carries attributes).
A URL	The URL can point to an image, text file, or HTML file to be included at this point.
A counter	A counter for numbering elements on the page (discussed in the next section).
`atrr(x)`	The value of an attribute named *x* that is carried on that element (this is of more use to languages other than XHTML).
`open-quote`	Inserts the appropriate opening quote symbol (see the "Quotation Marks" section later in this chapter).
`close-quote`	Inserts the appropriate closing quote symbol (see the "Quotation Marks" section later in this chapter).
`no-open-quote`	Do not use any opening quotes.
`no-close-quote`	Do not use a closing quote (of particular use in prose where one person is speaking for a long while and style dictates the quote is closed only on the last paragraph).

Counters

You have already seen how you can create a number list using the `<ol>` element, so the concept of automatic numbering is not new. The `counter()` function is different from numbered lists because you can create a counter that increments each time a browser comes across any specified element — not just an `<li>` element.

The idea is particularly helpful if you want to automatically number sections of a document without them being a list. It also means that items will automatically be renumbered if extra elements are added or removed (without having to go into the document and manually renumber each item).

In order to see how it works, we will create an example where the sections of a document are going to be numbered using the `counter()` function. Here is the XHTML (`ch08_eg22.html`):

```
<body>
<h1> Introducing Web Technologies</h1>
  <h2>Introducing HTML</h2>
  <h2>Introducing CSS</h2>
  <h2>Introducing XHTML</h2>
<h1> Structure of Documents</h1>
  <h2>Text</h2>
  <h2>Lists</h2>
  <h2>Tables</h2>
  <h2>Forms</h2>
</body>
```

The example is going to contain two counters, one called `chapter` and the other called `section`. Each time an `<h1>` element comes up, the chapter counter will be incremented by 1, and each time the `<h2>` element comes up, the section counter will be incremented by 1.

Furthermore, each time the browser comes across an `<h1>` element, it will insert the word "Chapter" and the number in the counter before the content of the `<h1>` element. Meanwhile, each time the browser comes across an `<h2>` element, it will display the number of the chapter counter, then a period or full stop, and then the value of the section counter.

The result should look like Figure 8-22.

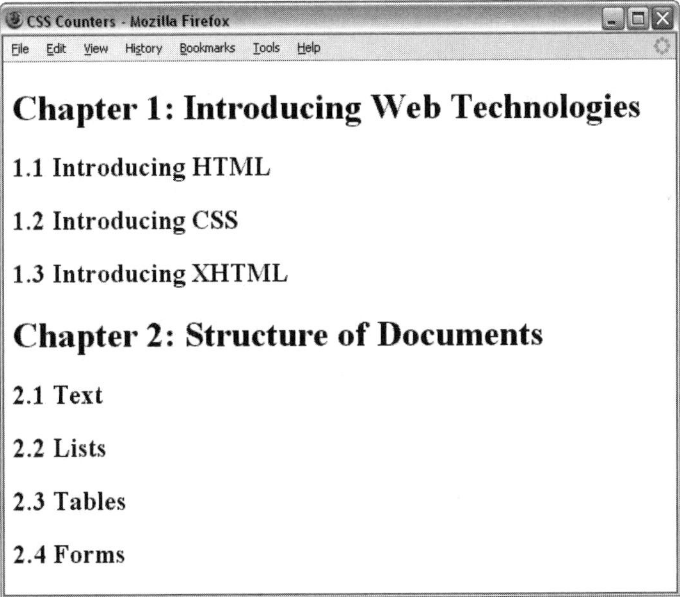

Figure 8-22

Let's take a look at how this works. First, it is worth noting that you use the counter-reset property on the <body> element to create the chapter and section counters and set them to zero.

```
body {counter-reset: chapter; counter-reset: section;}
```

Then there are the CSS rules using the :before pseudo-class to insert the automatic numbering of sections. First look at the rule that adds the word Chapter and the chapter number before every <h1> element; if you look at the content property, the value has a set of quotes containing the word Chapter, followed by the counter() function (inside the brackets you can see the name of the counter). After this, you can see another set of quotes containing the colon symbol followed by a space:

```
h1:before {content: "Chapter " counter(chapter) ": ";}
```

The content property that adds the section numbering before the <h2> elements starts with the counter() function calling the chapter counter and follows that with a period (or full stop) in quotes, then calls the counter() function again, this time with the section number:

```
h2:before { content: counter(chapter) "." counter
(section) " "; }
```

Each time the browser comes across an <h2> element, it should increment the section counter using the counter-increment property:

```
h2 {counter-increment: section; }
```

Each time the browser comes across an <h1> element, it should increment the chapter counter using the counter-increment property and reset the section counter:

```
h1 {counter-increment: chapter; counter-reset: section;}
```

When you put these rules together, they should look like this (ch08_eg22.css):

```
body {counter-reset: chapter; counter-reset: section;}
h1:before {content: "Chapter " counter(chapter) ": ";}
h2:before { content: counter(chapter) "." counter
(section) " "; }
h1 {counter-increment: chapter; counter-reset: section;}
h2 {counter-increment: section; }
```

The first version of IE to support the counter functions was IE8, although Firefox and Safari have enjoyed support for this feature for longer.

Quotation Marks

The content property can use the values open-quote and close-quote to add quote marks before and after occurrences of specified elements.

IE8 was the first version of Internet Explorer to support these properties (and it only works if the XHTML page contains a DOCTYPE declaration), although it has enjoyed support in Firefox for longer. Here is the XHTML for this example: (ch08_eg23.html):

```
<h1>Generated quotes</h1>
<p>Here are some quotes from Oscar Wilde:</p>
<blockquote>Consistency is the last refuge of the unimaginative.</blockquote>
<blockquote>If you want to tell people the truth, make them laugh,
otherwise they'll kill you.</blockquote>
<blockquote>It is a very sad thing that nowadays there is so little useless
information.</blockquote>
```

And now to add the quotes before and after the `<blockquotes>` element, use the following CSS (`ch08_eg23.css`):

```
blockquote:before {content: open-quote;}
blockquote:after {content: close-quote;}
```

You can see the result in Figure 8-23.

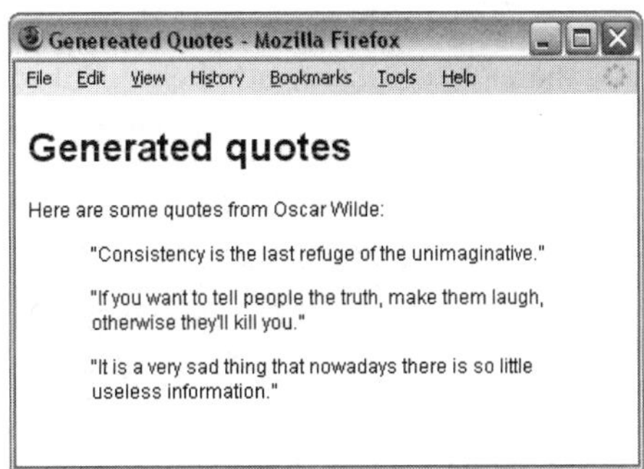

Figure 8-23

Miscellaneous Properties

There are a few very helpful properties that have not yet been covered, which you will look at next:

- The `cursor` property
- The `display` property
- The `visibility` property

The cursor Property

The `cursor` property allows you to specify the type of mouse cursor that should be displayed to the user. For example, when an image is used for a submit button on a form, this property is often used to change the cursor from an arrow to a hand, providing a visual clue to users that they can click on it.

Figure 8-24 shows you some of the cursor types that are available for you to use (although you will only see one at a time if you try the example out).

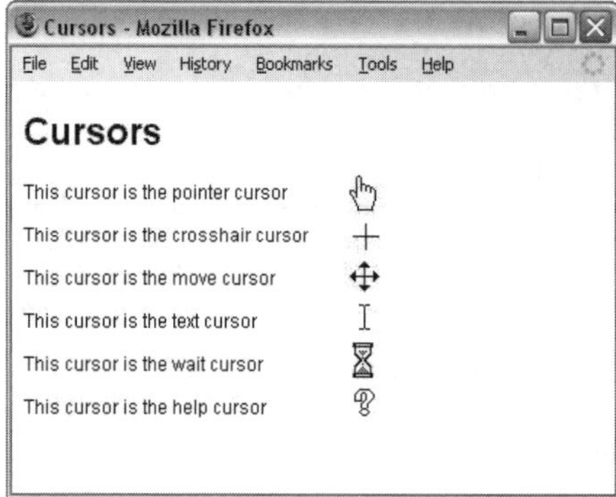

Figure 8-24

As a general rule, you should use these values only to add helpful information for users in places they would expect to see that cursor — for example, using a crosshair on a link may confuse users.

The table that follows shows possible values for the `cursor` property.

Value	Description
`auto`	Shape of the cursor depends on the context area it is over (a text cursor over text, a hand over a link, and so on).
`crosshair`	A crosshair or plus sign.
`default`	Usually an arrow.
`pointer`	A pointing hand.
`move`	A grasping hand (ideal if you are doing drag-and-drop script).

`e-resize`
`ne-resize`
`nw-resize`
`n-resize`
`se-resize`
`sw-resize`
`s-resize`
`w-resize`
	Indicate that an edge can be moved. For example, if you were stretching a box with the mouse, the `se-resize` cursor is used to indicate a movement starting from the southeast corner of the box.

Value	Description
`text`	Similar to the vertical bar I.
`wait`	An hourglass.
`help`	A question mark or balloon, ideal for use over help buttons.
`<url>`	The source of a cursor image file.

The display Property

The `display` property can be used to force an element to be either a block-level or inline box. For example, to make an inline element such as a link into a block-level box you would use the following:

```
a {display:block;}
```

Or you could make a block-level box such as a paragraph into an inline box like so:

```
p {display:inline;}
```

You may also want to use the value `none` to indicate that the box should not be displayed. When this value is used it does not take up any space on the page — it is treated as if it were not in the markup at all.

```
p {display:none;}
```

This property can take other values, but they are mainly for use with languages other than XHTML.

The visibility Property

The `visibility` property allows you to hide a box from view. When you give the `visibility` property a value of `hidden` you do not see the content of the element, but it still affects the layout of the page (it takes up the same amount of space that it would if you could see the element on the page — if you want to make something disappear without taking up space you should use the `display` property that you just met in the previous section). A common use of the `visibility` property would be to hide error messages that are displayed only if the user needs to see them. The `visibility` property can also take a value of `visible` to show the element (which is the default state for all elements).

Value	Purpose
`visible`	The box and its contents are shown to the user (the default state for all elements).
`hidden`	The box and its contents are made invisible, although they still affect the layout of the page.

For example, here are four paragraphs of text (`ch08_eg25.html`):

```
<body>
  <p>Here is a paragraph of text.</p>
  <p>Here is a paragraph of text.</p>
  <p class="invisible">This paragraph of text should be invisible.</p>
  <p>Here is a paragraph of text.</p>
</body>
```

Note that the third paragraph has a `class` attribute whose value indicates that it's part of the invisible class. Now look at the rule for this class (`ch08_eg25.css`):

```
p.invisible {visibility:hidden;}
```

You can see from Figure 8-25 that the invisible paragraph still takes up space, but it is not visible to the user.

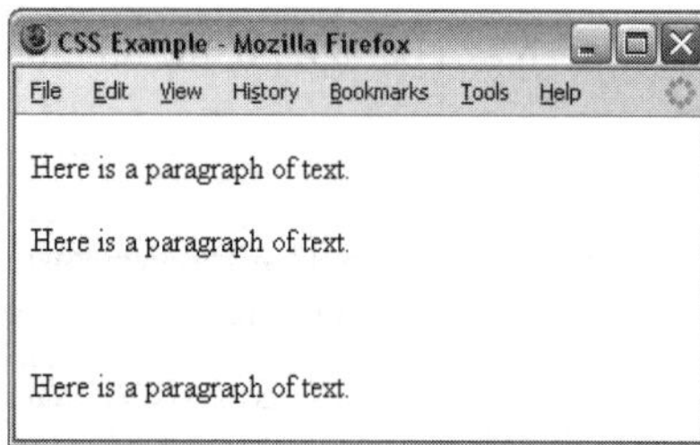

Figure 8-25

Remember that the source code will still contain whatever is in the invisible paragraph, so you should not use this to hide sensitive information such as credit card details or passwords.

Additional Rules

Before you move on to look at how you can use CSS to position elements on a page, let's take a look at three rules:

- `@import` imports another style sheet into the current style sheet.
- `!important` indicates that some rules should take precedence over others.
- `@charset` indicates the character set the style sheet uses.

The @import Rule: Modularized Style Sheets

The `@import` rule allows you to import styles from another style sheet. It should appear right at the start of the style sheet before any of the rules, and its value is a URL. It can be written in one of two ways:

```
@import "mystyle.css";
@import url("mystyle.css");
```

Either works fine. The significance of the `@import` rule is that it allows you to develop your style sheets with a modular approach. You can create separate style sheets for different aspects of your site. This is the concept I started to introduce in the last chapter when you created a style sheet for code styles. Now if you want to include those styles in any other style sheet you write, rather than repeating them you just use the `@import` rule to bring those rules into the style sheet you are writing.

Here is an example of a style sheet that imports the `codeStyles.css` style sheet from the last chapter (for convenience, this file has been copied into the folder for the code download for this chapter). This example is `ch08_eg26.css`:

```
@import "codeStyles.css"
body {
  background-color:#ffffff;
  font-family:arial, verdana, helvetica, sans-serif;}
h1 {font-size:24pt;}
```

As you can see, it does not contain many rules itself; the code styles have all been taken from the imported style sheet. Figure 8-26 shows a page that uses this style sheet that has imported the styles for the code (`ch08_eg26.html`).

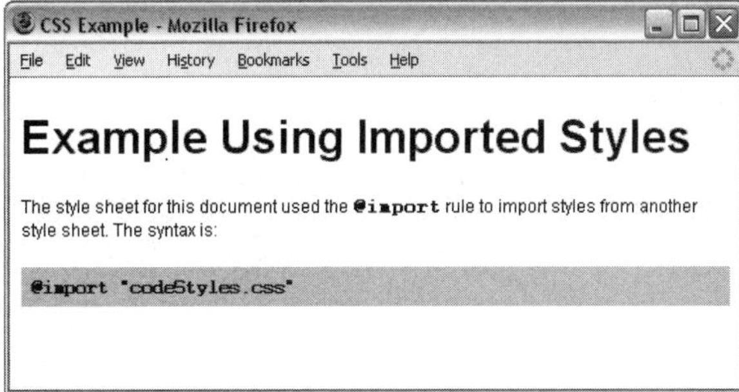

Figure 8-26

You might also consider developing modular style sheets that control appearance of forms, different layouts, and so on. If a style sheet contains a rule for one element (say the `<body>` element was given a black background color), this rule would take precedence over any conflicting rules that applied to imported style sheets (for example, if there was a rule in the imported style sheet indicating that the `<body>` element should be given a red background color).

The !important Rule

When there is a chance that two style-sheet rules might conflict with each other, you can use the `!important` rule to indicate that this particular rule should take precedence over others.

This can be helpful if you are developing modular style sheets and you want to ensure that a rule in the included style sheets takes precedence over any conflicting rules in the style sheet containing the `@import` rule (which would otherwise have taken precedence).

It can also be helpful when users have set their own style sheets. Part of the aim of separating style from content, using CSS to style web pages, was to make them more accessible to those with visual impairments. So after you have spent your valuable time learning about CSS and how to write your style sheets to make your sites attractive, I have to tell you that users can create their own style sheets, that can override your settings!

In reality, very few people do create their own CSS style sheets to view pages the way they want, but the ability is there, and was designed for those with disabilities. By default, your style sheet rather than theirs should be viewed; however, the user's style sheet can contain the `!important` rule, which says "override the site's style sheet for this property." For example, a user might use the rule like so:

```
p {font-size:18pt !important;
  font-weight:bold !important;}
```

There is nothing you can do to force the user to use your style sheet, but in practice, a very small percentage (if any) of your visitors will create their own style sheets, so you should not worry about it — it's covered here only so that you understand what the rule is and why you may come across it.

Note that in CSS1, the `!important` *rule allowed authors to overrule users' style sheets, but this was switched over in the second version.*

The @charset Rule

If you are writing your style sheet using a character set that features characters other than the basic Latin characters (the ASCII or ISO-8859-1 character sets), you might want to set the `@charset` rule at the top of your style sheet to indicate what character set the style sheet is written in.

The `@charset` rule must be written right at the beginning of the style sheet without even a space before it. The value is held in quotes and should be one of the language codes specified in Appendix G.

```
@charset "iso-8859-1"
```

Positioning and Layout with CSS

Up to this point, you have learned how the content of each element is represented in CSS using a box, and you've seen many of the properties you can use to affect the appearance of the box and its content. Now it's time to look at how to control where the boxes should be positioned within a page.

In CSS, there are three *positioning schemes* that allow you to control layout of a page: *normal*, *float*, and *absolute* positioning. In the following sections, you'll be seeing how you can use each of these to indicate where the content of an element should appear on the page.

While the CSS positioning schemes were not really intended to be a mechanism for controlling the layout of pages, they have become the standard way to lay out pages on the Web. For the rest of the chapter, we will be looking at *how* you can control where boxes appear on the page using CSS; then in the next chapter we will look at how to apply this knowledge to create attractive layouts.

Before CSS, web designers commonly used tables to control the layout of web pages. While you will still occasionally see tables used for this purpose, they were designed to contain tabular data, and you should aim to control layout of new pages using CSS instead. If you use CSS to control layout rather than tables your pages will be smaller (in terms of lines of code), easier to adapt to different devices, easier to redesign, faster to load, and more visible to search engines.

Normal Flow

By default, elements are laid out on the page using what is known as *normal flow*. In normal flow, the block-level elements within a page will flow from top to bottom (remember that each block-level element will appear as if it is on a new line), and inline elements will flow from left to right (because they do not start on a new line).

For example, each heading and paragraph should appear on a different line, whereas the contents of elements such as `<b>`, `<em>`, and `<span>` sit within a paragraph or other block-level element; they do not start on new lines.

Figure 8-27 illustrates this with three paragraphs, each of which is a block-level element sitting on top of the other. Inside each paragraph is an example of an inline element, in this case the `<b>` element (`ch08_eg27.html`).

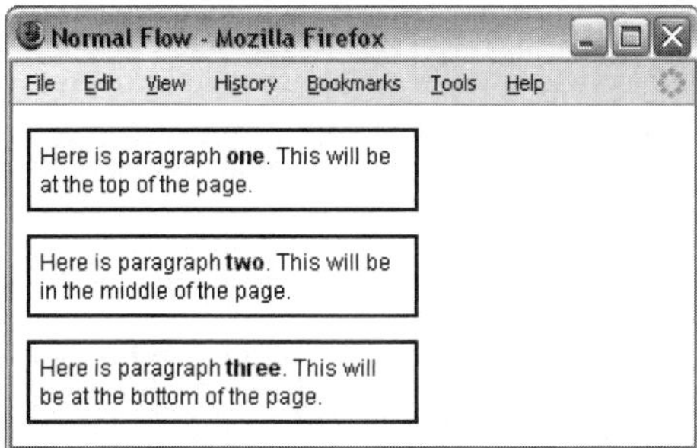

Figure 8-27

If you want the content of elements to appear in other places than where they would in normal flow, you have two properties to help you: `position` and `float`.

The position Property

The `position` property allows you to specify how you want to control the position for a box (and is generally used to take items out of normal flow). It can take the four values listed in the table that follows:

Value	Meaning
`static`	This is the same as normal flow, and is the default, so you will rarely (if ever) see it specified.
`relative`	The position of the box can be offset from where it would be if it were left in normal flow.
`absolute`	The box is positioned exactly using x and y coordinates from the top-left corner of the containing element.
`fixed`	The position is calculated from the top-left corner of a browser window and does not change position if the user scrolls the window.

You will see how these are used in the coming sections.

Box Offset Properties

As you'll see in the coming sections, when boxes have a `position` property whose value is `relative`, `absolute`, or `fixed`, they will also use *box offset* properties to indicate where these boxes should be positioned. The table that follows lists the `box offset` properties.

Property	Meaning
`top`	Offset position from the top of the containing element
`left`	Offset position from the left of the containing element
`bottom`	Offset position from the bottom of the containing element
`right`	Offset position from the right of the containing element

Each can take a value of a length, a percentage, or `auto`. Relative units, including percentages, are calculated with respect to the containing boxes' dimensions or properties.

Relative Positioning

Relative positioning allows you to move a box in relation to where it would appear in normal flow. For example, you might move a box 30 pixels down from where it would appear in normal flow, or 100 pixels to the right. It is displaced from where it would be in normal flow using the box offset properties.

Let's go back to the last example you met in the previous section when we were looking at normal flow and move the second paragraph using relative positioning, as shown in Figure 8-28.

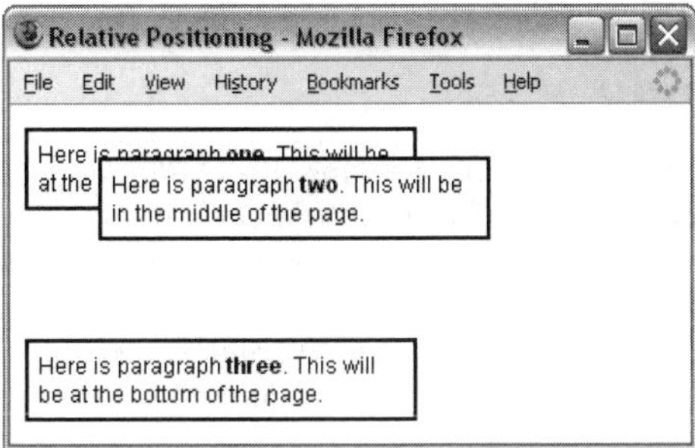

Figure 8-28

The second paragraph in this example is offset from where it would be in normal flow (where it was in the last example) by 40 pixels from the left and 40 pixels from the top — note the minus sign, which raises it above its position in normal flow (`ch08_eg28.css`).

```
p {border-style:solid;
  border-color:#000000;
  border-width:2px;
  padding:5px;
  background-color:#FFFFFF;}
p.two {
  position:relative;
  left: 40px;
  top: -40px;}
```

The value of the box offsets is most commonly given in pixels or a percentage.

You should specify only a left or right offset and a top or bottom offset. If you specify both left and right or both top and bottom, the right or bottom offset will be ignored.

When you are using relative positioning, you can end up with some boxes overlapping others, as in the previous example. Because you are offsetting a box relative to normal flow, if the offset is large enough, one box will end up on top of another. This may create an effect you are looking for; however, there are a couple of pitfalls you should be aware of:

- Unless you set a background for a box (either a background color or image) the box will be transparent by default, making any overlapping text an unreadable mess. In the preceding example, I used the `background-color` property to make the background of the paragraphs white and thereby prevent this from happening.
- The CSS specification does not say which element should appear on top when relatively positioned elements overlap each other, so there can be differences between browsers (although you can control this using the `z-index` property, which you will meet shortly).

Absolute Positioning

Absolute positioning takes an element out of normal flow, allowing you to fix its position. You can specify that an element's content should be absolutely positioned by giving it the `position` property with a value of `absolute`; then you use the box offset properties to position it where you want.

The box offsets fix the position of a box relative to the *containing block* — which is slightly different from a containing element because it is a containing element whose `position` property is set to `relative` or `fixed`.

Take a look at the following style sheet. This style sheet is for use with three paragraphs again, but this time the paragraphs are held within a `<div>` element that also uses absolute positioning (`ch20_eg29.css`):

```
div.page {
  position:absolute;
  left:50px;
  top: 100px;
  border-style:solid; border-width:2px; border-color:#000000;}
p {
  background-color:#FFFFFF;
  width:200px;
  padding:5px;
  border-style:solid; border-color:#000000; border-width:2px;}
p.two {
  position:absolute;
  left:50px;
  top: -25px;}
```

Figure 8-29 shows you what this would look like in a browser; as you can clearly see, the second paragraph is no longer in the middle of the page. The second paragraph element has been taken out of normal flow because the third paragraph is now in the place where the second paragraph would have been if it participated in normal flow. Furthermore, it even appears before the first paragraph and over to the right!

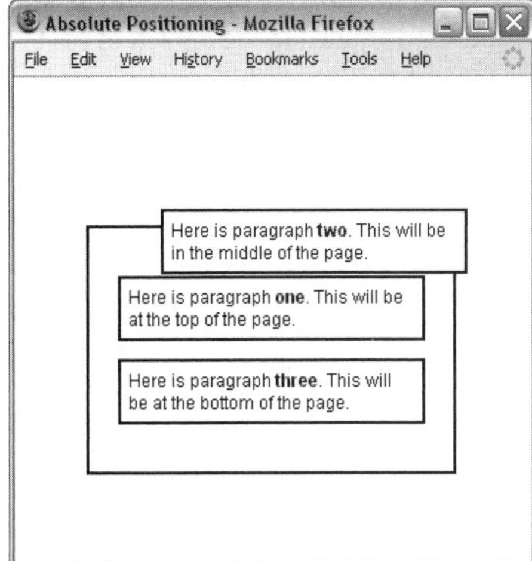

Figure 8-29

The presence of the `<div class="page">` element here is to show that the paragraph is being positioned according to the containing block — the absolutely positioned `<div>` element.

Absolutely positioned elements always come out above relatively positioned elements, as you see here, unless you use the `z-index` property (which you'll learn about later in this chapter).

It is also worth noting that, because absolutely positioned boxes are taken out of normal flow, even if two vertical margins meet, their margins do not collapse.

Fixed Positioning

The final value you need to be aware of for the `position` property is the value `fixed`. This value specifies that the content of the element should not only be completely removed from normal flow, but also that the box should not move when users scroll up or down a page.

While Firefox and Safari have offered support for fixed positioning for a while, IE7 was the first version of Internet Explorer to support it.

We'll use the following sample of XHTML from `ch08_eg30.html` to demonstrate fixed positioning. This example continues with several more paragraphs so that you can see the page scrolling while the content of the `<div>` element remains fixed at the top of the page:

```
<div class="header">Beginning Web Development</div>
<p class="one">This page has to contain several paragraphs so you can see
the effect of fixed positioning. Fixed positioning has been used on the
header so it does not move even when the rest of the page scrolls.</p>
```

Here you can see the style sheet for this example (`ch08_eg30.css`). The header has the `position` property with the value `fixed` and is positioned to the top left of the browser window:

```
div.header {
  position:fixed;
  top: 0px;
  left:0px;
  width:100%;
  padding:20px;
  font-size:28px;
  color:#ffffff; background-color:#666666;
  border-style:solid; border-width:2px; border-color:#000000;}
p {
  width:300px;
  padding:5px;
  color:#000000; background-color:#FFFFFF;
  border-style:solid; border-color:#000000; border-width:2px;}
p.one {margin-top:100px; }
```

Figure 8-30 shows you what this fixed header element looks like even though the user has scrolled halfway down the page.

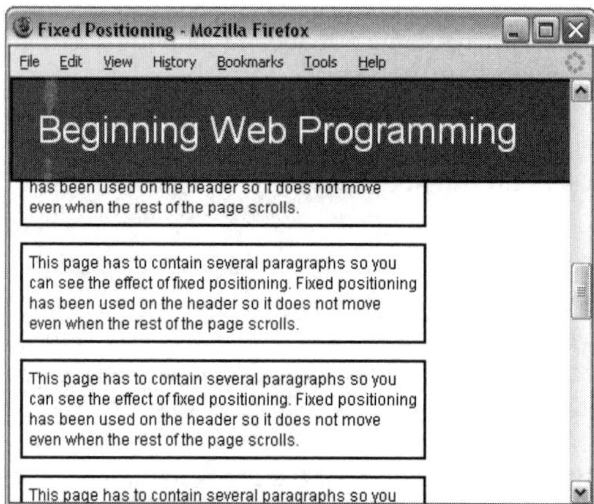

Figure 8-30

The z-index Property

Elements positioned using absolute and relative positioning often overlap other elements. When this happens the default behavior is to have the first elements underneath later ones. This is known as *stacking context*. You can specify which of the boxes appears on top using the `z-index` property. If you are familiar with graphic design packages, the stacking context is similar to using the "bring to top" and "send to back" features.

The value of the `z-index` property is a number, and the higher the number the nearer the top that element should be displayed (for example, an item with a `z-index` of 10 will appear on top of an item with a `z-index` of 5).

To better understand `z-index`, take a look at another example of absolute positioning — this time there are just three paragraphs (`ch08_eg31.css`):

```
<p class="one">Here is paragraph <b>one</b>. This will be at the top of the
page.</p>
<p class="two">Here is paragraph <b>two</b>. This will be underneath the
other elements.</p>
<p class="three">Here is paragraph <b>three</b>. This will be at the bottom
of the page.</p>
```

Each of these paragraphs shares common `width`, `background-color`, `padding`, and `border` properties, which are specified in the first rule (this saves us from having to repeat the same properties for each individual `<p>` element). Then each paragraph is positioned separately using absolute positioning. Because these paragraphs now all overlap, the `z-index` property is added to control which one appears on top; the higher the value, the nearer the top it ends up (`ch08_eg31.css`):

```
p {
  width:200px;
  background-color:#ffffff;
  padding:5px; margin:10px;
  border-style:solid; border-color:#000000; border-width:2px;}
p.one {
   z-index:3;
   position:absolute;
   left:0px; top:0px;}
p.two {
  z-index:1;
  position:absolute;
  left:150px; top: 25px;}
p.three {
   z-index:2;
   position:absolute;
   left:40px; top:35px;}
```

Figure 8-31 shows how the second paragraph now appears to be underneath the first and third paragraphs, and the first one remains on top.

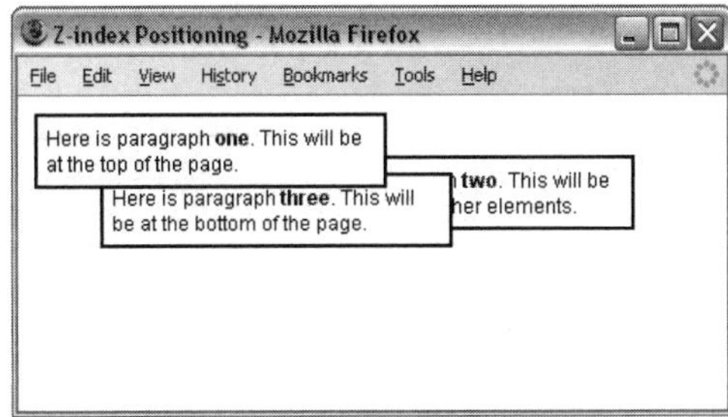

Figure 8-31

Floating Using the float Property

The `float` property allows you to take an element out of normal flow and place it as far to the left or right of a containing box as possible.

Anything else that lives in the containing element will flow around the element that is associated with the `float` property (just like text and other elements can flow around an image).

Whenever you specify a `float` property on an element, you must also set a `width` property indicating the width that the box should take up; otherwise, it will automatically take up 100 percent of the width of the containing box, leaving no space for things to flow around it and therefore making it appear just like a plain block-level element.

To indicate that you want a box floated either to the left or the right of the containing box, you set the `float` property, which can take one of the values listed in the table that follows.

Value	Purpose
`left`	The box is floated to the left of the containing element and the content of the containing element will flow to the right of it.
`right`	The box is floated to the right of the containing element and the content of the containing element will flow to the left of it.
`none`	The box is not floated and remains where it would have been positioned in normal flow.
`inherit`	The box takes the same property as its containing element.

When a box uses the `float` property, vertical margins will not be collapsed above or below it like block boxes in normal flow can be (because it has been taken out of normal flow). The floated box will be aligned with the top of the containing box.

Look at the following XHTML (`ch08_eg32.html`) and note how the first `<p>` element has a `class` attribute whose value is `pullQuote`:

```
<body>
  <h1>Heading</h1>
    <p class="pullQuote">Here is the pullquote. It will be removed from
    normal flow and appear on the right of the page.</p>
    <p>This is where the story starts and it will appear at the top of the
    page under the heading. You can think of it as the first paragraph of an
    article or story. In this example, the pull quote gets moved across to the
    right of the page. There will be another paragraph underneath.</p>

    <p>Here is another paragraph. This one will be at the bottom of the page.</p>

</body>
```

As this example shows, the first <p> element is taken out of the normal flow and placed to the right of the containing <body> element using the `float` property with a value of `right` (`ch08_eg32.css`):

```
body {
  color:#000000;
  background-color:#ffffff;
  font-size:12px;
  margin:10px;
  width:514px;
  border: 1px solid #000000;}
p {
  background-color:#FFFFFF;
  border:2px solid #000000;
  padding:5px;
  margin:5px;
  width:500px;}
.pullQuote {
  float:right;
  width:150px;}
```

You can see how the content of the first <p> element with the `class` attribute whose value is `pullQuote` ends up to the right of the page, with the content of the second paragraph flowing to the left and then underneath it, as shown in Figure 8-32.

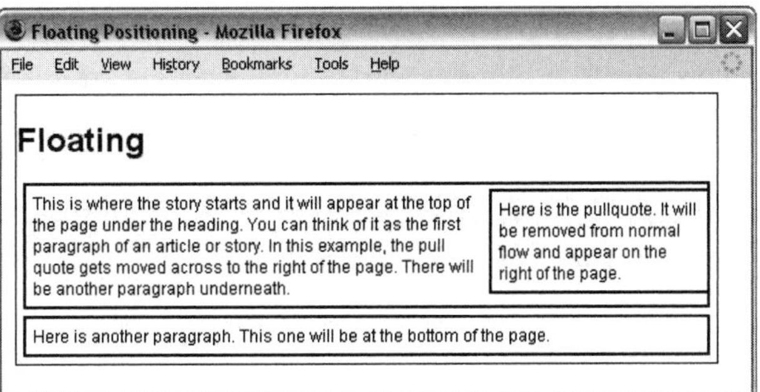

Figure 8-32

You will see lots more examples of how the `float` property works in the next chapter when you look at page layout.

The clear Property

The `clear` property is especially helpful when working with boxes that are floated. As you just saw in Figure 8-33, content can flow around a floated element; however, you might not want this to happen — you might prefer that nothing sit next to the floated element, and that surrounding content be pushed underneath the floated element. This is what the `clear` property is for, and the following table shows you the values that this property can take.

Value	Purpose
`left`	The element with the `clear` property cannot have content on the left hand side of it.
`right`	The element with the `clear` property cannot have content on the right hand side of it.
`both`	The element with the `clear` property cannot have content to the left or right of it.
`none`	Allows floating on either side.

Let's have a look at an example. Our XHTML page will use exactly the same structure as the last example, but this time the style sheet will ensure that nothing sits next to the pull quote.

To ensure that the second paragraph does not wrap around the pull quote, we use the `clear` property on the rule for the `<p>` elements indicating that nothing should appear to the left of it; you can see this new property is highlighted in the following code (`ch08_eg33.css`):

```
p {
  background-color:#FFFFFF;
  border:2px solid #000000;
  padding:5px;
  margin:5px;
  width:500px;
  clear:right}
```

Figure 8-33 shows you how the `clear` property works in this example, ensuring that the second and third paragraphs sit below the pull quote.

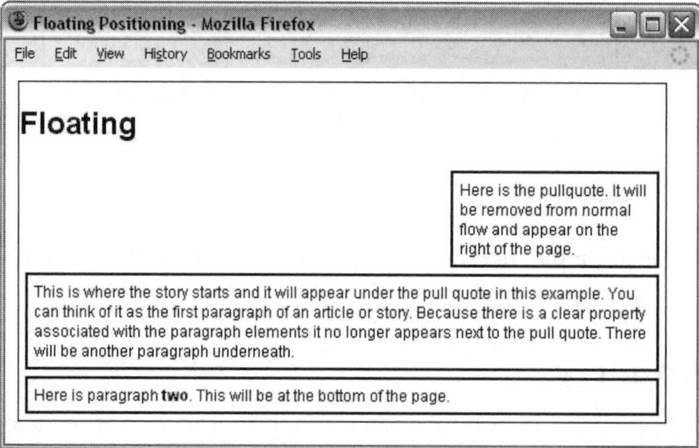

Figure 8-33

Try It Out A Sample Layout

In this Try It Out, you are going to create a sample page layout that uses a combination of the techniques you learned in this chapter to control the layout of the page using CSS.

The page you are going to work with is shown in Figure 8-34 without the style sheet attached.

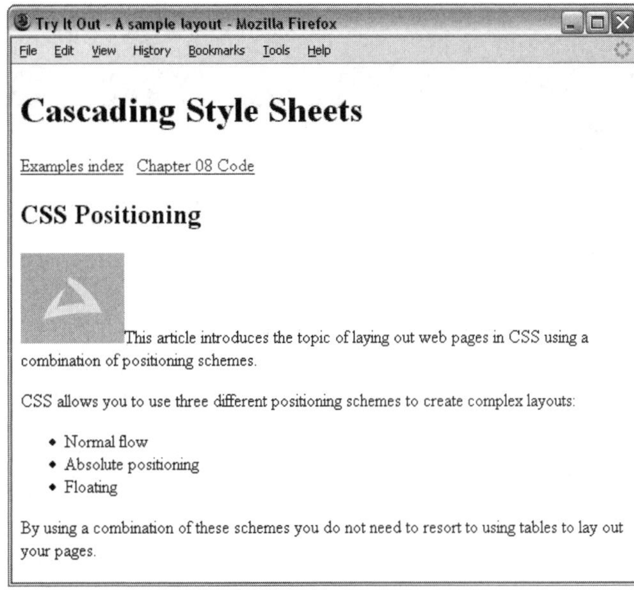

Figure 8-34

Here is the body of the XHTML code for this example (`samplePage.html`):

```
<body>
<h1>Cascading Style Sheets</h1>
  <div class="nav"><a href="../index.htm">Examples index</a>
      <a href="download.html">Chapter 8 Code</a></div>
<h2>CSS Positioning</h2>
  <p class="abstract"><img class="floatLeft" src="images/background.gif"
      alt="wrox logo" />This article introduces the topic of laying out
      web pages in CSS using a combination of positioning schemes.</p>
  <p>CSS allows you to use three different positioning schemes to create
     complex layouts:</p>
  <ul>
    <li>Normal flow</li>
    <li>Absolute positioning</li>
    <li>Floating</li>
  </ul>
  <p>By using a combination of these schemes you do not need to resort to
     using tables to lay out your pages.</p>
</body>
```

This example illustrates some of the issues that you need to be aware of with CSS — in particular, it is important to demonstrate that while you have seen some very helpful properties, some of them are only supported in the latest browsers. While you can design your site in such a way that it will work with most browsers, you might not be able to get some techniques to work in all the browsers you want it to — so you need to test your site thoroughly.

In Firefox, this Try It Out example will look like Figure 8-35; and you would get a similar result in IE7+.

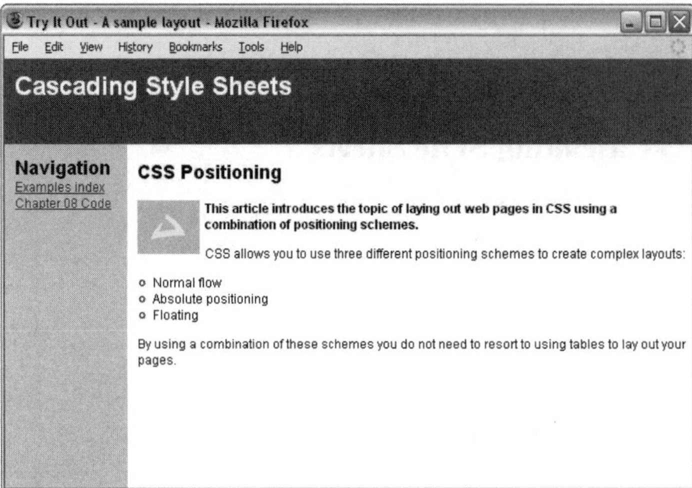

Figure 8-35

However, Figure 8-36 shows you what this page would look like in IE6. In particular note how there is no longer the word "navigation" before the links in the left, and how the heading "CSS Positioning" sits further down the page — so if you still have visitors coming to your site who use IE6, you need to consider which features will and won't work and check your page in IE6 before publishing the site.

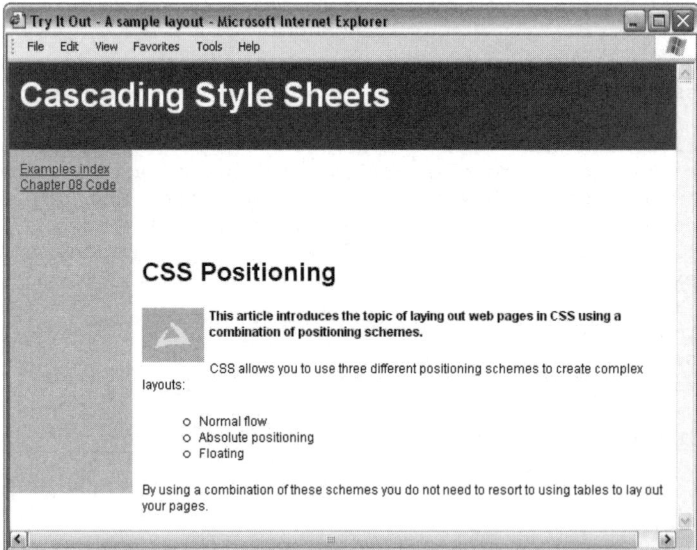

Figure 8-36

To start working on the CSS file for this page, start up your web-page editor and follow these steps:

1. Create a file called `samplePage.css`, add the elements from the XHTML page, and use class selectors where appropriate to identify each type of element. You should end up with a list like the one that follows; then you will be able to look at the rule for each element in turn.

```
body {}
h1 {}
div.nav {}
h2 {}
p {}
p.abstract {}
img {}
ul {}
```

2. First comes the rule for the `<body>` element, which just sets up some defaults for the page.

```
body {
    color:#000000;
    background-color:#ffffff;
    font-family:arial, verdana, sans-serif;
    font-size:12px;}
```

3. Next is the header for the site, which uses fixed positioning to take it out of normal flow and anchor it to the top of the page even if the user scrolls. It also has a `z-index` property to ensure that this heading remains on top of the navigation.

```
h1 {
  position:fixed;
  top:0px; left:0px;
  width:100%;
  color:#ffffff; background-color:#666666;
  padding:10px;
  height:60px;
  z-index:2;}
```

4. The navigation is also removed from normal flow because it is absolutely positioned. It is positioned 80 pixels from the top so that the links will not disappear underneath the page's heading when the page first loads. The navigation is placed in a box that is 100 pixels wide and 300 pixels high with a light gray background. As a visitor scrolls down the page, the navigation will go underneath the heading for the page because we have not specified a `z-index` property, and the heading has a `z-index` property with a value of `2`.

```
div.nav {
  position:absolute;
  top:80px; left:0px;
  width:100px;
  height:300px;
  padding:10px;
  background-color:#efefef;}
```

5. You may have noticed that the navigation bar contains the word "Navigation," which was not in the original HTML file. This style sheet uses the CSS `:before` pseudo-class to add this word in. You can see here that it also has other styles associated with it.

```
div.nav:before {
  content: "Navigation ";
  font-size:18px;
  font-weight:bold;}
```

6. Next is the rule for the `<h2>` element, which needs to be indented from the left because the navigation takes up the first 120 pixels to the left of it. It also has padding at the top to bring the text underneath the heading.

```
h2 {
  padding:80px 0px 0px 130px;}
```

7. Next are the two rules for paragraphs. The first rule is for all paragraphs, and the second one ensures that the abstract of the article is in bold. As with the `<h2>` element, all paragraphs need to be indented from the left.

```
p {padding-left:115px;}
p.abstract{font-weight:bold;}
```

8. The image that sits in the first paragraph is floated to the left of the text. As you can see, the text in the paragraph flows around the image. It also has a 5-pixel margin to the right.

```
img {
  float:left;
  width:60px;
  margin-right:5px;}
```

9. Finally, you have the rule for the unordered list element, which needs to be indented further than the paragraphs or level 2 heading. It also specifies the style of bullet to be used with the `list-style` property.

```
ul {
  clear:left;
  list-style:circle;
  padding-left:145px;}
```

10. Save your style sheet as `samplePage.css` and try loading the `samplePage.html` file that is going to use it.

Summary

In this chapter you learned the CSS properties that allow you to control lists, links, tables, outlines, and backgrounds with CSS. You then saw how CSS allows you to add content from the style sheet into the document. The `:before` and `:after` pseudo-classes allow you to add content before or after an element specified in the selector. This includes text, an image, or content from a file. You can even add automatic numbering or counting of any element using the `counter()` function and can manage complex sets of quotation marks (although not all browsers support all these functions yet).

You also learned how to use the `@import` rule to include rules from other style sheets into the current one and create modularized style sheets that allow you to re-use the same rules on different sites, while the `@charset` rule indicates which character set is being used in the style sheet.

Finally, this chapter looked at the three main positioning schemes in CSS: normal flow (and its offshoot relative positioning), absolute positioning (and its offshoot fixed positioning), and floating. These are powerful tools for controlling where the content of a document should appear; they complete the picture of separating style from content.

Exercises

The answers to all of the exercises are in Appendix A.

1. In this exercise, you create a linked table of contents that will sit at the top of a long document in an ordered list and link to the headings in the main part of the document.

   The XHTML file `exercise1.html` is provided with the download code for this book, ready for you to create the style sheet. Your style sheet should do the following:

   - Set the styles of all links including active and visited links
   - Make the contents of the list bold
   - Make the background of the list light gray and use padding to ensure the bullet points show
   - Make the width of the links box 250 pixels wide
   - Change the styles of heading bullet points to empty circles
   - Change the style of link bullet points to squares

   Your page should look something like Figure 8-37.

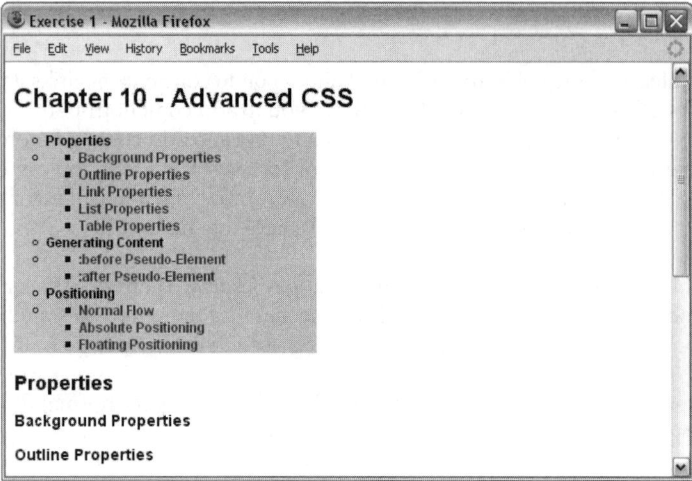

Figure 8-37

2. In this exercise, you test your CSS positioning skills. You should create a page that represents the links to the different sections of the chapter in a very different way. Each of the sections will be shown in a different block, and each block will be absolutely positioned in a diagonal top-left to bottom-right direction. The middle box should appear on top, as shown in the Figure 8-38.

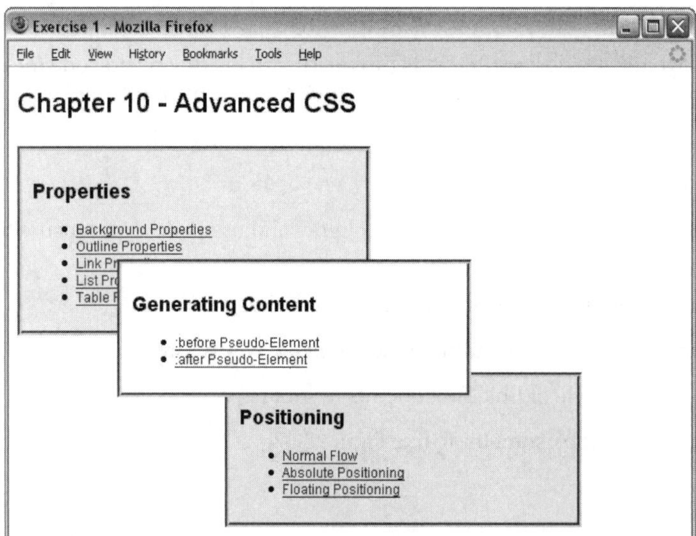

Figure 8-38

You can find the source XHTML file (`exercise2.html`) with the download code for this chapter.

Page Layout

This chapter is the first of two chapters about guiding you through the entire process of designing a site from start to finish.

There are a lot of people who have a web site simply because they think they should have one — they don't necessarily know what should be on it and for them the first reaction is often to copy other sites. So, before sketching out your first ideas of how the site might look, I am going to guide you through a process I use whenever I create a new web site. It helps the site owner understand what information should be on the site.

Having determined the content of your site, you can group the information into related chunks and create a *site map*. That site map shows each of the pages of your site, how they relate to each other, and what needs to appear on them.

Once you know what needs to appear on each page, then you can start to look at *page layout*, which involves the arrangement of the information on your pages.

Having determined what your page will look like, you need to translate your designs into code. This will involve learning how CSS can be used to control the position of content on your pages.

To wrap up the chapter we will take a look at the issues regarding developing web sites for use on mobile phones. Even if you do not think that you need to worry about users with mobile phones, you might reconsider when you find out that in some countries a fifth of Internet users access the Web via a mobile device.

This chapter is broadly grouped into six sections to reflect these topics:

- ❑ Understanding the aims of the site correctly, and getting the information to fulfill these aims
- ❑ Grouping the information into "elements" (such as logos, navigation, product information, contact information, and so on)
- ❑ Creating a site map, which shows how many pages you need and how they relate

- Deciding how to positioning the various elements within the page
- How to use CSS to position the elements on the page
- Developing for mobile phones

Once you have looked at the overall layout of the page in this chapter, Chapter 10 will go on to look at some more specific issues of designing the sections of each page, such as typography, design of menus, and creating usable forms.

Understanding the Site's Audience

Whether you are going to create a web site for yourself or are hoping to create sites for clients, in order for the design to be effective you need to be able to answer four questions about the audience for your site: who, why, what, and how often?

- **Who?** Who will visit the site?
- **Why?** Why have they come to your site? They probably want to achieve something . . .
- **What?** What sort of information do you think they would expect to find in order to satisfy their reason for coming to the site?
- **How often?** How often can you realistically expect them to visit?

The following sections will help you find out how to answer these questions, but first it is worth noting here that these questions are about your visitors and what *they* want from your site rather than what you (or your client) want from visitors.

Who Will Visit the Site?

Throughout the design process, you must keep one thing in mind: You need to design the page for the *target audience* of the site — not just yourself or the site owner.

If you ask a new client whom they are hoping to attract to their site, it is not uncommon for the answer to be along the lines of "the entire world." While it may be easier for people of all ages in all countries to visit a web site than it is for individuals to pop into a store or visit an exhibition, there are very few sites that will appeal to everyone.

Some of the following questions will help you define your target audience (some may be more relevant to your site than others):

- What is the age range of your target audience?
- Will your site appeal more to men or women?
- Which country do your visitors live in?
- Do they live in an urban area or rural area?
- What is the income level of the visitors?

- ❑ What level of education do they have?
- ❑ What is their marital or family status?
- ❑ What is their occupation?
- ❑ How many hours do they work per week?
- ❑ How often do they use the Web?

If your site is aimed at a business:

- ❑ What is the size of the company?
- ❑ What is the size of the department?
- ❑ What is the position on individuals in the company using the site?
- ❑ Will these individuals be using the item or information themselves?
- ❑ How large is the budget they control?

Once you have a better idea of who is coming to your site, you can invent five fictional visitors, sometimes referred to as *actors* or *personae,* representing the range of your target audience. For example, if you think your audience is composed of well-educated men and women between the ages of 20 and 40, with high earning potential, who regularly use the Web, you might end up with a list like this:

- ❑ Katie, female, 32, from San Diego, accountant, salary > $150k, uses Web two to three times a week.
- ❑ Ayo, male, 28, from Denver, attorney, salary > $100k, uses Web every day.
- ❑ Tim, male, 24, from New York, politics student, uses Web every day.
- ❑ Noriko, female, 38, from San Francisco, homemaker, trained accountant, household income > $150k, uses Web two to three times per week.
- ❑ Andrew, male, 35, from Chicago, attorney, salary > $120k, uses Web every day.

These fictional people, actors or personae, should become your friends. They can influence design decisions from simple things such as color palettes to more complicated issues such as the level of detail you offer when describing how to use the site. If in doubt, you can always come back and think, "What would Katie or Ayo want in this situation?"

Why Have They Visited Your Site?

While some people may happen across your site because they're browsing and see a link that they think is interesting, the majority of visitors arrive at your site for a reason. Your design should be influenced by the goals of users, and therefore you should try and list all the goals that people might have in mind when visiting the site.

It isn't possible to list every reason why people visit your site, but you are trying to get to the salient points, such as the following:

- A traveler wants to look at a hotel web site because he is creating a shortlist of hotels he may want to stay at in a city.
- A shopper wants to know the opening hours of her local store.
- A hobby-guitarist wants to look at a guitar web site to keep up to date with the latest guitars.
- An investor wants to see if a scientific research company has sold previous research, and therefore shows promise as an investment.
- A picture editor wants to look at a photographer's site to see work examples before deciding whether or not to hire the photographer.

To help determine why people are coming to your site, you should examine two basic categories of questions. The first category attempts to discover the underlying motivations of why visitors visit your site. The second category examines the specific goals of your visitors. In order to identify the underlying motivation for a visitor to come to your site you can ask questions such as:

- Is it to be entertained or to achieve a specific goal?
- Is the goal for personal or professional reasons?
- Would they see this as being essential or a luxury?

To find out the specific goals of visitors you can ask questions such as:

- Do they want general information/research (such as background on a topic/a company), or are they after something specific (such as a particular fact or information on a product)?
- Are they looking looking for the latest news or updates on a particular topic?
- Do they want to discover information about a specific product/service to help them decide whether to buy it?
- Do they want to buy a product or service they are already familiar with?
- Do they want information on ways to contact you? If so, can they visit you in person (which might require you to publish opening hours and a map of locations).

These questions will, of course, change from site to site, but whatever the question, it is also helpful to consider the *triggers* for visitors' coming — what made them come now.

Once you have a list of tasks that people might want to achieve when they visit your site, you need to prioritize the most important tasks that this web site should deal with. Allocate the most popular tasks to the fictional target audience members — for example:

- Katie bought a *product Y* several years ago; now she wants to purchase one from your site for a friend's birthday.
- Tim has read about your new *product X* in the press and wants to find out when it will be released in Canada.
- Ayo bought *product Z* five years ago, but it stopped working last week. Because it is out of warranty, he wants to get a phone number so that he can find out who might be able to repair it.

The combination of the typical personae of your target audience and the task each wants to achieve are sometimes referred to as *use cases*.

What Does a Visitor Need to Achieve a Goal?

Now that you have a list of reasons why people might be coming to your site, you need to work out what you need to offer in order to help them achieve their goal quickly and effectively. You should then prioritize the information from most important need-to-know through to things you would also like them to know, even if these are not essential to their goals.

The following questions may help you work out what information they need:

- ❑ Will they be familiar with your brand/subject area or do you need to introduce yourself?
- ❑ Will people be familiar with the product or service you are promoting, or do they need background information on it?
- ❑ What are the most important features of what you are offering?
- ❑ What is special about your product or service that differentiates it from the rival?

Consider for a moment when visitors are comparing your product or service with a rival; you will want to give them the key facts that they will be comparing against quickly and easily (otherwise you may not make the shortlist). Then you can highlight what distinguishes you from the competition, along with other background facts.

For example, if a traveler is considering whether to shortlist a hotel as a possible place to stay, this person may want to know what the hotel looks like, price, location, availability for the dates sought, and a phone number (since some people want to deal directly and not put a credit card number on the Web). If all this information isn't found, the prospective traveler is less likely to shortlist you. Once you have provided this information, you might like to add things that distinguish you from others, such as facilities at the hotel and what to do in the area.

You should aim to drill down as far as possible with your answers; for example, what information are you going to include about a product or service? A product will not only have a title, it could have a photo (or multiple photographs), description, dimensions, information about how and where it is made, typical uses for it, and so on. A service might require descriptions of the work involved, how long it takes to complete, what is required so the service can be performed, who will be performing the service, how they are qualified to perform the service, testimonials from people who have paid for this service, pictures of work done.

There are some kinds of goals that will require a lot less information. For example, someone who wants to find out the opening hours of your store will just want to know what time you open and close each day, and they do not want to search through products and offers to know if they can get there before you close.

The results of this task will vary hugely from site to site, but the process should always involve brainstorming everything your visitors will need to know, followed by a rationalized ordering and prioritization of this information.

How Often Will People Want to Visit?

The last important question about your audience is how often they are likely to come back.

There is a very simple reason for asking this: Some sites should change more often than others. If your site is about something that people do not need to keep coming back for, why spend a lot of time and money regularly adding new content to the site? For example, if you provide a service that people rarely use (from wedding services to double glazing), I would hope that the same person would not need to keep coming back to your site.

Conversely, if visitors have the potential to regularly return to the site, you will need to consider updating the content regularly so that they want to keep coming back.

Things You Want the Site to Do

By now you should have an idea of who is coming to your site, why they are coming, what they need in order to satisfy their reason for visiting, and when they might come back. This will probably be quite a long list already, but there is one more thing you need to add to it: information that the site owner wants on the site, but which might not be part of the list already.

This may include things that users could find useful when they arrive on the site (even though they may not have come for this reason), such as the ability to sign up for e-mail updates, subscribe to an RSS feed, search the site, enter a competition, or find out about your new upcoming product. It may also include information that is not really for the user (such as advertising).

Finally, if your list does not yet include such things, don't forget that you will want to include your logo or branding to most pages. You should also remember some boring yet necessary features such as a copyright notice, terms and conditions, and a privacy policy (the latter is important if you collect information about users or use a technology known as *cookies* for storing information on the user's computer).

Prioritizing Information

Now that you have a list of what your visitors want to achieve and what the site owner wants to achieve, you should start to prioritize that information. You have your fictional friends to help you work out which tasks are most important. If one of them has not already asked about a piece of information, or it will not help this person achieve a goal, it *may* be lower priority.

I have come across plenty of site owners who want to push messages that are not aligned with what the majority of visitors want to find out. With so many sites on the Web, if your site does not fulfill your visitors' requirements quickly and easily they will go elsewhere. I'm not saying you should ignore messages that the site owner wants featured, just that the needs of the visitors should usually be considered of paramount importance.

At this point you might also look at other sites that address a similar topic — the competition — and look at what they do and don't do well and whether these sites meet the needs of the people you expect to visit your site. One of the key points to think about here is what you can do differently or better — something that makes you look better than the competition (rather than just copying them).

Once you have every possible kind of information on your list, and you have prioritized it, you can trim your ideas back to what you are actually going to use for this web site. Remember that unused ideas can always be used in a future update of the site. (You do not need to use every idea when your site first launches.)

If you are working on a site for a client, it is good to get the client to agree to the aims of the site when you have defined them. Many clients can decide they want extra functionality added during the development of the site, so pinning down the aims from the start is important. If the client wants to then expand on these aims you can re-negotiate terms for these extra features (such as extra development time and extra expenses).

Grouping and Categorization

Now that you know what is going to appear on your site and the priority of such information, you should start to group together related information. If the site is advertising several products or services, these may be placed together in related groups of products or services, which can be split into subgroups. For example:

- You might group the information about how the company was formed and its history along with information about the company today in a general "about us" section. In this section, you might also include profiles of the people running the business.
- The different ways in which people can get in touch with you (phone, e-mail, fax, opening hours, maybe a map, and so on) and ideally a contact form could all be put in one "contact us" group.
- If a company has outside investors and is listed on the stock market, you might want to create a section for the investors, with company reports, information on the board of directors, and so on.

For most sites, you should try to create no more than six or seven sections. These sections will form the *primary* or *global navigation* items of your site. In addition to these items you will have the homepage. This method of grouping the site will make it much easier to navigate and understand.

Some of the sections will likely contain subsections with several pages of their own, and there may be more than seven subsections in each category. For example, a publisher might have more than seven genres of books in a books section (such as fiction, biography, reference, travel, and so on), or a cookery site may organize a recipes section by classes of ingredients or types of meals. These subsections form *secondary* or *category navigation*. In some cases, this can be split further into *tertiary* navigation.

Remember that your grouping should reflect what you expect the visitors to your site will want to do and the customers' understanding of your products, services, or subject. For example, if your customers are looking for a type of product on your site, will they be looking within a list of manufacturers or in a list of product types?

These categories and subcategories are like a table of contents and will form the basis of the navigation for your site — the sections will each need to take part in the main menu while the subsections will often form their own submenus. This organization is very important on web sites because they do not have the linear order a book does; users are far more likely to take different routes through a web site. The better organized your site, the more chance users will find what they are looking for.

Creating a Site Map

By now you should be getting a good idea of the sections and pages that are going to make up your site, so you should start drawing up a site map. You can do this with a pencil and paper, and it should end up looking something like either a family tree or folder list in Windows Explorer. You should start with the homepage for the site and all of the main categories at the top of the tree.

If any of the categories contain subcategories or more than one page, these pages should appear as children of the first page. For example, if one of your main categories is "products," then you might have this split into several subsections with a page about each item in those subsections.

You can see an example of a site map in Figure 9-1; you could draw this either vertically, as was done here, or horizontally (more like a family tree).

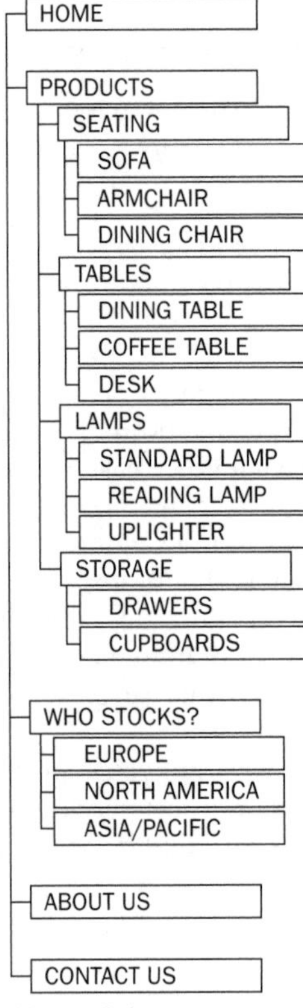

Figure 9-1

Once you have created a site map, you will know the following:

- ❑ How many pages are on your site
- ❑ What information will appear on each of those pages
- ❑ What links will appear on each page (and where those links point to)

Once you have created your site map, it is a good idea to try to look at the things that you initially expected to draw users to the site. You will also want to look at how users would navigate through the site map, step by step, to get to the information that you think they will need.

Identifying Key Elements for Each Page

Now that you know what pages will make up the site, go back to the groups of information and add these onto the relevant pages.

There will be some key items or *elements* that should appear on each page, such as a logo/branding, primary navigation, page headings, and a search box. Other information is more likely to appear on only one page, such as individual product details or terms and conditions.

When you are identifying the key elements of each page, several pages, may contain similar types of information. The structure of these pages should be very similar — for example, if you have lots of products listed on your site, each product page should use the same template so that visitors become aware of where to look for particular kinds of information.

> **You should create the list of the key elements of each page before you even start thinking about where to position them, although it is very helpful if you have an idea of how much space each element will take.**

These elements will reflect the aims of the site. But be warned: many clients will want to put everything on every page. You must show them how the organization and planning you have done will lead to a good design and simple navigation that avoids the need to put everything on each page. (You learn more about navigation in Chapter 10.) A site that is less cluttered yet easy to navigate is better than a site that has everything on each page because it is harder to find what you want on a page where there is too much information.

Page Size (and Screen Resolution)

Now that you have a site map to show the pages that make up the site, and a list of what should appear on each page, you are ready to start thinking about designing the pages.

When graphic designers create a page that is going to be printed they know the exact size of the paper their design will be printed on. On the Web, however, different visitors to your site will have different-sized monitors that work at different resolutions, which means that your web pages need to work on different-sized screens.

Understanding Screen Sizes

When thinking about screen sizes, you need to look at the resolution of screens: how many pixels are being displayed along the width and the height of the screen. For example, a screen running at a resolution of 1024 × 768 is 1,024 pixels wide and 768 pixels tall.

Most operating systems allow you to change the resolution that your screen is running at, and as technology has improved over the last decade the number of pixels available on a display has increased.

In January 2000, over 65 percent of web users had displays running at 800 × 600 pixels or less, and as a result most sites were designed to work on screens that were no wider than 800 pixels. Almost a decade later, around 95 percent of web users have a screen resolution of 1024 × 768 or higher and, as a result, sites have been getting wider, and sites are commonly designed for screens that are 1024 pixels wide.

Several sites provide statistics regarding screen resolution, such as `www.thecounter.com/stats/` and `www.w3schools.com/browsers/`. These sites also feature other helpful information such as the number of people using different browsers or operating systems.

(As you have probably guessed, mobile devices have much smaller screens, and we will deal with mobile devices separately later in the chapter.)

Deciding the Width of Your Page

As a general rule you will not want users to scroll horizontally, from left to right to view information on a web page, so you should probably make the width of your page fit within a screen that is 1024 pixels wide.

Even when a screen is 1024 pixels wide, you should not assume that you have this much space available for your designs because many browsers have a "window" which takes up space at the edges of the page, and on a long page there will be scroll bars which take up even more of the page. On a long page there will also be scrollbars that take extra pixels on the right-hand side of the window. Therefore, even if the screen is 1024 pixels wide, your design should allow space for the window and scroll bars; somewhere between 960 and 980 pixels is a more common width.

Deciding the Height of Your Page

While you should avoid expecting visitors to scroll horizontally, you can safely expect visitors to scroll up and down the page vertically to find the information they are looking for. However, it is very important that, when the page loads, the visitor has a good idea of what kind of information will be on that page without having to scroll.

The term *above the fold* is often used to refer to the part of the page that a visitor will see when the page loads before scrolling down. The term originates from newspaper design — newspapers are often folded in half so it's considered important to put key news items or photographs on the upper half of the front page.

Vertically, you need to account for the fact that a lot of users will have a menu or taskbar (such as the taskbar on Windows or the dock on Mac OS X) that will take up part of the screen's vertical height. You also have to consider the various toolbars that can appear in a browser window. Therefore, you should aim to ensure that the key points of a page appear in the top 570–600 pixels. Figure 9-2 shows you the vertical space taken up in my installation of Firefox on a PC.

Figure 9-2

Fixed-Width vs. Liquid Designs

You now know that you are looking to make your designs work within a page that is 960–980 pixels wide, and that a visitor should be able to understand what a page is about from the top 570–600 pixels. But you may have noticed that some designs stretch to fit the whole page as you increase the size of the browser window, and then contract again when you make the browser window smaller. This is known as a *liquid design*. By contrast, designs that force a page to a certain width or height are known as *fixed-width designs*.

Fixed-width designs like Figures 9-3 and 9-4 remain the same as you increase and shrink the size of the browser window, whereas the liquid layouts like Figures 9-5 and 9-6 stretch to fill the entire width of the browser window.

Fixed-width designs are commonly used where the designers want to retain control over exactly how the page looks. This is seen as particularly important when sites are heavily design-led (where the presentation of information on the site is particularly important) or when they feature a lot of text (because there is an optimal width for paragraphs of text). Good examples would be news sites such as `http://news.bbc.co.uk` shown in Figure 9-3 and `www.nytimes.com` shown in Figure 9-4.

Figure 9-3

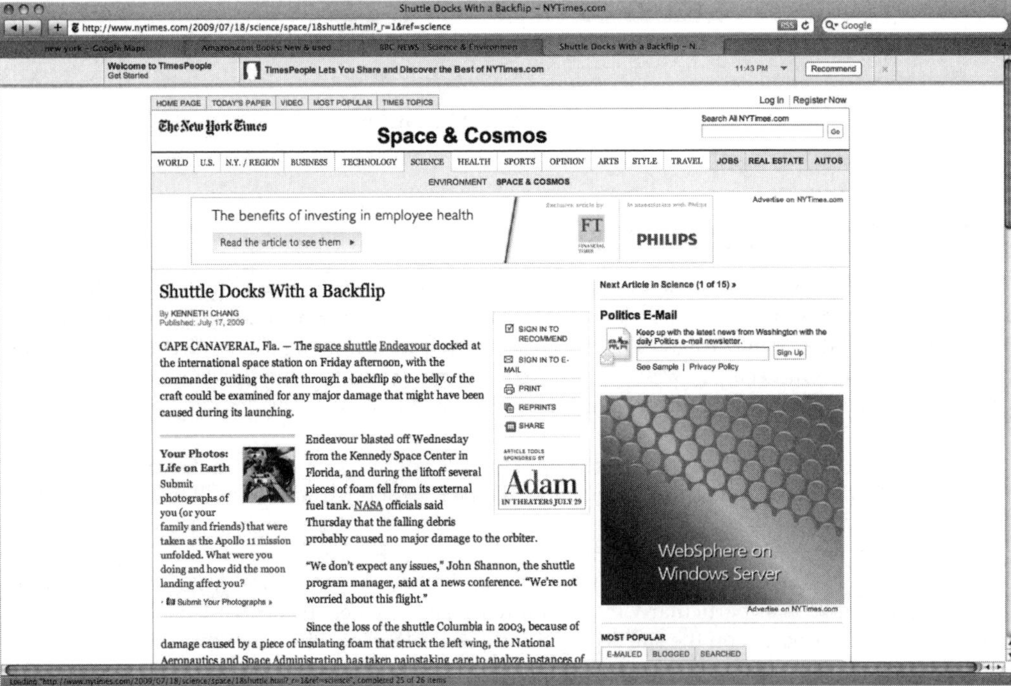

Figure 9-4

Liquid design is more likely to be featured on sites that are online tools or applications such as `maps.google.com` shown in Figure 9-5, and sites that feature a lot of lists such as `www.amazon.com` shown in Figure 9-6. With these pages, it is not as important for the designer to retain control over the width of the page; rather the user can change the size of the page.

Figure 9-5

Figure 9-6

Let's take a moment to look at how to control whether a page is a fixed-width or liquid layout.

Liquid (Stretchy) Page

In order to create a liquid layout that will stretch to fit the page, you specify proportions of a page using percentage values. For example, you might decide your page takes up 80 percent of the width of the browser, as in the example shown in Figure 9-7. If the user increases the size of the browser window, the page increases in size but retains the border around the outside.

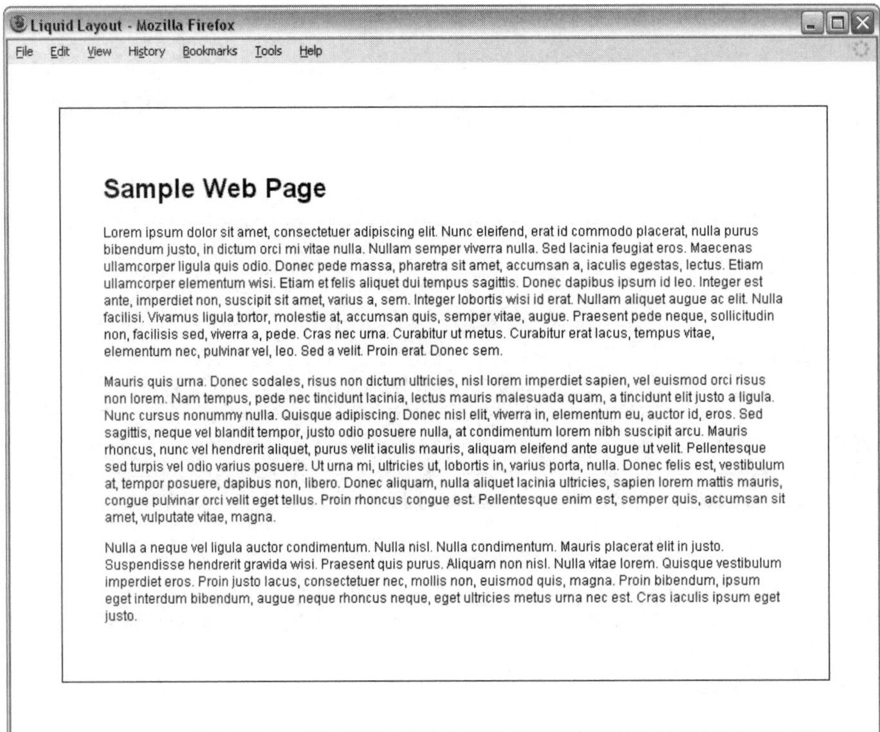

Figure 9-7

Here (`ch09_eg01.html`) you can see how this effect can be created using a `<div>` element, which acts as a container for the page:

```
<body>
  <div id="page">
    <!-- CONTENT OF PAGE GOES HERE -->
  </div>
</body>
```

The style sheet contains a rule for the `<div>` element, whose `id` attribute has a value of `page`, setting the `width` property to have a value of `80%` of the screen. A border is drawn around the edge so that you can see the box created by the `<div>` element. To make it more attractive, padding of 5% has been added inside the box to keep the content from the border (`ch09_eg01.css`):

```
div#page {
  width:80%;
  padding:5%;
  border:1px solid #666666;
  font-family:arial, verdana, sans-serif;
  font-size:12px;}
```

There are advantages and disadvantages to the liquid layout approach. The advantages are as follows:

- The page expands to fill the browser window and therefore does not leave large spaces around the page when there is a large window.
- If the user has a small window open in his or her browser, the page can contract to fit that window without the user having to scroll from left to right to view the content of the page.
- The design is tolerant of users setting font sizes larger than the designer intended, as the page layout can stretch.

The disadvantages are:

- If you do not control the width of sections of your page, the page can look different than you intended, and you can end up with unsightly gaps around certain elements or items that are squashed together.
- If the user has a very wide window, lines of text can become very long, and these become hard to read.
- If the user has a very narrow window, words may be squashed too small and you could end up with just a word or two on each line.
- If a fixed-width item (such as an image) is in a box that is too small to hold it (maybe the user has made the window small), it can overflow over the top of the text.

Fixed-Width Page

Fixed-width designs most commonly use pixels to indicate the width of the page. Fixed-width layouts allow designers much greater control over how their pages appear because the designer knows the size of the canvas; it cannot stretch and shrink as the users resize their windows. Even though a design might look a slightly different size on different resolution monitors, the proportions of elements on the page can remain the same. You can see an example of a fixed-width page in Figure 9-8. The code for this page (`ch09_eg02.html`) follows shortly.

While Figure 9-8 may look similar to Figure 9-7, if you try out the corresponding code, you will find that this example does not stretch to take up more of the browser window, unlike the previous example of a liquid layout.

Here you can see that we are using a `<div>` element again to hold the page, which carries an `id` attribute whose value is `page` (`ch09_eg02.html`); it is just the same as the XHTML in the last example:

```
<body>
  <div id="page">
     <!-- CONTENT OF PAGE GOES HERE -->
  </div>
</body>
```

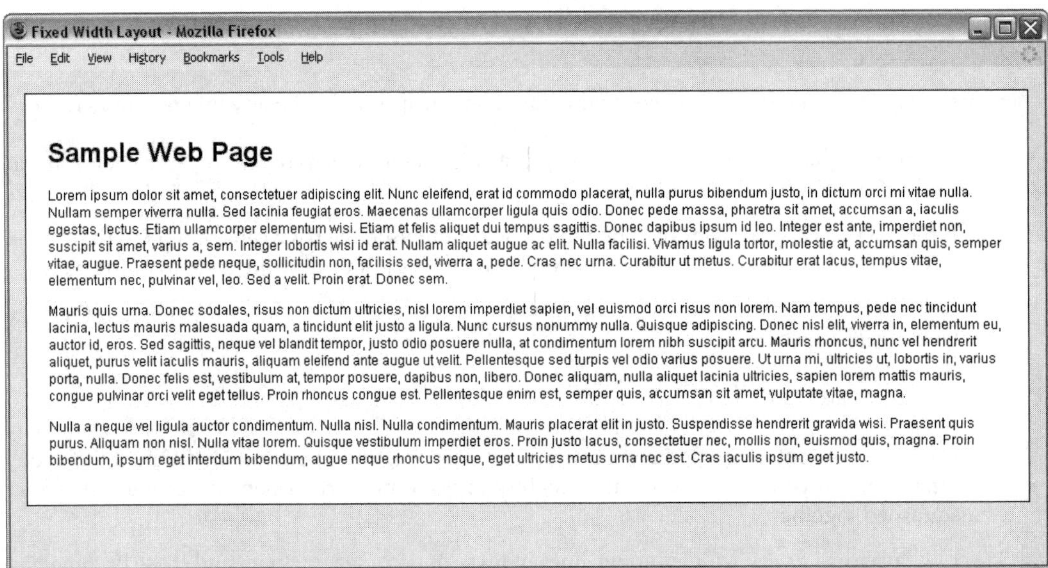

Figure 9-8

Now take a look at the CSS rules that correspond with this element (`ch09_eg02.css`):

```
div#page{
  width:880px;
  padding:20px;
  margin-left:auto;
  margin-right:auto;
  background-color:#ffffff;
  border:1px solid #666666;
  font-size:12px;}
  text-align:left;}
```

As you can see, the `width` property is used to fix the size of the page, and its value is specified in pixels. No matter how big or small the visitor's browser window is, this element remains the same size. If the user's browser is narrower than the layout specifies, horizontal scrollbars will appear, whereas if the window is wider than the layout specifies, there will be space to the side of the page.

You might also have noticed that the `margin-left` and `margin-right` properties have a value of `auto`, which ensures that the page is centered in the browser window in most browsers. Unfortunately, this does not work in Internet Explorer versions 5-7, therefore you also need to add a `text-align` property in a rule that applies to the `<body>` element; this should have a value of `center`. This ensures that the page sits in the middle of the window in IE. However, since the value of the `text-align` property is inherited by the page, if we did not add the `text-align` property to the page again (see the last line of this rule) the rest of the text in the page would be centered, so we align the text inside the page left.

As with the liquid design, there are both advantages and disadvantages to the fixed-width page approach.

The advantages are:

- Pixel values are accurate at controlling width and positioning of elements.
- The designer has far greater control over the appearance and position of items on the page.
- The size of an image will always remain the same relative to the rest of the page.
- You can control the lengths of lines of text regardless of the size of the user's window.

The disadvantages are:

- You can have a page sitting in the middle of a window with big gaps around it.
- If users browse at higher resolution than the page was designed for, the page can look smaller on their screens and can therefore be hard to read.
- If a user has font sizes set to a larger value, the text might not fit as intended in the allotted space.
- The design works best on devices that have size and resolution of screens similar to desktop computers.

Now that you've seen how to control the size of a page, you should look at designing the content.

Designing Pages

By now, you should know how many pages you have and the main *elements* that you need to fit on each page, and you might have decided whether you are going to use a fixed-width layout or a liquid layout. Now it's time to work out how the content is going to fit onto the page. All of this should happen before you start building your page.

> *It is important to distinguish between the use of the word elements in terms of designing pages (where it means items on the page such as navigation, branding, articles/products, and so on) and the more technical use of the word (because an element can also mean a pair of tags and their content, such as a* `<b>`*bold*`</b>` *element). Most of this section will refer to elements in terms of designing pages.*

Composition and Grids

Composition in any visual art (such as design, painting, or photography) is the placement or arrangement of visual elements — it is how they are organized on a page. In order to arrange the various items that need to appear on a web page, many designers use a *grid* (a set of lines, which are sometimes shaded in) and arrange the items that need to appear on a page according to the grid.

Figure 9-9 shows you the homepage of the web site for a leading UK newspaper.

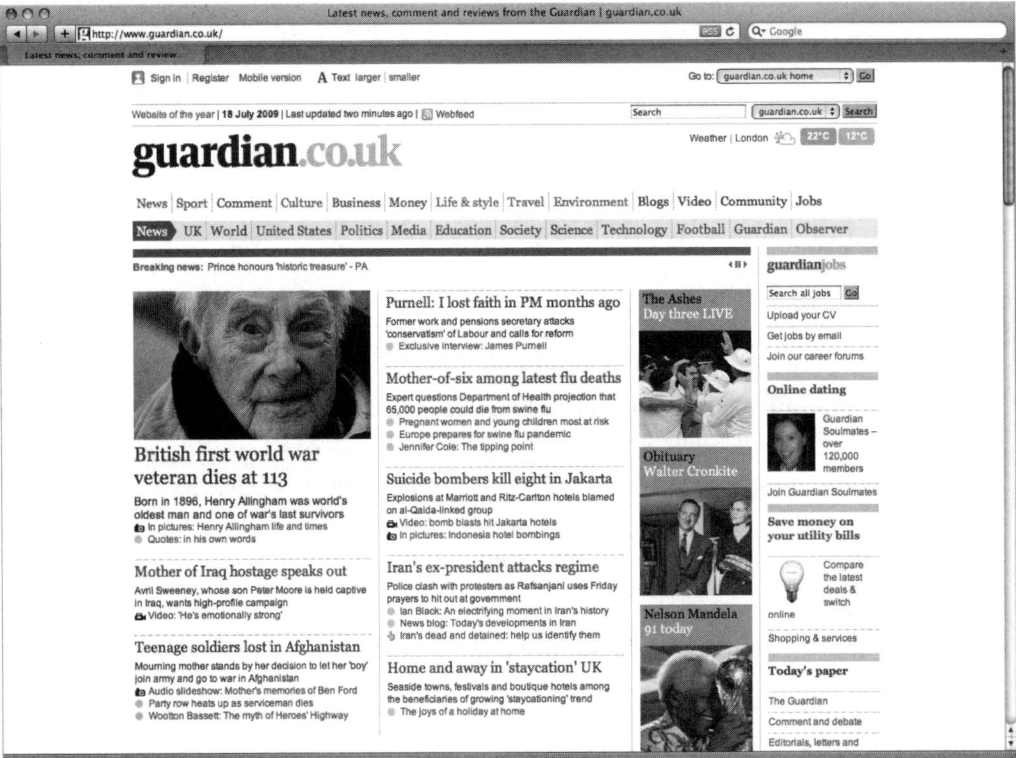

Figure 9-9

Figure 9-10 superimposes a set of vertical lines across the design to show you how this site was designed according to a grid system (in this grid the columns have been shaded in).

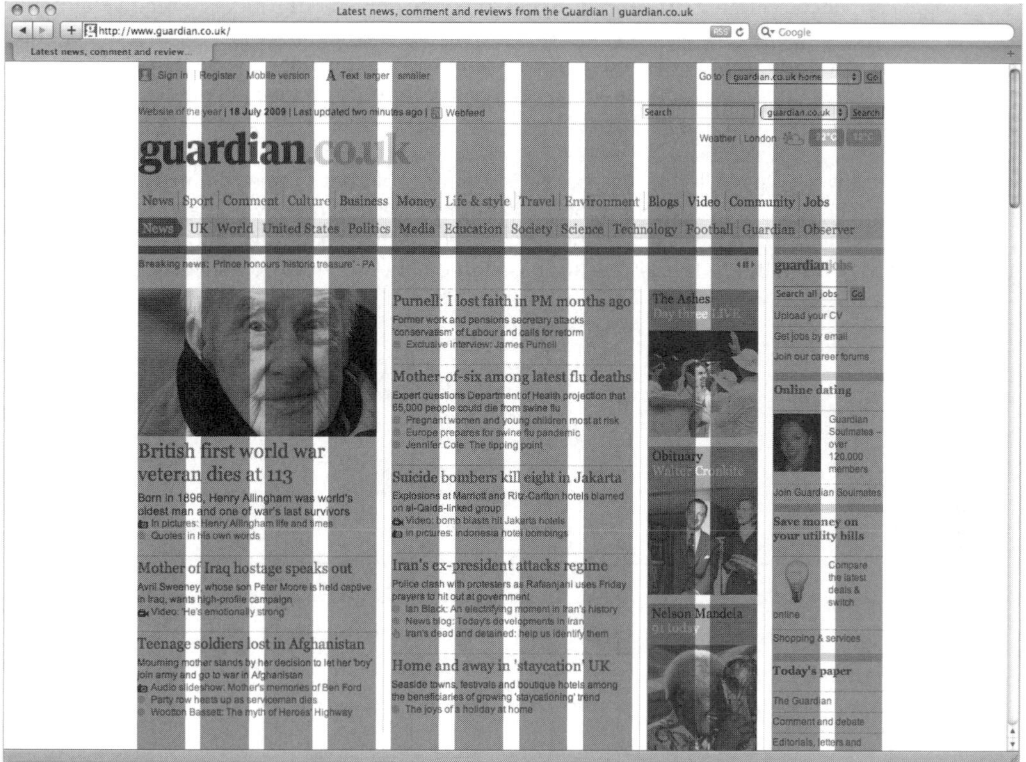

Figure 9-10

While good design is always subjective, a link between art and mathematics has existed for many centuries. For example, the *Golden Ratio* (also referred to as the Golden Section or Divine Section) has been used by many artists since the Renaissance, as its proportions are believed to be aesthetically pleasing. It is also widely found in nature and architecture, and has been studied by mathematicians as far back as Pythagoras and Euclid. The Golden Ratio is approximately 1.618, and it states that the sum of $a+b$ is to a as a is to b. For years, designers have created complex grids based upon this ratio (Figure 9-11).

$$\frac{a+b}{a} = \frac{a}{b}$$

100

161.8

Figure 9-11

It can become rather complicated to draw a grid based on the golden ratio, but a common alternative whose results are very similar is the *rule of thirds*, which is much easier to use. According to this rule, you should divide a workspace into thirds and align key points where the lines intersect (for example, portrait photographers often position the subject's eyes one third down on a portrait or the horizon on a landscape a third of the way down the picture).

If you apply this to a web page that is 960 pixels wide, you would have three columns of 320 pixels (or if the design were a liquid layout, 33 percent for each column). Vertical lines would also be drawn every 320 pixels to create a grid of boxes. Each of these boxes would then be divided into thirds. Figure 9-12 shows a grid based upon thirds; this grid is just based upon lines (they are not shaded).

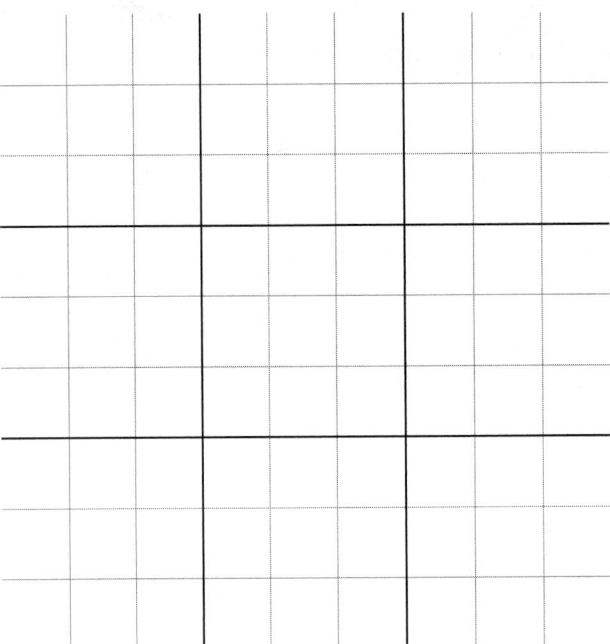

Figure 9-12

When you have columns in a design, you usually need a space between columns so that the text or images in one column do not run into the adjacent column (making the contents unreadable). The gap between columns is known as a gutter.

Personally, I prefer to design using grids that feature a gutter, like the one shown in Figure 9-13.

It can also help to start a design just using vertical lines at the beginning (before worrying about horizontal lines). Assuming we have decided to make our page 960 pixels wide, let's look at a couple of examples of vertical grids. Figure 9-13 shows a 12-column grid, where each column is 80 pixels wide and there is a 20-pixel gap between each column (plus 10 pixels to the left and right of the main page).

Figure 9-13

This grid can easily be used to create single column layouts or layouts with two equal-sized columns, as shown in Figure 9-14.

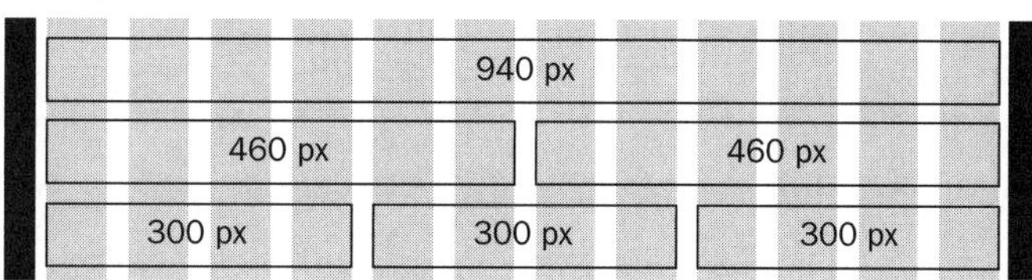

Figure 9-14

It can also be used to map out various other permutations of column widths, as shown in Figure 9-15.

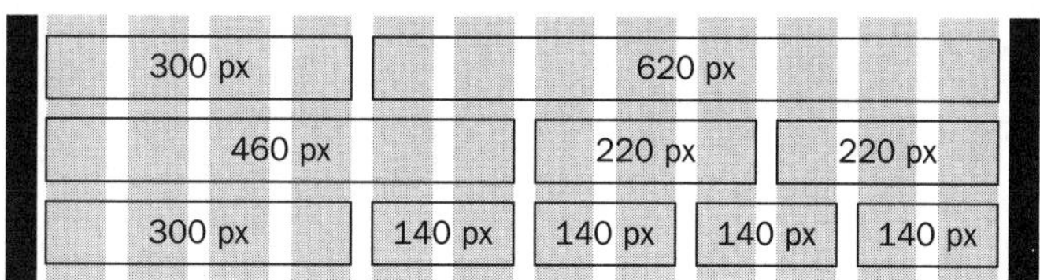

Figure 9-15

You may decide to create a grid with more columns. The following grid shown in Figure 9-16 has 16 columns rather than 12. As with the previous grid the page is 960 pixels wide, but each column is only 40 pixels wide and the gap (or gutter) between each is 20 pixels.

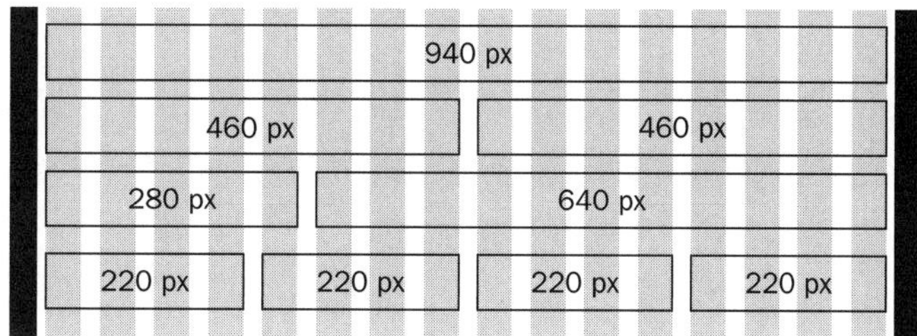

Figure 9-16

With both the 12- and 18-column grids, the number of columns was chosen because these divide equally into the width of the page, and because that number of columns offers flexible layouts. (The 12-column grid can be divided by 2, 3, 4, and 6, while the 18-column grid can be divided by 2, 3, 4, 6, and 9.)

If you can ensure that all of the boxes on your site align to a grid like this, your design will naturally look a lot better than a design that has blocks of different sizes that bear no direct relation to each other and where gaps between elements are of different sizes.

Let's turn our attention to the vertical lines — many designers will try to use the same *units of measurement* for vertical spaces. While this is not always possible (particularly further down the page), using vertical measurements that divide by the width of a single column will help make your designs more attractive. Figure 9-17 shows what the 12-column grid looks like with vertical lines set using the same distances.

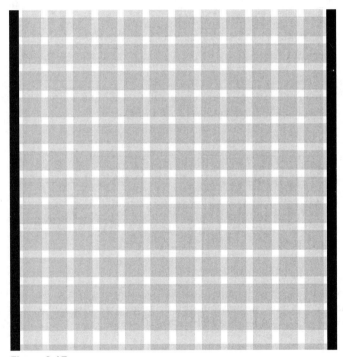

Figure 9-17

You may also choose the height of a box on the page by dividing the width by 1.618 (the golden ratio), because we already know that this is supposed to be an aesthetically pleasing size.

When setting up your grid, you should ensure that the grid can be applied to the entire site: the homepage, section pages, and individual item/article pages. Let's take a look at another couple of pages from the web site for the *Guardian* newspaper — Figure 9-18 shows you the homepage from the culture section, which is again based around three columns. Lower down the page, you can see that the columns are then divided in two to provide six columns:

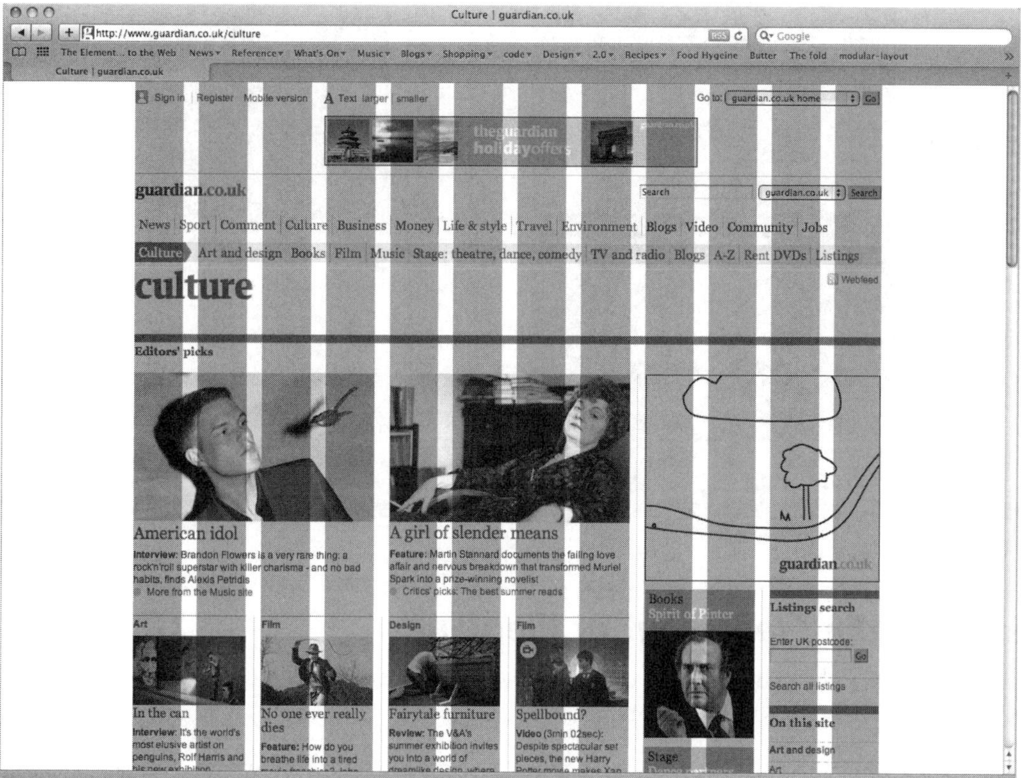

Figure 9-18

Figure 9-19 shows an individual article page; this time the main column of text is given more space (the main column is the one with the headline and the portrait photograph).

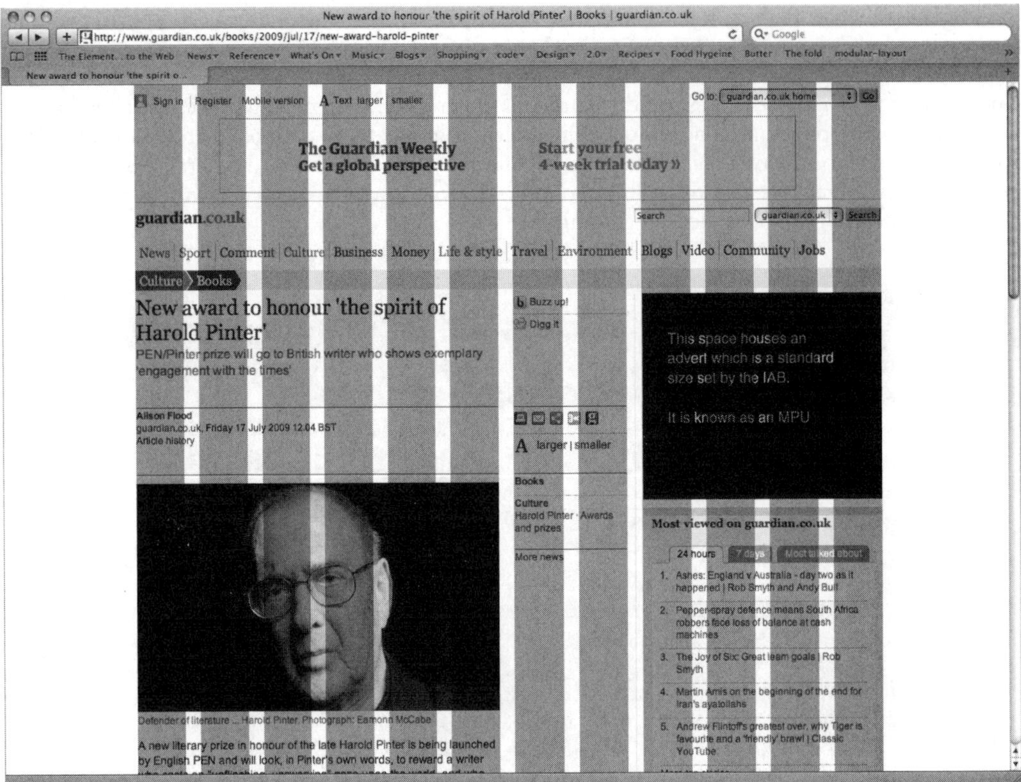

Figure 9-19

Sketching the Placement of Elements

You have looked at the grids designers use when creating layouts, so now it is time to start getting a feel for how the elements will be arranged on the grids.

At this point, you should just be using text, lines, and shading to sketch out where each element (such as the logo, primary navigation, headings and main bodies of text) sits on the page and how much space it gets. You should not be thinking yet about colors, fonts, backgrounds, images, or other design issues; rather, you should be focusing on the placement of information and creating a *visual hierarchy* to indicate the most important parts on each page.

While it may seem strange (and difficult at first) not to add visual presentation at this stage, it is important that you focus just on making sure you include all of the information a visitor needs and every item the user can interact with in order to give it the necessary space. This process is referred to as creating a *wire frame*. Figure 9-20 shows you an example of a basic wire frame for a web site (this figure is again based on the *Guardian* newspaper's site):

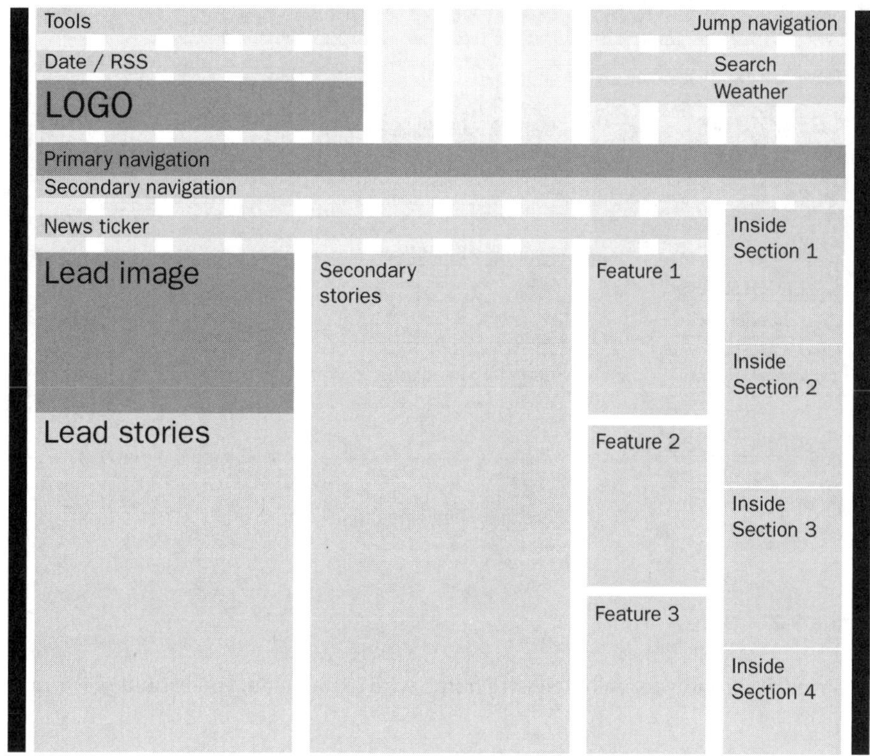

Figure 9-20

The wire frame of Figure 9-20 is very high-level; it does not yet show the parts of the page the user can interact with (such as navigation, buttons, and form controls). Nor does it give a guide of how much text might be shown for each item or the size of images.

Once you are happy with the general layout of information you should start to add some of this detail into the wire frame, as shown in Figure 9-21.

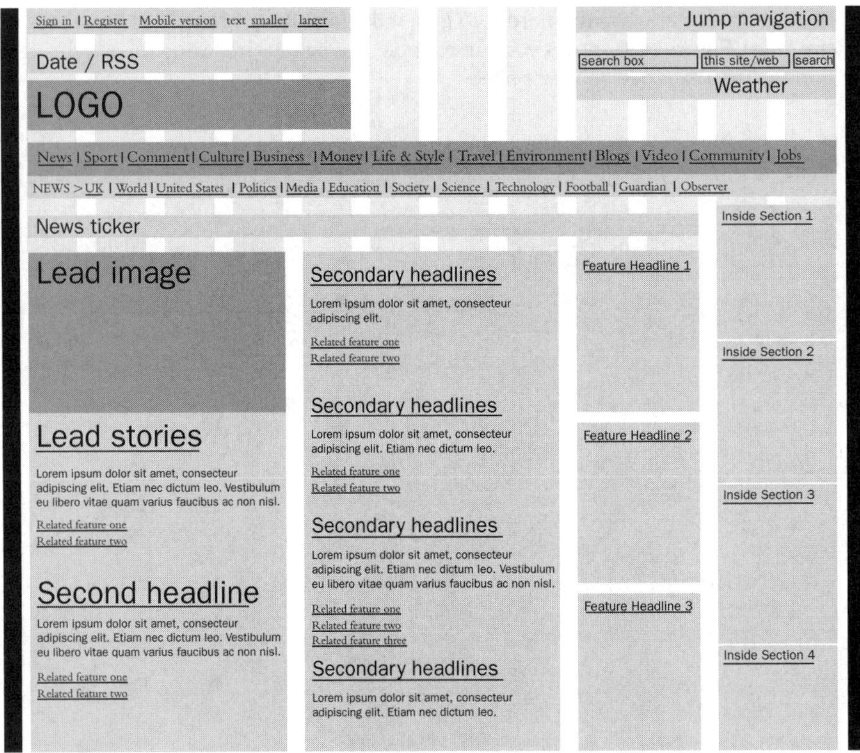

Figure 9-21

When you have the second version of the wire frame with extra detail, you should perform two very important checks:

- ❑ Go back to the target audience you identified earlier and ensure that they can achieve the tasks you allocated to each character you identified. Don't be surprised if you have to move some elements around on the page or if you have to add in an element or two that you missed from the initial list.
- ❑ Look at each page and decide whether a user coming to this page for the first time would be able to tell the purpose of this page from the part of the page that will appear above the fold. If not, you should arrange the items on the page so that a user would be able to determine what the page is about without scrolling.

You can see from the simple model in Figure 9-21 where the links go and how you can move about the site; however, you are not distracted by the design or look of the page. This is particularly important for two reasons:

- ❑ When you show users and clients a full design of the site, they tend to focus on the visual elements (such as fonts, choice of images, and colors) rather than the proposed function. A skeletal model ensures that the client focuses on the function and structure of the content and not how it is presented.
- ❑ If you do need to make changes, you can do so before the design or programming starts, which can save you from rewriting and/or redesigning much of the site later on.

The size and positioning of elements on a page is a valid part of the design process (not only the visual appearance but also the interface or interaction design — how the site handles). However, the process of wire-framing a design will help the user or client focus on what the site actually does and will help you finalize the functionality before starting to design the page. You may choose to tell the client that the exact positions of the elements in the wire frame may change, but that it is an indication of the content that will appear on those pages.

Common Page Elements and Templates

Branding theory states that consistency in how the brand is represented helps reinforce the brand. When it comes to web sites, any information that appears on more than one page should be presented in a consistent manner because it helps visitors:

- Identify the site from its appearance
- Learn how to use the site and find what they are looking for more quickly

You should formulate the consistent parts of the site early on in a design (because they are used on multiple pages). For example, the logo and primary navigation should be in the same place on every page. If you decide to put your primary navigation under the logo stretching from left to right, it should be under the logo stretching from left to right on every page. Likewise, if the sections of your site require subnavigation, this should be in the same place for each section of the site (even though the items in the subnavigation will change from section to section).

Here are some terms often used to describe parts of pages:

- **Headers:** The top part of the page on any site. In many cases the header will feature the logo and the primary navigation, which should be consistent across the entire site.
- **Footers:** Appear on the bottom of every page. They often contain things like copyright notices, privacy policy, and terms and conditions. Again, they should usually be consistent across the entire site.
- **Body and content:** Describe the main part of the page between the header and footer where the content sits.
- **Templates:** Describe a layout for several pages that look the same but contain different information. For example, an e-commerce site tends to use the same template to display each of its products, which helps the user know where to find things like the price, dimensions, and description of each product.

Grouping Elements

For most people, the more disconnected bits of information that are visible on a page at the same time, the harder the page is to understand. There are, however, several techniques you can use to group elements together and make it easier for people to understand pages. *Grouping* or *chunking* items together helps reduce the number of elements that the user sees on the page.

For example, look at Figure 9-22, which shows the BBC homepage (which I have personalized). There are over 65 links on this page, yet by grouping the items into related content areas (such as news, entertainment, and weather), it becomes much easier to digest the information on the page.

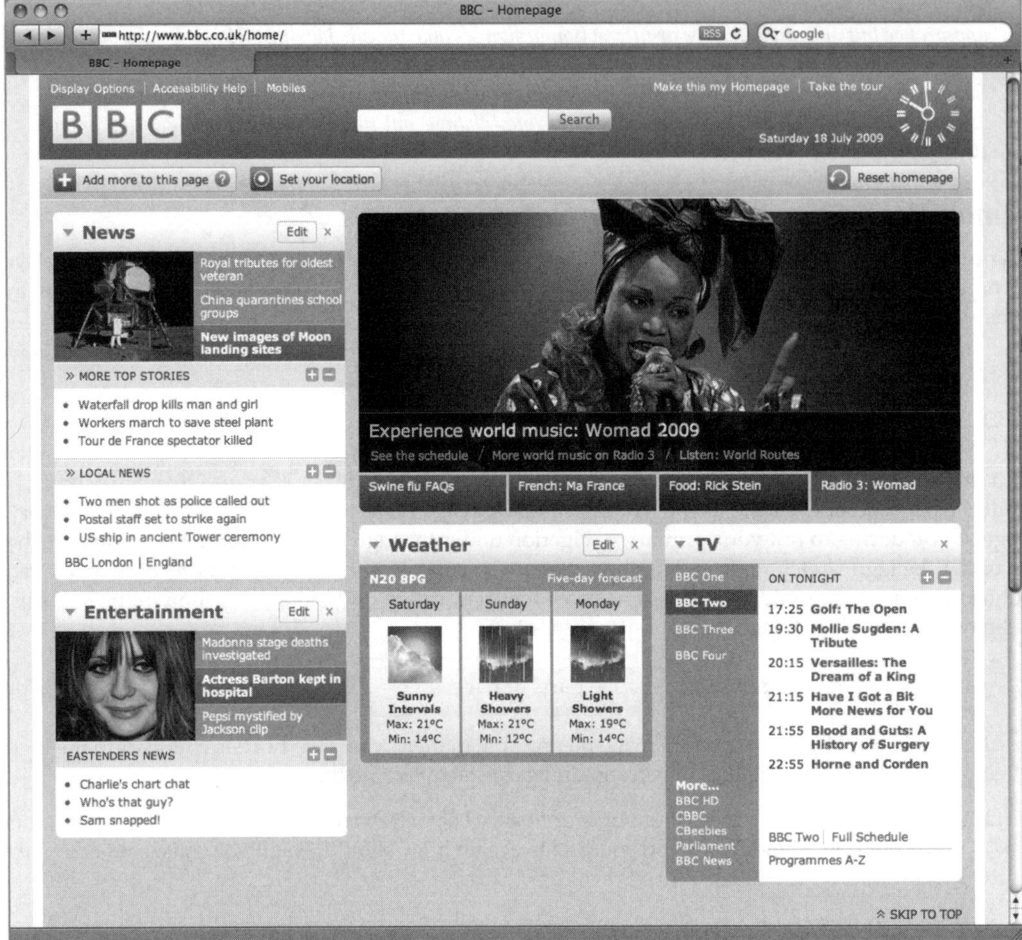

Figure 9-22

The following methods help make it clear to a user that several elements of a page are related:

- **Location:** Making sure that similar elements of the design are near to each other
- **Color:** Using blocks of background color to make it clear which items relate to each other
- **Borders and padding:** Creating a gap between one group of elements and other items on the page to indicate which are grouped together
- **Headings:** Giving related items a header, so that people know what will be in the block of information without necessarily reading each item in the block
- **Styles:** Using similar buttons for navigation items

Creating a Visual Hierarchy and Prioritizing Information on a Page

It is important to create a *visual hierarchy* in any design so that the most important item on the page is most prominent. There are several ways to do this; for example, you may allow the more important items:

- To take up more space
- Have more space between them and other items
- Use larger headings

The most important item on the page should be made immediately clear to the user. Looking again at the *Guardian* news homepage, you can see here that the main story is given more space than the secondary stories, which in turn are given more prominence than the features and inside sections on the right (Figure 9-23).

Figure 9-23

While it is tempting to put a lot of information on each page, if the screen is too cluttered it will be harder for the user to achieve the goal he or she had in mind when coming to your site. Therefore it is important to prioritize the information that appears on each page.

Generally speaking, the following items *should* be visible on every page, and they should be above the fold:

- **Branding/logo:** The company name or logo should appear on the same place in each page; it is commonly placed in the top left or top centered.
- **Primary navigation:** A link to the homepage and the main sections of the site — note that the homepage should almost always be the first item of navigation.
- **Any secondary navigation:** If the sections of the site are further divided into subsections, when you are in those sections you should be able to see enough of the navigation to tell that the subsections exist (although you do not need to be able to see all options).
- **Page headings:** With the exception of the homepage, every page should have a title or heading that quickly lets the user know what that page is about.
- **Content:** Ideally you want enough of the content of the page to be above the fold so that the users know whether this page is going to be relevant to them and, you hope, gets them involved with the content of the page before they have to start scrolling.
- **Search:** A way for users to search for the information they want if they do not see it immediately.

The items that *should not* need to appear on the portion of the page that's visible when the page loads are as follows:

- The detail of the rest of the page (for example, if you have a news article, it is only necessary to be able to view the headline and ideally a summary; the entire article does not need to fit in the top part of the page)
- Links to related information or other sites (things that are not essential to the point being discussed on this page)
- Items that are often required but rarely used, such as Copyright, Terms and Conditions, or Privacy Policy (these can generally go right at the bottom of the page)

The primary factor in prioritizing the items on the page should be letting visitors achieve what they came to do. Back in the early part of the chapter we talked about identifying the target audience of the site and generating some characters that represented typical visitors. We then went on to look at the tasks that these people would like to achieve. You should use this work to help prioritize the content on the site because the tasks people want to do most often should generally be prioritized above the less common ones. This is important because a lot of visitors will not scan the entire page and then choose the part that is most relevant to them; rather, they will select the first option that looks relevant to them and go with that before looking at the rest of the page — something known as *satisficing* (a mix of satisfying and sufficing). Remember that you can use a visual hierarchy (making some items more prominent than others) in order to help people notice the items you think they want to achieve first.

How Visitors Look at a Page

It is important to acknowledge that, no matter how much you would like your visitors to read every page on your site, and no matter how well written it is, they will not. Visitors scan web pages to find out whether that page is relevant to them.

During the initial scan of the page, when users determine if it is relevant to them, they will also select parts of the page that they will focus on. They are likely to give most attention to these areas rather than looking around for other information that might be relevant to them.

Research by a renowned web usability researcher and author, Jacob Nielsen, has indicated that people commonly scan a page using an "F" shape — starting with two horizontal stripes and then a vertical stripe (the shape and size of the F depend on your design, the type of page, and the amount of information on the page). Therefore, putting your primary navigation down the right-hand side of a page might not be a good idea; under the logo, left to right, might be better.

Now that you know people will scan the page, there are a few tactics you can use to make your site easier to scan:

- **Text should be concise in particular headings.** Where possible, the first couple of words in a heading or paragraph should describe the content the user would discover if he or she read on. Another renowned usability expert, Steve Krug, recommends that, when devising a web page, users look at the copy they started with and divide it in half. Then they should halve it again because most sites are far too wordy. By his own admission, the second one is an exaggeration, but his point is that most sites can get their message across in far fewer words if they really try.
- **Use subheadings to split up text.** If you have a lot of text, you should split it up with descriptive subheadings. Again make sure the first couple of words of the heading give the reader information about the content of the following text.
- **Use bolding and other styles.** Highlight keywords to help users scan pages for key terms, indicating whether the page is relevant to them.
- **Make links descriptive.** Where you have text links, ensure that the text describes what people will see if they click on the link. Links should also stand out from surrounding text (because many people will scan for links).
- **Stimulate users with visuals.** A lot of web users are attracted to (and navigate by) images. So if you have a list of articles or products on your site, thumbnails will help turn lists into something more visual and stimulating, in turn encouraging users to follow those links.

If you are designing a site for a company that's likely to want to change the main feature on a site regularly, you should consider allocating a part of the page for the company to control. You may give a proportion of the homepage (or homepages of the subcategories) to them for regularly changing features. For example, a shop might change the main section of a page every time there is an upcoming occasion it wants to market, such as religious holidays, New Year's, Valentine's Day, Mother's Day, Father's Day, start of school terms, and so on. It is usually better to give the company a section (or sections) of the page that it can edit rather than giving it free rein over the entire page (otherwise it may well be tempted to change the entire structure of the page even though visitors are used to it, and in doing so may break your grid). It is not uncommon for the person responsible for a company's web site to want to change the site more frequently than is necessary — this is often because this person spends more time looking at it than other visitors (and changing a site too often can frustrate visitors who get used to navigating a site in a particular way).

Homepages

First impressions do count, so your front page is very important. Unless you are working on a site for a company or subject that is a household name, it's important that a visitor be able to ascertain the main purpose of your site easily from the front page. Therefore, it is a good idea to feature a one-line description of the site prominently on the homepage (using no more than ten words — three to five is even better).

You then need to emphasize the tasks that users are most likely to want to come to the site to do — in order to help the most people find the information they came to see as quickly as possible.

You'll remember back to the beginning of the chapter where we talked about identifying personas for the target audience — specifying goals that each of these people would want to achieve, and prioritizing the importance of each of these goals — helping the personas achieve their goals should be the main focus of the homepage. You can also consider other things that might drive these personas into the site.

Because visitors tend to scan pages rather than reading all of their content, all headings and link names should begin with important keywords that help users understand what is in that section or link.

Also, because some people are very visual browsers and respond more to pictures than to text, you should consider the use of relevant photographs to help describe content in parts of a site and to encourage visitors to click on the links (you should also use descriptive text in the `alt` attribute on any `<img>` tags for those who cannot see the pictures).

It is crucial to remember that your front page should not solely cover what a company's marketing department wants it to cover that week or month. It's not just some advertising billboard they can use as they fancy — it must address the needs of the majority of visitors to the site. For example, the marketing department may want to push a new product, whereas most customers visiting the site want to find out about an older, more established one. If those users cannot find the information they came to the site looking for, the marketing department will not have as large an audience for the things they want to push. Balancing what the users want with what the company wants is extremely important — and users should not suffer.

Content Pages

Content pages are the meat of most sites; for example, on news sites they can contain articles, and on e-commerce sites they can contain details of each product. A content page should display the content in a way that makes it easy for the user to read the information.

As mentioned earlier, if you have several products or services, the information that you offer should fit in a template that is used for each content page and the presentation of information on these pages should be consistent for each item. For example, if you are dealing with clothes, a visitor should quickly and easily be able to look in the same place on each page in order to tell the colors and sizes in which a garment is available.

You should not make a page too busy because a clean presentation allows users to focus on the content. Even if you have a lot of information to fit on a page, group or chunk related information and make sure there is plenty of space between different elements.

Images should be relevant to the product, service, or topic in question and will usually look better if they are left- or right-aligned, with the text flowing around them. There should also be a gap between any images and the text that flows around them (set using margin properties in CSS).

If your site promotes products or services, these pages need to be action-oriented featuring a prominent "call to action." For example, if customers can buy the item they should be encouraged to do so with buttons that they can clearly click on with obvious titles such as "add to basket." If they have to inquire about a product or service before they can purchase it, then there should be a clear call to action for them to " inquire about this item." The inquiry could be a button or could feature a form for the visitor to fill in on the page.

Section Homepages

Between the homepage and the content pages there are often section homepages, particularly on larger sites. These are often necessary because:

- The section features too much information to fit on one page.
- There is not enough space on the homepage of that section to explain all the content that the user will find in this section.

There are usually two primary tasks that a section homepage needs to achieve:

- Let people know what content is in this section of the site. As with the homepage, a one-line description will often help users understand the section.
- Offer links to view the individual pages that they will find in this section of the site.

There is a rule that you may hear mentioned called the *three-click rule*, which states that people should be able to find the information they came to your site for in no more than three clicks (and that if users cannot find what they want within three clicks they will leave your site). As a result of this rule some larger sites have section homepages with a *huge* number of options for the user to pick from (otherwise they will not adhere to the three-click rule). More recent research has shown that users become frustrated if they have difficulty picking which link they need to follow, and that rather than setting an arbitrary limit of three clicks it is better to make their journey (and choice of what to click on) easy. If they have to click on five links to find what they want, it may well be less frustrating than getting there in three clicks if getting there in three clicks involved tougher decision making.

Selecting Images

The use of images has a huge impact on visitors' perceptions of a site. Attractive photographs and illustrations can make the difference between a below-average site and an attractive site (and a bad image on the homepage can create a poor impression which may discourage a user from delving deeper into the site).

It is not uncommon for those creating web sites to commission high-quality photographs and videos just for the sites (just as they might for adverts and brochures). Often these are not just photos of products; they are images that represent a lifestyle or portray an image the company is trying to associate with the brand. But shooting especially for the Web is not always necessary — sometimes a company will have photography it has already had taken for other marketing materials and you should consider using this.

You should also familiarize yourself with *stock photography* web sites (sites that sell images for use in marketing and PR). At the cheaper end of the market are sites such as `www.istockphoto.com` and `www.sxc.hu`, and at the more expensive end of the spectrum are sites such as `www.gettyimages.com` and `www.corbis.com`.

I would strongly advise against using clip art on your site as it generally looks quite amateurish. It's fine for a hobby site, but not ideal for a company web site.

Whatever image you use, you should ensure that you have the necessary copyright permission. If you do not, you could end up with either a court case, a heavy fine, or at the very least a letter telling you to remove the image (which would mean that you would have to redesign the site and explain your mistake to the client).

I have worked in the past with clients who have terrible logos that really bring down the look of the site, yet they are not interested in changing them. If you are unfortunate enough to come across such a logo, you are best off keeping the actual size of the logo relatively small; then you can rely on the company's colors to maintain the identity, and if the logo is graphical you can sometimes even add the company name in a larger plain font near the logo.

Things You May Need from a Client

When working on a site for a client, you should ask for the following *before* starting to design the site:

- An electronic copy of the company logo
- Branding guidelines (if the client has them), which will include things such as the company's color scheme, choice of typefaces, and other rules to help ensure that information representing the brand has a cohesive appearance
- Copies of brochures or leaflets that they have done (particularly if they do not have branding guidelines)

- Materials the client supposed to provide such as photographs
- Any text the client wants to write (preferably in electronic format which will allow you to copy and paste it rather than re-type it)

I generally avoid starting work on a site until the client has provided most of these things (otherwise you can spend lots of time on a project only to end up waiting a long time for the client to finish the copy or get some photographs taken).

Coding Your Design

Now that you have a good idea of how your page will be structured, it is time to start translating it into code.

In Chapter 8, you saw how the contents of an XHTML page appears in the order that you wrote it in the XHTML file; block-level elements such as headings and paragraphs would sit on top of each other, while inline elements such as images and emphasized text would sit alongside text and other inline elements. This is called normal flow.

In order to position elements on the page, we will be taking them out of normal flow. In particular, we will be using:

- The XHTML `<div>` element to group elements of our XHTML page into blocks or chunks
- The CSS `float` property to position these `<div>` elements to the left or the right of the page
- The CSS `width` property to set how wide the boxes should be (if you do not set a `width` property on a floated element, it takes up the full width of the page — just as it would in normal flow)
- The CSS `margin` property to separate blocks from each other

In this section, we are going to expand on that and learn how to create far more complex layouts. Before we delve into some sample layouts, there are a couple of points to note.

The IE Box Model Bug

You should always include a DOCTYPE declaration in your XHTML pages. If you do not, Internet Explorer will use a different version of the box model to all other browsers, and your pages will break or look bigger in Internet Explorer than they would in other browsers (Figure 9-24).

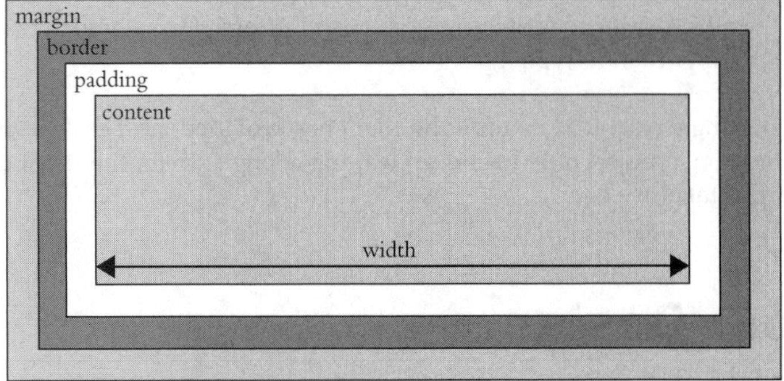

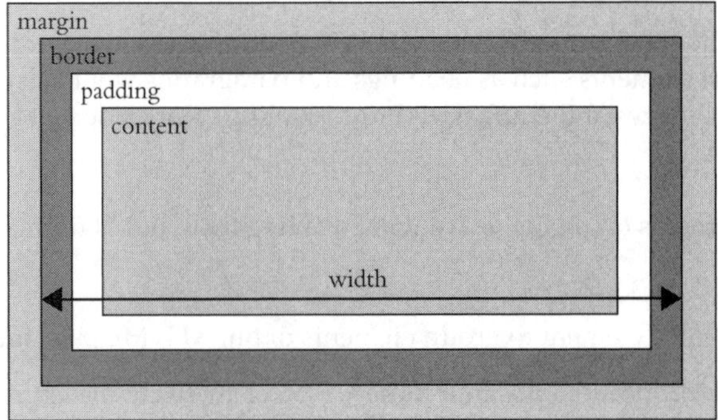

Figure 9-24

Including one of the following DOCTYPE declarations ensures that Internet Explorer version 6 and later will render the page correctly.

Here is the transitional XHTML DOCTYPE:

```
<!DOCTYPE html PUBLIC "-//W3C//DTD XHTML 1.0 Transitionalt//EN"
 "http://www.w3.org/TR/xhtml1/DTD/xhtml1-transitional.dtd">
```

And here is the strict XHTML DOCTYPE:

```
<!DOCTYPE html PUBLIC "-//W3C//DTD XHTML 1.0 Transitionalt//EN"
 "http://www.w3.org/TR/xhtml1/DTD/xhtml1-transitional.dtd">
```

Working with a Grid

If you have designed a page using a fixed-width grid, you can add the grid to the background of your pages while building them using the CSS `background-image` property. This will help you ensure that you align elements to the grid. To do this you will need a 1-pixel-tall version image of the grid which can then be repeated vertically.

Unfortunately, you cannot do this for liquid designs because you cannot vary the size and background image as the layout expands and contracts.

As an example, we will add the 12-column grid we were looking at earlier in the chapter to the background of the page, as shown in Figure 9-25.

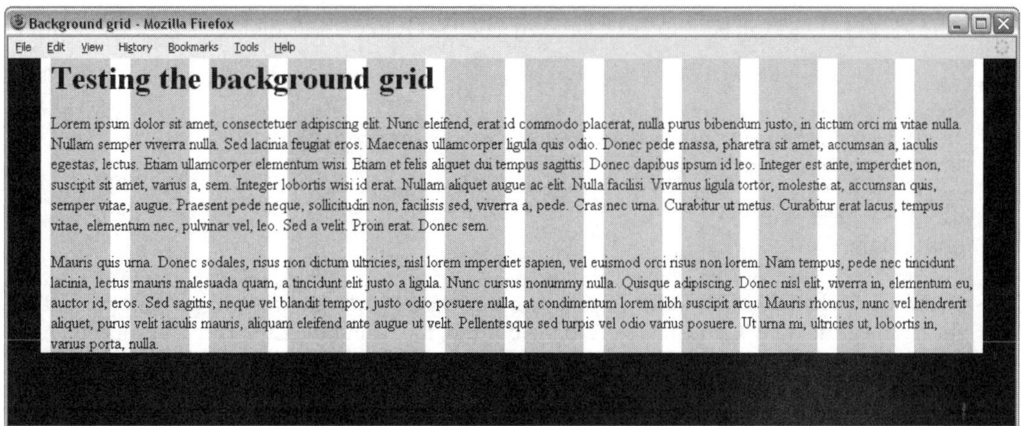

Figure 9-25

This example uses two `<div>` elements:

- The first has an `id` attribute whose value is `frame`; it will be the width of the grid.
- The second has an `id` attribute with a value of `page`; it is the width of the page less the gutter to the left and right.

Here is the code for `ch09_eg03.html`:

```
<body>
  <div id="frame">
    <div id="page">
      <h1>Testing the background grid</h1>
      <p>Lorem ipsum dolor sit amet...</p>
    </div>
  </div>
</body>
```

Now here is the CSS for this page (`ch09_eg03.css`). The first thing to note is that we set the `margin` property on the `<body>` element to `0px`. Otherwise, some browsers will add space inside the browser window and our site will not reach the top of the page. We also need to set the `text-align` property to have a value of `center`, so that the page frame will be centered in the middle of the page in IE versions 5 and 6.

```
body {
  background-color:#000000;
  margin:0px;}
  text-align:center;}
```

For the first of the <div> elements, we want to:

- Make it the width of the grid using the width property
- Add the grid to the back of the element using the background-image property, then use the background-repeat property to ensure that the grid repeats down the page
- Center the element using the margin-left and margin-right properties with a value of auto; and set text-align back to left (since we had set it to center on the <body> element).

```
#frame {
  width:960px;
  background-image:url("images/960px_12_col_grid.gif");
  background-repeat:repeat:y;
  margin-left:auto;
  margin-right:auto;}
  text-align:left;}
```

The second <div> element is not quite as wide as the frame because there is a 10-pixel gutter to the left and right on the grid. We will add 10 pixels to the bottom, too, using the CSS margin property.

```
#page {
  margin:0px 10px 10px 10px;
  background-color:#ffffff; }
```

In order to make the page look like the screenshot, you will need to set the margin of the <h1> element to 0px too — otherwise the browser will set space above the element and push the grid down the page.

Sometimes you may prefer to save an image of the entire page design and use this as a background image (effectively it would be like using code to trace over the boxes in your design).

Multi-Column Layouts

Now let's take a look at how to code some more complex layouts. We are going to start with a three-column layout, then look at a two-column layout, and finally add combinations of four and six columns as well.

Three-Column Layout

The first example we will look at features three columns, as well as a header, a navigation bar under the header, and a footer at the bottom of the page.

If you look at Figure 9-26 you can see the general layout of the page that we will be creating; there will be a header that takes up the full width of the page, followed by a navigation bar that will take up the full width of the page; under this will be three columns sitting next to each other, and finally a footer taking up the width of the page at the bottom.

Figure 9-26 is just intended to show you the structure of the page and how the XHTML elements you are about to meet map onto the layout (for example you can compare the code <div id="header"> header</div> in this figure to the code used to create that block. To see a screenshot of the finished example we are building, flick forward a couple of pages to see Figure 9-27.

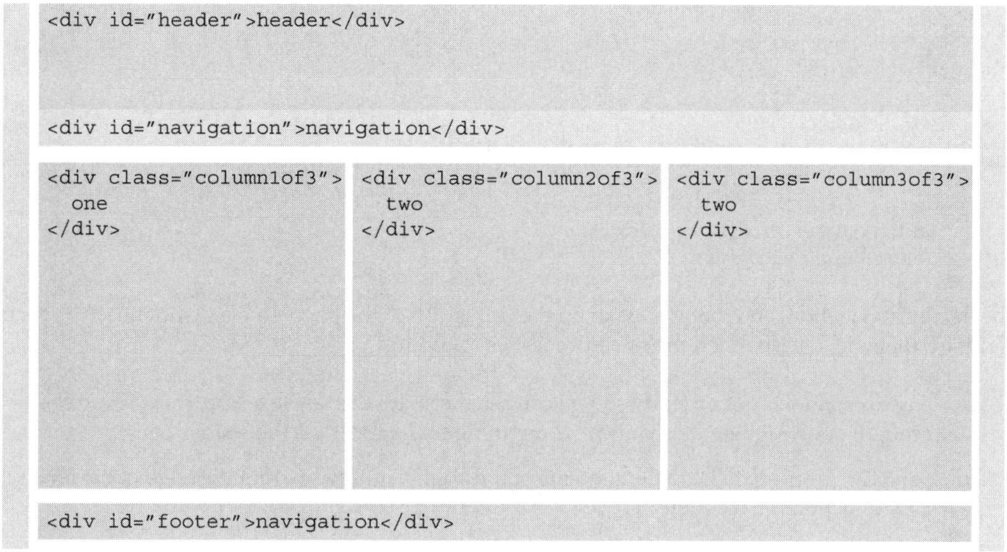

<div id="header">header</div>

<div id="navigation">navigation</div>

<div class="column1of3"> one </div>

<div class="column2of3"> two </div>

<div class="column3of3"> two </div>

<div id="footer">navigation</div>

Figure 9-26

Here you can see the code that generates a page with three columns that is similar to this structure (`ch09_eg04.html`). Note how the values for the `class` attributes on the columns indicate how many columns the page is divided into and which column is which. For example, the first column has a value of `column1of3`:

```
<body>
  <div id="frame">
    <div id="page">
      <div id="header">header</div>
      <div id="navigation">navigation</div>
      <div class="column1of3">column 1 of 3</div>
      <div class="column2of3">column 2 of 3</div>
      <div class="column3of3">column 3 of 3</div>
      <div id="footer">footer</div>
    </div>
  </div>
</body>
```

You could add other elements inside any of these `<div>` elements — for example, your header would likely contain an `<h1>` element with the name of the site, or an image containing the logo for the site. The navigation would contain `<a>` elements that would link to the pages of the site, and so on.

Now let's take a look at the CSS for this page (`ch09_eg04.css`). We can start with the rules for the `<body>` element and two `<div>` elements. These rules are virtually identical to the rules that contained the grid in the last example.

```
body {
  margin:0px;
  background-color:#000000;
  font-family:arial, verdana, sans-serif;}
  text-align:center;}
```

```
#frame {
  margin-left:auto;
  margin-right:auto;
  text-align:left;
  width:960px;
  background-image:url("images/960px_12_col_grid.gif");
  background-repeat:repeat-y;}
#page {
  padding:0px 10px 10px 10px;
  background-color:#ffffff;}
```

The header, navigation, and footer all take up the full width of the page, so we do not need to specify a width for them. I have provided the same properties for each:

- `background-color` property so you can see the space the box takes up; this also acts as a grouping or chunking mechanism for anything that appears in the header.
- `padding` property to keep the contents of these elements away from the edge of the box, which makes them more readable.
- `height` property to help the boxes sit nicely in the grid.

The footer also features a `clear` property, to ensure that it sits beneath the columns, and a `border` property on the top of the element to create a gap between the columns and the footer (you should not use the `margin` property and `clear` property on the same element because different browsers treat them in different ways).

```
#header {
  background-color:#cccccc;
  height:120px;
  padding:10px;}
#navigation {
  background-color:#efefef;
  height:40px;
  padding:10px;}
#footer {
  background-color:#cccccc;
  height:40px;
  padding:10px;
  clear:both;
  border-top:20px solid #ffffff;}
```

Finally, we come to the three columns. To make them sit nicely next to each other, use the following two properties:

- `float` to take the items out of normal flow.
- `width` to specify the width of the element that is being floated (if you do not specify a width the element will take up the full width of the container — just like the header, navigation, and footer do).

As with the header, navigation, and footer, the `background-color` property creates a chunk or group, the `padding` separates the content from the edge of the box making it more readable, and the `margin` on top of the boxes ensures that the boxes do not touch the navigation or other columns above them. The `height` property is only there for visual effect.

```
.column1of3, .column2of3, .column3of3 {
  float:left;
  width:280px;
  background-color:#cccccc;
  padding:10px;
  margin-top:20px;
  height:173px;}
```

Remember that the padding is added to the width of the box. Because we want the columns to be 300 pixels wide and to have 10 pixels of padding, the `width` property of the box should be set to `280px`.

There is one last property we need to set — the `margin` property — which adds the gutter that separates the boxes from each other. We only want to apply a gutter between the first and second columns, and between the second and third columns (because there is already a gutter to the left and right of the page). To achieve this, we will just set the `margin-right` property of the first and second columns.

```
.column1of3, .column2of3 {margin-right:20px;}
```

You can see the result in Figure 9-27, and you can try it out for yourself using the download code for the book. Note how you can still just about see the grid poking through the design between the navigation and the columns.

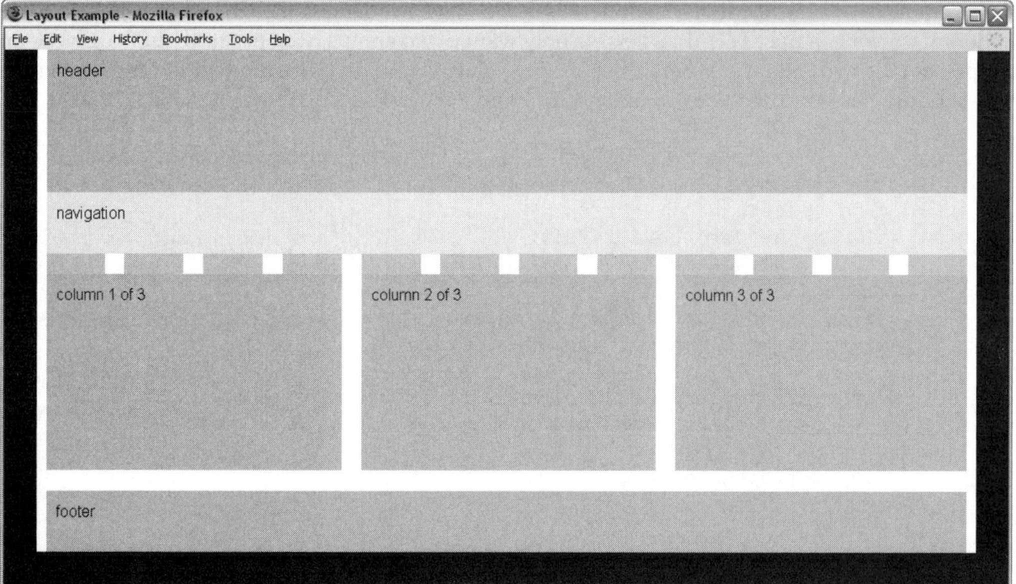

Figure 9-27

Two-Column Layouts

You've now seen a three-column layout, so let's look at how we could merge two columns and create a two-column grid. As Figure 9-28 shows, you could merge either columns 1 and 2 or columns 2 and 3.

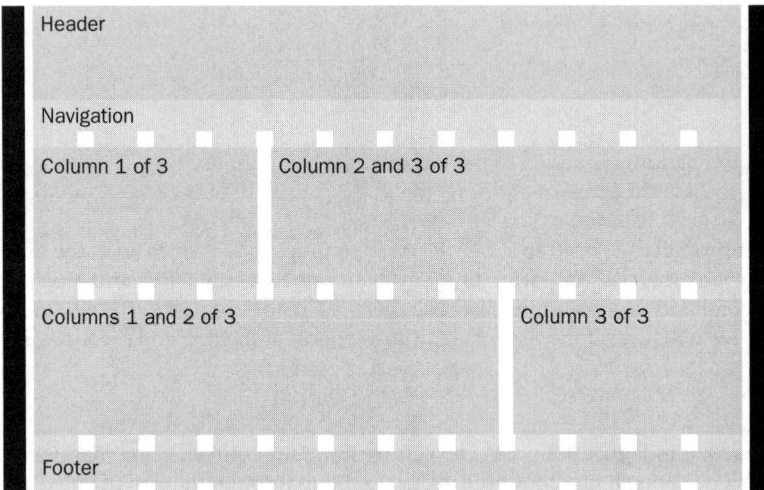

Figure 9-28

This example is very similar to the last one. We do not have to change much in the code to create these additions. Looking at the XHTML, when we only want two columns, we only have two `<div>` elements to represent the two columns. Where these `<div>` elements take up twice the width, we have two new values for the class attributes: `columns1and2of3` and `columns2and3of3` (`ch09_eg05.html`).

```
<body>
  <div id="frame">
    <div id="page">
      <div id="header">header</div>
      <div id="navigation">navigation</div>

      <div class="columns1and2of3">column 1 and 2 of 3</div>
      <div class="column3of3">column 3 of 3</div>

      <div class="column1of3">column 1 of 3</div>
      <div class="columns2and3of3">columns 2 and 3 of 3</div>

      <div id="footer">footer</div>
    </div>
  </div>
</body>
```

Now let's turn to the CSS. First we have to add a rule for these wider boxes; the only difference between this and the one for single columns is that the `width` property has a value of `600px` (`ch09_eg05.css`):

```
.columns1and2of3, .columns2and3of3 {
  float:left;
  width:600px;
  background-color:#cccccc;
  padding:10px;
  margin-top:20px;}
```

We also need to make sure that the new class representing the block that goes across columns 1 and 2 has a margin to the right, so we add the class selector to this line:

```
.column1of3, .column2of3, .columns1and2of3 {margin-right:20px;}
```

The result is shown in Figure 9-29.

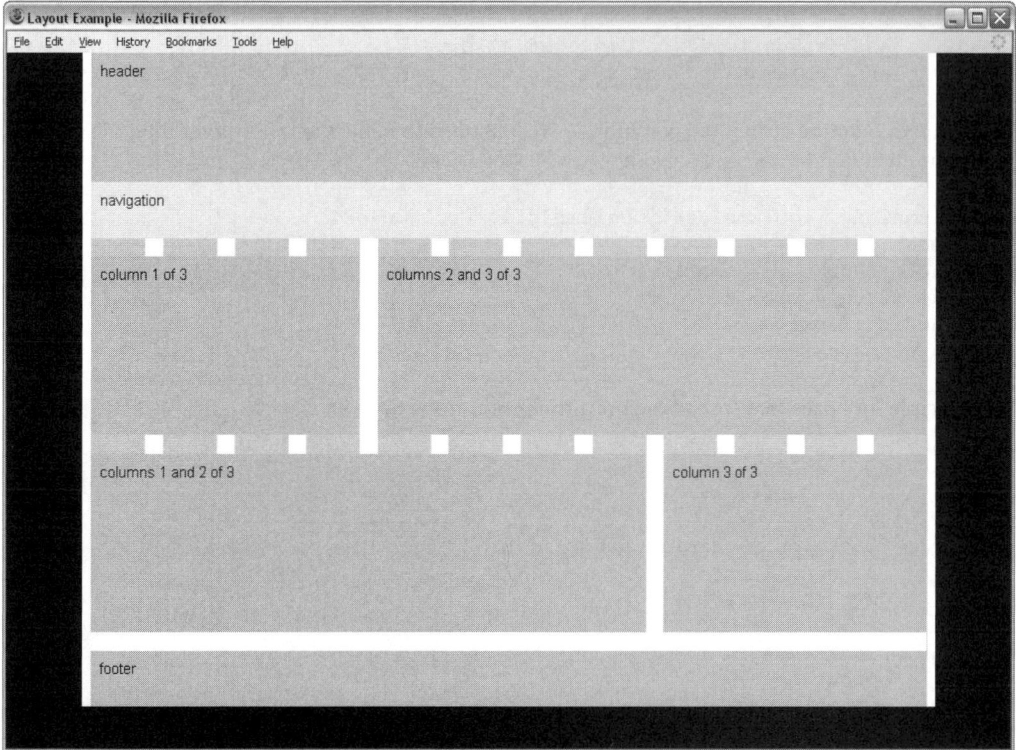

Figure 9-29

Four-Column Layouts

When I introduced the 960-pixel, 12-column grid, I pointed out that 12 could be divided by 2, 3, 4, and 6. Therefore, we can easily take this model and adapt it for four-column layouts. In this case the XHTML to create four columns might look like this (`ch09_eg06.html`):

```
<div class="column1of4">column 1 of 4</div>
<div class="column2of4">column 2 of 4</div>
<div class="column3of4">column 3 of 4</div>
<div class="column4of4">column 4 of 4</div>
```

You could have a class that represented the first two columns, and separate boxes for columns 3 and 4, like so:

```
<div class="columns1and2of4">columns 1 and 2 of 4</div>
<div class="column3of4">column 3 of 4</div>
<div class="column4of4">column 4 of 4</div>
```

Or you could have a class that created one box that spans columns 2, 3, and 4, like so:

```
<div class="column1of4">column 1 of 4</div>
<div class="columns2and3and4of4">columns 2 and 3 and 4 of 4</div>
```

Here is the CSS for the individual columns — we just need to make them narrower than the three-column layout (`ch09_eg06.css`):

```
.column1of4, .column2of4, .column3of4, .column4of4 {
  float:left;
  width:200px;
  background-color:#cccccc;
  padding:10px;
  margin-top:20px;}
```

The principle for boxes that spread over multiple columns is the same:

```
.columns1and2of4 {
        float:left;
        width:440px;
        background-color:#cccccc;
        padding:10px;
        margin-top:20px;}

.columns2and3and4of4 {
        float:left;
        width:680px;
        background-color:#cccccc;
        padding:10px;
        margin-top:20px;}
```

Again, we add a margin to the right of all elements except for those that fill up the right-most column:

```
.column1of4, .column2of4, .column3of4, .columns1and2of4 {margin-right:20px;}
```

You can see the result in Figure 9-30.

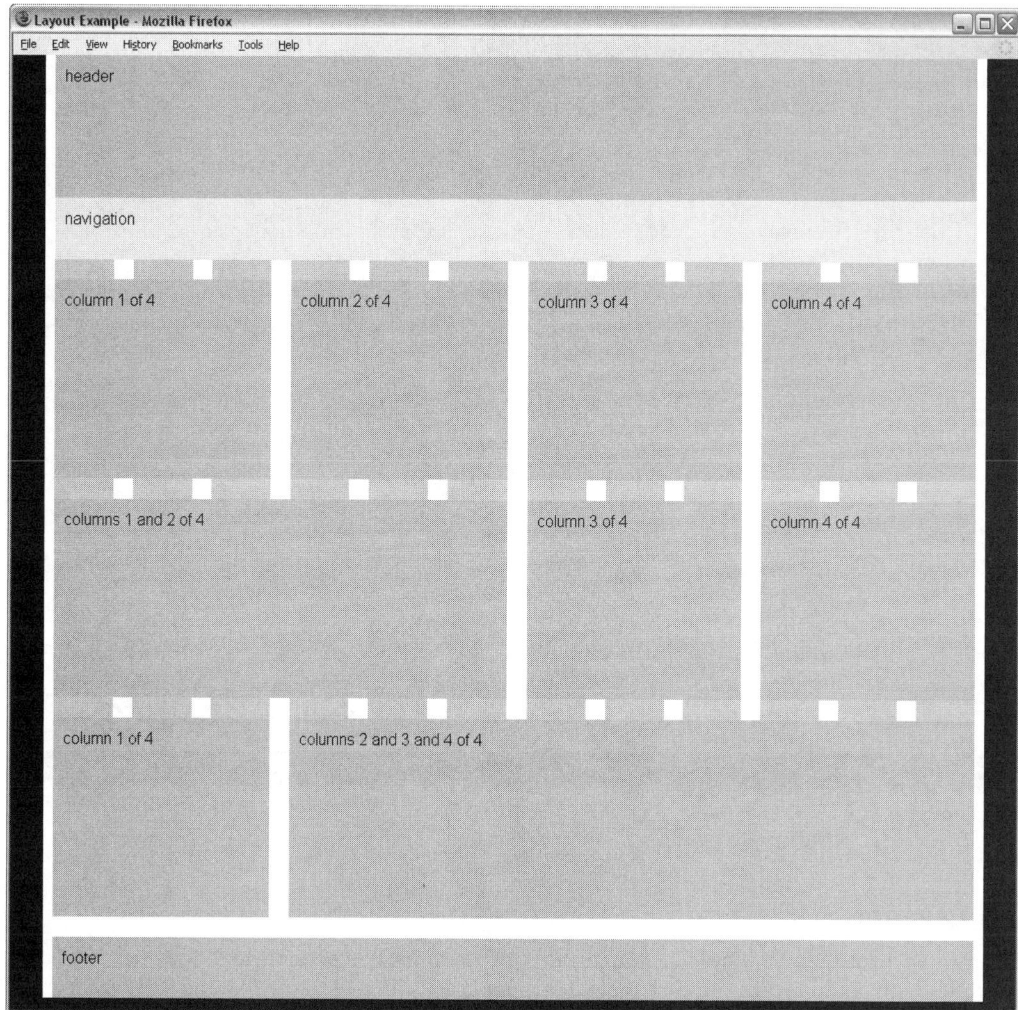

Figure 9-30

Six-Column Layouts

You can use the same principle yet again to create six-column layouts. Figure 9-31 shows you how two-, three-, and six-column layouts can all be made to work with this one grid. If you would like to look at the code for this example, it is provided with the rest of the code for this chapter; the files are `ch09_eg07.html` and `ch09_eg07.css`.

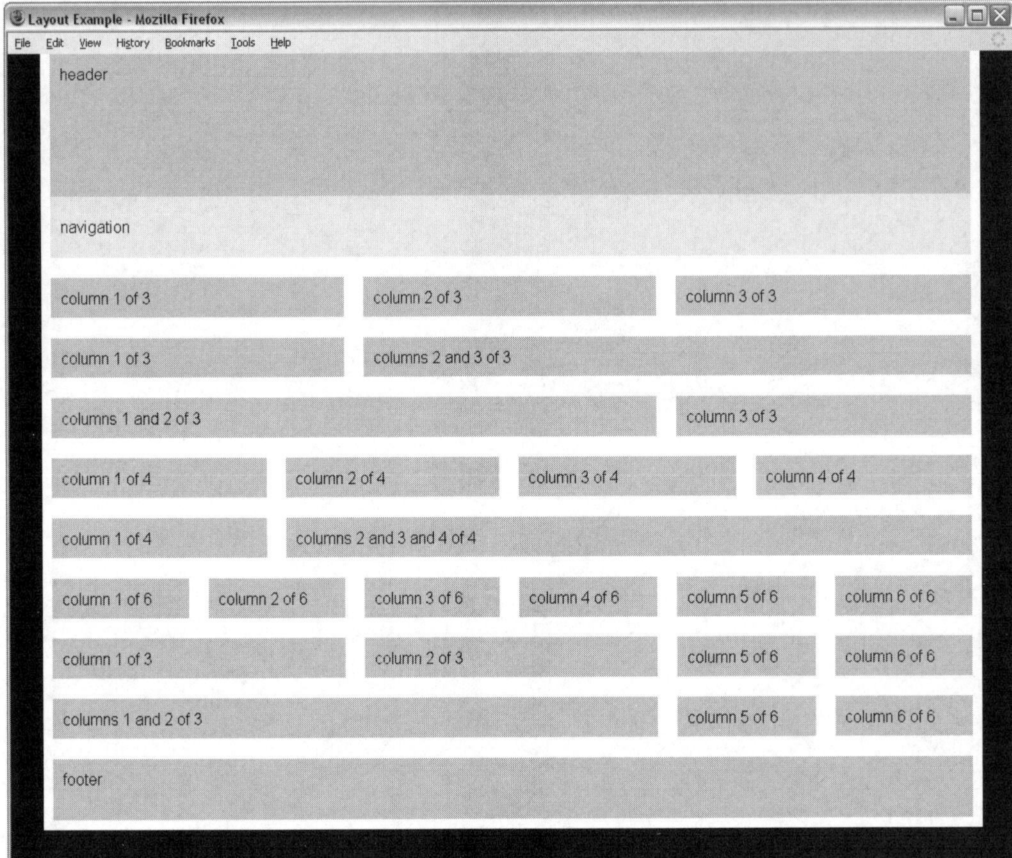

Figure 9-31

Liquid Layouts

So far we have looked at multiple-column fixed-width layouts. It is possible to follow the same principles with liquid layouts. In such cases, you simply have to make sure that the widths are specified using percentages rather than pixels.

Start with your layout grid and work out the percentage of each column. In the following table you can see the width of each column in pixels from the fixed-width design, and the percentage width we are using in the liquid design. Because the gutters on this page stretch to the edge of the browser window, we will make them the same size as the ones between columns.

Column	Pixel size in fixed-width design	Percentage size in liquid layout
Gutter 1	10px	2%
Column 1	300px	30%
Gutter 2	20px	2%
Column 2	300px	30%
Gutter 3	20px	2%
Column 3	300px	30%
Gutter 4	10px	2%
Total	960px	98%

If you have not already seen it, check the final row showing the totals at the bottom of this table. It shows that the entire width of the design is only going to take up 98 percent of the screen. You must leave 2 percent extra space to the right of the page because when browsers calculate percentages they round the size to the nearest pixel, and therefore if the design tried to take up 100 percent of the browser window, the total width might be more than is available (which could throw out the entire layout).

So, let's look at an example; this time the code does not need the two containing `<div>` elements, so it will just look like this (`ch09_eg08.html`):

```
<body>
  <div id="header">header</div>
  <div id="navigation">navigation</div>
  <div class="column1of3">column 1 of 3</div>
  <div class="column2of3">column 2 of 3</div>
  <div class="column3of3">column 3 of 3</div>
  <div id="footer">footer</div>
</div>
</div>
</body>
```

Now let's look at the CSS to go with this example. If you do not specify a width for a block-level element, it will take up the full width of the page. Therefore we do not need to set the width of the header, navigation, or footer (`ch09_eg08.css`).

```
#header {
  background-color:#cccccc;
  padding:10px;
  height:120px;}

#navigation {
  background-color:#efefef;
  padding:10px;
  height:40px;}
```

```
#footer {
  background-color:#cccccc;
  padding:10px;
  height:40px;
  clear:both;
  border-top:20px solid #ffffff;}
```

Looking back at the table, we still need to add Gutters 1, 2, and 3 to columns 1, 2, and 3 using the `margin-left` property with a value that is `2%`. We do not actually need to add Gutter 4 into the design because we have already allowed a little extra space to the right of the design.

We will also create padding in the boxes by giving the `padding` property a value of `1%`. Because the padding is added onto the width of the box, to create a box that takes up 30 percent of the screen, the `width` property for each column should have a value of `28%`.

```
/* 3 columns */
.column1of3, .column2of3, .column3of3 {
  float:left;
  width:28%;
  margin-left:2%;
  background-color:#cccccc;
  padding:1%;
  margin-top:20px;
  height:175px;}
```

You can see the result in Figure 9-32.

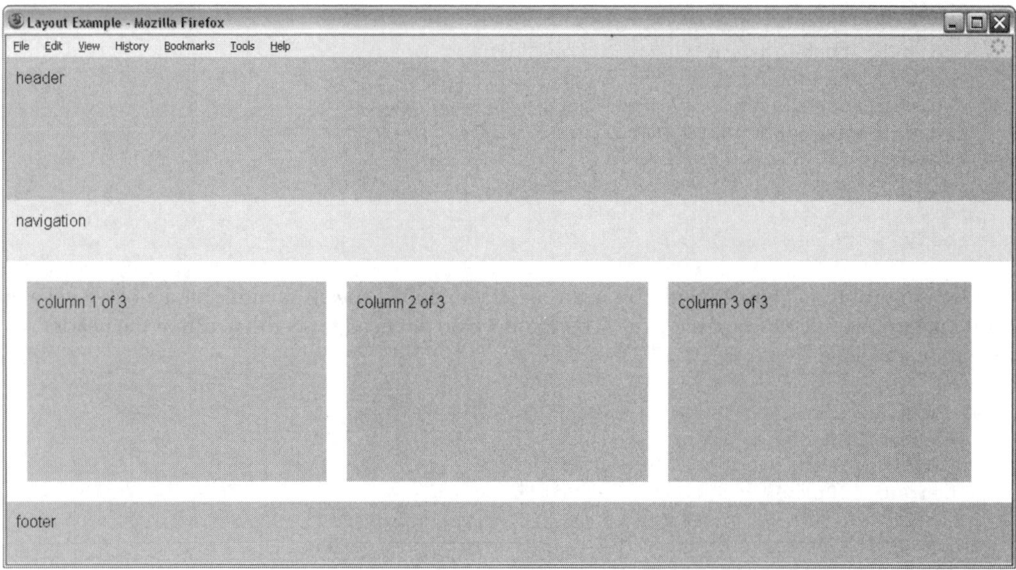

Figure 9-32

One of the issues with liquid layouts is that, because the user can shrink and increase the width of the boxes in the layout, the text may become too short or too long to read, and any fixed-width items (such as images) may end up poking out of boxes if they are too small.

In such cases, you can make use of the `min-width` and `max-width` attributes, which you read about in Chapter 7. Unfortunately, IE7 was the first version of Internet Explorer to support these properties. Luckily, the number of IE6 users is constantly shrinking, and since other browsers have supported these properties for longer, you should use them to help users whose browsers understand them (`ch09_eg09.css`).

```
.column1of3, .column2of3, .column3of3 {
  float:left;
  width:28%;
  margin-left:2%;
  background-color:#cccccc;
  padding:1%;
  margin-top:20px;
  height:175px;
  min-width:210px;
  max-width:400px;}
```

Once you specify a `min-width` property, if a user shrinks the window down quite small, you may find that content flows out of the boxes. You can use the `overflow` property to control what happens to content in such circumstances. Alternatively, you could put the three columns in a containing element and set a minimum width for that container element — wide enough to hold the minimum width of all three columns (`ch09_eg09.html`).

```
<div class="columns123">
  <div class="column1of3">
    <img src="images/golden_section.gif" width="200" height="75"
         alt="Golden Section" /> column 1 of 3
  </div>
  <div class="column2of3">column 2 of 3</div>
  <div class="column3of3">column 3 of 3</div>
</div>
```

Here is the rule that attaches the style to the new container element:

```
.columns123 {min-width:750px;}
```

You should also add the same minimum width to the other elements that take up the full width of the page since their width is calculated as the width of the browser window when the page loads, which means that these elements might not otherwise be as wide as the new container element.

Backgrounds That Reach the Bottom of the Page

One of the issues when you use the CSS `float` property to create columns is that when you specify a visible background color or border for the columns, each can look a different height. Let's add some content into the three-column layout you met earlier so you can see what happens:

```
<div class="column1of3">
 Lorem ipsum dolor sit amet, consectetur adipiscing elit.
```

```
  </div>
  <div class="column2of3">
    Lorem ipsum dolor sit amet, consectetur adipiscing elit.
    Quisque vel sem odio, et tincidunt magna. Nam malesuada justo non risus
    ullamcorper eget dignissim erat viverra.
  </div>
  <div class="column3of3">
    Lorem ipsum dolor sit amet, consectetur adipiscing elit.
    Quisque vel sem odio, et tincidunt magna. Nam malesuada justo non risus
    ullamcorper eget dignissim erat viverra. Mauris viverra massa ac libero
    feugiat tempor. Cras scelerisque fermentum dui et feugiat. Class aptent taciti
    sociosqu ad litora torquent per conubia nostra, per inceptos himenaeos.
  </div>
```

Figure 9-33 shows how the background for the box comes down only as far as the text (plus padding), which would not make for a very attractive design.

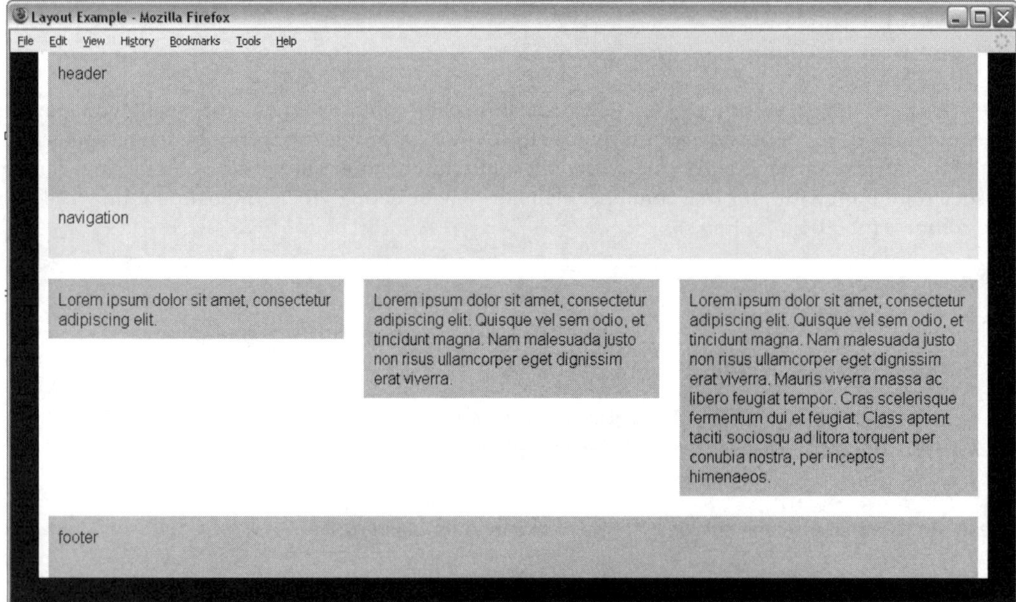

Figure 9-33

You have actually already seen a way around this problem, when we used the grid as a background image on the `<div>` element that had a `class` attribute whose value is `page`. By using a background image on the containing element, you can ensure that it applies to all columns, no matter how tall they are (`ch09_eg10.css`).

```
#frame {
  margin-left:auto;
  margin-right:auto;
  width:960px;
  background-color:#ffffff;
  background-image:url("images/960px_3column_background.gif");
  background-repeat:repeat-y;}
```

You can see the result in Figure 9-34.

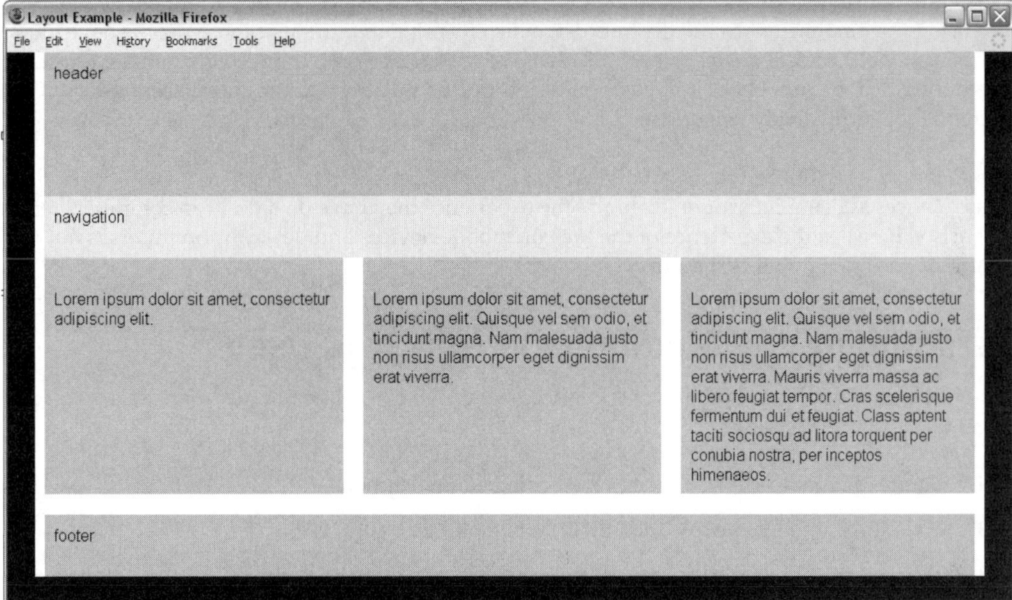

Figure 9-34

You are now well equipped to be creating well-thought-out sites and page layouts. If you are interested in finding out more about page layout, here are some good resources:

- **960.gs:** `http://960.gs/`
- **Blueprint:** `www.blueprintcss.org/`
- **YUI Grids:** `http://developer.yahoo.com/yui/grids/`

Before we finish looking at page layouts, we need to consider mobile phones that are used to access web pages.

Developing for Mobile Devices

Many people think that the use of the Web on mobile phones is not really relevant to them or their company, especially if they (or those in their peer group) do not use web services on their mobile phones. But two things are changing minds:

- The success of high-profile devices such as the Blackberry and iPhone
- Statistics that show how many people access web-based services on mobile phones

In 2009, the British government released statistics showing that 11 percent of UK mobile phone users were using their mobile to browse the Internet, which (bearing in mind that more people have mobile phones than web access) equates to over a fifth of web users accessing the Web via mobile devices. Considering that the number of mobile phones sold in 2008 outstripped the entire user base of PCs, this is a trend that is only likely to increase.

Despite the growing interest in the mobile Web, it is not uncommon for people to view the Web on mobile devices as being inferior or "behind" the experience they have on a desktop computer. Yet the comparison between the experience of the Web on mobile devices and desktop computers is not quite as straightforward as it might first seem.

Understanding the Medium and How It Is Used

When it comes to thinking about how people access the Web on mobile phones, there are some very important aspects to consider:

- **Context:** What the user is doing when using a mobile phone
- **Relationship:** How people treat their mobile phone
- **Capabilities:** The features and capabilities of mobile phones compared with desktop computers

Context: What Is the Mobile User Doing?

Mobile devices are being used on the move, often in a hurry, and sometimes one-handed. The result is that when mobile phones are used to access the Web, they are often used to achieve very different things than the same user might want to achieve in front of a desktop computer.

While people sit for hours in front of a desktop computer surfing the Web, when users are out and about, they are far less likely to be just surfing — rather they are more likely to want to do something specific (whether this is checking the local weather forecast, latest news headlines and sports results, or finding out the opening hours of a nearby shop).

It is important here to note that a laptop, even though it is portable, is often used in the same manner as a desktop, even if the user is in a coffee shop, a car park, or at an airport.

When you start to think about your site appearing on a mobile device, it is wise to go back to the beginning of this chapter and create a new set of actors or personae that reflects the typical visitors to your site via a mobile phone.

At the same time, you should be creating a new set of tasks that they might want to achieve, because the mobile user will often want to achieve different things than the desktop user would. For example, mobile users accessing a supermarket web site are more likely to look for the nearest store and its hours than they are to do their weekly grocery shopping on their phones.

Even if users want the same information that they might request when at a desktop computer (for example to check the latest sports results or weather forecast in their area), you should always consider whether they may benefit from the information being displayed in a very different way.

Relationship: How Do Users Treat Their Mobile Phones?

It is also worth comparing the relationship that people have with their mobile phones compared with desktop computers. It is far more common for people to have their own mobile phones whereas desktop computers are often shared between members of a family, or used at work and schools. This means that people have a more personal relationship with their mobile phones. It also means that it is possible to more accurately uniquely identify users and personalize services to them.

These devices are also usually carried around 24 hours a day, no matter where the owner is (they may be turned on silent, but rarely turned off).

Capabilities: How Do Features of Mobiles Compare with Desktop PCs?

Finally, we should compare capabilities of mobile phones and desktop computers. Here are some of the positive aspects of mobile phones that are not as apparent on desktop devices:

- **Allow for location specific services:** Because they can use triangulation or (where installed) GPS to identify location of users.
- **Have a built-in payment system:** Whether on contract or a pay-as-you-go scheme, the payment is integrated more than a desktop computer where a user must enter credit card information or set up an account with a service such as PayPal. The payment system is also available to those who are not old enough to have debit and credit cards. It has also been suggested that mobile phone owners are more used to (and willing to) pay for services accessed via their mobile than they are to pay for services accessed via a desktop computer.
- **Have a built-in camera:** Only a handful of desktop machines will have a camera built in, and those that do are still used in a desk-based setting (rather than being carried around all the time).
- **Are integrated with voice data:** Because they are phones as well, and although services such as Skype allow phone calls to be made through a computer, it is not inherent in the platform.
- **Have other features:** Such as SMS and MMS, which some users (particularly in Europe) use often.

Having said that, there are some inherent limitations with mobile devices:

- **Slower connection speeds:** The connection speeds of mobile phones consistently trail behind those offered by broadband connections.
- **Connection can be intermittent:** As users move about, for example when traveling in more isolated rural areas, or when going through tunnels in cities, their connection can be cut.
- **Screen are usually smaller:** Because screens are small, it is not possible for users to scan as much information to find out what they are looking for.
- **Input devices are harder to use:** Although many mobile users are adept at using their mobile phones, they are unlikely to achieve the same speed and accuracy of data input that they would achieve with a keyboard and mouse.
- **Less control over appearance:** Several phones will remove your choice of font, size of text, and background images to show them in a manner they see fit for the device.

Armed with this information, you can start to think about mobile development.

How to Approach Mobile Development

Often the key factors in deciding a mobile strategy will depend upon the resources a company has available for its web users and whether it has enough users to justify the expense of development. Broadly speaking, you can categorize the approaches in mobile development into one of three categories:

- Just have one main web site (no separate mobile site)
- Provide a different view of the content on your site to those with mobile phones
- Create an entirely new site for mobile users

Let's take a look at each of these options in turn.

Do Not Develop a Mobile Site

The cheapest and least time-intensive strategy for mobile development is simply to do nothing. Many mobile phones are adept at giving users access to the content on the site. Some larger touch-screen phones (such as the iPhone) are capable of cleverly resizing a web page to fit on the screen, then allow users to zoom into parts of the page. Other phones may change the way in which the page is presented in order to make it available on the size of screen they have (often overriding font sizes and image sizes).

The obvious drawback with this approach is that your content is not addressing the aims that visitors to a mobile site might have.

Provide an Alternative View of Your Site

A middle ground is to re-use the content that you have, but to present it in a manner that is easier for mobile users. In this middle ground there are two common options.

The first approach is to add a second style sheet to the same pages, so that mobile devices can use a separate set of CSS rules to control how the pages appear to them:

```
<link href="mobile.css" rel="stylesheet" type="text/css" media="handheld" />
```

This can help you use a different layout, change the dimensions of the page, and attempt to control colors and sizes of fonts.

Unfortunately, not all phones know to take this version of the style sheet, and those that do still have to download a page that is the same file size as the pages created for desktop computers (which means that they may take a long time to download).

I have seen style sheets for handheld devices that try to hide parts of the page (setting the CSS `display` property on those elements to `none`), which has the advantage that it makes the interface simpler, although it does not make the file size smaller.

The second approach is to use a different set of templates when someone arrives at your site via a mobile device. Rather than just using a new style sheet, some companies will use the same content, but design new pages to hold the information.

This approach allows a lot more flexibility because you can change the order in which items appear. You can also entirely remove some parts of the page (such as advertisements and secondary navigation), and therefore reduce bandwidth needed to load the pages.

Still, both of these methods still fail to address the context in which the phone is being used.

Create a Separate Mobile-Optimized with Its Own Content

If you have the resources available, users will often benefit from a site being specifically designed for use on a mobile phone. It allows you to address the requirements of users who are on the go (which are often different from those of a desktop PC user) and to understand the context in which visitors to your site use these devices.

A couple of good examples are `http://m.flickr.com/` (shown below in Figure 9-35) and `http://m.ebay.com/`(shown below in Figure 9-36). Both of these sites have been developed especially for mobile users (you should be able to access them from a desktop browser as well to get an idea of how they work). You may also note how the mobile version of Flickr also has a location-based option in the main navigation.

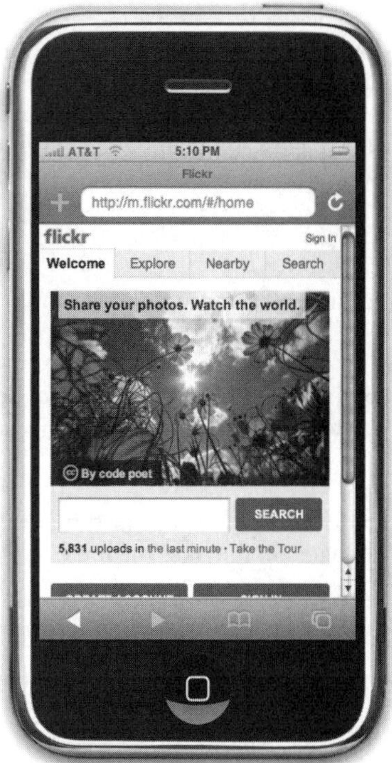

Figure 9-35

Figure 9-36

Should you have the opportunity to develop a site specifically for mobile users, it is very important to consider the function of these sites before addressing how they look. (Realistically the mobile offering is likely to look a lot more basic than the desktop site.) Also consider whether your users would benefit from features that are specific to mobile devices, such as location awareness (for example, a store might automatically show the closest locations), or the ability to send in pictures.

The first step is to look at the tasks you have identified as the most common ones that users will want to achieve on a mobile device and make them the first and most prominent offerings. In doing this, it is very important to retain focus on the main tasks and not try to give the mobile user every feature that is available on sites accessed by desktop computers. Content or features that are unlikely to be used on the go should be removed (or adapted into a form that will help mobile users).

Once you have worked out what it is that people want to achieve, and how you can meet their requirements, you can start to consider the practical aspects of your mobile site.

Building a Mobile Site

While there is not enough space in this book to go into this topic in great detail, and entire books have been written about building mobile web sites, I can give you some pointers regarding the key issues should you decide to create a site especially for mobile phones.

Domain Name

One of the most common questions regarding mobile development is whether to have a separate top-level domain name for the site because the `.mobi` top-level domain was created specifically for mobile devices.

In practice, a lot of companies have opted for a variation on their current address instead — for example, `m.domainname.com`, `mobile.domainname.com`, and `domainname.com/mobile`. In my opinion, the fewer taps a user has to make in order to reach a domain name on a mobile device, the better, which is why I tend to opt for the first of these options.

Device Detection

Device detection is a means by which the site attempts to tell whether a user is on a desktop computer or mobile phone, and then guide this user to the appropriate site.

Telling you how to do this is beyond the scope of this book, but the following two URLs should help you make a good start: `http://wurfl.sourceforge.net` or `www.andymoore.info`.

If you are able to offer device protection and send visitors to the mobile version of your site, it is a good idea to offer them a link to your full web site on the homepage. If they opt to use the full web site, you should aim to direct them to the same site in the future (when accessed from that phone).

Likewise, on your main web site, it is helpful to tell people that you have a mobile site, to make them more aware of its existence. You can also offer a link to the mobile version of the site.

Languages for Creating Mobile Web Sites

Most fairly recent phones that feature a web browser are capable of displaying XHTML and basic CSS. That doesn't mean that they will display them as you would expect. Some phones will show all text at the same size, and some will strip out styles that are not necessary (such as background images or colors). Others will show the more complex design.

Technically speaking, they tend to support one of two subsets of XHTML known as XHTML-Mobile Profile and XHTML Basic. A good rule of thumb, however, is just to stick to the most common XHTML features and then most phones will be able to handle it. Here is the DOCTYPE declaration for XHTML-Mobile Profile:

```
<!DOCTYPE html PUBLIC "-//WAPFORUM//DTD XHTML Mobile 1.0//EN"
 "http://www.wapforum.org/DTD/xhtml-mobile10.dtd">
```

While there is not enough space in this book to cover all the differences between XHTML-MP and XHTML, there are several resources on the Web that can help you with this, such as the Openwave developer's reference:

```
http://developer.openwave.com/documentation/xhtml_mp_css_reference/
```

Design Tips

Most new sites being created for mobile devices are targeting browsers that are between 240 and 320 pixels wide. The layout of these pages should generally be vertical pages that scroll down.

You still need white space in your designs so that they are easy to read. However, if you have too much white space, users will have to scroll more than necessary.

With the exception of touch phones such as the iPhone (and other larger screened phones), many of the browsers on mobile phones do not support the CSS float property, so your boxes are likely to be positioned one above the other, even if you tried to position them to the sides. Because block-level elements (by default) take up the full width of the page, they act like a liquid layout.

So, let's look at some specific issues regarding design for mobile devices.

Content

As we have already discussed, users are less likely to be just surfing the Web on a mobile phone; it is more likely that they are going to want to achieve tasks, and to do that quickly. Therefore:

- Use clear concise language. Content should be available in small bite-size chunks that are easy to digest.
- Use semantic markup, such as headings in `<hn>` elements, paragraphs in `<p>` elements, and so on.
- User fewer images and graphics to save on download speeds.
- Consider using the title of pages to indicate the action that a user should take.

Figure 9-37 shows the BBC news site on an iPhone; it uses less text and fewer images than the site for desktop computer users. The headlines are short and descriptive, while the page is designed to be long and thin (so users can scroll down to see more stories).

Color

Remember that many mobile phones are used outside where screens can be harder to read, and there is not often an easy way to adjust contrast. Therefore:

- ❑ Ensure that there is sufficient contrast in your designs.
- ❑ Avoid using backgrounds.

Figure 9-38 shows the simplified Amazon mobile homepage, which mainly features a search box for users to find the book or other product they are looking for. It is also worth noting on this example the link in the top left-hand corner to the "PC Site."

Figure 9-37

Figure 9-38

Navigation

Because those accessing the Web on a mobile device often want to achieve a task quickly, navigation is of primary importance — not only in helping them achieve their task as quickly as possible, but also because there is less space on the screen to show navigation options.

- Consider having the main navigation on the homepage only (with a link back to the homepage on every other page), or if you do have a navigation bar at the top of every page, have the minimum number of options you can.
- At the end of each page have home and back links, but don't repeat the links that appear on the bottom of the site used by desktop visitors (such as `about`, `help`, and `faq`).
- Consider using access keys for links (we discussed access keys in Chapter 5 when we were looking at Forms).

Figure 9-39 shows the result of a search on the Amazon mobile site. As you can see , there is a link back to the homepage at the top of the page (rather than a navigation bar), and this is followed by another small search box before showing the results.

Figure 9-39

Links

Although CSS allows you a lot of control over how links are presented, it is considered good practice on mobiles to keep links simple and obvious:

- Stick to black text and blue links, and avoid using other colors for links. Remember that many mobile phones are used outside where screens can be harder to read.
- Make it clear which link is active because it is harder to get the right link.
- For phones, while iPhone and the Mobile Opera browser automatically determine phone numbers, you can put phone numbers in `<a>` tags, with the `href` attribute starting with `tel`:

```
<a href="tel:+44 (0) 208 208 2080">+44 (0) 208 208 2080</a>
```

Forms

Filling in a form on a mobile phone is harder for most people than it would be on a desktop computer; not only might people be on the move, using one hand; they also have to contend with smaller buttons or input devices. Therefore you should avoid using form controls as much as possible:

- Consider using links instead of form controls.
- Do not mask passwords. The use of dots or asterisks on password inputs was to prevent people looking over the shoulder of the user from seeing the password entered; this is not so much of an issue on mobile devices (and it is easier to make mistakes when typing on a mobile device).
- If you have fields that only allow numbers (such as quantity fields), only allow people to enter numbers into these form fields (this technique is sometimes known as an input mask).
- Avoid logins unless absolutely necessary.

Testing

With the number of mobile devices available today, no one would expect you to test a mobile site on every available phone. Some developers choose to run a few phones with varying capabilities (switching one SIM card between them), but you can always ask friends to see if they can access a site for you and show you what it looks like on their phones.

You can also use the following emulators, which mimic the abilities of phones:

- dotMobi emulator — simulates Sony Ericsson K750 and Nokia N70 (`http://mtld.mobi/emulator.php`)
- Opera Mini Simulator (`www.operamini.com/`)
- Nokia Mobile Browser Simulator (`www.forum.nokia.com/`)
- Openwave phone simulator (`http://developer.openwave.com/dvl/tools_and_sdk/phone_simulator/`)
- iPhoney (`www.marketcircle.com/iphoney/`)
- Blackberry (`http://na.blackberry.com/eng/developers/resources/simulators.jsp`)

Another handy tool is the Firefox Web Developer Toolbar, which allows you to test pages on small screens (`https://addons.mozilla.org/en-US/firefox/addon/60`). This feature is available from the Miscellaneous menu, under the option Small Screen Rendering, as shown in Figure 9-40.

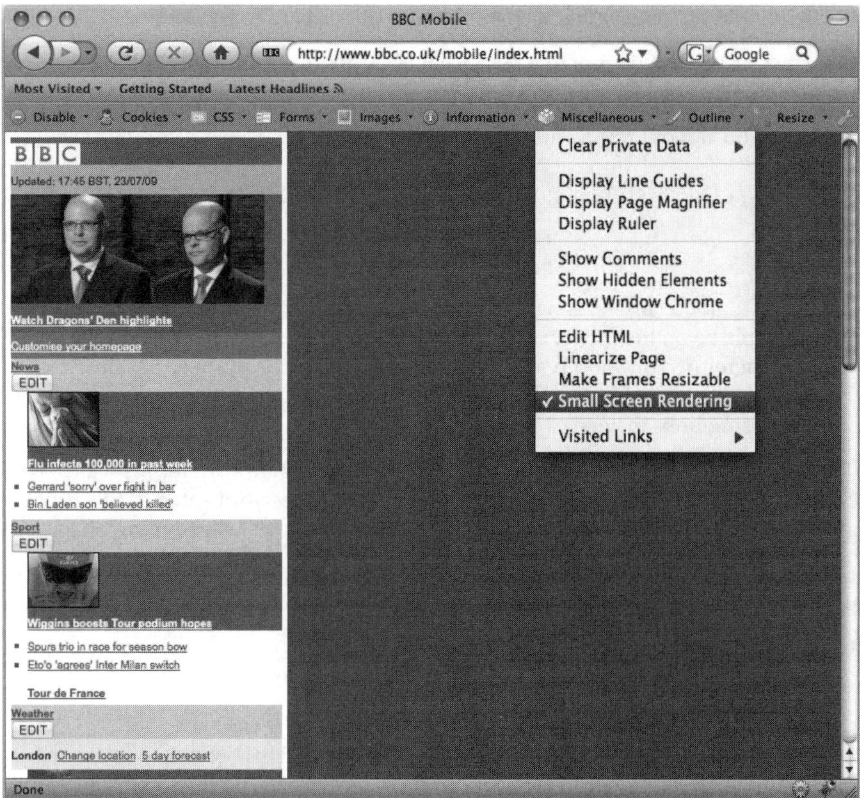

Figure 9-40

Once you know that your site is working, don't forget to test with real users (which is something we discuss in Chapter 13). It is also a good idea to validate your markup (also discussed in Chapter 13) because mobile phones are less forgiving of markup with errors than browsers such as IE, Firefox, and Safari on desktop computers. The W3C provides a tool for validating markup for mobiles here: `http://validator.w3.org/mobile/`.

Summary

This chapter introduced you to techniques for designing pages that are attractive and that meet the needs of those who visit them. You learned a process that helps you determine the information a visitor might expect to find on the site. You saw that this process involved creating fictional actors or personae who represented the typical audience, working out the tasks that these people would want to achieve, and determining the information needed to achieve those goals.

The information that visitors might expect to find was then added to the information that the site owners might want to convey (bearing in mind that the two may be different). The resulting list was then prioritized to determine the most important information on the site. From this, a site map is developed and the information is apportioned to the relevant pages.

The next step was to understand the issues regarding designing for screens — in particular, the difference between fixed-width and liquid layouts, whether your page should always stay the same size or expand and contract to fit the browser window.

Eventually the design or layout begins, and you saw how the use of a layout grid helps create a far more professional-looking layout compared with randomly selecting the size of parts of pages.

Some popular layout grids were then transformed into XHTML and CSS code, using floats to position the content on the page. This chapter demonstrated two-, three-, four-, and six-column layouts.

I hope the practical advice in this chapter makes it easier for you to design your web sites, and also helps you deal with those people or organizations you might be creating sites for. In the next chapter, we look at some more specific aspects within each page, such as typography, navigation, links, and forms.

Exercises

The answers to all the exercises are in Appendix A.

1. Take another look at the article page from the *Guardian* newspaper's web site; it is shown again in Figure 9-41. List all the different elements on the page that would have been listed in the design stage, and put them together in their relevant grouping or categories. For example, the main article section of the page might need a list like this:

```
Title
Summary
Author
Date
```

Figure 9-41

2. Try to recreate the structure of the page you can see in Figure 9-41. It sits in the 12-column 960-pixel grid we were using in this chapter, so you have seen much of the code you need already — you just need to assemble it correctly.

Design Issues

This chapter looks at design issues that affect specific aspects of your pages — typography, navigation, tables, and forms. Each is addressed in its own section, and each section contains helpful tips that will make your pages more attractive and easier to use.

First up is typography; you will see how carefully composing your text on the page makes it easier for people to read the words you have written and improves the clarity of your message.

Next, you look at the three main forms of navigation: menus, search, and links within pages. As you will see, a menu does not just offer a means for users to navigate your site; it also plays an important role in helping visitors understand what a site is about and how the information is organized.

If you have to add tabular data to your site, this section contains helpful guidelines to make your tables easier to read.

Finally, you will look at forms. I have yet to meet someone who enjoys filling out forms (particularly on the Web), so these techniques will increase the chances of your forms being completed (and completed with the right information).

While this chapter can't teach you how to be a great web page designer — that requires creativity, a good eye, and flair — it will show you some concepts that help create good designs and introduce you to some guidelines that will help you improve both the look and usability of your site.

Throughout this chapter I mention programs called screen readers. Screen readers are programs that read a page to a user. While screen readers are commonly used by those with visual impairments, they are likely to become more popular in other web-based scenarios, such as for those who want to access information while they are driving or doing something else that prevents them from actually reading a screen.

Typography

While typesetting used to be the domain of skilled craftsmen, the desktop publishing revolution, which started 25 years ago, has led us to the point where anyone can create a document on a standard PC in the home. This was followed by the Internet revolution, which has removed the need to print many messages because they can be seen on a screen.

While technology has allowed anyone to create documents on a home PC, the skills and experience of the typesetters who knew how to make type attractive and easy to read were not built into the new technology. But we can learn a lot from the experience of these craftsmen. Studying even the basics of typography can have a big impact on the design of your pages, and also on how many (and which) of your precious words are read.

Typography can be defined as the art of arranging text so that it is carefully *composed* on the page to create a readable, coherent, and visually satisfying whole that works invisibly. This means putting a lot of care and attention into typesetting in order to make your message clearer and help the reader navigate around the page with ease, but doing so in a manner that does not call readers' attention to what you are trying to do.

When you consider that web users commonly scan pages to find the information that they want, the value of good typography becomes even more apparent.

In this section, we will be looking at issues such as:

- Line length
- Relationship between sizes of letters
- Gaps between lines
- Spaces between letters and words
- Careful chunking
- Contrast
- Choice of fonts

Before you look at these issues in detail, it is worth clarifying a couple of terms typographers use:

- **Legible:** Text is legible if it is recognizable; for example, when a font gets too small it may no longer be legible.
- **Readable:** Text is readable if it is comfortable to read it for many minutes (without strain or difficulty).

A legible typeface can become unreadable through poor setting and placement, and a less legible typeface can be made more readable through good design.

Line Length — A Measure

A *measure* is the name typographers give to the number of characters in a single line of text.

It is generally considered that for a body of text (such as a news article), the line length should be between 45 and 75 characters including letters, spacing, and punctuation. If you have a narrow column, your measure should be less — around 30 to 50 characters.

At the end of each line of text, readers have to make an effort to accurately find the beginning of the next line, and they have to do this before the flow of the reading is lost. If a line is too long, it can be harder for the reader to scan back to the left-hand side of the page. If there are two few characters, the reader has to move onto the next line more often, causing too many breaks in the reading.

In a liquid layout you do not have control over the measure because users can increase and decrease the width of the writing as they change the size of the browser window. This is a key reason why text-heavy sites, such as news sites, often like to use fixed-width layouts.

With a fixed layout, you have greater ability to control the measure (although if the user changes the size of the font, it will affect the number of characters on each line). Figure 10-1 shows the BBC news site; as you can see, the main column (below the picture) has a measure of 45–75 words, and next to the picture and in the right-hand column the measure is less (30–50 characters).

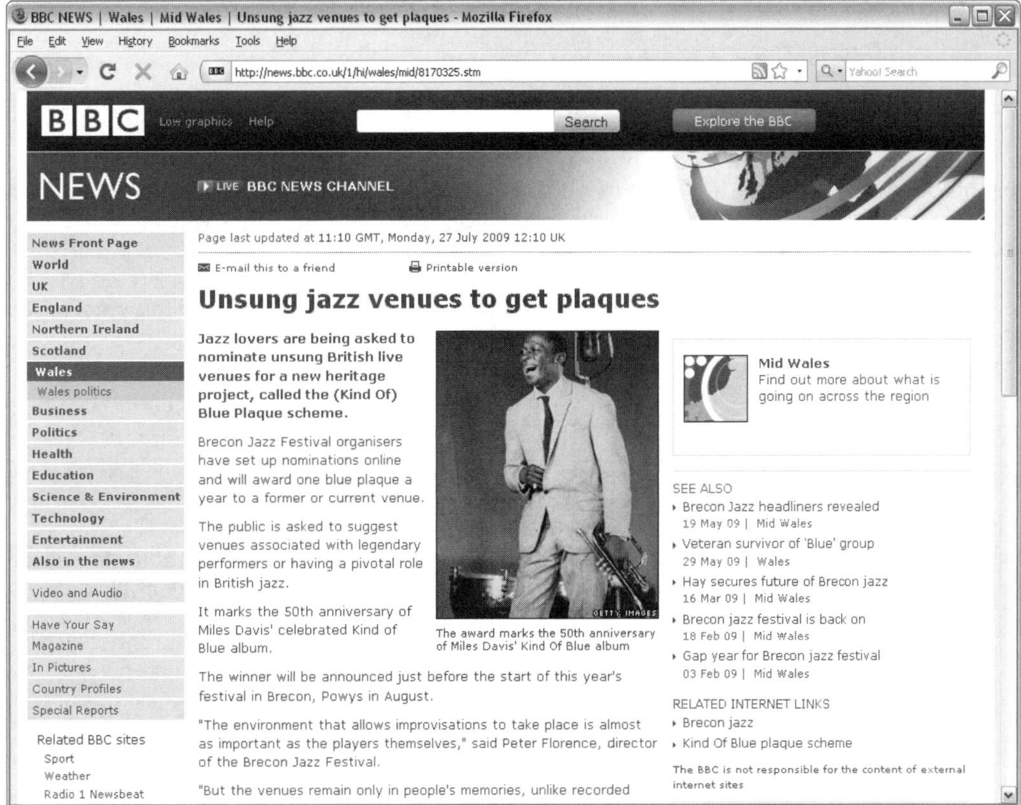

Figure 10-1

Font Sizes

You have probably come across the following series of typeface sizes in all kinds of programs, such as Word, Photoshop, or InDesign:

8pt 9pt 10pt 11pt 12pt 14pt 18pt 24pt 36pt 48pt 60pt 72pt

Such programs use the same sizes because they are set according to a scale or ratio, which was developed by European typographers in the sixteenth century.

Just as the shape of a rectangle based upon the golden ratio (with the square of its hypotenuse equal to the sum of its sides) looks pleasing to the eye, this scale of fonts works well and has changed little in the last 400 years.

Therefore, when you start designing pages, using these font sizes will help your pages look a lot more balanced.

You could choose settings in pixels that follow this scale of size, like so:

```
body    {font-size: 12px;}
h1      {font-size: 24px;}
h2      {font-size: 18px;}
h3      {font-size: 16px;}
h4      {font-size: 14px;}
```

Unfortunately, specifying font sizes in pixels is not very good for accessibility because Internet Explorer does not allow users to resize text when its size is specified in pixels. Therefore, you should aim to create a similar effect using percentages or ems as a unit of measurement because they will allow all users to change the size of the text.

Fortunately, the default size of text in all browsers is 16 pixels, so we can work from this point to create the correct size using percentages like so:

```
body    {font-size: 75%;}         /* 16 x .075  = 12 */
h1      {font-size: 200%;}        /* 12 x 2     = 24 */
h2      {font-size: 150%;}        /* 12 x 1.5   = 18 */
h3      {font-size: 133%;}        /* 12 x 1.333 = 16 */
h4      {font-size: 116%;}        /* 12 x 1.16  = 14 */
```

You could also use ems. Ems allow you to change the size of text relative to the size of the text element's parent element, so if the body of a web page is 16 pixels, to get a paragraph to render at 12px you use 0.75em:

```
body    {font-size: 100%;}         /* ensure IE scales correctly */
p       {font-size: 0.75em;}       /* 16 x 0.75  = 12 */
h1      {font-size: 1.5em;}        /* 16 x 1.5   = 24 */
h2      {font-size: 1.3em;}        /* 16 x 1.125 = 18 */
h3      {font-size: 0.875em;}      /* 16 x 0.875 = 14 */
```

You may have noticed in this example that there is a rule for the `<body>` element and the `<p>` element. The rule that applies to the `<body>` element is required because IE6 and IE7 exaggerate the smallness and largeness of the resized text without it, whereas the rule for the `<p>` element sets the size of the text in paragraphs to 12 pixels:

This may seem like a complicated way to calculate text sizes, but when you remember the importance of working to scale, and that this scale of sizes has been used for over 400 years, you should not need to work out too many of your own font scales for the moment.

As mentioned, the default size of text in a browser is 16 pixels, and traditionally the majority of sites have made the main body text smaller. Recently, however, a number of sites have started to leave the body text at the default size, suggesting that it increases readability (and that 11 or 12 pixel fonts are slightly too small).

```
body {font-size: 100%;}
h1   {font-size: 2em;}           /* 16 x 2     = 32  */
h2   {font-size: 1.5em;}         /* 16 x 1.5   = 24  */
h3   {font-size: 1.125em;}       /* 16 x 1.125 = 18  */
```

This can seem a little large at first, but it can certainly help readability. Figure 10-2 shows an example of a screenshot of `ch10_eg01.html`, which contains fonts sized using ems, with the scale starting at 12 pixels, whereas Figure 10-3 shows an example of a screenshot of `ch10_eg02.html`, which has a scale starting at 16 pixels. You can try these in your own browser to get a feel for the difference in text sizes.

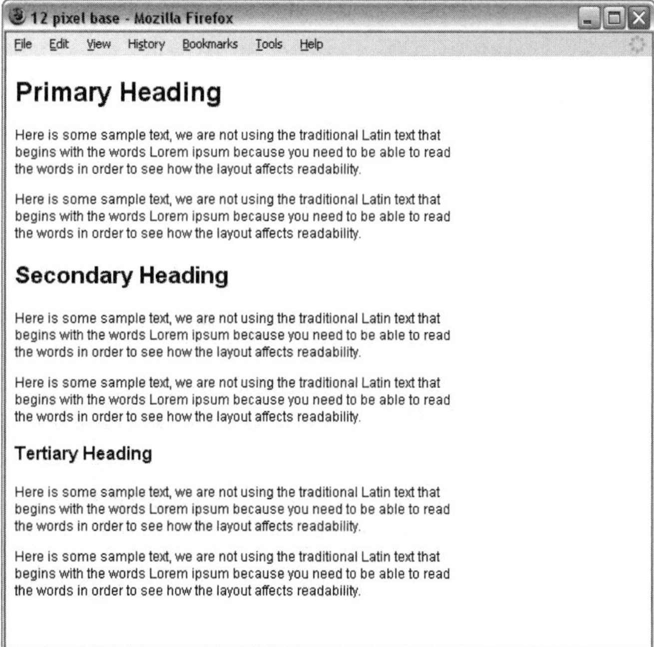

Figure 10-2

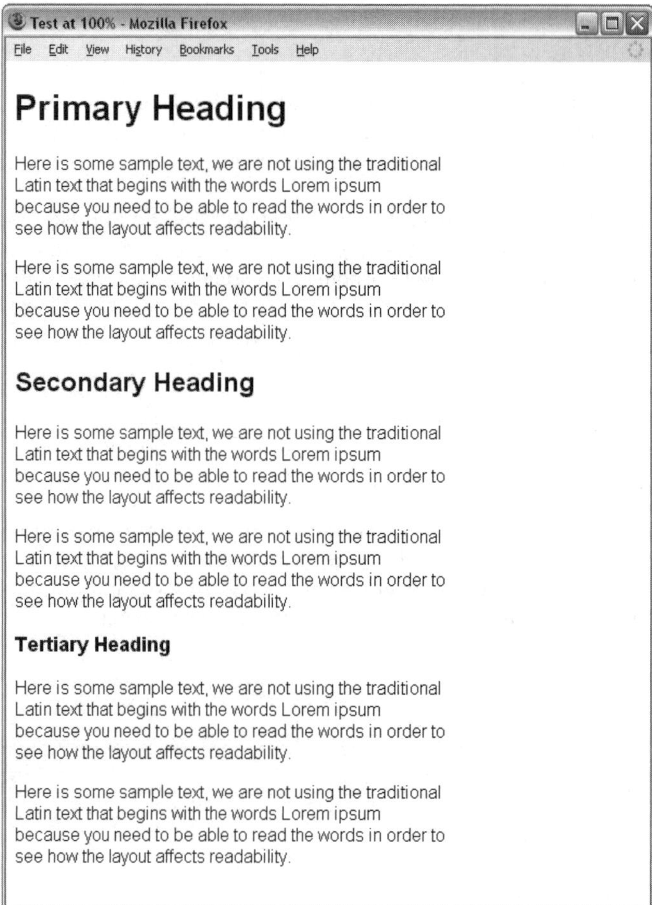

Figure 10-3

Choosing Fonts

In print, serif fonts tend to be easier to read for extended periods of time compared with sans-serif fonts. When reading books and long articles in a language with which we are familiar, good readers don't need to carefully look at the whole of each character, either focusing on the top half of characters or sometimes just on the general shape of familiar words.

On the Web, however, text is not as sharp as it is in print and the serifs on the font can make the characters less clear (because the screen has fewer dots per inch than print). As a result, most people find it easier to read longer passages of text in sans-serif fonts.

In practice, you are safe using either serif or sans-serif fonts as long as they are large enough to read.

When choosing which fonts (or typefaces) to use on a page, you should ensure that you consider which fonts users are likely to have installed on their computers; if users don't have your desired font installed on their computers your design will not show up in that font.

You can safely assume that the majority of users will have the following fonts installed:

- **Sans-serif:** Arial, Helvetica, Verdana
- **Serif:** Times, Times New Roman, Georgia
- **Monospace:** Courier, Courier New

You can suggest other fonts, in the hope that users have them installed, and at the end of the list you can put a generic font family, but remember that fonts can take up different amounts of space on the screen. So do check that your layout works in all choices of font.

Here you can see the font list from `ch10_eg03.html`:

```
h1, h2, h3, h4 {font-family: "gill sans", arial, sans-serif;font-weight:
normal;}
```

Figure 10-4 shows you what this looks like in Safari on a Mac with Gill Sans installed, and Figure 10-5 shows you the same page in Firefox on a PC that does not have Gill Sans installed.

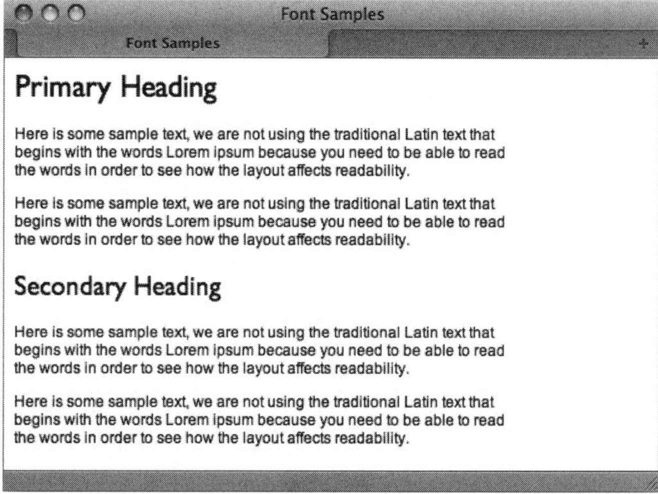

Figure 10-4

If you want to use a specific font for a logo, you should use an image instead. You can also look at sIFR (a technology that uses Flash) and Typekit as ways to include fonts that might not be installed on visitors' machines.

Line Height — Leading

Leading (pronounced *ledding*) is the vertical space between lines of text. Text sits on a baseline, and the height of letters such as a, e, and x are collectively known as the x height. The parts of letters that drop

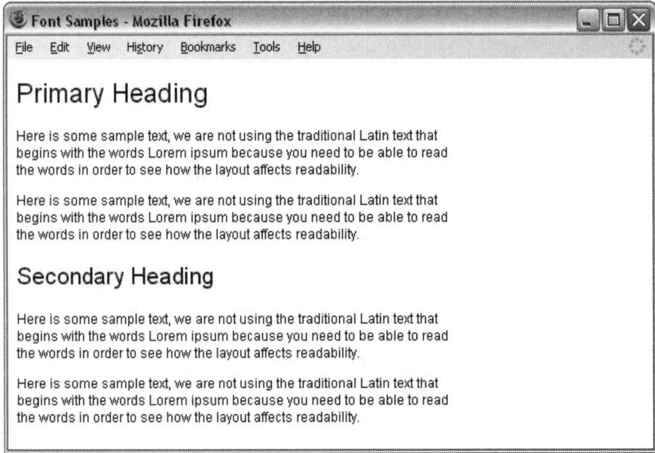

Figure 10-5

below the baseline are called descenders, while the bits that rise above the x height are known as ascenders. Leading is measured from the bottom of the descender on one line, to the top of the ascender on the next (Figure 10-6).

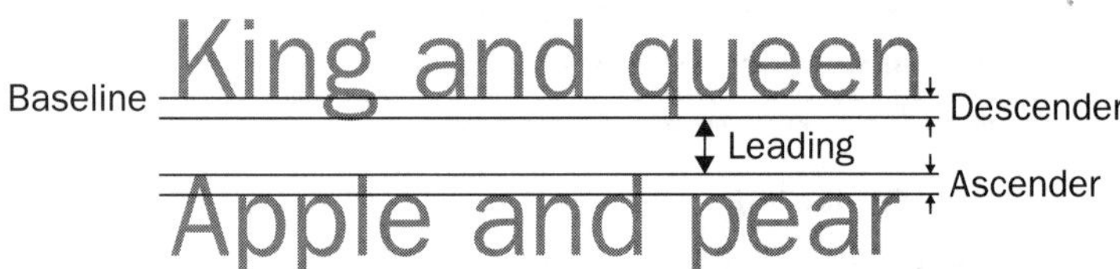

Figure 10-6

You can set the amount of leading in a document using the `line-height` property in CSS (when the line height is larger than the font size the gap created between each line of text acts as the leading, and the taller the line height the bigger the gap). Increasing the default amount of leading can make a block of text easier to read; if you look in Figure 10-7, the first paragraph is default size and the second paragraph has increased leading (`ch10_eg04.html`).

A good general guide for leading is that the vertical space between lines of text should be larger than the space between each word as this helps the eye move along the line instead of down the lines. Around 1.5 em is a good starting point.

When you use the `line-height` property in CSS, you should avoid specifying a value in pixels, because visitors can tell their browsers to increase the size of text on the page and doing so does not necessarily increase the line height as well (which means text can overlap). It is better to specify the line height using

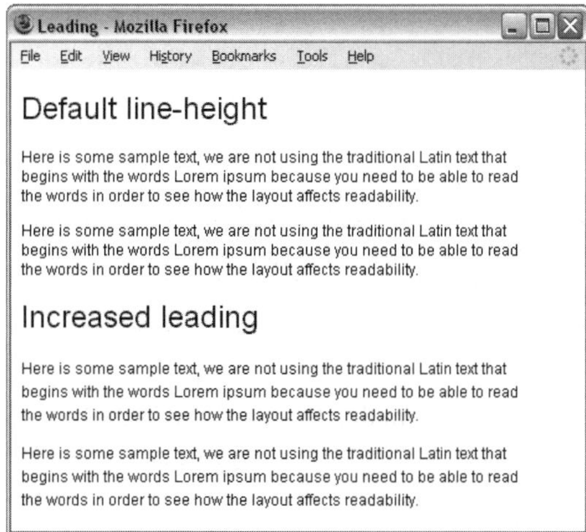

Figure 10-7

ems because they are relative to the size of font that the user has chosen. Here you can see the example of increased leading from example `ch10_eg04.html`:

```
p.adjusted {
    font-size: 12pt;
    line-height: 1.5em;}
```

If your measure is wider than suggested in the section on "Measure" (which recommended an upper limit of 75 characters), you can increase the leading to make it more readable.

CSS Resets

When you try to control designs to the pixel, as we do in this chapter, you could easily run into a complication because different browsers add different margins and padding to different elements. For example, the amount of padding inside the `<body>` element, the margins around `<hn>` elements, and so on, can be different from browser to browser.

The solution to this is adding rules to the beginning of your style sheet that set padding and margins of key elements to zero so that you are in complete control of them.

A popular set of rules for this is Eric Meyer's CSS Reset. The full version is available on his site at `http://meyerweb.com/eric/tools/css/reset/`. For the purposes of the examples in this chapter, you can make do with the following few lines which specify a long list of elements and set a handful of their properties:

```
html, body, div, span, applet, object, iframe,
h1, h2, h3, h4, h5, h6, p, blockquote, pre,
a, abbr, acronym, address, big, cite, code,
del, dfn, em, font, img, ins, kbd, q, s, samp,
small, strike, strong, sub, sup, tt, var,
```

```
b, u, i, center,
dl, dt, dd, ol, ul, li,
fieldset, form, label, legend,
table, caption, tbody, tfoot, thead, tr, th, td {
        margin: 0;
        padding: 0;
        border: 0;
        outline: 0;
        font-size: 100%;
        vertical-align: baseline;
        background: transparent;}
body {line-height: 1;}
```

You can either include these lines of code in the top of your style sheet or you could use the `@import` or `@include` command. In the next section, you see why this is so important.

Line Height — Baseline Grids

You have already seen vertical grids in the last chapter. Many typographers also use horizontal grids, known as *baseline grids,* and align the bottom of the main text to the grid. Figure 10-8 shows an example of a page where the text sits on a baseline grid (`ch10_eg05.html`).

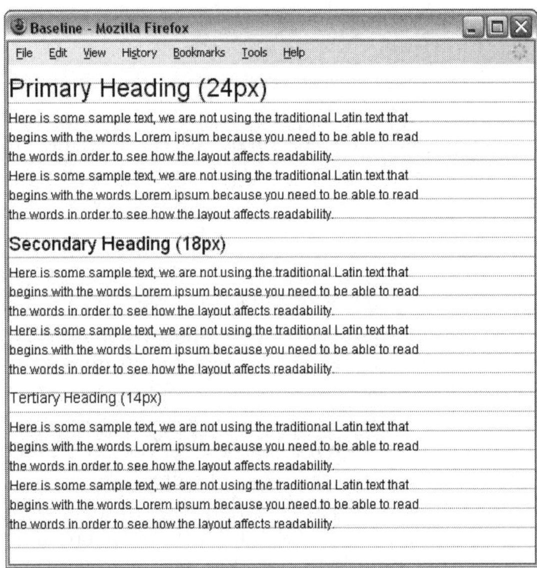

Figure 10-8

Getting to this point involves a few steps. First, you need to use some CSS reset rules to reset the size of margins and padding that a browser may add to certain elements by default (as we saw in the last section). Next you need to decide on the distance between the lines in the grid; this usually corresponds to the line height of the body text. The distance between the lines here is 18 pixels (and the text is

12 pixels), and to ensure the text lines up I created a GIF that is 1 pixel wide by 18 pixels tall, with a gray line on the bottom pixel, as shown in Figure 10-9.

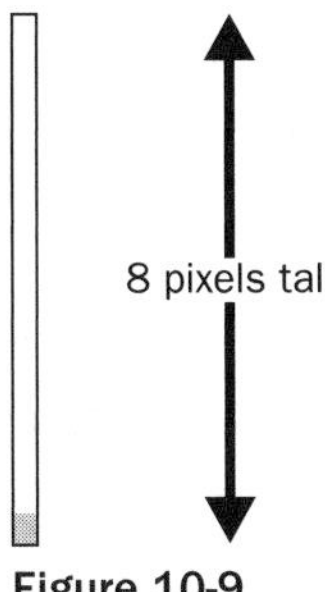

Figure 10-9

You can then make this image tile across the background of the browser to act as a guide while building the page. To do this you create a rule that applies to the `<body>` element using the `background-image` property. You may also have to add a little padding to the top of the document to start the first line on the grid.

```
body    {font-size:100%;          /* ensure IE scales correctly */
         background-image: url(images/baseline_grid.gif);
         padding-top:0.25em;}
```

Setting Headings on the Grid

When it comes to setting the headings on the grid, the easiest way is to just set the `line-height` property in CSS to a number that divides evenly into the grid height (this was shown in Figure 10-8).

```
p       {font-size:0.75em;         /* 16 x 0.75  = 12 */
         line-height:1.5em;}       /* 12 * 1.5   = 18 */
h1      {font-size:1.5em;          /* 16 x 1.5   = 24 */
         line-height:1.5em;}       /* 24 x 1.5   = 36 */
h2      {font-size:1.125em;        /* 16 x 1.125 = 18 */
         line-height:2em;}         /* 18 x 2     = 36 */
h3      {font-size:0.875em;        /* 16 x 0.875 = 14 */
         line-height:2.6em;}       /* 14 * 2.6   = 36 */
```

In practice, it is common to have a little more height above the headings than below; this can be achieved using the following calculation.

First, divide the baseline grid size by the font size:

For `<h1>` 18 ÷ 24 = 0.75

For `<h2>` 18 ÷ 18 = 1

For `<h3>` 18 ÷ 14 = 1.286

Then set the `line-height`, `margin-top`, and `margin-bottom` properties to the resulting value.

To create more margin above than below, adjust the values of the `margin-top` and `margin-bottom` properties, but make sure that they add up to the same amount. For example (`ch10_eg06.css`):

```
p       {font-size:0.75em;        /* 16 x 0.75  = 12 */
         line-height:1.5em;}      /* 12 x 1.5   = 18 */
h1      {font-size:1.5em;         /* 16 x 1.5   = 24 */
         line-height:0.75em;      /* 24 x 0.75  = 18 */
         margin-top:1.2em;
         margin-bottom:0.3em;}
h2      {font-size:1.125em;       /* 16 x 1.125 = 18 */
         line-height:1em;         /* 18 x 1     = 18 */
         margin-top:1.7em;
         margin-bottom:0.3em;}
h3      {font-size:0.875em;       /* 16 x 0.875 = 14 */
         line-height:1.286em;     /* 14 x 1.286 = 18 */
         margin-top:2.172em;
         margin-bottom:0.4em;}
```

When doing this, you need to be aware that browsers will round to the nearest pixel, so you will need to check the measurements against your background grid and adjust as necessary.

Aligning Other Items to the Grid

There are many reasons why you might like to have smaller text on the grid — a side column or captions under an image. There are two ways to keep this text on the grid:

- Have the same line height as your main body of text.
- Set the leading to be a fraction (such as two-thirds) of the grid height so it meets up again (every fourth line, in this case); this is known as *incremental leading*.

Here you can see the two techniques; the first sets the line height to the same as surrounding text, the second sets the line height to three-quarters of the height of the baseline grid, so that it will catch up every five lines. Using the second technique, you also need to add a margin to the top of the element to ensure that the first line sits on the grid (`ch10_eg07.html`).

```
.pull_quote {
        font-size: 0.92em;      /* 12 x 0.92 = 11 */
        line-height:1.64em;     /* 11 x 1.64 = 18 */
        float:right;
        width:100px;}
.pull_quote2 {
        font-size: 0.92em;       /* 12 x 0.92 = 11 */
        line-height: 1.2em;      /* 13 x 1.2 = 13.5 */
        margin-top: 0.2em;
        float:right;
        width:100px;}
```

You can see the result in Figure 10-10.

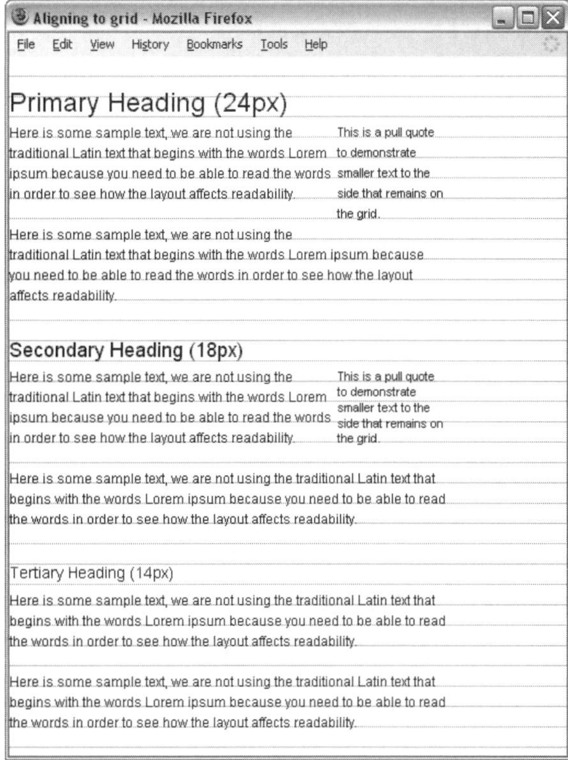

Figure 10-10

Just before we started to look at the grid, we reset the default padding and margins in CSS; this meant that two paragraphs would butt up next to each other. In Figure 10-10, margins have been added to the bottom of each paragraph to separate them when they sit next to each other.

The margin has only been added to the bottom of the paragraphs because the margin on the bottom of the headings is quite small and if there were a larger margin at the top of the paragraphs this would have taken precedence over the gap at the bottom of the heading and everything would have been thrown off-grid (because vertical margins collapse and only display the larger of the two).

To help keep items on the grid, it is also important to remember the following:

- Borders and padding on boxes can throw items off-grid; if you need to use these, adjust the margin around the element within the box to ensure the text sits on the grid.
- Borders and padding should be measured in the same unit as text so that, if a user resizes text, it sits on the grid.

Space Between Letters — Tracking

Tracking is the term typographers use to describe the space between letters. You can control the space between letters using the `letter-spacing` property in CSS.

For paragraphs of text in sentence case (where capitalization is the same as a normal sentence), you should not need to change the spacing between letters. (In fact, doing so may harm legibility.)

This feature can, however, be particularly helpful when dealing with headings or text that is all uppercase. This is because text in capital letters is harder to read than text in sentence case; in such cases giving the letter-spacing property a value of 0.1em can help improve legibility (`ch10_eg08.html`).

```
h1.header_spacing {letter-spacing:0.1em;}
```

You can see the difference in Figure 10-11.

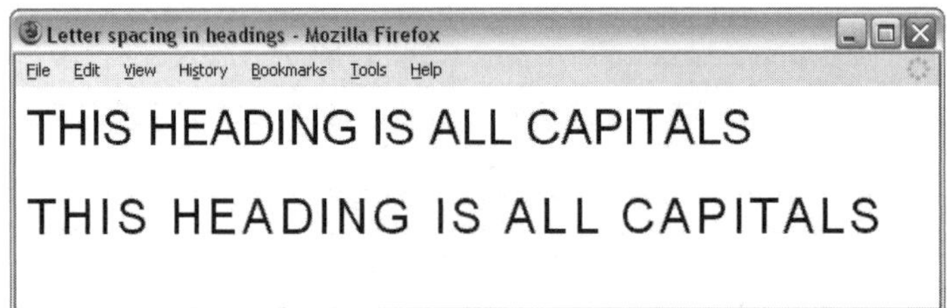

Figure 10-11

White Space

Because the amount of space you have on a screen is limited, it is tempting to put as much information on each page as possible. However, the space *between* items on a page can be just as important as the information itself; it will change the look of the page, its characteristics, its legibility, and how it is interpreted.

White space, or *negative space*, is the name given to the space between elements on a page, but it does not have to be white; it just signifies the gaps between items on the page. There are two types of white space, and it is important to pay attention to both:

- Macro white space is the space between the large elements on the page.
- Micro white space is the amount of space between things such as text, headings, and list items.

Figure 10-12 demonstrates macro white space, and how the use of white space between the big elements on a page lightens up the page, and gives it more space to breathe. Both of these examples are included in the download code in `ch10_eg09.html`).

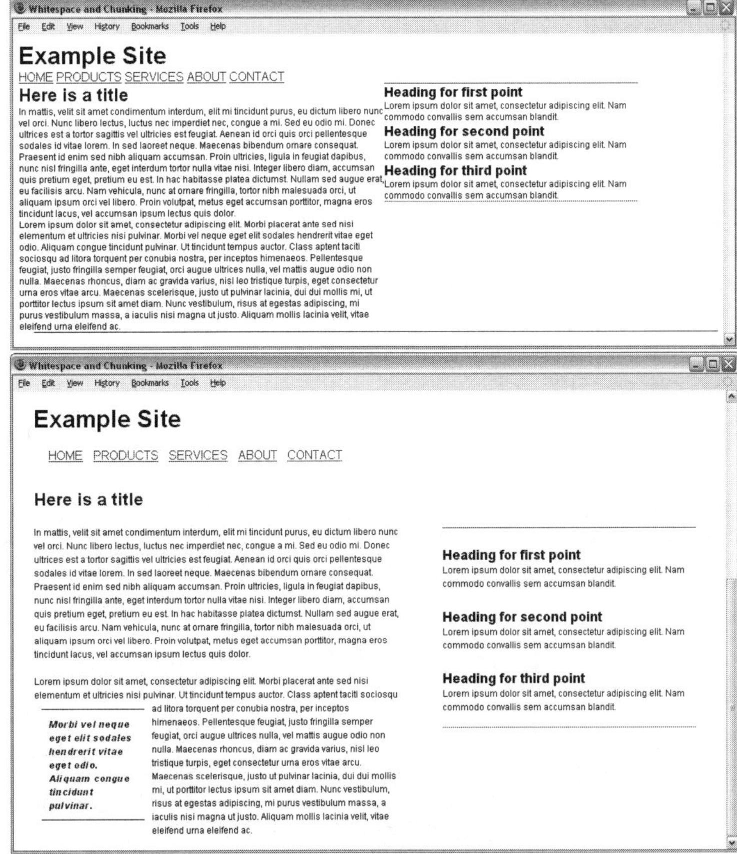

Figure 10-12

Meanwhile, Figure 10-13 (showing `ch10_eg10.html`) demonstrates the importance of setting the correct space between text; this is a good example of micro white space:

- On the left, there is no margin or padding on any element.
- In the middle, there are normal default margins, but this is all too evenly spaced.
- On the right, the headings have been bought closer to the text that relates to that heading.

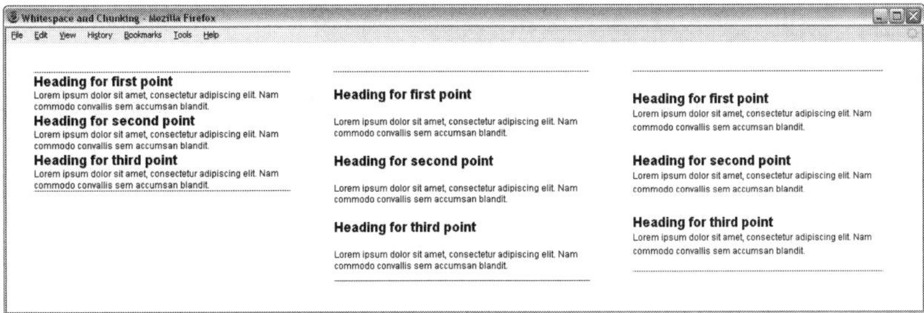

Figure 10-13

It is important to remember that if a page is too cluttered, it is harder to find what you are looking for, so do not be afraid to leave space in your designs, and if you are asked to move everything together (so that something else can be squeezed in) it is important to evaluate whether it affects the ability of visitors to scan the design for the information they need.

Chunking

Chunking, or grouping items together, is a very helpful tool in design. This was demonstrated well in Figure 10-12, where the use of white space puts related items together (headings with their corresponding text). Other common ways of chunking information include using a border on a box, or giving a box a background color. Figure 10-14 of the BBC homepage shows some good examples of chunking — putting related information in boxes.

Figure 10-14

The RadioTimes web site (see Figure 10-15) offers a good example of using background colors to group programs. The Architecture Association (see Figure 10-16) uses lines to indicate where groups of information sit together.

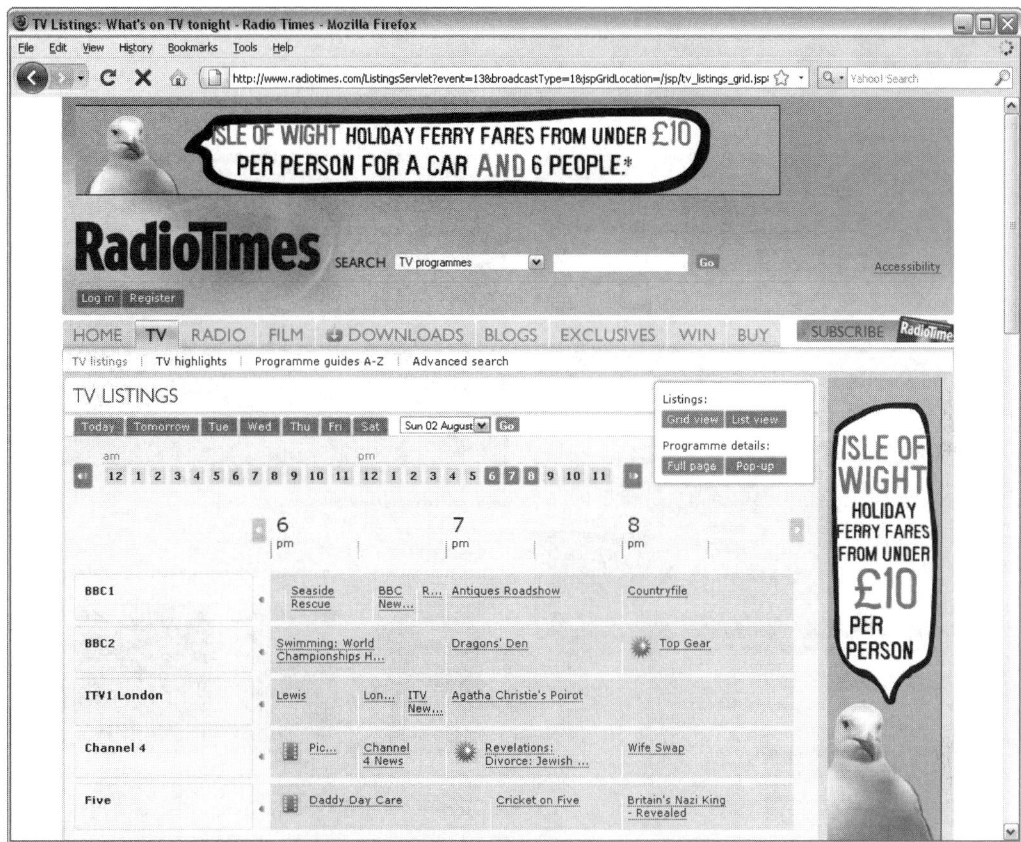

Figure 10-15

Contrast

It is very important to have enough contrast between any type and the background it is sitting on. It is not only people with color blindness and other visual impairments who suffer when there's a lack of contrast. Those with a bad monitor, or sunlight on their screens, may have more difficulty reading the content.

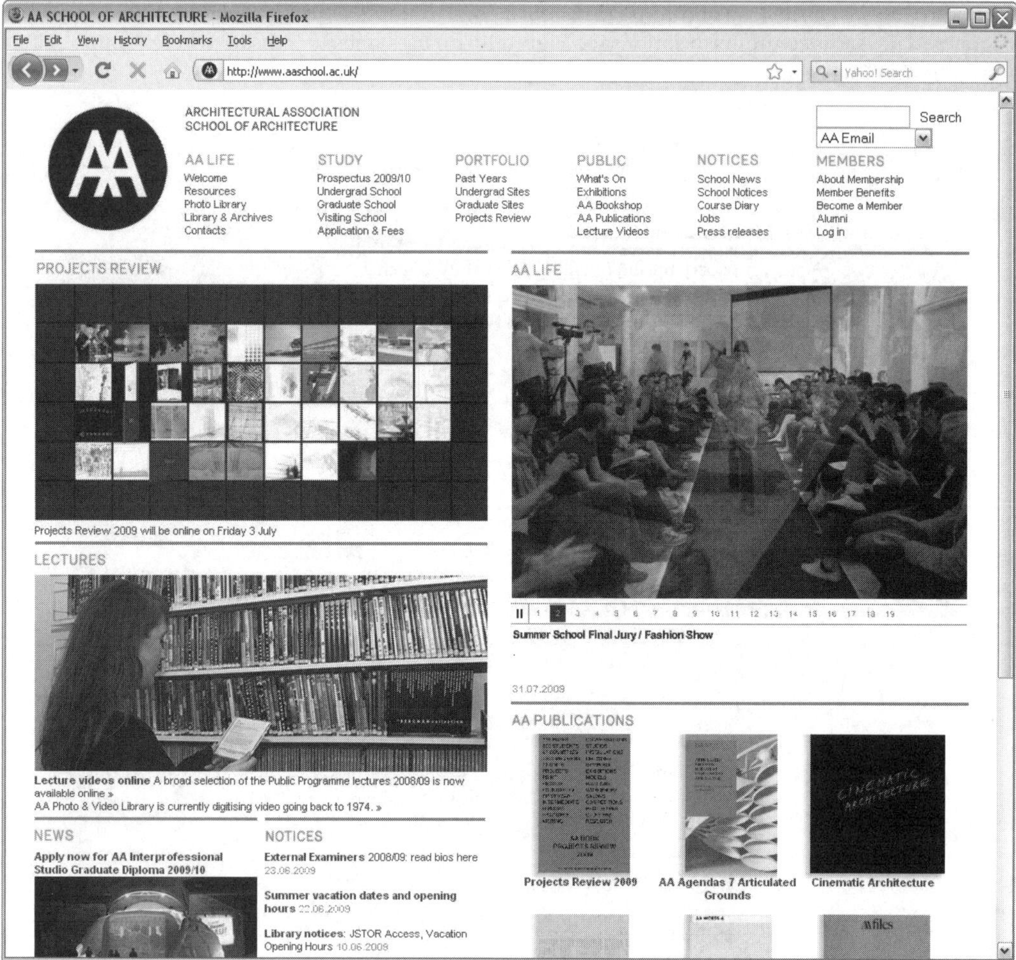

Figure 10-16

There is a very good tool for checking contrast at `www.snook.ca/technical/colour_contrast/colour.html`. You can see the foreground (or text) color on the left, the background color in the middle, and whether there is sufficient contrast on the right (Figure 10-17).

While it is important to have enough contrast in your designs, it is worth noting that if there is too much contrast, readability can suffer. For example, white text on a black background is hard to read for long periods of time because the contrast is higher than black text on a white background. If you do reverse out text, you can increase the leading and tracking, and decrease your font weight to make it easier to read. Figure 10-18 shows the difference between black text on white and reversing it out.

You can reduce the contrast in both of these examples to help make the text more readable. Rather than black on a white background, dark gray on a white background is easier to read, or even better, dark gray on an off-white (cream) background. Likewise, a light gray on a black background is easier to read than white on a black background.

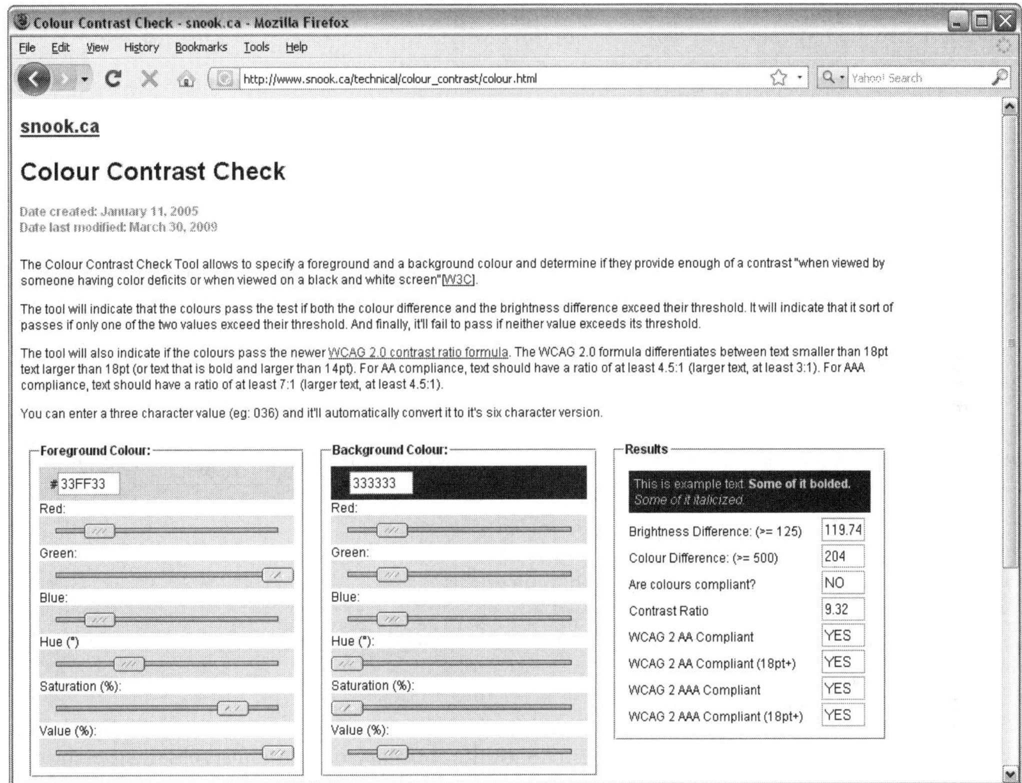

Figure 10-17

This example allows you to see how readable text is on different color backgrounds. The black text on white background should be more readable than text that is reversed out. A small amount of white text on a black background is not too difficult to read, but as the text gets long the readers eyes will find it harder.

This example allows you to see how readable text is on different color backgrounds. The black text on white background should be more readable than text that is reversed out. A small amount of white text on a black background is not too difficult to read, but as the text gets long the readers eyes will find it harder.

Figure 10-18

If you use a background image, you need to ensure that the image has low contrast; otherwise, you will find it hard to find a color that will be readable on top of it.

Navigation

A user will usually navigate your site in one of three ways:

- Using a menu that you provide
- Browsing through links provided in the middle of text and other parts of the page than the menu
- Searching for relevant items of information

In this section, you learn how to make it easier for users to get around your site using these three methods.

Menus

A menu is a key part of any web site that features more than one page. It doesn't just allow visitors to get where they want to go; a good menu also helps them to understand what your site is about and how it is organized.

As you saw in Chapter 9, a site may have more than one menu; it may have primary navigation, secondary navigation, and even tertiary navigation.

Usually, the primary menu appears either across the top of a site from left to right, or down the left side of the page.

Where you have primary and secondary navigation, sometimes both will be across the top of the site, or both down the left-hand side. Other times you might find primary navigation across the top and secondary navigation down the left-hand side.

The menu tends to be the main way in which users will navigate between sections of a site, and good menu design makes a big difference in how long they will spend on your site and whether or not they achieve what they came to achieve.

In this section, I introduce eight guiding rules:

- Menus should be concise.
- Menus should have clear labels.
- Menus should focus on what visitors want to achieve.

- ❑ Menus do not need to contain every link.
- ❑ Menus should provide context.
- ❑ Menus should be interactive.
- ❑ Menus should be consistent.
- ❑ If you use icons, add the text, too.

Menus Should Be Concise

Menus should be quick and easy to read, so you need to:

- ❑ Limit the number of options you have on the menu to no more than eight items.
- ❑ Choose single, descriptive words for each link.

Take a look at the three menus in Figure 10-19; none has more than eight options. Even Google, which has many more services than are shown here, has a "more" link for the options that are used less often (prioritizing what most users will want to do from this page).

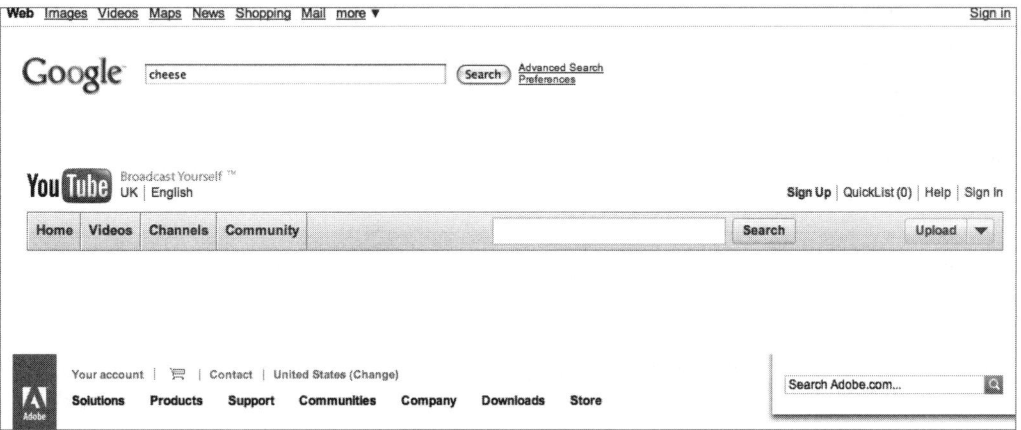

Figure 10-19

For a long time, many web designers thought you should be able to get to any page within three clicks. More recent research suggests that this is not necessarily the case; it is more important for each click to be easy — so that users do not have to think too much about what they want to do.

If you need lots of options, group some together and use secondary or tertiary navigation to split out options once the user has picked that first option.

Menus Should Have Clear Labels

The main navigation should allow the visitor to predict the kind of information that will be on the page. Therefore, the labels on any navigation should use language that the visitor will understand (not jargon).

If people might not know what is in a section, you can provide some extra description, as in the Stop Design site in Figure 10-20, or examples of what people might find in those sections, as in the Architectural Association site, also shown in Figure 10-20.

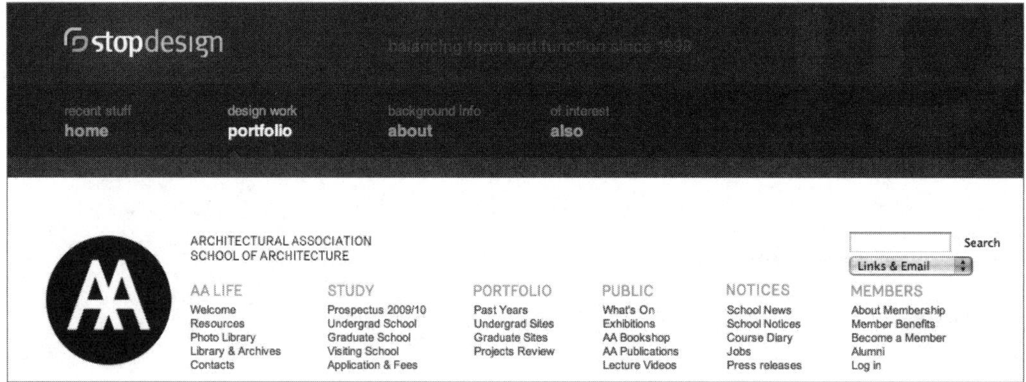

Figure 10-20

It is worth noting that in both of these examples, the main navigation still sticks out clearly, and the extra information is displayed in a more subtle way.

Once you have clicked on a navigation item, you should try to use the same word prominently in the heading for the following page; this reinforces to the users that they have arrived in the right place.

Menus Should Focus on What Visitors Want to Achieve

As we discussed in the last chapter, it is very important for any site to focus on what the *visitor* wants to achieve.

You can see in Figure 10-21 how the Red Cross has clear options to allow the user to join, give blood, donate, or volunteer, and the National Trust (a charity to protect and open historical houses and gardens) focuses on places to visit and events before fundraising.

To help focus on what visitors are likely to want to do, you can call upon the personae or actors that you defined in the last chapter to represent your target audience. By looking at the goals you decided that these people would want to achieve, you can test whether your navigation is going to allow users to achieve those goals.

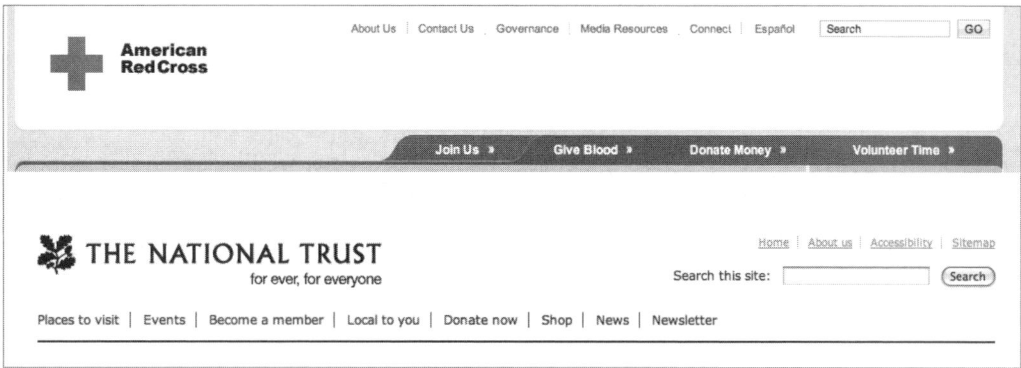

Figure 10-21

Sometimes you may find it helpful to offer different options for different kinds of users. In Figure 10-22, you can see that Dell and AT&T both create options for different types of customers (home, small business, and enterprise) so that they can offer products and services suited to them. You can also see a similar idea on the NASA web site, which has options for public, educators, students, and more.

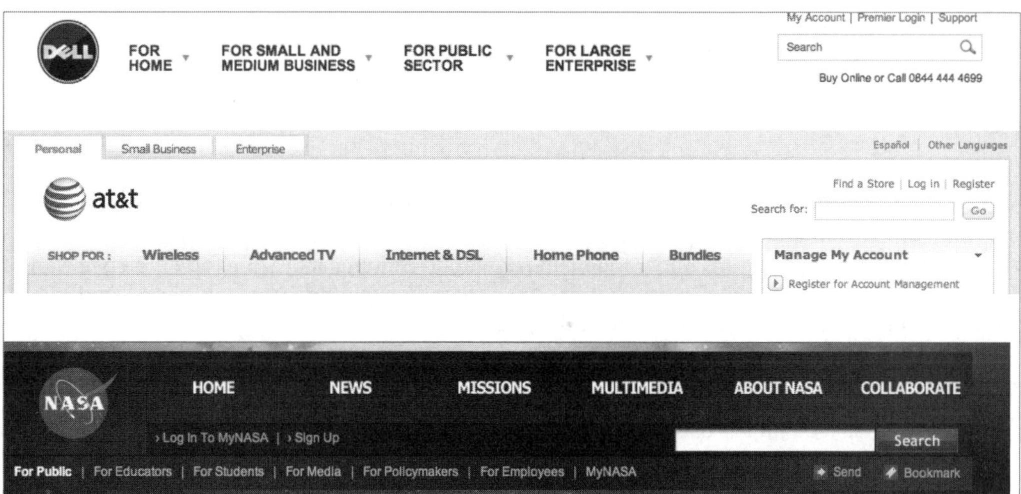

Figure 10-22

Menus Do Not Need to Contain Every Link

The main menu of your site should only reflect the sections or content of the site. Links to functions like those that follow can be kept separate:

- Login and register
- Shopping baskets and checkouts

- ❑ Search options
- ❑ Privacy policy, terms and conditions, press information, corporate information
- ❑ Tools such as bookmarking or printing a page

If you look at the British Gas menu in Figure 10-23, items that are not sections of the site are not in the main navigation (such as login, search, and contact). The Magento site does something similar, and although it breaks the rule about how many options should appear in the navigation, the main navigation nicely separates community areas of the site by putting them on a different background color.

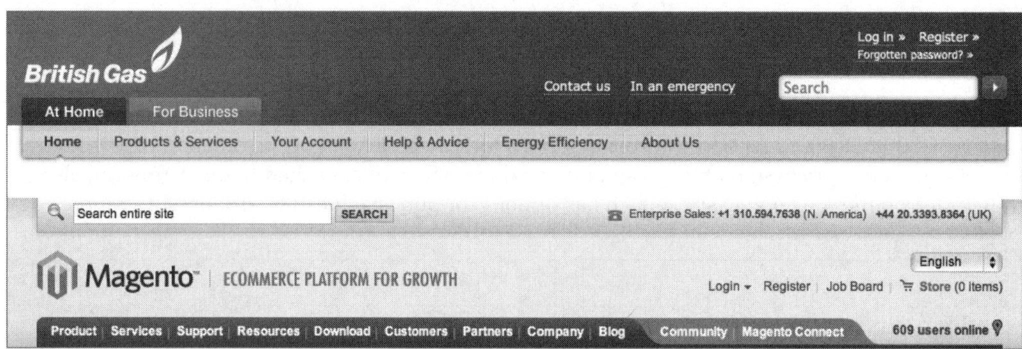

Figure 10-23

As already suggested, you might need to use secondary and tertiary navigation if you cannot fit everything in on your main navigation. Figure 10-24 shows a couple of examples from the *Telegraph,* whose secondary navigation sits under the main navigation running across the top of the page, and from Martha Stewart, where the primary navigation runs across the top of the page and the secondary navigation comes down the left-hand side of the page.

Menus Should Provide Context

It is important that a menu lets users know where they are at the moment. Popular tools for this include highlighting the current page using the following:

- ❑ **Color:** To show the current page, either changing the text or background as illustrated on the *Times* web site in Figure 10-25
- ❑ **Tabs:** As in the FedEx site in Figure 10-25 (this is a technique that Amazon made hugely popular, but no longer uses)
- ❑ **Underlining:** For the current option as shown in the Adaptive Path web site in Figure 10-25

It is worth noting that you should not rely solely on color because people who are color-blind would not necessarily be able to benefit.

Figure 10-24

Figure 10-25

You might also have noticed that the *Times* site adds a "breadcrumb" trail under the navigation to tell users where they are. This is a popular tool used on a lot of larger sites.

Menu Items Should Be Interactive

It is important that menu items are clearly separate from other content and that visitors know they can be clicked on.

It is also important to ensure that the links are big enough to click on, and that the link's appearance changes slightly when the mouse rolls over the it.

You can see three examples in Figure 10-26 — the Dyson site changes the color of text when you hover over it, the Apple site changes the background, and the B&Q site changes the background and also shows a range of options in that section.

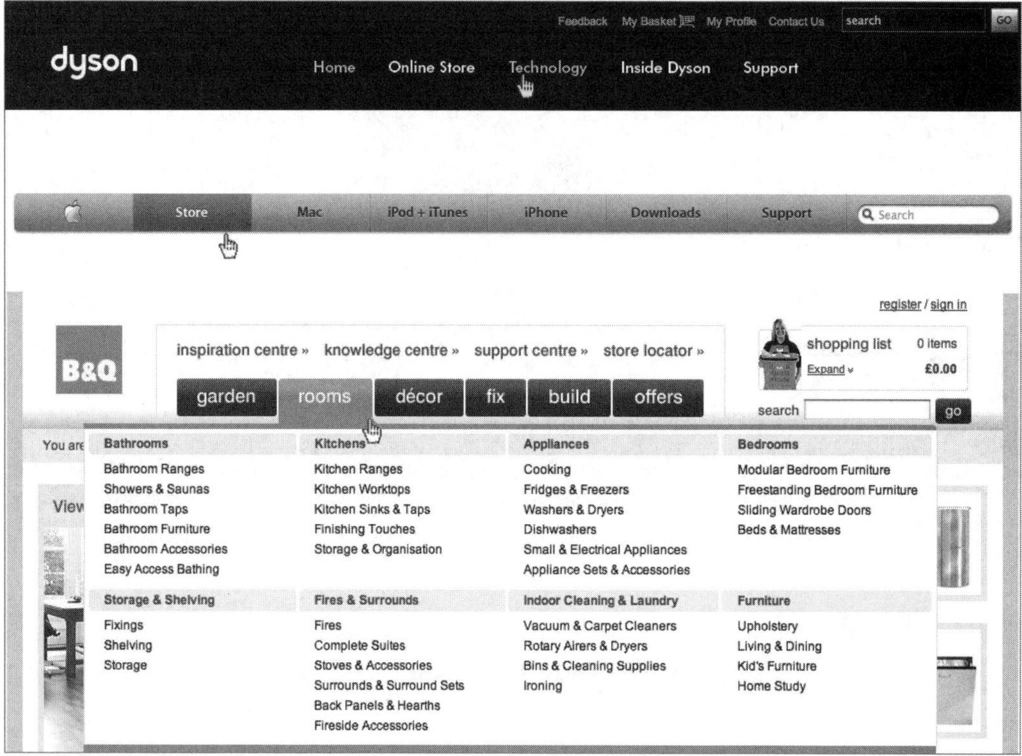

Figure 10-26

Menus Should Be Consistent Across All Pages

The more pages a site contains, the more navigation items you are going to require. As soon as you have to introduce submenus, the navigation becomes more complicated and will vary from page to page. It is very important that the primary navigation remains consistent across all pages.

The submenus in each section of your site should be in the same position on each page and have a similar look and feel, so that users know exactly where to go to navigate the site.

If You Use Icons, Provide a Text Equivalent, Too

It can be tempting to use icons in your navigation, but it is worth remembering that an icon that might seem obvious to you would not be so obvious to someone else. An icon of a house for Home, a magnifying glass for Search, a downward arrow for Download, or an envelope for Contact might all be commonly used, but it is always wise to offer a description in text, too.

Figure 10-27 shows a menu for the software called Coda from a company called Panic; its use of icons is accompanied by clear text. Below that, you can see the Apple menu — even for its search feature, Apple still adds the word "search" along with the magnifying glass icon.

Figure 10-27

Coding for Menus

You will often see menus coded as unordered lists because, semantically speaking, they are a list of links (`ch10_eg11.html`).

```
<ul id="navigation">
  <li><a href="/">Home</a></li>
  <li><a href="/products/">Products</a></li>
  <li><a href="/services/">Services</a></li>
  <li><a href="/about/">About</a></li>
  <li><a href="/contact/">Contact</a></li>
</ul>
```

In a moment we are going to turn this into a navigation menu like some of those we have seen in the examples. But first have a look at Figure 10-28 to see how it looks before you start to style it.

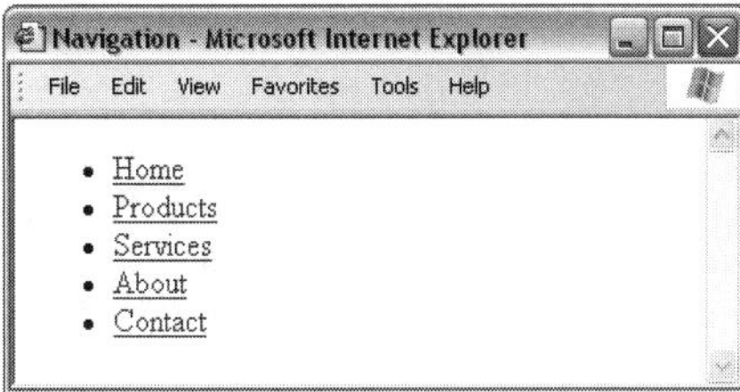

Figure 10-28

The first step is to remove the bullet-style marker and padding from the list, and set all the list items to be inline items so that they sit next to each other rather than on top of each other (`ch10_eg11.html`):

```
ul#navigation {
  list-style: none;
  margin: 0;}

ul#navigation li {
  display:inline;}
```

Figure 10-29 shows you that the links now sit next to each other.

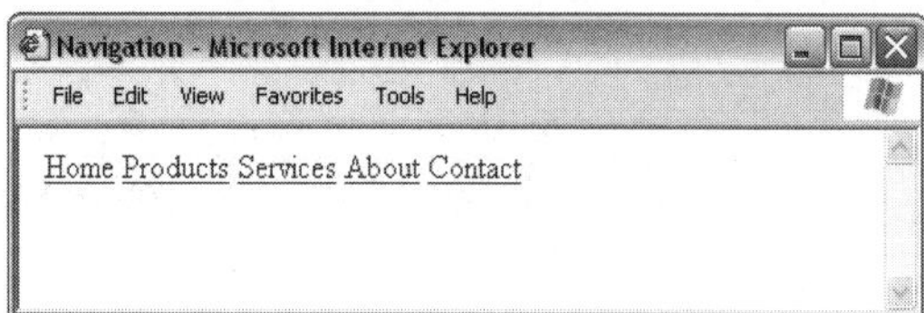

Figure 10-29

Next, let's change the default link styles to a new color text on a different background color, remove the underline, and make the text a larger font in a different typeface:

```
ul#navigation a {
  color:#ffffff;
  background-color:#000000;
  text-decoration:none;
  font-family:georgia, times, serif;
  font-size:1.126em;}
```

You can see the result in Figure 10-30.

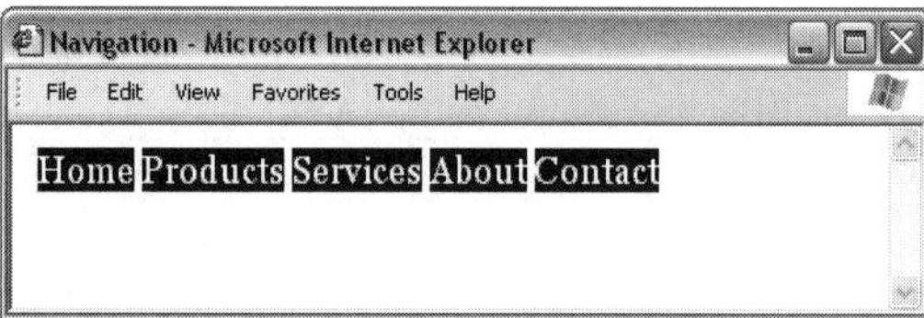

Figure 10-30

We can make this easier to use and more attractive by adding padding to the <a> elements — this will increase the clickable area. You could also add a border to the bottom of the boxes:

```
ul#navigation a {
  color:#ffffff;
  background-color:#000000;
```

```
    text-decoration:none;
    font-family:georgia, times, serif;
    font-size:1.126em;
    padding:10px;
    border-bottom:3px solid #ff6600;}
```

The last step in transforming the list is to create different hover states for the links:

```
ul#navigation a:hover {
    color:#000000;
    background-color:#ff6600;
    padding:10px;
    border-bottom:3px solid #000000;}
```

You can see the result in Figure 10-31.

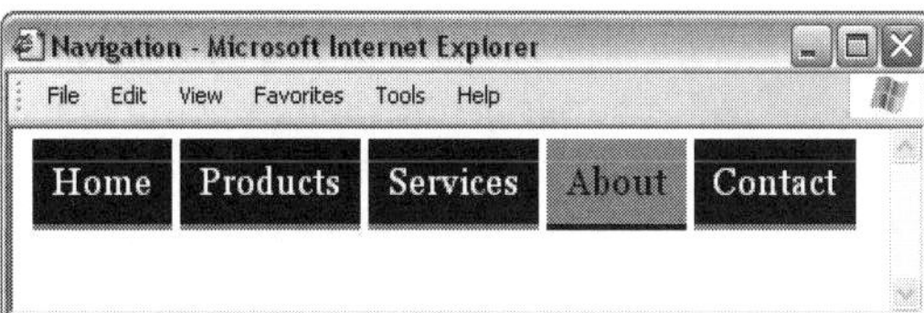

Figure 10-31

Links

In addition to the menus your visitors will be using to navigate the site, many web pages contain other hyperlinks in the text that makes up the body of the document. This short section addresses two topics regarding links that are not part of the main menu:

- Text links
- Images as links

Text Links

By default, text links tend to be blue and underlined. Some experts on usability suggest that all links should be left to their default appearance. However, from your experience of the Web, you probably know that using a color that's clearly different from the main text makes it easy enough for users to tell what text makes up a link.

You have just seen an example of how to change the color and appearance of links, and also how to change their state when someone hovers a mouse over the link.

When you use CSS to specify the color of links, the browser will not change the color of visited links anymore. To do this, you need to use the `:visited` pseudo class (`ch10_eg12.html`):

```
a {font-weight:bold; color:#ff0000; text-decoration:none;}
a:hover {color:#FF9900; text-decoration:underline; background-color:#f9f0f0;}
a:visited {color:#990000;}
```

As users hover over links, these links will be underlined, change color, and gain a background color. The visited links will be in a different shade, reminding users where they have been. You can see this best if you run the example available with the download code for the chapter (Figure10-32).

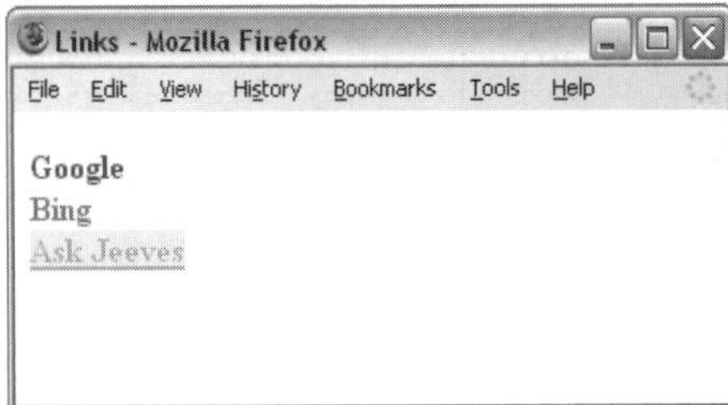

Figure 10-32

It is generally a bad idea to use a different weight of text when a user hovers over a link because this changes the width of the font, which in turn changes the position of words around it and makes it harder to read.

Images as Links

Images are often used as links in menus, advertisements, photos to click on, graphical icons, and so on. Whenever you use an image as a link you should use two attributes on the image:

- `alt ="description of image or text on image"`: Use this to tell users who cannot see the image what the image is or what it says.
- `title="where the link will take the user"`: Use this to show users a tooltip that says where the link will take them; this is also used by screen readers.
- If you do not use CSS to control the border of images that are links (and set them to "no border"), you should also add the `border` attribute: `border="0"`. If you don't use CSS to control borders or this attribute, you will get a border around the image in many browsers, which can look unsightly.

If you are using images as links, it is very helpful to design them in such a way that it is obvious to users where they can click. Figure 10-33 shows some image links from popular sites that have good button styles.

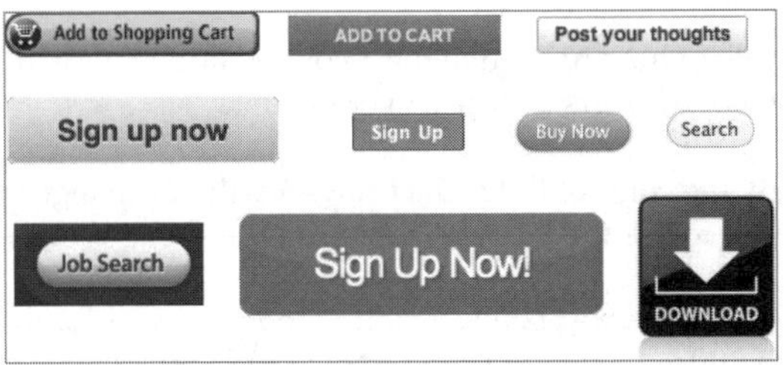

Figure 10-33

CSS Sprites

When creating graphical buttons, you will often want to use a second version of the image when a user hovers over it (known as a rollover state), to make it clear when someone is hovering over an image that can be clicked on.

Image rollovers were initially created using JavaScript to swap one image for another when the user hovers over it. Now, a much better technique is the use of *CSS sprites*. CSS sprites use one image to represent the different states of a button. When the page loads, one part of the image is shown to the user (the normal button style), then when the user hovers over the image, a different section of the image is shown (the rollover style).

Some CSS sprites take this even further and have one image that represents the different possible states that *all* the buttons on your site may have. We will take a look at our own example in a moment, but first, Figure 10-34 shows you examples of Google and Amazon's sprites: single images that represent several parts of their interface.

Another advantage of using sprites is that the browser is requesting only one image from the server, rather than many, which reduces the overhead on the web server.

To see how this works, take a look at Figure 10-35. We will be using this image to create three separate buttons with different states when the user hovers over them.

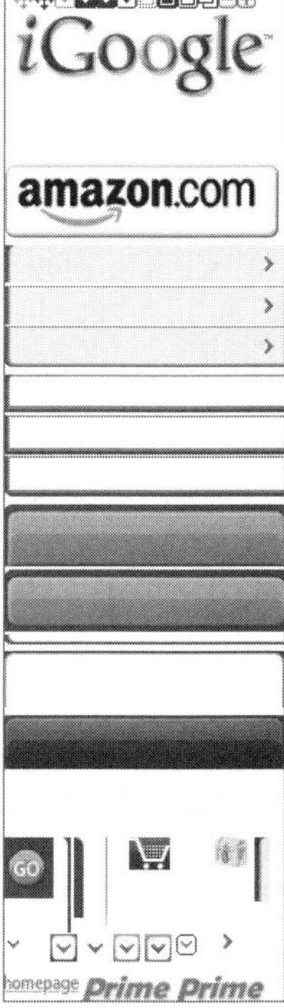

Figure 10-34

Figure 10-35

Here is the HTML for this example (`ch10_eg13.html`):

```
<ul id="navigation">
        <li><a class="buy" href="/buy/" title="Buy now">Buy now</a></li>
        <li><a class="more" href="/more/" title="View more">View more</a>
        </li>
        <li><a class="login" href="/login/" title="Login">Login</a></li>
</ul>
```

This does not need to be an unordered list; it could be any kind of element. The key point is that we will be setting each element to be as big as the button we want to appear. We will then use the CSS sprite as a background image for these elements.

By positioning the background image accurately, we can ensure that it shows the right image. And when the user hovers over a link, we change the position of the background image so that it shows the same button's rollover state.

```
#navigation li {
        list-style-type:none;
        font-size:2em;}

#navigation li a {
        background-image: url("images/buttons.jpg");
        background-repeat:no-repeat;
        display:block;
        width:200px;
        height:70px;
        text-indent: -900%;}

#navigation li a.buy {background-position:0px 0px;}
#navigation li a:hover.buy {background-position:0px -70px;}

#navigation li a.more {background-position:0px -140px;}
#navigation li a:hover.more {background-position:0px -210px;}

#navigation li a.login {background-position:0px -280px;}
#navigation li a:hover.login {background-position:0px -350px;}
```

Note how the same image is set as a background for all of these buttons. But the rules for each individual link use different `background-position` coordinates to show the part of the image that contains the relevant button. The hover state for these images then moves the background position to show the part of the image that has the hover state for that button. You can see the result in Figure 10-36.

Site Search Features

The third way a user can navigate your site is by using a search feature. A search feature allows users to immediately look for a keyword (or words) that relate to the information they are trying to find from your site. Searching can save users from having to learn your scheme for navigating the site and offers another way to find the information if they are having difficulty finding what they came for.

Figure 10-36

Search Features Make Sites More Usable

If you have only a few pages then your menu should be easy to understand, but as your site grows, search features become increasingly important.

Large commercial sites commonly store web pages in a database and can therefore use programming commands called *queries* to ask the database which pages contain the terms a user searched for.

For sites that do not use databases, the easiest way to add a search feature to your site is to use a third-party search utility to index your site for you.

Adding a Google Search to Your Site

When you search on Google, you can request results from just one domain by adding `site:`*`sitename.com`* to the search box. Using this functionality, you can create a form that will ask Google to search your site for whatever the visitor wants to find.

Here you can see an example of a form that searches the Wrox.com web site (`ch10_eg14.html`):

```
<form method="get" action="http://www.google.com/search">
  <input type="text" name="q" size="31" maxlength="255" value="" />
  <input type="submit" value="Search" />
  <input type="radio" name="sitesearch" value="wrox.com" />
</form>
```

Figure 10-37 shows you what happens if someone enters asp.net into the search box on this simple form.

Google also provides two services that allow you to format the results:

- A free service called Google Custom Search (`www.google.com/coop/cse/`)
- A fee-based service called Google Site Search (`www.google.com/sitesearch/`), which does not show ads

Another site that offers a search service is `www.atomz.com`.

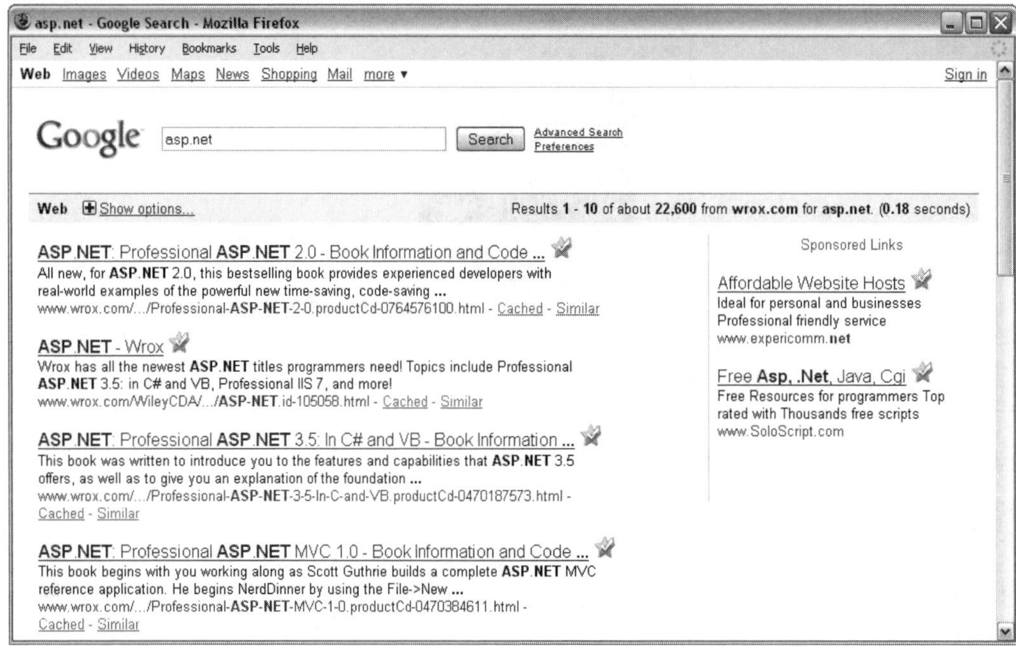

Figure 10-37

Tables

By their nature, tables often show a lot more information than one user will be interested in. A single visitor is likely to want to filter out a percentage of the information available. For example, if you are looking for train times, you want to know the times from your local station (not each station between you and the destination). By carefully designing your table, you can make it easier for people to find that information quickly.

There are some techniques that can make your tables a lot easier for users to read:

- Padding
- Headings
- Shading columns

In order to look at tables, we will be working with the example shown in Figure 10-38 (we are working toward creating a version of the table that you can see in `ch10_eg15.html`).

Padding

It is important to allow padding around each item so that there is space between each cell in the table (and between the content of the cell and any borders if they are used). When the content of table cells is allowed to touch either the edges of any cells or the neighboring cells, it becomes much harder

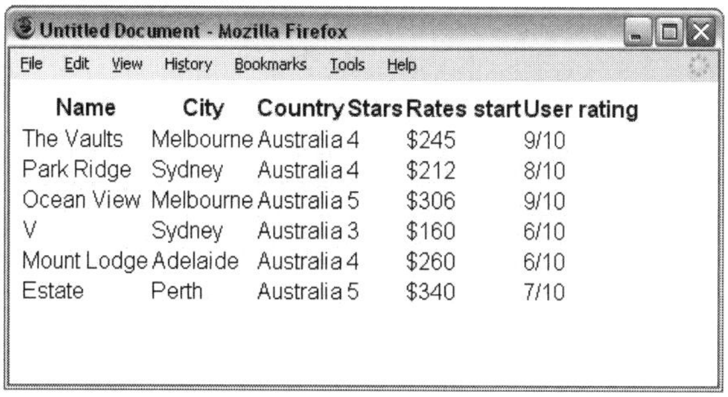

Untitled Document - Mozilla Firefox

File Edit View History Bookmarks Tools Help

Name	City	Country	Stars	Rates start	User rating
The Vaults	Melbourne	Australia	4	$245	9/10
Park Ridge	Sydney	Australia	4	$212	8/10
Ocean View	Melbourne	Australia	5	$306	9/10
V	Sydney	Australia	3	$160	6/10
Mount Lodge	Adelaide	Australia	4	$260	6/10
Estate	Perth	Australia	5	$340	7/10

Figure 10-38

to read. I tend to leave a little bit more space to the left and right of a column rather than above or beneath it. Here you can see a rule that adds padding to each `<td>` and `<th>` element:

```
th, td  {padding:10px 20px 8px 10px;}
```

Headings

All table headings should be in bold, which is the default style for the `<th>` element. I also tend to make headers uppercase and underline the headings with a dark line to separate the headings from the content:

```
th {
  border-bottom:2px solid #000000;
  text-transform:uppercase;
  background-color:#d6d6d6;
  text-align:left;}
```

You can see the difference in the table shown in Figure 10-39.

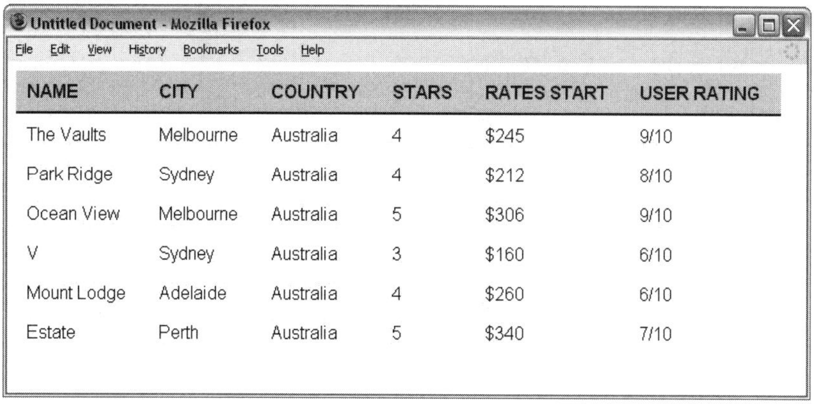

Untitled Document - Mozilla Firefox

File Edit View History Bookmarks Tools Help

NAME	CITY	COUNTRY	STARS	RATES START	USER RATING
The Vaults	Melbourne	Australia	4	$245	9/10
Park Ridge	Sydney	Australia	4	$212	8/10
Ocean View	Melbourne	Australia	5	$306	9/10
V	Sydney	Australia	3	$160	6/10
Mount Lodge	Adelaide	Australia	4	$260	6/10
Estate	Perth	Australia	5	$340	7/10

Figure 10-39

Shading Alternate Rows

Shading alternate rows will help users follow along the lines. You should only shade every other line, preferably using a slightly lighter shade than the heading, as shown in Figure 10-40.

You might also find it helpful to align numerical data to the right of the column and leave words aligned to the left.

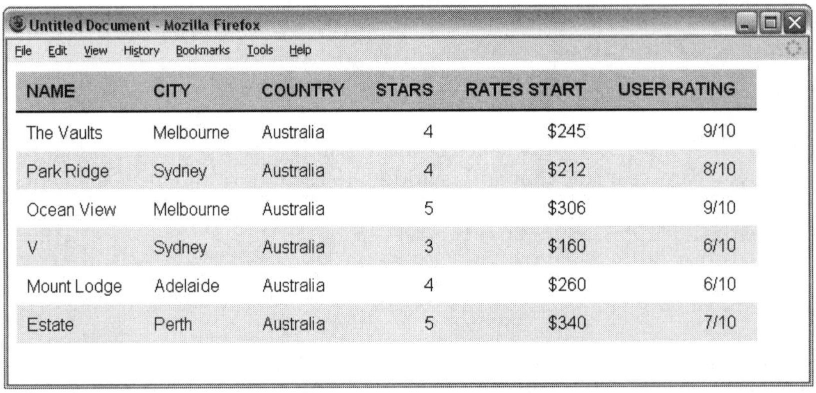

Untitled Document - Mozilla Firefox

File Edit View History Bookmarks Tools Help

NAME	CITY	COUNTRY	STARS	RATES START	USER RATING
The Vaults	Melbourne	Australia	4	$245	9/10
Park Ridge	Sydney	Australia	4	$212	8/10
Ocean View	Melbourne	Australia	5	$306	9/10
V	Sydney	Australia	3	$160	6/10
Mount Lodge	Adelaide	Australia	4	$260	6/10
Estate	Perth	Australia	5	$340	7/10

Figure 10-40

Remember that whatever background colors you use, there must be a good contrast between the background and the text in order for the user to be able to read it easily. The very light gray in this example is a good example of a color that does not dramatically affect the readability of the table itself.

If we put all of that together, the following is the CSS for the table you have been looking at:

```
th, td  {
  padding:8px 20px 8px 10px;
  margin:0px;}
th {
  border-bottom:2px solid #000000;
  text-transform:uppercase;background-color:#d6d6d6;
  text-align:left;}
.even{background-color:#efefef;}
.number {text-align:right;}
```

Forms

I have yet to meet anyone who enjoys filling in forms — especially on the Web. Therefore, if your site must include a form, good design is essential or people will not fill it in.

In this section, you learn about the following:

- What to do before designing the form
- How to design a form, select the right form controls, group them correctly, and label them
- How best to lay out a form

To illustrate the points in this section, you will see an example of a basic form that users have to fill in before they can register for an online service.

Before Designing the Form

Before you address how a form should really look, you need to do some preparation — this is just like the preparation you need to do before you start designing a site, although it should take less time.

Listing Required Information First

When designing a form, you should start out by creating a complete list of the information you require from a user. You might start with a general list with items such as login details, name, mailing address, and e-mail address, but you then need to make sure that you know what makes up each item. For example, do you need to get a user's first name and last name separately? If so these will have to be separate items on the form. What makes up the address: house number/name, street name, suburb, zip code, and so on? Which ones need to be separated from the others?

The following is a list of the information that is needed for our registration form:

- Login information
- User's name
- User's address
- User's contact details

When this is broken down, the exact information that's needed is as follows:

- **Login information:** Username and password
- **Name:** First name, last name
- **Land address:** Street address, city, zip code
- **Contact information:** E-mail address, area code, phone number

When you are creating forms, you should ask only for the information you really need to get a job done. When gathering information from visitors, it's very tempting to ask as many questions as you can; but the longer a form is, the less likely it is that users will complete it.

If you want to collect lots of nonessential information (for example, if you want to get a better idea of the demographic of visitors to your site), consider offering users an incentive to participate and answer the questions *after* they have registered/purchased an item. For example, if you want to know about their hobbies and interests, you might offer them an entry into a prize draw in return for answering a short survey, rather than forcing them to provide this information when first registering to use the site. Take a look at Figure 10-41, which shows the homepage for a blogging service called Tumblr; this is all you need to enter in order to start blogging on its platform.

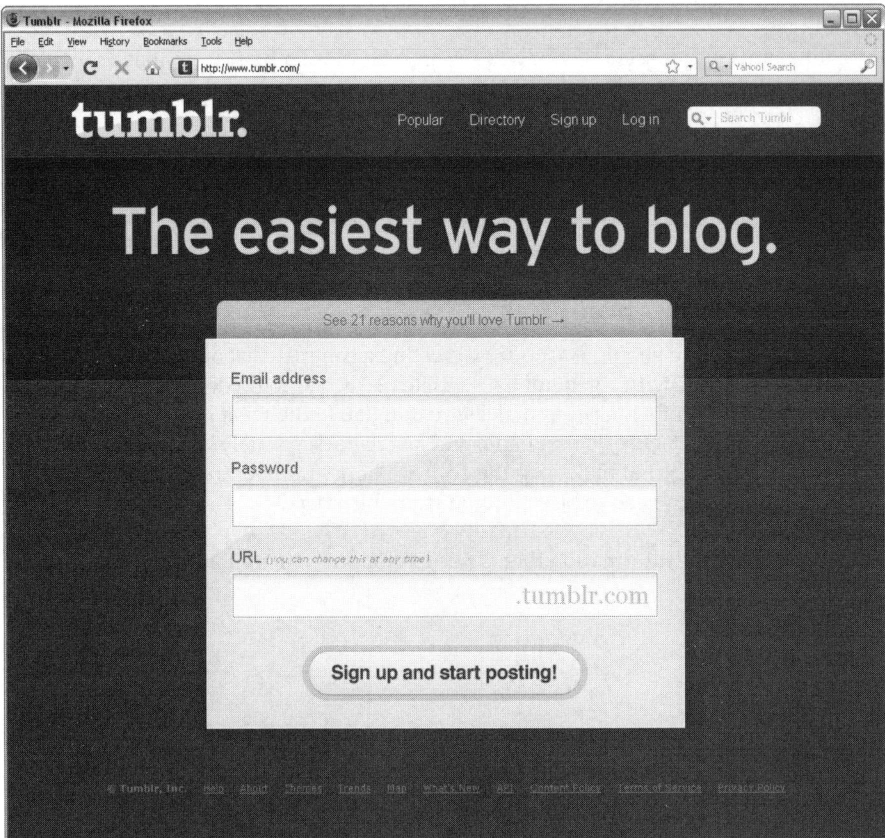

Figure 10-41

> **Note that when collecting and storing information about customers, you must also ensure that you meet the data protection laws of your country.**

Group Related Information

Once you know what information you want to collect from a visitor to your site, you need to look to see if there is a logical grouping to the information you require from visitors to help them understand the form.

If you find such a grouping in related information, you should make sure that these items go together in the form. In the example for this section, you could group the information like this:

- Name and e-mail address
- Login details
- Other contact details

In this example, the grouping is the same as the initial list of required information before it was broken down, but sometimes the grouping can be quite different.

Model Forms Users Are Familiar With

If you are creating an online application that represents a form that would previously have been filled in on paper *and* that your users would be familiar with, then you should make sure that your online form reflects that paper form. (If the form would not have been familiar to users this is not necessary.) If the goal of your application is to put existing software online, then it could also be modeled on the software interface.

The reason for modeling your form on something the user is familiar with is quite obvious: it makes it easier for the user to fill in. That is not to say that the layout of the form should be exactly the same (often paper forms cram too many questions into a small space). Rather, you should be asking similar questions in a similar order and grouping.

Are Users Going to Provide the Same Information Each Time?

Will users have to provide the same information each time they visit the site? Or will some data be stored in a database (or other application) and retrieved when they log in again? For example, if you are working on an online store, once the user has logged in, will the application remember the user's name, address, and contact details?

You should also consider how your form is going to be processed. If it's going to be processed by a human, the human can interpret the data the user enters, whereas if it goes straight into a database, users must be a lot more precise about the information they enter. This may affect your choice of form control required to collect the information.

What Else Needs to Appear on the Form?

Several forms contain extra information, such as shipping information, price lists, legal notices, and so on. Before you start designing the form, you should be aware of all the information that might be put on it, not just the form controls themselves.

Designing the Form

Now that you know what information must be captured by the form, you can design it. You can start by selecting the appropriate type of control and then grouping the controls together and labeling them. You can then add final touches to the layout of the form to control its presentation.

Selecting the Right Type of Form Control

You learned in Chapter 5 about the different types of form controls that you can use. It's important that you choose the correct type of form control for the information that you are trying to collect. Once you have decided which form control to use for each piece of information, you'll have an idea of the possible length and layout of the form.

Here are the types of form control you can choose from when you want a user to enter some text:

- If there is just one line of text, you use an `<input>` element whose `type` attribute has the value of `text`.
- If you want the user to enter more than one line of text you use the `<textarea>` element.
- If the information is sensitive (such as a credit card or password), use an `<input>` element whose `type` attribute has a value of `password`.

If you want the user to specify his or her choice from a limited number of options, you can use one of the following form controls:

- If the user can select only one option (from several), use a group of radio buttons (with the same name) or a drop-down select box.
- If the user can select multiple items, use checkboxes or a multiple select box.

Also consider how visitors would be used to giving this kind of information. For example, use a set of text inputs for each line of an address rather than, say, using a combination of a text input for the street name and a select box to indicate whether the street is a street, road, or avenue for the first line of the address.

Remember that each form control should use a name that describes its content. Rather than just arbitrary names such as `input1` and `input2`, you will also often see form control names that are given a prefix to describe what kind of form control they relate to:

- txt*Name* for text boxes and text areas
- rad*Name* for radio buttons
- chk*Name* for checkboxes
- sel*Name* for select boxes

Text Boxes

If you do not have a preset list of options for a visitor to pick from, textboxes tend to be the most natural way for users to offer information.

Where possible, you should allow users to enter text without having to scroll to see what they have typed. When you only want a short answer from a user, you can use a single-line text input, but when you want more information you should use a multi-line text area.

Users often take the size of the textbox to be an indication of the length of text that they should provide. In Figure 10-42 you can see an example where users are asked their favorite color and why they like this color. When you want users to provide more information, give them a larger area.

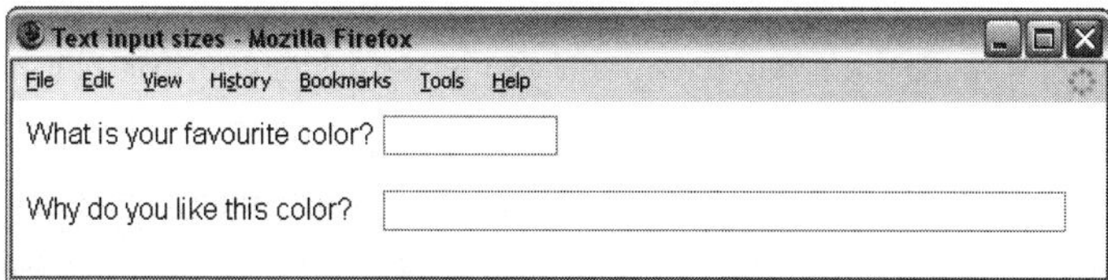

Figure 10-42

Radio Buttons and Checkboxes or Select Boxes

If you want a user to select *one* item from a fairly short list, you should consider using radio buttons rather than a drop-down list, because it allows the user to easily see all options at once.

Whenever you want a user to select *multiple* options from a list of options, checkboxes are usually a better approach.

If you are asking a user to agree to something (such as terms and conditions) you should always use a checkbox rather than a radio button because, once you have clicked on a radio button, you cannot click it again to deselect it if you want to change your mind (whereas you can click on a checkbox a second time to deselect it).

Both radio buttons and checkboxes also allow you to provide more information to the user than a drop-down list box or select box. A radio button or checkbox can have a long description next to it, whereas if you use a long description in a drop-down list or select box, the whole box grows wider. You can see an example of a long drop-down (which takes up the full width of the screen) and a set of radio buttons in Figure 10-43 (`ch10_eg16.html`).

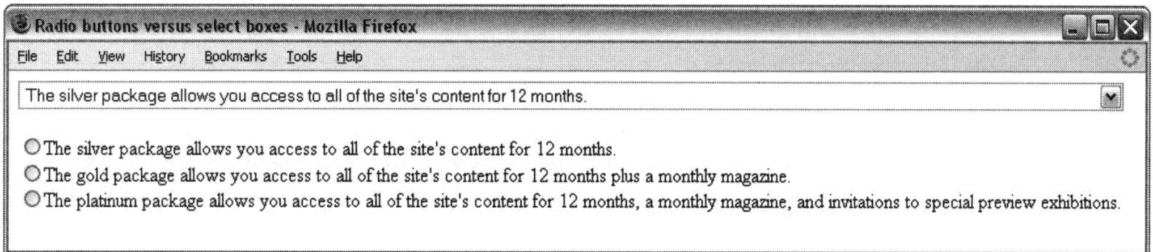

Figure 10-43

Select Boxes

Select boxes, also known as drop-down list boxes, save space on the screen, especially when there are lots of options. However, as Figure 10-43 shows, they do not look very good with long descriptions for each option because the width of a select box is the width of the widest option in it.

You should remember when providing a select box to include options for all users. For example, if you use a drop-down for U.S. states and you have visitors from outside the U.S., you should have at least one option for those who do not live in a U.S. state, even if the option is just "Outside U.S."

The order of items in a select box should reflect users' experience; for example, if you use month names, put them in chronological order, whereas if you use states or countries, alphabetical lists are easier to use.

If one (or a few options) within a long list are more popular or more likely to be chosen than other options, then you should put these at the top of the select box so that the user comes to them first.

Grouping Controls

Once you've decided what form controls you're going to use, you can start to put them on the page. As I already mentioned, the controls should be grouped together into related items of information — and the groups should reflect the users' understanding of the topic.

You can group form elements using white space (as discussed earlier in the chapter) by using the `<fieldset>` element or by splitting the form into several pages.

Using <fieldset> Elements

You already learned about the `<fieldset>` element in Chapter 5. It allows you to group sections of a form between the opening `<fieldset>` and closing `</fieldset>` tags. The fieldset can also carry a `<legend>` element directly after the opening `<fieldset>` tag to indicate a caption for the box.

For example, here is a form for a user to enter login details (`ch10_eg17.html`):

```
<form name="frmLogin" action="login.aspx" method="post">
  <fieldset>
    <legend>Login</legend>
      User name: <input type="text" size="12" name="txtUserName" /><br />
      Password: <input type="password" size="12" name="txtPassword" /><br />
      Confirm password: <input type="password" size="12"
              name="txtPasswordConfirmed" /><br />
      <input type="submit" value="Log in" />
  </fieldset>
</form>
```

Fieldsets were introduced in IE4, Netscape 6, and Firefox 1. Older browsers just ignore the `<fieldset>` and `<legend>` buttons if they do not understand them, so you can safely add these elements to all forms. You can see what this example looks like in Figure 10-44.

Figure 10-44

You can associate styles with the `<fieldset>` element, as in the following example (`ch10_eg17.css`):

```
fieldset {
  width:250px;
  padding:10px;
  font-size:12px;
  text-align:right;}
```

Note here how the `width` property has been set in the style sheet. This is particularly helpful to add to `<fieldset>` elements because they will otherwise stretch to the width of the browser window (or containing element).

Splitting a Form into Separate Pages

In some cases, long forms not only put off users but also make the form harder for the user to fill in. Therefore, if you have a long form, you can split it up into several pages to make it less intimidating and to group related information on a single page.

As a general guide, your form should be not much more than a "screenful" (at 1024 × 768 resolution) so the user does not have to scroll much.

If you split a form into separate pages, you should clearly indicate to the users how far they are through the form. In Figure 10-45, you can see a form that has been split up into four pages and a confirmation page.

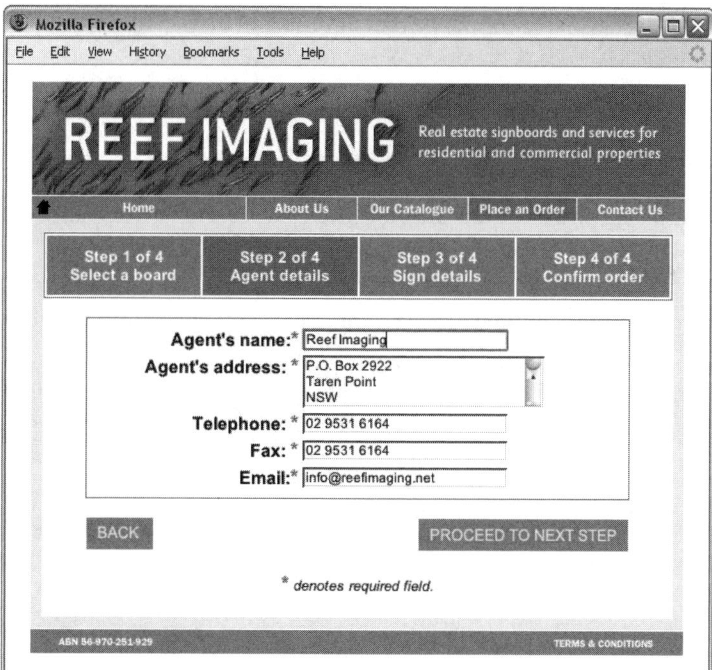

Figure 10-45

Splitting a form into several pages can introduce new complexities into the programming because the program has to remember what a user has entered between each form; however, there are several ways of doing this with a little extra effort. You will generally want users to go through these steps in order rather than allowing them to go between pages at random, so avoid links that allow them to jump to any page. When you split a form into separate pages, you should offer links for users to go back as well as forward. Figure 10-45 shows an example of a form that is split up across several pages; it clearly indicates which step you are currently on, and how many steps there are in the process.

Number Questions

If you have a lot of questions, as in an application form or an online test, you should number questions so that the users know where questions start and end. This can also be a help if you want to indicate to users that they should jump to another section of the form, because you can explicitly indicate which number question they should go to.

Layout of Forms

Ideally, a layout of a form should reflect what users would expect to see when dealing with such data. Their experience may have come from real-life experience (such as how they would write their address) or from common practice on other web sites.

Labeling Controls

The first issue concerned with layout of forms is the labeling of controls. It's very important that each control be clearly labeled so that users know what information they should be adding and where. There are two types of labels:

- Implicit labels that are normal text and markup next to the control
- Explicit labels that use the `<label>` element

You should consider the following as guidelines for where the label for an element should generally appear:

- **Text entry fields:** To the left of the input or directly above
- **Checkboxes and radio buttons:** To the right of the checkbox or radio button
- **Buttons:** On the button itself — its value

Implicit controls are the simplest way to label a control. To add an implicit label, you simply add text directly next to the label in question. For example (`ch10_eg18.html`):

```
First name: <input type="text" name="txtFirstName" size="12" /> <br />
Last name: <input type="text" name="txtLastName" size="12" /> <br />
E-mail address: <input type="text" name="txtEmail" size="12" /> <br />
<input type="submit" value="subscribe" />
```

You can see the result in Figure 10-46. The disadvantages with this approach are that:

- The form controls do not align with each other.
- You are not using the <label> element, which helps improve accessibility by allowing screen readers to associate a control with its label.

Figure 10-46

While <label> elements do require a little extra programming effort, it is generally a good idea to get into the habit of using them. You may remember from Chapter 5 that the <label> element must either contain the form control or use the `for` attribute whose value is the value of the `id` attribute on the form control.

Take a look at how we can improve this form by adding the <label> elements and adding a containing <div> for the corresponding form controls (`ch10_eg19.html`):

```
<label for="firstName">First name: </label>
<div class="control">
  <input type="text" name="txtFirstName" size="12" id="firstName" />
</div>
<label for="lastName">Last name: </label>
<div class="control">
  <input type="text" name="txtLastName" size="12" id="lastName" />
</div>
<label for="email">E-mail address: </label>
<div class="control">
  <input type="text" name="txtEmail" size="12" id="email" />
</div>
```

Now, using CSS we can set a `width` property and a `float` for both the <label> element and the <div> element so that each sits next to the other.

```
fieldset {
  font-size:12px;
  padding:10px;
  width:280px;
  line-height:2.4;}
```

```
label {
  float:left;
  width:100px;}

.control {
  float:left;
  width:150px;}
```

You can see the result in Figure 10-47.

Figure 10-47

Now let's have a look at an example of a form that allows users to indicate how they heard about a company. You should always use the `<label>` element on radio buttons and checkboxes because, when you do, the user can click on the label (as well as the radio button or checkbox) to select that item, and by increasing the clickable area you are making it easier for people to use the form (`ch10_eg20.html`):

```
<form name="frmExample" action="" method="post">
  <fieldset>
    <legend>How did you hear about us?</legend>
    <input type="radio" id="referrer1" name="radReferrer" value="Mouth" />
    <label for="referrer1" >Word of Mouth</label><br />
    <input type="radio" id="referrer2" name="radReferrer" value="Google" />
    <label for="referrer2" >Google Search</label><br />
    <input type="radio" id="referrer3" name="radReferrer"
    value="Magazine Ad" />
    <label for="referrer3" >Magazine Ad</label><br />
    <input type="radio" id="referrer4" name="radReferrer" value="Other" />
    <label for="referrer4" >Other</label>  
    <input type="text" value="txtOther" size="12" /><br />
    <input type="submit" value="Submit" />
  </fieldset>
</form>
```

You can see this form in Figure 10-48.

Figure 10-48

Remember that when choosing the prompt or the label for a form, you must choose words that will really mean something to users. What might be obvious to you might not be so clear to a visitor who is not as familiar with the topic as you — for example, a `productId` *number might be a unique identifying number for a product, but a customer can't be expected to know this or where to find it.*

Keeping Relevant Information Next to or Above Form Controls

By now you are getting the idea of how vital good labeling is to a user's understanding, so here are a couple of examples where the position of a label requires extra care. Take a look at the example in Figure 10-49, which is for a telephone number.

Figure 10-49

As you can see here, there is no indication what the separate boxes are for. While you or I might guess that one box is for the area code and the other for the main part of the number, users with screen readers are likely to be more confused by the presence of a second box because they can only listen to the form, not see it. Some users, especially those in a hurry, might try to put the whole number in just one textbox.

A far better approach to this example would be to indicate labels for the area code and the number, as shown in Figure 10-50.

Figure 10-50

This is much clearer for all, and you can see the code here (`ch10_eg21.html`):

```
<table>
  <tr>
    <td class="label">Phone number <span class="important">*</span></td>
    <td>Area code<input type="text" name="txtTelAreaCode" size="5" />
        Number<input type="text" name="txtTelNo" size="10" /></td>
  </tr>
</table>
```

Proper labeling is also very important when you have radio buttons or multiple choice buttons that express an option or rating. You can see a problematic example in Figure 10-51.

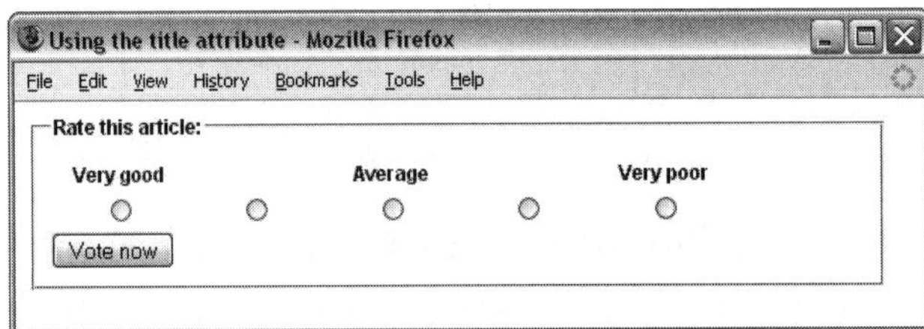

Figure 10-51

The code for this example puts the radio buttons and labels in a table. The problem with this example is not that the labels are not related to the correct radio buttons — as you can see in the following code, the `<label>` elements are used and associated with the correct table cells. The problem is that users with screen readers will hear labels for only three options, whereas there are really five options to choose from; you should be offering labels for each.

```
<table>
  <tr>
    <td><label for="VeryGood">Very good</label></td>
    <td></td>
    <td><label for="Average">Average</label></td>
    <td></td>
    <td><label for="VeryPoor">Very poor</label></td>
  </tr>
  <tr>
    <td><input type="radio" name="radRating" value="5" id="VeryGood"></td>
    <td><input type="radio" name="radRating" value="4" id="Good" /></td>
    <td><input type="radio" name="radRating" value="3" id="Average" /></td>
    <td><input type="radio" name="radRating" value="2" id="Poor" /></td>
    <td><input type="radio" name="radRating" value="1" id="VeryPoor" /></td>
  </tr>
</table>
```

If you really do not want to offer a text alternative for each of these items, a rather drastic alternative is to add labels for the items that have not yet been labeled and place a single-pixel transparent GIF with `alt` text inside the `<label>` element. The single-pixel image will not show up in a browser, but the `alt` text can be used to describe the purpose of the corresponding form control to visitors who reply upon screen readers, as shown here (`ch10_eg22.html`)

```
<table>
  <tr>
    <td><label for="VeryGood">Very good</label></td>
    <td><label for="Good"><img src="images/1px.gif" alt="This option
         has no label; its value is good" /></td>
    <td><label for="Average">Average</label></td>
    <td><label for="Poor"><img src="images/1px.gif" alt= "This option
         has no label; its value is poor" /></td>
    <td><label for="VeryPoor">Very poor</label></td>
  </tr>
  <tr>
    <td><input type="radio" name="radRating" value="5" id="VeryGood" /></td>
    <td><input type="radio" name="radRating" value="4" id="Good" /></td>
    <td><input type="radio" name="radRating" value="3" id="Average" /></td>
    <td><input type="radio" name="radRating" value="2" id="Poor" /></td>
    <td><input type="radio" name="radRating" value="1" id="VeryPoor" /></td>
  </tr>
</table>
```

You cannot actually see the difference between this example and the previous one, but you would be able to hear a difference if you were relying on a screen reader.

Required Information

A form will often include questions that a user must answer in order for it to be processed correctly. If a form control must be filled in, you should tell a user this. It is common practice to use one of the following techniques:

- Use an asterisk (*) to indicate required fields (usually in a different color) and, of course, include a note on the page that acts as a key indicating what the asterisk means.
- Write "required" next to the field (either in text or using an image).

You can see some examples in Figure 10-52.

Careful Placement of Buttons

You should be very careful about where you place buttons on a page. They should be close to the relevant part of the form; for example, in an online store the button to buy should be very clear and should be close to the product, as shown in Figure 10-53 on Etsy.

If you give the user more than one option, then the action that you think the user will want to take should always stand out more than other possible actions. For example if you have a Back or Previous button on a form, this should be less intrusive than the next button.

On a multi-page form, I would tend to put the previous button to the left, and the next button to the right (this mirrors the user's experience with the Back and Forward buttons on a browser window).

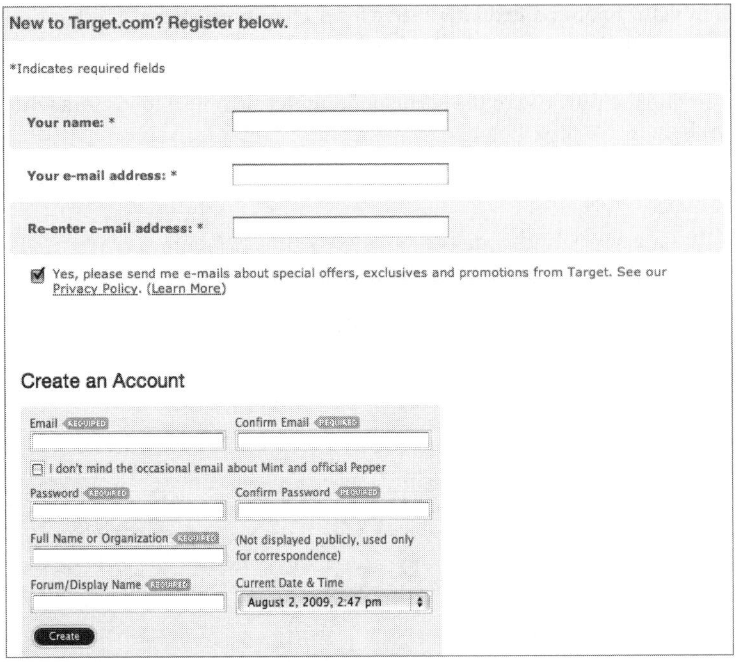

New to Target.com? Register below.

*Indicates required fields

Your name: *

Your e-mail address: *

Re-enter e-mail address: *

Yes, please send me e-mails about special offers, exclusives and promotions from Target. See our Privacy Policy. (Learn More)

Create an Account

Email REQUIRED

Confirm Email REQUIRED

I don't mind the occasional email about Mint and official Pepper

Password REQUIRED

Confirm Password REQUIRED

Full Name or Organization REQUIRED

(Not displayed publicly, used only for correspondence)

Forum/Display Name REQUIRED

Current Date & Time

August 2, 2009, 2:47 pm

Create

Figure 10-52

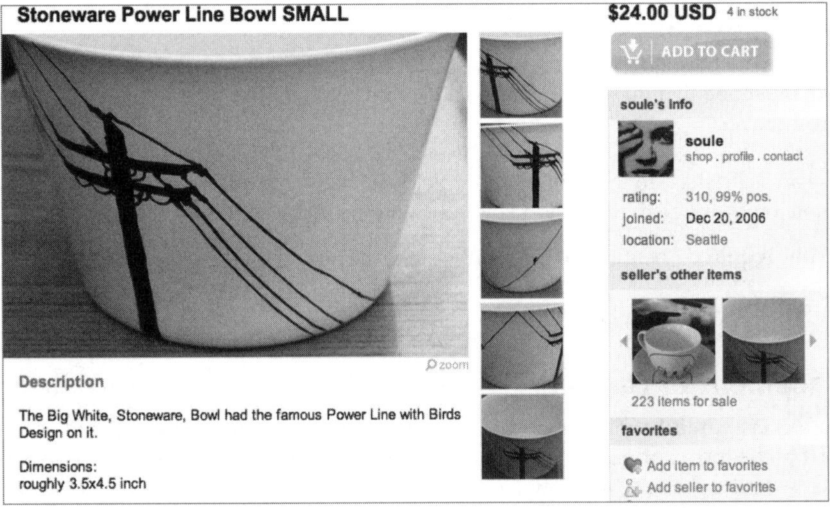

Figure 10-53

You can see an example of this in Figure 10-54.

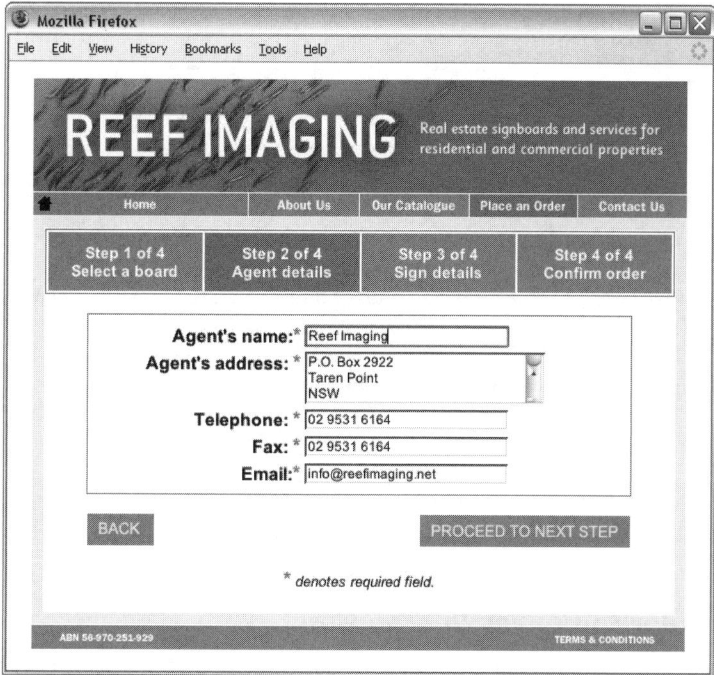

Figure 10-54

Using the title Attribute on Form Controls

One way to add extra information for users is to add a `title` attribute to the form control. When users put their cursors over the form control, the value of the `title` attribute appears as a tooltip. This is particularly helpful for clarifying the type of information that a user has to enter.

For example, here is a text input that requires a user to enter an authorization code. The `title` attribute clarifies where the authorization code comes from (`ch10_eg23.html`):

```
<form name="frmExample" action="" method="post">
  <fieldset>
    <legend>Enter your authorization code</legend>
    Code: 
    <input type="text" name="txtAuthCode" title="Enter the authorization
    code that was e-mailed when you registered." /></td>
  </fieldset>
</form>
```

You can see the result in Figure 10-55, with the tooltip showing as the user hovers over the text input.

Tab Index

Once you have created your form, you should check the tabbing order of form elements. Users should be able to use the Tab key on their keyboards to move between the form controls. If the order in which the

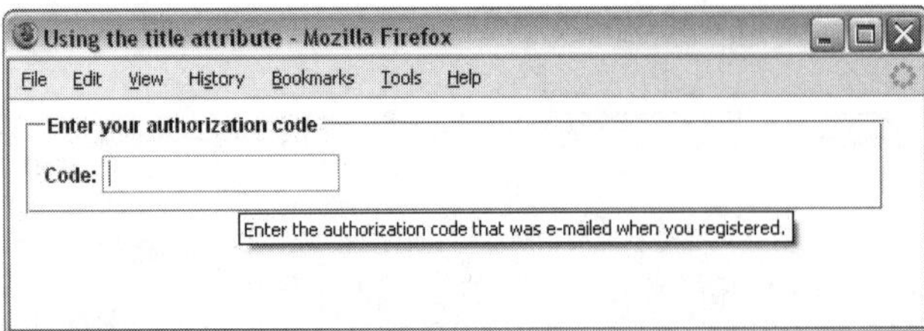

Figure 10-55

form controls gain focus is not the order in which you would expect to fill out the form, you should use the `tabindex` attribute, which can take a value of 0 to 32,767. (Chapter 5 covered this attribute in more detail.)

The `tabindex` attribute can be used on the following elements:

```
<a> <area> <button> <input> <object> <select> <textarea>
```

In Chapter 12, you will see an example of how you can automatically give focus to a form element when the page loads. You will also see how to affect the appearance of the form controls that currently have focus.

Don't Rely on Color to Convey Information

While color can be a very powerful tool in aiding the understanding of forms, you should never rely on a color alone to convey information, and you must ensure that there is enough contrast between colors to make the distinction clear.

Figure 10-56 shows an example of a form that uses color to indicate which items are required, but because this book is printed in black and white, you cannot tell which items have to be filled in.

Figure 10-56

This is easily solved, as shown in Figure 10-57, by adding the words required or an asterisk symbol with a key to indicate which items are mandatory (in addition to the use of color).

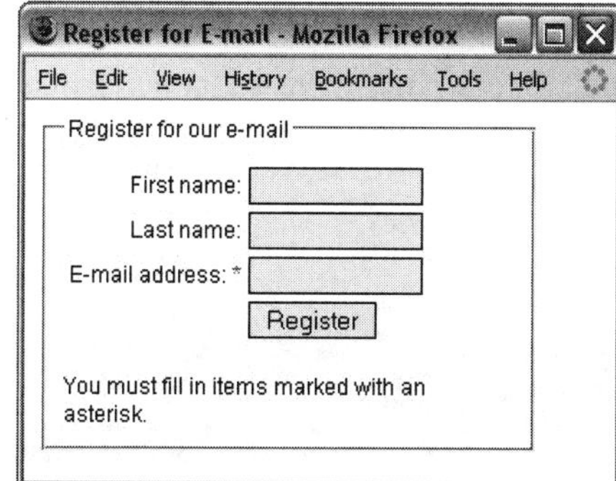

Figure 10-57

Using CSS with Form Elements

The use of CSS to control form elements has been increasingly popular, in particular to control borders and background colors of text inputs, text areas, and submit buttons, in order to create a more stylized form. Figure 10-58 shows a search form where the text input has been hugely transformed from the default text input.

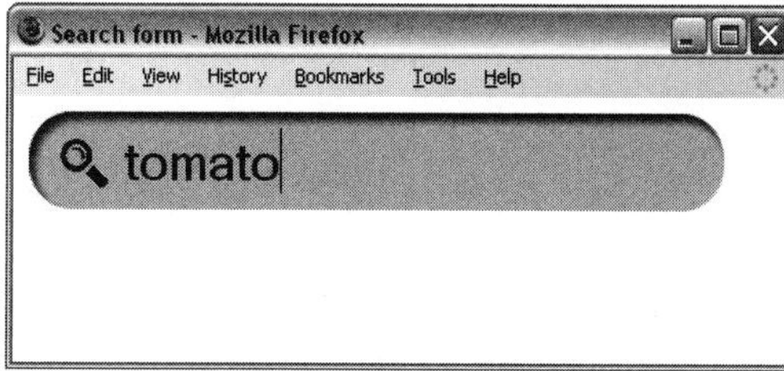

Figure 10-58

The following is the CSS style that is associated with the `<input>` elements (`ch10_eg24.html`):

```
input.search {
  width:335px;
  height:37px;
  padding:10px 10px 10px 55px;
  font-size:30px;
  background-image:url(images/background_search.gif);
  border:none;
  background-color:#cccccc;}

input:focus {
  outline: 0;}
```

If you use styles with form elements, you just have to make sure that you do not make the form harder to fill in by adding unnecessary style. As with any kind of text, if you do not have good contrast for text controls, they will be hard to read and users might enter the incorrect information.

Large Form Inputs

When a basic form is the main part of a page, there is a growing trend to increase the size of the form controls. Login screens and search boxes are good examples of where larger inputs are being used. Figure 10-59 shows you examples from WordPress and Dictionary.com.

Figure 10-59

Testing the Form

Once you have laid out your form, you then need to test the form. You will read more about testing a site in Chapter 13. Briefly, however, it is very helpful to watch people using your form once you have designed it to see how they interact with it.

The most important thing while doing this, and which you must remember, is that if you can see that a user is going to make a mistake, don't interrupt; watch what this person does, because it will teach you more about how the user expected the form to work.

Lazy Registration

One of the best ways to ensure that visitors engage with your site is to allow them to do what they came for. A growing trend in web design is that of lazy registration, where you allow people to get involved with your site with the fewest barriers possible. While you might not yet be ready to implement sites like these, it is interesting to be aware of the trend. For example, Doodle (`www.doodle.com`) allows you to start to schedule an event before signing up, and Posterous (`www.posterous.com`) allows you to start blogging by just sending an e-mail (Figure 10-60).

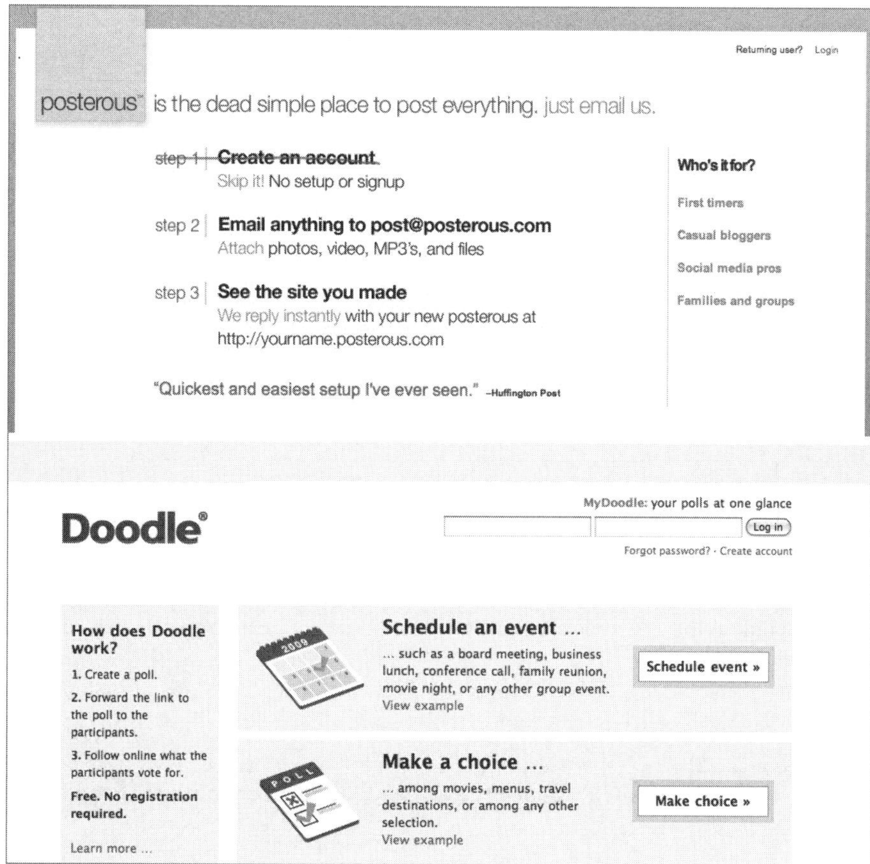

Figure 10-60

Try It Out A Site Registration Form

In this example, you are going to create a simple registration form for a web site. You will have to collect the information provided in the table that follows, using the form controls listed.

Information	Form control	Required
First name	Text input	Yes
Last name	Text input	Yes
E-mail address	Text input	Yes
Password for accessing the site	Password text input	Yes
Confirmation of password	Password text input	Yes
Register	Submit button	N/A

Figure 10-61 shows you what the form will look like when you are finished.

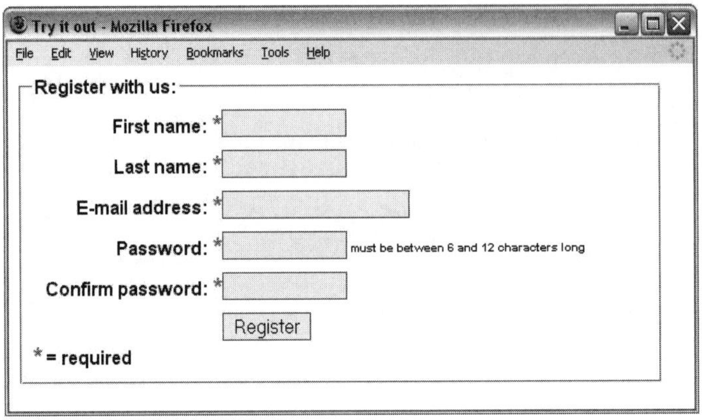

Figure 10-61

1. First set up the skeleton of the document, as you are probably used to doing by now. Don't forget the link to the CSS style sheet called `registration.css`. You can also add a `<form>` element:

```
<html>
  <head>
    <title>Try it out</title>
    <link rel="stylesheet" type="text/css" href="registration.css" />
  </head>
  <body>
  <form name="frmExample" action="register.aspx" method="post">
  </form>
  </body>
</html>
```

2. The form contains only five text inputs so it does not need splitting into separate groups, but it would be a good idea to put the whole thing in a `<fieldset>` element with a `<legend>`:

```
<form name="frmExample" action="" method="post">
<fieldset>
  <legend>Register with us:</legend>
</fieldset>
</form>
```

3. To control the presentation of the form, the inputs will be made to sit next to the labels by placing the form controls inside a `<div>` element, which has a `class` attribute whose value is `input`.

   The first row will contain a text input for the user's first name. You can add it like this just after the `<legend>` element:

```
<label for="fname">First name: <span class="required">*</span></label>
<div class="input">
      <input type="text" name="txtFirstName" id="fname" size="12" />
</div>
```

4. After the form control for the first name, add the text input for the last name and the e-mail address. You can make the size of the e-mail address text input a little larger than the other text inputs because this is likely to be longer (you do this by giving the `size` attribute a higher value than the other examples):

```
<label for="lname">Last name: <span class="required">*</span></label>
<div class="input">
    <input type="text" name="txtLastName" id="lname" size="12" />
</div>

<label for="email">E-mail address: <span class="required">*</span></label>
<div class="input">
    <input type="password" name="txtEmail" id="email" size="20" />
</div>
```

5. After these form controls, the final two controls users will have to fill in allow them to provide a password for the site and to confirm it. Both `<input>` elements have a `type` attribute whose value is `password`. In order to explain that the password should be between 6 and 12 characters long, a message has been added after the first password box in the right column. The reason for adding the note to the right of the password input is that it would throw out alignment of labels on the left if it were placed on the same side.

```
<label for="pwd">Password: <span class="required">*</span></label>
<div class="input">
    <input type="password" name="txtPassword" id="pwd" size="12" />
    <span class="small"> must be between 6 and 12 characters long</span>
</div>
<label for="pwdConf">Confirm password: <span class="required">*</span>
</label>
<div class="input">
    <input type="password" name="txtPasswordConf" id="pwdConf" size="12" />
</div>
```

6. A submit button has to be added to the end of the form. You put this in a `<div>` so that it can be positioned to the right side of the form. This is followed by the key to explain the purpose of the asterisk.

```
<div class="submit"><input type="submit" value="Register" /></div>
<span class="required">*</span> = required
```

7. Save this form as `registration.html`. Now let's have a look at the accompanying CSS file, `registration.css`. Here is the start:

```
body{
    color:#000000;
    background-color:#ffffff;
    font-family:arial, verdana, sans-serif;
    font-weight:bold;
    font-size:100%;}
```

8. Add some whitespace to the fieldset using the padding property and set its width to 550px.

```
fieldset {
    padding:10px;
    width:550px;}
```

9. You want to ensure that each <label> element sits to the left of its corresponding form control, so add a width and float property, then align the text to the right. The clear property can be used to ensure that each item starts on a new line, and the margin-bottom property will give some extra white space between the elements.

```
label {
    width:170px;
    float:left;
    text-align:right;
    clear:both;
    margin-bottom:10px;}
```

10. The <div> elements that hold the form controls have a class attribute whose value is input. Let's add a width and a float property to ensure they sit next to their labels.

```
.input {
    width:350px;
    float:left;}
```

11. To style the inputs themselves, you can add border and background styles. Because form controls do not inherit their size from the <body> element, you need to specify that again here to ensure that you have slightly larger than normal form controls.

```
input {
    border-style:solid;
    border-color:#666666;
    border-width:1px;
    background-color:#f2f2f2;
    font-size:100%;}
```

12. To make the form a little more interactive, when a form control has received focus, you can change the color of the border and background using the border and background properties.

```
input:focus {
    border-style:solid;
    border-color:#333333;
    border-width:1px;
    background-color:#ffffcc;}
```

13. To push the submit button onto a new line, you will use the clear property, and then to ensure it aligns with the other form controls, you can use the margin-left property.

```
.submit {
    clear:both;
    margin-left:170px;}
```

14. When the user hovers over the submit button, you can change the cursor style using the `cursor` property; this makes it even more clear that the user can click on the button.

```
.submit input{
    cursor:pointer;}
```

15. The final step is to set the styles for the required asterisks.

```
.small {font-size:10px;}

.required {
    font-weight:bold;
    font-size:20px;
    color:#ff0000;}
```

If you open the example in a browser, it should look like the screenshot shown in Figure 10-61 (at the start of this section).

Summary

In this chapter, you learned a lot more about web page layout. In Chapter 9, you looked at the general layout or structure of a page. In this chapter, you learned about issues regarding particular parts of pages: typography, navigation, tables, and forms — the bits that fill in that structure. From adding white space between elements on a page, such as text and images, to aligning parts of a form inside a table, you've seen lots of handy hints that will help you design better pages.

You have to remember, however, that there are no set rules that will make you a good designer — that will require practice. While you are practicing, it is a good idea to have a look at some of your favorite web sites and try to decide what about them you think works particularly well.

The only real restrictions you should impose upon yourself when designing a web page are what your audience would find attractive and easy to use. Remember that if you want your site to attract a lot of visitors, don't design the site just for yourself, and don't just design it for your clients; design it for expected visitors to the site.

Exercises

The answers to all of the exercises are in Appendix A.

1. In this exercise, you should add a second page to the Try It Out form at the end of the chapter (`registration.html`). The table that follows shows the new items you must add to the form.

You should also add the following:

- An indication at the top of the page as to how much of the form the user has completed
- A Back button and a Proceed button at the bottom (instead of the Submit button)

Information	Form control	Required
Address 1	Text input	Yes
Address 2	Text input	No
Town/Suburb	Text input	No
City/State	Text input	Yes
Zip code	Text input	Yes

When you have finished, the page should look something like Figure 10-62 (`registration2.html`).

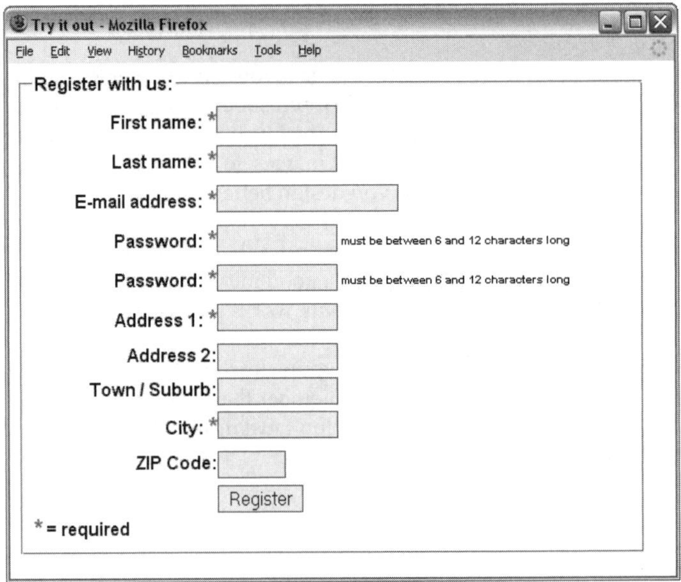

Figure 10-62

Learning JavaScript

There are many programming languages in existence today, and in this chapter, you will begin learning the basics of a programming language called JavaScript, which is by far the most common programming language used in web pages.

Although it is not possible to teach you everything there is to learn about JavaScript in one or two chapters, there are thousands of free scripts available on the Web that you can use. Therefore, the aim of this chapter is to teach you enough to start using these scripts in your web pages and to understand how they work. You should even be able to customize these scripts and write some basic scripts of your own based upon what you will learn in this and the following chapter. In addition, it will serve as a good introduction to general programming concepts.

Once you have covered the basics of JavaScript in this chapter, Chapter 12 will show you lots of examples that should both act as a library of helpful scripts you can use in your own pages and also clarify how the basic concepts you learned in this chapter work in practice.

As you will see, JavaScript gives web developers a programming language to use in web pages that allows them to perform tasks such as the following:

- Read elements from documents and write new elements and text into documents
- Manipulate or move text
- Perform mathematical calculations on data
- React to events, such as a user clicking a button
- Retrieve the current date and time from a user's computer or the last time a document was modified
- Determine the user's screen size, browser version, or screen resolution
- Perform actions based on conditions such as alerting users if they enter the wrong information into a form

You might need to read through this chapter more than once to get a good grasp of what you can do with JavaScript. Then, once you have seen the examples in the next chapter, you should have a better idea of its power. There is a lot to learn, but these two chapters should get you well on your way.

> **JavaScript is not the same as Java, which is a different programming language (although there are some similarities).**

What Is Programming About?

As you will see in this chapter, programming is largely about performing different types of *calculations* upon various types of data (including numbers, text and graphics). In all programming languages. you can perform tasks such as:

- Performing mathematical calculations on numbers such as addition, subtraction, multiplication, and division.
- Working with text to find out how long a sentence is, or where the first occurrence of a specified letter is within a section of text.
- Checking if one value (numbers or letters) matches another.
- Checking if one value is shorter or longer, lower or higher than another.
- Performing different actions based on whether a condition (or one of several conditions) is met. For example, if a user enters a number less than 10, a script or program can perform one action; otherwise it will perform a different action.
- Repeating an action a certain number of times or until a condition is met (such as a user pressing a button).

These actions might sound rather simple, but they can be combined so that they become complicated and powerful. As you will see, different sets of actions can be performed in different situations different numbers of times, to create a huge variety of results.

But before you can learn how to perform these kinds of calculations, first you need some data for the programming language to work with, and to know how the language can work with this data. For our purposes, the data we will be working will be the web page loaded in the browser at the time. When the browser loads a page, it stores it in an electronic form that programmers can then access through something known as an *interface*. The interface is a little like a predefined set of questions and commands. For example, you can ask questions like:

- What is the title of the page?
- What is the third item in the bulleted list whose `id` attribute has a value of `ToDoList`?
- What is the URL of the page in the first link on the page?

You can also use commands to tell the browser to change some of these values, or even add new elements into the page. The interface that works with web pages is called the *Document Object Model*. So, let's have a closer look at what an interface is and what an object model is?

In so-called *object-oriented* programming languages, real-life objects are represented (or modeled) using a set of *objects*, which form an *object model*. For example, a `car` object might represent a car, a `basket` object might represent a shopping basket, and a `document` object could represent a document such as a web page.

Each object can have a set of *properties* that describes aspects of the object. A `car` object might have properties that describe its color or engine size. A `basket` object might have properties that describe the number of items it contains or the value of those items. A `document` object has properties that describe the background color of the web page or the title of the page.

Then there are *methods*; each method describes an action that can be done to (or with) the object. For example, a method of an object representing a car might be to accelerate, or to change gear. A method of a shopping basket might be to add an item, or to recalculate the value of items in the basket. A method on a document could be to write a new line of text into the web page.

Finally, there are *events*; in a programming language, an event is the object putting up its hand and saying "*x* just happened," usually because a program might want to do something as a result of the event. For example, a `car` object might raise an event to say the ignition started, or that it is out of fuel. A `basket` might raise an event when an item is added to it, or when it is full. A document might raise an event when the user presses Submit on a form, or clicks a link. Furthermore, an event can also trigger actions; for example, if a car is out of fuel then the car will stop.

An object model is therefore a description of how a program can represent real-life entities using a set of objects, and it also specifies a set of methods, properties, and events an object may have.

All of the main browsers implement an object model called the *Document Object Model* that was devised to represent web pages. In this Document Object Model, the page as a whole is represented using a `document` object; then the links in that page are represented using a `links` object, the forms are represented in a `forms` object, images are represented using an `image` object, and so on.

So, the Document Object Model describes how you can:

- ❑ Get and set *properties* of a web page such as the background color.
- ❑ Call *methods* that perform actions such as writing a new line into a page.
- ❑ React to *events* such as a user pressing a Submit button on a form.

Web browsers implement the Document Object Model as a way for programming languages to access (and work with) the content of web pages. Once you have learned how the Document Object Model allows you to access and change web pages, you can then see how the programming language can ask the Document Object Model about the web page, perform calculations with the data it receives back, and then tell the browser to change something based upon these calculations.

If you think of the Document Object Model as an *interface* between the browser and the programming language, you can compare it to a remote control that acts as the interface between your TV and you. You know that pressing 1 on your remote control will turn your TV to channel 1, or that the volume-up button will increase the volume. If you call up the TV schedule, you can see what is on next, and you might choose to change the channel (or turn the TV off) as a result. Similarly, the Document Object Model is like the remote control that allows a programming language (such as JavaScript) to work with the browser (and the web page in that browser).

To take the remote control analogy a little further, it doesn't matter what language you speak; as long as someone presses the right button on the remote, the TV behaves in the same way. If you get a new TV, the core functions of the remote will be very similar. When working with the Document Object Model, it does not matter what language you program with. As long as you use the right properties and methods, the effect will be the same.

Also, under the covers, it does not matter how your remote tells the TV to turn up the volume, as long as the effect is the same (the volume goes up). Likewise, it doesn't matter how the browser retrieves the title of the page when you ask for it, or the background color of the page when you ask for that, as long as it returns it to you in the way you expect (which is specified in the Document Object Model).

The point of this analogy is that your script will achieve the same goal in any browser that implements the Document Object Model. It does not matter how a browser implements the Document Object Model, as long as you can ask it for properties, or to perform methods in the standard way set out in the Document Object Model, and you then get the results in an expected format. How the browser actually does the work under the hood does not matter.

In this chapter, you start by looking at how the Document Object Model allows you to work with a web page; then you look at JavaScript to see what you can do with this data and how you can use it to get and set values of the document, call methods, and respond to events.

How to Add a Script to Your Pages

JavaScript can either be embedded in a page or placed in an external script file (rather like CSS). But in order to work in the browser, the browser must have JavaScript enabled. (The major browsers allow users to disable JavaScript, although very few people do.)

You add scripts to your page inside the `<script>` element. The `type` attribute on the opening `<script>` tag indicates what scripting language will be found inside the element, so for JavaScript you use the value `text/JavaScript`.

There are several other scripting languages that do a very similar job to JavaScript (such as VBScript or Perl), but JavaScript is the main programming language used in web browsers.

Here you can see a very simple script that will write the words "My first JavaScript" into the page (`ch11_eg01.html`):

```
<html>
<body>
 <p>
  <script type="text/javascript">
    document.write("My first JavaScript")
  </script>
 </p>
</body>
</html>
```

In this case, we are using the `write()` method to add a new line of text into the web page (and the web page is represented using the `document` object). The text is added into the page where the script is written in the page. Figure 11-1 shows what this simple page would look like.

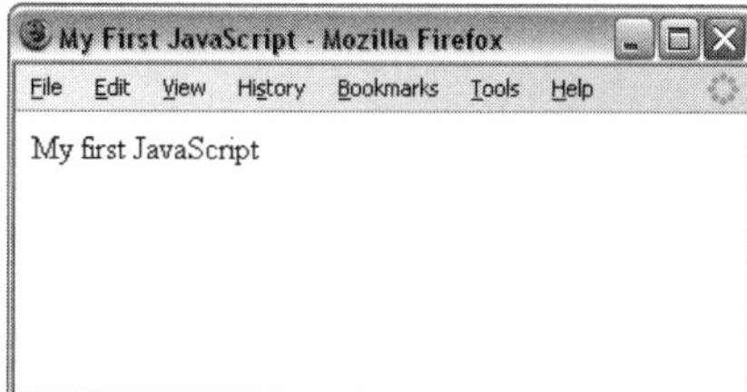

Figure 11-1

Where you put your JavaScript within a page is very important. If you put it in the body of a page — as in this example — then it will run (or *execute*) as the page loads. Sometimes, however, you will want a script ready to use as soon as the page has loaded, or you might want to use the same script in several parts of the page, in which case it tends to live inside the `<head>` element on the page (because scripts in the head of the page load before the page is displayed). Scripts that live in the head of a page are triggered (or *called*) by an event such as when the page finishes loading or when a visitor presses the submit button on a form.

You can also write JavaScript in external documents that have the file extension `.js` (just in the same way that you can write external style sheets). This is a particularly good option because:

- If your script is used by more than one page you do not need to repeat the script in each page that uses it.
- If you want to update your script you need only change it in one place.
- It makes the XHTML page cleaner and easier to read.

When you place your JavaScript in an external file, you need to use the `src` attribute on the `<script>` element; the value of the `src` attribute should be an absolute or relative URL pointing to the file containing the JavaScript. For example:

```
<script type="JavaScript" src="scripts/validation.js"></script>
```

So there are three places where you can put your JavaScripts, and a single XHTML document can use all three because there is no limit on the number of scripts one document can contain:

- **In the <head> of a page:** These scripts will be called when an event triggers them.
- **In the <body> of a page:** These scripts will run as the page loads.
- **In an external file:** If the link is placed inside the `<head>` element, the script is treated the same as when the script lives inside the head of the document waiting for an event to trigger it, whereas if it is placed in the `<body>` element it will act like a script in the body section and execute as the page loads.

Sometimes you will see examples of JavaScript written inside an XHTML comment.

```
<script type="text/javascript">
  <!--
    document.write("My first JavaScript")
  //-->
</script>
```

This was done because some old browsers do not support JavaScript, and therefore the comment hides the script from them. All browsers that support JavaScript just ignore these comments in the `<script>` element. Note how two forward slash characters (`//`) precede the closing characters of the XHTML comment. This is actually a JavaScript comment that prevents the JavaScript from trying to process the `-->` characters.

In XHTML, you should not use characters such as the angle brackets for anything other than tags. If you do, they are supposed to go in something known as a *CDATA section* (which tells the browser that the contents are not markup, and should not be processed as markup). Because JavaScript uses the angle brackets, even though it will not cause a problem in major browsers, you could put your scripts inside a CDATA section like this for technical accuracy (and to ensure that your page validates):

```
<script type="text/javascript">
//<![CDATA[
...
]]>
</script>
```

If you were to write a site that had to work on very old browsers, a good alternative to worrying about browsers that cannot support scripts is to use external scripts because if the browser cannot process the `<script>` element, it will not even try to load the document containing the script.

Comments in JavaScript

You can add comments to your JavaScript code in two ways. The first way, which you have already seen, allows you to comment out anything on that line after the comment marks. Here, anything on the same line after the two forward slash characters is treated as a comment:

```
<script type="text/javascript">
  document.write("My first JavaScript") // comment goes here
</script>
```

You can also comment out multiple lines using the following syntax, holding the comment between the opening characters `/*` and closing characters `*/` like so:

```
/* This whole section is commented
out so it is not treated as a part of
the script. */
```

This is similar to comments in CSS.

As with all code, it's good practice to comment your code clearly, even if you are the only person likely to be using it, because what may have seemed clear when you wrote a script may not be so obvious when you come back to it later.

The <noscript> Element

The `<noscript>` element offers alternative content for users who have disabled JavaScript. It can contain any XHTML content that the author wants to be seen in the browser if the user does not have JavaScript enabled.

Strictly speaking, the W3C's recommendations say that the content of this element should be displayed only when the browser does not support the scripting language required; however, the browser manufacturers have decided that it should also work when scripting is disabled.

Try It Out Creating an External JavaScript

You have already seen a basic example of a JavaScript that writes to a page. In this example, you will move that code to an external file. The external file is going to be used to write some text to the page.

1. Open your editor and type the following code:

```
document.write("Here is some text from an external file.");
```

2. Save this file as `external.js`.

3. Open a new page in your editor and add the following. Note that the `<script>` element is empty this time, but carries the `src` attribute whose value is the JavaScript file (just as it does on the `<img>` element). This may be a relative or full URL.

```
<html>
<body>
  <script src="external.js" type="text/JavaScript">
  </script>
  <noscript>This only shows if the browser has JavaScript turned off.
  </noscript>
</body>
</html>
```

4. Save this example as `ch11_eg02.html` and open it in your browser. You should see something like Figure 11-2.

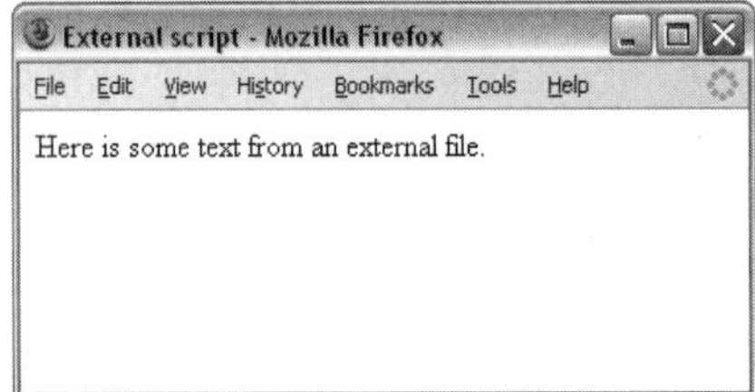

Figure 11-2

You can use this approach to include external JavaScripts in either the <head> or the <body> of a document. If you place them in the body of the document, as in this example, they are executed as the page loads — just as if the script were actually in the page there. If you place them in the head, then they will load when the page loads, and be triggered by an event.

I often use external JavaScript files for functions and place the <script> element in the head of the document because it allows me to re-use scripts on different sites I develop and ensures that the XHTML documents focus on content rather than being littered with scripts. You will see more of this approach later in the chapter.

The Document Object Model

As I mentioned at the start of the chapter, JavaScript by itself doesn't do much more than allow you to perform calculations or work with basic strings. In order to make a document more interactive, the script needs to be able to access the contents of the document and know when the user is interacting with it. The script does this by interacting with the browser by using the properties, methods and events set out in the interface called the Document Object Model.

The Document Object Model, or DOM, represents the web page that is loaded into the browser using a series of objects. The main object is the `document` object, which in turn contains several other child objects.

The DOM explains what *properties* of a document a script can retrieve and which ones it can alter; it also defines some *methods* that can be called to perform an action on the document.

Figure 11-3 shows you an illustration of the Level 0 HTML Document Object Model (as you will see shortly, there are different levels of the DOM).

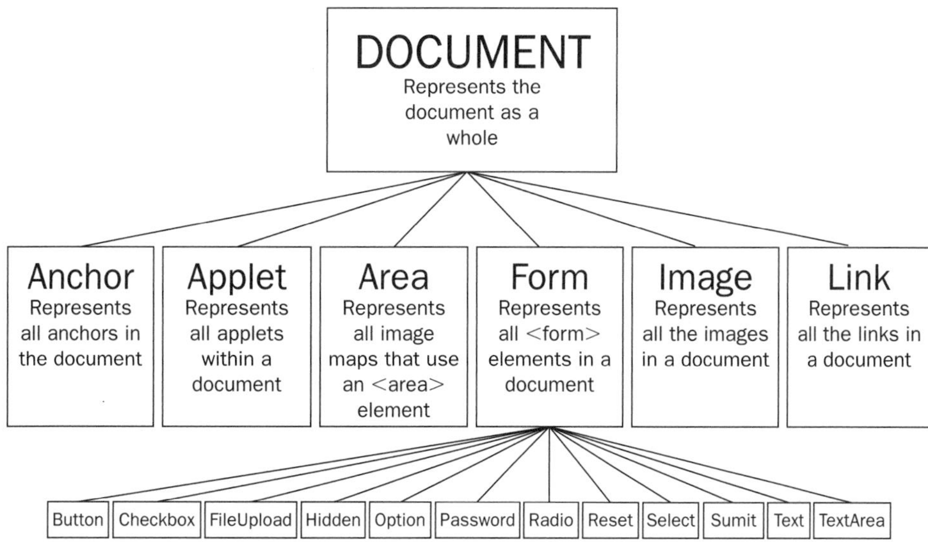

Figure 11-3

As you can see from Figure 11-3 the document object represents the whole document, and then each of the child objects represents a *collection* of similar tags within that document:

- The *anchor* collection represents all the anchors in a document that you can link to (`<a>` elements with a `name` attribute).
- The `applet` collection represents all the applets within a document.
- The `area` collection represents all the image maps that use an `<area>` element in the document.
- The `forms` collection contains all the `<form>` tags in the document.
- The `image` collection represents all the images in a document.
- The `link` collection represents all the hyperlinks within a page.

The `forms` collection also has child objects to represent each of the different types of form controls that can appear on a form: `Button`, `CheckBox`, `FileUpload`, `Hidden`, `Option`, `Password`, `Radio`, `Reset`, `Select`, `Submit`, `Text`, and `TextArea`.

To better understand how to access the document using the DOM, take a look at the following simple document, which contains one form and two links:

```
<h1>User Registration</h1>
<form name="frmLogin" action="login.aspx" method="post">
  Username <input type="text" name="txtUsername" size="12" /> <br />
  Password <input type="password" name="pwdPassword" size="12" /> <br />
  <input type="submit" value="Log In" />
</form>
<p>New user? <a href="register.aspx">Register here</a> |
 <a href="lostPassword.aspx">Retrieve password</a>.</p>
```

You can see this page in Figure 11-4.

Figure 11-4

The DOM would allow a script to access:

- The content of the form as part of the `forms` collection
- The two links as part of the `links` collection

Accessing Values Using Dot Notation

In order to access the different objects in the DOM, you list the objects in the tree shown in Figure 11-3, starting with the `document` object, working down to the object that holds the data you are after. Each object is separated by a period or full-stop character; hence, this is known as a *dot notation.*

For example, in order to access the first link in the document, you would want the `links` object, which is a child of the `document` object, so you could use something like this:

```
document.links[0].href
```

There are four parts of this statement, three of which are separated by periods, to get to the first link:

- The word `document` indicates I am accessing the `document` object.
- The word `links` corresponds to the `links` collection (after all, this example is to retrieve the value of the first link in the document).
- The `[0]` indicates that I want the first link in the document. Rather confusingly, the items of a collection are numbered from 0 rather than 1, which means the second link in the links collection is represented using `[1]`, the third using `[2]`, and so on.
- I have indicated that I want to retrieve the `href` property for this link.

Each object has different properties that correspond to that type of element; for example, links have properties such as the `href` property that accesses the value of the `href` attribute on this `<a>` element. Similarly, a `<textarea>` object has properties such as `cols`, `disabled`, `readOnly`, and `rows`, which correspond to the attributes on that element.

Rather than using the names of the type of object (such as forms and links), you can use the value of `name` attributes on the elements to navigate through the document. For example, the following line requests the value of the password box:

```
document.frmLogin.pwdPassword.value
```

Again, there are four parts to this statement:

- The `document` object comes first again as it represents the whole page (it is the top-level object).
- The name of the form, `frmLogin`.
- This is followed by the name of the form control, `pwdPassword`.
- Finally, the property I am interested in is the value of the password box, and this property is called `value`.

Both of these approaches enable you to navigate through a document, choosing the elements and properties of those elements you are interested in. Then you can retrieve those values, perform calculations upon them, and provide alternative values.

For the purpose of learning JavaScript, we are dealing with what is often called DOM Level 0 in this chapter because it works in most browsers. Its syntax was created before the W3C created its DOM Level 1, 2, and 3 recommendations (which get more complicated and have varying levels of support in different browsers). Once you are familiar with the basics, you can move on to look at these in more detail if you wish.

There is also a second type of object model, the Browser Object Model, which makes features of the browser available to the programmer, such as the `window` *object, which can be used to create new pop-up windows. The Browser Object Model can vary from browser to browser, although most browsers have common support for core functionality. You learn about the* `window` *object later in the chapter.*

The Document Object

In this section, we are going to take a closer look at the document object — this is the main object in the DOM and represents the document as a whole (and therefore allows you to access other child elements).

As you already know, an object can have properties that can tell you about the object, and methods to perform an action upon that object.

Once you understand how to work with one object, it's much easier to work with all kinds of objects — and you will come across many different types of objects when you start programming.

Properties of the Document Object

In the following table, you can see the properties of the document object. Several of these properties correspond to attributes that would be carried by the `<body>` element, which contains the document.

Many properties can be set as well as read. If you can set a property, it is known as a read/write property (because you can read it or write to it), whereas the ones you can only read are known as read-only. You can see which properties can be read and which can be written to in the last column of the table that follows.

Property Name	Purpose	Read/Write
`alinkColor`	Specifies link colors (like the deprecated `alink` attribute on the `<body>` element).	Read/write
`bgcolor`	Specifies background color (like the deprecated `bgcolor` attribute on the `<body>` element).	Read/write
`fgcolor`	Foreground/text color (like the deprecated `text` attribute of the `<body>` element).	Read/write
`lastModified`	The date the document was last modified. (This is usually sent by the web server in things known as HTTP headers that you do not see).	Read only
`linkColor`	Specifies link colors (like the deprecated `link` attribute of the `<body>` element).	Read/write
`referrer`	The URL of the page that users came from if they clicked a link. It is empty if there is no referrer.	Read only
`title`	The `title` of the page in the `<title>` element.	Read only (until IE 5 and Netscape 6 and later versions)
`vlinkColor`	The color of links that have been clicked on (like the deprecated `vlink` attribute of the `<body>` element).	Read/write

The properties that correspond to deprecated attributes of the `<body>` element should generally be avoided because CSS should be used to style text, links, and backgrounds.

To access any of the properties, again you use dot notation, so you can access the title of a document like so:

```
document.title
```

Or you could find out the date a document was last modified like so:

```
document.lastModified
```

Note that if the server does not support the `lastModified` property, IE will display the current date, while other browsers will often display `1 January 1970` (which is the date from which most computers calculate all dates).

Methods of the Document Object

Methods perform actions and are always written followed by a pair of brackets. Inside the brackets of some methods, you can see things known as *parameters* or *arguments*, which can affect what action the method takes.

For example, in the table that follows, you can see two methods that write new content into the web page. Both of these methods need to know what should be written into the page, so they take a string as an argument (a *string* is a sequence of characters that may include letters, numbers, spaces, and punctuation), and the string is what gets written into the page.

Method Name	Purpose
`write(string)`	Allows you to add text or elements into a document
`writeln(string)`	The same as `write()`, but adds a new line at the end of the output (as if you had pressed the Enter key after you had finished what you were writing)

You have already seen the `write()` method of the document object in `ch11_eg01.html`, which showed how it can be used to write content into a document:

```
document.write('This is a document');
```

You can also put something called an *expression* as a parameter of the `write()` method. For example, the following will write the text string `Page last modified on` followed by the last modified date of the document.

```
document.write('Page last modified on ' + document.lastModified);
```

You will see more about expressions later in the chapter, but in this case, the expression *evaluates* into (or results in) a string. For example, you might see something like `Page last modified on 12th December 2009`.

Now that you've seen the properties and methods of the `document` object, let's look at the properties and methods of some of the other objects, too.

The Forms Collection

The `forms` collection holds references corresponding to each of the `<form>` elements in the page. This might sound a little complicated, but you can probably imagine a web page that has more than one form — a login form, a registration form for new users, and a search box on the same page — the DOM deals with this by having a separate `form` object to represent each of the individual forms.

Imagine you want to use a script that can access the address of the page that the login form sends its data to. In the XHTML document you would be looking at the `action` attribute on the opening `<form>` tag. There is a corresponding `action` property on the `form` object, which holds the value of this attribute. So, you would need to access the `form` object that represented the login form, then retrieve the value of the property called `action`.

If the login form is the first form in the document, you might use the following index number to select the appropriate form and access the value of its `action` attribute (remember that index numbers start at 0 for the first form, 1 for the second form, 2 for the third, and so on):

```
document.forms[0].action
```

Alternatively, you can directly access that `form` object using its name (this is generally considered the preferred option because if another form were added to the page it could break the script):

```
document.frmLogin.action
```

The form that you select has its own object with properties and methods (each property generally corresponds to the attributes of the `<form>` element). Once you have seen the properties and methods of the forms, you will then see the objects, properties, and methods that correspond to the different types of form control.

Properties of the Form Objects

The following table lists the properties of the `form` objects; as you will see, most of them correspond to the attributes of the `<form>` element.

Property Name	Purpose	Read/Write
`action`	Specifies the value of the `action` attribute on the `<form>` element	Read/write
`length`	Gives the total number of form controls that are in this form	Read only
`method`	The value of the `method` attribute of the `<form>` element (either `get` or `post`)	Read/write
`name`	The value of the `name` attribute of the `<form>` element	Read only
`target`	The value of the `target` attribute of the `<form>` element	Read/write

Methods of the Form Objects

The following table lists the methods of the `form` objects.

Method Name	Purpose
`reset()`	Resets all `form` elements to their default values
`submit()`	Submits the form

A `<form>` element can have an attribute called `onsubmit` whose value is a script that should run when the user manually presses the Submit button. If JavaScript is used to submit a form, this attribute is ignored.

Form Elements

When you access a form, you usually want to access one or more of its elements. Each `<form>` element has an `elements` collection object as a property, which represents all of the elements in that form. This works in a similar way to the `forms` collection; it allows you to access the elements you want by `index` (an index being a number corresponding to their order in the document that starts with 0). Alternatively, you can use their names.

Here are some of the things you might want to do with the elements in a form:

- **Text fields:** Read data a user has entered or write new text to these elements.
- **Checkboxes and radio buttons:** Test if they are checked and check or uncheck them.
- **Buttons:** Disable them until a user has selected an option.
- **Select boxes:** Select an option or see which option the user has selected.

Properties of Form Elements

The following table lists the properties that correspond to the elements that may appear on a form.

Property	Applies to	Purpose	Read/Write
`checked`	Checkboxes and radio buttons	Returns `true` when checked or `false` when not	Read/write
`disabled`	All except hidden elements	Returns `true` when disabled and user cannot interact with it	Read/write
`form`	All elements	Returns a reference to the form it is part of	Read only
`length`	Select boxes	Number of options in the `<select>` element	Read only
`name`	All elements	Accesses the value of the `name` attribute of the element	Read only
`selectedIndex`	Select boxes	Returns the index number of the currently selected item	Read/write
`type`	All	Returns type of form control	Read only
`value`	All	Accesses the value attribute of the element or content of a text input	Read/write

If you want one of the form controls to be disabled until someone has performed an action — for example, if you want to disable the Submit button until the user has agreed to the terms and conditions — you should disable the form control in the script as the page loads, rather than disabling it in the form control itself using XHTML in case the user has turned off JavaScript (if this were the case, they would not be able to enable the Submit button). You will see more about this topic in Chapter 12.

Methods of Form Elements

The following table lists the methods of form elements.

Property Name	Applies to	Read/Write
`blur()`	All except hidden	Takes focus away from currently active element to next in tabbing order
`click()`	All except text	Simulates clicking the mouse over the element
`focus()`	All except hidden	Gives focus to the element
`select()`	Text elements except hidden	Selects the text in the element

Try It Out Collecting Form Data

In this example, you are going to retrieve the value of a textbox and write it into something known as a JavaScript alert box. The main purpose of the example is to show you how the value of the form can be retrieved, although it will also introduce you to an event and the JavaScript alert box.

The alert box is created using a method called `alert()` that is part of the JavaScript language (not the DOM). Alert boxes used to be very common on web sites, but you do not see them as much any more. However, in examples like this they are helpful to demonstrate how JavaScript can access documents.

The simple form will contain just one text input and a submit button. When you enter something into the textbox and click the submit button, the value you have entered in the textbox will appear in the alert box. You can see the page once the user has clicked the submit button in Figure 11-5.

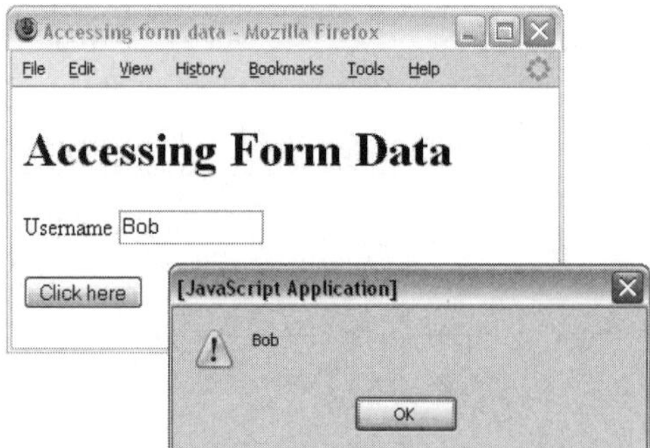

Figure 11-5

When you click OK, the alert box disappears.

1. Create a skeleton document for a Transitional XHTML page, and add a heading that explains what the example demonstrates:

```
<?xml version="1.0" encoding="UTF-8"?>
<!DOCTYPE html PUBLIC "-//W3C//DTD XHTML 1.0 Transitional//EN"
    "http://www.w3.org/TR/xhtml1/DTD/xhtml1-transitional.dtd">
<html xmlns="http://www.w3.org/1999/xhtml" lang="en">
<head>
  <title>Accessing form data</title>
</head>
<body>
  <h1>Accessing Form Data</h1>
</body>
</html>
```

2. Add a <form> element to the body of the document. The form should contain a text input for a username and a submit button, like so:

```
<body>
<h1>Accessing Form Data</h1>
<form name="frmLogin">
  Username <input type="text" name="txtUsername" size="12" /><br /><br />
  <input type="submit" value="Click here" />
</form>
</body>
```

3. Add the onsubmit attribute to the <form> element, and give it the following value:

```
<form name="frmLogin" onsubmit="alert(document.frmLogin.txtUsername.value)">
  Username <input type="text" name="txtUsername" size="12" /> <br />
  <input type="submit" value="Click here" />
</form>
```

Save the file as ch11_eg03.html, and open it in your browser. When you enter something into the text input and click Submit, you should see an alert box like that in Figure 11-5, which displays the value you entered into the textbox.

When the onsubmit event fires (which happens when the user clicks the Submit button), this simple line of script is run. In this case, the alert() method is called:

```
alert(document.frmLogin.txtUsername.value)
```

The alert(string) method allows you to write a string into the pop-up alert box. Like the write() method of the document object, which you saw earlier, the string does not need to be the actual text you want to display. In this example, rather than writing the same string to the alert box every time the script is run, whatever the user has entered into the text box will be written to the alert box.

You can see that inside the alert(), the text input has been selected using document.frmLogin .txtUsername along with the value property of this form control. So the value of the text input is written to the alert box.

As you have seen the `alert()` box takes a string as a parameter (just like the `write()` method you saw earlier), but we are not specifying the exact words to write out (rather we are telling the method to find out what the user entered). When you tell a method (such as the `alert()` method or the `write()` method) exactly what to write you put the value in double quote marks, but when you want the script to collect the information it is to display, you do not use the double quotes.

When the user clicks the Submit button, the `onsubmit` event fires, which creates the alert box that contains the value of the text input.

Images Collection

The `images` collection provides references to image objects, one representing each image in a document. These can again be referenced by name or by their index number in the collection. So the `src` attribute of the first image can be found using the index number like so:

```
document.images[0].src
```

or using its name; for example, if the image had a `name` attribute whose value was `imgHome`, you could access it using the following:

```
document.imgHome.src
```

There are no methods for the image objects in the Level 0 DOM, although there are several properties.

Properties of the Image Object

The following table lists the properties of the image object.

Property	Purpose	Read/Write
`border`	The `border` attribute of the `<img>` element, specifying the width of the border in pixels	Read/write
`complete`	Indicates whether an image has loaded successfully	Read only
`height`	The `height` attribute of the `<img>` element, specifying the height of the image in pixels	Read/write
`hspace`	The `hspace` attribute of the `<img>` element, specifying the gap above and below an image to separate it from its surrounding elements	Read/write
`lowsrc`	The `lowsrc` attribute of the `<img>` element (indicating a lower resolution version of the image)	Read/write
`name`	The `name` attribute of the `<img>` element	Read/write
`src`	The `src` attribute of the `<img>` element, indicating where the file is located	Read/write

Property	Purpose	Read/Write
vspace	The vspace attribute of the <img> element, specifying the gap to the left and right of an image to separate it from its surrounding elements	Read/write
width	The width attribute of the <img> element, specifying the width of the image in pixels	Read/write

Try It Out A Simple Image Rollover

In this example, you are going to see how to replace one image with another one when the user rolls over the image with the mouse. Most developers now use CSS to create image rollovers in their code, but this is a good way to demonstrate how to access image properties.

In this example, you are going to see two simple images, both saying "click here." When the page loads, the image will be in green with white writing, but as soon as the user hovers over the image, the script will access and change the src property of the image and change it to the image that is red with white writing.

1. Create the skeleton of a Transitional XHTML document:

```
<?xml version="1.0" encoding="UTF-8"?>
<!DOCTYPE html PUBLIC "-//W3C//DTD XHTML 1.0 Transitional//EN"
    "http://www.w3.org/TR/xhtml1/DTD/xhtml1-transitional.dtd">
<html xmlns="http://www.w3.org/1999/xhtml" lang="en">
<head>
  <title>Image Rollover</title>
</head>
<body>
</body>
</html>
```

2. Add the following link and image to the body of your document:

```
<p>Hover over the image with your mouse to see the simple rollover effect.
<br/>
<a href="">
  <img src="images/click_green.gif" width="100" height="50" border="0"
       alt="Example button" name="button" />
</a>
</p>
```

3. Now add the following onmouseover and onmouseout event handler attributes to the <a> element with the specified values:

```
<a href=""
   onmouseover="document.images.button.src='images/click_red.gif';"
   onmouseout="document.images.button.src='images/click_green.gif'">
```

When the user rolls over the image, the `onmouseover` event fires, and when the user moves off it again, the `onmouseout` event fires. This is why there are separate attributes that correspond to each of these events, and when one of these two events fires, the script held as a value for the corresponding attribute is executed.

The script in the `onmouseover` and `onmouseout` event handler attributes tells the browser to change the `src` attribute of the image, and therefore a different image is displayed to the user.

The first (`onmouseover`) indicates what should happen when the mouse is placed over the image; the second (`onmouseout`) indicates what should be done when the mouse is moved off the image.

When the user puts the mouse over an image, the `src` property of the image inside the link — named using the notation `document.images.button` — is changed.

4. Save this example as `ch11_eg4.html` and open it in your browser. Then roll your mouse over the image (without clicking it). You should see something like Figure 11-6 with the mouse over the image.

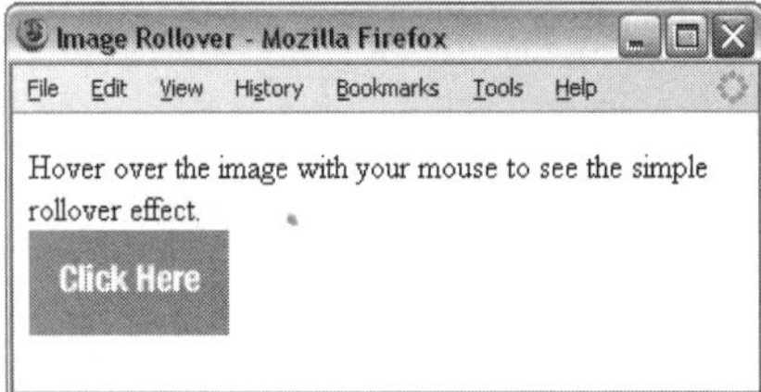

Figure 11-6

The `<img>` element must have a `name` attribute so that the image can be referenced in this way in the link (otherwise you would have to use its index in the images collection). It is generally best to use the name in situations like this, rather than the index of that image in the images collection, because if you were to add another image into the document before this one the whole script would need changing.

Note that if no event indicated what should happen when the user takes the mouse off the image, it would remain red rather than turning back to green. An image rollover script is a good example of changing or *setting* that property rather than just reading it.

Different Types of Objects

You will come across several types of objects in JavaScript, each of which is responsible for a related set of functionalities. For example, the `document` object has methods and properties that relate to the document; the `forms` collection, which is part of the `document` object, deals with information regarding forms; and so on. As you are about to see, there can be lots of different objects, each of which deals with a different set of functionalities and properties.

So, here are some of the types of objects you are likely to come across:

- **W3C DOM objects:** These are like those already covered in this chapter, although in more recent browsers several more objects are made available to allow you more control over a document.
- **Built-in objects:** Several objects are part of the JavaScript language itself. These include the `date` object, which deals with dates and times, and the `math` object, which provides mathematical functions. You will be learning more about these built-in objects later in the chapter.
- **Custom objects:** If you start to write advanced JavaScript, you might even start creating your own JavaScript objects that contain related functionality; for example, you might have a `validation` object that you have written just to use to validate your forms.

While it is not possible to cover the creation of custom objects in this chapter, you learn about the built-in objects later in this chapter.

Starting to Program with JavaScript

Now that you have seen how JavaScript is able to access a document in the web browser using the DOM, it is time to look at how you use these properties and methods in scripts.

As I mentioned earlier, a programming language mainly performs calculations. So here are the key concepts you need to learn in order to perform different types of calculations:

- A *variable* is used to store some information; it's like a little bit of the computer's memory where you can store numbers, strings (which are a series of characters), or references to objects. You can then perform calculations to alter the data held in variables within your code.
- *Operators* perform functions on variables. There are different types of operators — for example:
    - Arithmetic operators enable you to do things such as add (+) numbers together, or subtract (-) one from another (providing they are numbers).
    - Comparison operators enable you to compare two strings and see if one is the same as the other, or different (for example, whether *x* is equal to *y* or whether *a* is greater than *b*).
- *Functions* are parts of a script that are grouped together to perform a specific task. For example, you could have a function that calculates loan repayments, and when you tell the loan calculator function the information it needs (the amount of money to be borrowed, the number of years the loan will last, and the interest rate) the function will be able to return the monthly payment. Functions are objects in their own right and are very similar to things called methods; one of the key differences is that methods often belong to an object already, whereas functions are customized.
- *Conditional statements* allow you to perform different actions based upon a condition. For example, a condition might be whether a variable holding the current time is greater than 12. If the condition is true, code to write "Good Afternoon" might be run. Whereas, if it is less than 12, a different block of code saying "Good Morning" could be shown.

- *Loops* can be set up so that a block of code runs a specified number of times or until a condition is met. For example, you can use a loop to get a document to write your name 100 times.
- There are also several built-in JavaScript objects that have methods that are of practical use. For example, in the same way that the `document` object of the DOM has methods that allowed you to write to the document, the built-in JavaScript `date` object can tell you the date, time, or day of the week.

The following section looks at these key concepts in more detail.

Variables

Variables are used to store data. To store information in a variable, you can give the variable a name and put an equal sign between it and the value you want it to have. Here is an example:

```
userName = "Bob Stewart"
```

The variable is called `userName` and the value is `Bob Stewart`. If no value is given, then its value is *undefined*.

The script can access the value of the variable using its name (in this case `userName`). It can also change the value.

You can create a variable, but not store anything with it by using the `var` keyword; this is known as *declaring* a variable (unlike some other languages, you do not have to declare a variable before you can use it, although it is commonly considered good practice to do so).

```
var userName
```

There are a few rules you must remember about variables in JavaScript:

- They must begin with a letter or the underscore character.
- Variable names are case-sensitive.
- Avoid giving two variables the same name within the same document as one might override the value of the other, creating an error.
- Do not call two variables the same name, but use different cases to distinguish them (e.g., `username` and `UserName`) as this is a common source of confusion later.
- Try to use descriptive names for your variables. This makes your code easier to understand (and will help you debug your code if there is a problem with it).

Assigning a Value to a Variable

When you want to give a value to a variable, you put the variable name first, then an equal sign, and then on the right the value you want to assign to the variable. You have already seen values being assigned to these variables when they were declared a moment ago. So, here is an example of a variable being assigned a value and then the value being changed:

```
userName = "Bob Stewart"
userName = "Robert Stewart"
```

`userName` is now the equivalent of `Robert Stewart`.

Lifetime of a Variable

When you declare a variable in a function, it can be accessed only in that function. (You will learn about functions shortly.) After the function has run, you cannot call the variable again. Variables in functions are called *local variables*.

Because a local variable works only within a function, you can have different functions that contain variables of the same name (because each is recognized by that function only).

If you declare a variable using the `var` *keyword inside a function, it will use memory up only when the function is run, and once the function has finished it will not take up any memory.*

If you declare a variable outside a function, all the functions on your page can access it. The lifetime of these variables starts when they are declared and ends when the page is closed.

Local variables take up less memory and resources than page-level variables because they require only the memory during the time that the function runs, rather than having to be created and remembered for the life of the whole page.

Operators

The operator itself is a keyword or symbol that does something to a value when used in an *expression*. For example, the arithmetic operator + adds two values together.

The symbol is used in an expression with either one or two values and performs a calculation on the values to generate a result. For example, here is an expression that uses the multiplication operator:

```
area = (width * height)
```

An expression is just like a mathematical expression. The values are known as *operands*. Operators that require only one operand (or value) are sometimes referred to as *unary operators*, while those that require two values are sometimes called *binary operators*.

The different types of operators you will see in this section are:

- Arithmetic operators
- Assignment operators
- Comparison operators
- Logical operators
- String operators

You will see lots of examples of the operators in action both later in this chapter and in the next chapter. First, however, it's time to learn about each type of operator.

Arithmetic Operators

Arithmetic operators perform arithmetic operations upon operands. (Note that in the examples in the following table, x = 10.)

Symbol	Description	Example (x = 10)	Result
+	Addition	x+5	15
-	Subtraction	x-2	8
*	Multiplication	x*3	30
/	Division	x/2	5
%	Modulus (division remainder)	x%3	1
++	Increment (increments the variable by 1 — this technique is often used in counters)	x++	11
--	Decrement (decreases the variable by 1)	x--	9

Assignment Operators

The basic assignment operator is the equal sign, but do not take this to mean that it checks whether two values are equal. Rather, it's used to assign a value to the variable on the left of the equal sign, as you have seen in the previous section, which introduced variables.

The basic assignment operator can be combined with several other operators to allow you to assign a value to a variable *and* perform an operation in one step. For example, take a look at the following statement where there is an assignment operator and an arithmetic operator:

```
total = total - profit
```

This can be reduced to the following statement:

```
total -= profit
```

While it might not look like much, this kind of shorthand can save a lot of code if you have a lot of calculations like this (see table that follows) to perform.

Symbol	Example Using Shorthand	Equivalent Without Shorthand
`+=`	`x+=y`	`x=x+y`
`-=`	`x-=y`	`x=x-y`
`*=`	`x*=y`	`x=x*y`
`/=`	`x/=y`	`x=x/y`
`%=`	`x%=y`	`x=x%y`

Comparison Operators

As you can see in the table that follows, comparison operators compare two operands and then return either `true` or `false` based on whether the comparison is true or not.

Note that the comparison for checking whether two operands are equal is two equal signs (a single equal sign would be an assignment operator).

Operator	Description	Example
`==`	Equal to	1==2 returns `false` 3==3 returns `true`
`!=`	Not equal to	1!=2 returns `true` 3!=3 returns `false`
`>`	Greater than	1>2 returns `false` 3>3 returns `false` 3>2 returns `true`
`<`	Less than	1<2 returns `true` 3<3 returns `false` 3<1 returns `false`
`>=`	Greater than or equal to	1>=2 returns `false` 3>=2 returns `true` 3>=3 returns `true`
`<=`	Less than or equal to	1<=2 returns `true` 3<=3 returns `true` 3<=2 returns `false`

Logical or Boolean Operators

Logical or Boolean operators return one of two values: `true` or `false`. They are particularly helpful when you want to evaluate more than one expression at a time.

Operator	Name	Description	Example (where *x*=1 and *y*=2)
`&&`	And	Allows you to check if both of two conditions are met	`(x < 2 && y > 1)` Returns `true` (because both conditions are met)
`??`	Or	Allows you to check if one of two conditions are met	`(x < 2 ?? y < 2)` Returns `true` (because the first condition is met)
`!`	Not	Allows you to check if something is not the case	`! (x > y)` Returns `true` (because x is not more than y)

The two operands in a logical or Boolean operator evaluate to either `true` or `false`. For example, if `x=1` and `y=2`, then `x<2` is `true` and `y>1` is `true`. So the following expression:

```
(x<2 && y>1)
```

returns `true` because both of the operands evaluate to true (you can see more examples in the right-hand column of this table).

String Operator (Using + with Strings)

You can also add text to strings using the + operator. For example, here the + operator is being used to add two variables that are strings together:

```
firstName = "Bob"
lastName = "Stewart"
name = firstName + lastName
```

The value of the `name` variable would now be `Bob Stewart`. The process of adding two strings together is known as *concatenation*.

You can also compare strings using the comparison operators you just met. For example, you could check whether a user has entered a specific value into a text box. (You will see more about this topic when you look at the "Conditional Statements" section shortly.)

Functions

A function is made up of related code that performs a particular task. For example, a function could be written to calculate area given width and height. The function can then be called elsewhere in the script, or when an event fires.

Functions are either written in the `<head>` element or in an external file that is linked from inside the `<head>` element, which means that they can be reused in several places within the page.

How to Define a Function

There are three parts to creating or defining a function:

- Define a name for it.
- Indicate any values that might be required; these are known as arguments.
- Add statements to the body of the function.

For example, if you want to create a function to calculate the area of a rectangle, you might name the function `calculateArea()` (note that a function name should be followed by parentheses). In order to calculate the area, you need to know the rectangle's width and height, so these would be passed in as *arguments* (arguments are the information the function needs to do its job). Inside the body of the function (the part between the curly braces) are the *statements*, which indicate that area is equal to the width multiplied by the height (both of which have been passed into the function). The area is then returned.

```
function calculateArea(width, height) {
  area = width * height
  return area
}
```

If a function has no arguments it should still have parentheses after its name — for example, you might have a function that will run without any extra information passed as an argument such as, `logOut()`.

How To Call a Function

The `calculateArea()` function does nothing sitting on its own in the head of a document; it has to be *called*. In this example, you can call the function from a simple form using the `onclick` event, so that when the user clicks the Submit button the area will be calculated and shown in an alert box.

Here you can see that the form contains two text inputs for the width and height, and these are passed as arguments to the function like so (`ch11_eg05.html`):

```
<form name="frmArea" action="">
Enter the width and height of your rectangle to calculate the size:<br />
Width: <input type="text" name="txtWidth" size="5" /><br />
Height: <input type="text" name="txtHeight" size="5" /><br />
<input type="button" value="Calculate area"
  onclick="alert(calculateArea(document.frmArea.txtWidth.value,
  document.frmArea.txtHeight.value))" />
</form>
```

Take a closer look at what is happening when the `onclick` event fires. First, a JavaScript alert is being called, and then the `calculateArea()` function is being called inside the alert, so that the area is the value that is written to the alert box. Inside the parentheses where the `calculateArea()` function is being called, the two parameters being passed are the values of the width text box (`document.frmArea.txtWidth.value`) and the height text box (`document.frmArea.txtWidth.value`) using the dot notation you learned earlier in the section on the DOM.

The Return Statement

Functions that return a result must use the `return` statement. This statement specifies the value that will be returned to where the function was called. The `calculateArea()` function, for example, returned the area of the rectangle:

```
function calculateArea(width, height) {
  area = width * height
  return area
}
```

What is returned depends on the code inside the function; for example, our area function will return the area of the rectangle. By contrast, if you had a form where people could enter an e-mail address to sign up for a newsletter, you might use a function to check whether that person had entered a valid e-mail address before submitting the form. In that case, the function might just return `true` or `false` values.

What happens when the value is returned depends on how the function was called. With our function to calculate area, we could display the area to the user with some more JavaScript code. If we were checking whether an e-mail address was in a valid format before subscribing that e-mail address to a newsletter, the return value would determine whether the form was submitted or not.

Conditional Statements

Conditional statements allow you to take different actions depending upon different statements. There are three types of conditional statements you will learn about here:

- `if` statements, which are used when you want the script to execute if a condition is true
- `if...else` statements, which are used when you want to execute one set of code if a condition is true and another if it is false
- `switch` statements, which are used when you want to select one block of code from many depending on a situation

if Statements

`if` statements allow code to be executed when the condition specified is met; if the condition is true then the code in the curly braces is executed. Here is the syntax for an `if` statement:

```
if (condition)
{
  code to be executed if condition is true
}
```

For example, you might want to start your homepage with the text "Good Morning" if the time is in the morning. You could achieve this using the following script (`ch11_eg06.html`):

```
<script type="text/JavaScript">
  date = new Date();
  time = date.getHours();
  if (time < 12) {
    document.write('Good Morning');
  }
</script>
```

If you are executing only one statement (as we are here), the curly braces are not strictly required, so the following would do exactly the same job (although it is good practice to include them anyway as we did previously).

```
<script type="text/JavaScript">
  date = new Date();
  time = date.getHours();
  if (time < 12)
    document.write('Good Morning');
</script>
```

This example first creates a `date` object (which you learn about later in the chapter) and then calls the `getHours()` method of the `date` object to find the time in hours (using the 24-hour clock). If the time in hours is less than 12, then the script writes `Good Morning` to the page (if it is after 12, you will see a blank page because nothing is written to it).

if . . . else Statements

When you have two possible situations and you want to react differently for each, you can use an `if...else` statement. This means: "If the conditions specified are met, run the first block of code; otherwise run the second block." The syntax is as follows:

```
if (condition)
{
  code to be executed if condition is true
}
else
{
  code to be executed if condition is false
}
```

Returning to the previous example, you can write `Good Morning` if the time is before noon, and `Good Afternoon` if it is after noon (`ch11_eg07.html`).

```
<script type="text/JavaScript">
  date = new Date();
  time = date.getHours();
  if (time < 12) {
    document.write('Good Morning');
  }
  else {
    document.write('Good Afternoon');
  }
</script>
```

As you can imagine there are a lot of possibilities for using conditional statements.

switch Statements

A `switch` statement allows you to deal with several possible results of a condition. You have a single expression, which is usually a variable. This is evaluated immediately. The value of the expression is then compared with the values for each case in the structure. If there is a match, the block of code will execute.

Here is the syntax for a `switch` statement:

```
switch (expression)
{
case option1:
  code to be executed if expression is what is written in option1
  break;
case option2:
  code to be executed if expression is what is written in option2
  break;
case option3:
  code to be executed if expression is what is written in option3
  break;
default:
  code to be executed if expression is different from option1, option2,
  and option3
}
```

You use the `break` to prevent code from running into the next case automatically. For example, you might be checking what type of animal a user has entered into a textbox, and you want to write out different things to the screen depending upon what kind of animal is in the text input. Here is a form that appears on the page. When the user has entered an animal and clicks the button, the `checkAnimal()` function contained in the head of the document is called (`ch11_eg08.html`):

```
<p>Enter the name of your favorite type of animal that stars in a
cartoon:</p>
<form name="frmAnimal">
  <input type="text" name="txtAnimal" /><br />
  <input type="button" value="Check animal" onclick="checkAnimal()" />
</form>
```

Here is the function that contains the `switch` statement:

```
function checkAnimal() {
  switch (document.frmAnimal.txtAnimal.value){
    case "rabbit":
      alert("Watch out, it's Elmer Fudd!")
      break;
    case "coyote":
      alert("No match for the road runner - meep meep!")
      break;
    case "mouse":
      alert("Watch out Jerry, here comes Tom!")
      break;
    default : alert("Are you sure you picked an animal from a cartoon?");
  }
}
```

The final option — the default — is shown if none of the cases are met. You can see what this would look like when the user has entered **rabbit** into the textbox in Figure 11-7.

Note that, should the user enter text in a different case, it will not match the options in the `switch` statement. Because JavaScript is case-sensitive, if the letter's case does not match the value of the case in the `switch` statement, it will not be a match. You can solve this by making the text all lowercase in the first place before checking it using the `toLowerCase()` method of the built-in JavaScript string object, which you meet later in the chapter.

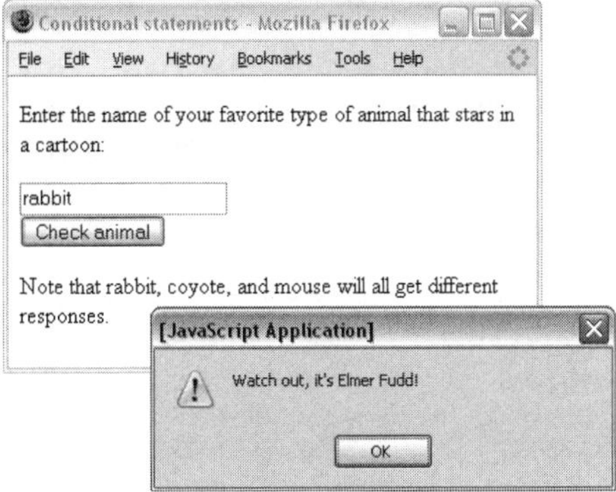

Figure 11-7

Looping

Looping statements are used to execute the same block of code a specified number of times (which is very handy because repetitive tasks are something that computers are particularly well suited to):

- A `while` loop runs the same block of code while or until a condition is true.
- A `do while` loop runs once before the condition is checked. If the condition is true, it will continue to run until the condition is false. (The difference between a `do` and a `do while` loop is that `do while` runs once whether or not the condition is met.)
- A `for` loop runs the same block of code a specified number of times (for example, five times).

while

In a `while` loop, a code block is executed if a condition is true and for as long as that condition remains true. The syntax is as follows:

```
while (condition)
{
  code to be executed
}
```

In the following example, you can see a `while` loop that shows the multiplication table for the number 3. This works based on a counter called `i`; every time the `while` script loops, the counter increments by one (this uses the `++` arithmetic operator, as you can see from the line that says `i++`). So, the first time the script runs the counter is 1, and the loop writes out the line 1 × 3 = 3; the next time it loops around the counter is 2, so the loop writes out 2 × 3 = 6. This continues until the condition — that *i* is no longer less than 11 — is true (`ch11_eg09.html`):

```
<script type="text/JavaScript">
i = 1
while (i < 11) {
 document.write(i + " x 3 = " + (i * 3) + "<br />" );
  i ++
}
</script>
```

You can see the result of this example in Figure 11-8.

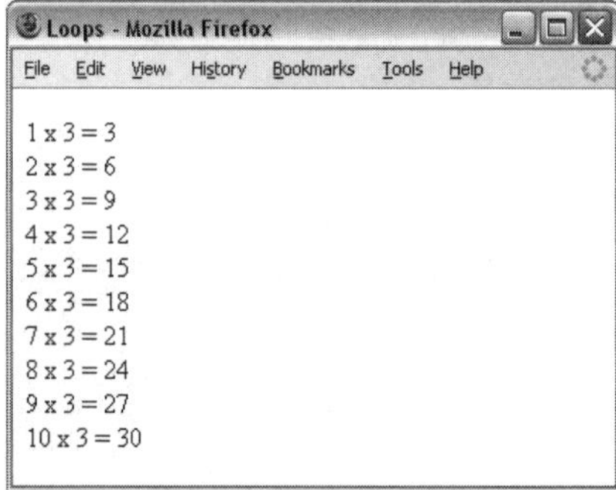

Figure 11-8

Before we go on to look at the next type of loop (a `do ... while` loop), it is worth noting that a `while` loop may never run at all (because the condition may not be true when it is called).

do . . . while

A `do ... while` loop executes a block of code once and then checks a condition. For as long as the condition is true, it continues to loop. So, whatever the condition, the loop runs at least once (as you can see the condition is after the instructions). Here is the syntax:

```
do
{
 code to be executed
}
while (condition)
```

For example, here is the example with the 3 times table again. The counter is set with an initial value of 12, which is higher than required in the condition, so you will see the sum 12 × 3 = 36 once, but nothing after that because when it comes to the condition, it has been met (ch11_eg10.html):

```
<script type="text/JavaScript">
i = 12
do {
 document.write(i + " x 3 = " + (i * 3) + "<br />" );
  i ++
}
while (i < 11)
</script>
```

Now, if you changed the value of the initial counter to 1, you would see that the script loops through the multiplication table as it did in the last example until it gets to 11.

for

The for statement executes a block of code a specified number of times. You use it when you want to specify how many times you want the code to be executed (rather than running while a particular condition is true/false). It is worth noting here that the number of times that the for loop runs could be specified by some other part of the code. First, here is the syntax (which always takes three arguments):

```
for (a; b; c)
{
 code to be executed
}
```

Now you need to look at what a, b, and c represent:

- a is evaluated before the loop is run, and is only evaluated once. It is ideal for assigning a value to a variable; for example, you might use it to set a counter to 0 using i=0.
- b should be a condition that indicates whether the loop should be run again; if it returns true the loop runs again. For example, you might use this to check whether the counter is less than 11.
- c is evaluated after the loop has run and can contain multiple expressions separated by a comma (for example, i++, j++;). For example, you might use it to increment the counter.

So if you come back to the 3 times table example again, it would be written something like this (ch11_eg11.html):

```
for (i=0; i<11; i++) {
 document.write(i + " x 3 = " + (i * 3) + "<br />" );
}
```

Let's look at the `for` statement in small chunks:

- `i=0` The counter is assigned to have a value of 0.
- `i<11` The loop should run if the value of the counter is less than 11.
- `i++` The counter is incremented by 1 every time the loop runs.

The assignment of the counter variable, the condition, and the incrementing of the counter all appear in the parentheses after the keyword `for`.

You can also assign several variables at once in the part corresponding to the letter `a` if you separate them with a comma, for example, `i = 0, j = 5;`. It is also worth noting that you can count downward with loops as well as up.

Infinite Loops and the break Statement

Note that, if you have an expression that always evaluates to `true` in any loop, you end up with something known as an *infinite loop*. These can tie up system resources and can even crash the computer, although some browsers try to detect infinite loops and then stop the loop.

You can, however, add a `break` statement to stop an infinite loop; here it is set to 100 (`ch11_eg12.html`):

```
for (i=0; /* no condition here */ ; i++) {
 document.write(i + " x 3 = " + (i * 3) + "<br />" );
  if (i == 100) {
   break;
  }
}
```

When the script gets to a `break` statement it simply stops running. This effectively prevents a loop from running too many times.

Events

All browsers are expected to support a set of events known as *intrinsic events* such as the `onload` event, which happens when a page has finished loading, `onclick` for when a user clicks on an element, and `onsubmit` for when a form is submitted. These events can be used to trigger a script.

You have already seen event handlers used as attributes on XHTML elements — such as the `onclick` attribute on an `<a>` element and the `onsubmit` attribute on the `<form>` element. The value of the attribute is the script that should be executed when the event occurs on that element (sometimes this will be a function in the `<head>` of the document).

There are two types of events that can be used to trigger scripts:

- Window events, which occur when something happens to a window. For example, a page loads or unloads (is replaced by another page or closed) or focus is being moved to or away from a window or frame.
- User events, which occur when the user interacts with elements in the page using a mouse (or other pointing device) or a keyboard, such as placing the mouse over an element, clicking on an element, or moving the mouse off an element.

For example, the `onmouseover` and `onmouseout` events can be used to change an image's `src` attribute and create a simple image rollover, as you saw earlier in the chapter:

```
<a href=""
  onmouseover="document.images.link.src='images/click_red.gif';"
  onmouseout="document.images.link.src='images/click_green.gif'">
  <img src="images/click_green.gif" width="100" height="50" border="0"
  name="link">
</a>
```

The table that follows provides a recap of the most common events you are likely to come across.

Event	Purpose	Applies To
`onload`	Document has finished loading (if used in a frameset, all frames have finished loading).	`<body>` `<frameset>`
`onunload`	Document is unloaded, or removed, from a window or frameset.	`<body>` `<frameset>`
`onclick`	Button on mouse (or other pointing device) has been clicked over the element.	Most elements
`ondblclick`	Button on mouse (or other pointing device) has been double-clicked over the element.	Most elements
`onmousedown`	Button on mouse (or other pointing device) has been depressed (but not released) over the element.	Most elements
`onmouseup`	Button on mouse (or other pointing device) has been released over the element.	Most elements
`onmouseover`	Cursor on mouse (or other pointing device) has been moved onto the element.	Most elements
`onmousemove`	Cursor on mouse (or other pointing device) has been moved while over the element.	Most elements
`onmouseout`	Cursor on mouse (or other pointing device) has been moved off the element.	Most elements

Continued

Event	Purpose	Applies To
onkeypress	A key is pressed and released.	Most elements
onkeydown	A key is held down.	Most elements
onkeyup	A key is released.	Most elements
onfocus	Element receives focus either by mouse (or other pointing device) clicking it, tabbing order giving focus to that element, or code giving focus to the element.	<a> <area> <button> <input> <label> <select> <textarea>
onblur	Element loses focus.	<a> <area> <button> <input> <label> <select> <textarea>
onsubmit	A form is submitted.	<form>
onreset	A form is reset.	<form>
onselect	User selects some text in a text field.	<input> <textarea>
onchange	A control loses input focus and its value has been changed since gaining focus.	<input> <select> <textarea>

You will see examples of these events used throughout this and the next chapter. You can also check which elements support which methods in Chapters 1 through 6 as those elements are discussed; almost every element can be associated with at least one event.

Built-in Objects

You learned about the `document` object at the beginning of the chapter and now it is time to see some of the objects that are built into the JavaScript language. You will see the methods that allow you to perform actions upon data, and properties that tell you something about the data.

String

The `string` object allows you to deal with strings of text. Before you can use a built-in object, you need to create an instance of that object. You create an instance of the `string` object by assigning it to a variable like so:

```
myString = new String('Here is some bold text')
```

The `string` object now contains the words "Here is some bold text" and this is stored in a variable called `myString`. Once you have this object in a variable, you can write the string to the document or perform actions upon it. For example, the following method writes the string as if it were in a `<b>` element:

```
document.write(myString.bold())
```

Note that if you viewed the source of this element, it would not actually have the `<b>` element in it; rather, you would see the JavaScript, so that a user who did not have JavaScript enabled would not see these words at all.

You can check the length of this string like so; the result will be the number of characters including spaces and punctuation (in this case 41):

```
MyString = new String("How many characters are in this sentence?")
alert(myString.length)
```

Before you can use the `string` object, remember you first have to create it and then give it a value.

Properties

The following table shows the main property for the `string` object and its purpose.

Property	Purpose
`length`	Returns the number of characters in a string.

Methods

The following table lists the methods for the `string` object and their purposes.

Method	Purpose
`anchor(name)`	Creates an anchor element (an `<a>` element with a `name` or `id` attribute rather than an `href` attribute).
`big()`	Displays text as if in a `<big>` element.
`bold()`	Displays text as if in a `<bold>` element.
`charAt(index)`	Returns the character at a specified position (for example, if you have a string that says "banana" and your method reads `charAt(2)`, then you will end up with the letter `n` — remember that indexes start at 0).
`fixed()`	Displays text as if in a `<tt>` element.
`fontcolor(color)`	Displays text as if in a `<font>` element with a `color` attribute.
`fontsize(fontsize)`	Displays text as if in a `<font>` element with a `size` attribute.

Continued

Method	Purpose
`indexOf(searchValue, [fromindex])`	Returns the position of the first occurrence of a specified character (or set of characters) inside another string. For example, if you have the word "banana" as your string, and you want to find the first occurrence of the letter `n` within "banana" you use `indexOf(n)`. If you supply a value for the `fromIndex` argument, the search will begin at that position. For example, you might want to start after the fourth character, in which case you could use `indexOf(n,3)`. The method returns `-1` if the string being searched for never occurs.
`italics()`	Displays text as if in an `<i>` element.
`lastIndexOf(searchValue, [fromIndex])`	Same as `indexOf()` method, but runs from right to left.
`link(targetURL)`	Creates a link in the document.
`small()`	Displays text as if in a `<small>` element.
`strike()`	Displays text as if in a `<strike>` element.
`sub()`	Displays text as if in a `<sub>` element.
`substr(start, [length])`	Returns the specified characters. 14,7 returns 7 characters, from the 14th character (starts at 0).
`substring(startPosition, endPosition)`	Returns the specified characters between the start and end index points. 7,14 returns all characters from the 7th up to but not including the 14th (starts at 0).
`sup()`	Displays text as if in a `<sup>` element.
`toLowerCase()`	Converts a string to lowercase.
`toUpperCase()`	Converts a string to uppercase.

Try It Out — Using the String Object

In this example, you see a subsection of a string collected and turned into all uppercase letters. The full string (at the beginning of the example) will hold the words "Learning about Built-in Objects is easy"; then the code just extracts the words "Built-in Objects" from the string, and finally it turns the selected part of the string into uppercase characters.

1. Create a skeleton XHTML document, like so:

```
<?xml version="1.0" ?>
<!DOCTYPE html PUBLIC "-//W3C//DTD XHTML 1.0 Transitional//EN"
    "http://www.w3.org/TR/xhtml1/DTD/xhtml1-transitional.dtd">
<html xmlns="http://www.w3.org/1999/xhtml" lang="en" xml:land="en">
<head>
  <title>String Object</title>
</head>
<body>
</body>
</html>
```

2. Because the code in this example is going to be run in only one place, the script can be added inside the body of the document, so add the <script> element and inside it write the following code:

```
<script type="text/JavaScript">
  myString = new String('Learning about Built-in Objects is easy')
  myString = myString.substring(15, 31)
  myString = myString.toUpperCase()
  document.write(myString)
</script>
```

Let's look at this a little closer. First you have to create an instance of the `string` object, which is assigned to the variable `myString`:

```
myString = new String('Learning about Built-in Objects is easy')
```

As it has been created, the string object has been made to hold the words `Learning about Built-in Objects is easy`. But, the idea of this exercise is just to select the words "Built-in Objects" so you use the `substring()` method to extract those words. The syntax is as follows:

```
substring(startPosition, endPosition)
```

So you select the `string` object (which is in the variable `myString`) and make its value the new substring you want (this is reassigning the value of the variable with the substring you want):

```
myString = myString.substring(15, 32)
```

This selects the string from the 16th character to the 33rd character — because it starts at position 0.

Next, you must convert the string to uppercase using the `toUpperCase()` method:

```
myString = myString.toUpperCase()
```

And finally you can write it to the document like so:

```
document.write(myString)
```

3. Save this file as `ch11_eg14.html` and when you open it in the browser, you should see the text shown in Figure 11-9.

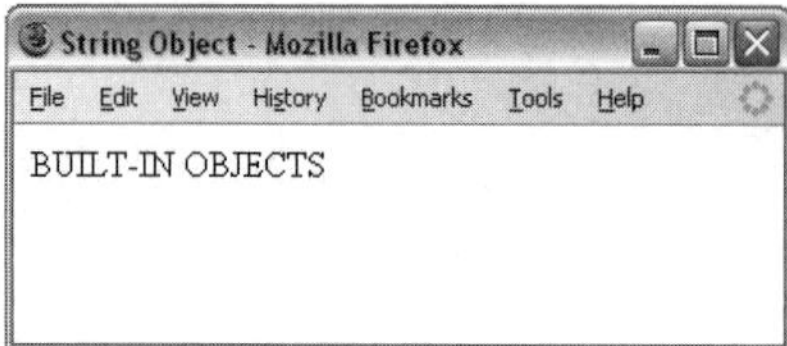

Figure 11-9

The result looks quite simple, but when you consider that the original string was `Learning about Built-in Objects is easy`, it now looks substantially different.

Date

The `date` object helps you work with dates and times. You create a new `date` object using the date constructor like so:

```
new Date()
```

You can create a `date` object set to a specific date or time, in which case you need to pass it one of four parameters:

- `milliseconds`: This value should be the number of milliseconds since 01/01/1970.
- `dateString`: Can be any date in a format recognized by the `parse()` method.
- `yr_num`, `mo_num`, `day_num`: Represents year, month, and day.
- `yr_num`, `mo_num`, `day_num`, `hr_num`, `min_num`, `seconds_num`, `ms_num`: Represents the years, days, hours, minutes, seconds, and milliseconds.

Here are some examples; the first uses milliseconds and will read `Thu Nov 27 05:33:20 UTC 1975`:

```
var birthDate = new Date(8298400000)
document.write(birthDate)
```

The second uses a `dateString`, and will read `Wed Apr 16 00:00:00 UTC+0100 1975`:

```
var birthDate = new Date("April 16, 1975")
document.write(birthDate)
```

The third uses `yr_num`, `mo_num`, and `day_num`, and will read `Mon May 12 00:00:00 UTC+0100 1975`:

```
var birthDate = new Date(1975, 4, 28)
document.write(birthDate)
```

There are a few things to watch out for:

- The first confusing thing you might notice here is that the number 4 corresponds to the month of May! That makes January 0. Similarly, when working with days, Sunday is treated as 0.
- You might find that you get different time zones than I do. I am based in London, so I run on Greenwich Mean Time (GMT) or Coordinated Universal Time (UTC). All the date object's workings are performed using UTC, even though your computer may display a time that is consistent with your time zone.
- While you can add or subtract dates, your result will end up in milliseconds. For example, if I wanted to find out the number of days until the end of the year, I might use something like this:

```
var today = new Date()
var newYear = new Date(2010,11,31)
var daysRemaining = (newYear - today)
document.write(daysRemaining)
```

The problem with this is that you end up with a result that is very long (plus if you read this during 2010 or minus if you read it after 2010). With 86,400,000 milliseconds in each day, you are likely to see a very large figure.

So, you need to divide the `daysRemaining` by the number of milliseconds in the day (`86400000`) to find the number of days (`ch11_eg15.html`):

```
var today = new Date()
var newYear = new Date(2010,11,31)
var daysRemaining = (newYear - today)
daysRemaining = daysRemaining/86400000
document.write(daysRemaining)
```

When you use the `date` object, you need to bear in mind that a user's computer click may well be inaccurate and the fact that different users could be in various time zones.

The following table shows some commonly used methods of the `date` object.

Method	Purpose
`date()`	Returns a `Date` object
`getDate()`	Returns the date of a `Date` object (from 1 to 31)
`getDay()`	Returns the day of a `Date` object (from 0 to 6; 0=Sunday, 1=Monday, and so on)
`getMonth()`	Returns the month of a `Date` object (from 0 to 11; 0=January, 1=February, and so on)
`getFullYear()`	Returns the year of a `Date` object (four digits)
`getYear()`	Returns the year of a `Date` object using only two digits (from 0 to 99)

Continued

Method	Purpose
`getHours()`	Returns the hours of a `Date` object (from 0 to 23)
`getMinutes()`	Returns the minutes of a `Date` object (from 0 to 59)
`getSeconds()`	Returns the seconds of a `Date` object (from 0 to 59)
`getTime()`	Returns the number of milliseconds since midnight 1/1/1970
`getTimezoneOffset()`	Returns the time difference between the user's computer and GMT
`parse()`	Returns a string date value that holds the number of milliseconds since January 01 1970 00:00:00
`setDate()`	Sets the date of the month in the `Date` object (from 1 to 31)
`setFullYear()`	Sets the year in the `Date` object (four digits)
`setHours()`	Sets the hours in the `Date` object (from 0 to 23)
`setMinutes()`	Sets the minutes in the `Date` object (from 0 to 59)
`setMonth()`	Sets the months in the `Date` object (from 0 to 11; 0=January, 1=February)
`setSeconds()`	Sets the seconds in the `Date` object (from 0 to 59)
`setTime()`	Sets the milliseconds after 1/1/1970
`setYear()`	Sets the year in the `Date` object (00 to 99)
`toGMTString()`	Converts the `Date` object to a string, set to GMT time zone
`toLocaleString()`	Converts the `Date` object to a string, set to the current time zone of the user
`toString()`	Converts the `Date` object to a string

Many of the methods in the table that follows were then added offering support for the universal (UTC) time, which takes the format `Day Month Date, hh,mm,ss UTC Year`.

Method	Purpose
`getUTCDate()`	Returns the date of a `Date` object in universal (UTC) time
`getUTCDay()`	Returns the day of a `Date` object in universal time
`getUTCMonth()`	Returns the month of a `Date` object in universal time
`getUTCFullYear()`	Returns the four-digit year of a `Date` object in universal time
`getUTCHours()`	Returns the hour of a `Date` object in universal time

Method	Purpose
`getUTCMinutes()`	Returns the minutes of a `Date` object in universal time
`getUTCSeconds()`	Returns the seconds of a `Date` object in universal time
`getUTCMilliseconds()`	Returns the milliseconds of a `Date` object in universal time
`setUTCDate()`	Sets the date in the `Date` object in universal time (from 1 to 31)
`setUTCDay()`	Sets the day in the `Date` object in universal time (from 0 to 6; Sunday=0, Monday=1, and so on)
`setUTCMonth()`	Sets the month in the `Date` object in universal time (from 0 to 11; 0=January, 1=February)
`setUTCFullYear()`	Sets the year in the `Date` object in universal time (four digits)
`setUTCHour()`	Sets the hour in the `Date` object in universal time (from 0 to 23)
`setUTCMinutes()`	Sets the minutes in the `Date` object in universal time (from 0 to 59)
`setUTCSeconds()`	Sets the seconds in the `Date` object in universal time (from 0 to 59)
`setUTCMilliseconds()`	Sets the milliseconds in the `Date` object in universal time (from 0 to 999)

Math

The `math` object helps in working with numbers. It has properties for mathematical constants and methods representing mathematical functions such as the Tangent and Sine functions.

For example, the following sets a variable called `numberPI` to hold the constant of pi and then write it to the screen (`ch11_eg16.html`):

```
numberPI = Math.PI
document.write (numberPI)
```

The following example rounds pi to the nearest whole number (integer) and writes it to the screen (also shown in `ch11_eg16.html`):

```
numberPI = Math.PI
numberPI = Math.round(numberPI)
document.write (numberPI)
```

Properties

The following table lists the properties of the `math` object.

Property	Purpose
`E`	Returns the base of a natural logarithm
`LN2`	Returns the natural logarithm of 2
`LN10`	Returns the natural logarithm of 10
`LOG2E`	Returns the base-2 logarithm of E
`LOG10E`	Returns the base-10 logarithm of E
`PI`	Returns pi
`SQRT1_2`	Returns 1 divided by the square root of 2
`SQRT2`	Returns the square root of 2

Methods

The following table lists the methods for the `math` object.

Method	Purpose
`abs(x)`	Returns the absolute value of *x*
`acos(x)`	Returns the arccosine of *x*
`asin(x)`	Returns the arcsine of *x*
`atan(x)`	Returns the arctangent of *x*
`atan2(y,x)`	Returns the angle from the x-axis to a point
`ceil(x)`	Returns the nearest integer greater than or equal to *x*
`cos(x)`	Returns the cosine of *x*
`exp(x)`	Returns the value of E raised to the power of *x*
`floor(x)`	Returns the nearest integer less than or equal to *x*
`log(x)`	Returns the natural log of *x*
`max(x,y)`	Returns the number with the highest value of *x* and *y*
`min(x,y)`	Returns the number with the lowest value of *x* and *y*
`pow(x,y)`	Returns the value of the number *x* raised to the power of *y*
`random()`	Returns a random number between 0 and 1

Method	Purpose
`round(x)`	Rounds *x* to the nearest integer
`sin(x)`	Returns the sine of *x*
`sqrt(x)`	Returns the square root of *x*
`tan(x)`	Returns the tangent of *x*

Array

An *array* is like a special variable. It's special because it can hold more than one value, and these values can be accessed individually. Arrays are particularly helpful when you want to store a group of values in the same variable rather than having separate variables for each value. You may want to do this because all the values correspond to one particular item, or just for the convenience of having several values in the same variable rather than in differently named variables; or it might be because you do not know how many items of information are going to be stored (for example, you might store the items that would appear in a shopping basket in an array). You often see arrays used in conjunction with loops, where the loop is used to add information into an array or read it from the array.

You need to use a *constructor* with an `array` object, so you can create an array by specifying either the name of the array and how many values it will hold or by adding all the data straight into the array. For example, here is an array that is created with three items; it holds the names of musical instruments:

```
instruments = new Array("guitar", "drums", "piano")
```

The items in the array can be referred to by a number that reflects the order in which they are stored in the array. The number is an index, so it begins at 0. For example, you can refer to the guitar as `instruments[0]`, the drums as `instruments[1]`, and so on.

An array does need to know how many items you want to store in it, but you do not need to provide values for each item in the array when it is created; you can just indicate how many items you want to be able to store (to confuse matters, this value does not start at 0 so it will create three elements not four):

```
instruments = new Array(3)
```

This number is stored in the `length` property of the `array` object and the contents are not actually assigned yet. If you want to increase the size of an array, you can just assign a new value to the `length` property that is higher than the current length.

Here is an example that creates an array with five items and then checks how many items are in the array using the `length` property:

```
fruit = new Array("apple", "banana", "orange", "mango", "lemon")
document.write(fruit.length)
```

Here is an example of the `toString()` method, which converts the array to a string.

```
document.write('These are ' + fruit.toString())
```

Keeping the related information in the one variable tends to be easier than having five variables, such as `fruit1`, `fruit2`, `fruit3`, `fruit4`, and `fruit5`. Using one array like this also takes up less memory than storing five separate variables, and in situations when you might have varying numbers of fruit it allows the variable to grow and shrink in accordance with your requirements (rather than creating ten variables, half of which might be empty).

Methods

The table that follows lists the methods of an array:

Method	Purpose
`concat()`	Joins (or concatenates) two or more arrays to create one new one
`join(separator)`	Joins all of the elements of an array together separated by the character specified as a separator (the default is a comma)
`reverse()`	Returns the array with items in reverse order
`slice()`	Returns a selected part of the array (if you do not need it all)
`sort()`	Returns a sorted array, sorted by alphabetical or numerical order

Window

Every browser window and frame has a corresponding `window` object that is created with every instance of a `<body>` or `<frameset>` element.

For example, you can change the text that appears in the browser's status bar using the `status` property of the `window` object. To do this, first you need to add a function in the head that is going to be triggered when the page loads, and then you use this function to indicate what should appear in the status bar:

```
<script type="text/javascript">
  function statusBarText()
  {
    window.status = "Did you see me down here?"
  }
</script>
```

You then call this function from the `<body>` element's `onload` event, like so:

```
<body onload="statusBarText()">
```

Properties

The table that follows lists the properties of the `window` object.

Property	Purpose
`closed`	A Boolean determining if a window has been closed. If it has, the value returned is `true`.
`defaultStatus`	Defines the default message displayed in a browser window's status bar (usually at the bottom of the page on the left).
`document`	The document object contained in that window.
`frames`	An array containing references to all named child frames in the current window.
`history`	A history object that contains details and URLs visited from that window (mainly for use in creating back and forward buttons like those in the browser).
`location`	The location object; the URL of the current window.
`name`	The window's name.
`status`	Can be set at any time to define a temporary message displayed in the status bar; for example, you could change the message in the status bar when a user hovers over a link by using it with an `onmouseover` event on that link.
`statusbar`	The status bar has a property that indicates whether the status bar is visible. The value is a Boolean `true` or `false` — for example, `window.statusbar[.visible=false]`.
`toolbar`	The toolbar has a property that indicates whether the scrollbar is visible or not. Its value is a Boolean `true` or `false` — for example, `window.toolbar[.visible=false]`. This can be set only when you create the new window.
`top`	A reference for the topmost browser window if several windows are open on the desktop.
`window`	The current window or frame.

Methods

The table that follows lists the methods of the `window` object.

Method	Purpose
`alert()`	Displays an alert box containing a message and an OK button.
`back()`	Same effect as the browser's Back button.
`blur()`	Removes focus from the current window.

Continued

Method	Purpose
`close()`	Closes the current window or another window if a reference to another window is supplied.
`confirm()`	Brings up a dialog box asking users to confirm that they want to perform an action with either OK or Cancel as the options. They return `true` and `false`, respectively.
`focus()`	Gives focus to the specified window and brings it to the top of others.
`forward()`	Equivalent to clicking the browser's Forward button.
`home()`	Takes users to their browser's designated homepage.
`moveBy(horizontalPixels, verticalPixels)`	Moves the window by the specified number of pixels in relation to current coordinates.
`moveTo(Xpostion, Yposition)`	Moves the top left of the window to the specified x-y coordinates.
`open(URL, name [,features])`	Opens a new browser window (this method is covered in more detail in the next chapter).
`print()`	Prints the content of the current window (or brings up the browser's print dialog).
`prompt()`	Creates a dialog box for the user to enter an input.
`stop()`	Same effect as clicking the Stop button in the browser.

Writing JavaScript

You need to be aware of a few points when you start writing JavaScript:

- JavaScript is case-sensitive, so a variable called `myVariable` is different than a variable called `MYVARIABLE`, and both are different than a variable called `myvariable`.
- When you come across symbols such as `(`, `{`, `[`, `"`, and `'` they must have a closing symbol to match: `'`, `"`, `]`, `}`, and `)`. (Note how the first bracket opened is the last one to be closed, which is why the closing symbols are in reverse order here.)
- Like XHTML, JavaScript ignores extra spaces, so you can add white space to your script to make it more readable. The following two lines are equivalent, even though there are more spaces in the second line:

```
myVariable="some value"
myVariable = "some value"
```

- If you have a large string, you can break it up with a backslash, as you can see here:

```
document.write("My first \
  JavaScript example")
```

- But you must not break anything other than strings, so this would be wrong:

```
document.write \
  ("My first JavaScript example")
```

- You can insert special characters such as ″,′, ;, and &, which are otherwise reserved (because they have a special meaning in JavaScript), by using a backslash before them like so:

```
document.write("I want to use a \"quote\" mark \& an ampersand.")
```

  This writes out the following line to the browser:

```
I want to use a "quote" mark & an ampersand.
```

- If you have ever used a full programming language such as C++ or Java, you know they require a semicolon at the end of each line. This is optional in JavaScript unless you want to put more than one statement on a line.

A Word About Data Types

By now you should be getting the idea that you can do different things with different types of data. For example, you can add numbers together but you cannot mathematically add the letter *A* to the letter *B*. Some forms of data require that you are able to deal with numbers that have decimal places (floating point numbers); currency is a common example. Other types of data have inherent limitations; for example, if I am dealing with dates and time, I want to be able to add hours to certain types of data without getting 25:30 as a time (even though I often wish I could add more hours to a day).

Different types of data (letters, whole numbers, decimal numbers, dates) are known to have different *data types*; these allow programs to manage the different types of data in different ways. For example, if you use the + operator with a string, it concatenates two strings, whereas if it is used with numbers, it adds the two numbers together. Some programming languages require that you specifically indicate what type of data a variable is going to hold and require you to be able to convert between types. While JavaScript supports different data types, as you are about to see, it handles conversion between types itself, so you never need to worry about telling JavaScript that a certain type of data is a date or a *string* (a string being a set of characters that may include letters and numbers).

There are three simple data types in JavaScript:

- **Number:** Used to perform arithmetic operations (addition, subtraction, multiplication, and division). Any whole number or decimal number that does not appear between quotation marks is considered a number.
- **String:** Used to handle text. It is a set of characters (including numbers, spaces, and punctuation) enclosed by quotation marks.
- **Boolean:** A Boolean value has only two possible values: `true` and `false`. This data allows you to perform logical operations and check whether something is true or false.

You may also come across two other data types:

- **Null:** Indicates that a value does not exist. This is written using the keyword `null`. This is an important value because it explicitly states that no value has been given. This can mean a very different thing from a string that just contains a space or a zero.
- **Undefined:** Indicates a situation where the value has not been defined previously in code and uses the JavaScript keyword `undefined`. You might remember that if you declare a variable but do not give it a value, the variable is said to be undefined (you are particularly likely to see this when something is not right in your code).

Keywords

You may have noticed that there are several keywords in JavaScript that perform functions, such as `break`, `for`, `if`, and `while`, all of which have special meaning; therefore, these words should not be used in variable, function, method, or object names. The following is a list of the keywords that you should avoid using (some of these are not actually used yet, but are reserved for future use):

```
abstract boolean break byte case catch char class const
continue default do double else extends false final
finally float for function goto if implements import
in instanceof int interface long native new null
package private protected public return short static
super switch synchronized this throw throws transient
true try var void while with
```

Summary

This chapter has introduced you to a lot of new concepts: objects, methods, properties, events, arrays, functions, interfaces, object models, data types, and keywords. While it's a lot to take in all at once, by the time you have looked at some of the examples in the next chapter it should be a lot clearer. After reading that chapter, you can read through this chapter again and you should be able to understand more examples of what can be achieved with JavaScript.

You started off by looking at how you can access information from a document using the Document Object Model (this chapter focused on the Level 0 DOM).

Once you have figured out how to get information from a document, you can use JavaScript to perform calculations upon the data in the document. JavaScript mainly performs calculations using features such as the following:

- Variables (which store information in memory)
- Operators (such as arithmetic and comparison operators)
- Functions (which live in the `<head>` of a document and contain code that is called by an event)
- Conditional statements (to handle choices of actions based on different circumstances)
- Loops (to repeat statements until a condition has been met)

As you will see in Chapter 12, these simple concepts can be brought together to create quite powerful results. In particular, when you see some of the validation scripts that will check the form data users enter, you will see some quite advanced JavaScript, and you will have a good idea of how basic building blocks can create complex structures.

Finally, you looked at a number of other objects made available through JavaScript; you met the `string`, `date`, `math`, `array`, and `window` objects. Each object contains related functionality; each has properties that tell you about the object (such as the date, the time, the size of window, or length of string), and methods that allow you to do things with this data stored in the object.

I hope you are starting to get a grasp of how JavaScript can help you add interactivity to your pages, but you will really get to see how it does this in the next chapter when you delve into examples of JavaScript libraries and look at examples that will really help you make use of JavaScript.

Exercises

1. Create a script to write out the multiplication table for the number 5 from 1 to 20 using a `while` loop.
2. Modify `ch11_eg06.html` so that it can say one of three things:
    - "Good Morning" to visitors coming to the page before 12 P.M. (using an `if` statement).
    - "Good Afternoon" to visitors coming to the page between 12 and 6 P.M. — again using an `if` statement. (Hint: You might need to use a logical operator.)
    - "Good Evening" to visitors coming to the page after 6 P.M. up until midnight (again using an `if` statement).

Working with JavaScript

You learned the key concepts behind the JavaScript language in Chapter 11; in this chapter, you see how these concepts come together in working scripts. By looking at several examples, you learn different ways in which JavaScript can interact with your web pages, some helpful coding practices for writing your own JavaScripts, and some shortcuts to creating interactive pages. The chapter is roughly split into two sections:

- **Creating your own basic scripts:** The first section focuses on how to write your own basic scripts. Most of these examples work with form elements.
- **Using pre-written JavaScript libraries:** The second section focuses on a number of scripts that have already been written and shows you how you can add powerful and complex features to your site with just a few lines of code.

By the end of the chapter, not only will you have learned a lot about using JavaScript in your pages, but you will also have seen many helpful tools and techniques you can use in your own pages.

Practical Tips for Writing Scripts

Before you start looking at the examples, I'd like to share a few practical hints on developing JavaScripts that should save you time.

Has Someone Already Written This Script?

There are thousands of free JavaScripts already on the Web, so before you start writing a script from scratch, it is worth searching to see if someone has already done all the hard work for you. Here are a couple of sites that will help you get going (and don't forget you can search using a search engine such as Google, too):

- `www.HotScripts.com`
- `www.JavaScriptKit.com`

- `www.webreference.com/programming/javascript/`
- `http://JavaScript.Internet.com`

Of course, for some tasks you will have to write your own script, but you may still find that someone has written a script that does something similar (and could learn something just by looking at how they approached the problem).

You will see more about this topic near the end of the chapter when you look at using existing JavaScript libraries.

Reusable Functions

Along with reusing other people's scripts and folders, you can also write code that you can reuse yourself. For example, you might build several sites that use a similar form that allows people to contact the site owners. On each contact form there might be several fields that are required, and you might decide to write a script to ensure that people fill in the required fields. Rather than writing a new script for each site, you can create a script that you can use on any contact form you write.

So, you should aim to make your code as reusable as possible, rather than writing a script that will only work with one page. You will see examples of this shortly.

Using External JavaScript Files

Whenever you are going to use a script in more than one page it's a good idea to place it in an external JavaScript file (a technique you learned about at the beginning of Chapter 11). For example, if you wanted to create a newsletter signup form on each page of your site, then you might use a script to check that the text entered into the e-mail address box is in a valid e-mail format. Rather than including this script on every page, if the script lives in an external JavaScript file:

- You do not have to copy and paste the same code into several files.
- The file size of the pages is smaller because the JavaScript is in one file that is included on each page rather than repeated in multiple pages.
- If you need to change something about the script, you need to change only the one script, not every page that uses it.

Place Scripts in a Scripts Folder

When you use external scripts you should create a special `scripts` folder — just as you would an `images` folder. This helps improve the organization of your site and your directory structure. Whenever you need to look at or change a script, you know exactly where it will be.

You should also use intuitive names for your script files so that you can find them quickly and easily.

Form Validation

Form validation is one of the most common tasks performed using JavaScript. You have likely come across forms on the Web that have shown you a prompt when you have not entered a value into a field that requires one, or when you have entered the wrong kind of value; this is because the form has been *validated*. That is, a script has checked to see whether the text you have entered or choices you have made match some rules that the programmer has written into the page. For example, if you are expected to enter an e-mail address, these validation rules may check what you entered to ensure that it contains an `@` symbol and at least one period or full stop. These kinds of rules help ensure that the data provided by users meets the requirements of the application before being submitted.

When to Validate

Validation can happen in two places: in the browser using JavaScript, and on the server using one of several languages such as ASP.NET or PHP. In fact, applications that collect important information using a form (such as e-commerce orders) are usually validated both in the browser *and* on the server. You may wonder why forms are validated in the browser if they will only get checked again when they reach the server; the reason is that it helps the user enter the correct data required for the job without the form being sent to the server, being processed, and then being sent back again if there are any errors. This has two key advantages:

- It's quicker for the user because the form does not need to be sent to the server, processed, and returned to the user with any relevant error messages.
- It saves the load on the server because some errors will get caught before the form is submitted.

It is very important to validate on the server because you cannot guarantee that the user has JavaScript enabled in his or her browser, and if a user entered a wrong value into a database or other program it could prevent the entire application from running properly. (It is also possible for hackers to bypass JavaScript if they are intending to send some incorrect information.)

What You Can Check For

When it comes to validating a form you cannot always check whether users have given you the correct information, but you can check whether they have given you some information in the correct format. For example, you cannot ensure that the user has entered his or her correct phone number; the user could be entering anyone's phone number, but you can check that it's a number rather than letters or other characters, and you can check that the number contains a minimum number of digits. As another example, you can't ensure someone has entered a real e-mail address rather than a false address, but you can check that whatever was entered followed the general structure of an e-mail address (including an `@` sign and a period, and that it is at least seven characters long). So JavaScript form validation is a case of minimizing the possibility of user errors by validating form controls.

When it comes to form controls that allow users to indicate their choice from a selection of options (such as checkboxes, drop-down select boxes, and radio buttons), you can use JavaScript to check that a user has selected one of the options (for example, to check that a user has checked the terms and conditions).

How to Check a Form

There are several ways in which you can check a form. Usually when the user presses the submit button on a form, it triggers the `onsubmit` event handler on the `<form>` element, which in turn calls a validation function stored either in a separate script or in the head of the document. The function must then return `true` in order for the form to be sent, or, if an error is encountered, the function returns `false` and the user's form will not be sent — at which point the form should indicate to the user where there is a problem with the information the user entered.

> *If you use a validation function that is called by the* `onsubmit` *event handler, but the user's browser does not support JavaScript, then the form will still be submitted without the validation checks taking place.*

In the validation functions you meet in this chapter, the first task will be to set a variable that can be returned to say whether the script found errors or not. At first, this is set to `true` (indicating that the form can be sent because problems were found); then as the script checks the values the user has entered, if the function finds an error this value can be turned to `false` to prevent the form from being submitted.

Some forms also check values as the user moves between form fields — in which case the values the user entered are passed to a function that checks that specific form control using the `onblur` event (which fires when that form control loses focus).

Checking Text Fields

You have probably seen forms on web sites that ask you to provide a username and password, and then to re-enter the password to make sure you did not mistype something. It might resemble Figure 12-1.

Figure 12-1

Let's take a look at the code for this form, and how it calls the JavaScript that will validate what the user has entered (`ch12_eg01.html`).

```
<form name="frmRegister" method="post" action="register.aspx"
  onsubmit="return validate(this);">
  <div>
    <label for="txtUserName">Username:</label>
```

```
    <input type="text" name="txtUserName" id="txtUserName" size="12" />
  </div>
  <div>
    <label for="txtPassword">Password: </label>
    <input type="password" name="txtPassword" id="txtPassword" size="12" />
  </div>
  <div>
    <label for="txtPassword2">Confirm your password:</label>
    <input type="password" name="txtPassword2" id="txtPassword2" size="12"/>
  </div>
  <div>
    <input type="submit" value="Log in" />
  </div>
</form>
```

The opening `<form>` tag has an `onsubmit` attribute; when the user presses the submit button on the form, the script specified in this attribute will be run.

```
<form name="frmRegister" method="post" action="register.aspx"
  onsubmit="return validate(this);">
```

In this case, when the user presses the submit button, a function called `validate()` will run. Before the name of the function is the keyword `return`; this indicates that the `validate()` function will return a value of `true` or `false` (in order for the form to be submitted, the function must return `true`; if it returns `false` the form is not submitted).

The `validate()` function we are writing will take one parameter; it tells the function the form that you want to process. So, inside the parentheses of the `validate()` function, you can see the word `this`, which indicates that *this* is the form you wish to validate (as opposed to any other form that might appear on the page).

With a login form like this one, you might want to check a few things:

- That the username is of a minimum length
- That the password is of a minimum length
- That the two passwords match

In this section, you are going to look at two different ways to approach the `validate()` function:

- Creating a single function to check the form
- Creating re-usable functions that are called by this function

In both cases, the `validate()` function will live in the `<head>` element, and will start by setting a variable called `returnValue` to `true`; if no errors are found this will be the value that the function returns, which will in turn allow the form to be sent. If an error is met, the variable will be set to `false`, and the form will not send.

Single Function Approach

The first approach we will look at to validate this form is to write a validation script especially for this one form, where all of the rules live inside the one function (`ch12_eg01.html`).

The function will be called `validate()` and it will expect to be told which form it is working with as a parameter of the function:

```
function validate(form) {
```

This is why the `onsubmit` attribute of the `<form>` element used the keyword `this` when calling the function, indicating that *this* is the form it wanted to process.

In the script, you want to collect the values that the user entered into the text controls and store these in variables. You identify the form controls within the page one by one, using the dot notation you met in the last chapter. You then collect the value the user typed into that control using the `value` property:

```
function validate(form) {
  var returnValue = true;
  var username = form.txtUserName.value;
  var password1 = form.txtPassword.value;
  var password2 = form.txtPassword2.value;
```

Because we have told the function which form we are working with, the dot notation can start with `form` rather than `document.frmRegister`; the following two lines would do exactly the same thing:

```
var username = document.frmRegister.txtUserName.value;
var username = form.txtUserName.value;
```

Now you can start to check whether the data that was entered by the user meets the criteria you require for the form to be submitted. First you can check whether the username is at least six characters long. The value the user entered into the username form control is already stored in a variable called `username`, and because it is a string (a set of letters or numbers), you can use the `length` property to tell how long it is.

If the username is not long enough, you will need to take action, so you place your validation test in an `if` statement. The following states that if the `length` of the variable is less than six characters long, the code in curly braces will be run:

```
if (username.length < 6) {
  username is less than 6 characters so do something
}
```

In this case, if it is less than six characters long, you will do three things:

- Set the variable `returnValue` to `false`, so that the form will not be submitted.
- Tell the user what has happened so that he or she can correct the error. For this example, we will use the JavaScript `alert()` function to create an alert box (like the ones you met in the last chapter) containing a message for the user.
- Pass focus back to this item (using the JavaScript `focus()` method) on the form so that the user can change what he or she had put in this form.

Here you can see the `if` statement with all of these actions:

```
if(username.length < 6) {
  returnValue = false;
  alert("Your username must be at least\n6 characters long.\n
  Please try again.");
  frmRegister.txtUserName.focus();
}
```

The alert box used to be a very popular way to show users errors on their forms (as it is a very simple technique of providing feedback). These days, it is more popular to write an error message into the page itself; however, this is more complicated, so you will see how to do that later in the chapter.

You may have noticed `\n` *in the middle of the error message; this creates a line break in JavaScript.*

Next you want to check the length of the first password. To do this, you can use the same approach. But if the password is not long enough you will empty both password controls, and give focus to the first password box:

```
if (password1.length < 6) {
  returnValue = false;
  alert("Your password must be at least\n6 characters long.\n
    Please try again.");
  frmRegister.txtPassword.value = "";
  frmRegister.txtPassword2.value = "";
  frmRegister.txtPassword.focus();
}
```

If the code has gotten this far, the username and first password are both long enough. Now, you just have to check whether the value of the first password box is the same as the second one, as shown here. Remember that the `!=` operator used in this condition means "not equal," so the `if` statement will take action if the value of `password1` does not equal that of `password2`.

```
if (password1.value != password2.value) {
  returnValue = false;
  alter("Your password entries did not match.\nPlease try again.");
  frmRegister.txtPassword.value = "";
  frmRegister.txtPassword2.value = "";
  frmRegister.txtPassword.focus();
}
```

You can see here that when the user has entered passwords that do not match, the user is shown an alert box with an error message reporting that the password entries did not match. Also, the contents of both password inputs are cleared and the focus is passed back to the first password box.

Because a password input will show dots or asterisks rather than the characters, when a user makes a mistake with a password input, he or she will not be able to see where the mistake is. This is why I clear password boxes when a user has made a mistake in them.

The only thing left to do in this function is return the value of the `returnValue` variable — which will be `true` if all the conditions are met or `false` if not.

```
return returnValue;
}
```

Here is the function in its entirety (`ch12_eg01.html`):

```
function validate(form) {

  var returnValue = true;

  var username = form.txtUserName.value;
  var password1 = form.txtPassword.value;
  var password2 = form.txtPassword2.value;

if(username.length < 6) {
  returnValue = false;
  alert("Your username must be at least\n6 characters long.\n
  Please try again.");
  document.frmRegister.txtUserName.focus();
}

if (password1.length < 6) {
  returnValue = false;
  alert("Your password must be at least\n6 characters long.\n
  Please try again.");
  document.frmRegister.txtPassword.value = "";
  document.frmRegister.txtPassword2.value = "";
  document.frmRegister.txtPassword.focus();
}

if (password1 != password2) {
  returnValue = false;
  alert("Your password entries did not match.\nPlease try again.");
  document.frmRegister.txtPassword.value = "";
  document.frmRegister.txtPassword2.value = "";
  document.frmRegister.txtPassword.focus();
}
  return returnValue;
}
```

In Figure 12-2 you can see the result if the user's password is not long enough.

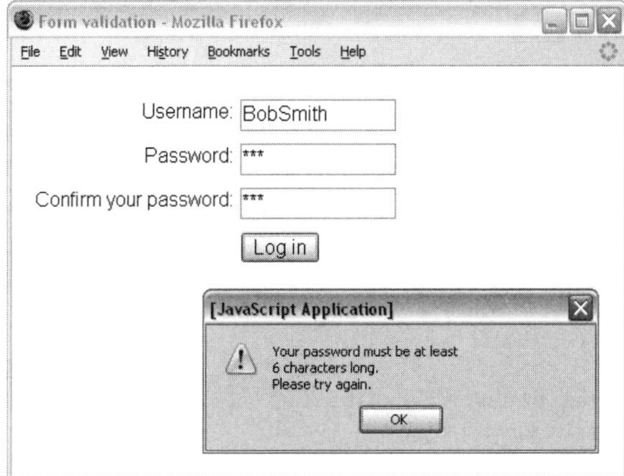

Figure 12-2

This example should have given you a good idea of how to check what a user has entered into a form against a set of rules.

Re-Usable Functions Approach

While the example you just saw works fine, you can save time and effort by writing code that you can re-use. For example, many programmers have a single JavaScript file that will contain a set of form validation functions they can use in any form that they write. These functions can check for things like the following:

- Whether the user has entered text that is longer than the minimum required length as demonstrated with the username and password in the last example
- Whether the text entered by the user consists only of numbers (no other characters) — which could be handy for telephone numbers or for asking customers the quantity of goods they want in an e-commerce store
- Whether, when you are requesting an e-mail address, the user has entered that address in the correct form

JavaScript files that contain functions that can be re-used are often known as JavaScript libraries. Let's look at the same form again, but develop a validation approach that utilizes this approach.

Using the second approach, we still have to write a `validate()` function for each form, but the function is much shorter than the last one you saw. Its job is to pass values from the form to functions in the

JavaScript validation library that does the real validation work. So, this time our `validate()` function will call two other functions in the JavaScript library:

- `validateConfirmPassword()` will check that the two password fields match.
- `validateMinimumLength()` will ensure that the user has entered a minimum number of characters for the form field.

You will look at these functions in a moment, but first let's look at the `validate()` function that calls them (which lives in the same page as the form); its job is to pass values from the form to the library functions. If there is an error, it will then prevent the submission of the form, and will tell the user the error message. Before you look at each line of the function individually, here is the entire function:

```
function validate(form) {
  var returnValue = "";
  returnValue += validateConfirmPassword(form.txtPassword,
      form.txtPassword2,
      'Your passwords did not match');
  returnValue += validateMinimumLength(form.txtPassword, 6,
      'Your password must be at least 6 characters long');
  returnValue += validateMinimumLength(form.txtUserName, 6,
      'Your username must be at least 6 characters long');
  if (returnValue != "") {
    return false;
  }
  return true;
}
```

Let's take a closer look at this; it starts with the function name. The function takes one parameter, the form it has to validate, which is given in parentheses.

```
function validate(form) {
```

Then a variable called `returnValue` is declared; this time, rather than being set to `true`, it is set to an empty string using empty quotes.

```
var returnValue = "";
```

You then make three calls to functions, each of which checks a different aspect of the form. We'll look at each of these in turn in a moment. If these functions find a problem (because the user has not entered what you wanted), the functions will return an error. You may remember from the last chapter that += adds a value onto an existing variable, so if the function returns an error the error message is appended to the variable `returnValue`; if there is not an error, nothing will be added to the variable.

First you can see we're calling the `validateConfirmPassword()` function. We tell it the two password controls that we want it to check using the dot notation, along with the error message we want to display if the fields do not match.

```
returnValue += validateConfirmPassword(form.txtPassword, form.txtPassword2,
      'Your passwords did not match');
```

Because the `validateConfirmPassword()` function will return the error message if the passwords do not match, we will know if there is a problem because the `returnValue` attribute will contain this error message; it will no longer be empty.

We then call the `validateMinimumLength()` function to check the length of the first password control. Here we are passing in the form control to check, the minimum number of characters the user can enter for that form control, and the error message to show if the form control is not that length.

```
returnValue += validateMinimumLength(form.txtPassword, 6,
    'Your password must be at least 6 characters long');
```

We then check that the username entered is more than six characters. To do this we call the `validateMinimumLength()` function a second time. Here you can already start to see the benefits of code re-use; rather than repeating the entire function again we are using the same function we just used a second time, but this time we are telling it to check a different form control and display a different error message if there is a problem.

```
returnValue += validateMinimumLength(form.txtUserName, 6,
    'Your username must be at least 6 characters long');
```

Having checked these three aspects of the form, if there is a problem `returnValue` will no longer be empty. The following `if` statement says if `returnValue` is not empty, the `validate()` function should return `false` to say that the form should not be submitted. Otherwise, if it is blank, we can return `true`, which will allow the form to be submitted.

```
if (returnValue != "") {
  return false;
}
return true;
```

You might notice that we start with the rules that apply to the last items in the form, and work backwards to the rules that apply to the first form controls. We do this because, when there is an error, we want to return focus to the form field with the error (just as we did in the first example). If there is more than one error, we want the user to start at the top of the form, and work through it correcting all errors, so we want the last error that the script *processes* to be the first one that the user will see.

As you will see in a moment, when these functions find an error, not only do they give focus to that form element, they also write the error message into the page, which means we need to change the form in the XHTML page slightly. Let's look at the form again; this time there are empty `<span>` elements after the form controls. These will hold any error messages that are returned. When designing your form, it is important to leave enough space in the page for these error messages. It is also *very* important that there be no spaces between the closing of the `<input />` tag and the start of the `<span>` tag; otherwise, the form will not work.

```
<form name="frmRegister" method="post" action="register.aspx"
  onsubmit="return validate(this);">
  <div>
    <label for="txtUserName">Username:</label>
    <input type="text" id="txtUserName" size="12" /><span
       class="message"></span>
  </div>
  <div>
    <label for="txtPassword">Password: </label>
    <input type="password" id="txtPassword" size="12" /><span
       class="message"></span>
  </div>
  <div>
    <label for="txtPassword2">Confirm your password:</label>
    <input type="password" id="txtPassword2" size="12" /><span
       class="message"></span>
  </div>
  <div>
    <input type="submit" value="Log in" />
  </div>
</form>
```

So, now let's take a look at the function that will check that a user has entered a minimum number of characters into a specified form field.

```
function validateMinimumLength (control, length, errormessage) {
  var error="";
  document.getElementById(control.id).nextSibling.innerHTML="";
  if (control.value.length < length) {
    error = errormessage;
    document.getElementById(control.id).nextSibling.innerHTML=errormessage;
    document.getElementById(control.id).focus();
    }
  return error;
}
```

We are passing three things into the function so that it can perform its calculation:

- The form control we want to check
- The length of the text we expect the user to have entered
- An error message we will show to the user if the control is not long enough

```
function validateMinimumLength (control, length, errormessage) {
```

You can see in the brackets the words `control`, `length`, and `errormessage`. Inside the function, we can use these words to refer to the values passed into the function when it was called. For example, look at this line:

```
if (control.value.length < length) {
```

We have an `if` statement checking whether the length of the control passed in (`control`) is less than the minimum number of characters we will allow (`length`).

If the user has not entered enough characters, we set the value of a variable called `error` (which was declared in the second line of the function) to contain the error message.

```
error = errormessage;
```

We then write the error message into the extra `<span>` element we added after each form control to display the problem.

```
document.getElementById(control.id).nextSibling.innerHTML=errormessage;
```

There is a lot going on in this one line, so let's break it down:

- `control.id` gives you the value of the `id` attribute of the form control that you are working with.
- `document.getElementById(control.id)` gives you the form control you are working with (the `getElementById()` method returns an element given an `id` attribute, and you have just seen how to get the value of the `id` attribute for the form control you are working with using `control.id`).
- `nextSibling` returns the next element after this form control, which is the `<span>` element following it that will hold the error message.
- `innerHTML=errormessage` adds the error message inside that `<span>` element.

If there is a problem, we also give the form control with the problem focus:

```
document.getElementById(control.id).focus();
```

We then return the error back to the `validate()` function in the page with the form (so that it can prevent the form from being submitted). Before looking at how we pass the error back, you may have noticed this line of code, which appears before the `if` statement that checks the length of the value entered into the form control:

```
document.getElementById(control.id).nextSibling.innerHTML="";
```

Its purpose is to ensure the `<span>` element next to the form control is blank. We need to do this because, once a form has been submitted and errors have been spotted, the user may resubmit the form again — in which case we need to clear any error messages, and then check the form control again, and only if there is still a problem display the error message again.

As you might imagine, if you are creating a lot of sites, with many forms, the ability to re-use validation functions saves you from having to code each form again and again.

Figure 12-3 shows the error message generated when the user has not entered a value for the username.

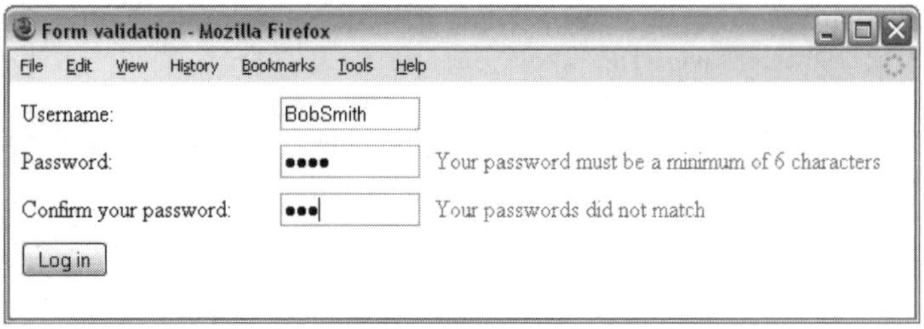

Figure 12-3

The replace() Method

Now that you have seen examples of how to validate text fields using a single function and using re-usable functions, it's time to look at some other ways that you can work with text inputs.

The JavaScript `replace()` method often comes in handy with text inputs because it allows you to replace certain characters with other characters. The simplest way to use the `replace()` method is to use the following syntax:

```
string.replace(oldSubString, newSubString);
```

For example, imagine you had a variable called `message`. The following line would look at this variable and replace instances of the letters "bad" with the letters "good":

```
message.replace('bad', 'good');
```

Let's add this into a form so you can see it working; we have a `<textarea>` that contains the sentence "I think it would be a bad idea to make a badge." When the user clicks on the button, we will replace the letters `bad` with the word `good`. Rather than creating a function to demonstrate this, we can simply put the script we want to run in the `onclick` event of the button (`ch12_eg03.html`).

```
<form name="myForm">
  Message: <textarea name="myTextArea" id="myTextArea" cols="40" rows="10">
  I think it would be a bad idea to make a badge.</textarea>
  <input type="button" value="Replace characters bad"
         onclick="document.myForm.myTextArea.value =
         document.myForm.myTextArea.value.replace('bad', 'good');" />
</form>
```

If you look at the value of the `onclick` attribute, it takes whatever was in the text area and replaces any occurrence of the letters `bad` with the letters `good`. Figure 12-4 shows you what this might look like after the user has pressed the button once.

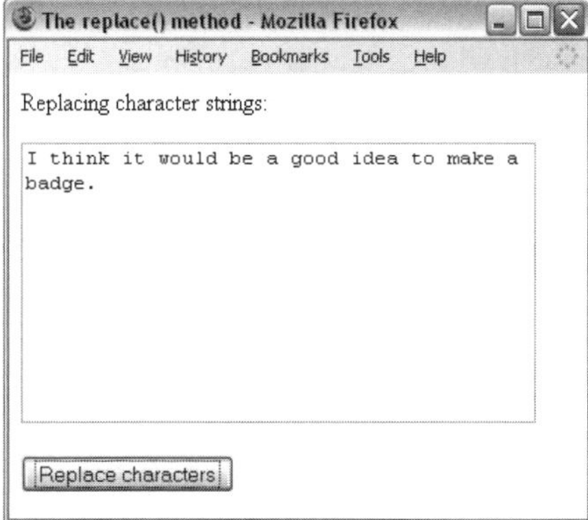

Figure 12-4

There is something interesting to note here. The `replace()` function replaces the *first* instance of the string `bad`. If the button were pressed again, you would see another issue: the word "badge" would turn into "goodge". We can address both of these issues using something known as a *Regular Expression* inside the `replace()` function.

Regular Expressions

Regular Expressions provide a very powerful way to find a particular string, although the downside of this power is that they can become quite complicated. For example, look at this modified example of the `replace()` method we were just looking at (`ch12_eg04.html`):

```
replace(/\bbad\b/gi, 'good');
```

There are four things going on in this Regular Expression; let's build up to this expression, starting with the letters `bad` that we want to replace:

- `/bad/` The forward slashes around the string `bad` indicate that it is looking for a match for that string.
- `/bad/g` The `g` after the second slash (known as a *flag*) indicates that the document is looking for a global match across the whole of the string (without the `g` flag, only the first match in the string is replaced).
- `/bad/gi` The `i` flag indicates that it should be a case-insensitive match (so the string `bad` should be replaced in any mix of characters in upper- and lowercase).
- `/\bbad\b/gi` The `\b` on either side of the string `bad` indicates a word boundary — each specifies that you just want to look for whole words — so the string will be replaced only if the string `bad` is a word on its own. The letters `bad` in the word `badge` would not be replaced because the regular expression says there should be a word boundary on both sides of the letters `bad`. (You cannot just check for the presence of a space on either side of the letters `bad`, because there might be punctuation next to one of the letters.)

Using Regular Expressions, you could also match more than one string using the pipestem character; the following example looks for a match with `bad`, `terrible`, or `awful`:

```
/bad|terrible|awful/
```

Note that if you want to search for any of the following characters, they must be escaped because they have special meanings in Regular Expressions:

```
\ | ( ) [ { ^ $ * + ? .
```

If you want to escape these characters, they must be preceded by a backslash (for example `/\ \ /` matches a backslash and `/\$/` matches a dollar sign).

The table that follows lists some other interesting characters used in regular expressions.

Expression	Meaning
`\n`	Linefeed
`\r`	Carriage return
`\t`	Tab
`\v`	Vertical tab
`\f`	Form-feed
`\d`	A digit (same as `[0-9]`, which means any digit 0 through 9)
`\D`	A non-digit (same as `[^0-9]` where ^ means not)
`\w`	A word (alphanumeric) character (same as `[a-zA-Z_0-9]`)
`\W`	A non-word character (same as `[^a-zA-Z_0-9]`)
`\s`	A white-space character (same as `[\t\v\n\r\f]`)
`\S`	A non–white-space character (same as `[^\t\v\n\r\f]`)

For a slightly more complex example, if you wanted to replace all carriage returns or linefeeds with the `<br />` tag, you could use the following (`ch12_eg05.html`):

```
replace(/\r|\n|\r\n|\n\r|/g),'<br />');"
```

In this case, the `replace()` method is looking for either linefeeds using `\n` or carriage returns using `\r`. Then these are being replaced with `<br />`. Figure 12-5 shows you what this example could look like with the carriage returns and line feeds replaced with `<br />` tags. If you needed to replace carriage returns or line feeds with the `<br />` element, it is more likely that task would be done behind the scenes when the form is submitted, rather that giving the user a button to replace these characters. But it does illustrate how to use the `replace()` function with a Regular Expression.

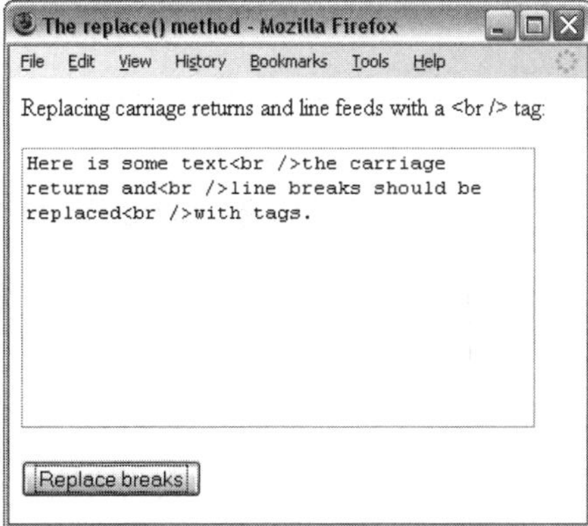

Figure 12-5

Testing Characters Using test() and Regular Expressions

Regular Expressions really come into their own when you need to test whether strings entered by users conform to a pattern. For example, Regular Expressions can be used to test whether the string follows a pattern for e-mail addresses, for an amount of currency, or for a phone number.

To check whether a value a user has entered matches a regular expression, you can use the `test()` method, which takes two parameters: the Regular Expression and the value the user entered. The `test()` method returns `true` if the value entered by the user matches the regular expression, and `false` if it does not.

Here is an example of a function that checks whether a user entered a currency (`ch12_eg06.html`). We will look at it line by line in a moment:

```
function validate(form) {
  var returnValue = true;
  var amountEntered = form.txtAmount.value;

  if (!/^\d+(\.\d{1,2})?$/.test(amountEntered))
  {
    alert("You did not enter an amount of money");
    document.frmCurrency.txtAmount.focus();
    returnValue = false;
  }

return returnValue;
}
```

To start, a variable called `returnValue` is set to `true`; this is what will be returned from the function unless we find an error. Then a variable is set to hold the value the user entered into the form:

```
  var returnValue = true;
  var amountEntered = form.txtAmount.value;
```

Next, we have to test whether the value the user entered is a currency. We will use the `test()` method with the following regular expression:

```
/^\d+(\.\d{1,2})?$/
```

The `test()` method is used inside an `if` statement; note that the first exclamation mark is there to say "If the test fails, perform an action":

```
if (!/^\d+(\.\d{1,2})?$/.test(amountEntered)){
```

If the test fails, we have to tell the user, give the focus back to that form control, and set the variable `returnValue` to have a value of `false`.

```
    alert("You did not enter an amount of money");
    document.frmCurrency.txtAmount.focus();
    returnValue = false;
```

Here is the simple form to test this example:

```
<form name="myForm" onsubmit="return validate(this);"
      action="money.aspx" method="get">
  Enter an amount of money here $
  <input type="text" name="txtAmount" id="txtAmount" size="7" />
  <input type="submit" value="Check format" />
</form>
```

Figure 12-6 shows this form in action.

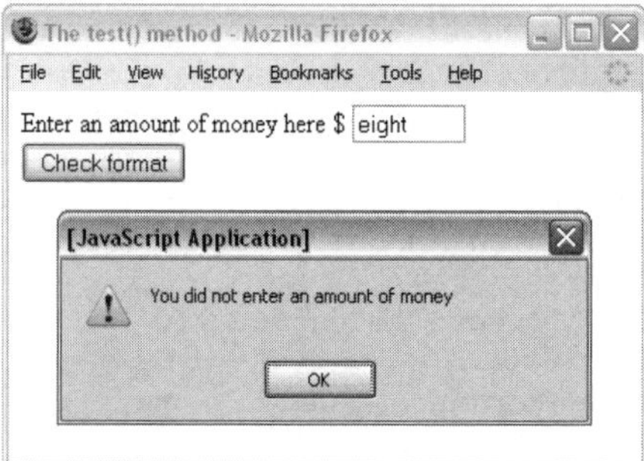

Figure 12-6

Regular Expressions are not the easiest thing to learn to write, and there are entire books devoted to writing complex expressions. However, the table that follows lists some helpful ones that you can use to get you started.

Test for	Description	Regular Expression
White space	No white-space characters.	`\S/;`
Alphabetic characters	No characters of the alphabet or the hyphen, period, or comma may appear in the string.	`/[^a-z \-\.']/gi;`
Alphanumeric characters	No letters or number may appear in the string.	`/[^a-z0-9]/gi;`
Credit card details	A 16-digit credit card number following the pattern XXXX XXXX XXXX XXXX.	`/^\d{4}([-]?\d{4}){3}$/;`
Decimal number	A number with a decimal place.	`/^\d+(\.\d+)?$/;`
Currency	A group of one or more digits followed by an optional group consisting of a decimal point plus one or two digits.	`/^\d+(\.\d\{1,2})?$/;`
E-mail address	An e-mail address.	`/^\w(\.?[\w-])*@\w(\.?[\w-])*\.[a-z]{2,6}(\.[a-z]{2})?$/i;`

Select Box Options

When you want to work with a drop-down select box, the `select` object (which represents the select box) has a very helpful property called `selectedIndex`, which tells you which option the user has selected.

Because this is an index, it will start at 0, so if the user has selected the first option, the `selectedIndex` property will have a value of `0`. If the user selects the second option, the `selectedIndex` property will be given a value of `1`, the third will be given a value of `2`, and so on.

By default, if the user does not change the value that the control has when the page loads, the value will be `0` for a standard select box (because the first option is automatically selected when the form loads). In a multiple select box (which allows users to select more than one option from the list), the default value will be `1` if none of the options are selected (which indicates that the user has not selected any option).

Look at the following simple select box; the first option in this select box asks the user to select a suit of cards (ch12_eg07.html):

```
<form name="frmCards" action="cards.aspx" method="get"
      onsubmit="return validate(this)">
  <select name="selCards" id="selCards">
    <option>Select a suit of cards</option>
    <option value="hearts">Hearts</option>
    <option value="diamonds">Diamonds</option>
    <option value="spades">Spades</option>
    <option value="clubs">Clubs</option>
  </select>
  <input type="submit" value="Send selection" />
</form>
```

Now, to check that one of the suits of cards has been selected, you have the `validate()` function, which will have been passed the `form` object as a parameter. In the case of this example, if the `selectedIndex` property of the object representing the select box has a value of `0`, then you have to alert the users that an option has not been selected and ask them to do so.

```
function validate(form) {
  var returnValue = true;
  var selectedOption = form.selCards.selectedIndex;
  if (selectedOption==0)
  {
    returnValue = false
    alert("Please select a suit of cards.");
  }
  return returnValue;
}
```

In Figure 12-7, you can see the warning if the user has not selected a suit of cards.

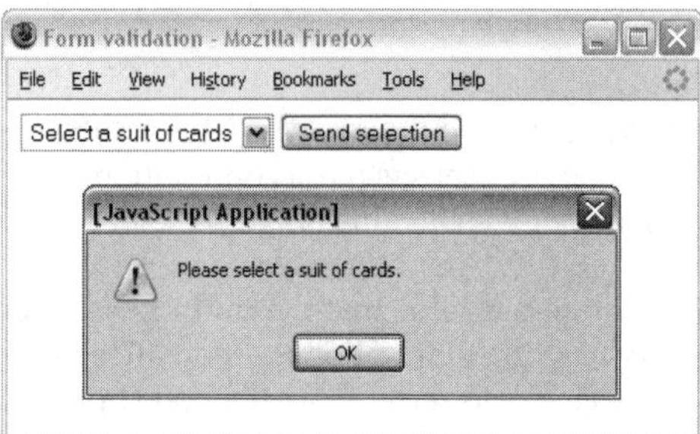

Figure 12-7

If you wanted to access the `value` attribute on the selected option (rather than its index number) you would use the following syntax:

```
form.selCards.options[selected].value
```

This is because you need to look at which of the [option] elements was selected to get its value rather than just the index number of the selected element.

Radio Buttons

A group of radio buttons is different from other form controls in that only one option from a group can be selected at a time, and all members of the group share a value for the name attribute. Scripts that interact with radio buttons usually want to either check that one of the options has been selected, or find out which of the options has been selected.

A set of radio buttons is represented as an array in JavaScript, and in order to find out which one was selected, you need to loop through the array, looking at the checked property of each radio button. If it is selected, the value will be true and false if not. For example, the following is a form with four radio buttons (ch12_eg08.html):

```
<form name="frmCards" action="cards.aspx" method="post"
      onsubmit="return validateForm(this)" >
  <p>Please select a suit of cards.</p>
  <p><input type="radio" name="radSuit" value="hearts" /> Hearts</p>
  <p><input type="radio" name="radSuit" value="diamonds" /> Diamonds</p>
  <p><input type="radio" name="radSuit" value="spades" /> Spades</p>
  <p><input type="radio" name="radSuit" value="clubs" /> Clubs</p>
  <p><input type="submit" value="Submit choice" /></p>
</form>
```

In order to loop through each of the radio buttons in the collection and see which one has a checked property, you will use a for loop.

The following function uses a variable I will call radioChosen to indicate whether one of the radio buttons has been chosen. Its value starts off as false, and if a button has been chosen the value is set to true. Once the loop has gone through each of the radio buttons, an if statement tests whether one of the options has been selected by looking at the value of this variable:

```
function validate(form) {
   var radioButtons = form.radSuit;
   var radioChosen = false;
   for (var i=0; i<radioButtons.length; i++) {
    if (radioButtons[i].checked)
     {
       radioChosen=true;
       returnValue=true;
     }
   }
   if (radioChosen == false) {
     returnValue = false;
     alert("You did not select a suit of cards");
   }
return returnValue;
}
```

While the order of attributes on an element should not matter in XHTML, there was a bug in Netscape 6 and some versions of Mozilla, which means it will show a `checked` property of the radio button only if the `type` attribute is the first attribute given on the `<input />` element.

You can see the result in Figure 12-8.

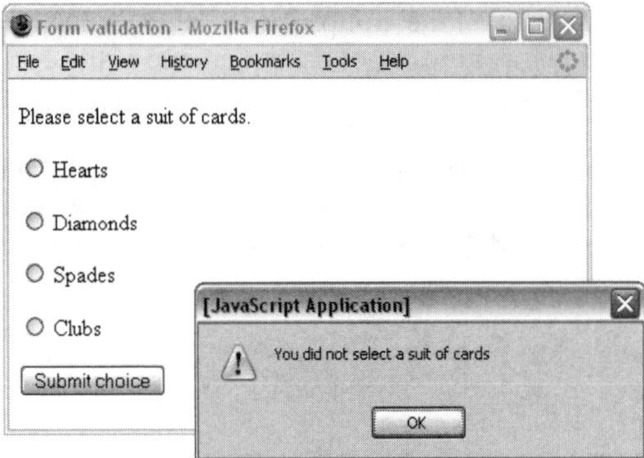

Figure 12-8

Another way to ensure that one of the options is selected is to preselect an option when the page loads.

Checkboxes

Checkboxes allow a user to select zero, one, or more items from a set of choices (they are not mutually exclusive as radio buttons are). As with radio buttons, when a group of checkboxes share the same name they are made available in JavaScript as an array.

The following is a slight change to the last example using checkboxes instead of radio buttons, and the user can select more than one suit of cards (`ch12_eg09.html`):

```
<form name="frmCards" action="cards.aspx" method="post">
  <p>Please select one or more suits of cards.</p>
  <p><input type="checkbox" name="chkSuit" value="hearts" /> Hearts</p>
  <p><input type="checkbox" name="chkSuit" value="diamonds" /> Diamonds</p>
  <p><input type="checkbox" name="chkSuit" value="spades" /> Spades</p>
  <p><input type="checkbox" name="chkSuit" value="clubs" /> Clubs</p>
  <p><input type="button" value="Count checkboxes"
      onclick="countCheckboxes(frmCards.chkSuit)" /></p>
</form>
```

The following is the function that counts how many checkboxes have been selected and displays that number to the user. As with the last example, if no checkboxes have been selected, you can alert the user that she must select an option value.

```
function countCheckboxes(field) {
  var intCount = 0
  for (var i = 0; i < field.length; i++) {
     if (field[i].checked)
         intCount++; }
  alert("You selected " + intCount + " checkbox(es)");
}
```

You can see the form in Figure 12-9 where the user has selected two checkboxes.

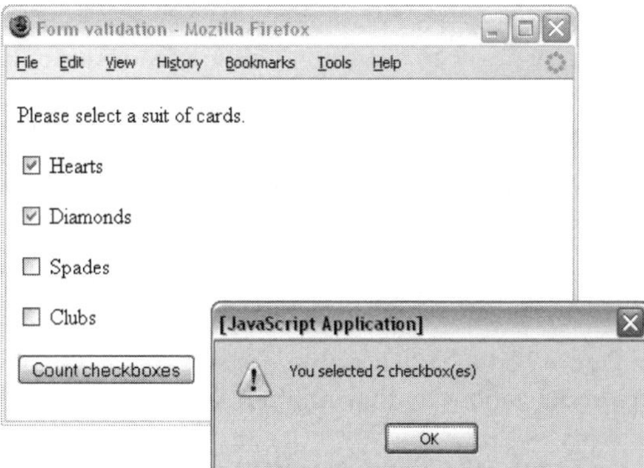

Figure 12-9

Preventing a Form Submission Until a Checkbox Has Been Selected

If you want to ensure that a single checkbox has been selected — for example, if you want a user to agree to certain terms and conditions — you can do so by adding a function to the `onsubmit` event handler similar to those you have seen already. The function checks whether the checkbox has been checked, and if the function returns `true` the form will be submitted. If the function returns `false`, the user would be prompted to check the box. The function might look like this (`ch12_eg10.html`):

```
function checkCheckBox(myForm){
  if (myForm.agree.checked == false )
  {
    alert('You must agree to terms and conditions to continue');
    return false;
  } else
    return true;
}
```

Another technique you may sometimes see is to use script to simply disable the Submit button until users have clicked the box to say that they agree with the terms and conditions.

If you use a script to disable a form control until a user has clicked on an option, you should disable the control in the script when the page loads rather than using the `disabled` *attribute on the element itself. This is important for those who do not have JavaScript enabled in their browsers. If you use the* `disabled` *attribute on a* `<form>` *element and users do not have JavaScript enabled, they will never be able to use that form control. However, if you have used a script to disable it when the page loads, then you know that the script will be able to re-enable the form control when the user clicks the appropriate box. This is a great reminder that JavaScript should be used to enhance usability of pages and should not be required in order to use a page.*

The following is a very simple page with a form. When the page loads, the Submit button is disabled in the `onload` event. If the user clicks the `chkAgree` checkbox, then the Submit button will be re-enabled (`ch12_eg10.html`):

```
<body onload="document.frmAgree.btnSubmit.disabled=true">
<form name="frmAgree" action="test.aspx" method="post">
I understand that this software has no liability:
<input type="checkbox" value="0" name="chkAgree" id="chkAgree"
       onclick="document.frmAgree.btnSubmit.disabled=false" />
<input type="submit" name="btnSubmit" value="Go to download" /><br />
<p>You will not be able to submit this form unless you agree to the
   <a href="terms.html">terms and conditions</a> and check the terms and
   conditions box.</p>
</form>
</body>
```

You can see this example in Figure 12-10. Note how there is an explanation of why the Submit button might be disabled. This helps users understand why they might not be able to click the Submit button.

This technique can also be used with other form controls — you will see an example that enables a text input later in the chapter.

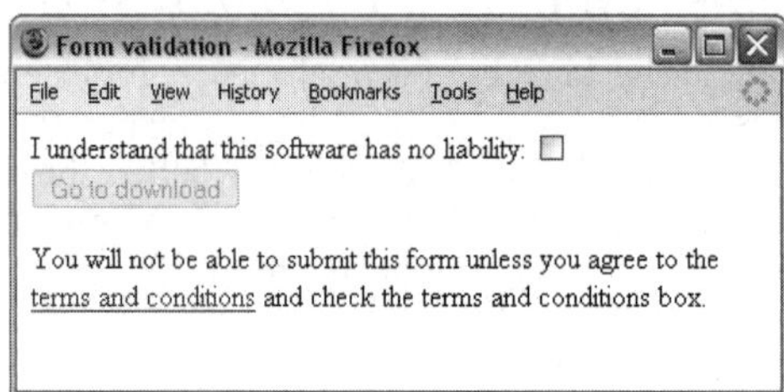

Figure 12-10

Form Enhancements

The examples you are going to meet in this section do not actually help you validate a form; rather, they simply enhance the usability of a form.

Focus on First Form Item

If a lot of users are likely to interact with your page using a form, you can give focus to that text box when the page loads so that users do not have to move their mouse, click the text input, and then move their hands back to the keyboard before they enter any text. You might choose to do this on a page where there is a prominent login box or an option to search your site.

To give focus to the first text input on a form, simply add an `onload` event handler to the `<body>` element of the document. This handler selects the form control that you want to highlight and uses the `focus()` method of that control to give it focus, as follows (`ch12_eg11.html`):

```
<body onload="document.myForm.myTextBox.focus();">
```

When the page loads, the cursor should be flashing in the form control that you have selected, ready for the user to enter some text as shown in Figure 12-11 (some browsers may also have other ways of indicating an active text box, such as a highlighted border or shaded background).

Note that the `onload` event fires when the complete page has loaded (not as soon as the browser loads that individual element). This is worth bearing in mind because, if you have a very complicated page that takes a long time to load, this might not be a great option for the user; the focus might not be passed to the form until after the user has already had a chance to start typing in that field.

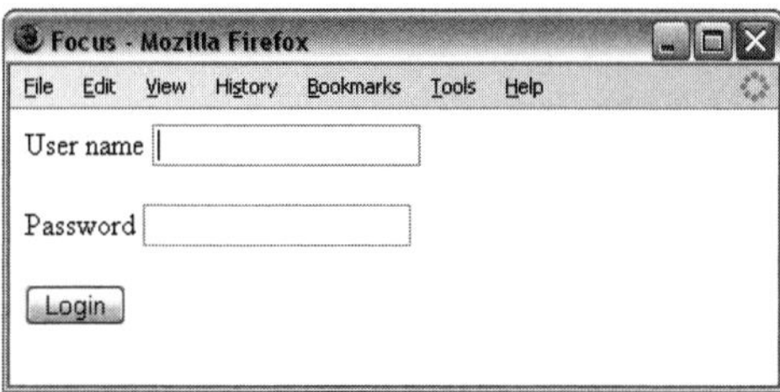

Figure 12-11

Auto-Tabbing Between Fields

The `focus()` method can also be used to pass the focus of one control to another control. For example, if one of the controls on a form is to provide a date of birth in MM/DD/YYYY format, then you can move focus between the three boxes as soon as the user enters a month, and then again once the user has entered a day (`ch12_eg12.html`):

```
<form name="frmDOB">
  Enter your date of birth:<br />
  <input name="txtMonth" id="txtMonth" size="3" maxlength="2"
       onkeyup="if(this.value.length>=2)
       this.form.txtDay.focus();"/>
  <input name="txtDay" id="txtDay" size="3" maxlength="2"
       onkeyup="if(this.value.length>=2)
       this.form.txtYear.focus();" />
  <input name="txtYear" id="txtYear" size="5" maxlength="4"
       onkeyup="if(this.value.length>=4)
       this.form.submit.focus();" />
  <input type="submit" name="submit" value="Send" />
</form>
```

This example uses the `onkeyup` event handler to check that the length of the text the user has entered is equal to or greater than the required number of characters for that field. If the user has entered the required number of characters, the focus is moved to the next box.

Note how the length of the text input is discovered using `this.value.length`. The `this` keyword indicates the current form control, whereas the `value` property indicates the value entered for the control. Then the `length` property returns the length of the value entered for the control. This is a quicker way of determining the length of the value in the current form control than the full path, which would be as follows:

```
document.fromDOB.txtMonth.value.length
```

The other advantage of using the `this` *keyword rather than the full path is that the code would work if you copied and pasted these controls into a different form, as you have not hard-coded the name of the form.*

You can see this example in Figure 12-12; the user has entered an appropriate number of digits in one field so the focus is moved on to the next.

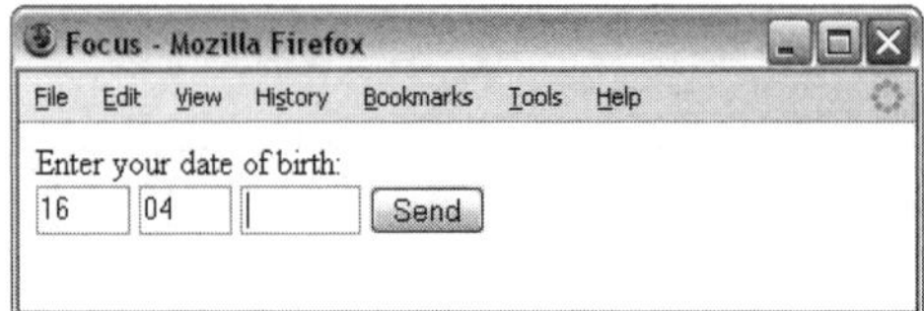

Figure 12-12

You might have noticed that the value of the `size` attribute is also one digit larger than the maximum length of the field to ensure that there is enough space for all of the characters (otherwise the width of the control can sometimes be slightly too small to see all of the characters at once).

If you use this technique, it is always worth testing the form on a few users to check if it is acting as an enhancement. This is important because some web users have become used to pressing the tab key very quickly after entering short numbers (such as individual components of dates of birth) to take them to the next form control.

I have also seen this technique used to allow users to enter their credit card details using four blocks of four codes. While 16 digits is the most common length for a credit card number, and they are often printed in blocks of 4 digits, some Visa cards, for example, contain 13 digits and some American Express cards use 15 digits. So this is not a good idea.

Disabling a Text Input

Sometimes you will want to disable a text input until a certain condition has been met — just as the Submit button was disabled until the user clicked the checkbox to agree to terms and conditions in Figure 12-10.

This example features a form that asks users how they heard about the site; radio buttons are used for several options such as Friend, TV ad, magazine ad, and Other. If the user selects the Other option, the text input next to that option allows the user to indicate how they heard about the site. You can see the form in Figure 12-13.

In this example, it's not just a case of enabling the text box when the user selects the other radio button; you really need to check the value of each radio button as it is selected — after all, if the user selects Other as his or her first choice, but then changes her mind and selects TV or one of the other options, you will want to disable the text input and change its value again. Therefore, each time the user selects a radio button, a function in the head of the document is called that is responsible for enabling and disabling the control and setting values.

Figure 12-13

First, here is the form that gives users the options (`ch12_eg13.html`). Note how the text input is disabled using the `onload` event handler of the `<body>` element and that the text input does not use the `disabled` attribute (this is the same as the earlier example with the Submit button).

```
<body onload="document.frmReferrer.txtOther.disabled=true;
              document.frmReferrer.txtOther.value='not applicable' ">
<h2>How did you hear about us?</h2>
<form name="frmReferrer">
  <input type="radio" name="radHear" value="1"
         onclick="handleOther(this.value);" />From a friend<br />
  <input type="radio" name="radHear" value="2"
         onclick="handleOther(this.value);" />TV Ad<br />
  <input type="radio" name="radHear" value="3"
         onclick="handleOther(this.value);" />Magazine Ad<br />
  <input type="radio" name="radHear" value="4"
         onclick="handleOther(this.value);" />Newspaper Ad<br />
  <input type="radio" name="radHear" value="5"
         onclick="handleOther(this.value);" />Internet<br />
  <input type="radio" name="radHear" value="other"
         onclick="handleOther(this.value);" />Other... Please specify:
  <input type="text" name="txtOther" />
</form>
```

As you can see from this form, every time the user selects one of the options on this form, the `onclick` event calls a function called `handleOther()`. This function is passed the value of the form control as a parameter.

Looking at the function, you can see a simple `if...else` statement that checks whether the value of the selected form control is equal to the text `other` (remember that checking whether one value is equal to another value uses two equal signs because the single equal sign is used to set a variable). If the value of the selected radio button is "other," the textbox's `disabled` property is set to `false`, and the value cleared. For all other options the textbox is disabled and its value set to `not applicable`.

```
function handleOther(strRadio) {
  if (strRadio == "other") {
    document.frmReferrer.txtOther.disabled = false;
    document.frmReferrer.txtOther.value = '';
  }
  else {
    document.frmReferrer.txtOther.disabled = true;
    document.frmReferrer.txtOther.value = 'not applicable';
  }
}
```

Case Conversion

There are times when it is helpful to change the case of text a user has entered to make it all uppercase or all lowercase — in particular because JavaScript is case-sensitive. To change the case of text, there are two built-in methods of JavaScript's `string` object:

- `toLowerCase()`
- `toUpperCase()`

To demonstrate, here is an example of a text input that changes case as focus moves away from the text input (`ch12_eg14.html`):

```
<form>
  <input type="text" name="case" size="20"
         onblur="this.value=this.value.toLowerCase();" />
</form>
```

If your form data is being sent to a server, it is generally considered better practice to make these changes on the server because they are less distracting for users — a form that changes letter case as you use it can appear a little odd to users.

Trimming Spaces from Beginning and End of Fields

You might want to remove spaces (white space) from the beginning or end of a form field for many reasons, even simply because the user did not intend to enter it there. The technique I will demonstrate here uses the `substring()` method of the `String` object, whose syntax is:

```
substring(startPosition, endPosition)
```

This method returns the part of the string specified by the start and end points — if no end position is given, then the default is the end of the string. The start and end positions are zero-based, so the first character is 0. For example, if you have a string that says `Welcome`, then the method `substring(0, 1)` returns the letter `W`.

First we will look at removing white space from the start of a string. To do this the `substring()` method will be called upon twice. First you use the `substring()` method to retrieve the first letter that the user has entered into a text control. If this character is a space, you can then call the `substring()` method a second time to remove the space.

So the first call to the `substring()` goes in a `while` loop like so:

```
while (this.value.substring(0,1) == ' ')
```

The second time the `substring()` method is called, it selects the value of the control from the second character to the end of the string (ignoring the first character). This is set to be the new value for the form control; so you have removed the first character, which was a space:

```
this.value = this.value.substring(1, this.value.length);
```

This whole process of checking whether the first character is a blank, and then removing it if it is, will be called using the `onblur` event handler; so when focus moves away from the form control, the process starts. Here you can see the entire process using the `while` loop to indicate that, for as long as the first character is a blank, it should be removed using the second call to the `substring()` method (`ch12_eg15.html`).

```
<form>
  <input type="text" name="txtName" size="100"
    value=" Enter text leaving whitespace at start. Then change focus."
    onblur="while (this.value.substring(0,1) == ' ')
    this.value = this.value.substring(1, this.value.length);" /><br />
</form>
```

To trim any trailing spaces, the process is similar but reversed. The first `substring()` method collects the last character of the string, and if it is blank removes it, as follows:

```
<form>
<input type="text" name="txtName" size="100"
       value="Enter text leaving whitespace at end. Then change focus. "
       onblur="while (this.value.substring
           (this.value.length-1,this.value.length) == ' ')
           this.value = this.value.substring(0, this.value.length-1);" /><br/>
</form>
```

As long as you are not targeting browsers as old as Netscape 4 and IE4, you can alternatively use a Regular Expression to trim the spaces, as follows:

```
<form>
  <input type="text" name="removeLeadingAndTrailingSpace" size="100"
    value=" Enter text with white space, then change focus. "
    onblur="this.value=this.value.replace(/^\ \s+/, '').replace(/\s+$/,'');"
  /><br />
</form>
```

This removes both trailing and leading spaces.

Regular Expressions are quite a large topic in themselves and were introduced earlier in this chapter. If you want to learn more about them, refer to *Beginning JavaScript, 2nd Edition* by Paul Wilton (Wrox, 2000).

Selecting All the Content of a Text Area

If you want to allow users to select the entire contents of a text area (so they don't have to manually select all the text with the mouse), you can use the `focus()` and `select()` methods.

In this example, the `selectAll()` function takes one parameter — the form control that you want to select the content of (`ch12_eg16.html`):

```
<html>
<head><title>Select whole text area</title>
<script language="JavaScript">
  function selectAll(strControl) {
    strControl.focus();
    strControl.select();
  }
</script>
</head>
<body>
  <form name="myForm">
    <textarea name="myTextArea" rows="5" cols="20">This is some
text</textarea>
    <input type="button" name="btnSelectAll" value="Select all"
           onclick="selectAll(document.myForm.myTextArea);" />
  </form>
</body>
</head>
</html>
```

The button that allows the user to select all has an `onclick` event handler to call the `selectAll()` function and tell it which control it is whose contents should be selected.

The `selectAll()` function first gives that form control focus using the `focus()` method and then selects its content using the `select()` method, because the form control must gain focus before it can have its content selected. The same method would also work on a single-line text input and a password field.

Check and Uncheck All Checkboxes

If there are several checkboxes in a group of checkboxes, it can be helpful to allow users to select or clear a whole group of checkboxes at once. The following are two functions that allow precisely this:

```
function check(field) {
  for (var i = 0; i < field.length; i++) {
    field[i].checked = true;}
}
function uncheck(field) {
  for (var i = 0; i < field.length; i++) {
    field[i].checked = false; }
}
```

In order for these functions to work, more than one checkbox must be in the group. You then add two buttons that call the check or uncheck functions, passing in the array of checkbox elements that share the same, name such as the following (`ch12_eg17.html`):

```
<form name="frmSnacks" action="">
   Your basket order<br />
   <input type="checkbox" name="basketItem" value="1" />Chocolate
   cookies<br />
   <input type="checkbox" name="basketItem" value="2" />Potato chips<br />
   <input type="checkbox" name="basketItem" value="3" />Cola<br />
   <input type="checkbox" name="basketItem" value="4" />Cheese<br />
   <input type="checkbox" name="basketItem" value="5" />Candy bar<br /><br
/>
   <input type="button" value="Select All"
          onclick="check(document.frmSnacks.basketItem);" />

   <input type="button" value="Deselect All"
          onclick="uncheck(document.frmSnacks.basketItem);" />
</form>
```

You can see how this form appears in Figure 12-14.

Figure 12-14

This could also be combined into a single function, which could be called from the same button, such as the following:

```
function checkUncheckAll(field) {
 var theForm = field.form, i = 0;
 for(i=0; i<theForm.length;i++){
   if(theForm[i].type == 'checkbox' && theForm[i].name != 'checkall'){
   theForm[i].checked = field.checked;
   }
  }
}
```

Try It Out An E-mail Form

Having seen lots of examples of how to work with forms, it is time to try to put some of these techniques together. In this exercise you are going to create an e-mail form that has a few interesting features. It checks that all fields have an entry of some kind, and uses a Regular Expression to check the structure of an e-mail address. The form also includes a quick address book that contains addresses of potential recipients of the e-mail. Figure 12-15 shows you what the form is going to look like.

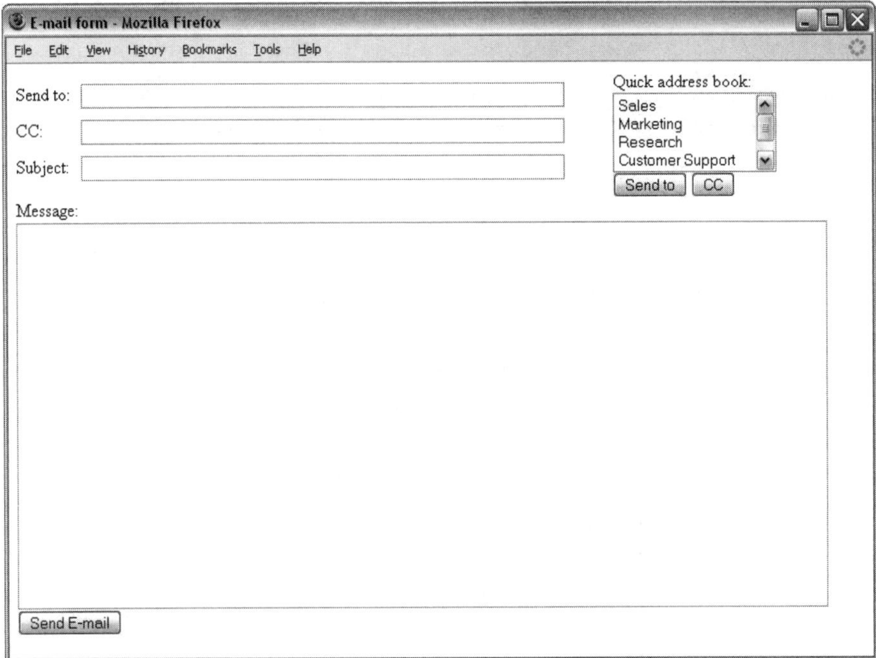

Figure 12-15

1. Create a skeleton XHTML document with <head>, <title>, and <body> elements.

```
<?xml version="1.0" encoding="UTF-8"?>
<!DOCTYPE html PUBLIC "-//W3C//DTD XHTML 1.0 Transitional//EN"
    "http://www.w3.org/TR/xhtml1/DTD/xhtml1-transitional.dtd">
<html xmlns="http://www.w3.org/1999/xhtml" lang="en">
<head>
  <title>E-mail form</title>
</head>
<body>
  </body>
</html>
```

2. In the body of the document, add the <form> element and two <div> elements. The first <div> holds the To, CC, and Subject fields, while the second holds the quick address. Note

how there is an empty <span> element next to the form controls; this will hold any error messages.

```
<form name="frmEmail" onsubmit="return validate(this)" action="success.html"
      method ="post">
  <div id="toCCsubject">

    <label>Send to:</label>
    <input type="text" size="50" name="txtTo" id="txtTo" /><span
      class="error"></span>

    <label>CC:</label>
    <input type="text" size="50" name="txtCC" id="txtCC" /><span
       class="error"></span>

    <label>Subject:</label>
    <input type="text" size="50" name="txtSubject" id="txtSubject" /><span
      class="error"></span>

  </div>
  <div id="addressBook">
    <! – quick address book will go here – ></td>
  </div>
```

3. Next you need to add the quick address book into the second <div> element. The address book uses a multiple-line select box. Underneath it are two buttons: one to add addresses to the `txtTo` field and one to add addresses to the `txtCC` field. Both of these buttons call the `add()` function when clicked:

```
Quick address book:<br />
<select size="4" name="selectList1" style="width:150px">
  <option value="sales@example.org">Sales</option>
  <option value="marketing@example.org">Marketing</option>
  <option value="research@example.org">Research</option>
  <option value="support@example.org">Customer Support</option>
  <option value="it@example.org">IT</option>
</select><br />
<input type="button" onclick="add(txtTo, document.frmEmail.selectList1);"
       value="Send to" />
<input type="button" onclick="add(txtCC, document.frmEmail.selectList1);"
       value="CC" />
```

4. Add the message <textarea> element and a `Send E-mail` button (and close the </form> element):

```
<div class="message">
  Message:<br />
  <textarea name="txtMessage" rows="20" cols="115"></textarea><br />
  <input type="submit" value="Send E-mail" />
</div>
</form>
```

5. Now that the form itself is complete, we can start to look at the script. The `add()` function adds e-mail addresses from the address book into the To or CC fields (if there is already an address in there, the semicolon is added to separate out multiple addresses).

   The `add()` function takes two parameters:

   - `objInput`: The field that the selected address is being sent to
   - `objList`: The select box list that contains the e-mail addresses

   This function starts by collecting the value of the selected item, using the `selectedIndex` property of the select box, and placing it in a variable called `strGroup`. Next it checks whether the form field the address is being added to is empty; if it is, the e-mail address stored in the `strGroup` attribute is added to the field. If the `To` or `CC` field is not empty, a semicolon and a space will be added before the e-mail address because this is the usual delimiter for multiple e-mail addresses:

```
function add(objInput, objList){
var strGroup = objList.options[objList.selectedIndex].value;
  if (objInput.value == "")
  {
     objInput.value = strGroup
  }
  else
  {
     objInput.value += ('; ' + strGroup)
  }
}
```

6. Now, let's add the second function — the `validate()` function, which you can see is quite long:

```
function validate(form) {

  var returnValue = true;
  var sendTo = form.txtTo.value;
  var cc = form.txtCC.value;
  var subject = form.txtSubject.value;
  var message = form.txtMessage.value;
  var rxEmail=/^\w(\.?[\w-])*@\w(\.?[\w-])*\.[a-z]{2,6}(\.[a-z]{2})?$/i;

  document.getElementById("txtTo").nextSibling.innerHTML="";

  if (sendTo == "")  {
    returnValue = false;
      document.getElementById("txtTo").nextSibling.innerHTML=
        "There are no email addresses in the To field";
    document.getElementById("txtTo").focus();
  }
  else {
    var arrTo = sendTo.split("; ");
```

```
    for (var i=0; i<(arrTo.length); i++) {
      if (!rxEmail.test(arrTo[i]))
      {
        returnValue = false;
        document.getElementById("txtTo").nextSibling.innerHTML=
          "The e-mail address(es) provided does not appear to be valid";
        document.getElementById("txtTo").focus();
      }
    }
  }


  document.getElementById("txtCC").nextSibling.innerHTML="";
  if (sendTo != "")
  {
    var arrCC = cc.split("; ");
    document.getElementById("txtCC").nextSibling.innerHTML="";

    for (var i=0; i<(arrCC.length); i++) {
      if (!rxEmail.test(arrCC[i]))
        {
          returnValue = false;
          document.getElementById("txtCC").nextSibling.innerHTML=
            "The e-mail address(es) provided does not appear to be valid";
          document.getElementById("txtCC").focus();
        }
      }
    }

  document.getElementById("txtSubject").nextSibling.innerHTML="";
  if (subject == "")
  {
    returnValue = false;
      document.getElementById("txtSubject").nextSibling.innerHTML=
        "There is no subject line for this e-mail";
      document.getElementById("txtSubject").focus();
  }

  document.getElementById("txtMessage").nextSibling.innerHTML="";
  if (message=="")
  {
    returnValue = false;
      document.getElementById("txtMessage").nextSibling.innerHTML=
        "There is no message for this e-mail";
      document.getElementById("txtMessage").focus();
  }


return returnValue;
}
```

The `validate()` function is quite a bit more complex, so let's break it down and look at it step by step. It starts off by setting a `returnValue` variable to `true` and collecting the form's values into variables:

```
function validate(form) {
  var returnValue = true;
  var sendTo = form.txtTo.value;
  var cc = form.txtCC.value;
  var subject = form.txtSubject.value;
  var message = form.txtMessage.value;
  var rxEmail=/^\w(\.?[\w-])*@\w(\.?[\w-])*\.[a-z]{2,6}(\.[a-z]{2})?$/i;
```

The first task for the validate form is to check whether the user has entered an e-mail into the To field, and if so check that the e-mail address is valid. Since we will be writing any errors into the `<span>` elements that follow the form fields, we need to empty any content from the `<span>` element that follows the To field (because we are about to recheck the values the user has entered, and if the user has corrected an earlier mistake we do not want to leave an error message there).

The real checks appear in an `if ... else` statement; it then checks whether the user has entered a value into the To field. If there is no value, it sets the `returnValue` attribute to `false`, adds an error into the `<span>` element following the field, and passes focus to the To field.

```
if (sendTo == "")  {
    returnValue = false;
    document.getElementById("txtTo").nextSibling.innerHTML="There are no email
    addresses in the To field";
    document.getElementById("txtTo").focus();
  }
```

The `validate` function gets more interesting when it comes to checking that valid e-mail addresses have been entered into the form. The Regular Expression that's used to check the e-mail addresses was stored in a variable at the top of the page — this time called `rxEmail`:

```
var rxEmail=/^\w(\.?[\w-])*@\w(\.?[\w-])*\.[a-z]{2,6}(\.[a-z]{2})?$/i;
```

In order to check that the e-mail addresses entered are valid, the `To` field gets split into an array using the `split()` method of the `String` object. This function will take a string and split it into separate values whenever it comes across a specified character or set of characters. In this case, the method looks for any instances of a semicolon followed by a space, and wherever it finds these it creates a new item in the array.

```
var arrTo = sendTo.split("; ");
```

Imagine having the following e-mail addresses (note that this is just to illustrate the `split()` method; it is not part of the code):

```
sales@example.com; accounts@example.com; marketing@example.com
```

These would be split into the following array (again, this is not part of the code from the example):

```
arrTo[0] = "sales@example.com"
arrTo[1] = "accounts@example.com"
arrTo[2] = "marketing@example.com"
```

So now there has to be a `for` loop in the code that will go through each e-mail address in the array and check that it follows the pattern described in the Regular Expression. The `for` loop has three parameters; the first sets a counter called `i` to be `0`, checks that the counter is less than the number of items in the array, and finally increments the counter. Inside the loop is an `if` statement that checks whether the e-mail address matches the Regular Expression using the `test()` method; if it does not, it will set the `returnValue` to `false` and add a message to the page to indicate that the value does not seem to be a valid e-mail address:

```
for (var i=0; i<(arrTo.length); i++) {
      if (!rxEmail.test(arrTo[i]))
      {
        returnValue = false;
        document.getElementById("txtTo").nextSibling.innerHTML="The e-mail
        address(es) provided does not appear to be valid";
        document.getElementById("txtTo").focus();
      }
    }
```

After this, you can see a similar setup for the CC field:

```
document.getElementById("txtCC").nextSibling.innerHTML="";
if (sendTo != "")
{
  var arrCC = cc.split("; ");
  document.getElementById("txtCC").nextSibling.innerHTML="";

  for (var i=0; i<(arrCC.length); i++) {
    if (!rxEmail.test(arrCC[i]))
      {
        returnValue = false;
        document.getElementById("txtCC").nextSibling.innerHTML=
          "The e-mail address(es) provided does not appear to be valid";
        document.getElementById("txtCC").focus();
      }
    }
  }
```

The last checks ensure that something was entered into the subject and message inputs:

```
document.getElementById("txtSubject").nextSibling.innerHTML="";
  if (subject == "")
  {
    returnValue = false;
      document.getElementById("txtSubject").nextSibling.innerHTML=
        "There is no subject line for this e-mail";
    document.getElementById("txtSubject").focus();
```

```
    }

    document.getElementById("txtMessage").nextSibling.innerHTML="";
    if (message=="")
    {
      returnValue = false;
        document.getElementById("txtMessage").nextSibling.innerHTML=
          "There is no message for this e-mail";
      document.getElementById("txtMessage").focus();
    }
```

Finally we return the `returnValue` attribute to indicate whether the form can be submitted.

```
  return returnValue;
  }
```

7. Save the file as `emailform.html`, and when you open it in the browser window it should resemble the example you saw in Figure 12-15.

Now you have an example of a form that has more than one function. It uses JavaScript to create a quick address book and validates the entries to stop the user from trying to send an e-mail address that is not valid.

JavaScript Libraries

The examples you have seen so far in this chapter have been designed to give you a better understanding of how JavaScript can be integrated into your XHTML documents — how events (such as a user hovering over, or clicking on, an element) can be used to trigger JavaScript functions.

In the case of the form validation script, you have seen an example of how to include an external JavaScript into a page with one line of code, and how the functionality of that script can be used in multiple web pages. This demonstrated that if you write a script carefully, once the work has been done, you can use it again and again in other pages with minimum effort.

JavaScript files that contain functions that you want to use in several pages are often referred to as *JavaScript libraries* (because, once you have included the file in your page, you can borrow its functionality).

In this section, you are going to meet several scripts that offer functionality you might want to use in several of your web pages. For example, you will see how to create:

- Animated effects and drag-and-drop lists
- Lightboxes and modal windows
- Sortable tables
- Calendar controls
- Auto-completing text inputs

Each of these example scripts is built on top of a one of the major JavaScript libraries that you will see used again and again if you explore other examples on the Web. So, the examples you meet in this chapter are built upon:

- Scriptaculous (which is actually built on top of another JavaScript library called Prototype)
- JQuery
- MochiKit
- Yahoo User Interface (YUI)

While you will meet several helpful scripts before the end of this chapter, the real purpose of this section is to illustrate how you can easily integrate this type of JavaScript code (that someone else has written) into your pages to offer complex functionality with minimum effort.

I have included versions of each of these libraries with the code download for this chapter. If you look in the code folder for Chapter 12, you will see inside the scripts folder that there are folders called `scriptaculous`, `mochikit`, *and* `yui` *(each folder corresponding to the three libraries you will be using). It is worth, however, checking the web sites for each of these libraries as they may have been updated since this book was written.*

Animated Effects Using Scriptaculous

To start with, I am going to show you some basic animation effects that can be created using a JavaScript library called Scriptaculous, which is built on top of another JavaScript library called Prototype. I have included a copy of Scriptaculous 1.8.2 and Prototype 1.6.0 with the code download for this chapter; however, you can check for more recent versions and download your own copy of these files from `http://script.aculo.us/`.

Scriptaculous can help you with many kinds of tasks: animation, adding drag-and-drop functionality, building editing tools, and creating autocompleting text inputs. It also includes utilities to help create DOM fragments. But in this section, you will just focus on some of the animation effects. (You will see examples of drag-and-drop and autocompleting text inputs later in the chapter.)

Scriptaculous contains many functions that help you create different types of animations. The first example is going to feature four of these animated effects, and it will demonstrate how easily you can add powerful features into your page with very little code. You can see what this page will look like in Figure 12-16, although you really need to try the example to see the actual animation by opening `ch12_eg18.html` in your browser.

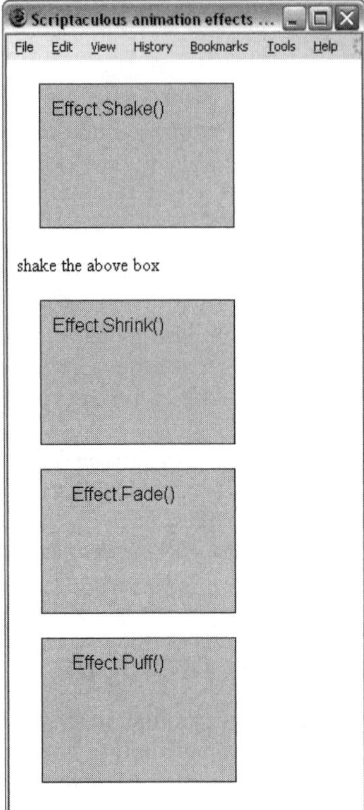

Figure 12-16

As you may remember from the last chapter, JavaScript programmers use objects to represent real life objects or concepts. In the case of the Scriptaculous library, the animated effects are handled by an object called `Effect`. There are different types of effects, which are each called using different methods. For example, to create a shaking effect you need to call the `Shake()` method of the `Effect` object. To create a fading effect you use the `Fade()` method of the `Effect` object. Some of these methods can take different parameters that allow you to vary how the effect works.

In order to use the animated effects and other features of the Scriptaculous library, you need to add both the `prototype.js` library and the `scriptaculous.js` library, which I have placed in a folder called `scriptaculous`:

```
<script src="scripts/scriptaculous/prototype.js"
  type="text/javascript"></script>
<script src="scripts/scriptaculous/scriptaculous.js"
   type="text/javascript"></script>
```

In the body of the page, there is a box to demonstrate each effect; when you click on the box, the effect is triggered. Each box is created using a `<div>` element, inside which I have written the name of the `Effect` object and the method that box will demonstrate. Let's start by looking at the first box, which demonstrates the shake effect:

```
<div id="effect-shake" onclick="Effect.Shake(this)">
  Effect.Shake()
</div>
```

As you already know, the event attributes allow events to trigger JavaScripts. In this example, the `onclick` event causes the `Effect` object's `Shake()` method to be called. As with the forms you looked at earlier, the keyword `this` (which you can see inside the parentheses of the `Shake()` method) indicates that we want to create a shake animation for this element.

If you wanted the effect to be triggered by the user interacting with a different element, you could pass the `Shake()` method the `id` of the box you want to shake. For example, here is a simple link; when the user clicks on the words "shake the above box," the first box will shake.

```
<a onclick="Effect.Shake('effect-shake')">
  shake the above box
</a>
```

Let's look at the second example, which shrinks the box when you click on it until it vanishes. It is very similar but this time we are calling the `Shrink()` method of the `Effect` object.

```
<div id="demo-effect-shrink" onclick="Effect.Shrink(this);">
    Effect.Shrink
</div>
```

Because the box disappears once it has shrunk, you can call the `Appear()` method of the `Effect` object to make it re-appear. You cannot call this method right away; otherwise, you will not be able to see the effect working, so you can call this method after a set period using the `setTimeout()` method of the `window` object (this is a JavaScript object, not one created by one of the JavaScript libraries). In this case, the `Appear()` method is called after 2500 milliseconds.

```
<div id="demo-effect-shrink" onclick="Effect.Shrink(this);
window.setTimeout('Effect.Appear(\'effect-shrink\')',2500);">
```

Here are the other two effects:

```
<div id="effect-fade" onclick="Effect.Fade(this);
    window.setTimeout('Effect.Appear(\'effect-fade\')',2500);">
      Effect.Fade()
</div>

<div id="effect-puff" onclick="Effect.Puff(this);
    window.setTimeout('Effect.Appear(\'effect-puff\')',2500);">
      Effect.Puff()
</div>
```

You do not need to know *how* the Script creates these effects; all you need to know is the syntax of the method that calls each effect.

As you can see, this is a very simple way of creating animated effects using JavaScript; one that lots of other scripts make use of.

Drag-and-Drop Sortable Lists Using Scriptaculous

Having seen how simple it is to create some animations using Scriptaculous, let's have a look at an example of something you might want to do in a user interface: create drag-and-drop lists. You may have seen some sites where you can re-order lists (such as "to do" lists or top 10 lists) just by dragging and dropping the elements.

You can see the example you are going to build in Figure 12-17; when the page loaded, the boxes were in numerical order. However, they have now been dragged and dropped to a different order.

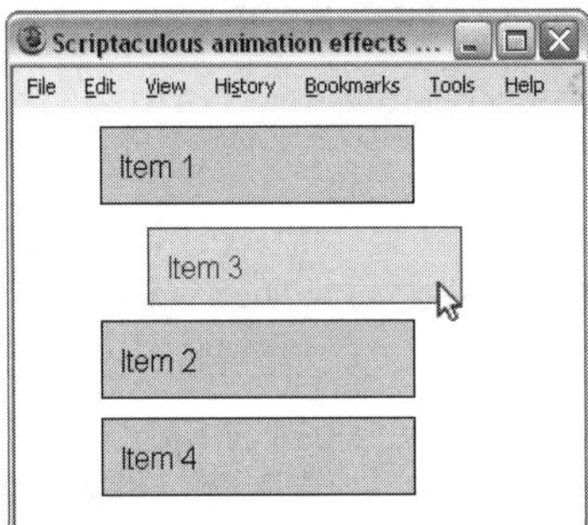

Figure 12-17

In this example (`ch12_eg19.html`), you need to include the Scriptaculous and Prototype libraries again. Then you have a simple unordered list (there are some CSS rules in the head of the document that control the presentation of the list to make each list item appear in its own box).

```
<script src="scripts/prototype.js" type="text/javascript"></script>
<script src="scripts/scriptaculous.js" type="text/javascript"></script>
<style type="text/css">
  li {border;1px solid #000000; padding:10px; margin-top:10px;
  font-family:arial, verdana, sans-serif;background-color:#d6d6d6;
  list-style-type:none; width:150px;}
</style>
</head>
<body>
<ul id="items_list">
   <li id="item_1">Item 1</li>
   <li id="item_2">Item 2</li>
   <li id="item_3">Item 3</li>
   <li id="item_4">Item 4</li>
</ul>
```

In order to make this list sortable, you just need to add one `<script>` element after the list:

```
<script type="text/javascript" language="javascript">
   Sortable.create("items_list",{dropOnEmpty:true,constraint:false});
</script>
```

Here you are using the `Sortable` object that is part of the Scriptaculous library, and calling its `create()` method to turn the list into a sortable one. The `create()` method takes two parameters:

- The first is the value for the `id` attribute of the unordered list element, in this case `items_list`.
- The second features options that describe how the sortable list should work. The first of the options specified here is `dropOnEmpty` with a value of `true` to indicate that element should only be dropped between elements, not on top of another one, and the `constraint` property, which is set to `false`. (If this were left off or `true` it would allow items to be moved along a vertical axis only, whereas set to `false` you can move the list items to the left or right while dragging them).

This kind of drag-and-drop list is often linked to some kind of functionality that will update a database (such as allowing users to re-order a "to do" or preference list), which would involve a script on the server written in a language such as ASP.NET or PHP code. However, this example does demonstrate something that is achieved very easily with just a few lines of code, thanks to the Scriptaculous library.

Creating a Lightbox

A lightbox is the term given to an image (or set of images) that opens up in the foreground of the browser without reloading the page. The image appears in the middle of the browser window, and the rest of the page is often dulled out. Figure 12-18 shows an example of a lightbox activated on a page (`ch12_eg20.html`).

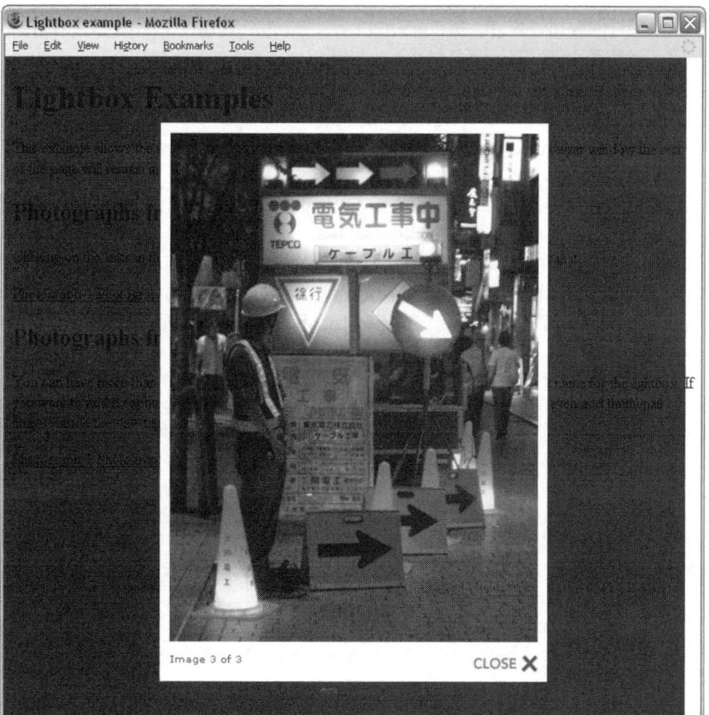

Figure 12-18

The script we will be looking at in this section is called Lightbox2, and was written by Lokesh Dhakar. It is based on the Prototype and Scriptaculous libraries so we will include them as well as the lightbox script.

So, to create a lightbox, first you add in the following three scripts (`ch12_eg20.html`):

```
<script type="text/javascript" src="scripts/scriptaculous/prototype.js">
</script>
<script type="text/javascript"
    src="scripts/scriptaculous/scriptaculous.js?load=effects,builder"></
script>
<script type="text/javascript" src="scripts/lightbox.js"></script>
```

There are also some CSS styles that are used in the lightbox, so you can either link to this style sheet or include the rules from it in your own style sheet:

```
<link rel="stylesheet" href="css/lightbox.css" type="text/css"
    media="screen" />
```

Finally, you create a link to each of the images in the lightbox; here you can see a lightbox that contains three images:

```
<a href="images/image-1.jpg" rel="lightbox[Japan]">Picture 1</a>
<a href="images/image-2.jpg" rel="lightbox[Japan]">Picture 2</a>
<a href="images/image-3.jpg" rel="lightbox[Japan]">Picture 3</a>
```

Note the use of the `rel` attribute on the links; this uses the keyword `lightbox`, followed by a name for the `lightbox` in square brackets. This lightbox is called `Japan`.

Inside the link, you can have anything. There is just some simple text in this example, although you could include a thumbnail image to represent each of the larger images.

You do not have to indicate the size of the image, as the script will automatically determine this and resize the lightbox to fit the image.

You can also have multiple lightboxes on the same page as long as you give each lightbox a different name; here you can see a second lightbox added with photographs from Paris:

```
<h1>Images from Japan</h1>
<a href="images/Japan1.jpg" rel="lightbox[Japan]">Picture 1</a>
<a href="images/Japan2.jpg" rel="lightbox[Japan]">Picture 2</a>
<a href="images/Japan3.jpg" rel="lightbox[Japan]">Picture 3</a>
<h1>Images from Paris</h1>
<a href="images/Paris1.jpg" rel="lightbox[Paris]">Picture 1</a>
<a href="images/Paris2.jpg" rel="lightbox[Paris]">Picture 2</a>
<a href="images/Paris3.jpg" rel="lightbox[Paris]">Picture 3</a>
```

This is just one of many examples of lightbox scripts you would find if you searched for a lightbox script (other popular examples include Thickbox, Fancybox, and JQuery Lightbox).

This is a similar technique you may have seen used to create modal dialog boxes.

Creating a Modal Window

A modal window is a "child" window that you have to interact with before you can go back to the main window. You have probably seen modal windows on web sites you have visited; they are often used for login or contact forms, and their appearance is similar to the lightbox that you just saw (with a grayed-out page). You can see the example we are going to create in Figure 12-19.

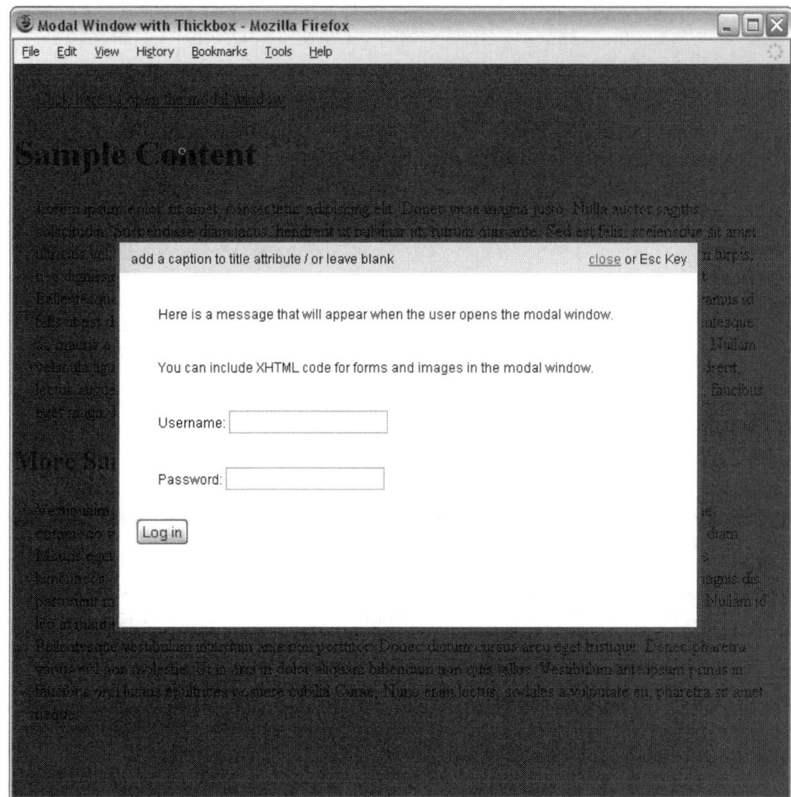

Figure 12-19

The example of a modal window we will look at uses a script called Thickbox written by Cody Lindley; this example is built on another of the main JavaScript libraries called JQuery.

To re-create this example, first you need to include the JQuery library along with the Thickbox script and style sheet in the head of your document like so (`ch12_eg21.html`):

```
<script type="text/javascript"
    src="scripts/jquery/jquery-1.3.2.js"></script>
<script type="text/javascript" src="scripts/thickbox/thickbox.js"></script>
<link rel="stylesheet" href="scripts/thickbox/thickbox.css"
    type="text/css" media="screen" />
```

Next, you can write the content that you want to appear in the modal window:

```
<div id="myOnPageContent"><p>
  Here is a message that will appear when the user opens the modal window.
</p></div>
```

You do not want this to show when the page loads, so add the following style sheet rule into the header of the page (or your style sheet):

```
<style type="text/css">#myOnPageContent {display:none;}</style>
```

Finally, you can add a link that will open up the modal window. To do this, we will use an `<a>` element, although you could trigger it using the `onload` event of the document (to bring the window up when the page first loads), or you could use a form element.

There are a few things to note about this `<a>` element, starting with the `class` attribute whose value is `thickbox`:

```
<a class="thickbox"
  href="#TB_inline?height=300&width=500&inlineId=myOnPageContent"
  title="add a caption to title attribute / or leave blank">link</a>
```

As you can see, the value of the `href` attribute is quite long. Let's break that down:

- `#TB_inline?` is used to trigger the lightbox.
- `height` and `width` specify the height and width of the box in pixels. You can adjust these depending on the size of your message.
- `inlineID` is used to specify the value of the `id` attribute of the element that contains the message to appear in the modal window. In our case, the `<div>` element containing the message for the modal window was `myOnPageContent`.

You may also have noticed that the link used a `title` attribute whose value appeared as a title at the top of the modal window.

Again this demonstrates how you can add a powerful technique to your page with very little code.

Sortable Tables with MochiKit

In this example, you will create a *sortable table*, which means you can re-order the contents of the table by clicking on the heading for each column. This kind of feature is particularly helpful when dealing with a long table where different users might want to sort the data in different ways (according to different column headings).

Figure 12-20 illustrates a table of employees; the up arrow next to the "Date started" table heading indicates that the table's contents are being ordered by the date the employee started (in ascending order). If you clicked on the heading "Name" you would be able to sort the table by alphabetical order of employee names.

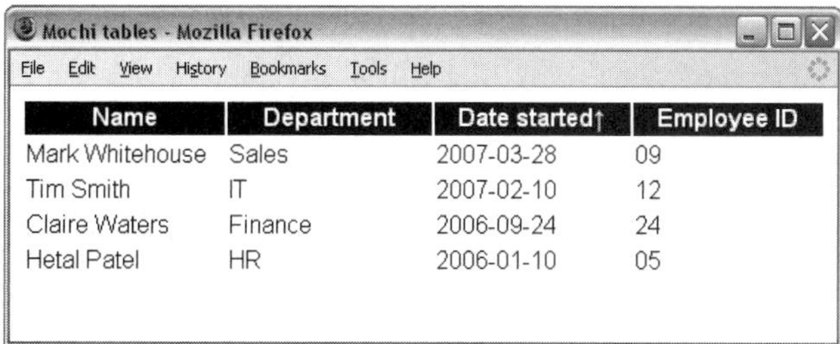

Figure 12-20

This example uses another JavaScript library — MochiKit. By looking at examples that use different libraries, you can see how easy it is to work with the various libraries (which offer different functionality). You can download the latest version of MochiKit from `www.mochikit.com/`, although I have included version 1.3.1 with the download code for this chapter.

In order to create a sortable table, you again need to include two scripts; the first is for the `MochiKit.js` JavaScript library, and the second is for the `sortable_tables.js` file (`ch12_eg22.html`).

```
<script type="text/javascript"
   src="scripts/MochiKit/MochiKit.js"></script>
<script type="text/javascript"
  src="scripts/MochiKit/examples/sortable_tables/sortable_tables.js">
</script>
```

Next, I have added a couple of CSS styles to distinguish the headers from the columns and to set the font used:

```
<style type="text/css">
  th, td {font-family:arial, verdana, sans-serif;}
  th {background-color:#000000;width:200px;color:#ffffff;}
</style>
```

Now let's look at the actual table; there are just three things you need to add to your table so that you can sort the contents by clicking on the headings:

- The `<table>` element needs an `id` attribute whose value is `sortable_table`.
- For each column, the `<th>` (table heading) elements need to have an attribute called `mochi:sortcolumn` (we will look at the values this attribute takes after you have seen the code).
- The first row of `<td>` elements needs to have `mochi:content` (again we will look at the values for this attribute after you have seen the code).

So here is the table with these additions:

```
<table id="sortable_table" class="datagrid">
  <thead>
    <tr>
      <th mochi:sortcolumn="name str">Name</th>
      <th mochi:sortcolumn="department str">Department</th>
      <th mochi:sortcolumn="datestarted isoDate">Date started</th>
      <th mochi:sortcolumn="extension str">Employee ID</th>
    </tr>
  </thead>
  <tbody>
    <tr mochi:repeat="item domains">
      <td mochi:content="item.name">Tim Smith</td>
      <td mochi:content="item.department">IT</td>
      <td mochi:content="item.datestarted">2007-02-10</td>
      <td mochi:content="item.extension">12</td>
    </tr>
    <tr>
      <td>Claire Waters</td>
      <td>Finance</td>
      <td>2006-09-24</td>
      <td>24</td>
    </tr>
    <tr>
      <td>Hetal Patel</td>
      <td>HR</td>
      <td>2006-01-10</td>
      <td>05</td>
    </tr>
    <tr>
      <td>Mark Whitehouse</td>
      <td>Sales</td>
      <td>2007-03-28</td>
      <td>09</td>
    </tr>
  </tbody>
</table>
```

The `<th>` elements carry the `mochi:sortcolumn` attribute, which contains two items of information separated by a space:

- A unique ID for that column.
- The format of the data in that column. This can be `str` if the data is a string or `isoDate` for a date in the format shown.

Now take a look at the first row of data because the `<td>` elements in this row carry `mochi:content` attributes. Again these are made up of two items, this time separated by a period or full stop:

- The keyword `item`
- The unique ID for the column that was specified in the `mochi:sortcolumn` attribute in the corresponding header

As with the other examples in this section, it is best to try it using the download code so you can see how it works and understand how easy it can be to add quite complex functionality to a table — creating an effect similar to the Sort Data options in Excel, which are useful when dealing with large amounts of data.

Creating Calendars with YUI

The fourth and final JavaScript library you will be looking at is the Yahoo User Interface library; it is the largest of the three libraries, with all kinds of functionality split into many separate scripts. I have only included a subset of version 2.7.0 of the YUI library with the code download for this chapter (the full version is over 11MB in size); however, you can download the full and latest version from `http://developer.yahoo.com/yui/`. Broadly speaking, the YUI is split into four sections:

- At the heart of the YUI there are three scripts: the Yahoo Global Object, the DOM Collection, and the Event Utility. When using the library, sometimes you will only need to include one or two of these scripts; other times you will need all three.
- Then there are library utilities, which provide functionality that you might use in many tasks, such as libraries that help you create animated effects, drag-and-drop functionality, and image loading. When one of these scripts requires functionality from one of the core scripts, you are told in the accompanying documentation.
- At the other end of the spectrum, the library contains scripts to create individual kinds of user interface controls, such as calendars, color pickers, image carousels, and a text editor. There are helpful "cheat sheets" that show you how to quickly create each of these user interface components.
- Finally, there is a set of CSS style sheets, which you might need to use with some of the UI controls in order to make them appear as you want.

In this section, we are going to see how to use the YUI to add a Calendar to your web page with just a few lines of code. Figure 12-21 shows what the calendar will look like.

Figure 12-21

To start, you have to include three core JavaScript files from the YUI library:

```
<script type="text/javascript" src="scripts/yui/yahoo/yahoo.js"></script>
<script type="text/javascript" src="scripts/yui/event/event.js" ></script>
<script type="text/javascript" src="scripts/yui/dom/dom.js" ></script>
```

Next, you need to add the `calendar.js` script, which is used to create the calendar (`ch12_eg23.html`).

```
<script type="text/javascript"
  src="scripts/yui/build/calendar/calendar.js"></script>
```

For this example, you will also include one of the css files that is included with the YUI download:

```
<link type="text/css" rel="stylesheet"
href="scripts/YUI/skins/sam/calendar.css">
```

In the body of the page, you need to add a `<div>` element, which will be populated by the calendar.

```
<div id="cal1Container"></div>
```

Finally, you add in the script, which calls the YUI library, and fills the `<div>` element with the calendar.

```
<script>
    YAHOO.namespace("example.calendar");
      YAHOO.example.calendar.init = function() {
      YAHOO.example.calendar.cal1 =
        new YAHOO.widget.Calendar("cal1","cal1Container");
      YAHOO.example.calendar.cal1.render();
    }
  YAHOO.util.Event.onDOMReady(YAHOO.example.calendar.init);
</script>
```

Rather like some of the other examples in this section, this is likely to be tied into some other kind of functionality, such as a holiday booking form where you are specifying dates you want to travel or an events list where you are looking at what is happening on a particular date. But this does demonstrate how libraries can be used to add significant functionality to your pages with ease.

Auto-Completing Text Inputs with YUI

The final example you will look at in this section allows you to create a text input where users are offered suggestions of options they might be trying to type. The example allows you to enter the name of a U.S. state, and as you start typing suggestions will appear as to which state you are trying to enter.

You can see what the input will look like in Figure 12-22.

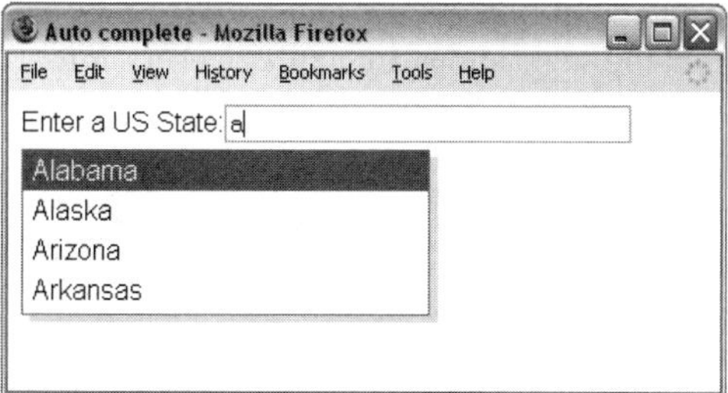

Figure 12-22

To start with in this example (`ch12_eg24.html`), you include the three core JavaScript files:

```
<script type="text/javascript" src="scripts/yui/yahoo/yahoo.js"></script>
<script type="text/javascript" src="scripts/yui/event/event.js"></script>
<script type="text/javascript" src="scripts/yui/dom/dom.js"></script>
```

Then you add the animation and data source library utilities.

```
<script type="text/javascript"
    src="scripts/yui/animation/animation.js"></script>
<script type="text/javascript"
    src="scripts/yui/datasource/datasource.js"></script>
```

Finally, you add in the `autocomplete.js` JavaScript file:

```
<script type="text/javascript"
    src="scripts/yui/automcomplete/automcomplete.js"></script>
```

Then, in the body of the page, you add the text input and a `<div>` that will contain suggestions of what you are trying to type in.

```
Select a US state:
<input id="myInput" type="text">
<div id="myContainer"></div>
```

Next, a JavaScript array is created with all of the possibilities that someone might be trying to enter.

```
<script type="text/javascript">
YAHOO.example.arrayStates = [
    "Alabama",
    "Alaska",
    "Arizona",
    "Arkansas",
    "California",
    "Colorado",
    // other states go here
];
</script>
```

Finally, the JavaScript is added to the page that ties the text input form control to the array, and calls the Auto-Complete function so that the suggestions are made as users enter their cursors into the text input.

```
<script type="text/javascript">
YAHOO.example.ACJSArray = new function() {
    // Instantiate first JS Array DataSource
    this.oACDS = new YAHOO.widget.DS_JSArray(YAHOO.example.statesArray);
    // Instantiate first AutoComplete
    this.oAutoComp =
      new YAHOO.widget.AutoComplete('statesinput','myContainer',
        this.oACDS);
    this.oAutoComp.prehighlightClassName = "yui-ac-prehighlight";
    this.oAutoComp.typeAhead = true;
    this.oAutoComp.useShadow = true;
    this.oAutoComp.minQueryLength = 0;
    this.oAutoComp.textboxFocusEvent.subscribe(function(){
        var sInputValue = YAHOO.util.Dom.get('statesinput').value;
        if(sInputValue.length === 0) {
            var oSelf = this;
            setTimeout(function(){oSelf.sendQuery(sInputValue);},0);
        }
    });

};
</script>
```

Again, you can see that by following a simple example made available with a JavaScript toolkit, you can significantly enhance the usability or functionality of your page (without the need to write all of the code to do the job from scratch).

There are many more JavaScript libraries on the Web, each of which has different functionality, and each of which is continually being developed and refined, so it is worthwhile taking some time to look at the different libraries that are available, and checking in with your favorites every so often to see how they have been updated.

Summary

In this chapter, you have seen many uses for JavaScript, and you should now have a better understanding of how to apply it. With the help of these scripts you should now be able to use these and other scripts in your page. You should also have an idea of how you can tailor or even write your own scripts.

You have seen how you can help a user fill in a form correctly by providing validation. For example, you might check to make sure required fields have something in them or that an e-mail address follows the expected pattern. This saves users time by telling them what they have to do before a page gets sent to a server, processed, and then returned with errors. The validation examples highlight the access the DOM gives to document content, so that you can perform operations on the values users provide.

You also saw how the DOM can help make a form generally more usable by putting the focus on appropriate parts of the form and manipulating the text users have entered, by removing or replacing certain characters.

Finally, you took a look at some popular JavaScript libraries: Scriptaculous, JQuery, MochiKit, and the Yahoo User Interface Library. JavaScript libraries offer sophisticated functionality that you can easily drop into your pages with just a few lines of code, and are the basis for many of the scripts available on the web that allow you to add complex functionality to your site with minimum effort.

Exercises

There is only one exercise for this chapter because it is quite a long one. The answers to all the exercises are in Appendix A.

1. Your task is to create a validation function for the competition form in Figure 12-23.

   The function should check that the user has done the following things:

   - Entered his or her name
   - Provided a valid e-mail address
   - Selected one of the radio buttons as an answer to the question
   - Given an answer for the tiebreaker question, which is no more than 20 words

These should be in the order that the controls appear on the form.

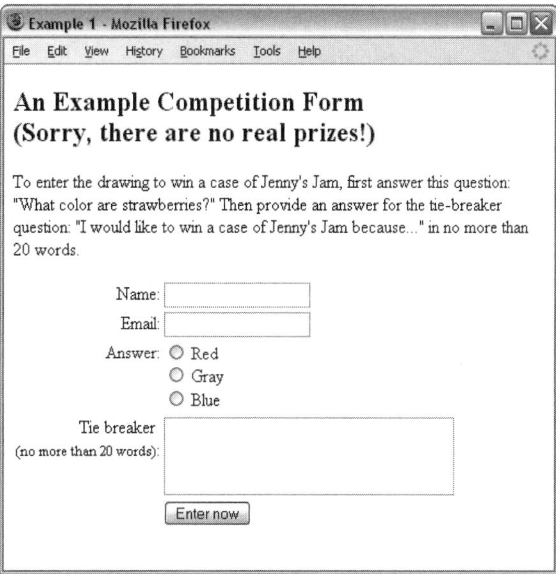

Figure 12-23

Here is the code for the form:

```
<form name="frmCompetition" action="competition.aspx" method="post"
onsubmit="return validate(this);">
<h2>An Example Competition Form <br />(Sorry, there are no real
prizes!)</h2>
<p> To enter the drawing to win a case of Jenny's Jam, first answer
this question: "What color are strawberries?" Then provide an answer for
the tie-breaker question: "I would like to win a case of Jenny's Jam
because..." in no more than 20 words.</p>
<table>
  <tr>
    <td class="formTitle">Name: </td>
    <td><input type="text" name="txtName" size="18" /></td>
  </tr>
  <tr>
    <td class="formTitle">Email: </td>
    <td><input type="text" name="txtEmail" size="18" /></td>
  </tr>
  <tr>
    <td class="formTitle">Answer: </td>
    <td><input type="radio" name="radAnswer" value="Red" /> Red<br />
          <input type="radio" name="radAnswer" value="Gray" /> Gray<br />
          <input type="radio" name="radAnswer" value="Blue" /> Blue
    </td>
    </tr>
   <tr>
     <td class="formTitle">Tie breaker <br/ ><small>(no more than 20 words)
     </small>: </td>
     <td><textarea name="txtTieBreaker" cols="30" rows="3"/></textarea>
     </td>
   </tr>
   <tr>
     <td class="formTitle"></td>
     <td><input type="submit" value="Enter now" /></td>
   </tr>
</table>
</form>
```

Putting Your Site on the Web

Once you've created your web site, you'll want to make it available for everyone to see. In this chapter, you are going to look at preparing your site for the public, putting it on the Web, and telling people about it once it is live.

You will learn some checks and tests to perform before you put your site on the Web including validating your documents, checking links, and ensuring that the site works in different browsers.

When you are ready to share your site with the public, you will need to arrange *hosting*. In order to help you choose the right hosting company and, indeed, the right package from a hosting company, you need to learn the key terminology used by these companies. Therefore, I will explain what terms such as shared and dedicated hosting are, how much space or bandwidth you need, and so on.

Once your site is ready for the public to see, you will then want to ensure they know about it! You will want to ensure that it is indexed by the major search engines, such as Google and Yahoo. You might also consider a number of other strategies to let people know you are out there, such as pay-per-click advertising (from the likes of Google's AdWords or Yahoo! Search Marketing). After putting all the hard work into creating a site, you want it to be a success.

When visitors come to your site, you can learn a lot, such as how many people have looked at the site, which pages are most popular, and how visitors found your site. Web analytics helps you track and decipher this information, and I will introduce you to a web analytics tool from Google called Google Analytics, which is free.

We will finish up by looking at some other technologies that you might like to consider learning once you are comfortable with what you have covered in this book.

But before you look at all of this, you need to learn one final element that provides information about documents and their content — the `<meta>` element.

In this chapter, you learn how to do the following:

- Use the `<meta>` element
- Perform tests to ensure your site will work as you intended
- Find a *host* to make sure your site can be accessed by everyone on the Web
- Move your site from your computer to your host's web server using FTP
- Submit your site to search engines
- Increase visitor numbers
- Use pay-per-click advertising
- Discover other technologies you might like to look at next
- Control different versions of your site so that you can make changes without making mistakes

Meta Tags

Before you start looking at how to test your site, you need to learn about one last tag — the `<meta>` tag. Meta tags live in the `<head>` rather than the `<body>` of a document and contain information *about* a document (rather than information that is part of the document that you would see in the browser window). The information can be used for a number of purposes including helping search engines index your site, specifying the author of a document, and, if the document is time-sensitive, specifying when the page should expire.

The `<meta>` element is an empty element and so does not have a closing tag. Instead, `<meta>` elements carry information within attributes, so you need a forward slash character at the end of the element. For example, here is a `<meta>` element that provides a description of a computer bookshop web site:

```
<meta name="description" content="Buy computer programming books
    to learn HTML, XHTML, JavaScript, ASP.Net, PHP" />
```

The `<meta>` element can take eight attributes, four of which are universal attributes — `dir`, `lang`, `xml:lang`, and `title`. The other four, however, are specific to the `<meta>` element:

- `schema`
- `name`
- `content`
- `http-equiv`

The `name` and `content` attributes tend to be used together, as do the `http-equiv` and `content` attributes. These pairings will be addressed next.

name and content Attributes

The `name` and `content` attributes specify properties of the entire page. The value of the `name` attribute is the property you are setting, and the value of the `content` attribute is the setting that you want to give this property.

Here you can see a `<meta>` element where the `name` attribute indicates that you are going to specify a `description` for the page, and the `content` attribute is where this description of the page goes:

```
<meta name="description" content="Buy computer programming books to
learn HTML, XHTML, JavaScript, ASP.Net, PHP" />
```

The value of the `name` attribute can be anything; no restrictions are published in any standards. Therefore, if you need to add your own information about a document and its content, you can use this element. Some predefined values for this attribute that are commonly used are:

- `description`: Specifies a description of the page
- `keywords`: Contains a list of comma-separated keywords that a user might search on to find the page
- `robots`: Indicates how search engines should index the page

The `description` and `keywords` properties can be used by programs called crawlers, bots, or spiders, which most search engines use to help index web sites. Therefore, they're worth adding to any web page. These programs go through web sites, adding information to the databases used by the search engines, following links as they come across them, indexing those pages, and so on — this is how search engines manage to index so many sites.

Using name with a Value of description

You have already seen an example of giving the `name` attribute a value of `description`, and using the `content` property to specify a sentence that describes the site. Some search engines display the value of the `description` property in their search results.

A description should be a maximum of 200 characters long, although some search engines, such as Google, display only the first 100 characters. Therefore, you should try to get across the main content in the first 100 characters.

For example, here is the `<meta>` tag showing the description of the Wrox Press homepage (at the time this book was being written):

```
<meta name="description" content="Wrox.com has all the coding and
programming resources you need. Find books, articles, and other IT content,
programmer to programmer (p2p) forums, and free code downloads!" />
```

And here is the description that you will see if you type Wrox into Google:

"Wrox.com has all the coding and programming resources you need. Find books, articles, and other IT content, programmer to programmer (p2p) forums. . . ."

Using name with a Value of keywords

The `keywords` property was created to supply a list of words that a search engine could use to index the site. In practice, search engines take very little (if any) notice of this anymore, although many sites will still provide keywords in this manner. For example, an online computer bookstore might use keywords such as this:

```
<meta name="keywords" content="computer, programming, books, web, asp,
asp.net, C#, vb, visual basic, c++, Java, Linux, XML, professional,
developer, html, html, css, xslt, access, sql, php, mysql" />
```

A rough guideline to the limit of the text should be around 200 characters. You should never use words that do not directly relate to the content of the site. Ideally, the same keywords should also appear in the text for that page.

You could also use the `lang` attribute in conjunction with the description and keywords to indicate the language they are using, or to offer keywords in multiple languages. For example, here are the keywords in U.S. English:

```
<meta name="keywords" content="computer, programming, books"
lang="en-us" />
```

And again in French:

```
<meta name="keywords" content="livres, ordinatteur, programmation"
lang="fr" />
```

And finally in German:

```
<meta name="keywords" content="programmieren, bucher, computers"
lang="de" />
```

Using name with a Value of robots

As I mentioned earlier, many search engines use programs to index web pages on their behalf. You can use the `name` attribute with a value of `robots` to prevent one of these programs from indexing a page or from following links on the page (because many of these programs follow the links they find on your site and index those, too). For example, you probably would not want a search engine to index any pages that you are still developing, or which you use to administer the site.

Here you can see that the `<meta>` element tells search engines not to index the current page or to follow any of the links on it to index those.

```
<meta name="robots" content="noindex, nofollow" />
```

The content attribute can have the values shown in the table that follows.

Value	Meaning
all	Index all pages.
none	Index no pages.
index	Index this page.
noindex	Do not index this page.
follow	Follow links from this page.
nofollow	Do not follow links from this page.

By default the values would be all, index, and follow, allowing web crawlers to follow any link and index all pages.

If you want to prevent pages from being indexed you should use this technique in conjunction with a file called robots.txt, which is discussed in the "robots.txt" section later in this chapter.

http-equiv and content

The http-equiv and content attributes are paired together to set *HTTP header* values. Every time a web browser requests a page, HTTP headers are sent with the request, and each time the server responds sending a page back to the client, it adds HTTP headers back to the client:

- The headers sent from a browser to a server when it requests a page contain information such as the type of browser, the operating system, the screen resolution, the date, the formats the browser will accept, and other information about the user's configuration.
- The headers returned from a server to a web browser contain information such as the type of web server, the date and time the page was sent, and the date and time the page was last modified.

Of course, the headers *can* contain much more information, and using the <meta> tags is one way of adding new headers to be sent with the document. For example, you might want to add a header to indicate when the page should expire (no longer be valid) — which is especially helpful if the document contains things such as special offer prices which you know will expire on a certain date — or to refresh a page after a period of time.

Expiring Pages

It can be important to expire pages because browsers have something known as a *cache*, a space on the hard drive where they store pages of web sites you have visited. If you go back to a site you have already visited, the browser can load some (or all) of the page from the cache rather than having to retrieve the whole page again. This is done because it can make the page load quicker (since the browser does not have to collect as much data).

Here you can see a <meta> tag that will cause the page to expire on Friday, April 16, 2011, at 11:59 (and 59 seconds) p.m. Note that the date must follow the format shown.

```
<meta http-equiv="expires" content="Fri, 16 April 2011 23:59:59 GMT" />
```

If this were included in a document and the user tried to load the page after the expiry date, then the browser would not use the cached version; rather it would try to find a fresh copy from the server. This helps ensure that users get the latest copies of documents and thereby prevents people from using out-of-date information.

Preventing a Browser from Caching a Page

You can prevent some browsers from caching a page altogether using the value `pragma` for the `http-equiv` attribute and a value of `no-cache` for the `content` attribute like so:

```
<meta http-equiv="pragma" content="no-cache" />
```

Refreshing and Redirecting Pages

You can set a page to refresh after a certain number of seconds using the following `<meta>` tag, which gives the `http-equiv` attribute a value of `refresh`:

```
<meta http-equiv="refresh"
content="10;URL=http://www.wrox.com/latest.aspx" />
```

This will cause the page to refresh itself after 10 seconds. You can see the number of seconds given as the first part of the value for the `content` attribute, which is followed by a semicolon, the keyword URL, an equal sign, and the address of the page to be refreshed.

You can even refresh to a different page. For example, if your site moves from one domain to another, you can leave a page up for visitors who go to the old domain saying that you have moved and that the user will be redirected automatically in five seconds.

When you use this technique to reload the same page it is referred to as *refreshing* the page, while sending the user to a new page or site is called *redirecting* the user.

It is generally considered bad practice to refresh entire pages, in particular because someone might be in the middle of reading the page when you refresh it. It is important to bear in mind that some people will not read a page at the same speed as others (especially if they have a screen reader to read the page to them, in which case the page's automatically refreshing would be very frustrating). The one exception to this rule would be sites such as sports results, online chat applications, or auction sites where parts of the page refresh so that the user has the latest information — although this kind of refresh is done using very different techniques.

Specifying the Author Name

You can set the name of the author of the document using a value of `author` for the `http-equiv` attribute and then using the author's name as the value of the `content` attribute, like so:

```
<meta http-equiv="author" content="Jon Duckett" />
```

Setting the Character Encoding

Character encodings indicate the character encoding that was used to store the characters within a file. You can specify the encoding used in a document with a `<meta>` tag whose `http-equiv` attribute has a value of Content-Type. The value of the content attribute should then be the character encoding used to save the document; for example:

```
<meta http-equiv="Content-Type" content="ISO-8859-1" />
```

Here you can see that the document was written using the ISO-8859-1 encoding. You will see more about character encodings in Appendix E.

The scheme Attribute

The scheme attribute is not yet widely supported, although it was created to allow web page authors to specify a scheme or format for a property value. For example, if you are working with dates, you can write them in several ways. In the U.S., the date format is commonly written mm-dd-yyyy, whereas in Europe it is written dd-mm-yyyy. So, you might use the scheme attribute to indicate a date format. In the U.S., you could use the following:

```
<meta scheme="usa" name="date" content="04-16-1975" />
```

In Europe, you might use the following:

```
<meta scheme="Europe" name="date" content="16-04-75" />
```

The use of the scheme attribute does assume that the processing application understands the value of the scheme attribute and name attribute — and given that the mainstream browsers would not understand this, it would fall upon either a script or a custom application to interpret the use of this element.

Having taken a look at the <meta> element, it is time to start preparing your site for the public to visit.

Testing Your Site

Most web page authors build their first sites on their desktop or laptop computer. The site usually works well on that machine, but different visitors to the site will be using different operating systems and browsers, viewing the pages on different-sized monitors, and connecting to the Internet with different connection speeds. With all this in mind, it is sensible to perform some tests on the site before setting your site loose for everyone to look at.

So, the two stages of testing are as follows:

- **Pre-publishing tests:** These are performed on your computer before asking anyone else to look at the site.
- **Pre-release tests:** Performed on the site exactly as it will be published on the Web (on a web server).

These tests help ensure that as many people as possible view your site as you intended them to.

Validating HTML, XHTML, and CSS

One of the best ways to ensure a site will work on the majority of browsers is to validate your code and make sure that you have stuck to the rules of the language. A *validator* will check things such as whether you have closed all tags correctly, that the attributes you have used are actually allowed on that element, and so on. All it takes is for you to miss something as simple as one closing `</td>` tag and, while the page may look fine on your browser, it will not necessarily work on someone else's computer.

It is helpful to try to validate the first page you build of each site, as it is quite tempting to copy and paste parts of your code from one file to the other and use your first page as a template for other pages of the site. If you have an error in your template page and you use it to create all the other sites before you test it, you might have to amend every page.

As discussed in Chapter 1, each version of HTML and XHTML has a set of rules that govern that version of the language, known as a DTD or schema. A validator can check whether a web page obeys the rules of that DTD or schema. Therefore, by validating your pages you will know if you have left out a tag or other important part of the markup. It is the DOCTYPE declaration at the start of your page that will tell a validation tool which DTD or schema your page should match the rules of.

The W3C (the body that oversees development of HTML, XHTML, and CSS) has a free online validation tool at `http://validator.w3.org/`. It allows you to enter a URL for a site or upload a page from your computer as shown in Figure 13-1.

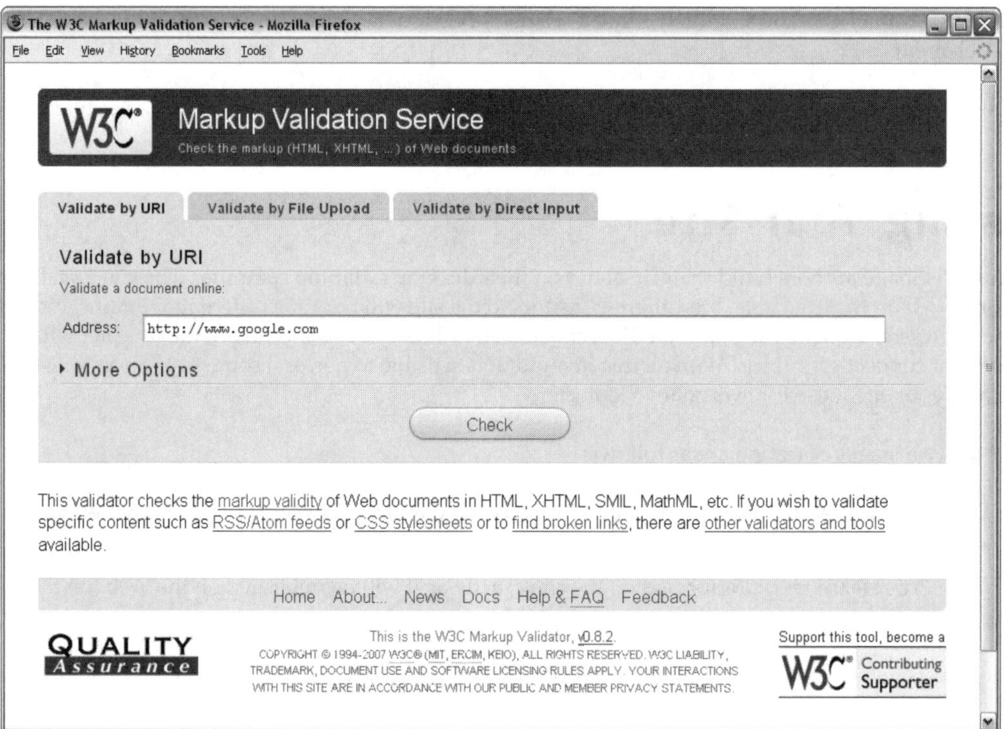

Figure 13-1

It will then tell you if there are errors in your document; you can see examples of this in Figure 13-2.

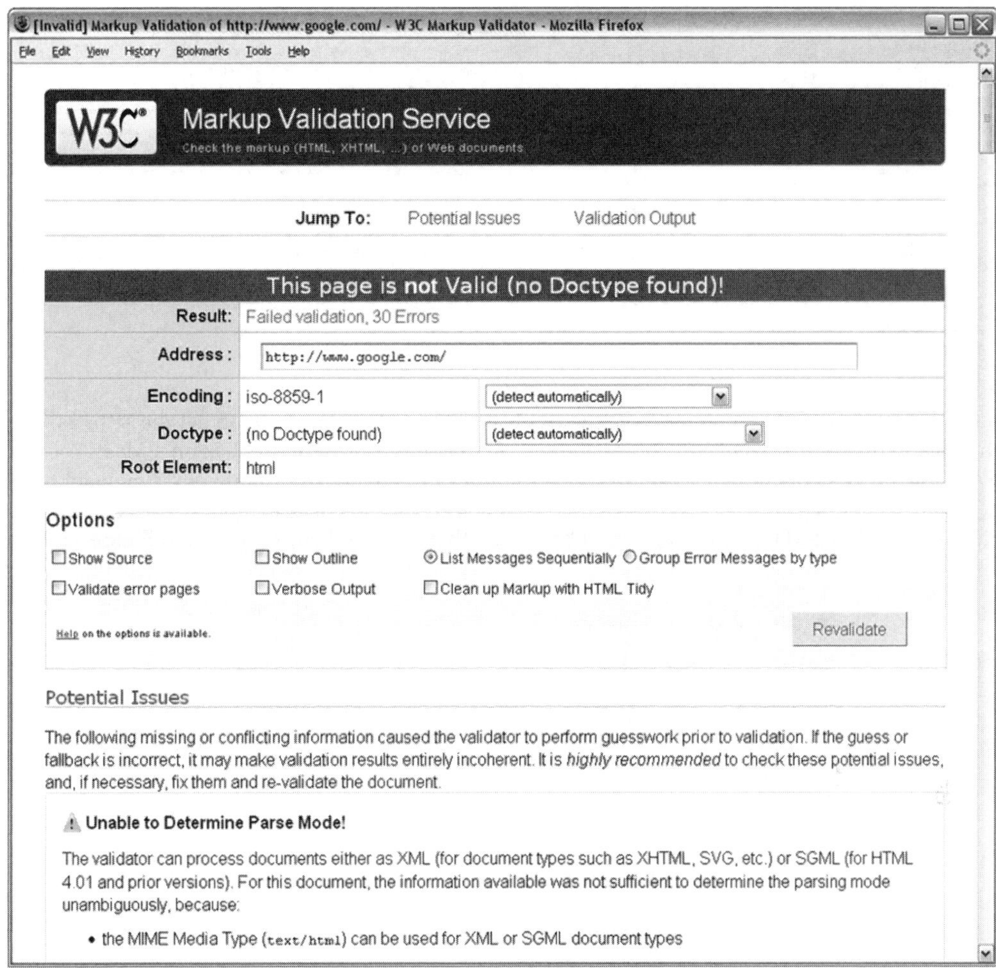

Figure 13-2

While the W3C validation tool is very helpful — and free — having to validate each page individually can take a while.

Many web page authoring tools, such as Dreamweaver, contain tools that allow you to validate your entire site.

Dreamweaver (which appears to be the most popular authoring tool among web professionals) introduced good validation features for XHTML pages in its Dreamweaver MX version (far better than the validation offered by earlier versions of Dreamweaver). Validating a page is as simple as saving it and then pressing Shift+F6; you should see errors appear in the results panel, as in Figure 13-3.

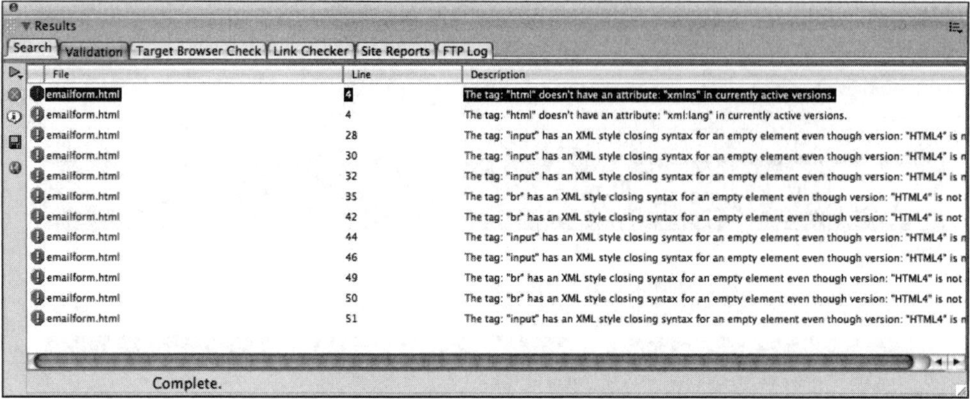

Figure 13-3

For this to work correctly you must have the right settings in Dreamweaver. To get the settings, you can right-click in the results panel and choose the setting dialog box (or Option-click on a Mac). You will then see a whole range of document standards appear in the new Preferences dialog box. You want to make sure that each option is unchecked except the version you want to check against. So, if you are trying to validate Transitional XHTML 1.0, you must have only that box checked, as shown in Figure 13-4.

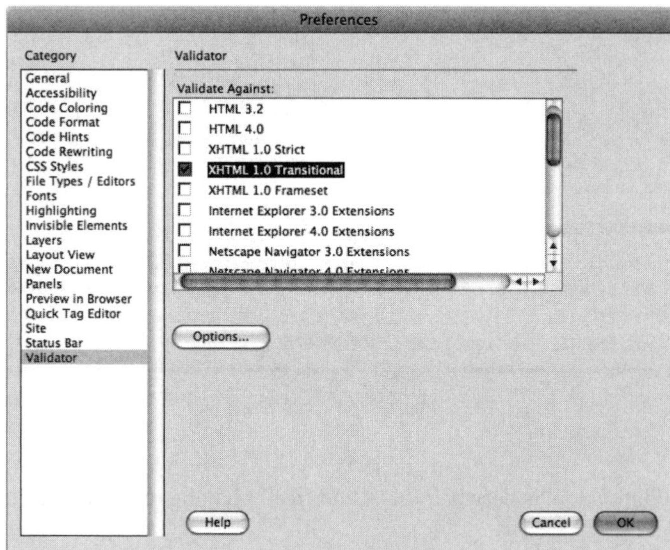

Figure 13-4

Link Checking

It is important to check your links both before your site goes live and after you have published it on the Web. There are several online tools to help you check links; some of them charge, although there are some free link-checking services such as:

- The W3C's link checker at `http://validator.w3.org/checklink/`
- HTMLHELP's Link Valet at `www.htmlhelp.com/tools/valet/`

You can also use the Link Valet tool to check whether any site you link to has been changed since a specified date. This can be very helpful because an external site might restructure its pages, and the old URL will no longer be valid, or it might start publishing content you no longer wish to link to.

In Figure 13-5, you can see the results of a single page validated with the W3C's link validator.

The results from these services might appear quite verbose, but you should be able to tell which links are bad by looking for some kind of highlighting — which tends to be in red for broken or questionable links.

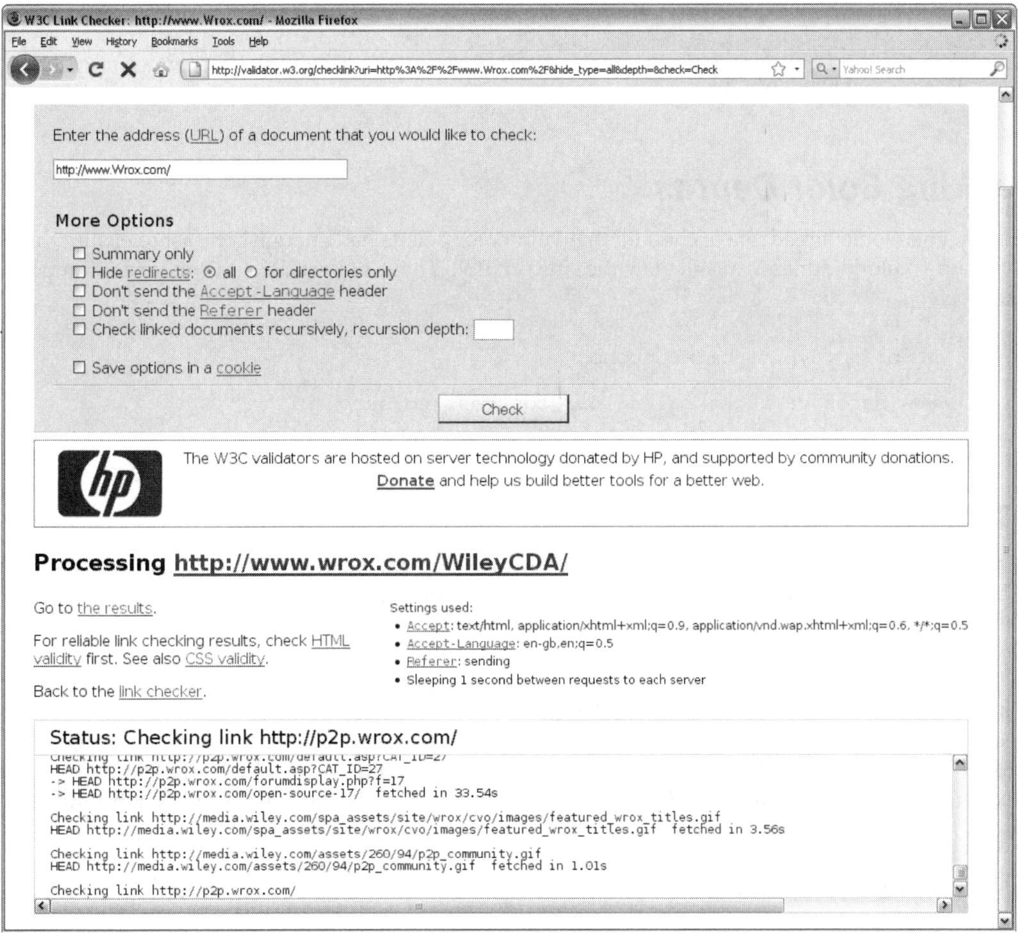

Figure 13-5

Dreamweaver also contains its own link-checking tool. You can access this from the Results menu or by pressing Control+Shift+F9.

There are options to check a page, a folder, or a whole site. Once Dreamweaver has found your broken links you can fix them in either the Results window or the Properties window as shown in Figure 13-6 (or by going into the code for the relevant page).

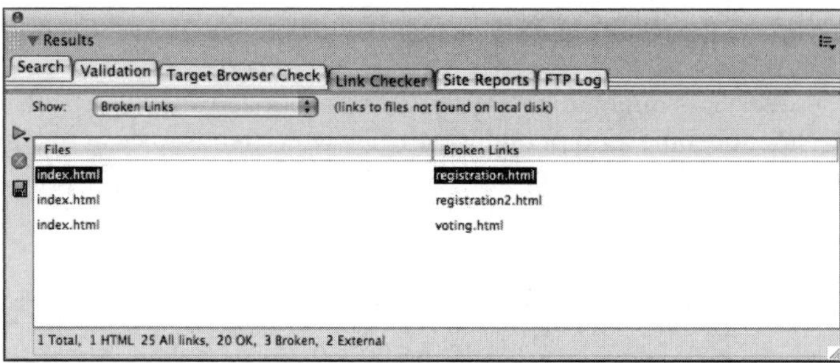

Figure 13-6

Checking Color Depths

Ideally you would already have checked that your color palette had enough contrast to ensure those who suffer colorblindness can still view the site. But if you have not yet done this there are some handy tools here:

- `http://graybit.com/main.php`
- `www.snook.ca/technical/colour_contrast/colour.html`
- `www.vischeck.com/vischeck/vischeckURL.php`

Accessibility Checkers

Chapter 14 contains a list of techniques to help ensure that your site meets accessibility requirements. This not only helps make sure you reach any potential audience that may suffer from visual or physical disabilities, but also has the benefit that your site is likely to work better on the ever-increasing range of devices that can be used to access the Web.

There are some online tools that help check whether your site meets some of the accessibility requirements, although they cannot check for all aspects of accessibility. For example, these tools can check whether you have used `alt` attributes on each image, but they cannot tell whether the alternative text will make sense to someone who cannot see the image. Here are two of the online tools that you can use to help check whether your site is accessible:

- `www.webaim.org/resources/wave/`
- `www.section508.info/`

A very good reference on the topic of accessibility is *Web Accessibility: Web Standards and Regulatory Compliance* by Jim Thatcher, et al. (Friends of Ed, 2006).

Checking in Different Versions of Browsers

Even if you write your pages to the letter as far as the recommendations go and your pages validate perfectly, different versions of browsers on different operating systems behave differently. The page that looked perfect on your monitor just doesn't look the same on a friend's or colleague's monitor. So, you should always try to test your web page on as many different browsers and platforms as possible. You should, at the very least, have the latest versions of Internet Explorer and Firefox on your computer, and ideally Opera and Safari too.

I would also recommend checking your site in Internet Explorer 6. (At the time of this writing, I was working on a popular web site that still had 16 percent of visitors using IE6, and it does not always show your site as you might expect.) Unfortunately, you are able to install only one version of Internet Explorer on a single computer (unless you have a partition running a second version of Windows or run a Windows emulator), and you are likely to want the latest version for day-to-day use. If you have an old PC lying around, you can keep older versions of browsers on that and use it to test your pages once you have built them. If you need to download an old version of a browser, try `http://browsers.evolt.org/`.

Some web sites and services offer to take screenshots of each page of your web site on many different versions of several makes of browser for you, so that you can check how the pages appear in different browsers. However, this can be quite expensive and time consuming. Examples include:

- `http://browsershots.org/`
- `www.browsercam.com/`
- `http://browserlab.adobe.com/`

Another great way to check that a site is working is to ask all your friends to check it before it goes live. At least one or two of them will have different browsers or operating systems, if you're lucky. Ask them to check what it looks like and send you a screenshot of a couple of pages in their browser. If you want to, you can even offer a small prize to one lucky tester as an incentive for them to test your site.

Pilot Testing

If you are able to, get people who have not been involved in the project to test your site before it is released to the public. This is important because what might seem perfectly obvious to you is not always so clear to someone who is coming to the site for the first time. By the time you have built the site, you will be so close to the designs and workings that it will be very difficult to look at it with the same objectivity as someone who has never seen it.

You want to sit your participants down in front of the site and ask them to perform the tasks. Ideally, the people performing this kind of test on your site would be your target audience.

In Chapter 9, you may remember that we discussed the idea of creating personae that reflect your target audience, and that these actors should have roles that they want to achieve when coming to your site.

You can use these roles again when testing your site. For example, you might have a site that sells bikes and you could ask users to complete the following tasks:

- ❑ Find a bike they think would be suitable for their 8-year-old daughter
- ❑ Work out how much a particular model of bike costs
- ❑ Find out how to visit the store and when it's open
- ❑ Check whether a helmet meets a certain safety standard

You should only ask each tester to perform around five tasks; any more than this and they will be getting used to the layout and operation of the site.

You should just watch what the users do. You must resist all temptation to intervene at any point, even if you want to ask what someone is trying to do or want to tell them how to get to something you think they are trying to find. (As soon as you start talking to them, you affect their normal behavior — and you won't learn as much.)

Watching where people go to achieve these tasks, how long they spend on each page, and how they navigate can teach you a lot about your site.

Some people prefer to watch silently while participants perform these tasks. Others ask participants to talk their way through what they are doing. In this second scenario (sometimes known as the talking-aloud protocol), you need to make sure that users talk their way through every thought process. You often get broken sentences, but you can get an idea of what you expect of them by performing the task first yourself on a different site. Here is an example of a transcript you might end up with:

1. "I'm supposed to look for a bike for Julia."
2. "Looking at . . . home, store . . . "
3. "Clicking on store . . . "
4. "List of brands appears on the left, not heard of many of these."
5. "Pictures on right saying men's bikes, women's bikes, boys' bikes, girls' bikes . . . ?"
6. "Click on picture for girls' bikes . . . "
7. "Shows ages, so click on 'first bikes' . . . "
8. "Looking at pictures . . . "
9. "This one looks good; click on that picture . . . "
10. "Doesn't do anything . . . thought it would show more information about it . . . "
11. "Click on Raleigh Butterfly."
12. "There, that one looks fine."

You could consider setting up a video camera over the user's shoulder so that you can see the screen and also record their voice, as long as it doesn't put the user off too much. Again you must resist the temptation to interrupt if users are doing something that is not what you think they should be doing in order to achieve the task — after all, in this example you learned that the user expected to be able to click on the image of the bike to see more details, but couldn't.

If you have the time and budget, then there is a lot more you can do in terms of testing. But many web developers avoid doing any testing because they feel that they do not have the time and budget, and if you find yourself in this situation, you can find out a lot about your site and how it will be used by simply watching a small group of people perform basic tasks.

Proofreading

If you are working on a commercial site, it can often help to hire a proofreader to check all your text. Silly typos can affect people's impression of the site you built and make both you (and the client, if you are developing the site for someone else) look less professional.

If your client finds errors throughout the site, you appear careless — even if the client supplied the error-ridden copy for the site.

Taking the Leap to Live

Your site should now be ready for the public to view it, so in this section we will look at how to get it on the Web. In order to do this you will need to get a domain name and hosting space, and you will have to transfer the site to the new server using an FTP program.

Getting a Domain Name

The *domain name* is the part of the web address you commonly see after the letters `www`. For example, Wrox Press uses the domain name `wrox.com`, whereas Amazon uses the domain name `amazon.com` in the U.S., `amazon.co.uk` in the U.K., `amazon.de` in Germany, and so on.

You can register your domain name with a domain registration company, of which there are hundreds; just search on your favorite search engine and you will find plenty. Most companies go for the suffix `.com`, but several other suffixes are available. For example, there are country-specific domain suffixes (also known as *top-level domains*) such as `.co.uk` for the UK, `.de` for Germany, `.com.au` for Australia, and `.ru` for Russia. You should choose a country-specific domain only if you are based in that country. Indeed, some domain names can only be bought by people with registered companies in that country. Then there are also suffixes such as `.me.uk`, which is for personal sites; `.info`, which is for information-based sites; and `.org`, which is for registered organizations. (Unless you are working for a large multi-national corporation, you do not need to purchase all available suffixes for your domain name.)

Before you register your name, you need to see if it is available; all domain name registration companies should have a form that allows you to search to see if your domain name is available. You might find this a frustrating process, as an incredibly high proportion of the `.com` domain names you might think of have been taken already, as well as most popular words (even combinations of popular words).

You might also like to check that the name of your site is not very similar to that of someone you would not want to be associated with, just in case the user mistypes the URL. For example, you would not want a children's site to have a very similar URL to an adult-content site.

You can order your domain name without actually having a site ready; this is known as *domain parking*. You order the name as soon as you know you are going to create the site (after all, you will probably want to use the URL in the site design, and will therefore need to order it before you start designing the site), but you do not put anything up there until you have built the site.

Several domain-name registration companies also offer *hosting* (hosting is covered in the next section), but you do not (generally speaking) have to order your domain name from the same people that host your site. You can get the domain name registration company to point the domain to your hosting company's servers (usually there is a control panel on the site you registered the name with where you specify where your domain name actually points).

Your domain name should be easy to remember. Avoid names that are so long that users will find them hard to remember or too long to type in. For example, if you were called the Sydney Slate Roofing Services Limited, you might choose a domain such as `www.SydneySlate.com` rather than `www.SydneySlateRoofingServicesLimited.com`.

When you register the domain name, you will also be able to use this for your e-mail addresses. For example, if you choose the domain `www.example.com`, then no one else will be able to use the e-mail address `bob@example.com` without your permission. (Unfortunately, it is possible for spammers to make e-mails *appear* as if they come from your domain, simply by changing the "from" address in their e-mail programs, and there is nothing you can do to prevent this.)

Hosting

You already know that in order to view a web page, a browser requests a page from a web server. The web server is a special computer that is constantly connected to the Internet.

When you access a page using a domain name, such as `www.example.com/`, something called a *name server* changes the name into a number. The number (known as an IP address) uniquely identifies a machine on the Web and this machine holds your web site.

So when you are ready to put your site out on the Web, you are going to need some space on a web server. Hundreds of companies will allow you to put your web site on their servers and will, of course, charge you for the service. The service is known as *web hosting* because the company hosts your site for you.

Some ISPs will give you a small amount of web space free when you choose them to access the Internet. There are also other sites that offer free hosting (these are often paid for by the use of pop-up advertisements that appear when your pages load). For a personal site you may need only a small amount of web space and you might be prepared to put up with any pop-up ads that come with the free service. For commercial sites, however, it is better to choose some paid hosting — which can still be very cheap but will not serve advertisements.

Key Considerations for Choosing a Host

As I said, literally hundreds of companies offer web hosting, and it can seem like a minefield deciding which to go with. Following is a discussion of the key points you need to understand and consider when choosing a site (these points are listed here in alphabetical order, rather than in order of importance):

- **Backups:** You should check whether your host performs backups on your sites and, if so, how often. A backup is simply a copy of the site taken in case there is a problem with the computer it is on.

  Some companies will only create backups so that they can restore your web site in the event of a server breaking down. Others will also allow you access to backups (which can be handy if you accidentally break the site, because you can go to the backup and get an older version that you know worked).

If your site changes regularly, you will want to look for frequent backups (daily at least), and you would want the hosting provider to do this automatically. But if the site does not change regularly, you may be prepared to create a backup yourself, and do it less often.

- **Bandwidth:** This is the amount of data you are allowed to use on your site. If the average size of one of your web pages is 75KB including images, and you get 100 visitors to your site per month, with each visitor looking at 10 pages, you will need at least 75000kb (or 75MB) of bandwidth per month. In reality, you will find that hosts often allow a lot more than this, but it gives you an idea of how to calculate bandwidth.

  The tricky part of deciding how much bandwidth you will need is to judge how successful your site will be. You can never predict how popular your site will be, and if it is mentioned in a popular newspaper or magazine, it can suddenly get a lot more traffic. Most hosting companies will charge you an extra fee if you exceed the bandwidth allocated on your account, and their web site will usually tell you how much bandwidth you have used in a month.

- **Country:** You might want to consider which country your site is hosted in. It is best to host the site in the same country where you expect the majority of your visitors to be because the data has less distance to travel, which should make your site appear to those users more quickly. If you are setting up a site for an Australian market, for example, you would ideally host the site in Australia as it would be quicker for Australian visitors to load the pages than if it were hosted in Europe. In practice, however, you are rarely likely to see *much* of a performance difference.

- **Data centers:** Data centers are where the hosting company will have its servers (and it may be a different building from where the company's offices are). A lot of companies say that they have multimillion-dollar data centers, but this does not necessarily mean your hosting company is a big operation, because most hosting companies hire space in a large data center that is shared by many companies.

- **Disk space:** This is the amount of space you get to store files on the computer that serves your site. You will usually see a figure given in MB (megabytes) or GB (gigabytes) The disk space governs how large your site can be; you must have more disk space than the total size of all of the XHTML, CSS, script files, and images that make up your site. You can check how large your web site is by simply looking at the size of the folder that your site is in (as long as you do not have any other files in that folder).

- **E-mail accounts:** Hosting companies generally provide e-mail services with web hosting. You need to consider two factors here: the size of mailbox you are allowed, and the number of mailboxes you are given. Some hosts give you unlimited mailboxes but set a maximum amount of storage space across all of them, so if you have five mailboxes and only 100 megabytes of space to share among them, each account can hold only 20MB at capacity. Some hosting companies allow you only a few mailboxes, but will allow a fixed amount for each mailbox (say 100MB each). Finally, some hosting companies allow you to take up the amount of space you have allocated for your domain with mail, so the only limit is your storage limit.

- **Shared versus dedicated hosting:** The cheaper web hosting is nearly always provided on what is known as a *shared host*. This means that your web site is on the same physical computer as many other sites. Because the smaller sites do not have as many visitors, the computer can easily cope with hosting several sites. However, larger sites that receive many thousands of visitors a day or serve large files (such as music downloads or a lot of heavy graphics) require extra bandwidth and take up more resources on that server. When visitors to your site start to request a lot of large files, the amount of data you are sending to them could exceed the bandwidth limit set on your account, and this is likely to result in increased charges. Therefore, if your site becomes extremely popular, it may be less expensive to get your own server, which is known as a *dedicated server* because it is dedicated to your use.

Some of the very popular sites on the Web are actually hosted across several servers — the site may be so busy that one computer alone cannot handle the traffic, or one machine may require maintenance so there are others to take the strain. Banks, large online stores, and multinational corporations are examples of sites that would use this kind of setup — known by many names including a *load-balanced server* or *cluster of servers*, a *web farm*, or a *cloud platform*.

Some companies will offer to host your site on a cluster or cloud, which means that they have several sites on the same *set* of servers (generally this is more reliable than having several sites on one single server).

Don't be put off by this talk about dedicated or load-balanced servers. Generally, if your site is so popular that you require your own dedicated server, you should be making enough money from it to warrant the extra cost.

- **Statistics packages:** Every time a user requests a file from your site, the web server can store certain details about the user — for example, the IP address, browser version, language of the operating system, and so on. This information comes in the HTTP headers from the browser, and is stored in what is known as a *log file*. Statistics packages can look at the log files that contain this information and interpret some very useful information from them. For example, you can see how many pages you have served to visitors, what users typed into search engines to find you, and what the most common page people leave your site from is. All this information helps you understand what users are doing on your site and can help you improve the site and the number of visitors it receives. You learn more about statistics packages later in the chapter.
- **Uptime:** Uptime refers to the percentage of time your web server is working and available for people to look at your site. You will generally see figures such as 99 percent uptime, which means that, on average, 99 out of every 100 minutes your site will be available. But then that also means that your site might be down for 1 percent of the time, which could be 87.6 hours per year, or *four days*. If your site is your main source of income, you should find an alternative with more uptime.

Unless you are a running a *very* large company, it is rarely worth the investment of running your own servers because you are likely to need someone capable of administering the machines and taking care of them on a regular basis. If you decide that you do need your own dedicated servers, several hosting companies will manage a server on your behalf, updating it with new patches for the operating system to fix security holes when needed — this is known as a *managed dedicated server*. While this is still expensive, you will generally find it cheaper than hiring someone yourself to manage your servers.

Putting Your Site on a Server Using FTP

Once you have paid for some space on a web server, you need to be able to get the files that make up your web site onto this computer — which can be on the other side of the world. The most efficient way to do this is using *FTP*.

FTP stands for File Transfer Protocol. The Internet uses a number of different protocols for sending different types of information. For example, HTTP (Hypertext Transfer Protocol) is used for transmitting hypertext files, which are better known as web pages (that's why most web addresses start with http://).

FTP is a protocol used to transfer binary files across the Internet and is much quicker at sending whole web sites to a server than HTTP.

Most hosting providers actually require that you use FTP to transfer your pages onto their servers, which means that you need an FTP program (sometimes referred to as an FTP client) to put your files on a server.

FTP programs usually have two windows, each with a file explorer. One represents the files and folders on your computer; the other represents the folders on the web server. In Figure 13-7, you can see the folders on my computer, and on the right you can see those on a web server.

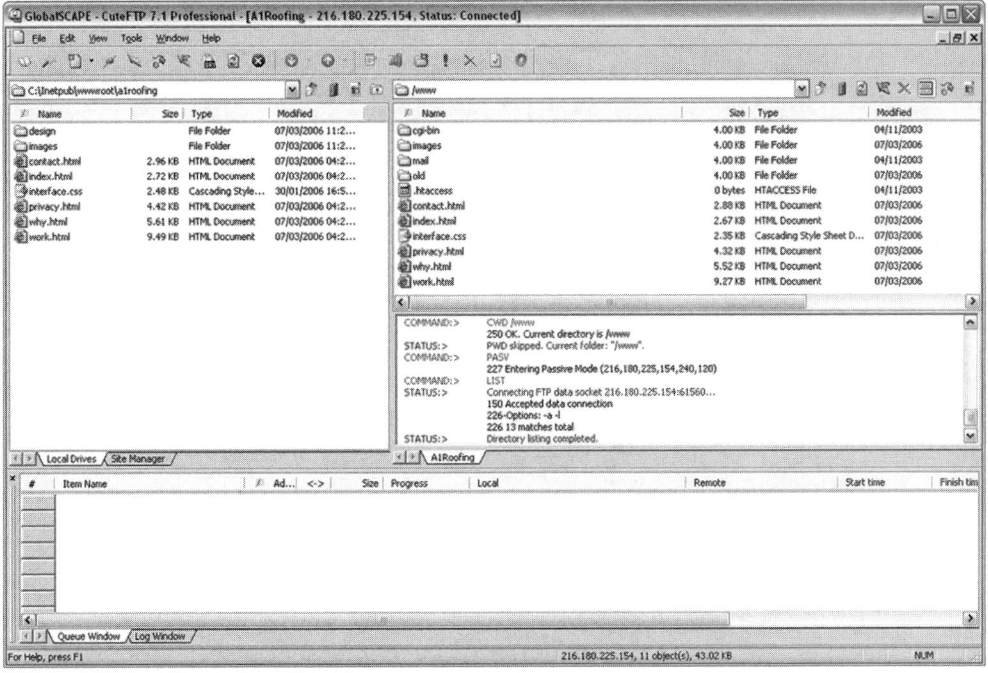

Figure 13-7

The table that follows shows some of the most popular FTP programs.

Product Name	URL	OS
FireFTP	`http://fireftp.mozdev.org/`	Windows and Mac OS X
Cute FTP	`www.cuteftp.com/`	Windows and Mac OS X
FTPX	`www.ftpx.com/`	Windows
Fetch	`www.fetchsoftworks.com/`	Mac
Transmit	`www.panic.com/transmit/`	Mac

Each of the programs is slightly different, but they all follow similar principles.

When you register with a host, this host will send you details of how to FTP your site to its servers. This will include:

- An FTP address (such as `ftp.example.com`)
- An FTP username (usually the same as your username for the domain)
- An FTP password (usually the same as your password for the domain)

Figure 13-8 shows you how these are entered into the FTP program called Transmit on a Mac.

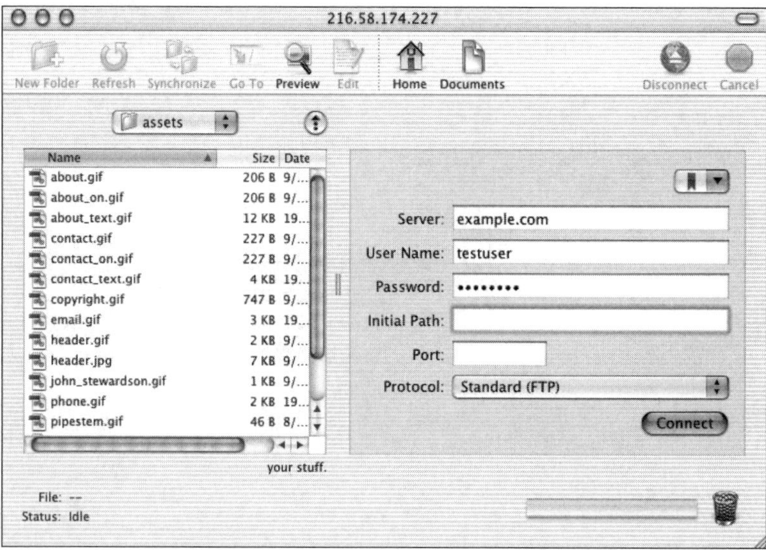

Figure 13-8

Some hosting companies allow you to use a variant of FTP called SFTP or secure FTP. This is considered to be more secure than standard FTP because the username and password are encrypted when they are sent to the server. If your host supports this option, it is a good idea to use it.

The Importance of Directory Structure and Relative URLs

Because a lot of people develop their first site on a desktop or a laptop computer they often use relative URLs for all links, images, style sheets and scripts, rather than absolute ones (because they do not have a full URL for the site yet). This is very helpful because it means that the links will work on a web server of the hosting company without any changes.

When developing a site on your desktop machine, the address bar of your browser might contain something like this:

```
C:\Documents and Settings\administrator\websites\examplesite\index.html
```

But when you are ready to make the switch to the new site, you are going to want it to appear here:

```
http://www.example.com/index.html
```

If you are using relative URLs to link to all of your other pages, images, script files, and so on, then moving a site to a new folder or even a new URL will not be a problem. However, if you hard-code your paths, you may find that links, images, and other files do not load. For example, suppose you used an image for the logo of your site, and used the full file path in the `src` attribute, like so:

```
<img src=" C:\Documents and Settings\administrator\websites\
examplesite\mages\our_logo.gif" alt="Our Logo" />
```

This image would not be loaded when you move the site to a server. It is better to use something like this:

```
<img src="images/our_logo.gif" alt="our logo" />
```

Now, as long as the `images` folder is within the directory that this page lives in, the image will be loaded, no matter where the site is moved.

Now that your site is on the server where the public can see it, you should check your pages thoroughly again to ensure they appear as you intended. Remember to check that all of the links work and that the images and other files are loading. You should consider running a link checking tool (like the ones discussed earlier in this chapter) again to help check whether links are working. Once you are happy that the site is functioning properly, you can start to tell the world about it.

Telling the World about Your Site

Now that you have built your site and put it up on the Web, you want people to discover it. When creating a web site, many people take the "build it and they will come" approach, expecting people to just find their site (perhaps through search engines such as Google). There are, however, many things you can do to help promote your site and significantly increase the number of people who will see it.

There are whole books devoted to web marketing (and many web sites), but here are some pointers for how to make more people aware of your site.

Always Mention Your URL

The first thing to do is to mention your URL wherever you can. For a start, if you have any printed material, from business cards and letterheads to brochures, posters and adverts, include your URL on them. Likewise, ensure that you have it on your e-mail signature.

Content Is King

Entertaining or informative content is one of the best reasons for people to come to your site. If you are able to, creating regular content not only gives people more reasons to come to your site (because you are regularly adding new material that may be of interest to new people), but it also gives people who have found your site a reason to come back regularly.

If you want people to come back regularly, it is important to give people an idea of how often the site is updated. This can be done through some fairly simple means such as adding the date that the items are published under headlines (as you see on many blogs), or by spelling out how often the site is updated.

If you have any particularly interesting or noteworthy news that you think would benefit from a Press Release, then you can consider writing one and submitting it to a PR news service such as PR Web (`www.PRweb.com`). Other journalists and bloggers may pick up on your article and mention it.

Some site owners will allow other web sites to republish content that they have written in return for a link back to their web site. If you want to do this you can tell visitors that this is an option at the bottom of your articles, and go out and offer your content to other sites.

Forums, Communities, and Social Networks

Many industries and hobbies have their own forums and online communities. You can also find groups of people interested in the same topic on social networks, such as Facebook and LinkedIn.

If you become a part of any online community that is relevant to your site, you can build your profile amongst the community. By having your URL on the signature and profile page of sites you post to, or on your social network profile pages, more people become aware of your site, and they may be regularly reminded of it.

It is very important when becoming part of an online community that you do not just post messages when you have something to say about your site or have added something new to it. As with any community you should get involved in the conversations and reply to other people's posts offering advice where you can (giving back to the community, not just using it to promote your site).

Check for Trade Sites and Directories

Many trades and hobbies have at least one site that lists all other sites in that field. Try to find out if there are any sites that relate to the subject of your site and ask those sites to link to you.

Some trade directories charge for listings; if this is the case ask their monthly traffic and average number of visits you can expect per month from your listing before handing over any money. You may then want to suggest a trial period before handing over a full year's subscription (you will see how to track how many people come from such sites shortly).

Reciprocal Links

Many smaller sites offer reciprocal links; that is, they will link to you in return for your linking to them. It is a way for everyone to boost traffic. If you do this, make sure that you are not putting someone on the front page of your site when they are going to put a link to you tucked away on a page that few people will come across — the term is *reciprocal linking*, after all.

While it is good to have as many people linking to your site as possible, you will tend to get better trafic from sites that cover topics relating to the subject of your site.

Look at Your Competition

Use a few search engines to search for competing sites or company names and see who is linking to and talking about them — the sites that link to your competitors may well link to you, too, if you ask.

Make It Easy for People to Link to You

You have probably seen links like those shown in Figure 13-9 on many web pages, encouraging users to bookmark a page on services such as Delicious or Stumble Upon, or to vote for the page on sites like Digg.

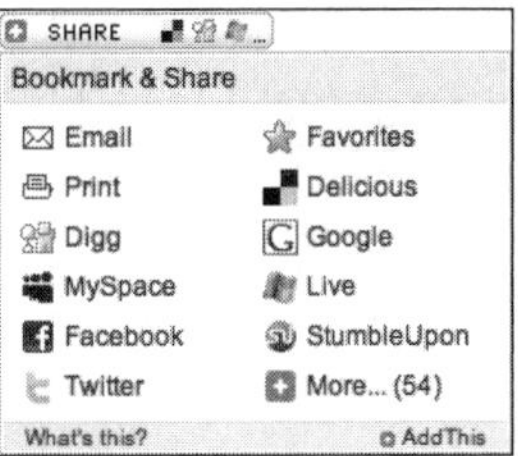

Figure 13-9

While most of the sites shown in this button in Figure 13-9 will have pages that describe how to link to each of them individually, a far simpler and quicker way to add these options to your site is using a web site called `www.addthis.com/` (this site provides very simple tools to create a link like this encouraging visitors to share the site with others).

You can also provide a page with buttons or banners that make it easy for other sites to link to you. This is more likely to happen with hobby sites than with commercial ventures, but people who create sites in their spare time will often link to other special-interest sites. If you provide them with attractive images, and show them the code to add the images and links to their site, they are more likely to include these ads. Figure 13-10 shows some examples from the Oxfam web site.

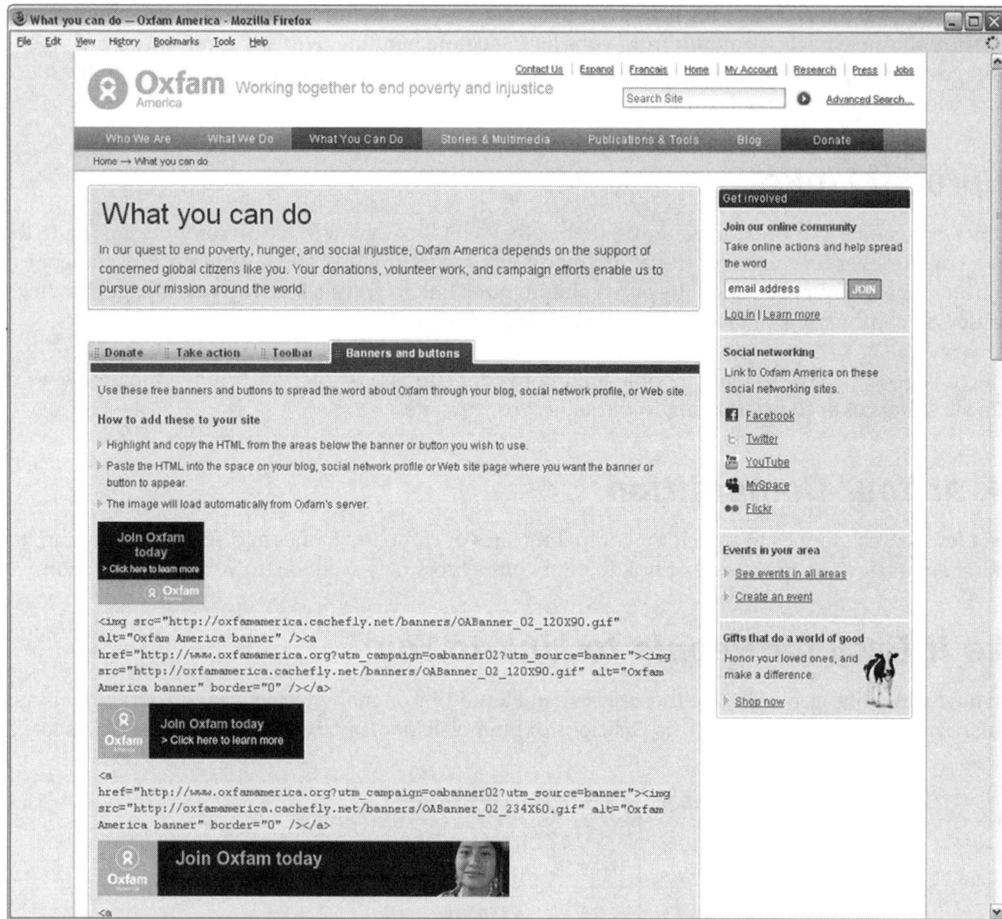

Figure 13-10

Pay-per-click Advertising

When you have searched on Google you will probably have noticed the links down the right-hand side of the page like those in Figure 13-11.

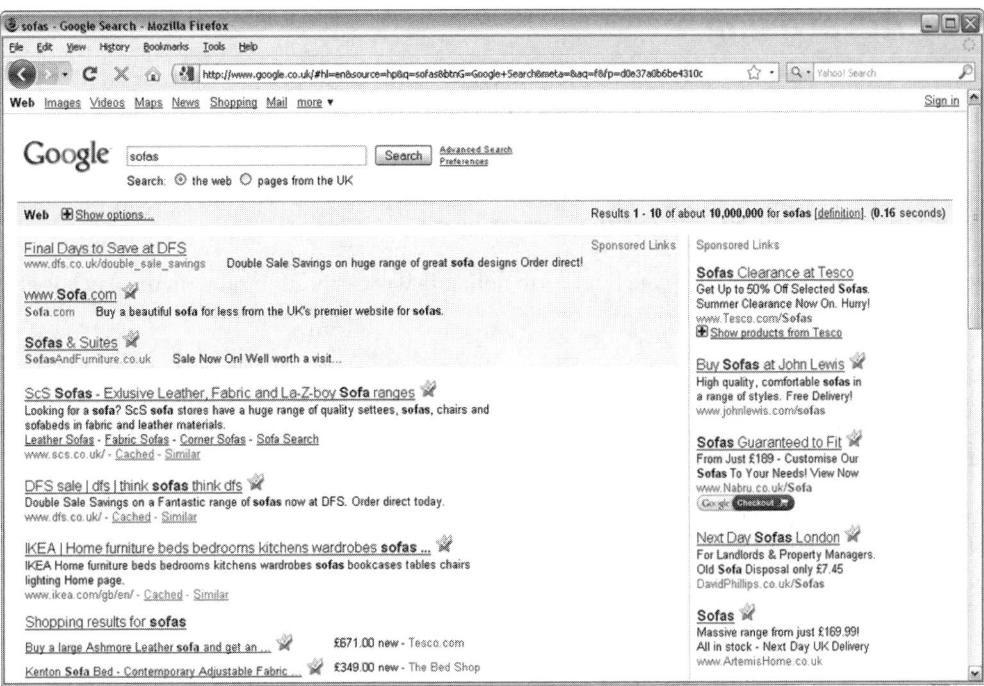

Figure 13-11

These are examples of what is known as pay-per-click advertisements, so called because the advertiser only pays each time someone clicks on the ad.

Google's pay-per-click advertising system is called AdWords, and in order to advertise, you specify a set of keywords that relate to your site (and create your ad copy). The ad will only appear when someone searches on one of these keywords.

There are two main factors that determine the order in which your advertisements will appear:

- The amount you are prepared to pay each time someone clicks the ad.
- The number of people who actually click on your ad. If users do not click the ad, then it slips down in position no matter how much you pay, because Google stands to make more money if ten people click a cheaper link than if one person clicks a slightly more expensive link. Also Google wants to remain as relevant as possible to visitors, so it will prioritize the most popular links.

This can be a very cost-effective way to generate traffic to your site. Yahoo offers a similar service called Yahoo! Search Marketing, and Microsoft has a system called adCenter.

Display Advertising

Display advertising is a term used to describe advertisements where you pay for your ad to appear on a particular site. It is most commonly associated with banner ads.

Companies are charged for display ads in two common ways. First, there is the cost-per-thousand impressions confusingly named CPM (which stands for cost per mille). Second, you may be charged to occupy a space on a page on a per month or per year basis.

If you do take out display advertising it is worth noting that click-through rates on display ads are very low.

Remember that a lot of web users are immune to advertising and just scan pages to find what they really want. If you are going to create a banner, make sure it's visually attractive and gives people a clear incentive for clicking on it. You want people to want to click on your ad so it's worth the money you are spending to have it appear on other sites.

Some current thinking suggests that online display ads are more suited to brand awareness than achieving specific actions such as getting people to visit your site, because click-through rates are very low. It is not uncommon for display ads to have less than 1 percent of the people viewing the ad visiting the site.

Create an E-mail Newsletter

If you have regularly changing content, consider adding an e-mail newsletter feature to your site. By encouraging people to sign up for e-mail updates you can regularly remind them about your site and tell them what has changed.

Some good tools for creating and managing e-mail lists are:

- `www.CampaignMonitor.com`
- `www.MailChimp.com`

Both of these tools not only help you send e-mails to visitors, but also help you create subscription forms so that visitors can easily sign up to your newsletter.

Near the form where people can subscribe to your newsletter, it is a good idea to explain to visitors the incentives for signing up and tell them the benefits of giving you their e-mail address.

You can also consider approaching other complimentary companies to see if they would mention you in their newsletter in return for a mention on yours.

Now that people are coming (you hope) to your site, you can learn a lot about what they are doing on the site and how they found you.

Understanding Your Visitors

As soon as you have people coming to your site, you should start looking at how they found you, what they are looking at, the operating system and browser they are using, and when they are leaving.

There are two main ways to learn about the visitors to your site:

- **Log file analysis**, which studies log files on your server
- **Analytics software**, which requires you to add a couple of lines of script into each page of your web sites so that they can record information to a database

When any file is requested from a server, it can create a log file to record information about the browser that requested the page. Many hosting companies will then provide tools that allow you to analyze these log files and give you information about your visitors (which tool they offer varies between hosting companies but the tools will offer similar features).

Analytics software uses a script that records similar information to that available in log files into a database. It also provides tools to analyze this information.

Personally, I install analytics software for all sites I develop. For most small and medium sized sites, I use Google Analytics, which is a free service offered by Google (`www.Google.com/analytics`). The terms used in site analysis can be confusing; for example, you may have heard people say that a site gets 10,000 *hits*. This can be quite misleading. The term "hit" refers to the number of files that have been downloaded from the site — and every image counts as a file in this total as well as the XHTML pages. Thus, a single web page with nine images will equal ten hits (and some graphics-intensive pages can have over 30 images for each page that is served). Therefore, it is generally more helpful to look at *page views* rather than hits, as this represents the number of pages that have been viewed on your site.

You may also come across the term "visits." You should be aware, however, that different statistics packages calculate visits in different ways. Some count every visitor using the same IP address as the same person — so if there are ten people, all of whom work in the same building, looking at the same site at once, then that might look like only one user instead of ten. Different packages also tend to count visits as different lengths of times; some packages remember an IP address for a whole day, so if the same person comes to the site in the morning and then again in the evening it is counted as just one visit. Others will remember the IP address for only 15 minutes.

You will also find that some advertisers will ask for the number of unique visitors you receive each month — again different statistics packages can count unique users in different ways, so this figure can be a little misleading.

Figure 13-12 shows you an example of a report from Google Analytics.

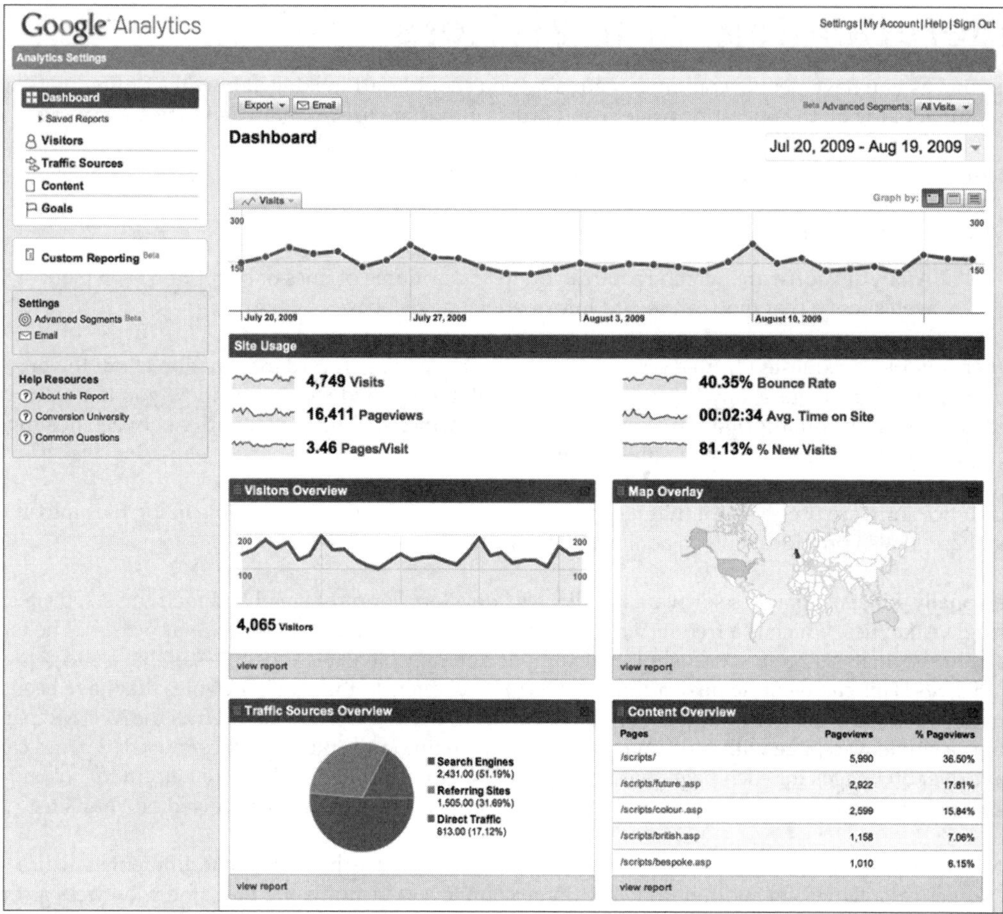

Figure 13-12

Ten Things to Check in Google Analytics

There is an incredible amount of information available, but here are ten things I always look at first when studying a Google Analytics report for a site:

1. **Pageviews:** This shows the total number of pages all visitors have viewed on your site.
2. **Visits:** This shows the number of times people have visited your site over a given period.
3. **Unique visits:** This totals the number of visitors who have visited the web site over a given period, with each visitor counted only once. This is important because when compared with total visits you can get a good idea of how many people are returning to your site regularly.

4. **Referrers:** These are the sites that are sending visitors to your site, and will include a mix of sites that link to you and search engines. If a site is sending you a lot of traffic, you might like to get in touch and see if you can work together to ensure that the traffic keeps flowing.
5. **Search terms:** These are the terms that people are entering into a search engine such as Google before visiting your site. This can be particularly helpful in letting you know how visitors describe the things they are looking for (because visitors often use very different terminology to site owners).
6. **User's browser, operating system, and screen resolution:** This is important because it shows you which browsers and operating systems you should be checking your site on.
7. **Top content:** This shows the most popular pages and sections of your site.
8. **Top entry pages:** This shows the most popular pages that people first see when coming to your site (you can often find that referrers and search engines send visitors to specific pages on your site rather than the homepage).
9. **Top exit pages:** This shows the pages that people left on (if a lot of people are leaving on the same page, then it is probably a good idea to consider changing that page).
10. **Bounce rate:** This is the number of people who left on the same page they arrived on (if a lot of people are leaving from the same page they arrived on, it suggests that the content is not what people were looking for *or* that the page did not sufficiently encourage people to look around after they arrived at the page and to explore more).

Google Analytics lets you specify the timeframe you want to look at this data for. I find that looking at monthly reports gives me a good overview and starting point for a site's traffic.

You can also instruct it to e-mail you reports on a daily, weekly, or monthly basis, which saves you having to log in to check the statistics each day.

Measuring Everything

The ability to track where visitors come from using tools such as Google Analytics means that in addition to discovering where people are coming from, you can also measure the success of marketing activity, which allows you to determine the return on your investment (ROI).

In addition to ascertaining whether your marketing investment has paid off in terms of financial cost, you should also consider the time it took you to initiate the marketing activity. For example, you may spend $100 in a month on Google AdWords and it could take you half a day to set it up, write your ads, and check in again a few times while the ads are running. In this instance, it may be more cost-effective to spend 10 minutes writing to a few bloggers who might create a lot more traffic for you at no cost.

So, wherever you can, try to ensure that you are able to measure the performance of each kind of marketing and awareness activity you perform. In addition to looking at referrers, Google Analytics allows you to add the following extra information to your URL so that you can measure the effectiveness of links.

Term	Description	Query String Property
Campaign source	The referring site	`utm_source`
Campaign medium	Such as blog, e-mail, PPC, display	`utm_medium`
Campaign term	Keywords for the campaign	`utm_term`
Campaign content	Used to differentiate multiple links from similar campaigns	`utm_content`
Campaign name	A readable term you can use to determine the source	`utm_campaign`

There is a handy tool that Google offers to add these links to your URL — just search for Google Analytics URL Builder. Here is an example of a URL with additions to say that a display advert had been added to `www.referrer.com` for a campaign about cheddar cheese:

```
http://www.example.com/?utm_source=referrer.org&utm_medium=display&utm_term
=cheese&utm_content=cheddar&utm_campaign=taste%2Bthe%20cheese
```

What Next?

You've learned all about XHTML and CSS, made a good start at learning JavaScript, and learned how to put your site live on the Web. That is probably enough for now, so you might wonder why there is a section entitled "What Next?" This section covers two topics:

- ❑ Tools you can use to add powerful features to your site, using knowledge you already have
- ❑ What technologies might be appropriate to learn next

So, the first part of this final section will look at services provided on the Web that you can use to enhance your site. You learn about blogs, discussion groups or forums, search, and e-mail newsletters. While these might all sound complicated — and they are advanced features — they can be remarkably easy to implement and you will see how they can be powerful and impressive features on any site.

The second will then look at some other technologies you might like to consider learning.

Tools

There are lots of companies and individuals who create software that you can use on your web site: blogs, message boards, content management systems, e-mail newsletters — the list is (almost) endless. They allow you to add complex features to your site that would take a lot of time and experience to create yourself. Many web design firms use off-the-shelf software, and customize it for their clients (rather than building applications from scratch).

You may find some of these tools will help you create a more advanced web site, and what you have learned in this book will help you take control of the appearance of these tools and make them fit in with the sites you design.

Generally the tools discussed in this section are provided in one of two ways (or sometimes both):

- **Services:** The software is run on platforms that are hosted and managed by the company that sells the service. You will get a unique log on to the service.
- **Code:** Those that provide the code for you to run on your own web site.

Some companies charge for a license to use the software on your site, but there are also a lot of free options out there.

Many hosting companies will allow you to add some of the software discussed in this section to your site using what are known as "one-click-installations," where you only need to press one button on the control panel for your web site to have them install the tools.

Blogs

The word "blog" is short for *weblog*. Blogs were initially devised as a way to add online journals or diaries to a personal web site. The idea behind blogs was to allow users to easily add new entries or *posts* to their web site without having to manually code the page (sometimes called *one-click publishing*).

The posts are added to the site in a chronological order, and while they are often used for online diaries or journals, they have been used for a wide variety of other purposes, such as a way for people to add news, posts about a topic of shared interest, links, and so on to their site.

Some blogging platforms are very simple to use. For example, to set up a Posterous blog, you just e-mail them with your first post, and they reply once the service has been set up for you with details of how to work with the platform. Here are some examples of hosted blogging services:

- `www.posterous.com`
- `www.tumblr.com`
- `www.blogger.com`

Some other blogging platforms offer a lot more functionality, although the extra power comes at a price of them being more complex to learn. Both of these are provided as software (although Wordpress.com offers a hosted version of WordPress, too):

- `www.wordpress.org`
- `www.movabletype.org`

Both of these blogging platforms actually offer far more functionality that makes them entire content management systems (applications that make it easier for non-programmers to upload and edit the content of their web site). Individual developers have also extended these platforms with more features and functions (such as events calendars, advertising tools, mailing lists, and more).

Discussion Boards or Forums

Discussion boards or forums allow users to post questions or comments and then have other users reply to them. They are a great way to add a community feeling to your site, and also provide new content to your site without adding it yourself. They can also attract visitors back to your site at regular intervals.

You may choose to break down your subject area into different sub-topics. For example, if you were running a site about a particular type of car you might have one discussion group for technical questions and answers about fixing problems with that model of car, you might have another forum that allows users to indicate when they are buying or selling parts for that car, and a third area for general chat about the cars.

One of the great things about discussion boards is that, if your site gets known for answering questions, people will come to that site whenever they have a problem. You may well have to start the community off by answering all the questions yourself, but with luck, other members will soon start adding their thoughts.

There is more forum software available to install on your own server than there are services. The following table shows you some examples:

Product	Web site	Format
PHPBB	`www.phpBB.com`	PHP Code
VBulletin	`www.vbulletin.com/`	PHP Code
AspNetForum	`www.jitbit.com/asp-net-forum.aspx`	ASP.NET Code
Active Forums	`www.activemodules.com/products/activeforums.aspx`	ASP.NET Code
Zeta Boards	`www.zetaboards.com/`	Hosted
Pro Boards	`www.proboards.com/`	Hosted

You should be aware that you may be held legally responsible for what people write on your discussion board. If someone takes offense to something written on a board or forum on your site, you can be held accountable as the publisher of the content on the Web — even if you do not share the opinion of the person who wrote the item.

Some discussion boards get around this by allowing the owner to moderate each post (read it before allowing it to go on the site); others simply regularly check the site for offensive material and remove any posts they consider offensive as soon as possible.

Adding a Search Utility

As mentioned in Chapter 10, you might want to add a search utility to your site. In Chapter 10, you saw that you can add a Google search utility to your site, and you can even customize the search by going to `www.google.com/coop/cse/`. Another site that offers a free customizable search service is the Atomz service at `www.Atomz.com/`.

The addition of a search facility to your site can mean the difference between users finding what they hoped to find or simply giving up and leaving. With both the Google and Atomz services, you are given the code for a form that will allow users to send queries to the respective company's web site. The company's servers will then return a page to your users with the results of the search. Both services allow you to create custom headers for the page so that it contains your branding, although the company's servers generate the results.

Creating an E-mail Newsletter

Getting visitors to sign up to an e-mail newsletter is a great way to remind people of your site and drive regular traffic. The problem with e-mail newsletters is sending attractive campaigns out to the people who have signed up.

The e-mail programs that you run on your desktop or laptop computers will not allow you to create the kind of attractive e-mails that many companies send out (which are created in HTML). To send HTML e-mails you can look at a third-party service.

I also tend to recommend using an e-mail service rather than installing e-mail software on your server because the e-mail services will have a lot higher delivery rates. If you send bulk e-mails from a server used for shared hosting, it is less likely that your e-mails will get through to the intended recipients.

Such services charge based on the size of your e-mail list, and some have an additional charge per newsletter you send. Two popular services (which were introduced earlier in the section on promoting your site) are:

- `www.CampaignMonitor.com/`
- `www.MailChimp.com/`

It is important to remember that people must subscribe to receive your newsletter. You cannot just upload all of the contacts from your address book to these services. To help increase subscribers, most e-mail services will provide forms which you can drop into your site that allow people who visit your site to subscribe to your newsletter.

You should also be aware that e-mail clients are not as advanced as web browsers. Therefore you should not use external CSS style sheets; rather you should use inline CSS rules in the `style` attribute on those elements or old-style HTML markup that can control presentation of elements (which is covered in the appendix on deprecated markup). Finally, you should never be tempted to use scripts or videos in e-mails, although you can link to web pages that use both.

Introducing Other Technologies

This section provides an introduction to some other technologies, what they can do, and how you can make use of them on web sites. I hope this helps you decide what technology you might want to start learning next when you have gained experience with everything you've learned in this book.

Server-Side Web Programming: ASP.NET and PHP

You've already seen the very basics of what a programming language such as JavaScript can do in a browser, but when a programming language is used on a web server, it becomes even more powerful.

Any time you want to collect information from a visitor to your site and return a page that is customized for that visitor, you will want to look at server-side programming. Here are some examples of applications where different users will need different pages:

- **Shopping online:** Users browse through a catalog of products and select which ones they want. Their choices are often reflected in a shopping basket displayed on each page. After they have chosen what they want, they provide their payment details and contact/delivery details. At the same time, the people running the store are likely to have a browser-based interface that allows them to add new products to the site (rather than having to create each new page and link to it individually).
- **Checking train times:** The user enters the point he or she is traveling from and the destination, along with preferred travel times. The application then creates a page that contains the requested journey times.
- **Discussion boards and forums:** The examples you have already seen mentioned in this chapter of discussion boards and forums rely on another company's server-side programming and code to handle all of the posts.
- **Searching for content on a site:** The user enters a term into a form that he or she wants to search, which is then sent to the application on the server. The application creates a page that contains results the user inquired about.

One thing that all these types of applications have in common is that the scripts on the server are being used to store information in, and read information out of, a database. (You can think of a database being a little like a set of spreadsheets where information is stored for use in many kinds of applications.) You will learn more about this shortly in the section "Content Management."

Choosing a Server-Side Language

You can work in several different server-side languages and environments, such as ASP.NET and PHP, both of which offer very similar capabilities. Generally speaking (although there are exceptions to the rule):

- ASP.NET runs on Microsoft IIS and Windows servers.
- PHP runs on UNIX servers.

You can code these pages on your desktop computer with the right software installed, but you will want to host the finished web site on a web server.

> *The first applications created using a script on a server were known as CGI scripts. You may still see* `CGI` *or* `CGI-bin` *in the URL of some applications. However, the languages discussed here are in far higher demand.*

Different developers will have different opinions about which language to choose. Most people learn one language and environment and stick to it (although to a certain degree it is much simpler to learn a second language and environment when you already understand one and know what can be done with server-side scripting languages).

If you are learning a technology in order to get a job, then it's a good idea to keep an eye on job advertisements. You will be able to track the technologies employers are asking for and also (if you look regularly) you will be able to see the emerging technologies early on — first there will be only one or two mentions of these technologies, and then the mentions will come more regularly. Job ads can therefore be quite a good barometer for technologies you should consider learning. (And if your boss catches you looking at job ads, you've got a great excuse — you're just researching which technologies are going to be more popular in the near future.)

Content Management

One of the key aspects of many sites is a *content management system*. This is actually a fancy name for something that will allow you to easily update the content of your web site without actually having to create a new page for each new article, posting, or product for sale.

Content management systems tend to be based on a relational database. Relational databases contain one or more tables, each of which is like a spreadsheet. Figure 13-13 shows you a database used on a site about music. (This "example" site is adapted from an actual one.)

Data in Table 'articles'

articleid	posted	lastupdate	headline	headlinedate	startdate	enddate	source	summary	articleurl	article	priority
2	2005/08/17	2005/08/17	Help/FAQ		2005/08/17 00:00	9999/12/31 00:00		Here are the answ		<Long Text>	9
3	2005/08/17	2005/08/17	How2		2005/08/17 00:00	9999/12/31 00:00		Not entirely sure w		<Long Text>	9
4	2005/08/17	2005/08/17	Jargon Buster		2005/08/17 00:00	9999/12/31 00:00		Slang which the yo		<Long Text>	9
5	2005/08/17	2005/08/17	Affiliates		2005/08/17 00:00	9999/12/31 00:00		Welcome there affi		<Long Text>	9
6	2005/08/17	2005/08/17	About Us & Meet th		2005/08/17 00:00	9999/12/31 00:00		So, who are the Mu		<Long Text>	9
7	2005/08/17	2005/08/17	Terms and Conditio		2005/08/17 00:00	9999/12/31 00:00		 		<Long Text>	9
8	2005/08/17	2005/08/17	Prize Draw Rules	Thursday, Novemb	2005/08/17 00:00	9999/12/31 00:00		Here are the rules I		<Long Text>	9
9	2005/08/17	2005/08/17	Privacy Policy		2005/08/17 00:00	9999/12/31 00:00		So, you want to kn		<Long Text>	9
10	2005/08/17	2005/08/17	Site Map and RSS F		2005/08/17 00:00	9999/12/31 00:00		Here's an overview		<Long Text>	9
11	2005/08/17	2005/08/17	Advertise on Music		2005/08/17 00:00	9999/12/31 00:00		Give us your mone		If you would like to	9
1001	2005/11/06	2005/11/06	IMESH is the first P	Sunday, November	2005/11/06 18:37	9999/12/31 00:00		Everybody is a look		<Long Text>	3
1002	2005/11/08	2005/11/08	John Lennon Catal	Tuesday, Novembe	2005/11/08 07:59	9999/12/31 00:00		FIRST DIGITAL REL		<Long Text>	1
1003	2005/11/24	2005/11/24	Bestival, Isle of Wi	Thursday, Novemb	2005/11/24 04:55	9999/12/31 00:00		Ben Osbourne mus		<Long Text>	1
1004	2005/11/25	2005/11/25	PREVIEW: A ROCK	Friday, November	2005/11/25 05:00	2006/02/25 05:00		A new exhibition of		<Long Text>	1
1005	2005/11/28	2005/11/28	Robbie spurns Cou	Monday, November	2005/11/28 07:38	9999/12/31 00:00		Courtney Love's&n		<Long Text>	1
1006	2005/08/18	2005/08/18	Leonard Cohen Bar	Thursday, August	2005/08/18 00:00	2005/12/18 00:00	BBC News	Singer Leonard Coh		<Long Text>	9
1007	2005/08/18	2005/08/18	Madonna Album De	Thursday, August	2005/08/18 00:00	2005/12/18 00:00	BBC News	Press for Madonna'		<Long Text>	9
1008	2005/08/18	2005/08/18	EU Online Deal Nea	Thursday, August	2005/08/18 00:00	2005/12/18 00:00	BBC News	Belgium and the Ne		<Long Text>	9
1018	2005/10/25	2005/10/25	The Game Fights Th	Wednesday, Nover	2005/10/25 00:00	2005/12/26 00:00		Just when you thou		<Long Text>	1
1019	2005/11/02	2005/11/02	Depeche Mode Car	Wednesday, Nover	2005/11/02 00:00	9999/12/31 00:00		Depeche Mode hav		<Long Text>	9
1020	2005/11/28	2005/11/28	Glitter Faces Death	Monday, November	2005/11/24 15:40	9999/12/31 00:00		Gary Glitter has be		<Long Text>	9
1021	2005/11/28	2005/11/28	Jessica Simpson an	Monday, November	2005/11/24 15:59	9999/12/31 00:00		3 years then Knox		<Long Text>	9
1022	2005/11/28	2005/11/28	Ozzies are Dumb	Monday, November	2005/11/27 16:15	9999/12/31 00:00		Daniel Radcliffe has		<Long Text>	9
1023	2005/11/28	2005/11/28	Sony BMG launch n	Monday, November	2005/11/28 17:23	9999/12/31 00:00		Sony BMG is to laur		<P>Sony BMG is to	9
1024	2005/11/28	2005/11/28	Sony BMG, Disney	Monday, November	2005/11/26 17:35	9999/12/31 00:00		Music industry seek		Music industry seek	9
1025	2005/11/28	2005/11/28	Madonna owns Eur	Monday, November	2005/11/28 17:40	9999/12/31 00:00		Madonna is the firs		Madonna is t	9
1026	2005/11/28	2005/11/28	Jonathan Ross for	Monday, November	2005/11/28 17:44	9999/12/31 00:00		Jonathan Ross is h		<P>Jonathan Ross	9
1027	2005/12/06	2005/12/06	MTV revamp	Tuesday, Decembe	2005/12/06 03:47	9999/12/31 00:00		MTV launches new		<P>MTV have just	9
1028	2005/12/06	2005/12/06	Doherty Vs Gallagh	Tuesday, Decembe	2005/12/06 03:56	9999/12/31 00:00		Lisa Moorish has Li		<Long Text>	2
1029	2005/12/06	2005/12/06	The hills are alive w	Tuesday, Decembe	2005/12/06 04:09	9999/12/31 00:00		Tesco plans a launc		<Long Text>	9
1030	2005/12/06	2005/12/06	Epitaph for Hell is f	Tuesday, Decembe	2005/12/06 04:37	9999/12/31 00:00		UK's Hell is for Herc		<Long Text>	9
1031	2005/12/06	2005/12/06	Daddy Fresh Launc	Tuesday, Decembe	2005/12/06 05:18	2006/12/06 05:18		Daddy Fresh Launc		<Long Text>	9
1032	2005/12/06	2005/12/06	PRESS RELEASE: K	Tuesday, Decembe	2005/12/06 05:27	2006/12/06 05:27		PRESS RELEASE: K		<Long Text>	9
1033	2005/12/06	2005/12/06	Festival: The Night	Tuesday, Decembe	2005/12/06 05:35	9999/12/31 00:00		The Nightmare bef		<Long Text>	9
1034	2005/12/06	2005/12/06	Feeder postpone d	Tuesday, Decembe	2005/12/06 09:38	2006/03/06 09:38		Grant from Feeder		<P>Feeder's Lond	9
1035	2005/12/06	2005/12/06	Grassroots gig pre	Tuesday, Decembe	2005/12/05 11:00	2005/12/09 11:00		GRASSROOTS XMA		<Long Text>	9
1036	2005/12/06	2005/12/06	Elton to replace Mo	Tuesday, Decembe	2005/12/31 11:10	9999/12/31 00:00		Elton John and Dav		<P>Elton John anc	9
1037	2005/12/07	2005/12/07	Robbie is Not Gay	Wednesday, Decer	2005/12/07 03:52	2006/12/07 03:52		ROBBIE IS NOT GA		Robbie is NOT GAY	9
1038	2005/12/07	2005/12/07	My Space turns to	Wednesday, Decer	2005/12/07 03:55	9999/12/31 00:00		According to the FT		According to the FT	9
1039	2005/12/07	2005/12/07	Please rise Sir Terr	Wednesday, Decer	2005/12/07 04:03	9999/12/31 00:00		Terry Wogan has b		<P>'In the name o	9
1040	2005/12/07	2005/12/07	PODCAST is voted	Wednesday, Decer	2005/12/07 04:10	9999/12/31 00:00		Podcast has been c		<P>Podcast has be	9
1041	2005/12/07	2005/12/07	Indie Licence for Pc	Wednesday, Decer	2005/12/06 04:16	9999/12/31 00:00		Podcasts get licenc		<Long Text>	9
1042	2005/12/07	2005/12/07	Lyric sites get Ceas	Wednesday, Decer	2005/12/07 06:19	9999/12/31 00:00		Warner/Chappell h		<P>Warner/Chapp	9
1043	2005/12/07	2005/12/07	MP3 toilet seat	Wednesday, Decer	2005/12/07 06:26	9999/12/31 00:00		Those crazy Japan		<P>Upon reporting	9
1071	2005/12/12	2005/12/12	Williams - Pinball	Monday, December	2005/12/13 06:18	9999/12/31 00:00		<STRONG>Williams		<Long Text>	4
1073	2005/12/12	2005/12/12	Fink - 'Pretty Little	Monday, December	2005/12/12 06:43	9999/12/31 00:00		Fink - 'Pretty Little		<Long Text>	9
1074	2005/12/12	2005/12/12	Scuba - 'Words/ Th	Monday, December	2005/12/12 06:55	9999/12/31 00:00		Scuba - 'Words/ Th		<Long Text>	9
1075	2005/12/12	2005/12/12	Parker Frisby/Hiltm	Monday, December	2005/12/12 07:07	9999/12/31 00:00		Parker Frisby/ Hiltm		<Long Text>	1
1076	2005/12/12	2005/12/12	Touché - Interview	Monday, December	2005/12/12 07:49	9999/12/31 00:00		Ben Osborne interv		<Long Text>	9

Figure 13-13

You can see that there are several rows in this table, each containing the details of a different advertisement. The columns each contain different information about the article in that row:

- `articleid` is a number used to uniquely identify each article in the system.
- `posted` is the date the article was posted.
- `lastupdate` is the date that the article was last updated.
- `headline` is the headline for the article.
- `headlinedate` is the date that the article says it was written on.
- `startdate` is the date the article should be published on.
- `enddate` is the date that the article should stop being available on the site (several of the articles have the date set to the 31 December 9999 — so if the site is still around then, the managers will have to do something about the dates, but until then the article will remain published).

This table actually contains a lot more fields, but this gives you an idea of how the information is stored. When users come to the site that uses this database, they will navigate through categories to find the items they are interested in. Rather than having a page containing the details of each article, the site contains only one page that displays all news articles, called `article.aspx`. This is like a template for all the articles, and the title, headline date, and article are added into the page at the same place in each article. You can see an example of an article in Figure 13-14.

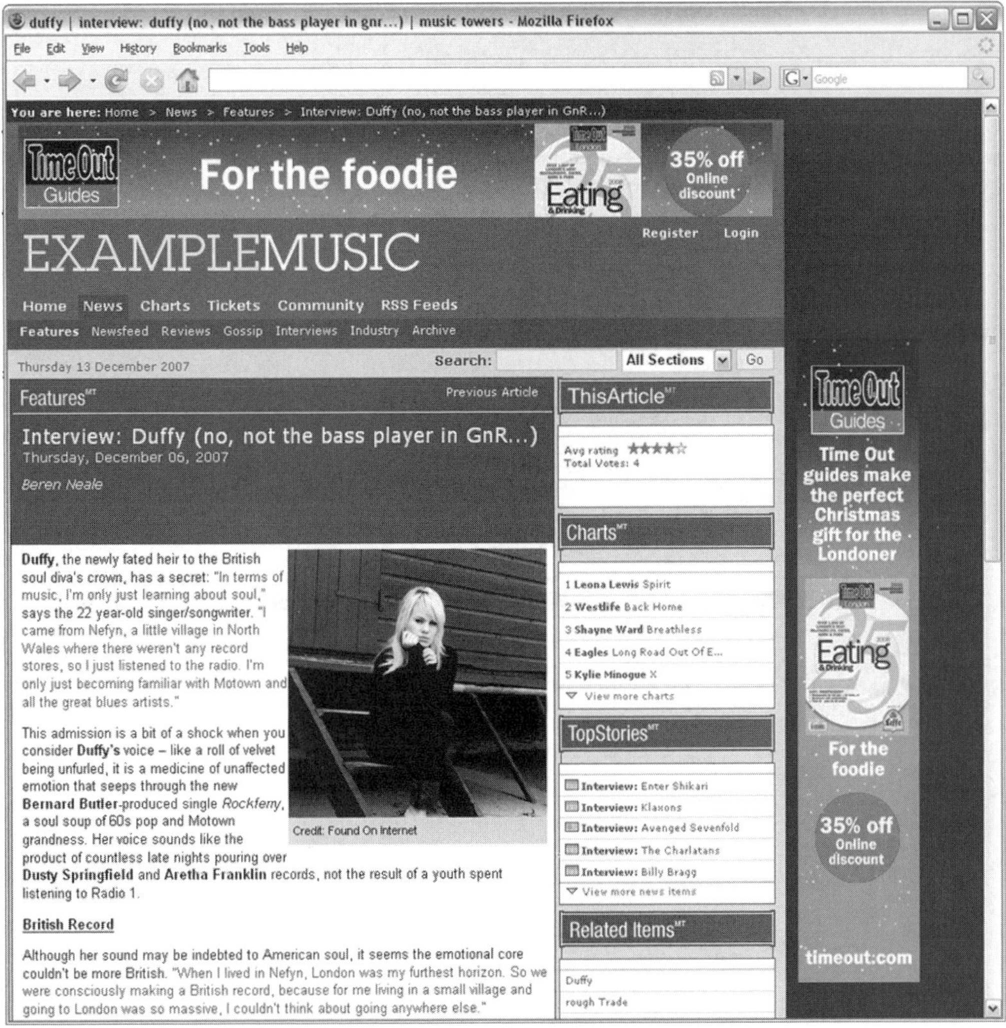

Figure 13-14

The structure of the URL for this article is the key to how this template-based system works:

```
http://www.example.com/news/features/article.aspx?a=1496
```

The `article.aspx` page is requested, and when it is requested, the article identifier `1496` is also requested. This corresponds with the number in the first column of the table in Figure 13-13. All the details of this article are then placed into the template. So, where the text says "Thursday December 6, 2007" this is the headline date field from the database.

Some sites contain the headlines in the URL rather than an article ID, for example:

```
http://www.example.com/news/features/Interview-Duffy-(no-not-the-bass-player-in-GnR)
```

Here you can see that the title of the article is used in the URL rather than the ID, which is known as URL rewriting. Behind the scenes, the URL is compared to the database, and it will know to return the article whose headline matches the end part of the URL.

This approach is also what makes it possible for many authors to update the same site without having to know how to code each individual page. They simply log into an administration tool that allows them to submit articles using a simple form. Figure 13-15 shows one of the pages that enables users to enter new articles.

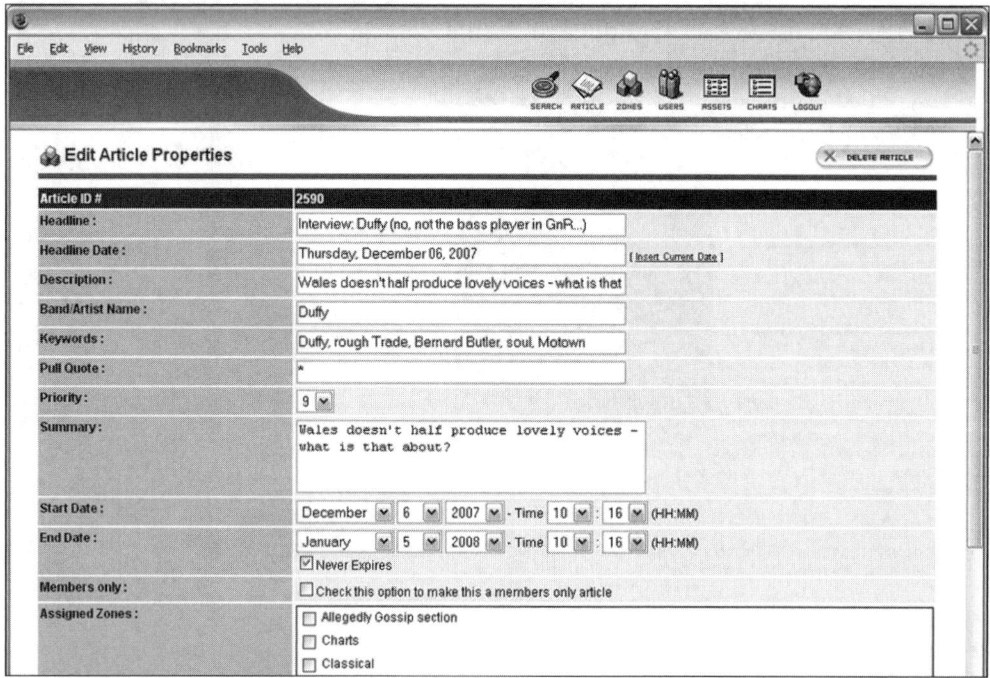

Figure 13-15

This approach of storing content in a database is employed in many different types of sites. For example, auction sites such as eBay store each item for sale in a row of a database; likewise, e-commerce stores tend to store product details in a database, with each product stored in a row of one of the tables. When these sites use a row of a table for each article or product, new articles or products can be added to the database using XHTML forms (rather than having to hand-code pages or manually update the database).

Flash

Flash is used on web sites for animated content, audio, and video. In order to view Flash files, users need the free Flash plug-in — known as the Flash Player — installed on their computers. Statistics from several sources suggest that over 90 percent of the computers connected to the Web have this installed.

In order to create Flash files, you need to purchase a special authoring tool made by Adobe. If you are considering learning Flash, you can download a free trial version from the Adobe web site to start practicing. It is a very powerful tool, and there are lots of examples of what you can do using Flash at the following sites:

- `www.adobe.com/products/flash/`
- `www.flashkit.com/gallery/`

Very few sites need to be designed completely in Flash. It is much more common to see parts of pages created in Flash (such as banner ads and animations). This is partly because it is much quicker to develop a site in XHTML and partly because fewer people have the skills to integrate Flash with databases than do with XHTML.

Learning Graphics Packages

Learning how to deal with text, illustrations, photos, and images correctly is very important if you are going to be involved with designing web pages as well as coding them. There are two key types of graphics packages you might want to learn:

- A photo editing and manipulation package such as Adobe Photoshop or the "lite" version, Photoshop Elements.
- A vector art package such as Adobe Illustrator or Macromedia Freehand. These work with vector graphics (line drawings created using coordinates), which are then filled in with colors.

Adobe Photoshop is by far the most popular graphics program used for developing web graphics, and a lot of people use this program to design entire sites. You need only look at job ads for web designers and you'll see that knowing Photoshop is often a prerequisite.

Photoshop not only allows you to work with photos, but it can also be used to create text and logos (although an experienced designer would usually favor a vector graphics program when it comes to creating logos and diagrams from scratch). It will then take these images and create optimized versions of them ready for the Web with smaller file sizes for quicker downloads.

When working in Photoshop, you can create an image built up from many layers — each layer is like a piece of clear film over the first image you start with, allowing you to make changes on top of the image.

When you have experience with a photo package, you might want to learn a vector image package, especially if you are going to be creating lots of logos or diagrams. Vector packages are of little use when it comes to working with photos, but they are great for doing line-based work. By their nature, vector graphics scale very well, and logos are often created in a vector format because they allow you to scale a logo to a large size for a poster or shrink it down for a small web graphic. By contrast, if you blow up a bitmapped image (the type used in Photoshop) to a very large size it will look grainy — you will be able to see all of the pixels that make up the image.

Of course, there are many other technologies you could learn, but the ones discussed in this section offer you the next logical steps in your web development career. If you want to work more with graphics, Photoshop or Flash are a good place to start. If you want to work more on programming, consider moving onto a server-side programming language.

Summary

In this chapter, you have seen how to prepare your web site for a waiting world. You started off learning about the `<meta>` tags that you can use to add content *about* your documents (such as the author, expiration date, or default scripting language) — hence the name `<meta>` *tags*; they contain information about the web page rather than being part of the content of the page.

You then learned about different sorts of tests that you should perform on your pages. These tests included validating your pages (to make sure that your markup is written according to the relevant recommendations and that you are following the rules you should), checking links to make sure all of them work and are not pointing to the wrong place, and checking that your site meets accessibility guidelines.

Next, you looked at the potential minefield of choosing a host on whose servers you can put your web site. This ever-changing market is hard to keep up with, but it can be well worth checking on a few hosts rather than going with the first one you find. New deals with more storage, greater bandwidth, larger mailboxes, and newer features are coming out all the time, so it pays to shop around.

Once your site is live, you will want people to come and look at it. You should try to attract new visitors through a combination of techniques, and this is an ongoing process that requires regular attention.

You can also gain valuable information about your visitors by using statistics packages that analyze your log files, working out how people came across your site, how many pages they looked at, what terms they searched on in search engines to arrive at your site, and so on.

The final part of the chapter looked at where you can go next with your site. You saw that there are services such as blogs, discussion boards, and search features that have already been developed by companies that allow you to integrate these services into your site. If you are interested in programming, you should consider learning a server-side language such as ASP.NET or PHP. Alternatively, if you are more interested in the visual appearance and design of sites you should consider learning a graphics program such as Adobe Photoshop, and possibly some animation software such as Flash.

This book has covered a lot, and the best way to make sure you have understood it properly is to get out there and build some sites. Perhaps you can create a site about a hobby or interest of yours, or maybe you can create a site for friends who run their own small business.

Remember that if you like the way someone has done something on a site (perhaps you like the layout, or the size and type of font used) you can simply go to the View menu on your browser and select the option to display the source for the page. While you should never copy someone else's design or layout, you can learn a lot from looking at how other people have built their sites. But remember that they might not be using XHTML; a lot of pages are out there that were built using earlier versions of HTML. HTML is not as strict about how you write your pages, and there are a lot of coders who are not as aware of such things as which elements require closing brackets, when to use quotes for attributes, or how to use CSS well.

While this more relaxed way of coding may seem easier, by being strict with how you use markup, separating as much of your markup from styling as possible, and using JavaScript only to enhance pages, you end up with pages that will be available to more browsers and more people for a longer time.

Checklists

This final chapter contains checklists on some helpful topics. The checklists are not intended to be exhaustive and turn you into an expert on each of these topics (as there are entire books devoted to the subjects of these checklists). Rather, the purpose is to show the key points, and bring together some of the things you have learned throughout the book. There are four checklists, covering:

- Search engine optimization
- Accessibility
- Differences between HTML and XHTML
- HTML 5

Search Engine Optimization Checklist

On any successful site, a good proportion of traffic will come from search engines. In order for people to find you on a search engine, you want to be as near the top of their search results as possible.

The techniques you can use to improve your visibility in search engines are known as *Search Engine Optimization* or *SEO* for short, and can be grouped in two ways:

- Things you can do on the site (on-page)
- Things that appear on other people's sites (off-page)

We will mainly be focusing on the former because you have a lot more control over what appears on the pages of your own site (although mentions will be made of off-page techniques).

On-Page Techniques

Before you can start optimizing your site for search engines, you need to determine what terms users would type into a search engine in order to find your site; these are known as *keywords* and *key phrases.*

You then need to include these keywords and phrases in the copy for your site. There are four places where it is important for these words and phrases to appear:

- ❑ **Title of the page:** This is specified in the `<title>` element, which you met in Chapter 1. It appears at the top of the browser window (above all the toolbars).
- ❑ **Description of the page:** This is added using the `<meta>` tag, which you met in Chapter 13. While it is not visible in the page, it is often shown in the results pages of search engines.
- ❑ **Headings:** You met the `<h1>` to `<h6>` tags in Chapter 1; they are used to help structure the page, providing headings that describe what will be found in the subsequent sections.
- ❑ **Body text:** This is the copy that appears in the `<body>` of the page, for example in paragraphs, lists, and links.

It is important to remember that search engines rely on text; they cannot see what is in images (other than in the alt text that you provide on images and in filenames). Therefore, if you can incorporate the keywords and phrases that you have identified into these four parts of your pages, your site is more likely to get picked up by search engines.

You can further help the search engines by carefully structuring your documents, and using semantic markup. A good way to add structure to your pages is to organize the sections of pages using headings that describe what will be found in the following paragraphs, lists, images, and forms. Furthermore, elements such as the `<address>`, `<cite>`, `<code>`, and `<em>` elements help describe the information that will be found inside those elements.

When working with search engines, it is important to remember that you should not try to fool them (for example, do not try to squeeze extra keywords onto your page by writing them in the same color as the background of the page). Search engines know a lot of ways in which people try to fool them, and they will penalize you for this kind of behavior. You should also avoid free (or paid) tools that promise to submit your site to hundreds of search engines.

I hope that all of the preceding information seems straightforward and easy to implement. For many people, the biggest problem regarding SEO is in identifying the keywords and phrases that they should be using in the first place, and that is what we will be focusing on in this checklist.

Identifying Keywords and Phrases

When choosing keywords and phrases, it is very important to remember that in most cases, it is important to focus not just on attracting volumes of users, but also on attracting the right kind of visitors. For example, if you are creating a site for a service that is offered locally, such as slate roofing, then you probably are not interested in people who:

- ❑ Do not live in the same geographic area you work in
- ❑ Have a roof made of tiles or shingles
- ❑ Live in apartment blocks (and do not have roofs of their own)

Therefore, getting 10,000 people to visit you by searching for "new roof" is not likely to be as valuable to you as getting 100 people who are looking for "slate roof Chicago."

It is also important that the page people find in the search engine has a title and description that relates to the keywords people are using when they search, because the titles and descriptions are commonly displayed in search engine results. If users do not think the page looks relevant (by looking at the information the search engine returns), they are less likely to click on the link to your page.

So, in order to come up with the search terms you are going to use on your site, use the steps in the following sections.

Brainstorm for Words People Might Search On

List every individual word you think people might search under when looking for your site.

Select Five to Ten Major Keywords

From your brainstorming list, select 5–10 major keywords, most of which will be single words (although you may have a couple of phrases, such as "slate roof").

Write these 5–10 major keywords in columns because you are going to create lists underneath them.

List Other Keywords and Phrases That Correspond to Your Major Keywords

Now that you have your list of major keywords, you can go back to your brainstorming session and expand upon the 5–10 major keywords you selected. List keywords and phrases that closely correspond to these major keywords.

You might find it helpful to look up synonyms of words in your list and also the root words of terms (for example, you might add light to a list that covers lighting).

It is also important to consider more generic terms such as buy, download, free, info, or tips, if you think that potential visitors might be hoping for one of these.

You should be looking for a total of around 20–30 popular phrases that you think your target audience will search for.

If you have a phrase that contains words such as "the" or "and," do not skip that word in the phrase. For example, "chicken and mushroom pie" should not become "chicken mushroom pie."

Look Up Related Words (Not Exact Matches)

Sometimes people will search for terms that are not exactly what your site offers, but they are close enough for your site to be relevant to that visitor. For example, thinking back to our café example, we might add restaurant and coffee shop to the lists.

If there are some terms that are not exact matches, but are relevant and related to the content of your site, add them under the major keywords.

Determine the Popularity of Terms

Use one of the following web-based tools to look up the words and phrases on your list.

- ❑ **Keyword Discovery:** `www.keyworddiscovery.com/`
- ❑ **Wordtracker:** `www.wordtracker.com/`

These tools both show alternative options for search terms. They also show the number of times people have searched for these words.

When you look at the alternative options for search terms on these sites, you want to look at the top 10 variations, and see how many are relevant — if several of the top 10 variations on the term apply to your site, then this should be a *core term* (and you should list the top 10 variations with it).

Prioritize the Core Terms

To determine the priority of the core terms that you have found, you need to look at the number of searches each core term got, and compare this number with how closely you think that search meets your target audience. At first this will require you to judge which terms you think might be most relevant to your audience, but as your site grows you will be able to use analytics software to discover how people are really finding your site.

If a search term generates 10,000 visitors, but only 10 percent would be interested in the content of your site, that term is not as valuable as a term that attracts just 5,000 viewers of whom 50 percent would be interested in your content.

Location

If the information, service or product your site offers is location-dependent, then the location should be added to your core terms.

The location you choose to include might not just be the name of the town that your business is based in. If you have customers across the state, county, or region that you work in, you might like to use those names, too (after all, more people might search on the name of the region than on your specific town).

Mapping Core Terms to Pages

Now you need to take each of the core terms (and its variations) and map them to the most relevant page.

Most of the core terms will match to internal pages. You might have more than one page focused on one core term, but you should not try to get more than one core term per page (or one core term plus location).

Homepages

The two or three most general (rather than specific) and the most popular core terms should be prime targets for the homepage.

Whenever you are looking at your on-page techniques for search engine optimization, it is important to measure the success of your efforts. This involves not only looking at things such as your page rank in Google, but also using analytics software to see which terms people are searching on most frequently in order to find your site (a topic which was introduced in Chapter 13).

Off-Page Techniques

When search engines calculate where to position your site on a list of search results, the major search engines will consider the number of sites that link to you.

The search engines are not just looking for any site that links to you, but rather for sites that contain terms similar to those that people are entering into search engines in order to find your site. For example, a search engine would not consider a link from an acupuncture site to a site about slate roofing as having the importance of a link between a building projects site and a site about slate roofing.

Search engines also look at the words that appear between the opening `<a>` tag and the closing `</a>` tag. If the text in the link contains keywords, the search engines will consider that link more relevant than one that just says something like "Click here."

If you use analytics software on your site, then you will be able to see which sites are linking to you. You can then use this information to find more sites that cover similar topics and see if they would like to cover you, too.

Accessibility Checklist

Accessibility is about ensuring that as many people as possible can access your web pages. Traditionally, writing on accessibility has focused on people who may have disabilities such as vision impairments (and therefore use screen readers to read the content of web sites to them). Others might have poor motor control and find it hard to use a mouse. However, it is increasingly becoming apparent that accessibility techniques apply to people who simply do not use a standard desktop PC to access web pages — for example, those on mobile devices who might not be able to use a mouse or view as many images at the same time.

Entire books have been written on accessible design for the Web, but this checklist will help ensure that your site meets basic accessibility requirements, and points you to the relevant part of the book where each of these topics was discussed.

Setting Up Your Document

When creating any new document, you should:

- ❑ Use a DOCTYPE declaration to indicate which version of HTML or XHTML you are using.
- ❑ Specify the language of your document on the `<body>` element. If the language changes in the middle of the text, specify it with the `lang` or `xml:lang` attributes.

Structural and Semantic Markup

In Chapter 1, you met lots of elements that are used to mark up text. You should always try to use these elements to add structure and semantic information to the words on the page. Where possible:

- ❑ Use the different levels of headings `<h1>` through `<h6>` to organize and add structure to your pages.
- ❑ Use elements for the purpose they were created, not just for visual effects (use CSS to control presentation of documents).
- ❑ Use any elements available that describe the purpose or meaning of words in your page; for example, use the `<acronym>` element when you have an acronym on the page, use the `<address>` element when you have an mail address to write out, and the `<code>` element when you are writing code.
- ❑ Try to use relative units of measurement for your text (rather than absolute sizes) so that users can easily increase and decrease the size of the text in their browser.

Links and Navigation

As you saw in Chapter 2, links are one of the key things that differentiate the Web from other media. Your links need to be as accessible as possible so that people can navigate your site. When you are creating links:

- ❑ Ensure that your links stand out on the page so visitors can easily see where they should be clicking and thus can skim the page for links.
- ❑ Use text or images inside the link that will describe what visitors will see if they click the link (do not just use terms such as "click here"). If you use images inside a link, it is important to ensure that the alt text describes what users will see if they click the link.
- ❑ You can use the `title` attribute on an `<a>` element to provide additional information to a visitor.
- ❑ In Chapter 5 you saw how forms can make use of keyboard shortcuts to help visitors navigate the form. Keyboard shortcuts could also be used to link to other parts of pages.
- ❑ Avoid opening links in new windows as this can often confuse users who either do not see the new window opening, or end up with more windows open than they wanted.
- ❑ Avoid links and interactive elements that require a user to have fine control over the mouse (or other pointing device).

Images and Multimedia

Images, audio, and video (as you saw in Chapter 3) can really bring a page to life. But assistive technologies used by those who have vision impairments are unable to describe the content of an image, audio file, or video. Therefore, there is one key rule for all kinds of multimedia content: Always provide a text description for non-text content. To achieve this:

- ❑ Provide an `alt` attribute for every image, and ensure that the text you specify as a value of the `alt` attribute describes the content of that image to a visitor. The only exception to this rule is when the image does not convey any meaning (perhaps it is just a decorative element). In this case you still use the `alt` attribute, but you do not give it a value.
- ❑ If the image is quite complex and the description does not fit nicely into the `alt` attribute (for example, if you have an information graphic), you can use the `longdesc` attribute to specify where a longer description is, or use a letter D inside a normal link that points to a longer description.
- ❑ If you have video or audio track, provide a text-based transcript (either on the same page or link to it).
- ❑ If you use an image map, offer a text-based alternative to the image links.
- ❑ If you provide any animated content, ensure that there is an easy way for the visitor to pause or stop that content.
- ❑ You should also avoid using animated content that could induce a seizure (for example, strobed content). If you do want to include such content, there should be a clear warning before that content, which the user should be forced to read and agree to.

Color

Color is an important part of any web site, but color blindness is far more prevalent than most web designers realize. When creating a page, color can help add information and organize the page. However:

- ❑ No information on the page should be conveyed by color alone.
- ❑ There must be sufficient contrast between backgrounds and text so that the user can read the content. (You saw tools for checking this in Chapter 13.)

Tables

We looked at creating tables in Chapter 4. When you create a table you should:

- ❑ Use `<th>` elements for all headings.
- ❑ Describe the content of the table using the `<caption>` element.
- ❑ In complex tables, use the `scope` and `headers` attributes to describe which cells each heading corresponds to.
- ❑ Not use tables as a way to control layout of entire pages.

Forms

Chapter 5 introduced forms, which you will need to use if you want to collect information from visitors to your site. I then discussed them again in the chapters that covered JavaScript. Some instructions for their use follow:

- ❑ Use the `<label>` element to indicate the label for each individual type of form element.
- ❑ If a user makes an error, where possible write the error next to the appropriate form field, and give that form element focus so the user can correct the element.
- ❑ Make use of the `<fieldset>` and `<legend>` elements to group form controls into related functionality.
- ❑ Access keys can help users navigate long forms.

Style Sheets

You looked at CSS in Chapters 7 and 8. Using CSS to control the presentation of a document will automatically help improve accessibility of the page (because style sheets can be overruled by a user when necessary). But you should still:

- ❑ Use relative measurements rather than absolute measurements (or pixels) where possible (particularly for text).
- ❑ Organize the page so it can still be read without style sheets.
- ❑ Ensure that you have provided enough contrast in colors so that any text can easily be read.
- ❑ Aim to design for device independence, or use CSS to provide alternative style sheets for multiple devices.

JavaScript

JavaScript was covered in Chapters 11 and 12. It is important that your pages work even if the user does not have JavaScript enabled. Here are some instructions that help ensure your scripts do not compromise the accessibility of pages:

- ❑ If you need to use JavaScript on your pages (and they will not work without it), then you should use the `<noscript>` element to provide an explanation that the page will not work if the visitor does not have JavaScript enabled.
- ❑ Do not automatically refresh pages (and if you provide this feature, allow visitors the option to turn it off).
- ❑ Do not use JavaScript to redirect people from one page to another.
- ❑ Ensure that your scripts can be controlled with accessible/assistive technologies (such as screen readers).

Skip Links

One topic not covered in the main part of the book is the creation of skip links. These are links that allow people who use screen readers (rather than visual browsers) to skip over the common content that appears on every page, such as the header and main navigation. Imagine that you are browsing the Web using technology that reads every single page to you; you can see that on sites where you viewed many pages, it would not take long to get tired of hearing the same header repeatedly every time you moved to a new page.

The solution to this problem is a technique generally known as *skip links* or *skip navigation*. It simply involves creating links to specific parts of the page, such as the main content, and then hiding those links from users who are browsing visually using CSS. For example, take a look at the following links after the opening body element:

```
<body>
  <div class="skip-links">
    <a href="#content">skip to main content</a>
    <a href="#search">skip to search</a>
    <a href="#footer">skip to footer</a>
  </div>
```

These links correspond to `id` attributes of `<a>` elements in the relevant sections of the page. For example, the first `<h1>` element might look like this:

```
<h1><a id="#content">Introduction to Accessibility</h1>
```

The links at the top of the page are hidden using a CSS rule like this so that visitors using a normal visual browser do not see the skip links:

```
.skip-links {display:none;}
```

This makes browsing a site much more pleasant for those who are having the site read to them.

Differences Between HTML and XHTML

Most of this book covers XHTML. But having learned XHTML, you are now able to code in HTML, too, because XHTML is HTML 4 written using stricter rules. The sections that follow summarize the differences between HTML and XHTML.

All Tag Names and Attribute Names Must Be Written in Lowercase

In HTML you could use a mix of uppercase and lowercase characters:

```
<P>Here is a <b>bold</b> word in a paragraph</P>.
```

In XHTML, all tag names and attribute names must be written in lowercase:

```
<p>Here is a <b>bold</b> word in a paragraph</p>.
```

All Attributes Must Have a Value Given in Double Quotation Marks

In HTML, you could have attributes that did not have a value, and the values did not need to be in quotation marks:

```
<form method=post>
```

In XHTML, all attributes must have a value (the value can just be the name of the attribute if no other is given), and they must be given in double quotation marks:

```
<form method="post">
```

Elements Must Nest; There Must Be No Overlapping

In HTML, you may find that some elements are not placed entirely within one element; the opening tag may sit inside one element and be closed outside that element:

```
<p>Here is a paragraph, the second half <b>will be in bold.</b></p>
```

In XHTML, if an opening tag sits inside another element, the closing tag must also sit within the same element:

```
<p>Here is a paragraph, the second half <b>will be in bold.</b></p>
```

Empty Elements Must Contain a Closing Slash

In HTML, you might see an empty element written like this:

```
<img src="images/test.gif" alt="Test image">
```

In XHTML, there should be a forward slash character before the closing angled bracket to indicate that the element is empty:

```
<img src="images/test.gif" alt="Test image" />
```

Scripts Should Live in a CDATA Section

In HTML, scripts and style elements could be included in a document, even if they included characters such as `&` or <:

```
<script type="text/javascript">
test(value1, value2) {
  if ((value1 < value2) && (value1.length > 5)) {
    x = true;
  }
}
</script>
```

In XHTML, scripts should live inside a CDATA section like so:

```
<script type="text/javascript">
<![CDATA[
test(value1, value2) {
  if ((value1 < value2) && (value1.length > 5)) {
    x = true;
  }
}
]]>
</script>
```

HTML 5

Having reached the end of a book on HTML 4.01 and XHTML, you might not expect to see an additional section showing HTML 5. But HTML 5 will be the next major version of HTML, designed to replace HTML 4.01 and XHTML.

Realistically, it is expected that the work on HTML 5 will take several years before it is finished and released; however, some browsers are already implementing some features of HTML 5 (such as new browser-side database and caching mechanisms, APIs that help add audio and video to pages or that facilitate drag-and-drop functionality, and some new elements that help add semantic information to pages).

The purpose of this section is therefore just to give you a hint of how HTML will be developing in the future.

Language Compatibility in HTML 5

In order to be backwards compatible with earlier versions of HTML, the markup of HTML 5 will not be as strict as that of XHTML.

Authors can used mixed case in tags and attributes (rather than all lowercase), closing elements may be missed, and not all attributes need to have values or be given in quotes.

There will be a new doctype declaration:

```
<!DOCTYPE html>
```

Stylistic Markup Will Be Removed

Certain deprecated elements are being removed, including `<big>`, `<center>`, `<font>`, `<s>`, `<strike>`, `<tt>`, and `<u>` because these effects should be achieved by CSS. Frames and their associated markup are also being removed (although the `<iframe>` element is likely to remain part of the specification).

Presentational attributes such as `align`, `background`, `bgcolor`, `border`, `cellpadding`, `cellspacing`, `char`, `compact`, `height`, `marginheight`, `nowrap`, `size`, `type`, and `width` are all being removed.

Having said this, in practice browsers are still likely to support these older elements so that they can render older pages, which means that these elements may still work.

New Semantic Elements

There are several new elements and attributes that reflect the typical use of modern sites. Several of these are semantic replacements for the generic `<div>` and `<span>` elements that are used to group parts of pages. Here are a few examples:

- ❑ `<nav>` for a section of the page that shows navigation
- ❑ `<header>` for the header of a page with introductory or navigational content
- ❑ `<footer>` for footer information such as copyright and author information
- ❑ `<article>` to represent an independent piece of a document such as a blog entry or newspaper article
- ❑ `<section>` to act as a generic section of a document or application (it has to be a logical section; the element should not just be used to add styling to a group of elements, which remains the job of the `<div>` element)
- ❑ `<hgroup>` to contain the header of an individual section
- ❑ `<aside>` to represent something that is only slightly related to the rest of the content
- ❑ `<figure>` to associate a caption with a graphic or video (for example)

```
<figure>
  <video src="BobsFirstBirthday.ogv"></video>
  <legend>A video of Bob's first Birthday</legend>
</figure>
```

- ❑ `<progress>` to represent the completion of a task
- ❑ `<command>` to represent a command a user can invoke
- ❑ `<time>` to represent a date or time

To see how this new markup might be used in practice, let's look at an example of how you might create a page today using `<div>` elements to group together parts of the page, and then we can look at how these new elements in HTML 5 would be used to recreate the same page:

```
<div id="header">
  <div id="navigation"></div>
</div>
<div class="article">
  <div class="section"</div>
  <div class="section"</div>
  <div class="section"</div>
</div>
<div class="side_widget"></div>
<div id="footer"></div>
```

Now, if we look at how the same structure might be represented in HTML 5 you can see that the new elements add semantic information that explains what will be found in that section of the markup, rather than just grouping elements using a generic `<div>` element:

```
<header>
  <nav></nav>
</header>
<article>
  <section></section>
  <section></section>
  <section></section>
</article>
<footer></footer>
```

New Values for the <input> Element's type Attribute

The `<input>` element can take new values for the `type` attribute, including:

- `tel` for a telephone number (a single line text box with no breaks)
- `search` for a search input (a single line text box with no breaks)
- `url` for a path to a page or other resource on the web
- `email` for an e-mail address or list of e-mail addresses
- `datetime` for a date and time (year, month, day, hour, minute, second, fraction of second, with time zone set to UTC)
- `date` for a date (year, month and day with no time zone)
- `month` for a date with a year and a month (no time zone)
- `week` for a date consisting of a week number and year (no time zone)
- `datetime-local` for a date with year, month, day, hour, minute, second, fraction of a second, with time zone
- `number` for a numerical value
- `range` for a numerical value with extra information that indicates a range of number (adding `min` and `max` attributes to describe the range)
- `color` for a color specified using a hex code or three numbers ranging from 0 to 255

New Multimedia Elements

Other new elements provide ways to integrate specific types of content, such as the `<audio>` and `<video>` element, without relying on plug-ins. The `<audio>` element will allow MP3s to be embedded into the page; the `<video>` element is more controversial at the time of this writing, as browser manufacturers are struggling to agree on one common format that all browsers will support.

HTML 5 will also be able to use SVG and MathML inline.

New APIs

In addition to the Document Object Model (which you learned about in Chapter 11, which introduced JavaScript), new interfaces are being developed that cover the following:

- **Offline storage of data:** Allows the browser to store information locally; this is already being used for things such as managing e-mail when you are not connected.
- **Geolocation:** Allows the browser to identify where you are, which then enables featuers such as searches to be localized.
- **Canvas:** Allows you to create two-dimensional drawings using JavaScript, which could have many applications from creating graphs and information graphics to producing interactive animations.
- **Timed media playback:** Allows the browser to access and play time-based media such as audio and video, as well as showing the states of the files (such as whether they are ready to play or not, and whether they are loading).
- **Drag and drop:** Provides an event-based system for dragging and dropping elements of a page.
- **Cross-document messaging:** Allows part of a page to communicate with another part of the page or even a different window, without the entire page being refreshed. For example, you might have a text editor for creating a new blog post in one part of the page and a live preview of what that page will look like in another (where updates are shown in real time, without needing to refresh the page).

All the information in this section is still subject to change over the next few years until those working on the HTML 5 specification have finished it. Once the specification has become final, it is likely that many visitors to sites you develop will still be using older browsers, so you may not be able to use these new features for another few years. Having said this, many browsers are starting to implement some of the features discussed in this section, and you should be able to experiment with them over the next few years as they develop.

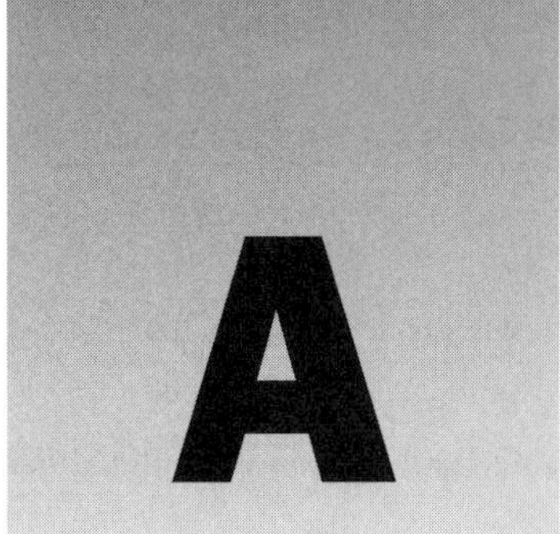

Answers to Exercises

This appendix covers the answers to each of the exercises at the end of each chapter.

Chapter 1

Exercise 1

Mark up the following sentence with the relevant presentational elements.

> The 1st time the **bold** man wrote in *italics*, he underlined several key words.

Answer

The sentence uses superscript, bold, italic, and underlined presentational elements.

```
<p>The 1<sup>st</sup> time the bold man wrote in <i>italics</i>, he
<u>underlined</u> several key words.</p>
```

Exercise 2

Mark up the following list, with inserted and deleted content:

Ricotta pancake ingredients:

- 1 ~~1/2~~ 3/4 cups ricotta
- 3/4 cup milk
- 4 eggs
- 1 cup plain white flour
- 1 teaspoon baking powder

- ~~75g~~ 50g butter
- pinch of salt

Answer

Here is the bulleted list with elements that show which content has been inserted and deleted:

```
<h1>Ricotta pancake ingredients:</h1>
<ul>
  <li>1 <del>1/2</del><ins>3/4</ins> cups ricotta</li>
  <li>3/4 cup milk</li>
  <li>4 eggs</li>
  <li>1 cup plain <ins>white</ins> flour</li>
  <li>1 teaspoon baking powder</li>
  <li><del>75g</del><ins>50g</ins> butter</li>
  <li>pinch of salt</li>
</ul>
```

Chapter 2

Exercise 1

Look back at the Try It Out example where you created a menu, and create a new page that links directly to each course on the menu. Then add a link to the main Wrox web site (`www.wrox.com`). The page should look something like Figure A-1.

Figure A-1

Answer

Here is the page with links to the menu first, and then a link to the Wrox Press web site:

```
<?xml version="1.0" encoding="iso-8859-1"?>
<!DOCTYPE html PUBLIC "-//W3C//DTD XHTML 1.0 Transitional//EN"
  "http://www.w3.org/TR/xhtml1/DTD/xhtml1-transitional.dtd">
<html xmlns="http://www.w3.org/1999/xhtml">
<head>
  <title>Links to Example Cafe and Wrox.com</title>
  <meta http-equiv="Content-Type" content="text/html; charset=iso-8859-1"/>
</head>
<body>
```

```
    <h1>Links to Example Cafe</h1>
    <p>
      <a href="http://www.examplecafe.com/menu.html#starters">Starters</a> |
      <a href="http://www.examplecafe.com/menu.html#mains">Main Courses</a> |
      <a href="http://www.examplecafe.com/menu.html#desserts">Desserts</a>
    </p>
    <p>This is an example taken from a book published by
      <a href="http://www.wrox.com">Wrox Press</a>
    </p>.
  </body>
  </html>
```

Exercise 2

Go back to the pages in the sample application and make sure that you have updated the navigation for each page.

Answer

Navigation for the homepage:

```
<div>
    HOME
    <a href="menu.html">MENU</a>
    <a href="recipes.html">RECIPES</a>
    <a href="contact.html">CONTACT</a>
</div>
```

Navigation for the menu page:

```
<div>
    <a href="index.html">HOME</a>
    MENU
    <a href="recipes.html">RECIPES</a>
    <a href="contact.html">CONTACT</a>
  </div>
```

Navigation for the recipes page:

```
<div>
    <a href="index.html">HOME</a>
    <a href="menu.html">MENU</a>
    RECIPES
    <a href="contact.html">CONTACT</a>
  </div>
```

Navigation for the contact page:

```
<div>
    <a href="index.html">HOME</a>
    <a href="menu.html">MENU</a>
    <a href="recipes.html">RECIPES</a>
    CONTACT
  </div>
```

Chapter 3

Exercise 1

Add the images of icons that represent a diary, a camera, and a newspaper to the following example. All of the images are provided in the `images` folder in the download code for Chapter 3.

```
<h1>Icons</h1>
<p>Here is an icon used to represent a diary.</p>
<img src="images/diary.gif" alt="Diary" width="150" height="120" /><br />

<p>Here is an icon used to represent a picture.</p>
Camera image goes here<br />

<p>Here is an icon used to represent a news item.</p>
Newspaper image goes here<br />
```

Your finished page should resemble Figure A-2.

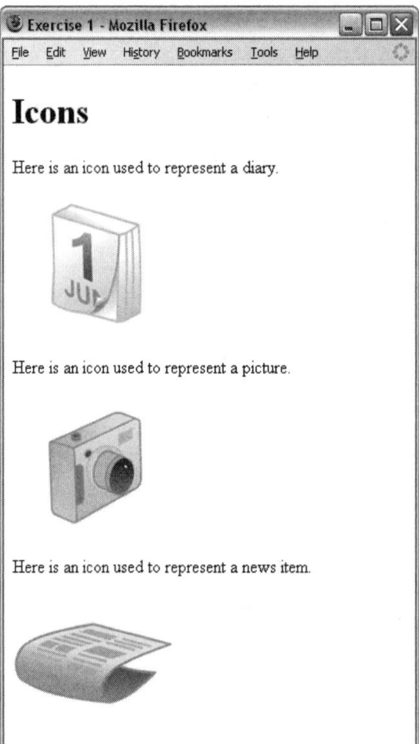

Figure A-2

Answer

Here is the code for this page:

```
<?xml version="1.0" ?>
<!DOCTYPE html PUBLIC "-//W3C//DTD XHTML 1.0 Strict//EN"
 "http://www.w3.org/TR/xhtml1/DTD/xhtml1-strict.dtd">
<html xmlns="http://www.w3.org/1999/xhtml" lang="en" xml:lang="en">

<head>
  <title>Exercise 1</title>
</head>

<body>
  <h1>Icons</h1>
  <p>Here is an icon used to represent a diary.</p>
  <img src="images/diary.gif" alt="Diary" width="150" height="120" /><br />

  <p>Here is an icon used to represent a picture.</p>
  <img src="images/picture.gif" alt="Picture" width="150" height="120" /><br />

  <p>Here is an icon used to represent a news item.</p>
  <img src="images/news.gif" alt="news" width="150" height="120" /><br />

</body>
</html>
```

Exercise 2

Look at the images shown in Figures A-3 and A-4 and decide whether you are more likely to get smaller file sizes and better quality images if you save them as JPEGs or GIFs.

Figure A-3

Figure A-4

Answer

As discussed in Chapter 3, images with large, flat areas of color, such as Image 1 where we see only the silhouette of the people, compress better as GIFs than JPEGs, while JPEGs are better for saving photographic images where there is greater variety of colors and more difference in the shades of different colors.

- Image 1 (Figure A-3): GIF or PNG (you may remember that PNGs are a replacement for GIFs)
- Image 2 (Figure A-4): JPEG.

Exercise 3

Go through the files for the sample application and replace the main heading with the logo on each page. On every page except for the homepage, make sure that the image links back to the `index.html` page.

Answer

The new heading should look like this:

```
<a id="top" href="index.html">
  <img src="images/logo.gif" alt="example cafe" width="194" height="80" />
</a>
```

Chapter 4

Exercise 1

Where should the `<caption>` element for a table be placed in the document and, by default, where is it displayed?

Answer

The <caption> element should appear after the opening <table> element but before the first <tr> element.

Exercise 2

In what order would the cells in Figure A-5 be read out by a screen reader?

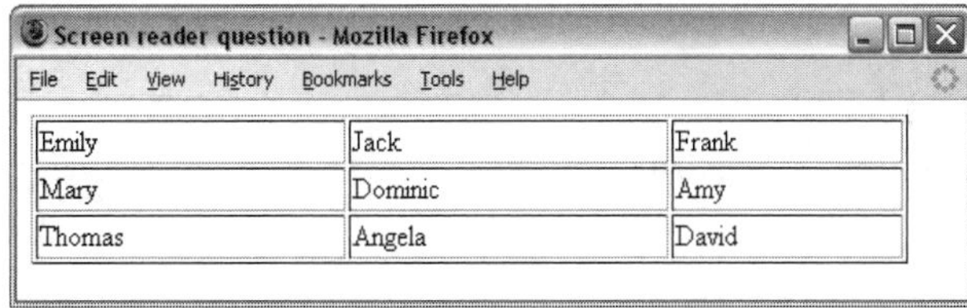

Emily	Jack	Frank
Mary	Dominic	Amy
Thomas	Angela	David

Figure A-5

Answer

The names would be read in the following order: Emily, Jack, Frank, Mary, Dominic, Amy, Thomas, Angela, and David.

Exercise 3

Create a table to hold the data shown in Figure A-6. To give you a couple of clues, the document must be Transitional XHTML 1.0 because the `width` attribute is used on the cells of the first row of the table. You have also seen examples of how the border is generated in this chapter, using another deprecated attribute, but on the <table> element rather than the cells.

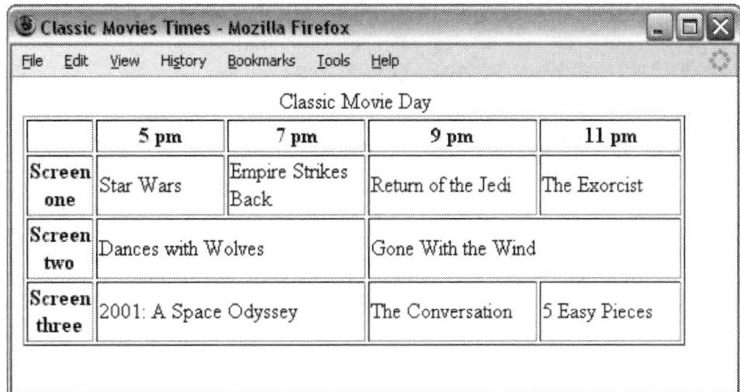

Classic Movie Day

	5 pm	7 pm	9 pm	11 pm
Screen one	Star Wars	Empire Strikes Back	Return of the Jedi	The Exorcist
Screen two	Dances with Wolves		Gone With the Wind	
Screen three	2001: A Space Odyssey		The Conversation	5 Easy Pieces

Figure A-6

Answer

Here is the code for the cinema timetable (`ch04_exercise3.html`):

```
<?xml version="1.0" encoding="UTF-8"?>
<!DOCTYPE html PUBLIC "-//W3C//DTD XHTML 1.0 Transitional//EN"
 "http://www.w3.org/TR/xhtml1/DTD/xhtml1-transitional.dtd">
<html xmlns="http://www.w3.org/1999/xhtml" lang="en">

<head>
  <title>Classic Movies Times</title>
</head>

<body>
<table border="1" width="500">
<caption>Classic Movie Day</caption>
  <tr>
    <th></th>
    <th width="200">5 pm</th>
    <th width="200">7 pm</th>
    <th width="200">9 pm</th>
    <th width="200">11 pm</th>
  </tr>
  <tr>
    <th>Screen one</th>
    <td>Star Wars</td>
    <td>Empire Strikes Back</td>
    <td>Return of the Jedi</td>
    <td>The Exorcist</td>
  </tr>
  <tr>
    <th>Screen two</th>
    <td colspan="2">Dances with Wolves</td>
    <td colspan="2">Gone With the Wind</td>
  </tr>
  <tr>
    <th>Screen three</th>
    <td colspan="2">2001: A Space Odyssey</td>
    <td>The Conversation</td>
    <td>5 Easy Pieces</td>
  </tr>
</table>

</body>
</html>
```

Chapter 5

Exercise 1

Create an e-mail feedback form that looks like the one shown in Figure A-7.

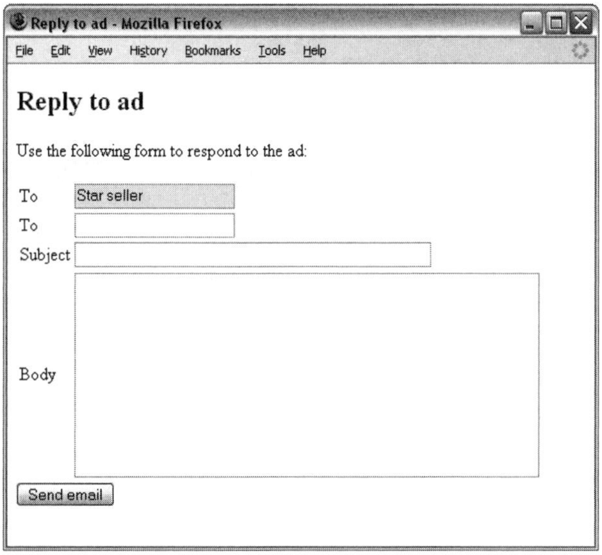

Figure A-7

Note that the first textbox is a `readonly` textbox so that the user cannot alter the name of the person the mail is being sent to, and that `readonly` textboxes are displayed in different ways on different browsers (in this example you can see the text input is grayed out, whereas on some other browsers you might just see a lighter border around the text input).

Answer

Here is the code for the feedback form:

```
<?xml version="1.0" encoding="UTF-8"?>
<!DOCTYPE html PUBLIC "-//W3C//DTD XHTML 1.0 Transitional//EN"
 "http://www.w3.org/TR/xhtml1/DTD/xhtml1-transitional.dtd">
<html xmlns="http://www.w3.org/1999/xhtml" lang="en">

<head>
  <title>Reply to ad</title>
</head>

<body>
<h2>Reply to ad</h2>
<p>Use the following form to respond to the ad:</p>

<form action="http://www.example.com/ads/respond.aspx" method="post"
      name="frmRespondToAd">
<table>
  <tr>
    <td><label for="emailTo">To</label></td>
    <td><input type="text" name="txtTo" readonly="readonly" id="emailTo"
         size="20" value="Star Seller" /></td>
  </tr>
```

```
    <tr>
      <td><label for="emailFrom">To</label></td>
      <td><input type="text" name="txtFrom" id="emailFrom" size="20" /></td>
    </tr>
    <tr>
      <td><label for="emailSubject">Subject</label></td>
      <td><input type="text" name="txtSubject" id="emailSubject"
          size="50" /></td>
    </tr>
    <tr>
      <td><label for="emailBody">Body</label></td>
      <td><textarea name="txtBody" id="emailBody" cols="50" rows="10">
          </textarea></td>
    </tr>
  </table>
    <input type="submit" value="Send email" />

  </form>

  </body>
  </html>
```

Exercise 2

Create a voting or ranking form that looks like the one shown in Figure A-8.

Figure A-8

Note that the following `<style>` element was added to the `<head>` of the document to make each column of the table the same fixed width, with text aligned in the center.

```
<head>
  <title>Voting</title>
  <style type="text/css">td {width:100; text-align:center;}</style>
</head>
```

Answer

Here is the code for the voting form. Note how the checked attribute is used on the middle value for this form so that it loads with an average score (in case the form is submitted without a value selected):

```
<?xml version="1.0" ?>
<!DOCTYPE html PUBLIC "-//W3C//DTD XHTML 1.0 Transitional//EN"
 "http://www.w3.org/TR/xhtml1/DTD/xhtml1-transitional.dtd">
<html xmlns="http://www.w3.org/1999/xhtml" lang="en">

<head>
  <title>Voting</title>
  <style type="text/css">td {width:100; text-align:center;}</style>
</head>

<body>
<h2>Register your opinion</h2>
<p>How well do you rate the information on this site (where 1 is
    very poor and 5 is very good)?</p>

<form action="http://www.example.com/ads/respond.aspx" method="get"
       name="frmRespondToAd">

<table>
  <tr>
    <td><input type="radio" name="radVote" value="1" id="vpoor" /></td>
    <td><input type="radio" name="radVote" value="2" id="poor" /></td>
    <td><input type="radio" name="radVote" value="3" id="average"
         checked="checked" /></td>
    <td><input type="radio" name="radVote" value="4" id="good" /></td>
    <td><input type="radio" name="radVote" value="5" id="vgood" /></td>
  </tr>
  <tr>
    <td><label for="vpoor">1 <br />Very Poor</label></td>
    <td><label for="poor">2 <br />Poor</label></td>
    <td><label for="average">3 <br />Average</label></td>
    <td><label for="good">4 <br />Good</label></td>
    <td><label for="vgood">5 <br />Very Good</label></td>
  </tr>
</table>
<input type="submit" value="Vote now" />
</form>

</body>
</html>
```

Chapter 6

Exercise 1

Create a frameset like the one shown in Figure A-9, where clicking a fruit loads a new page in the main window. When the page loads in the main window, it will carry the details for the appropriate fruit (to save time, you can use the images and fruit description pages in the code download, but try to create the frameset and navigation on your own).

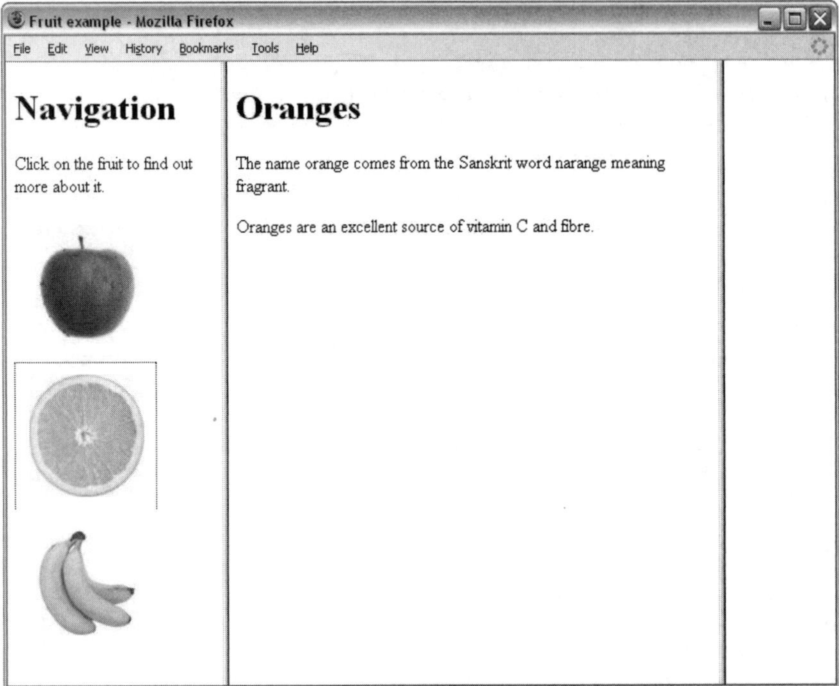

Figure A-9

Answer

The first example required five files:

- A frameset document
- A navigation document
- The apple page
- The orange page
- The banana page

Here is the frameset document (`ch06_exercise1.html`):

```
<?xml version="1.0" encoding="iso-8859-1"?>
<!DOCTYPE html PUBLIC "-//W3C//DTD XHTML 1.0 Frameset//EN"
 "http://www.w3.org/TR/xhtml1/DTD/xhtml1-frameset.dtd">
<html>
<head>
  <title>Fruit example</title>
```

```
</head>

<frameset cols="200, 450, *">
  <frame src="frames/fruitNav.html" />
  <frame name="main_frame" src="frames/apple.html" />

  <noframes><body>This site makes use of a technology called frames.
  Unfortunately the browser you are using does not support this technology.
  We recommend that you update your browser. We apologize for any
  inconvenience this causes.
  </body></noframes>

</frameset>

</html>
```

This is a frameset document type, which contains two columns that are a fixed size, and then the remainder of the window is left blank (hence there are only `<frame>` elements for the first two columns). Note how the second `<frame>` element carries the `name` attribute so that the links in the navigation frame can load in that part of the page.

Here is the navigation pane (`fruitNav.html`):

```
<?xml version="1.0" encoding="iso-8859-1"?>
<!DOCTYPE html PUBLIC "-//W3C//DTD XHTML 1.0 Transitional//EN"
"http://www.w3.org/TR/xhtml1/DTD/xhtml1-transitional.dtd">
<html xmlns="http://www.w3.org/1999/xhtml">
<head>
  <title>Navigation</title>
  <style type="text/css">img {border-style:none; border-width:0px;}</style>
</head>
<body>

<h1> Navigation </h1>
<p>Click on the fruit to find out more about it.</p>
<a href="../frames/apple.html" target="main_frame"><img src="../images/
   apple.jpg" alt="apple" /></a>
<a href="../frames/orange.html" target="main_frame"><img src="../images/
   orange.jpg" alt="orange" /></a>
<a href="../frames/banana.html" target="main_frame"><img src="../images/
   banana.jpg" alt="banana" /></a>
</body>
</html>
```

This is a normal XHTML document; the only things of note in this document are the `target` attributes on the links to indicate that the link should open in the other frame, and the `<style>` element in the `<head>`.

The pages about the fruit (`apple.html`, `orange.html`, and `banana.html`) are all the same except for their text content. Here is `apple.html`:

```
<?xml version="1.0" encoding="iso-8859-1"?>
<!DOCTYPE html PUBLIC "-//W3C//DTD XHTML 1.0 Transitional//EN"
"http://www.w3.org/TR/xhtml1/DTD/xhtml1-transitional.dtd">
<html xmlns="http://www.w3.org/1999/xhtml">
<head>
  <title>Apple</title>
</head>

<body>
  <h1>Apples</h1>

  <p>Apples come in different colors, and there are over 7500 varieties
  of apples.</p>

  <p>An apple contains about 5g of fiber (1/5 recommended daily
  average).</p>

</body>
</html>
```

Exercise 2

Re-create the `<iframe>` element shown in Figure A-10 (where you can load two different documents inside the iframe window in the current page).

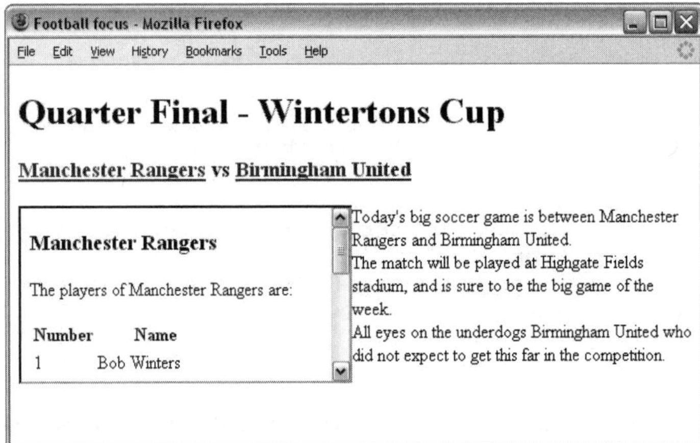

Figure A-10

Answer

The inline frame example requires four files:

- `ch06_exercise2.html` contains the page that you load.
- `teamA.html` contains the names of players in Team A.

- teamB.html contains the names of players in Team B.
- clickForTeam.html is what loads in the iframe before the user clicks either team.

First up is ch06_exercise2.html, which contains the <iframe> element. It is a normal XHTML document, with two links that carry the target attribute so that they can indicate which frame the document that they link to should go into.

```
<?xml version="1.0" encoding="iso-8859-1"?>
<!DOCTYPE html PUBLIC "-//W3C//DTD XHTML 1.0 Transitional//EN"
  "http://www.w3.org/TR/xhtml1/DTD/xhtml1-transitional.dtd">
<html xmlns="http://www.w3.org/1999/xhtml">
<head>
  <title>Football focus</title>
</head>
<body>
<h1>Quarter Final - Wintertons Cup</h1>
<h3>
  <a href="frames/teamA.html" target="iframe">Manchester Rangers</a>
  vs
  <a href="frames/teamB.html" target="iframe">Birmingham United</a>
</h3>
  <p>
   <iframe name="iframe" width="300" height="150"
   src="frames/clickForTeams.html" align="left" ></iframe>

   Today's big soccer game is between Manchester Rangers and Birmingham
   United. The match will be played at Highgate Fields stadium, and is
   Sure to be the big game of the week, with all eyes on the underdogs
   Birmingham United who did not expect to get this far in the
   competition.
  </p>
</body>
</html>
```

As you can see from the <iframe> element, it carries an src attribute that indicates that a page called clickForTeams.html should load into the iframe when the page loads. This is just a plain XHTML page:

```
<?xml version="1.0" encoding="iso-8859-1"?>
<!DOCTYPE html PUBLIC "-//W3C//DTD XHTML 1.0 Transitional//EN"
  "http://www.w3.org/TR/xhtml1/DTD/xhtml1-transitional.dtd">
<html xmlns="http://www.w3.org/1999/xhtml">
<head>
  <title>Teams</title>
</head>
<body>
<h3>Click on a team name to load their players here</h3>
</body>
</html>
```

Now here is the page `teamB.html`, which contains a table for the players in the starting lineup of the team. The page `teamA.html` is exactly the same, just with different players.

```
<?xml version="1.0" encoding="iso-8859-1"?>
<!DOCTYPE html PUBLIC "-//W3C//DTD XHTML 1.0 Transitional//EN"
  "http://www.w3.org/TR/xhtml1/DTD/xhtml1-transitional.dtd">
<html xmlns="http://www.w3.org/1999/xhtml">
<head>
  <title>Team B</title>
</head>
<body>
<h3>Birmingham United</h3>
  <p>The players of Birmingham United are</p>:
  <table>
    <tr><th>Number</th><th>Name</th></tr>
    <tr><td>1</td><td>Chris Warner</td></tr>
    <tr><td>2</td><td>Felix Thomlinson</td></tr>
    <tr><td>3</td><td>Barry Carr</td></tr>
    <tr><td>4</td><td>Mike Patterson</td></tr>
    <tr><td>5</td><td>Richard Neilson</td></tr>
    <tr><td>6</td><td>Brian Childer</td></tr>
    <tr><td>7</td><td>Micky Stephens</td></tr>
    <tr><td>8</td><td>Richard Brooks</td></tr>
    <tr><td>9</td><td>Nick Evans</td></tr>
    <tr><td>10</td><td>Joseph Barton</td></tr>
    <tr><td>11</td><td>Rob Bishop</td></tr>
  </table>
</body>
</html>
```

Chapter 7

Exercise 1

In the exercises for this chapter, you are going to continue to work on the Example Café web site:

a. First, open the `index.html` page and add a `<div>` element just inside the opening `<body>` tag and the closing `</body>` tag, and give the element an `id` attribute whose value is `page`. Repeat this for each page of the site.

b. Now, in the style sheet add a rule that gives this element a margin, border, and padding so that it looks like the border in Figure A-11.

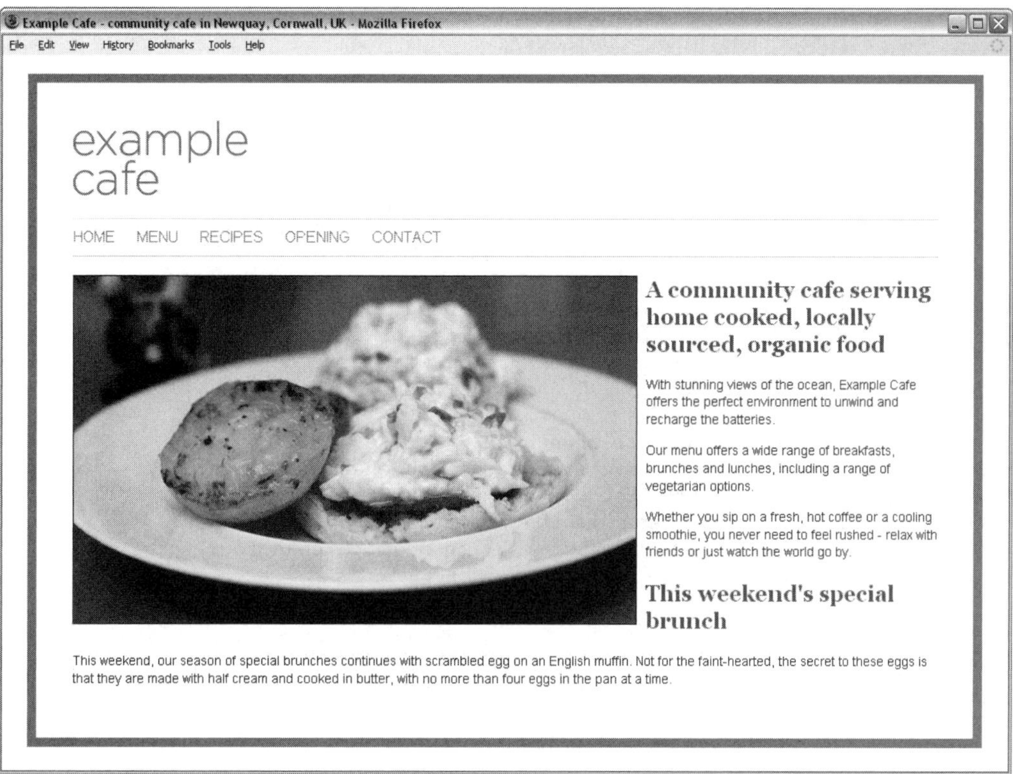

Figure A-11

Answer

First, here is the XHTML for the homepage; you can see the new <div> element has been highlighted:

```
<?xml version="1.0" encoding="iso-8859-1"?>
<!DOCTYPE html PUBLIC "-//W3C//DTD XHTML 1.0 Transitional//EN"
  "http://www.w3.org/TR/xhtml1/DTD/xhtml1-transitional.dtd">
<html xmlns="http://www.w3.org/1999/xhtml">
<head>
  <title>Example Cafe - community cafe in Newquay, Cornwall, UK</title>
  <link rel="stylesheet" type="text/css" href="css/interface.css" />
  <meta http-equiv="Content-Type" content="text/html; charset=iso-8859-1"/>
</head>

<body>
<div id="page">

  <a id="top"><img src="images/logo.gif"
    alt="example cafe" width="194" height="80" />
  <div id="navigation">
    HOME
    <a href="menu.html">MENU</a>
    <a href="recipes.html">RECIPES</a>
```

```
        <a href="opening.html">OPENING</a>
        <a href="contact.html">CONTACT</a>
      </div>

      <img src="images/scrambled_eggs.jpg" width="622" height="370"
        alt="Photo of scrambled eggs on an English muffin" align="left" />
      <h2>A community cafe serving home cooked, locally sourced,
        organic food</h2>
      <p>With stunning views of the ocean, Example Cafe offers the perfect
        environment to unwind and recharge the batteries.</p>
      <p>Our menu offers a wide range of breakfasts, brunches and lunches,
        including a range of vegetarian options.</p>
      <p>Whether you sip on a fresh, hot coffee or a cooling smoothie,
        you never need to feel rushed - relax with friends or just watch
        the world go by.</p>

      <h2>This weekend's special brunch</h2>
      <p>This weekend, our season of special brunches continues with scrambled
        egg on an English muffin. Not for the faint-hearted,
        the secret to these eggs is that they are made with
        half cream and cooked in butter, with no more than four eggs
        in the pan at a time.</p>

    </div>
    </body>
    </html>
```

Now here is the CSS rule that creates the blue border:

```
#page {
       width:960px;
       border:10px solid #3399cc;
       padding:40px;
       margin:20px;}
```

Exercise 2

Create a CSS rule that will make the following changes to the navigation:

a. Add a single-pixel gray border on the top and bottom.

b. Give it 20 pixels of margin above and below the gray lines.

c. Give it 10 pixels of padding on the top and bottom in the box.

d. Add a margin to the right of each link in the navigation.

Answer

The first three changes (for points a, b, and c) can be handled using one CSS rule. The rule will need to control four properties:

- The `border-top` and `border-bottom` properties add a single-pixel gray line above and below the navigation
- The `padding` property adds space between the lines and the items in the navigation
- The `margin` property adds a bit of space above and below the gray lines

Then the `margin-right` property can be used to add space to the right of each individual link.

```
#navigation {
        border-top:1px solid #d6d6d6;
        border-bottom:1px solid #d6d6d6;
        padding:10px 0px 10px 0px;
        margin:20px 0px 20px 0px;}

#navigation a {
        color:#3399cc;
        text-decoration:none;
        margin-right:20px;}
```

Exercise 3

Give the main image on the homepage a `class` attribute whose value is `main_image`, and then create a rule that gives the image a single-pixel black border, and also give the image a 10-pixel margin on the right and bottom sides of the image.

Answer

Here is the new CSS rule that controls the appearance of the image:

```
.main_image {
        border:1px solid #000000;
        margin:0px 10px 10px 0px;}
```

Exercise 4

Increase the gaps between each line of text to 1.3 em.

Answer

You can add the `line-height` property to the rule that controls the `<p>` elements to change the gap between the text, which typesetters refer to as leading.

```
p {
        color:#333333;
        font-size:90%;
        line-height:1.3em;}
```

Exercise 5

Take a look at the following XHTML page:

```
<?xml version="1.0" encoding="iso-8859-1"?>
<!DOCTYPE html PUBLIC "-//W3C//DTD XHTML 1.0 Transitional//EN"
    "http://www.w3.org/TR/xhtml1/DTD/xhtml1-transitional.dtd">
<html xmlns="http://www.w3.org/1999/xhtml" lang="en">
<head>
  <title>Font test</title>
  <link rel="stylesheet" type="text/css" href="ch07_exercise5.css" />
</head>
<body>
<table>
  <tr>
    <th>Quantity</th>
    <th>Ingredient</th>
  </tr>
  <tr class="odd">
    <td>3</td>
    <td>Eggs</td>
  </tr>
  <tr>
    <td>100ml</td>
    <td>Milk</td>
  </tr>
  <tr class="odd">
    <td>200g</td>
    <td>Spinach</td>
   </tr>
   <tr>
     <td>1 pinch</td>
     <td>Cinnamon</td>
   </tr>
 </table>
</body>
</html>
```

Now create the `ch07_exercise5.css` style sheet, which makes this example look like it does in Figure A-12.

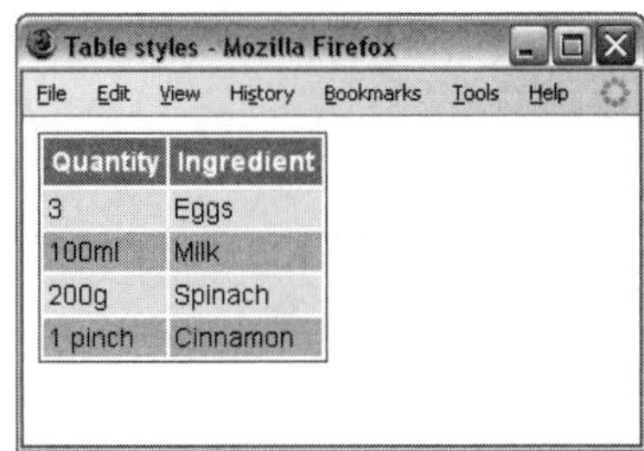

Figure A-12

Don't worry about getting the sizes exactly the same as the screenshot, but do make sure you have padding in the cells and a border around the outside. The white border is created by default in IE and you find out how to remove this in Chapter 8.

Answer

First you need to add a style rule for the either the `<body>` element or all elements using the universal selector `*`, which indicates that the rule applies to all elements. As I mentioned in the chapter, I always set the `background-color` property of the `<body>` element on a site in case the user has set it to another value. You can also set the `font-family` and `font-size` properties to control how the text appears.

```
body {
  background-color:#ffffff;
  font-family:arial, verdana, sans-serif;
  font-size:14px;}
```

In order to give the entire table a single-pixel, dark gray border, you can use the following style rules (or you could just use the `border` property shorthand):

```
table {
  border-style:solid;
  border-width:1px;
  border-color:#666666;}
```

The table headings have a dark background with light writing; the font is also bold. In addition, there is no border to the headings (note how the shorthand `border` property is used this time) and the cells have padding:

```
th {
  color:#ffffff;
  background-color:#999999;
  font-weight:bold;
  border:none;
  padding:4px;}
```

By default, the table rows will have a light background color:

```
tr {background-color:#cccccc;}
```

To alternate the colors of the rows, the `<tr>` elements that have a `class` attribute whose value is `odd` will have a different background color:

```
tr.odd {background-color:#efefef;}
```

Finally, we should give two pixels of padding to each table cell, and ensure that the color of the text in the cells is black.

```
td {
  color:#000000;
  padding:2px;}
```

Chapter 8

Exercise 1

In this exercise, you create a linked table of contents that will sit at the top of a long document in an ordered list and link to the headings in the main part of the document.

The XHTML file `ch08_exercise1.html` is provided with the download code for this book, ready for you to create the style sheet. Your style sheet should do the following:

- Set the styles of all links including active and visited links
- Make the contents of the list bold
- Make the background of the list light gray and use padding to ensure the bullet points show
- Make the width of the links box 250 pixels wide
- Change the style of heading bullet points to empty circles
- Change the style of link bullet points to squares

Your page should look something like Figure A-13.

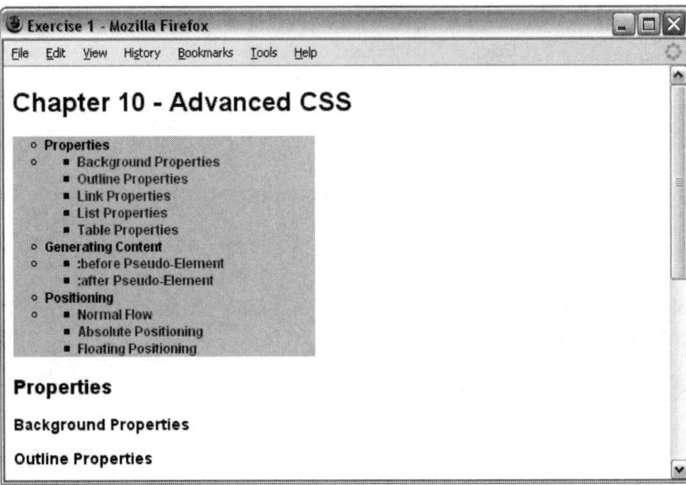

Figure A-13

Answer

To start off, you can create a rule that applies to the `<body>` element to control the background color of the page and the font used.

```
body {
  background-color:#ffffff;
  font-family:arial, verdana, sans-serif;
  font-size:12px;}
```

There were several tasks that related to the list of bullet points that make up the contents. If you look at the following rule, you can see it starts by setting the background color of the list to a light gray. This is followed by a property that sets the default style of bullet points to empty circles. Then all the text is made bold. The fourth property sets the padding to the left of the list. Finally, the width of the lists are set to 250 pixels wide.

```
ul {
  background-color:#d6d6d6;
  list-style:circle;
  font-weight:bold;
  padding-left:30px;
  width:250px;}
```

The links to the sections are in nested unordered lists, and there are a couple of properties you need to set for these lists. First, you have to set the bullet points to squares. Second, because all unordered lists have a gray background and are 250 pixels wide, the nested lists would end up poking out to the right-hand side if you did not make them less wide.

```
ul ul {
  list-style:square;
  width:220px;}
```

The final item on the list was to set the styles of all links including active and visited links, which requires another four rules:

```
a:link {
  color:#0033ff;;
  text-decoration:none;}
a:visited {
  color:#0066ff;
  text-decoration:none;}
a:active {
  text-decoration:underline;}
a:link:hover {
  color:#003399;
  background-color:#e9e9e9;
  text-decoration:underline;}
```

Exercise 2

In this exercise, you test your CSS positioning skills. You should create a page that represents the links to the different sections of the chapter in a very different way. Each of the sections will be shown in a different block, and each block will be absolutely positioned in a diagonal top left to bottom right direction. The middle box should appear on top, as shown in the Figure A-14.

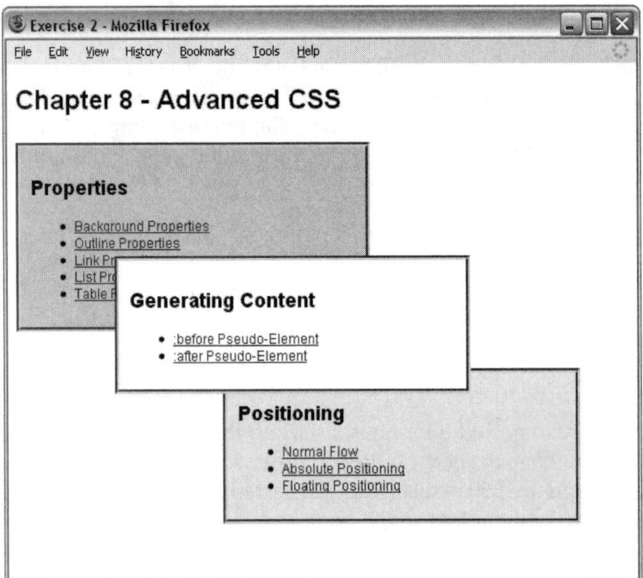

Figure A-14

You can find the source XHTML file (`ch08_exercise2.html`) with the download code for this chapter.

Answer

To begin, you set the background color for the entire page and default font in a rule that applies to the `<body>` element.

```
body {
  background-color:#ffffff;
  font-family:arial, verdana, sans-serif;
  font-size:12px;}
```

Next, you can set a rule that applies to all of the `<div>` elements. Even though you will be changing the background color of two of the boxes, whenever boxes are taken out of normal flow there is a risk that they will overlap, so you should give them a background color (because by default boxes have no background).

You can also set some common properties, adding padding to each box, as well as a border and the width of the boxes.

```
div {
  background-color:#ffffff;
  padding:10px;
  border-style:groove; border-width:4px; border-color:#999999;
  width:300px;}
```

Finally, you simply position each of the boxes. Because the containing element is the <body> element, you position each box from the top-left corner of the browser window.

```
div.page1 {
  position:absolute;
  top:70px;
  z-index:2;
  background-color:#d6d6d6;}

div.page2 {
  position:absolute;
  top:170px; left:100px;
  z-index:3;}

div.page3 {
  position:absolute;
  top:270px; left:200px;
  z-index:1;
  background-color:#efefef;}
```

Chapter 9

Exercise 1

Take another look at the article page from the *Guardian* newspaper's web site; it is shown again in Figure A-15. List all the different elements on the page that would have been listed in the design stage, and put them together in their relevant grouping or categories. For example, the main article section of the page might need a list like this:

```
Title
Summary
Author
Date
```

Figure A-15

Answer

It should look something like the following list (although there will be some slight differences depending on the level of detail you have gone into and the names you have chosen).

```
Header
        Sign in / Register
        Link to mobile site
        Text size
        Drop down select box of links to other parts of site

Advert
```

```
Site name / link to home page
Search

Navigation
       News, Sport, Comment, Culture, Business, Money, Life & Style,
       Travel, Environment, Blogs, Video, Community, Jobs

Breadcrumb trail

Article

Title
Summary
Author
Date
Article history
Main photograph
Photograph caption
Article body

Social media links
       Buzz Up, Digg

Tools
       Print, Send to friend, Share, Clip, Contact

Change text size

Related article links

Most viewed articles
       Last 24 hours, last 7 days, most talked about

Best sellers from shop
```

Exercise 2

Try to recreate the structure of the page you can see in Figure A-15. It sits in the 12-column 960-pixel grid we were using in this chapter, so you have seen much of the code you need already—you just need to assemble it correctly.

Answer

The code in `ch09_eg07.html` and `ch09_eg07.css` shows several configurations for columns on the grid, and covers most of what you need for the example.

What is missing from this example is a CSS class that splits the page into two, which is needed because the main article only takes up half of the page. You also need to add a margin to the right-hand side of the first column. The new rules should look like this:

```
.column1of2, .column2of2 {
        float:left;
        width:440px;
        background-color:#cccccc;
        padding:10px;
        margin-top:20px;}

.column1of2 {margin-right:20px;}
```

Now, you have all of the combinations of columns that you need; you can start to build up the structure that is shown in Figure A-15.

If you look at the main article, which takes up half of the page, we will use the new class we created for that. Next to that is a column that takes up one-sixth of the page, so we will use the appropriate column for that—`column4of6`. The final column there takes up one-third of the page, so we use the class `column3of3` to represent that one. It is important to remember that, in all of these classes, the column to the right is different than the others because it does not have a margin to the right. And for clarity, it helps to use the class that represents the element's position.

At the top of the page, all of the elements either take up the full width of the page, or fit into thirds of a page.

```
<?xml version="1.0" ?>
<!DOCTYPE html PUBLIC "-//W3C//DTD XHTML 1.0 Transitionalt//EN"
 "http://www.w3.org/TR/xhtml1/DTD/xhtml1-transitional.dtd">
<html xmlns="http://www.w3.org/1999/xhtml" lang="en" xml:lang="en">
  <head>
    <title>Layout Example</title>
    <link rel="stylesheet" type="text/css" href="ch09_exercise2.css" />
  </head>
  <body>
    <div id="frame">
          <div id="page">

        <div class="columns1and2of3 clear">sign in / register /
          text size</div>
        <div class="column3of3">go to... site sections</div>

        <div id="header clear">ad</div>

        <div class="column1of3 clear">site name</div>
        <div class="column2of3">empty</div>
        <div class="column3of3">search</div>

        <div id="navigation clear">navigation and breadcrumb</div>

        <div class="column1of2 clear">article</div>
```

```
            <div class="column4of6">socia media links, tools, and other
              links</div>
            <div class="column3of3">most viewed articles and best sellers from
              the shop</div>

                <div class="clear"></div>

          </div>
        </div>
      </body>
    </html>
```

Chapter 10

Exercise 1

In this exercise, you should add a second page to the Try It Out form at the end of the chapter (`registration.html`). The table that follows shows the new items you must add to the form.

You should also add the following:

- An indication at the top of the page as to how much of the form the user has completed
- A Back button and a Proceed button at the bottom (instead of the Submit button)

Information	Form control	Required
Address 1	Text input	Yes
Address 2	Text input	No
Town/Suburb	Text input	No
City/State	Text input	Yes
Zip code	Text input	Yes

When you have finished, the page should look something like Figure A-16.

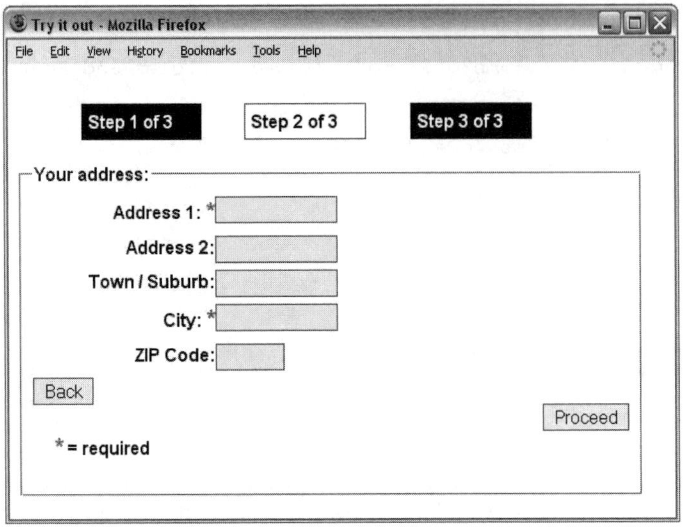

Figure A-16

Answer

To start, you need to add indicators to show how far the user is through the form. You are indicating that they are at step 2 of 3. So you create an element to contain each of the steps.

If you are following the same approach as you did in the last chapter, you could use a `<div>` element for each of these steps and call these `column1of3`, `column2of3`, and `column3of3`, or you could just create one class that represents all of them, called `step`.

In this case, however, you will use an unordered list for each of the steps rather than a `<div>` element since they are related points.

```
<ul class="steps">
  <li>Step 1 of 3</li>
  <li class="on">Step 2 of 3</li>
  <li>Step 3 of 3</li>
</ul>
```

Because you are going to use the CSS `float` property to make these list items sit next to each other, and because the form is in normal flow, the form might end up sitting next to the three steps unless you use the CSS `clear` property. When you come to the CSS, you will create a CSS rule that will use the `clear` property, and attach it to any element that has a `class` attribute whose value is `clear`.

```
<br class="clear" />
```

Then there is the main part of the form, which collects the address details. You will change the `<legend>` for the fieldset at the same time as adding the address fields:

```
<form name="frmExample" action="" method="post">
<fieldset>
<legend>Your address:</legend>

<label for="address1">Address 1: <span class="required">*</span></label>
<div class="input">
  <input type="text" name="txtAddress1" id="address1" size="12" />
</div>

<label for="address2">Address 2: </label>
<div class="input">
  <input type="text" name="txtAddress2" id="address2" size="12" />
</div>

<label for="town">Town / Suburb: </label>
<div class="input">
  <input type="text" name="txtTown" id="town" size="12" />
</div>

<label for="city">City: <span class="required">*</span></label>
<div class="input">
  <input type="text" name="txtCity" id="city" size="12" />
</div>

<label for="zip">ZIP Code: </label>
<div class="input">
  <input type="text" name="txtZIP" id="zip" size="5" />
</div>
```

Finally, you have to add in the Back and Proceed buttons that link between the pages.

```
  <br class="clear" />

  <span class="back"><input type="submit" value="Back" /></span>
  <span class="next"><input type="submit" value="Proceed" /></span>

  <div class="clear"><span class="required">*</span> = required</div>

</fieldset>

</form>
```

In the CSS, you need to add five new rules to the style sheet. To start off, you set the styles for the unordered list that represents the steps.

```
.steps {list-style-type:none;}
.steps li {display:inline; float:left; width:100px; margin:20px;
       padding:5px; color:#ffffff; background-color:#000000;
       border:1px solid #000000;}
.steps .on {border: 1px solid #666666; background-color:#efefef;
       color:#000000; background-color:#ffffff;}
```

You also need to add the class that describes how to clear content that comes after floated elements:

```
.clear {clear:both;margin:20px;}
```

Finally, in order to make the next button sit to the right of the form, you need to float that element to the right of the fieldset:

```
.next {float:right;}
```

Chapter 11

Exercise 1

Create a script to write out the multiplication table for the number 5 from 1 to 20 using a `while` loop.

Answer

The exercise is based around a counter (to work out where you are in your tables); each time the code is run, the counter increments by 1. So, you need to make sure the counter can go up to 20, rather than 10. This goes in the condition of the `while` loop:

```
while (i < 21) {
```

Then you need to change the multiplier, which is both written out and used in the calculation:

```
document.write(i + " x 5 = " + (i * 5) + "<br />" );
```

The final code should look like this:

```
<script type="text/JavaScript">
i = 1
while (i < 21) {
 document.write(i + " x 5 = " + (i * 5) + "<br />" );
  i ++
}
</script>
```

As you can see, this code is no longer than the loop in `ch11_eg09.html`, but it writes out twice the numbers, which really shows you the power of using loops in your code.

Exercise 2

Modify `ch11_eg06.html` so that it can say one of three things:

- "Good Morning" to visitors coming to the page before 12 p.m. (using an `if` statement).
- "Good Afternoon" to visitors coming to the page between 12 and 6 p.m., again using an `if` statement. (Hint: You might need to use a logical operator.)

- "Good Evening" to visitors coming to the page after 6 p.m. up until midnight (again using an `if` statement).

Answer

This script needs to use the `getHours()` method of the date object to determine the time and then uses `if` statements to check the appropriate time for each statement presented to the user.

Note how the afternoon uses a logical operator to check that it is after 12 but before 6 p.m.

```
<script type="text/JavaScript">
  date = new Date();
  time = date.getHours();

  if (time < 12)
  document.write('Good Morning');

  if (time >= 12 && time < 18)
  document.write('Good Afternoon')

  if (time >= 18)
  document.write('Good Evening');
</script>
```

Chapter 12

Exercise 1

Your task is to create a validation function for the competition form in Figure A-17.

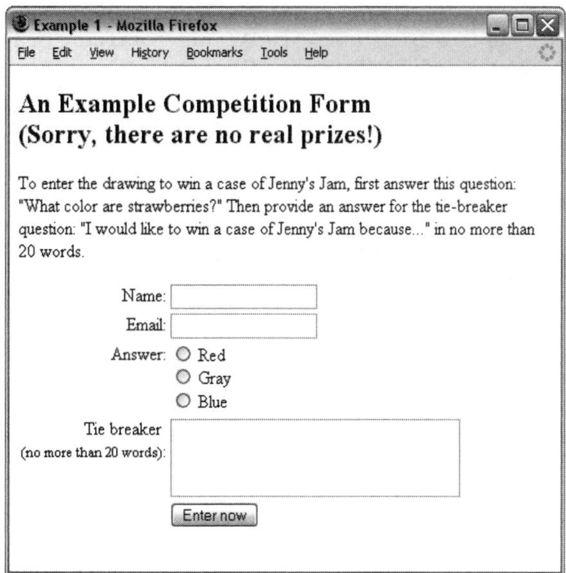

Figure A-17

The function should check that the user has done the following things:

- Entered his or her name
- Provided a valid e-mail address
- Selected one of the radio buttons as an answer to the question
- Given an answer for the tiebreaker question and that it is no more than 20 words

These should be in the order that the controls appear on the form.

Here is the code for the form:

```
<form name="frmCompetition" action="competition.aspx" method="post"
    onsubmit="return validate(this);">
<h2>An Example Competition Form <br />(Sorry, there are no real
prizes!)</h2>
<p> To enter the drawing to win a case of Jenny's Jam, first answer
  this question: "What color are strawberries?" Then provide an answer for
  the tie-breaker question: "I would like to win a case of Jenny's Jam
  because..." in no more than 20 words.</p>
<table>
  <tr>
    <td class="formTitle">Name: </td>
    <td><input type="text" name="txtName" size="18" /></td>
  </tr>
  <tr>
    <td class="formTitle">Email: </td>
    <td><input type="text" name="txtEmail" size="18" /></td>
  </tr>
  <tr>
    <td class="formTitle">Answer: </td>
    <td><input type="radio" name="radAnswer" value="Red" /> Red<br />
          <input type="radio" name="radAnswer" value="Gray" /> Gray<br />
          <input type="radio" name="radAnswer" value="Blue" /> Blue
    </td>
  </tr>
  <tr>
    <td class="formTitle">Tie breaker <br/ ><small>(no more than 20 words)
    </small>:
</td>
    <td><textarea name="txtTieBreaker" cols="30" rows="3" /></textarea></td>
  </tr>
  <tr>
    <td class="formTitle"></td>
    <td><input type="submit" value="Enter now" /></td>
  </tr>
</table>

</form>
```

Answer

The `validate()` function for this example uses techniques you learned about in Chapter 12. It starts off by setting a variable called `returnValue` that will either be `true` or `false` when the function finishes running—it starts off with a value of `true`, which is switched to `false` if any of the form fields fail to meet the requirements.

```
<script type="text/JavaScript">

  function validate(form) {
    var returnValue = true
```

First you have to check whether the value of the `txtName` field has a value in it:

```
var name=form.txtName.value
if (name=="")
  {
    returnValue = false;
    alert("You must enter a name")
    document.frmCompetition.txtName.focus();
  }
```

Next you have to check whether the e-mail address follows the format it is supposed to. If the address is empty, it will not match the regular expression; therefore you do not need to check if the control is empty first:

```
var email=form.txtEmail.value
var rxEmail = /^\ w(\.?[\w-])*@\w(\.?[\w-])*\.[a-z]{2,6}(\.[a-z]{2})?$/i;

if (!rxEmail.test(email))
  {
    returnValue = false;
    alert("You must enter a valid email address")
    document.frmCompetition.txtEmail.focus()
  }
```

Next you must loop through the radio buttons to see if an answer was provided. This involves looping through the buttons and testing whether each button has the `checked` property. If a radio button has been checked then a variable (in this case called `radioChosen`) is changed to have a value of `true`. Once all of the radio buttons have been looped through, there is a conditional `if` statement checking whether the value of this attribute is `true` or `false`.

```
var radioChosen = false;
var radioButtons = form.radAnswer;
for (var i=0; i<radioButtons.length; i++) {
if (radioButtons[i].checked)
  {
  radioChosen=true;
  }
}

if (radioChosen == false) {
  returnValue = false;
  alert("You did not answer the question");
}
```

Finally, you come to the <textarea> element and the tiebreaker. This one needs to have a value, but must not be longer than 20 words. To start then, it is checked to see if it has any value at all:

```
var tieBreaker=form.txtTieBreaker.value
if (tieBreaker=="")
  {
    returnValue = false;
    alert("You must enter an answer for the tie breaker")
    document.frmCompetition.txtTieBreaker.focus();
  }
```

Then the value entered is split into separate words using the `split()` function of the string object and a regular expression. Because the `split()` function splits the string after spaces, you can check how many words were entered simply by finding out the length of the array created by the `split()` function. Because the array is zero-based, you need to find out whether the number of items in the array is less than or equal to 20. If there are too many words, the user is warned and told how many words she entered in order to help her make the response shorter.

```
var tieBreakerWords = tieBreaker.split(/\s+/g);
wordCount = tieBreakerWords.length;

if (wordCount > 20) {
  returnValue = false;
  alert("Your tie breaker answer must be no more than 20 words. You entered"
  +wordCount+ "words.");
  document.frmCompetition.txtTieBreaker.focus();
}
```

That is the final test and the `returnValue` (either `true` or `false`) indicates whether the form will be submitted or not.

```
  return returnValue
}

</script>
```

There were no exercises in Chapters 13 or 14.

XHTML Element Reference

This appendix is a quick reference to the elements that are in the HTML and XHTML recommendations. They are listed with the attributes each element can carry and a brief description of their purpose.

Please be aware that this appendix features deprecated elements, which are marked with the word "deprecated" next to them; you should avoid using these elements where possible because they are marked for removal from future specifications.

There are also several elements that are used just to control the presentation of documents, without describing their contents or the structure of the information in the document. You should avoid using these elements, and aim to use CSS to control the presentation of your documents instead.

When an element has only been introduced recently, I will note the first version of Internet Explorer (IE) and Firefox (FF) to support the element next to the element's name, starting with IE6 and FF2.

Finally, all attribute values should be given inside double quotation marks, and any attribute listed without a value should have the name of the attribute repeated as its value in order to be XHTML-compliant — for example, `disabled = "disabled"`.

Core Attributes

Unless otherwise stated, the core attributes can be used with all of the elements in this appendix.

`class = name`	Specifies a class for the element to associate it with rules in a style sheet
`dir = ltr | rtl`	Specifies the direction for rendering text (left to right or right to left)

(continued)

`id = name`	Defines a unique identification value for that element within the document
`lang = language`	Specifies the (human) language for the content of the element
`onclick = script`	Specifies a script to be called when the user clicks the mouse over this element
`ondblclick = script`	Specifies a script to be called when the user double-clicks the mouse over this element
`onkeydown = script`	Specifies a script to be called when the user presses a key while this element has focus
`onkeypress = script`	Specifies a script to be called when the user presses and releases a key while this element has focus
`onkeyup = script`	Specifies a script to be called when the user releases a key while this element has focus
`onmousedown = script`	Specifies a script to be called when the user presses the mouse button while the cursor is over this element's content
`onmousemove = script`	Specifies a script to be called when the user moves the mouse cursor while over this element's content
`onmouseout = script`	Specifies a script to be called when the mouse has been over an element, and has moved outside of its border so that it is no longer over the element
`onmouseover = script`	Specifies a script to be called when the mouse is moved over this element's content
`onmouseup = script`	Specifies a script to be called when the user releases a mouse button while the cursor is over this element's content
`style = style`	Specifies an inline CSS style rule for the element
`title = string`	Specifies a title for the element
`xml:lang`	Specifies the (human) language for the content of the element

<a>

Defines a link. The `href` or `name` attribute must be specified.

`accesskey = key_character`	Defines a hotkey/keyboard shortcut for this anchor
`charset = encoding`	Specifies a character set used to encode the target document

`coords = x_y coordinates`	Specifies a list of coordinates indicating the shape of a link in an image map
`href = url`	Specifies the URL of the hyperlink target
`hreflang = language_code`	Specifies the language encoding for the target of the link
`rel = relationship (same | next | parent | previous | string)`	Indicates the relationship of the current document to the target document
`rev = relationship`	Indicates the reverse relationship of the target document to this one
`shape = circ | circle | poly | polygon | rect | rectangle`	Defines the shape of a region in an image map
`tabindex = number`	Defines this element's position in the tabbing order
`target = <window_name> | _parent | _blank | _top | _self`	Defines the name of the frame or window that should load the linked document
`type = MIME_type`	Defines the MIME type of the target

<abbr>

Indicates that the content of the element is an abbreviation.

<acronym>

Indicates that the content of the element is an acronym.

<address>

Indicates that the content of the element is an address.

<applet> (Deprecated)

Used to place a Java applet or executable code in the page.

Takes only the attributes listed in the table that follows.

align = top | middle | bottom | left | right | absmiddle | baseline | absbottom | texttop	Aligns the applet within the containing element
alt = text	Specifies alternative text to replace the <applet> for browsers that support the element, but are unable to execute it
archive = url	Specifies a class archive that must be downloaded to the browser and searched for
class = name	Specifies a class for the element to associate it with rules in a style sheet
code = classname	Specifies the class name of the code (required)
codebase = url	Specifies a URL from which the code can be downloaded
height = number	Specifies the height of the <applet> in pixels
hspace = number	Specifies the width to allow to the left and right of the <applet> in pixels
id = name	Specifies a unique ID for the element
name = name	Specifies the name of this instance of the applet
object = data	Specifies the filename of the compiled code to run
vspace = number	Specifies the height to allow to the top and bottom of the <applet> in pixels
width = number	Specifies the width of the <applet> in pixels

<area>

Used to specify coordinates for a clickable area or hotspot in an image map.

`accesskey = key_character`	Defines a hotkey/keyboard shortcut for this area
`alt = text`	Specifies alternative text for the area if the image cannot be loaded
`coords = string`	Specifies a list of coordinates for the area
`href = url`	Specifies the URL of the hyperlink target
`name = string`	Specifies a name for the element that can be used to identify it
`nohref`	Specifies that there is not a document associated with the area
`shape = circ | circle | poly | polygon | rect | rectangle`	Defines the shape of a region
`tabindex = number`	Defines this element's position in the tabbing order
`target = <window_name> | _parent | _blank | _top| _self`	Defines the name of the frame or window that should load the linked document

<b>

The content of the element should be displayed in a bold font.

<base>

Specifies a base URL for the links in a document.

Supports only the attributes listed in the table that follows.

`href = url`	Specifies the URL of the base for the links in this document
`id = id`	Specifies a unique identifier for the element
`target = <window_name> | _parent | _blank | _top | _self`	Defines the name of the frame or window that should load the linked document

<basefont> (Deprecated)

Specifies a base font to be the default font when rendering a document.

Supports only the attributes listed in the table that follows.

`color = color`	Specifies the color of text in this element
`face = font_family_name`	Specifies the font family in this element
`size = value`	Specifies the size of the font (required)

<bdo>

Turns off the bidirectional rendering algorithm for selected fragments of text.

`dir = ltr | rtl`	Specifies the font family in this element

<big>

Renders text in a font size larger than its containing element.

<blockquote>

The content of the element is a quotation. Usually used for a paragraph quote or longer (otherwise use the <q> element).

`cite = url`	Specifies a URL for the source of the quote

<body>

Specifies the start and end of the body section of a page.

`alink = color`	Specifies the color of active links
`background = url`	Specifies the URL for a background image to be used as wallpaper for the background of the whole document
`bgcolor = color`	Specifies a background color for the document

bgproperties = fixed	Image does not scroll with document content
link = color	Specifies the color of unvisited links
onload = script event handler	Specifies a script to run when the page loads
onunload = script event handler	Specifies a script to run when the page is unloaded
text = color	Specifies a color for the text in the document
vlink = color	Specifies the color of visited links

Inserts a line break.

Supports only the attributes listed in the table that follows.

class = name	Specifies a class for the element to associate it with rules in a style sheet
clear = left | right | none | all	Breaks the flow of the page and moves the break down until the specified margin is clear
id = id	Specifies a unique identifier for this element
style = style	Specifies inline CSS style rules for this element
title = string	Specifies a title for this element

<button>

Creates an HTML button. Any enclosed markup is used as the button's caption.

accesskey = key_character	Defines a hotkey/keyboard shortcut for this element
disabled = disabled	Disables the button, preventing user intervention
name = name	Specifies a name for the form control passed to the form's processing application as part of the name/value pair (required)

(continued)

`onblur = script`	Specifies a script to run when the mouse moves off the button
`onfocus = script`	Specifies a script to run when the element gains focus
`tabindex = number`	Defines this element's position in the tabbing order
`type = button | submit | reset`	Specifies the type of button
`value = string`	Specifies the value of the parameter sent to the processing application as part of the name/value pair (required)

<caption>

The content of this element specifies a caption to be placed next to a table.

`align = top|bottom | right | left`	For IE this specifies the horizontal alignment of the caption; in Netscape it sets vertical position
`valign = bottom | top`	Specifies the vertical position of the caption

<center> (Deprecated)

The content of this element (and child elements) should be centered on the page.

<cite>

The content of the element is a citation and tends to be rendered in italics.

<code>

The content of the element is code and should be rendered in a fixed-width font.

<col>

Specifies column-based defaults for a table.

`align = center | left | right | justify | char`	Specifies the alignment of the column
`bgcolor = color`	Specifies a background color for the column

`char = string`	Specifies the alignment character for text within the cells
`charoff = string`	Specifies the offset character that the alignment character is set to
`span = number`	Number of columns affected by the `<col>` tag
`valign = bottom | top`	Specifies the vertical alignment of content within the element
`width = number`	Specifies the width of the column in pixels

<colgroup>

Used to contain a group of columns.

`align = center | left | right | justify | char`	Specifies the horizontal alignment of content within the column
`bgcolor = color`	Specifies the background color for the group of columns
`char = string`	Specifies the alignment character for text within the cells
`charoff = string`	Specifies the offset character that the alignment character is set to
`valign = bottom | top`	Specifies the vertical alignment of content within the element
`width = number`	Specifies the width of the column group in pixels

<dd>

The definition of an item in a definition list. This is usually indented from other text.

<del>

The content of the element has been marked as having been deleted from an earlier version of the document.

`cite = url`	Specifies a URL for justification of deletion
`datetime = date`	Specifies the date and time it was deleted

<dfn>

Defines an instance of a term.

<dir> (Deprecated)

The content of the element is rendered in a directory-style file list.

`type = bullet`	Specifies the type of bullet used to display the list

<div>

A containing element to hold other elements, defining a section of a page. This is a block-level container.

`align = center | left | right`	Specifies the alignment of text within the `<div>` element
`nowrap = nowrap`	Prevents word-wrapping within this `<div>` element

<dl>

Denotes a definition list.

`compact = compact`	Makes the list more vertically compact

<dt>

Denotes a definition term within a definition list.

<em>

The element content is emphasized text, and is usually rendered in an italic font.

<embed>

Embeds files in a page that require another supporting application.

`align = absbottom | absmiddle | baseline | bottom | left | middle | right | texttop | top`	Specifies the alignment within the containing element
`border = number`	Specifies the width of the border around the embedded object in pixels
`height = number`	Specifies the height of the embedded object in pixels
`hidden = hidden`	Specifies that the embedded object should be hidden
`hspace = number`	Specifies the amount of additional space to be added to the left and right of the embedded object
`name = name`	Specifies a name for the embedded object
`palette=foreground | background`	Sets foreground and background colors of the embedded object
`pluginspage = url`	Specifies the URL of the page where the plug-in associated with the object can be downloaded
`src = url`	Specifies the URL of the data to be used by the object
`type = MIME_type`	Specifies the MIME type of the data used by the object
`units = en | ems | pixels`	Sets units for height and width attributes
`vpsace = number`	Specifies the amount of additional space to be added above and below the embedded object
`width = number`	Specifies the width of the embedded object in pixels

<fieldset>

Creates a box around the contained elements indicating that they are related items in a form.

`align = center | left | right`	Specifies the alignment of the group of elements
`tabindex = number`	Defines this `<fieldset>`'s position in the tabbing order

<font> (Deprecated)

Specifies the typeface, size, and color of the font to be used for text within the element.

`color = color`	Specifies the color of text in this element
`face = font_family_list`	Specifies the family of font to be used for the text in this element
`size = value`	Specifies the size of the text used in this element

<form>

Containing element for form controls and elements.

`accept-charset = list`	Specifies a list of accepted character sets the processing application can handle
`action = url`	Specifies the URL of the processing application that will handle the form
`enctype = encoding`	Specifies the encoding method for form values
`method = get | post`	Specifies how the data gets sent from the browser to the processing application
`onreset = script`	Specifies a script that is run when the form values are reset
`onsubmit = script`	Specifies a script that is run before the form is submitted
`target = <window_name> | _parent | _blank | _top | _self`	Defines the name of the frame or window that should load the results of the form

<frame>

Specifies a frame within a frameset.

Supports only the attributes listed in the table that follows.

`[event_name] = script`	The intrinsic events supported by most elements
`bordercolor = color`	Specifies the color of the border of the frame

`class = name`	Specifies a class name to associate styles with the element
`frameborder = no | yes | 0 | 1`	Specifies the presence or absence of a frame border
`id = string`	Specifies a unique value for the element
`lang = language_type`	Specifies the language used for the content of the frame
`longdesc = url`	Specifies a URL for a description of the content of the frame
`marginheight = number`	Specifies the height of the margin for the frame in pixels
`marginwidth = number`	Specifies the width of the margin for the image in pixels
`noresize = noresize`	Specifies that the frame cannot be resized
`scrolling = auto | yes | no`	Specifies whether the frame can have scrollbars if the content does not fit in the space in the browser
`style = style`	Specifies inline CSS style rules
`src = url`	Specifies a URL for the location of the content for that frame
`title = title`	Specifies a title for the frame

<noframes>

The content of this element should be displayed if the browser does not support frames.

<frameset>

Specifies a frameset containing multiple frames (and possibly other nested framesets). This element replaces the `<body>` element in a document.

`border = number`	Specifies the width of the borders for each frame in the frameset
`bordercolor = color`	Specifies the color of the borders for frames in the frameset

(continued)

`cols = list`	Specifies the number of columns in the frameset allowing you to control layout of the frameset
`frameborder = no | yes | 0 | 1`	Specifies whether borders will be present for the frames in this frameset
`framespacing = number`	Specifies the space between each frame in pixels
`onblur = script`	Specifies a script to run when the mouse moves off the frameset
`onload = script`	Specifies a script to run when the frameset loads
`onunload = script`	Specifies a script to run when the frameset is unloaded
`rows = number`	Specifies the number of rows in a frameset allowing you to control the layout of the frameset

<head>

Container element for heading information *about* the document; its content will not be displayed in the browser.

Supports only the attributes listed in the table that follows.

`class = classname`	Specifies a class to associate style rules with this element
`dir = ltr | rtl`	Specifies the direction of text within this element
`Id = string`	Specifies a unique identifier for this element
`lang = language_type`	Specifies the language used in this element
`profile = url`	Specifies a URL for a profile of the document
`xml:lang = language_type`	Specifies the language used in this element

<hn>

Headings from `<h1>` (largest) through `<h6>` (smallest).

`align = left | center | right`	Specifies the horizontal alignment of the header within its containing element

<hr />

Creates a horizontal rule across the page (or containing element).

Supports only the attributes listed in the table that follows.

`[event_name] = script`	The intrinsic events supported by most elements
`align = center | left | right`	Specifies the horizontal alignment of the rule
`class = classname`	Specifies a class for the element to associate it with rules in a style sheet
`color = color`	Specifies the color of the horizontal rule
`dir = ltr | rtl`	Specifies the direction of the text
`id = string`	Specifies a unique identifier for this element
`noshade = noshade`	Specifies that there should not be a 3D shading on the rule
`style = string`	Specifies inline CSS style rules for the element
`title = string`	Specifies a title for the element
`width = number`	Specifies the width of the rule in pixels or as a percentage of the containing element

<html>

Containing element for an HTML or XHTML page.

`class = classname`	Specifies a class for the element to associate it with rules in a style sheet
`dir = ltr | rtl`	Specifies the direction of the text within the element
`id = string`	Specifies a unique identifier for this element
`lang = language_type`	Specifies the language used in this element
`version = url`	Specifies the version of HTML used in the document — replaced by the DOCTYPE declaration in XHTML
`xmlns = uri`	Specifies namespaces used in XHTML documents
`xml:lang = language_type`	Specifies the language used in this element

<i>

The content of this element should be rendered in an italic font.

<iframe>

Creates an inline floating frame within a page.

`align = absbottom | absmiddle | baseline | bottom | top | left | middle | right | texttop | top`	Specifies the alignment of the frame in relation to surrounding content or margins
`frameborder = no | yes | 0 | 1`	Specifies the presence of a border: `1` enables borders, `0` disables them
`height = number`	Specifies the height of the frame in pixels
`longdesc = url`	Specifies a URL for a description of the content of the frame
`Marginheight = number`	Specifies the space above and below the frame and surrounding content in pixels
`marginwidth = number`	Specifies the space to the left and right of the frame and surrounding content in pixels
`scrolling = auto | yes | no`	Specifies whether scrollbars should be allowed to appear if the content is too large for the frame
`src = url`	Specifies the URL of the file to be displayed in the frame
`width = number`	Specifies the width of the frame in pixels

<img>

Embeds an image within a document.

`align = absbottom | absmiddle | baseline | bottom | top | left | middle | right | texttop | top`	Specifies the alignment of the image in relation to the content that surrounds it
`alt = text`	Specifies alternative text if the application is unable to load the image (required); also used in accessibility devices
`border = number`	Specifies the width of the border of the image in pixels — you must use this property if the image is a link, to prevent borders from appearing

`height = number`	Specifies the height of the image in pixels
`hspace = number`	Specifies the amount of additional space to be added to the left and right of the image
`ismap = ismap`	Specifies whether the image is a server-side image map
`longdesc = url`	Specifies a URL for a description of the content of the image
`loop = number`	Specifies the number of times the video should be played; can take a value of `infinite`
`lowsrc = url`	Specifies a URL for a low-resolution version of the image that can be displayed while the full image is loading
`name = name`	Specifies a name for the element
`onabort = script`	Specifies a script to run if loading of the image is aborted
`onerror = script`	Specifies a script to run if there is an error loading the image
`onload = script`	Specifies a script to run when the image has loaded
`src = url`	Specifies the URL of the image
`usemap = url`	Specifies the map containing coordinates and links that define the links for the image (server-side image map)
`vspace = number`	Specifies the amount of additional space to be added above and below the image
`width = name`	Specifies the width of the image

<input type="button">

Creates a form input control that is a button a user can click.

`accesskey = key_character`	Defines a hotkey/keyboard shortcut for the button
`disabled = disabled`	Disables the button, preventing user intervention
`name = name`	Specifies a name for the form control passed to the form's processing application as part of the name/value pair (required)
`tabindex = number`	Defines this element's position in the tabbing order
`value = string`	Specifies the value of the parameter sent to the processing application as part of the name/value pair

<input type="checkbox">

Creates a form input control that is a checkbox a user can check.

`accesskey = key_character`	Defines a hotkey/keyboard shortcut for the checkbox
`checked = checked`	Specifies that the checkbox is checked (can be used to make the checkbox selected by default)
`disabled = disabled`	Disables the checkbox, preventing user intervention
`name = name`	Specifies a name for the form control passed to the form's processing application as part of the name/value pair (required)
`readonly = readonly`	Prevents user from modifying content
`tabindex = number`	Defines this element's position in the tabbing order
`value = string`	Specifies the value of the control sent to the processing application as part of the name/value pair

<input type="file">

Creates a form input control that allows a user to select a file.

`accesskey = key_character`	Defines a hotkey/keyboard shortcut for this file input
`disabled = disabled`	Disables the file upload control, preventing user intervention
`maxlength = number`	Maximum number of characters the user may enter
`name = name`	Specifies a name for the form control passed to the form's processing application as part of the name/value pair (required)
`onblur = script`	Specifies a script to run when the mouse leaves the control
`onchange = script`	Specifies a script to run when the value of the element changes
`onfocus = script`	Specifies a script to run when the element gains focus
`readonly = readonly`	Prevents user from modifying content
`size = number`	Specifies the number of characters to display for the element

`tabindex = number`	Defines this element's position in the tabbing order
`value = string`	Specifies the value of the control sent to the processing application as part of the name/value pair

<input type="hidden">

Creates a form input control, similar to a text input, but is hidden from the user's view (although the value can still be seen if the user views the source for the page).

`name = name`	Specifies a name for the form control passed to the form's processing application as part of the name/value pair (required)
`value = string`	Specifies the value of the control sent to the processing application as part of the name/value pair

<input type="image">

Creates a form input control that is like a button or submit control, but uses an image instead of a button.

`accesskey = key_character`	Defines a hotkey/keyboard shortcut for this image button
`align = center | left | right`	Specifies the alignment of the image
`alt = string`	Provides alternative text for the image
`border = number`	Specifies the width of the border in pixels
`disabled = disabled`	Disables the image button, preventing user intervention
`name = name`	Specifies a name for the form control passed to the form's processing application as part of the name/value pair (required)
`src = url`	Specifies the source of the image
`readonly = readonly`	Prevents user from modifying content
`tabindex = number`	Defines this element's position in the tabbing order
`value = string`	Specifies the value of the control sent to the processing application as part of the name/value pair

<input type="password">

Creates a form input control that is like a single-line text input control but shows asterisks or bullet marks rather than the characters to prevent an onlooker from seeing the values a user has entered. This should be used for sensitive information — although you should note that the values get passed to the servers as plain text. (If you have sensitive information, you should still consider making submissions safe using a technique such as SSL.)

`accesskey = key_character`	Defines a hotkey/keyboard shortcut for this element
`disabled = disabled`	Disables the text input, preventing user intervention
`maxlength = number`	Maximum number of characters the user can enter
`name = name`	Specifies a name for the form control passed to the form's processing application as part of the name/value pair (required)
`onblur = script`	Specifies a script to run when the mouse moves off the element
`onchange = script`	Specifies a script to run when the value of the element changes
`onfocus = script`	Specifies a script to run when the element gains focus
`onselect = script`	Specifies a script to run when the user selects this element
`readonly = readonly`	Prevents user from modifying content
`size = number`	Specifies the width of the input in numbers of characters
`tabindex = number`	Defines this element's position in the tabbing order
`value = string`	Specifies the value of the control sent to the processing application as part of the name/value pair

<input type="radio">

Creates a form input control that is a radio button. These appear in groups that share the same value for the `name` attribute and create mutually exclusive groups of values (only one of the radio buttons in the group can be selected).

`accesskey = key_character`	Defines a hotkey/keyboard shortcut for this radio button
`checked = checked`	Specifies that the default condition for this radio button is checked

`disabled = disabled`	Disables the radio button, preventing user intervention
`name = name`	Specifies a name for the form control passed to the form's processing application as part of the name/value pair (required)
`readonly = readonly`	Prevents user from modifying content
`tabindex = number`	Defines this element's position in the tabbing order
`value = string`	Specifies the value of the control sent to the processing application as part of the name/value pair

<input type="reset">

Creates a form input control that is a button to reset the values of the form to the same values present when the page loaded.

`accesskey = key_character`	Defines a hotkey/keyboard shortcut for this button
`disabled = disabled`	Disables the button, preventing user intervention
`tabindex = number`	Defines this element's position in the tabbing order
`value = string`	Specifies the value of the control sent to the processing application as part of the name/value pair

<input type="submit">

Creates a form input control that is a Submit button to send the form values to the server.

`accesskey = key_character`	Defines a hotkey/keyboard shortcut for this element
`disabled = disabled`	Disables the button, preventing user intervention
`name = name`	Specifies a name for the form control passed to the form's processing application as part of the name/value pair
`tabindex = number`	Defines this element's position in the tabbing order
`value = string`	Specifies the value of the control sent to the processing application as part of the name/value pair

<input type="text">

Creates a form input control that is a single-line text input.

`accesskey = key_character`	Defines a hotkey/keyboard shortcut for this element
`disabled = disabled`	Disables the text input, preventing user intervention
`maxlength = number`	Maximum number of characters the user can enter
`name = name`	Specifies a name for the form control passed to the form's processing application as part of the name/value pair (required)
`onblur = script`	Specifies a script to run when the mouse moves off the element
`onchange = script`	Specifies a script to run when the value of the element changes
`onfocus = script`	Specifies a script to run when the element gains focus
`onselect = script`	Specifies a script to run when the element is selected
`readonly = readonly`	Prevents user from modifying content
`size = number`	Specifies the width of the control in characters
`tabindex = number`	Defines this element's position in the tabbing order
`value = string`	Specifies the value of the control sent to the processing application as part of the name/value pair

<ins>

The content of the element has been added since an earlier version of the document.

`cite = url`	Specifies a URL indicating why the content was added
`datetime = date`	Specifies a date and time for the addition of content

<isindex> (Deprecated)

Creates a single-line text input; you should use the `<input>` element instead. Only the attributes listed in the table that follows are supported.

accesskey = key_character	Defines a hotkey/keyboard shortcut for this element
action = url	IE specifies only the URL of the search application
class = classname	Specifies a class for the element to associate it with rules in a style sheet
dir = ltr | rtl	Specifies the direction of the text within the element
id = string	Specifies a unique identifier for this element
lang = language_type	Specifies the language used in this element
prompt = string	Specifies an alternative prompt for the field input
style = string	Specifies inline CSS style rules for the element
tabindex = number	Defines this element's position in the tabbing order
title = string	Specifies a title for the element
xml:lang = language_type	Specifies the language used in this element

<kbd>

The content of the element is something that should be entered on a keyboard, and is rendered in a fixed-width font.

<label>

The content of the element is used as a label for a form element.

accesskey = key_character	Defines a hotkey/keyboard shortcut for this element
for = name	Specifies the value of the id attribute for the element it is a label for
onblur = script	Specifies a script to run when the mouse moves off the label
onfocus = string	Specifies a script to run when the label gains focus

<legend>

The content of this element is the title text to place in a `<fieldset>`. It could be used in HTML 5 to provide a title for `<figure>` and `<details>` elements.

accesskey = key_character	Defines a hotkey/keyboard shortcut for this element
align = top | left | bottom | right	Specifies the position of the legend in relation to the fieldset

<li>

The content of this element is an item in a list. The element is referred to as a line item. For appropriate attributes, see the parent element for that kind of list (`<ul>`, `<ol>`, `<menu>`).

type = bullet_type	Specifies the type of bullet used to display the list items
value = number	Specifies the number the list will start with

<link>

Defines a link between the document and another resource. Often used to include style sheets in documents.

Takes only the attributes listed in the table that follows.

charset = character_set	Specifies a character set used to encode the linked file
href = url	Specifies the URL of the linked document
hreflang = language_type	Specifies the language encoding for the target of the link
media = list	Types of media the document is intended for
rel = same | next | parent | previous | string	Indicates the relationship of the document to the target document
rev = relation	Indicates the reverse relationship of the target document to this one
type = type	Specifies the MIME type of the document being linked to

<map>

Creates a client-side image map and specifies a collection of clickable areas or hotspots.

`name = string`	Name of the map (required)

<menu> (Deprecated)

Creates a menu list and renders the child elements as individual items. Replaced by lists (`<ol>` and `<ul>`). Deprecated in HTML 4.01.

<meta>

Allows for information about the document or instructions for the browser; these are not displayed to the user.

Takes only the attributes listed in the table that follows.

`charset = character_set`	Specifies a character set used to encode the document
`content= meta_content`	Specifies the value for the meta-information
`dir = ltr | rtl`	Specifies the direction of the text within the element
`http-equiv = string`	Specifies the HTTP equivalent name for the meta-information; causes the server to include the name and content in the HTTP header
`lang = language_type`	Specifies the language used in this element
`name = string`	Specifies the name of the meta-information
`scheme = scheme`	Specifies the profile scheme used to interpret the property
`xml:lang = language_type`	Specifies the language used in this element

<noframes>

The content of the element is displayed for browsers that do not support frames.

<noscript>

The content of the element is displayed for browsers that do not support the script. Most browsers will also display this content if scripting is disabled.

<object>

Adds an object or non-HTML control to the page. Will be the standard way of including images in the future.

`align = absbottom | absmiddle | baseline | bottom | left | middle | right | texttop | top`	Specifies the position of an object in relation to surrounding text
`archive = url`	Specifies a list of URLs for archives or resources used by the object
`border = number`	Specifies the width of the border in pixels
`classid = url`	Specifies the URL of the object
`codebase = url`	Specifies the URL of the code required to run the object
`codetype = MIME-type`	Specifies the MIME type of the code base
`data = url`	Specifies the data for the object
`declare`	Declares an object without instantiating it
`height = number`	Specifies the height of the object in pixels
`hspace = number`	Specifies the amount of additional space to be added to the left and right of the embedded object
`name = name`	Specifies a name for the object
`shapes = shapes`	Specifies that the object has shaped hyperlinks
`standby = string`	Defines a message to display while the object is loading
`tabindex = number`	Defines this element's position in the tabbing order
`type = MIME type`	Specifies the MIME type for the object's data
`usemap = url`	Defines an image map for use with the object
`vspace = number`	Specifies the amount of additional space to be added above and below the embedded object
`width = number`	Specifies the object's width in pixels

<ol>

Creates an ordered or numbered list.

compact = compact	Attempts to make the list more vertically compact
start = number	Specifies the number with which the list should start
type = bullet_type	Specifies the type of bullet used to display the list items

<optgroup>

Used to group `<option>` elements in a select box.

disabled = disabled	Disables the group, preventing user intervention
label = string	Specifies a label for the option group

<option>

Contains one choice in a drop-down list or select box.

disabled = disabled	Disables the option, preventing user intervention
label = string	Specifies a label for the option
selected = selected	Indicates that the option should be selected by default when the page loads
value = string	Specifies the value of this option in the form control sent to the processing application as part of the name/value pair

<p>

The content of this element is a paragraph.

align = center | left | right	Specifies the alignment of the text within the paragraph

<param>

Used as a child of an `<object>` or `<applet>` element to set properties of the object. See the `<object>` or `<applet>` elements for details.

<pre>

The content of this element is rendered in a fixed-width type that retains the formatting (such as spaces and line breaks) in the code.

`width = number`	Specifies the width of the preformatted area in pixels

<q>

The content of the element is a short quotation.

`cite = url`	Specifies the URL for the content of the quote in question

<s> *(Deprecated)*

The content of the element should be rendered with strikethrough.

<samp>

The content of the element is a sample code listing. Usually rendered in a smaller fixed-width font.

<script>

The content of the element is a script code that the browser should execute.

`charset = encoding`	Specifies a character set used to encode the script
`defer = defer`	Defers execution of the script
`language = name`	Specifies the language used in this element
`src = url`	URL for the location of the script file
`type = encoding`	Specifies the MIME type of the script

<select>

Creates a select or drop-down list box.

`disabled = disabled`	Disables the select box, preventing user intervention
`multiple = multiple`	Permits selection of multiple items from the list
`name = name`	Specifies a name for the form control passed to the form's processing application as part of the name/value pair (required)
`onblur = script`	Specifies a script to run when the mouse moves off the control
`onchange = script`	Specifies a script to run when the value of the element changes
`onfocus = script`	Specifies a script to run when the element gains focus
`size = number`	Specifies the number of items that may appear at once
`tabindex = number`	Defines this element's position in the tabbing order

<small>

The content of this element should be displayed in a smaller font than its containing element.

<span>

Used as a grouping element for inline elements (as opposed to block-level elements); also allows for the definition of non-standard attributes for text on a page.

<strike> (Deprecated)

The content of this element should be rendered in strikethrough.

<strong>

The content of this element has strong emphasis and should be rendered in a bold typeface.

<style>

Contains CSS style rules that apply to that page.

<sub>

The content of this element is displayed as subscript.

<sup>

The content of this element is rendered as superscript.

<table>

Creates a table.

`align = center | left | right`	Specifies the alignment of the table within its content
`background = url`	Specifies a URL for a background image
`bgcolor = color`	Specifies a background color for the table
`border = number`	Specifies the width of the border in pixels
`bordercolor = color`	Specifies the color of the border
`bordercolordark = color`	Specifies the darker border color
`bordercolorlight = color`	Specifies the lighter border color
`cellpadding = number`	Specifies the distance between the border and its content in pixels
`cellspacing = number`	Specifies the distance between the cells in pixels
`cols = number`	Specifies the number of columns in the table
`frame = above | below | border | box | hsides | lhs | rhs | void | vsides`	Defines where the borders are displayed
`height = number`	Specifies the height of the table in pixels
`hspace = number`	Specifies the amount of additional space to be added to the left and right of the table
`nowrap = nowrap`	Prevents the content of the table from wrapping
`rules = all | cols | groups | none | rows`	Specifies where the inner dividers are drawn
`summary = string`	Offers a summary description of the table
`valign = bottom | top`	Specifies the alignment of content in the table
`vspace = number`	Specifies the amount of additional space to be added above and below the table
`width = number`	Specifies the width of the table in pixels

<tbody>

Denotes the body section of a table.

`align = center | left | right`	Specifies the alignment of the content of the body of the table
`char = string`	Specifies an offset character for alignment
`charoff = string`	Specifies the offset within the cells from the offset character
`valign = bottom | top`	Specifies the vertical alignment of content in the body of the table
`width = number`	Specifies the width of the table body in pixels

<td>

Creates a cell of a table.

`abbr = string`	Specifies an abbreviation for the cell's content
`align = center | left | right`	Specifies the alignment of the content of the cell
`axis = string`	Specifies a name for a related group of cells
`background = url`	Specifies a URL for a background image for the cell
`bgcolor = color`	Specifies the background color of the cell
`border = number`	Specifies the border width of the cell in pixels
`bordercolor = color`	Specifies the border color of the cell
`bordercolordark= color`	Specifies the dark border color of the cell
`bordercolorlight= color`	Specifies the light border color of the cell
`char = string`	Specifies the cell alignment character
`charoff = string`	Specifies the offset from the cell alignment character
`colspan = number`	Specifies the number of columns this cell spans
`headers = string`	Specifies the names of header cells associated with this cell
`height = number`	Specifies the height of the cell in pixels

(continued)

`nowrap = nowrap`	Prevents the content of the cell from wrapping
`rowspan = number`	Specifies the number of rows the cell spans
`scope = row | col | rowgroup | colgroup`	Specifies the scope of a header cell
`valign = bottom | top`	Specifies vertical alignment of the content of the cell
`width = number`	Specifies the width of the cell in pixels

<textarea>

Creates a multiple-line text input control in a form.

`accesskey= key_character`	Defines a hotkey/keyboard shortcut for this form control
`cols = number`	Specifies the number of columns of characters the text area should be (the width in characters)
`disabled = disabled`	Disables the text area, preventing user intervention
`name = string`	Specifies a name for the form control passed to the form's processing application as part of the name/value pair (required)
`onblur = script`	Specifies a script to run when the mouse moves off the text area
`onchange = script`	Specifies a script to run when the value of the element changes
`onfocus = script`	Specifies a script to run when the element gains focus
`onselect = script`	Specifies a script to run when the text area is selected
`readonly = readonly`	Prevents the user from modifying content
`rows = number`	Specifies the number of rows of text that should appear in the text area without the scrollbar appearing
`tabindex = number`	Defines this element's position in the tabbing order
`wrap = physical _ vertical _ off`	Specifies whether the text in a text area should wrap or continue on the same line when width of text area is reached

<tfoot>

Denotes row or rows of a table to be used as a footer for the table.

`align = center | left | right`	Specifies the alignment of the content of the footer of the table
`char = string`	Specifies an offset character for alignment
`charoff = string`	Specifies the offset within the cells from the offset character
`valign = bottom | top`	Specifies the vertical alignment of content in the foot of the table
`width = number`	Specifies the width of the table body in pixels

<thead>

Denotes row or rows of a table to be used as a header for the table.

`align = center | left | right`	Specifies the alignment of the content of the head of the table
`char = string`	Specifies an offset character for alignment
`charoff = string`	Specifies the offset within the cells of the alignment position
`valign = bottom | top`	Specifies the vertical alignment of content in the head of the table
`width = number`	Specifies the width of the table body in pixels

<th>

Denotes a header cell of a table. By default, content is often shown in bold font.

`abbr = string`	Specifies an abbreviation for the cell's content
`align = center | left | right`	Specifies the alignment of the content of the cell
`axis = string`	Specifies a name for a related group of cells
`background = url`	Specifies a URL for a background image for the cell

(continued)

bgcolor = color	Specifies the background color of the cell
border = number	Specifies the border width of the cell in pixels
bordercolor = color	Specifies the border color of the cell
bordercolordark= color	Specifies the dark border color of the cell
bordercolorlight= color	Specifies the light border color of the cell
char = string	Specifies the cell alignment character
charoff = string	Specifies the offset from the cell alignment character
colspan = number	Specifies the number of columns this cell spans
headers = string	Specifies the names of header cells associated with this cell
height = number	Specifies the height of the cell in pixels
nowrap	Prevents the content of the cell from wrapping
rowspan = number	Specifies the number of rows the cell spans
scope = row | col | rowgroup | colgroup	Specifies the scope of a header cell
valign = bottom | top	Specifies vertical alignment of the content of the cell
width = number	Specifies the width of the cell in pixels

<title>

The content of this element is the title of the document and will usually be rendered in the top title bar of the browser; it may only live in the head of the page. Supports only the attributes listed in the table that follows.

dir = ltr | rtl	Specifies the direction of the text within the element
id = string	Specifies a unique identifier for this element
lang = language_type	Specifies the language used in this element
xml:lang = language_type	Specifies the language used in this element

<tr>

Denotes a row of a table.

align = center | left | right	Specifies the alignment of the content of the row
background = url	Specifies a URL for a background image for the row
bgcolor = color	Specifies the background color of the row
border = number	Specifies the border width of the row in pixels
bordercolor = color	Specifies the border color of the row
bordercolordark= color	Specifies the dark border color of the row
bordercolorlight= color	Specifies the light border color of the row
char = string	Specifies the row alignment character
charoff = string	Specifies the offset from the row alignment character
nowrap = nowrap	Prevents the content of the cell from wrapping
valign = bottom | top	Specifies vertical alignment of the content of the cell

<tt>

The content of this element is rendered in a fixed-width font, as if on a teletype device.

<u> (Deprecated)

The content of this element is rendered with underlined text.

<ul>

Creates an unordered list.

compact = compact	Attempts to make the list more compact vertically
type = bullet_type	Specifies the type of bullet used to display the list items

<var>

The content of this element is a programming variable, and is usually rendered in a small fixed-width font.

CSS Properties

This appendix is a reference to the main CSS properties that you will be using to control the appearance of your documents.

For each property covered, you will first see a very brief description of the property and then an example of its usage. This is followed by two tables: the one on the left shows the possible values the property can take along with the first versions of Internet Explorer and Firefox to support these values, and the table on the right indicates whether the property can be inherited, what the default value for the property is, and which elements it applies to.

While browsers may support the `inherit` value of many properties, if the browser is unable to set the property to some other value in the first place (perhaps because that value is not supported), then the `inherit` value is of little use.

At the end of the appendix are units of measurement.

Font Properties

The font properties allow you to change the appearance of a typeface.

font

Allows you to set several font properties at the same time, separated by spaces. You can specify `font-size`, `line-height`, `font-family`, `font-style`, `font-variant`, and `font-weight` in this one property.

```
font {color:#ff0000; arial, verdana, sans-serif; 12pt;}
```

Value	IE	FF	Inherited	Yes
[font-family]	3	1	Default	n/a
[font-size]	3	1	Applies to	All elements
[font-style]	3	1		
[font-variant]	4	1		
[font-weight]	3	1		
[line-height]	3	1		
`inherit`	8	1		

font-family

Allows you to specify the typefaces you want to use. Can take multiple values separated by commas, starting with your first preference, then your second choice, and ending with a generic font-family (`serif`, `sans-serif`, `cursive`, `fantasy`, or `monospace`).

```
p {font-family:arial, verdana, sans-serif;}
```

Value	IE	FF	Inherited	Yes
[generic family]	3	1	Default	Set by browser
[specific family]	3	1	Applies to	All elements
`inherit`	8	1		

font-size

Allows you to specify a size of font. The `font-size` property has its own specific values:

- **Absolute sizes:** `xx-small`, `x-small`, `small`, `medium`, `large`, `x-large`, `xx-large`
- **Relative sizes:** `larger`, `smaller`
- **Percentage:** Percentage of the parent font
- **Length:** A unit of measurement (as described at end of the appendix)

Value	IE	FF	Inherited	Yes
[absolute size]	3	1	Default	`medium`
[relative size]	4	1	Applies to	All elements
[percent]	3	1		
[length]	3	1		
`inherit`	8	1		

font-size-adjust

Allows you to adjust the aspect value of a font, which is the ratio between the height of a lowercase letter *x* in the font and the height of the font.

```
{font-size-adjust:0.5;}
```

Value	IE	FF	Inherited	Yes
[number]	-	-	Default	Specific to font
none	-	-	Applies to	All elements
inherit	-	1		

font-stretch

Allows you to specify the width of the letters in a font (not the size between them).

- **Relative values:** `normal`, `wider`, `narrower`
- **Fixed values:** `ultra-condensed`, `extra-condensed`, `condensed`, `semi-condensed`, `semi-expanded`, `expanded`, `extra-expanded`, `ultra-expanded`

```
p {font-family:courier; font-stretch:semi-condensed;}
```

Value	IE	FF	Inherited	Yes
[relative]	-	-	Default	Specific to font
[fixed]	-	-	Applies to	All elements
inherit	-	1		

font-style

Applies styling to a font. If the specified version of the font is available, it will be used; otherwise, the browser will render it.

```
p {font-style:italic;}
```

Value	IE	FF	Inherited	Yes
normal	3	1	Default	normal
italic	3	1	Applies to	All elements
oblique	4	1		
inherit	8	1		

font-variant

Creates capital letters that are the same size as normal lowercase letters.

Value	IE	FF	Inherited	Yes
`normal`	4	1	Default	`normal`
`small-caps`	4	1	Applies to	All elements
`inherit`	8	1		

font-weight

Specifies the thickness of the text — its "boldness."

- **Absolute values:** `normal`, `bold`
- **Relative values:** `bolder`, `lighter`
- **Numeric value:** Between 0 and 100

```
p {font-weight:bold;}
```

Value	IE	FF	Inherited	Yes
[absolute]	3	1	Default	`normal`
[relative]	4	1	Applies to	All elements
[number 1-100]	4	1		
`inherit`	8	1		

Text Properties

Text properties change the appearance and layout of text in general (as opposed to the font).

letter-spacing

Specifies the distance between letters as a unit of length.

```
p {letter-spacing:1em;}
```

Value	IE	FF	Inherited	Yes
[length]	4	1	Default	`normal`
`normal`	4	1	Applies to	All elements
`inherit`	8	1		

text-align

Specifies whether text is aligned `left`, `right`, `center`, or `justified`.

```
p {text-align:center}
```

Value	IE	FF	Inherited	Yes
`left`	3	1	Default	Depends on user agent and element (usually `left` except for `<th>` elements, which are `center`)
`right`	3	1	Applies to	All elements
`center`	3	1		
`justify`	4	1		
`inherit`	8	1		

text-decoration

Specifies whether text should have an `underline`, `overline`, `line-through`, or `blink` appearance.

```
p {text-decoration:underline;}
```

Value	IE	FF	Inherited	No
`none`	3	1	Default	`none`
`underline`	3	1	Applies to	All elements
`overline`	4	1		
`line-through`	3	1		
`blink`	-	1		
`inherit`	8	1		

text-indent

Specifies the indentation in length or as a percentage of the parent element's width.

```
p {text-indent:3em;}
```

Value	IE	FF	Inherited	Yes
[length]	4	1	Default	`0`
[percentage]	4	1	Applies to	Block elements
`inherit`	8	1		

text-shadow

Creates a drop shadow for the text. It should take three lengths; the first two specify X and Y coordinates for the offset of the drop shadow, while the third specifies a blur effect. This is then followed by a color, which can be a name or a hex value.

```
.dropShadow {text-shadow: 0.3em 0.3em 0.5em black}
```

Value	IE	FF	Inherited	No
[shadow effects]	-	3.1b	Default	none
none	-	3.1b	Applies to	All elements
inherit	-	1		

(Also supported in Safari 3, Chrome 2 and Opera 9.6 and higher.)

text-transform

Specifies capitalization of text in an element:

- none: Removes inherited settings.
- uppercase: All characters are uppercase.
- lowercase: All characters are lowercase.
- capitalize: First letter of each word is capitalized.

```
p {text-transform:uppercase;}
```

Value	IE	FF	Inherited	Yes
none	4	1	Default	none
uppercase	4	1	Applies to	All elements
lowercase	4	1		
capitalize	4	1		
inherit	8	1		

white-space

This indicates how white space should be dealt with:

- `normal`: White space should be collapsed.
- `pre`: White space should be preserved.
- `nowrap`: Text should not be broken to a new line except with the `<br />` element.

```
p {white-space:pre;}
```

Value	IE	FF	Inherited	Yes
`normal`	5.5	1	Default	`normal`
`pre`	5.5	1	Applies to	Block elements
`nowrap`	5.5	1		
`inherit`	8	1		

word-spacing

This specifies the gap between words:

```
p {word-spacing:2em;}
```

Value	IE	FF	Inherited	Yes
`normal`	6	1	Default	`normal`
[length]	6	1	Applies to	All elements
`inherit`	8	1		

Color and Background Properties

The following properties allow you to change the colors and backgrounds of both the page and other boxes.

background

This is shorthand for specifying background properties for `color`, `url`, `repeat`, `scroll`, and `position`; separated by a space. By default, the background is transparent.

```
body {background: #efefef url("images/background.gif"); }
```

Value	IE	FF	Inherited	No
[background-attachment]	4	1	Default	Not defined (by default background is transparent)
[background-color]	3	1	Applies to	All elements
[background-image]	3	1		
[background-position]	4	1		
[background-repeat]	3	1		
`inherit`	-	1		

background-attachment

This specifies whether a background image should be fixed in one position or scroll along the page:

```
body {background-attachment:fixed;
      background-image: url("images/background.gif");}
```

Value	IE	FF	Inherited	No
`fixed`	4	1	Default	`scroll`
`scroll`	4	1	Applies to	All elements
`inherit`	8	1		

background-color

Sets the color of the background. This can be a single color or two colors blended together. Colors can be specified as a color name, hex value, or RGB value. By default the box will be transparent.

```
body {background-color:#efefef;}
```

Value	IE	FF	Inherited	No
[color]	4	1	Default	`transparent`
`transparent`	4	1	Applies to	All elements
`inherit`	8	1		

background-image

This specifies an image to be used as a background, which by default will be tiled. Value is a URL for the image.

```
body {background-image: url("images/background.gif");}
```

Value	IE	FF	Inherited	No
[url]	4	1	Default	none
none	4	1	Applies to	All elements
inherit	8	1		

background-position

Specifies where a background image should be placed in the page, from the top-left corner. Values can be an absolute distance, percentage, or one of the keywords. If only one value is given, it is assumed to be horizontal.

- Keywords available are: `top`, `bottom`, `left`, `right`, `center`

```
body {background-position:center;
      background-image: url("images/background.gif");}
```

Value	IE	FF	Inherited	No
[length - x y]	4	1	Default	top, left
[percentage - x% y%]	4	1	Applies to	Block-level elements
top	4	1		
left	4	1		
bottom	4	1		
right	4	1		
center	4	1		
inherit	8	1		

background-repeat

Specifies if a background image should be repeated, and if so in which directions. Values are `repeat` to repeat horizontally and vertically, `repeat-x` to just repeat horizontally, `repeat-y` to just repeat vertically, and `no-repeat` to prevent it from repeating.

Value	IE	FF	Inherited	No
`repeat`	4	1	Default	`none`
`repeat-x`	4	1	Applies to	All elements
`repeat-y`	4	1		
`no-repeat`	4	1		
`inherit`	8	1		

background-positionX

Position of a background image to run horizontally across the page. Values are the same as for `background-position` (default: `top`).

background-positionY

Position of a background image to run vertically down the page. Values are the same as for `background-position` (default: `left`).

Border properties

The border properties allow you to control the appearance and size of a border around any box.

border (border-bottom, border-left, border-top, border-right)

This is shorthand for specifying `border-style`, `border-width`, and `border-color` properties.

Value	IE	FF	Inherited	No
[border-style]	4	1	Default	`none, medium, none`
[border-width]	4	1	Applies to	All elements
[border-color]	4	1		
`inherit`	8	1		

border-style (border-bottom-style, border-left-style, border-top-style, border-right-style)

This specifies the style of line that should surround a block box.

```
div.page {border-style:solid;}
```

Value	IE	FF	Inherited	No
none	4	1	Default	none
dotted	5.5	1	Applies to	All elements
dashed	5.5	1		
solid	4	1		
double	4	1		
groove	4	1		
ridge	4	1		
inset	4	1		
outset	4	1		
hidden	-	-		
inherit	8	1		

border-width (border-bottom-width, border-left-width, border-top-width, border-right-width)

Specifies the width of a border line; can be a width or a keyword.

```
div.page {border-width:2px;}
```

Value	IE	FF	Inherited	No
[length]	4	1	Default	medium
thin	4	1	Applies to	All elements
medium	4	1		
thick	4	1		
inherit	8	1		

border-color (border-bottom-color, border-left-color, border-top-color, border-right-color)

Specifies the color of a border; values can be a color name, hex code, or RGB value.

```
table {border-color:#000000;}
```

Value	IE	FF	Inherited	No
[color value]	4	1	Default	`none`
`inherit`	8	1	Applies to	All elements

Dimensions

The dimensions properties allow you to specify the size that boxes should be.

height

Specifies the vertical height of a block element.

```
table {height:400px;}
```

Value	IE	FF	Inherited	No
`auto`	4	1	Default	`auto`
[length]	4	1	Applies to	Block-level elements
[percentage]	4	1		
`inherit`	8	1		

width

Specifies the horizontal width of an element.

```
td {width:150px;}
```

Value	IE	FF	Inherited	No
`auto`	4	1	Default	`auto`
[length]	4	1	Applies to	Block level elements
[percentage]	4	1		
`inherit`	8	1		

line-height

This specifies the height of a line of text. It is a way of controlling leading (space between multiple lines of text) because the line height may be more or less than the size of the font.

```
p {line-height:18px;}
```

Value	IE	FF	Inherited	Yes
`normal`	3	1	Default	Depends on browser
[number]	4	1	Applies to	All elements
[length]	3	1		
[percentage]	3	1		
`inherit`	8	1		

max-height

This specifies the maximum height of a block-level element (same values as for `height`).

```
td {max-height:200px;}
```

Value	IE	FF	Inherited	No
`auto`	7	1	Default	`auto`
[length]	7	1	Applies to	Block-level elements
[percentage]	7	1		
`inherit`	8	1		

max-width

This specifies the maximum width of a block-level element (same values as for `width`).

```
td {max-width:400px;}
```

Value	IE	FF	Inherited	No
`auto`	7	1	Default	`auto`
[length]	7	1	Applies to	Block elements
[percentage]	7	1		
`inherit`	8	1		

min-height

This specifies the minimum height of a block-level element (same values as for `height`).

```
td {min-height:100px;}
```

Value	IE	FF	Inherited	No
`auto`	7	1	Default	`auto`
[length]	7	1	Applies to	Block-level elements
[percentage]	7	1		
`inherit`	8	1		

min-width

This specifies the minimum width of a block-level element (same values as for `width`).

```
td {min-width:200px;}
```

Value	IE	FF	Inherited	No
`auto`	7	1	Default	`auto`
[length]	7	1	Applies to	Block elements
[percentage]	7	1		
`inherit`	8	1		

Margin Properties

Margin properties allow you to specify a margin around a box and therefore create a gap between elements' borders.

margin (margin-bottom, margin-left, margin-top, margin-right)

This specifies the width of a margin around a box.

```
p {margin:15px;}
```

Value	IE	FF	Inherited	No
auto	3	1	Default	0
[length]	3	1	Applies to	All elements
[percentage — relative to parent element]	3	1		
inherit	8	1		

Padding Properties

Padding properties set the distance between the border of an element and its content. They are important for adding white space to documents (in particular table cells).

padding (padding-bottom, padding-left, padding-right, padding-top)

This specifies the distance between an element's border and its content.

```
td {padding:20px;}
```

Value	IE	FF	Inherited	No
auto	4	1	Default	zero
[length]	4	1	Applies to	All elements
[percentage — relative to parent element]	4	1		
inherit	8	1		

List Properties

List properties affect the presentation of bulleted, numbered, and definition lists.

list-style

This is shorthand allowing you to specify `list-style-position` and `list-style-type`.

```
ul {list-style: inside disc}
```

Value	IE	FF	Inherited	Yes
`<position>`	4	1	Default	Depends on browser
`<type>`	4	1	Applies to	List elements
`<image>`	4	1		
`inherit`	8	1		

list-style-position

This specifies whether the marker should be placed inside each item of a list or to the left of them.

```
ul {list-style-position:inside;}
```

Value	IE	FF	Inherited	Yes
`inside`	4	1	Default	`outside`
`outside`	4	1	Applies to	List elements
`inherit`	8	1		

list-style-type

This indicates the type of bullet or numbering that a bullet should use.

```
ul {list-style-type:circle;}
```

Value	IE	FF	Inherited	Yes
`None`	4	1	Default	`disc`
`disc (default)`	4	1	Applies to	List elements
`circle`	4	1		
`square`	4	1		
`decimal`	4	1		
`decimal-leading-zero`	-	-		
`lower-alpha`	4	1		
`upper-alpha`	4	1		
`lower-roman`	4	1		
`upper-roman`	4	1		

Additional numbered list styles are available in CSS, but unfortunately they are not supported in IE7, Netscape 7, or Firefox 2.

`hebrew`	Traditional Hebrew numbering
`georgian`	Traditional Georgian numbering (an, ban, gan, . . . , he, tan, in, in-an, . . .)
`armenian`	Traditional Armenian numbering
`cjk-ideographic`	Plain ideographic numbers
`hiragana`	(a, i, u, e, o, ka, ki, . . .)
`katakana`	(A, I, U, E, O, KA, KI, . . .)
`hiragana-iroha`	(i, ro, ha, ni, ho, he, to, . . .)
`katakana-iroha`	(I, RO, HA, NI, HO, HE, TO, . . .)

marker-offset

This specifies the space between a list item and its marker.

```
ol {marker-offset:2em;}
```

Value	IE	FF	Inherited	No
[length]	7	1	Default	`auto`
`auto`	7	1	Applies to	Marker elements
`inherit`	8	1		

Positioning Properties

Positioning properties allow you to use CSS for positioning boxes on the page.

position

Specifies the positioning schema that should be used for an element. When an element is positioned, you also need to use the box-offset properties covered next (`top`, `left`, `bottom`, and `right`). Note that you should not use `top` and `bottom` or `left` and `right` together (if you do, `top` and `left` take priority).

- `absolute` can be fixed on the canvas in a specific position from its containing element (which is another absolutely positioned element); it will also move when the user scrolls the page.
- `static` will fix it on the page in the same place and keep it there even when the user scrolls.
- `relative` will be placed offset in relation to its normal position.
- `fixed` will fix it on the background of the page and not move when the user scrolls.

```
p.article{position:absolute; top:10px; left:20px;
```

Value	IE	FF	Inherited	No
`absolute`	4	1	Default	`static`
`relative`	4	1	Applies to	All elements
`static`	4	1		
`fixed`	7	1		
`inherit`	8	1		

top

This sets the vertical position of an element from the top of the window or containing element.

Value	IE	FF	Inherited	No
auto	4	1	Default	auto
[length]	4	1	Applies to	Positioned elements
[percentage — relative to parent's height]	4	1		
inherit	8	1		

left

This sets the horizontal position of an element from the left of the window or containing element.

Value	IE	FF	Inherited	No
auto	4	1	Default	auto
[length]	4	1	Applies to	Positioned elements
[percentage — relative to parent's width]	4	1		
inherit	8	1		

bottom

This sets the vertical position of an element from the bottom of the window or containing element.

Value	IE	FF	Inherited	No
auto	5	1	Default	auto
[length]	5	1	Applies to	Positioned elements
[percentage — relative to parent's height]	5	1		
inherit	8	1		

right

This sets the horizontal position of an element from the right of the window or containing element.

Value	IE	FF	Inherited	No
auto	5	1	Default	auto
[length]	5	1	Applies to	Positioned elements
[percentage — relative to parent's width]	5	1		
inherit	8	1		

vertical-align

This sets the vertical positioning of an inline element:

- `baseline` aligns element with base of parent.
- `middle` aligns midpoint of element with half the height of parent.
- `sub` makes element subscript.
- `super` makes element superscript.
- `text-top` aligns element with the top of parent element's font.
- `text-bottom` aligns element with the bottom of parent element's font.
- `top` aligns top of element with the top of tallest element on current line.
- `bottom` aligns element with the bottom of lowest element on the current line.

```
span.superscript {vertical-align:super;}
```

Value	IE	N	Inherited	No
baseline	4	1	Default	baseline
middle	4	1	Applies to	Inline elements
sub	4	1		
super	4	1		
text-top	4	1		
text-bottom	4	1		

Value	IE	N	Inherited	No
`top`	4	1		
`bottom`	4	1		
[percentage relative to line height]	8	1		
[length]	-	-		
`inherit`	8	1		

z-index

Controls which overlapping element appears to be on top. Positive and negative numbers are permitted.

```
p {position:absolute; top:10px; left:20px; z-index:3;}
```

Value	IE	FF	Inherited	No
`auto`	4	1	Default	Depends on position of element in XHTML source document
[number]	4	1		
`inherit`	8	1	Applies to	Positioned elements

clip

Controls which part of an element is visible. Parts outside the clip are not visible. If value is `rect()`, it takes the following form:

- `rect([top] [right] [bottom] [left])`

```
rect(25 100 100 25)
```

Value	IE	FF	Inherited	No
`auto`	4	1	Default	`auto`
`rect`	4	1	Applies to	Block elements
`inherit`	8	1		

overflow

This specifies how a container element will display content that is too large for its containing element.

```
p {width:200px; height:200px; overflow:scroll;}
```

Value	IE	FF	Inherited	No
auto	4	1	Default	visible
hidden	4	1	Applies to	Block elements
visible	4	1		
scroll	4	1		
inherit	8	6		

overflow-x

Same as `overflow`, but only for the horizontal x-axis. First supported in IE5.

overflow-y

Same as `overflow`, but only for the vertical y-axis. First supported in IE5.

Outline Properties

Outlines act like borders, but do not take up any space — they sit on top of the canvas.

Outline (outline-color, outline-style, outline-width)

Shortcut for the `outline-color`, `outline-style`, and `outline-width` properties:

```
outline {solid #ff0000 2px}
```

Note that `outline-color`, `outline-style`, and `outline-width` take the same values as `border-color`, `border-style`, and `border-width`.

Value	IE	FF	Inherited	No
outline-color	8	1.5	Default	none
outline-style	8	1.5	Applies to	All elements
outline-width	8	1.5		
outline	8	1.5		

Table Properties

Table properties allow you to affect the style of tables, rows, and cells.

border-collapse

This specifies the border model that the table should use (whether adjacent borders should be collapsed into one value or kept separate).

```
table {border-collapse:separate;}
```

Value	IE	FF	Inherited	Yes
collapse	5	1	Default	collapse
separate	5	1	Applies to	Table and inline elements
inherit	8	1		

border-spacing

This specifies the distance between adjacent cells' borders.

```
table {border-spacing:2px;}
```

Value	IE	FF	Inherited	Yes
[length]	8	1	Default	0
inherit	8	1	Applies to	Table and inline elements

caption-side

This indicates which side of a table a caption should be placed on.

```
caption {caption-side:bottom;}
```

Value	IE	FF	Inherited	Yes
top	8	1	Default	top
left	8	1	Applies to	<caption> elements in <table> elements
bottom	8	1		
right	8	1		
inherit	8	1		

empty-cells

This specifies whether borders should be displayed if a cell is empty.

```
td, th {empty-cells:hide;}
```

Value	IE	FF	Inherited	Yes
show	5	1	Default	show
hide	5	1	Applies to	Table cell elements
inherit	8	1		

table-layout

Specifies how the browser should calculate the layout of a table; can affect the speed of rendering a large or graphics-intensive table.

Value	IE	FF	Inherited	No
auto	5	1	Default	auto
fixed	5	1	Applies to	Table and inline elements
inherit	8	6		

Classification Properties

Classification properties affect how the boxes in the box model are rendered.

clear

Forces elements, which would normally wrap around an aligned element, to be displayed below it. Value indicates which side may not touch an aligned element.

```
p {clear:left;}
```

Value	IE	FF	Inherited	No
none	4	1	Default	none
both	4	1	Applies to	All elements
left	4	1		
right	4	1		
inherit	8	1		

display

Specifies how an element is rendered, if at all. If set to `none` the element is not rendered and it does not take up any space. This property can also force an inline element to be displayed as a block or vice versa.

```
span.important {display:block;}
```

Value	IE	FF	Inherited	Yes
none	4	1	Default	inline
inline	5	1	Applies to	All elements
block	5	1		
list-item	5	1		
inherit	8	1		

While the default value of this property is `inline`, browsers tend to treat the element depending on its inherent display type. Block-level elements, such as headings and paragraphs, get treated as if the default were `block`, whereas inline elements such as `<i>`, `<b>`, or `<span>` get treated as `inline`.

float

Subsequent elements should be wrapped to the left or right of the element, rather than below.

```
img.featuredItem {float:left;}
```

Value	IE	FF	Inherited	No
none	4	1	Default	none
left	4	1	Applies to	All elements
right	4	1		
inherit	8	1		

visibility

Specifies whether an element should be displayed or hidden. Even if hidden, elements take up space on the page, but are transparent.

Value	IE	FF	Inherited	No
`visible`	4	1	Default	`inherit`
`show`	8	1	Applies to	All elements
`hidden`	4	1		
`hide`	8	1		
`collapse`	8	1		
`inherit`	8	1		

Internationalization Properties

Internationalization properties affect how text is rendered in different languages.

direction

Specifies the direction of text from left to right or right to left. This should be used in association with the `unicode-bidi` property.

```
td.word{direction:rtl; unicode-bidi:bidi-override;}
```

Value	IE	FF	Inherited	Yes
`ltr`	5	1	Default	`ltr`
`rtl`	5	1	Applies to	All elements
`inherit`	8	1		

unicode-bidi

The `unicode-bidi` property allows you to override Unicode's built-in directionality settings for languages.

```
td.word{unicode-bidi:bidi-override; direction:rtl; }
```

Value	IE	FF	Inherited	No
`normal`	5	2	Default	`normal`
`embed`	5	2	Applies to	All elements
`bidi-override`	5	2		
`inherit`	8	2		

Lengths

Following are the unit measurements for lengths that can be used in CSS.

Absolute Lengths

Unit	IE	FF
cm	3	1
in	3	1
mm	3	1
pc	3	1
pt	3	1

Relative Lengths

Unit	IE	FF
em	4	1
ex	4	1
px	3	1

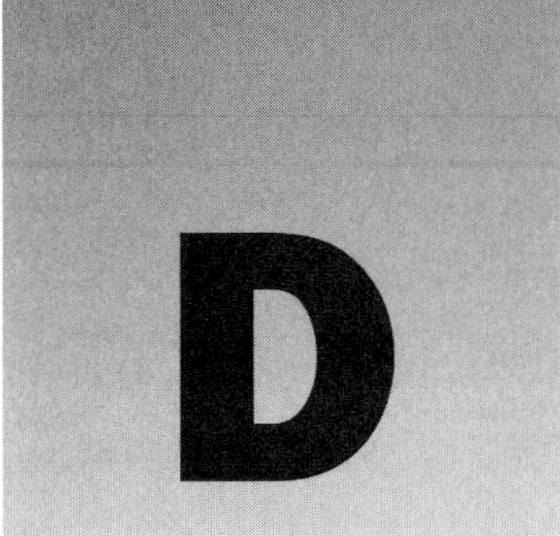

Color Names and Values

The first thing you need to learn about color is how to specify exactly the color you want; after all, there are a lot of different hues, tones, and shades and it's important you choose the right ones.

In XHTML there are two key ways of specifying a color:

- **Hex codes:** These are six-digit codes representing the amount of red, green, and blue that make up the color, preceded by a pound or hash sign # (for example, `#333333`).
- **Color names:** A set of names that represent over 200 colors, such as `red`, `lightslategray`, and `fuchsia`.

In addition, when writing CSS style sheets you can also specify colors using RGB color values. Here, numbers between 0 and 255 represent the amount of red, green, and blue that make up each color.

Using Hex Codes to Specify Colors

When you start using *hexadecimal codes* (or hex codes for short), they can be a little daunting because they use a mix of numbers and letters to represent colors. While we are used to numbers that are represented with 10 digits (0-9), hexadecimal codes are represented with 16 digits (0-9 and A-F). The table that follows provides some examples of colors and their hex values; we will come back to look at Understanding Hex Codes shortly, once you've seen what they're trying to represent.

Color	Hexadecimal Code
Black	#000000
White	#FFFFFF
Red	#FF0000
Green	#00FF00
Blue	#0000FF
Purple	#800080

The idea that colors are represented by a mix of numbers and letters might seem a little strange, but what follows the # sign is actually the amount of red, green, and blue that make up the color. The format for hex codes is as follows:

```
#rrggbb
```

As you might already know, the screens on computer monitors are made up of thousands of tiny squares called pixels (if you look very closely at your monitor you should be able to see them). When it is not turned on, the screen is black because it does not emit any light. When it is turned on, a picture is created because each pixel can be a different color. Every one of these colors is expressed in terms of a mix of red, green, and blue (just like a television screen).

It's hardly surprising, therefore, that you specify colors in the amounts of red, green, and blue that are required to make a given color. The values of red, green, and blue required to make a color are specified using numbers between 0 and 255, so when red, green, and blue all have a value of 0 you get black, whereas if each has a value of 255 you get white. If red is given a value of 255, and green and blue have a value of 0, you get red. You can make other colors by mixing the amounts of red, green, and blue as well — for example if red and blue are given values of 255 and blue a value of 0, you get pink.

You may have seen that some software represents colors using three sets of numbers between 0 and 255. Figure D-1 shows the color window in Adobe Photoshop.

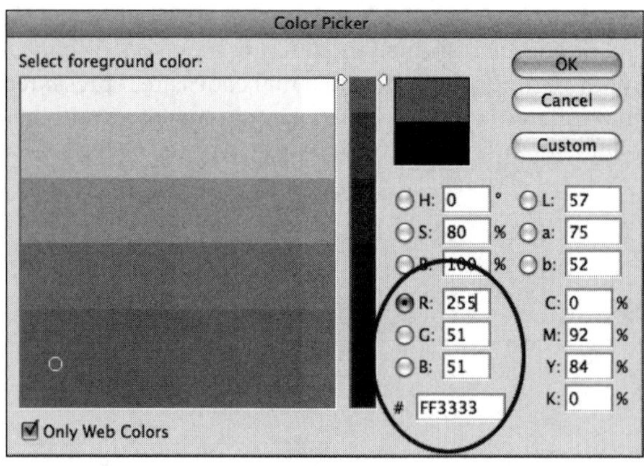

Figure D-1

The hexadecimal codes used on the Web for color are a direct translation of these values between 0 and 255, except they use two characters, not three, to represent the numbers between 0 and 255. For example, FF represents 255 and 00 represents 0.

When designing a site, you can use a tool such as Photoshop or a number of free resources on the Web to find hex codes for colors:

- `www.colorschemer.com/`
- `www.colourlovers.com/colors/add`

However, if you really want to understand how hex codes work, you need to understand how computers store information, so read on in the following section.

Understanding Hex Codes

You may have heard people say that computers store all their information in 0s and 1s, and while it may sound hard to believe, it's true! The smallest unit of information a computer stores in is known as a *bit*, and a bit can have only one of two values:

- 0, which means off (or false)
- 1, which means on (or true)

These two values on their own will not store much information, but if you combine 4 bits together, you can get 16 different values. For example, using combinations of four 0s and 1s, you can represent the digits 0 through 9 (and still have values to spare):

```
0000 0001 0010 0011 0100 0101 0110 0111 1000 1001 1010 1011 1100 1101 1110 1111
  0    1    2    3    4    5    6    7    8    9    -    -    -    -    -    -
```

Four bits can be replaced by a single hexadecimal digit. There are 16 digits in hexadecimal numbers to represent the 16 possible values of four 0s and 1s:

```
0000 0001 0010 0011 0100 0101 0110 0111 1000 1001 1010 1011 1100 1101 1110 1111
  0    1    2    3    4    5    6    7    8    9    A    B    C    D    E    F
```

0 is the smallest; F is the largest.

Still, computers need to work with more than 16 possible values, so they tend to store information in even larger segments. A group of 8 bits is known as a *byte*. A byte can therefore be represented using just two hexadecimal digits. For example:

```
Binary          0100     1111
Hexadecimal      4         F
```

This gives 256 possible combinations of 0s and 1s (16 × 16), plenty for the characters of the English language, and that is why colors are represented in numbers between 0 and 255.

So, while hexadecimal codes for web colors may appear a little complicated, I think you would agree that `#4F4F4F` is a lot easier to read than `010011110100111101001111`. The following table shows some more hexadecimal codes and their corresponding decimal numbers.

Hexadecimal	Decimal
00	0
33	51
66	102
99	153
AA	170
BB	187
CC	204
DD	221
EE	238
FF	255

Using Color Names to Specify Colors

Rather than using hex values to specify colors, you can also use the names of many colors such as red, green, and white to specify the color you want. There are more than 200 different color names supported by IE, Firefox, and Safari, all of which are listed at the end of this appendix.

Although names might sound a lot easier to understand than hex codes, some of the colors are easier to remember than others, and remembering which color corresponds to each of the 200 names is very difficult. Here is a sample of some of the color names:

```
aqua, beige, coral, darkcyan, firebrick, green, honeydew, indianred,
lavenderblush, maroon, navy, oldlace, palegreen, red, saddlebrown,
tan, white, yellow
```

Furthermore, if you do jobs for larger companies, such companies often want to specify very exact colors that represent their brand, and their color might not have an HTML name. Indeed, when clients specify the color they want, they usually specify a hex code.

Given that hex codes give you many more choices of shades, tints, and hues of colors than color names, and bearing in mind that a lot of companies ask for specific colors to represent their company, hex codes tend to be the choice of web professionals.

Color Name and Number Reference

The following table shows the color names supported by the main browsers, and their corresponding hex values. It is worth noting, however, that these are browser extensions, not part of the HTML or XHTML recommendations.

Color Name	Hex Value	Color Name	Hex Value
aliceblue	#f0f8ff	darkgoldenrod	#b8860b
antiquewhite	#faebd7	darkgray	#a9a9a9
aqua	#00ffff	darkgreen	#006400
aquamarine	#7fffd4	darkkhaki	#bdb76b
azure	#f0ffff	darkmagenta	#8b008b
beige	#f5f5dc	darkolivegreen	#556b2f
bisque	#ffe4c4	darkorange	#ff8b04
black	#000000	darkorchid	#9932cc
blanchedalmond	#ffebcd	darkred	#8b0000
blue	#0000ff	darksalmon	#e9967a
blueviolet	#8a2be2	darkseagreen	#8fbc8f
brown	#a52a2a	darkslateblue	#483d8b
burlywood	#deb887	darkslategray	#2f4f4f
cadetblue	#5f9ea0	darkturquoise	#00ced1
chartreuse	#7fff00	darkviolet	#9400d3
chocolate	#d2691e	deeppink	#ff1493
coral	#ff7f50	deepskyblue	#00bfff
cornflowerblue	#6495ed	dimgray	#696969
cornsilk	#fff8dc	dodgerblue	#1e90ff
crimson	#dc143c	firebrick	#b22222
cyan	#00ffff	floralwhite	#fffaf0
darkblue	#00008b	forestgreen	#228b22
darkcyan	#008b8b	fuchsia	#ff00ff

Continued

Color Name	Hex Value
gainsboro	#dcdcdc
ghostwhite	#f8f8ff
gold	#ffd700
goldenrod	#daa520
gray	#808080
green	#008000
greenyellow	#adff2f
honeydew	#f0fff0
hotpink	#ff69b4
indianred	#cd5c5c
indigo	#4b0082
ivory	#fffff0
khaki	#f0e68c
lavender	#e6e6fa
lavenderblush	#fff0f5
lawngreen	#7cfb04
lemonchiffon	#fffacd
lightblue	#add8e6
lightcoral	#f08080
lightcyan	#e0ffff
lightgoldenrodyellow	#fafad2
lightgreen	#90ee90
lightgrey	#d3d3d3
lightpink	#ffb6c1
lightsalmon	#ffa07a
lightseagreen	#20b2aa
lightskyblue	#87cefa
lightslategray	#778899

Color Name	Hex Value
lightsteelblue	#b0c4de
lightyellow	#ffffe0
lime	#00ff00
limegreen	#32cd32
linen	#faf0e6
magenta	#ff00ff
maroon	#800000
mediumaquamarine	#66cdaa
mediumblue	#0000cd
mediumorchid	#ba55d3
mediumpurple	#9370db
mediumseagreen	#3cb371
mediumslateblue	#7b68ee
mediumspringgreen	#00fa9a
mediumturquoise	#48d1cc
mediumvioletred	#c71585
midnightblue	#191970
mintcream	#f5fffa
mistyrose	#ffe4e1
moccasin	#ffe4b5
navajowhite	#ffdead
navy	#000080
oldlace	#fdf5e6
olive	#808000
olivedrab	#6b8e23
orange	#ffa500
orangered	#ff4500
orchid	#da70d6

Color Name	Hex Value	Color Name	Hex Value
palegoldenrod	#eee8aa	sienna	#a0522d
palegreen	#98fb98	silver	#c0c0c0
paleturquoise	#afeeee	skyblue	#87ceeb
palevioletred	#db7093	slateblue	#6a5acd
papayawhip	#ffefd5	slategray	#708090
peachpuff	#ffdab9	snow	#fffafa
peru	#cd853f	springgreen	#00ff7f
pink	#ffc0cb	steelblue	#4682b4
plum	#dda0dd	tan	#d2b48c
powderblue	#b0e0e6	teal	#008080
purple	#800080	thistle	#d8bfd8
red	#ff0000	tomato	#ff6347
rosybrown	#bc8f8f	turquoise	#40e0d0
royalblue	#4169e1	violet	#ee82ee
saddlebrown	#8b4513	wheat	#f5deb3
salmon	#fa8072	white	#ffffff
sandybrown	#f4a460	whitesmoke	#f5f5f5
seagreen	#2e8b57	yellow	#ffff00
seashell	#fff5ee	yellowgreen	#9acd32

Character Encodings

In Appendix D, I discussed how computers store information, how a character-encoding scheme is a table that translates between characters, and how they are stored in the computer.

The most common character set (or character encoding) in use on computers is ASCII (The American Standard Code for Information Interchange), and it is probably the most widely used character set for encoding text electronically. You can expect all computers browsing the Web to understand ASCII.

Character Set	Description
ASCII	American Standard Code for Information Interchange, which is used on most computers

The problem with ASCII is that it supports only the upper- and lowercase Latin alphabet, the numbers 0–9, and some extra characters: a total of 128 characters in all. Here are the printable characters of ASCII (the other characters are things such as line feeds and carriage-return characters).

<table>
<tr><td></td><td>!</td><td>"</td><td>#</td><td>$</td><td>%</td><td>&</td><td>'</td><td>(</td><td>)</td><td>*</td><td>+</td><td>,</td><td>-</td><td>.</td><td>/</td></tr>
<tr><td>0</td><td>1</td><td>2</td><td>3</td><td>4</td><td>5</td><td>6</td><td>7</td><td>8</td><td>9</td><td>:</td><td>;</td><td><</td><td>=</td><td>></td><td>?</td></tr>
<tr><td>@</td><td>A</td><td>B</td><td>C</td><td>D</td><td>E</td><td>F</td><td>G</td><td>H</td><td>I</td><td>J</td><td>K</td><td>L</td><td>M</td><td>N</td><td>O</td></tr>
<tr><td>P</td><td>Q</td><td>R</td><td>S</td><td>T</td><td>U</td><td>V</td><td>W</td><td>X</td><td>Y</td><td>Z</td><td>[</td><td>\</td><td>]</td><td>^</td><td>_</td></tr>
<tr><td>`</td><td>a</td><td>b</td><td>c</td><td>d</td><td>e</td><td>f</td><td>g</td><td>h</td><td>i</td><td>j</td><td>k</td><td>l</td><td>m</td><td>n</td><td>o</td></tr>
<tr><td>p</td><td>q</td><td>r</td><td>s</td><td>t</td><td>u</td><td>v</td><td>w</td><td>x</td><td>y</td><td>z</td><td>{</td><td>|</td><td>}</td><td>~</td><td></td></tr>
</table>

However, many languages use either accented Latin characters or completely different alphabets. ASCII does not address these characters, so you need to learn about character encodings if you want to use any non-ASCII characters.

Character encodings are also particularly important if you want to use symbols, as these cannot be guaranteed to transfer properly between different encodings (from some dashes to some quotation mark characters). If you do not indicate the character encoding the document is written in, some of the special characters might not display.

The International Standards Organization created a range of character sets to deal with different national characters. ISO-8859-1 is commonly used in Western versions of authoring tools such as Macromedia Dreamweaver, as well as applications such as Windows Notepad.

Character Set	Description
ISO-8859-1	Latin alphabet part 1 Covering North America, Western Europe, Latin America, the Caribbean, Canada, Africa
ISO-8859-2	Latin alphabet part 2 Covering Eastern Europe including Bosnian, Croatian, Czech, Hungarian, Polish, Romanian, Serbian (in Latin transcription), Serbocroatian, Slovak, Slovenian, Upper Sorbian, and Lower Sorbian
ISO-8859-3	Latin alphabet part 3 Covering SE Europe, Esperanto, Maltese, Turkish, and miscellaneous others
ISO-8859-4	Latin alphabet part 4 Covering Scandinavia/Baltics (and others not in ISO-8859-1)
ISO-8859-5	Latin/Cyrillic alphabet part 5
ISO-8859-6	Latin/Arabic alphabet part 6
ISO-8859-7	Latin/Greek alphabet part 7
ISO-8859-8	Latin/Hebrew alphabet part 8
ISO-8859-9	Latin 5 alphabet part 9 (same as ISO-8859-1 except Turkish characters replace Icelandic ones)
ISO-8859-10	Latin 6 Lappish, Nordic, and Eskimo
ISO-8859-15	The same as ISO-8859-1 but with more characters added
ISO-8859-16	Latin 10 Covering SE Europe Albanian, Croatian, Hungarian, Polish, Romanian and Slovenian, plus can be used in French, German, Italian, and Irish Gaelic
ISO-2022-JP	Latin/Japanese alphabet part 1
ISO-2022-JP-2	Latin/Japanese alphabet part 2
ISO-2022-KR	Latin/Korean alphabet part 1

It is helpful to note that the first 128 characters of ISO-8859-1 match those of ASCII, so you can safely use those characters as you would in ASCII.

The *Unicode* Consortium was then set up to devise a way to show *all* characters of different languages, rather than have these different incompatible character codes for different languages.

Therefore, if you want to create documents that use characters from multiple character sets, you will be able to do so using the single Unicode character encodings. Furthermore, users should be able to view documents written in different character sets, providing their processor (and fonts) support the Unicode standards, no matter what platform they are on or which country they are in. By having the single character encoding, you can reduce software development costs because the programs do not need to be designed to support multiple character encodings.

One problem with Unicode is that a lot of older programs were written to support only 8-bit character sets (limiting them to 256 characters), which is nowhere near the number required for all languages.

Unicode therefore specifies encodings that can deal with a string in special ways so as to make enough space for the huge character set it encompasses. These are known as UTF-8, UTF-16, and UTF-32.

Character Set	Description
UTF-8	A Unicode Translation Format that comes in 8-bit units. That is, it comes in *bytes*. A character in UTF-8 can be from 1 to 4 bytes long, making UTF-8 variable width.
UTF-16	A Unicode Translation Format that comes in 16-bit units. That is, it comes in *shorts*. It can be 1 or 2 shorts long, making UTF-16 variable width.
UTF-32	A Unicode Translation Format that comes in 32-bit units. That is, it comes in *longs*. It is a fixed-width format and is always 1 "long" in length.

The first 256 characters of Unicode character sets correspond to the 256 characters of ISO-8859-1.

By default, HTML 4 processors should support UTF-8, and XML processors are supposed to support UTF-8 and UTF-16; therefore, all XHTML-compliant processors should also support UTF-16 (as XHTML is an application of XML).

For more information on internationalization and different character sets and encodings, see `www.i18nguy.com/`.

Special Characters

Some characters are reserved in XHTML; for example, you cannot use the greater-than and less-than signs or angle brackets within your text because the browser could mistake them for markup. XHTML processors must support the five special characters listed in the table that follows.

Symbol	Description	Entity Name	Number Code
&	Ampersand	&	&
<	Less than	<	<
>	Greater than	>	>
"	Double quote	"	"
	Non-breaking space		

To write an element and attribute into your page so that the code is shown to the user rather than being processed by the browser (for example, as `<div id="character">`), you would write:

```
&lt;div id=&quot;character&quot;&gt;
```

There is also a long list of special characters that HTML 4.0–aware processors should support. In order for these to appear in your document, you can use either the numerical code or the entity name. For example, to insert a copyright symbol you can use either of the following:

```
&copy; 2008
&#169; 2008
```

Appendix F: Special Characters

The special characters have been split into the following sections:

- Character Entity References for ISO 8859-1 Characters
- Character Entity References for Symbols, Mathematical Symbols, and Greek Letters
- Character Entity References for Markup-Significant and Internationalization Characters

They are taken from the W3C website at `www.w3.org/TR/REC-html40/sgml/entities.html`.

Character Entity References for ISO 8859-1 Characters

Symbol	Description	Entity Name	Number Code
	No-break space = non-breaking space		
¡	Inverted exclamation mark	¡	¡
¢	Cent sign	¢	¢
£	Pound sign	£	£
¤	Currency sign	¤	¤
¥	Yen sign = yuan sign	¥	¥
¦	Broken bar = broken vertical bar	¦	¦
§	Section sign	§	§
¨	Diaeresis = spacing diaeresis	¨	¨
©	Copyright sign	©	©
ª	Feminine ordinal indicator	ª	ª
«	Left-pointing double angle quotation mark = left-pointing guillemet	«	«
¬	Not sign	¬	¬
SHY	Soft hyphen = discretionary hyphen		
®	Registered sign = registered trademark sign	®	®
¯	Macron = spacing macron = overline = APL overbar	¯	¯
°	Degree sign	°	°
±	Plus-minus sign = plus-or-minus sign	±	±
^{2}	Superscript two = superscript digit two = squared	²	²

Symbol	Description	Entity Name	Number Code
³	Superscript three = superscript digit three = cubed	³	³
´	Acute accent = spacing acute	´	´
µ	Micro sign	µ	µ
¶	Pilcrow sign = paragraph sign	¶	¶
·	Middle dot = Georgian comma = Greek middle dot	·	·
¸	Cedilla = spacing cedilla	¸	¸
¹	Superscript one = superscript digit one	¹	¹
º	Masculine ordinal indicator	º	º
»	Right-pointing double angle quotation mark = right pointing guillemet	»	»
¼	Vulgar fraction one-quarter = fraction one-quarter	¼	¼
½	Vulgar fraction one-half = fraction one-half	½	½
¾	Vulgar fraction three-quarters = fraction three-quarters	¾	¾
¿	Inverted question mark = turned question mark	¿	¿
À	Latin capital letter A with grave = Latin capital letter A grave	À	À
Á	Latin capital letter A with acute	Á	Á
Â	Latin capital letter A with circumflex	Â	Â
Ã	Latin capital letter A with tilde	Ã	Ã
Ä	Latin capital letter A with diaeresis	Ä	Ä
Å	Latin capital letter A with ring above = Latin capital letter A ring	Å	Å
Æ	Latin capital letter AE = Latin capital ligature AE	Æ	Æ
Ç	Latin capital letter C with cedilla	Ç	Ç
È	Latin capital letter E with grave	È	È
É	Latin capital letter E with acute	É	É
Ê	Latin capital letter E with circumflex	Ê	Ê

(continued)

Symbol	Description	Entity Name	Number Code
Ë	Latin capital letter E with diaeresis	Ë	Ë
Ì	Latin capital letter I with grave	Ì	Ì
Í	Latin capital letter I with acute	Í	Í
Î	Latin capital letter I with circumflex	Î	Î
Ï	Latin capital letter I with diaeresis	Ï	Ï
Ð	Latin capital letter ETH	Ð	Ð
Ñ	Latin capital letter N with tilde	Ñ	Ñ
Ò	Latin capital letter O with grave	Ò	Ò
Ó	Latin capital letter O with acute	Ó	Ó
Ô	Latin capital letter O with circumflex	Ô	Ô
Õ	Latin capital letter O with tilde	Õ	Õ
Ö	Latin capital letter O with diaeresis	Ö	Ö
×	Multiplication sign	×	×
Ø	Latin capital letter O with stroke = Latin capital letter O slash	Ø	Ø
Ù	Latin capital letter U with grave	Ù	Ù
Ú	Latin capital letter U with acute	Ú	Ú
Û	Latin capital letter U with circumflex	Û	Û
Ü	Latin capital letter U with diaeresis	Ü	Ü
Ý	Latin capital letter Y with acute	Ý	Ý
Þ	Latin capital letter THORN	Þ	Þ
ß	Latin small letter sharp s = ess-zed	ß	ß
à	Latin small letter a with grave = Latin small letter a grave	à	à
á	Latin small letter a with acute	á	á
â	Latin small letter a with circumflex	â	â

Symbol	Description	Entity Name	Number Code
ã	Latin small letter a with tilde	ã	ã
ä	Latin small letter a with diaeresis	ä	ä
å	Latin small letter a with ring above = Latin small letter a ring	å	å
æ	Latin small letter ae = Latin small ligature ae	æ	æ
ç	Latin small letter c with cedilla	ç	ç
è	Latin small letter e with grave	è	è
é	Latin small letter e with acute	é	é
ê	Latin small letter e with circumflex	ê	ê
ë	Latin small letter e with diaeresis	ë	ë
ì	Latin small letter i with grave	ì	ì
í	Latin small letter i with acute	í	í
î	Latin small letter i with circumflex	î	î
ï	Latin small letter i with diaeresis	ï	ï
ð	Latin small letter eth	ð	ð
ñ	Latin small letter n with tilde	ñ	ñ
ò	Latin small letter o with grave	ò	ò
ó	Latin small letter o with acute	ó	ó
ô	Latin small letter o with circumflex	ô	ô
õ	Latin small letter o with tilde	õ	õ
ö	Latin small letter o with diaeresis	ö	ö
÷	Division sign	÷	÷
ø	Latin small letter o with stroke = Latin small letter o slash	ø	ø
ù	Latin small letter u with grave	ù	ù
ú	Latin small letter u with acute	ú	ú
û	Latin small letter u with circumflex	û	û

(continued)

Symbol	Description	Entity Name	Number Code
ü	Latin small letter u with diaeresis	ü	ü
ý	Latin small letter y with acute	ý	ý
þ	Latin small letter thorn	þ	þ
ÿ	Latin small letter y with diaeresis	ÿ	ÿ

Character Entity References for Symbols, Mathematical Symbols, and Greek Letters

Symbol	Description	Entity Name	Number Code
Latin Extended-B			
ƒ	Latin small f with hook = function = florin	ƒ	ƒ
Greek			
Α	Greek capital letter alpha	Α	Α
Β	Greek capital letter beta	Β	Β
Γ	Greek capital letter gamma	Γ	Γ
Δ	Greek capital letter delta	Δ	Δ
Ε	Greek capital letter epsilon	Ε	Ε
Ζ	Greek capital letter zeta	Ζ	Ζ
Η	Greek capital letter eta	Η	Η
Θ	Greek capital letter theta	Θ	Θ
Ι	Greek capital letter iota	Ι	Ι
Κ	Greek capital letter kappa	Κ	Κ
Λ	Greek capital letter lambda	Λ	Λ
Μ	Greek capital letter mu	&Mu	Μ
Ν	Greek capital letter nu	Ν	Ν

Symbol	Description	Entity Name	Number Code
Ξ	Greek capital letter xi	Ξ	Ξ
Ο	Greek capital letter omicron	Ο	Ο
Π	Greek capital letter pi	Π	Π
Ρ	Greek capital letter rho	Ρ	Ρ
Σ	Greek capital letter sigma	Σ	Σ
Τ	Greek capital letter tau	Τ	Τ
Υ	Greek capital letter upsilon	Υ	Υ
Φ	Greek capital letter phi	Φ	Φ
Χ	Greek capital letter chi	Χ	Χ
Ψ	Greek capital letter psi	Ψ	Ψ
Ω	Greek capital letter omega	Ω	Ω
α	Greek small letter alpha	α	α
β	Greek small letter beta	β	β
γ	Greek small letter gamma	γ	γ
δ	Greek small letter delta	δ	δ
ε	Greek small letter epsilon	ε	ε
ζ	Greek small letter zeta	ζ	ζ
η	Greek small letter eta	η	η
θ	Greek small letter theta	θ	θ
ι	Greek small letter iota	ι	ι
κ	Greek small letter kappa	κ	κ
λ	Greek small letter lambda	λ	λ
μ	Greek small letter mu	μ	μ
ν	Greek small letter nu	ν	ν
ξ	Greek small letter xi	ξ	ξ
ο	Greek small letter omicron	ο	ο

(continued)

Symbol	Description	Entity Name	Number Code
π	Greek small letter pi	π	π
ρ	Greek small letter rho	ρ	ρ
ς	Greek small letter final sigma	ς	ς
σ	Greek small letter sigma	σ	σ
τ	Greek small letter tau	τ	τ
υ	Greek small letter upsilon	υ	υ
φ	Greek small letter phi	φ	φ
χ	Greek small letter chi	χ	χ
ψ	Greek small letter psi	ψ	ψ
ω	Greek small letter omega	ω	ω
θ	Greek small letter theta symbol	ϑ	ϑ
ϒ	Greek upsilon with hook symbol	ϒ	ϒ
ϖ	Greek pi symbol	ϖ	ϖ
General Punctuation			
•	Bullet = black small circle	•	•
…	Horizontal ellipsis = three dot leader	…	…
′	Prime = minutes = feet	′	′
″	Double prime = seconds = inches	″	″
‾	Overline = spacing overscore	‾	‾
⁄	Fraction slash	⁄	⁄
Letterlike Symbols			
℘	Script capital P = power set = Weierstrass p	℘	℘
ℑ	Blackletter capital I = imaginary part	ℑ	ℑ
ℜ	Blackletter capital R = real part symbol	ℜ	ℜ
™	Trademark sign	™	™

Symbol	Description	Entity Name	Number Code
ℵ	Alef symbol = first transfinite cardinal	ℵ	ℵ
Arrows			
←	Left arrow	←	←
↑	Up arrow	↑	↑
→	Right arrow	→	→
↓	Down arrow	↓	↓
↔	Left-right arrow	↔	↔
↵	Down arrow with corner leftward = carriage return	↵	↵
⇐	Left double arrow	⇐	⇐
⇑	Up double arrow	⇑	⇑
⇒	Right double arrow	⇒	⇒
⇓	Down double arrow	⇓	⇓
⇔	Left-right double arrow	⇔	⇔
Mathematical Operators			
∀	For all	∀	∀
∂	Partial differential	&part ;	∂
∃	There exists	∃	∃
∅	Empty set = null set = diameter	∅	∅
∇	Nabla = backward difference	∇	∇
∈	Element of	∈	∈
∉	Not an element of	∉	∉
∋	Contains as member	∋	∋
∏	n-ary product = product sign	∏	∏
∑	n-ary summation	∑	∑

(continued)

Symbol	Description	Entity Name	Number Code
−	Minus sign	−	−
∗	Asterisk operator	∗	∗
√	Square root = radical sign	√	√
∝	Proportional to	∝	∝
∞	Infinity	∞	∞
∠	Angle	∠	∠
∧	Logical and = wedge	∧	∧
∨	Logical or = vee	&or ;	∨
∩	Intersection = cap	∩	∩
∪	Union = cup	∪	∪
∫	Integral	∫	∫
∴	Therefore	∴	∴
∼	Tilde operator = varies with = similar to	∼	∼
≅	Approximately equal to	≅	≅
≈	Almost equal to = asymptotic to	≈	≈
≠	Not equal to	≠	≠
≡	Identical to	≡	≡
≤	Less than or equal to	≤	≤
≥	Greater than or equal to	≥	≥
⊂	Subset of	⊂	⊂
⊃	Superset of	⊃	⊃
⊄	Not a subset of	⊄	⊄
⊆	Subset of or equal to	⊆	⊆
⊇	Superset of or equal to	⊇	⊇
⊕	Circled plus = direct sum	⊕	⊕
⊗	Circled times = vector product	⊗	⊗

Symbol	Description	Entity Name	Number Code
⊥	Up tack = orthogonal to = perpendicular	⊥	⊥
·	Dot operator	⋅	⋅
Miscellaneous Technical			
⌈	Left ceiling = apl upstile	⌈	⌈
⌉	Right ceiling	⌉	⌉
⌊	Left floor = apl downstile	⌊	⌊
⌋	Right floor	⌋	⌋
〈	Left-pointing angle bracket = bra	⟨	〈
〉	Right-pointing angle bracket = ket	⟩	〉
Geometric Shape			
◊	Lozenge	◊	◊
Miscellaneous Symbols			
♠	Black spade suit	♠	♠
♣	Black club suit = shamrock	♣	♣
♥	Black heart suit = valentine	♥	♥
♦	Black diamond suit	♦	♦

Markup-Significant and Internationalization Characters

Symbol	Description	Entity Name	Number Code
"	Quotation mark = APL quote	"	"
&	Ampersand	&	&
<	Less-than sign	<	<
>	Greater-than sign	>	>

(continued)

Symbol	Description	Entity Name	Number Code
Œ	Latin capital ligature OE	Œ	Œ
œ	Latin small ligature oe	œ	œ
Š	Latin capital letter S with caron	Š	Š
š	Latin small letter s with caron	š	š
Ÿ	Latin capital letter Y with diaeresis	Ÿ	Ÿ
Spacing Modifiers			
ˆ	Modifier letter circumflex accent	ˆ	ˆ
˜	Small tilde	˜	˜
General Punctuation			
	En space		
	Em space		
	Thin space		
ZW NJ	Zero width non-joiner	‌	‌
ZW J	Zero width joiner	‍	‍
LRM	Left-to-right mark	‎	‎
RLM	Right-to-left mark	‏	‏
–	En dash	–	–
—	Em dash	—	—
’	Left single quotation mark	‘	‘
‘	Right single quotation mark	’	’
‚	Single low-9 quotation mark	‚	‚
“	Left double quotation mark	“	“
”	Right double quotation mark	”	”
„	Double low-9 quotation mark	„	„
†	Dagger	†	†
‡	Double dagger	‡	‡

Symbol	Description	Entity Name	Number Code
‰	Per mille sign	‰	‰
‹	Single left-pointing angle quotation mark (proposed, but not yet standardized)	‹	‹
›	Single right-pointing angle quotation mark (proposed, but not yet standardized)	›	›
€	Euro sign	€	€

Language Codes

The following table shows the two-letter ISO 639 language codes that are used to declare the language of a document in the `lang` and `xml:lang` attributes. It covers many of the world's major languages.

Country	ISO Code	Country	ISO Code
Abkhazian	AB	Bhutani	DZ
Afan (Oromo)	OM	Bihari	BH
Afar	AA	Bislama	BI
Afrikaans	AF	Breton	BR
Albanian	SQ	Bulgarian	BG
Amharic	AM	Burmese	MY
Arabic	AR	Byelorussian	BE
Armenian	HY	Cambodian	KM
Assamese	AS	Catalan	CA
Aymara	AY	Chinese	ZH
Azerbaijani	AZ	Corsican	CO
Bashkir	BA	Croatian	HR
Basque	EU	Czech	CS
Bengali; Bangla	BN	Danish	DA

Continued

Country	ISO Code	Country	ISO Code
Dutch	NL	Japanese	JA
English	EN	Javanese	JV
Esperanto	EO	Kannada	KN
Estonian	ET	Kashmiri	KS
Faroese	FO	Kazakh	KK
Fiji	FJ	Kinyarwanda	RW
Finnish	FI	Kirghiz	KY
French	FR	Korean	KO
Frisian	FY	Kurdish	KU
Galician	GL	Kurundi	RN
Georgian	KA	Laothian	LO
German	DE	Latin	LA
Greek	EL	Latvian; Lettish	LV
Greenlandic	KL	Lingala	LN
Guarani	GN	Lithuanian	LT
Gujarati	GU	Macedonian	MK
Hausa	HA	Malagasy	MG
Hebrew	HE	Malay	MS
Hindi	HI	Malayalam	ML
Hungarian	HU	Maltese	MT
Icelandic	IS	Maori	MI
Indonesian	ID	Marathi	MR
Interlingua	IA	Moldavian	MO
Interlingue	IE	Mongolian	MN
Inuktitut	IU	Nauru	NA
Inupiak	IK	Nepali	NE
Irish	GA	Norwegian	NO
Italian	IT	Occitan	OC

Country	ISO Code	Country	ISO Code
Oriya	OR	Swedish	SV
Pashto; Pushto	PS	Tagalog	TL
Persian (Farsi)	FA	Tajik	TG
Polish	PL	Tamil	TA
Portuguese	PT	Tatar	TT
Punjabi	PA	Telugu	TE
Quechua	QU	Thai	TH
Rhaeto-Romance	RM	Tibetan	BO
Romanian	RO	Tigrinya	TI
Russian	RU	Tonga	TO
Samoan	SM	Tsonga	TS
Sangho	SG	Turkish	TR
Sanskrit	SA	Turkmen	TK
Scots Gaelic	GD	Twi	TW
Serbian	SR	Uigur	UG
Serbo-Croatian	SH	Ukrainian	UK
Sesotho	ST	Urdu	UR
Setswana	TN	Uzbek	UZ
Shona	SN	Vietnamese	VI
Sindhi	SD	Volapuk	VO
Singhalese	SI	Welsh	CY
Siswati	SS	Wolof	WO
Slovak	SK	Xhosa	XH
Slovenian	SL	Yiddish	YI
Somali	SO	Yoruba	YO
Spanish	ES	Zhuang	ZA
Sudanese	SU	Zulu	ZU
Swahili	SW		

MIME Media Types

You have seen the `type` attribute used throughout this book on a number of elements, the value of which is a MIME media type.

MIME (Multipurpose Internet Mail Extension) media types were originally devised so that e-mails could include information other than plain text. MIME media types indicate the following things:

- How the parts of a message, such as text and attachments, are combined into the message
- The way in which each part of the message is specified
- The way the items are encoded for transmission so that even software that was designed to work only with ASCII text can process the message

As you have seen, however, MIME types are not just for use with e-mail; they were adopted by web servers as a way to tell web browsers what type of material was being sent to them so that they could cope with that kind of file correctly.

MIME content types consist of two parts:

- A main type
- A sub-type

The main type is separated from the sub-type by a forward slash character—for example, `text/html` for HTML.

This appendix is organized by the main types:

- `text`
- `image`
- `multipart`
- `audio`

- video
- message
- model
- application

For example, the text main type contains types of plain-text files, such as:

- text/plain for plain text files
- text/html for HTML files
- text/rtf for text files using rich text formatting

MIME types are officially supposed to be assigned and listed by the Internet Assigned Numbers Authority (IANA).

Many of the popular MIME types in this list (all those that begin with "x-") are not assigned by the IANA and do not have official status. (Having said that, I should mention that some of these are very popular and browsers support them, such as audio/x-mp3. You can see the list of official MIME types at www.iana.org/assignments/media-types/).

Those preceded with .vnd are vendor-specific.

The most popular MIME types are listed in this appendix in a bold typeface to help you find them.

text

Note that, when specifying the MIME type of a content-type field (for example in a <meta> element), you can also indicate the character set for the text being used. For example:

```
content-type:text/plain; charset=iso-8859-1
```

If you do not specify a character set, the default is US-ASCII.

calendar	**plain**
css	prs.fallenstein.rst
directory	prs.lines.tag
enriched	rfc822-headers
html	richtext
parityfec	**rtf**

sgml	vnd.IPTC.NITF
t140	vnd.latex-z
tab-separated-values	vnd.motorola.reflex
uri-list	vnd.ms-mediapackage
vnd.abc	vnd.net2phone.commcenter.command
vnd.curl	vnd.sun.j2me.app-descriptor
vnd.DMClientScript	vnd.wap.si
vnd.fly	vnd.wap.sl
vnd.fmi.flexstor	vnd.wap.wml
vnd.in3d.3dml	vnd.wap.wmlscript
vnd.in3d.spot	**xml**
vnd.IPTC.NewsML	**xml-external-parsed-entity**

image

bmp	tiff-fx
cgm	vnd.cns.inf2
g3fax	vnd.djvu
gif	vnd.dwg
ief	vnd.dxf
jpeg	vnd.fastbidsheet
naplps	vnd.fpx
png	vnd.fst
prs.btif	vnd.fujixerox.edmics-mmr
prs.pti	vnd.fujixerox.edmics-rlc
t38	vnd.globalgraphics.pgb
tiff	vnd.microsoft.icon

Continued

(continued)

vnd.mix	vnd.svf
vnd.ms-modi	vnd.wap.wbmp
vnd.net-fpx	vnd.xiff
vnd.sealed.png	**x-portable-pixmap**
vnd.sealedmedia.softseal.gif	**x-xbitmap**
vnd.sealedmedia.softseal.jpg	

multipart

alternative	mixed
appledouble	parallel
byteranges	related
digest	report
encrypted	signed
form-data	voice-message
header-set	

audio

32kadpcm	EVRC
AMR	EVRC0
AMR-WB	EVRC-QCP
basic	G722
CN	G.722.1
DAT12	G723
dsr-es201108	G726-16
DVI4	G726-24

G726-32	SMV-QCP
G726-40	telephone-event
G728	tone
G729	VDVI
G729D	vnd.3gpp.iufp
G729E	vnd.cisco.nse
GSM	vnd.cns.anp1
GSM-EFR	vnd.cns.inf1
L8	vnd.digital-winds
L16	vnd.everad.plj
L20	vnd.lucent.voice
L24	vnd.nokia.mobile-xmf
LPC	vnd.nortel.vbk
MPA	vnd.nuera.ecelp4800
MP4A-LATM	vnd.nuera.ecelp7470
mpa-robust	vnd.nuera.ecelp9600
mpeg	vnd.octel.sbc
mpeg4-generic	vnd.qcelp — deprecated, use audio/qcelp
parityfec	vnd.rhetorex.32kadpcm
PCMA	vnd.sealedmedia.softseal.mpeg
PCMU	vnd.vmx.cvsd
prs.sid	**x-aiff**
QCELP	**x-midi**
RED	**x-mod**
SMV	**x-mp3**
SMV0	**x-wav**

video

BMPEG	parityfec
BT656	pointer
CelB	**quicktime**
DV	SMPTE292M
H261	vnd.fvt
H263	vnd.motorola.video
H263-1998	vnd.motorola.videop
H263-2000	vnd.mpegurl
JPEG	vnd.nokia.interleaved-multimedia
MP1S	vnd.objectvideo
MP2P	vnd.sealed.mpeg1
MP2T	vnd.sealed.mpeg4
MP4V-ES	vnd.sealed.swf
MPV	vnd.sealedmedia.softseal.mov
mpeg	vnd.vivo
mpeg4-generic	**x-sgi-movie**
nv	**x-msvideo**

message

CPIM	partial
delivery-status	rfc822
disposition-notification	s-http
external-body	sip
http	sipfrag
news	

model

iges	vnd.gtw
mesh	vnd.mts
vnd.dwf	vnd.parasolid.transmit.binary
vnd.flatland.3dml	vnd.parasolid.transmit.text
vnd.gdl	vnd.vtu
vnd.gs-gdl	**vrml**

application

activemessage	EDI-X12
andrew-inset	EDIFACT
applefile	eshop
atomicmail	font-tdpfr
batch-SMTP	http
beep+xml	hyperstudio
cals-1840	iges
cnrp+xml	index
commonground	index.cmd
cpl+xml	index.obj
cybercash	index.response
dca-rft	index.vnd
dec-dx	iotp
dicom	ipp
dvcs	isup
EDI-Consent	mac-binhex40

Continued

(continued)

macwriteii	prs.nprend
marc	prs.plucker
mathematica	qsig
mpeg4-generic	reginfo+xml
msword	remote-printing
news-message-id	riscos
news-transmission	rtf
ocsp-request	sdp
ocsp-response	set-payment
octet-stream	set-payment-initiation
oda	set-registration
ogg	set-registration-initiation
parityfec	sgml
pdf	sgml-open-catalog
pgp-encrypted	sieve
pgp-keys	slate
pgp-signature	timestamp-query
pidf+xml	timestamp-reply
pkcs10	tve-trigger
pkcs7-mime	vemmi
pkcs7-signature	vnd.3gpp.pic-bw-large
pkix-cert	vnd.3gpp.pic-bw-small
pkix-crl	vnd.3gpp.pic-bw-var
pkix-pkipath	vnd.3gpp.sms
pkixcmp	vnd.3M.Post-it-Notes
postscript	vnd.accpac.simply.aso
prs.alvestrand.titrax-sheet	vnd.accpac.simply.imp
prs.cww	vnd.acucobol

vnd.acucorp	vnd.dreamfactory
vnd.adobe.xfdf	vnd.dxr
vnd.aether.imp	vnd.ecdis-update
vnd.amiga.ami	vnd.ecowin.chart
vnd.anser-web-certificate-issue-initiation	vnd.ecowin.filerequest
vnd.anser-web-funds-transfer-initiation	vnd.ecowin.fileupdate
vnd.audiograph	vnd.ecowin.series
vnd.blueice.multipass	vnd.ecowin.seriesrequest
vnd.bmi	vnd.ecowin.seriesupdate
vnd.businessobjects	vnd.enliven
vnd.canon-cpdl	vnd.epson.esf
vnd.canon-lips	vnd.epson.msf
vnd.cinderella	vnd.epson.quickanime
vnd.claymore	vnd.epson.salt
vnd.commerce-battelle	vnd.epson.ssf
vnd.commonspace	vnd.ericsson.quickcall
vnd.contact.cmsg	vnd.eudora.data
vnd.cosmocaller	vnd.fdf
vnd.criticaltools.wbs+xml	vnd.ffsns
vnd.ctc-posml	vnd.fints
vnd.cups-postscript	vnd.FloGraphIt
vnd.cups-raster	vnd.framemaker
vnd.cups-raw	vnd.fsc.weblaunch
vnd.curl	vnd.fujitsu.oasys
vnd.cybank	vnd.fujitsu.oasys2
vnd.data-vision.rdz	vnd.fujitsu.oasys3
vnd.dna	vnd.fujitsu.oasysgp
vnd.dpgraph	vnd.fujitsu.oasysprs

Continued

(continued)

vnd.fujixerox.ddd	vnd.informix-visionary
vnd.fujixerox.docuworks	vnd.intercon.formnet
vnd.fujixerox.docuworks.binder	vnd.intertrust.digibox
vnd.fut-misnet	vnd.intertrust.nncp
vnd.genomatix.tuxedo	vnd.intu.qbo
vnd.grafeq	vnd.intu.qfx
vnd.groove-account	vnd.ipunplugged.rcprofile
vnd.groove-help	vnd.irepository.package+xml
vnd.groove-identity-message	vnd.is-xpr
vnd.groove-injector	vnd.japannet-directory-service
vnd.groove-tool-message	vnd.japannet-jpnstore-wakeup
vnd.groove-tool-template	vnd.japannet-payment-wakeup
vnd.groove-vcard	vnd.japannet-registration
vnd.hbci	vnd.japannet-registration-wakeup
vnd.hhe.lesson-player	vnd.japannet-setstore-wakeup
vnd.hp-HPGL	vnd.japannet-verification
vnd.hp-hpid	vnd.japannet-verification-wakeup
vnd.hp-hps	vnd.jisp
vnd.hp-PCL	vnd.kde.karbon
vnd.hp-PCLXL	vnd.kde.kchart
vnd.httphone	vnd.kde.kformula
vnd.hzn-3d-crossword	vnd.kde.kivio
vnd.ibm.afplinedata	vnd.kde.kontour
vnd.ibm.electronic-media	vnd.kde.kpresenter
vnd.ibm.MiniPay	vnd.kde.kspread
vnd.ibm.modcap	vnd.kde.kword
vnd.ibm.rights-management	vnd.kenameaapp
vnd.ibm.secure-container	vnd.kidspiration

vnd.koan	vnd.mophun.certificate
vnd.liberty-request+xml	vnd.sss-ntf
vnd.llamagraphics.life-balance.desktop	vnd.street-stream
vnd.llamagraphics.life-balance .exchange+xml	vnd.svd
vnd.lotus-1-2-3	vnd.swiftview-ics
vnd.lotus-approach	vnd.triscape.mxs
vnd.lotus-freelance	vnd.trueapp
vnd.lotus-notes	vnd.truedoc
vnd.lotus-organizer	vnd.ufdl
vnd.lotus-screencam	vnd.uiq.theme
vnd.lotus-wordpro	vnd.uplanet.alert
vnd.mcd	vnd.uplanet.alert-wbxml
vnd.mediastation.cdkey	vnd.uplanet.bearer-choice
vnd.meridian-slingshot	vnd.uplanet.bearer-choice-wbxml
vnd.micrografx.flo	vnd.uplanet.cacheop
vnd.micrografx.igx	vnd.uplanet.cacheop-wbxml
vnd.mif	vnd.uplanet.channel
vnd.minisoft-hp3000-save	vnd.uplanet.channel-wbxml
vnd.mitsubishi.misty-guard.trustweb	vnd.uplanet.list
vnd.Mobius.DAF	vnd.uplanet.list-wbxml
vnd.Mobius.DIS	vnd.uplanet.listcmd
vnd.Mobius.MBK	vnd.uplanet.listcmd-wbxml
vnd.Mobius.MQY	vnd.uplanet.signal
vnd.Mobius.MSL	vnd.vcx
vnd.Mobius.PLC	vnd.vectorworks
vnd.Mobius.TXF	vnd.vidsoft.vidconference
vnd.mophun.application	vnd.visio

Continued

(continued)

vnd.visionary	vnd.yellowriver-custom-menu
vnd.vividence.scriptfile	watcherinfo+xml
vnd.vsf	whoispp-query
vnd.wap.sic	whoispp-response
vnd.wap.slc	wita
vnd.wap.wbxml	wordperfect5.1
vnd.wap.wmlc	x-debian-package
vnd.wap.wmlscriptc	x-gzip
vnd.webturbo	x-java
vnd.wqd	x-javascript
vnd.wrq-hp3000-labelled	x-msaccess
vnd.wt.stf	x-msexcel
vnd.wv.csp+wbxml	x-mspowerpoint
vnd.wv.csp+xml	x-rpm
vnd.wv.ssp+xml	x-zip
vnd.xara	x400-bp
vnd.xfdl	xhtml+xml
vnd.yamaha.hv-dic	xml
vnd.yamaha.hv-script	xml-dtd
vnd.yamaha.hv-voice	xml-external-parsed-entity
vnd.yamaha.smaf-audio	zip
vnd.yamaha.smaf-phrase	

Deprecated and Browser-Specific Markup

As the versions of HTML and XHTML have developed, quite a lot of markup has been *deprecated*, which is the W3C's way of alerting web developers that is is likely to be removed from future versions of HTML and XHTML and that web-page authors should stop using it (although there is an acknowledgment that some people may still need to use it for a while). Where markup is deprecated, there is usually an acceptable alternative way to achieve the same goal (in many cases using CSS).

You can still use quite a lot of the deprecated markup that you meet in this chapter when using the Transitional XHTML DOCTYPE, but Strict XHTML has already removed most of the elements and attributes that affect presentation of elements.

I have included the details of these elements and attributes in this book, despite the fact that the markup is deprecated or out of date, because you are likely to come across it in other people's code, and on very rare occasions you might need to resort to using some of this markup in order to get a specific job done.

In addition to deprecated markup, I will introduce some of the browser-specific markup that you may come across. This is markup that browser manufacturers added to their browsers to allow users to do more things than they could in competing browsers — but these browser-specific elements and attributes never made it into the HTML recommendations, and are therefore referred to as *browser-specific markup*.

This appendix covers the following:

- ❑ Elements and attributes that have been deprecated in recent versions of HTML and XHTML
- ❑ Specification of font appearances without using CSS
- ❑ Control of backgrounds without using CSS

- Control of presentations of links, lists, and tables without using CSS
- Elements and attributes that control the formatting of a document
- Elements, attributes, and styles that Microsoft added to IE (but that are not supported by other browser manufacturers)

Before you look at any of this markup, however, here's a quick word on why a good part of this appendix is deprecated markup.

Why Deprecated Markup Exists

In the introduction to this book, I explained how XHTML 1.0 was created after HTML had reached version 4.01. The elements and attributes are virtually identical, but the syntax of XHTML is much stricter (for example, you must use lowercase letters in tag names, attributes must be enclosed in double quotes, and so on).

Up to that point, with each version of HTML, new elements and attributes were added and old ones removed. These changes have been necessary because web-page authors have wanted to create increasingly complicated pages, and also because there has been an increasing drive to separate the content of web pages from the rules that describe how the page should be displayed.

In older versions of HTML, before CSS was introduced, HTML contained markup that could be used to control the presentation of a web page (such as the `<font>` element that would control the font used in a document, or the `bgcolor` attribute that would set the background color of a page).

When CSS was introduced to style web pages, all of the HTML markup that had previously controlled how a page would appear could be removed. (This is a big source of deprecated markup.)

When your web pages just focus on the content (the words themselves), its structure (the headings and paragraphs), and its meaning (using elements that indicate their contents are an address or a quote), you end up with much simpler documents. You can also present the same document in different ways, which is particularly helpful considering that there are an increasing number of different devices being used to access the Web (from mobile phones to game consoles), all of which have different-sized screens and abilities, which may need styling in different ways.

Older Pages Break Many Rules

You should be aware that a lot of the pages you see on the Web probably break a lot of the rules you have learned in this book so far. You will see element and attribute names in upper- and lowercase, you will see missing quotation marks on attribute values, even attributes without values, and you will see elements that do not have closing tags. You will see pages without `DOCTYPE` declarations and pages littered with deprecated markup. Keep in mind, however, that many of the pages that break the rules you have learned might have been written when the rules were not as strict, and at the time of writing the code may have been perfectly acceptable. Indeed, the fact that web browsers would try to show pages even if the markup contained errors (and that they would skip over tags that they did not understand) significantly helped the adoption of HTML, because it helped people who did not program to develop web pages far more easily than languages that showed complex error messages when they encountered something they didn't understand.

It wasn't just humans who wrote code that might be frowned upon these days. The early versions of authoring tools such as Microsoft FrontPage and Macromedia Dreamweaver sometimes generated code that had strange capitalization or missing quotation marks, and featured attributes without values. This does not make it okay to follow their lead; the first versions of these programs were written before XHTML came along with its stricter rules.

Having said all this, it is also worth noting that when HTML 5 comes out (which is unlikely to be before 2011), it will probably relax some of the rules imposed by XHTML (for example it is likely to allow authors to mix upper- and lowercase again, and they might not need to close all elements). Having said that, I think that there will still be advantages to learning code using the stricter XHTML syntax. For example, many of the tools written to work with XML can also be used with XHTML. These might not work if you have written HTML 5 pages that do not adhere to the stricter XHTML syntax.

Even if a page with bad or deprecated markup renders fine in your browser, it's still wise to avoid this markup because your pages are less likely to appear as you intended on the increasing number of devices being used on the Web.

Fonts

In this section, you learn about several elements (and their attributes) that affect the appearance of text and fonts, all of which have been deprecated.

The <font> Element

The `<font>` element was introduced in HTML 3.2 and deprecated in HTML 4.0. It allows you to indicate the typeface, size, and color of font the browser should display between the opening `<font>` and closing `</font>` tags. You could probably find many sites that are still littered with `<font>` tags, one for each time you see the style of text change on the page.

The following table shows the three attributes the `<font>` element relies upon:

Attribute Name	Use	Values
`face`	Specify the typeface that should be used	Name of the typeface to use (can include more than one name in order of preference)
`size`	Specify the size of the font	A number between 1 and 7 where 1 is the smallest font size and 7 is the largest font size
`color`	Specify the color of the font	A color name or hex value (see Appendix D)

The following is an example of how the `<font>` element would have been used (`ai_eg01.html`). You can see that there are three occurrences of the `<font>` element:

```
<html>
  <head>
    <title>Example of &lt;font&gt; Element</title>
  </head>
  <body>
    <p>This is the browser's default font.</p>
    <font face="arial, verdana, sans-serif" size="2">
      <h1>Example of the &lt;font&gt; Element</h1>
        <p><font size="4" color="darkgray">Here is some size 3 writing
        in the color called darkgray. The typeface is determined by the
        previous &lt;font&gt; element that contains this paragraph.</font></p>
        <p><font face="courier" size="2" color="#000000">Now here is a courier
        font, size 2, in black</font></p>
    </font>
  </body>
</html>
```

The result of this example is shown in Figure I-1.

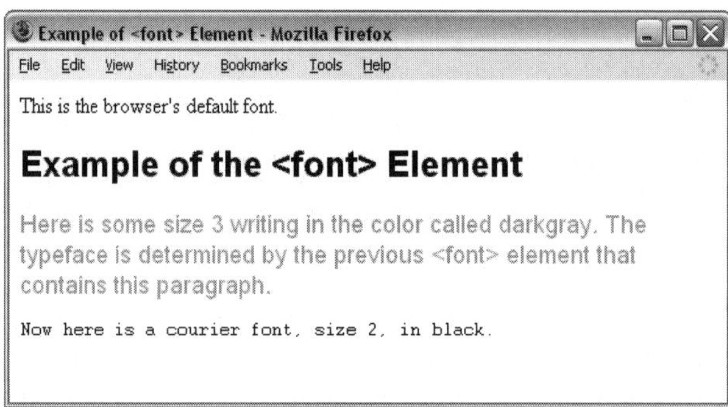

Figure I-1

As you can see from Figure I-1, all the writing within a `<font>` element follows the rules laid down in the attributes that you can see on the opening `<font>` tag. The first paragraph is in the browser's default font (which is probably a size 3 Times family font in black). The first `<font>` element appears directly after this paragraph and contains the rest of the page, therefore acting like a default setting for the rest of the page, which should appear in an Arial typeface.

As you can see, the name of the Arial typeface is followed by the typeface Verdana; this is supposed to be a second choice if Arial is not available. Then if Verdana is not available, the browser's default sans-serif font should be used:

```
<font face="arial, verdana, sans-serif" size="2">
```

This `<font>` element also indicates that the default size of the text in the rest of the document should be size 2. Note that this `<font>` element does not override the size of the `<h1>` element, but it does affect the typeface used — the heading is written in Arial.

While this <font> element is acting as a default for most of the page, if you want a particular part of the page to have any other font properties, you can indicate so in another <font> element.

You can see in the second paragraph that color and the size of the font are changed to dark gray and size 4.

```
<p><font size="4" color="darkgray">Here is some size 4 darkgray
      writing</font></p>
```

The third paragraph then uses a different typeface, a smaller size, and black:

```
<p><font face="courier" size="2" color="#000000">Now here is a courier
      font, size 2, in back</font></p>
```

Note that you may have to use <font> elements inside <td> and <th> elements, as the styles specified outside tables are not inherited by the text inside cells. Figure I-2 shows you the different font sizes from 1 to 7 (ai_eg02.html).

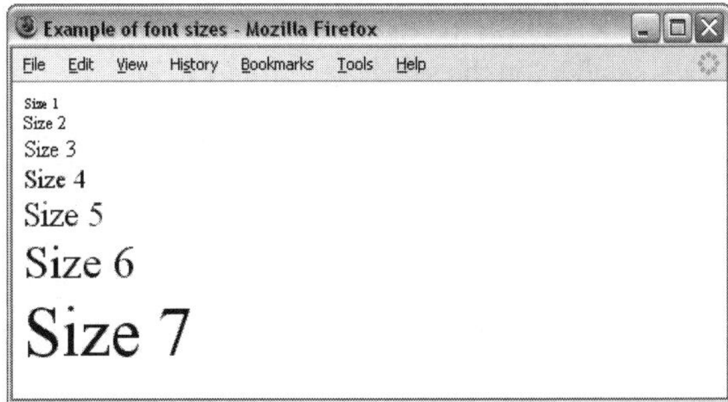

Figure I-2

Font sizes can change slightly from browser to browser, so you cannot rely on them to be exactly the same number of pixels tall or wide in a layout.

The preferred method with CSS would be to use the font-family, font-size, and color properties on the element containing the text that you wanted to style. You learned about these CSS properties in Chapter 7.

The text Attribute

The text attribute is used on the <body> element to indicate the default color for text in the document; it was deprecated in HTML 4. Its value should be either a color name or a hex color. For example (ai_eg03.html):

```
<body text="#999999">
  This text should be in a different color than the next bit
    <font color="#000000">which is black</font>, and now back to gray.
</body>
```

You can see the result in Figure I-3.

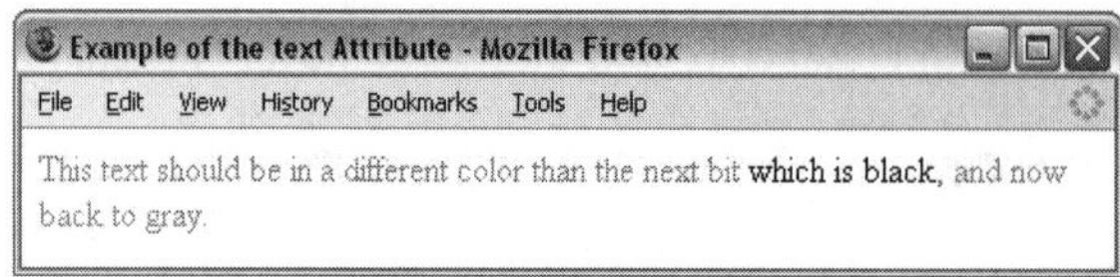

Figure I-3

The <basefont> Element

The `<basefont>` element is supposed to set a default font size, color, and typeface for the page. You can then use the `<font>` elements to override the `<basefont>` settings. However, this is not supported in Firefox or Safari, and other browsers do not always obey the settings in tables or headings.

The attributes that the `<basefont>` element takes are exactly the same as for the `<font>` element, which you've just seen. And again, elements such as the heading elements will retain their own size.

You can also set the size of fonts relative to the size of the `<basefont>` by giving them a value of `+1` for a size larger or `-2` for two sizes smaller (on the same scale from 1 to 7).

You can see these effects by revisiting the last example, and making some changes — the changes are highlighted (`ai_eg04.html`):

```
<html>
  <head>
    <title>Example of &lt;basefont&gt; Element</title>
  </head>
  <body>
    <basefont face="arial, verdana, sans-serif" size="2" color="#999999">
    <p>This is the page's default font.</p>
      <h2>Example of the &lt;basefont&gt; Element</h2>
      <p><font size="+4" color="333333">Here is some dark gray text
            four sizes  larger</font></p>
      <p><font face="courier" size="-1" color="#000000">Here is a courier
            font, a size smaller, in black</font></p>
  </body>
</html>
```

You can see the result in Figure I-4, shown in Internet Explorer (because the example does not work in Firefox or Safari).

As you can see, the default font now takes on the properties specified in the `<basefont>` element; it is gray, size 2, and uses the Arial typeface.

The paragraph after the `<h2>` element uses a font size four sizes larger than the default size and is gray text, whereas the following paragraph uses a font one size smaller than the default font — you can also see that the color of this font is black (overriding the default).

Figure I-4

Because this element was deprecated in HTML 4, the preferred option is to use CSS styles attached to the `<body>` element to set default font properties for the document.

The <s> and <strike> Elements

Both the `<s>` and `<strike>` elements were added to HTML in version 3.2 and deprecated in version 4. They indicate that their content should have a strikethrough style. For example (`ai_eg05.html`):

```
<s>This text will have a line through it</s><br/>
<strike>This text will also have a line through it.</strike>
```

You can see the results in Figure I-5.

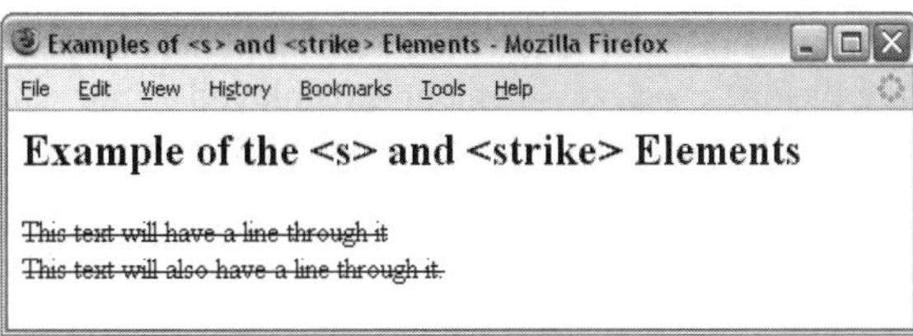

Figure I-5

You should now use the `text-decoration` property in CSS, with a value of `line-through`, unless you are trying to indicate deleted content, in which case you should use the `<del>` element.

The <u> Element

The `<u>` element renders its content underlined. It was introduced in HTML 3.2 and deprecated in version 4.

```
<u>This text should be underlined.</u>
```

You can see the effect in Figure I-6.

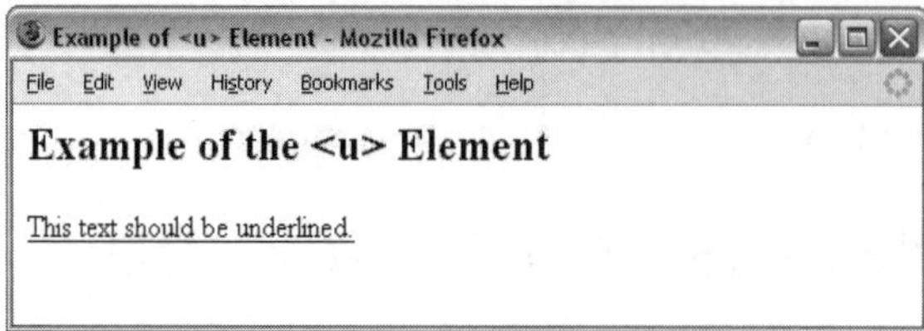

Figure I-6

You should now use the `text-decoration` property in CSS with a value of `underline` unless you are trying to indicate added content (when a document has been revised), in which case you should use the `<ins>` element.

The <listing>, <plaintext>, and <xmp> Elements

These three elements are all obsolete; they were introduced in HTML 2 and removed from HTML 4. They are included here only because you may come across them in old examples.

All three elements display text in a monospaced font as the `<pre>` element does.

The `<xmp>` element was designed for a short snippet of example code, and cannot contain any other markup; any characters such as angle brackets in element names get displayed as if they are text, so you do not need to use escape characters for them. The HTML 2 specification suggested that the author use a maximum limit of 80 characters on any one line.

The `<listing>` element, meanwhile, has a recommended limit of 132 characters per line, and tends to display text in a small font.

The `<plaintext>` tag indicates that *anything* following it should appear as plain text, even markup. Because everything following the `<plaintext>` element is displayed as normal text, including tags, there is no closing tag (if you tried to use a `</plaintext>` tag, it too would be displayed as normal text).

Here is an example of these three elements (`ai_eg07.html`):

```
<body>
  <h2>Example of the &lt;listing&gt;, &lt;plaintext&gt;, and &lt;xmp&gt;
      Elements</h2>
  <listing>These words are written inside a &lt;listing&gt; element.</listing>
  <xmp>These words are written inside an <xmp> element.</xmp>
  <plaintext>These words are written inside a <plaintext>
      element.
</body>
```

You can see the result in Figure I-7. Note how the escape characters in the `<xmp>` element are ignored and not escaped (this could also contain angle brackets and they would display normally). You will also see the closing `</body>` and `</html>` tags because anything after the opening `<plaintext>` tag is treated as plain text.

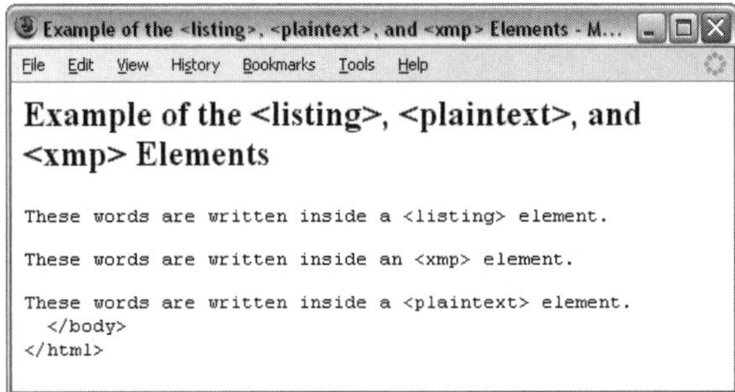

Figure I-7

The replacements in XHTML are `<pre>` and `<samp>`.

Backgrounds

There were two attributes in HTML that would allow you to change the background of a whole page or part of it:

- `bgcolor`, which allowed you to specify a background color on the `<body>` and various table elements
- `background`, which allowed you to specify a background image on the `<body>` element

The bgcolor Attribute

The `bgcolor` attribute allowed you to specify a background color for the whole document, or just part of it. It could be used on the following elements:

```
<body> <table> <tr> <th> <td>
```

The value of the attribute should be a color name or hex color, as described in Appendix D.

The following is an example of a document using some different background colors (`ai_eg08.html`):

```
<html>
  <head>
    <title>Example of bgcolor Attribute</title>
  </head>
  <body bgcolor="#efefef">
      <h2>Example of the bgcolor Attribute</h2>
      <table bgcolor="#999999">
        <tr>
          <th bgcolor="#cccccc">Heading One</th>
          <th bgcolor="#cccccc">Heading Two</th>
        </tr>
        <tr bgcolor="#f2f2f2">
```

```
            <td>Cell One</td>
            <td>Cell Two</td>
          </tr>
          <tr>
            <td>Cell Three</td>
            <td>Cell Four</td>
          </tr>
  </body>
</html>
```

You can see this page in Figure I-8.

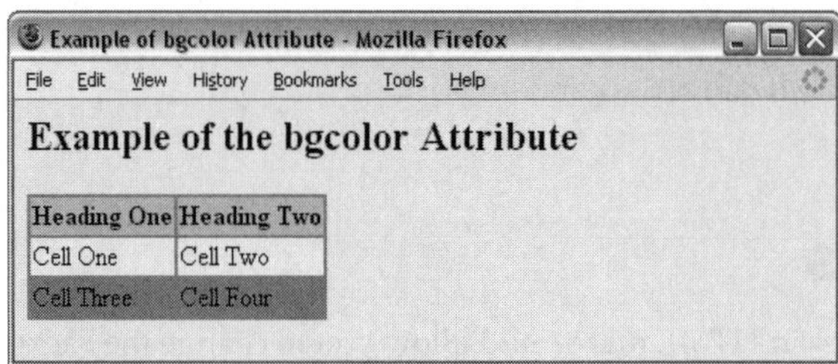

Figure I-8

The page has a very light gray background color specified on the `<body>` element. The table then has a background color, which you can see on the bottom row and all around the edges of the table. This is the default color for the table. Then you can see that the `bgcolor` attribute is used both on the `<th>` elements (the table headings) and the following `<tr>` element that contains the first row.

The preferred method of changing background colors now is to use the `background-color` property in CSS.

The background Attribute

The `background` attribute allowed you to specify a background image for the whole page, and its value should be the URL to the background image (which can be an absolute or relative URL). Netscape and Microsoft also allowed this attribute to be used on tables to create a background image for the tables.

Here you can see an example of the `background` attribute being used (`ai_eg09.html`):

```
<html>
  <head>
    <title>Example of background Attribute</title>
  </head>
  <body background="images/background_large.gif" bgcolor="#f2f2f2">
      <h2>Example of the background Attribute</h2>
  </body>
</html>
```

Note that the `bgcolor` attribute has also been used on the `<body>` element, which will be used if the image cannot be found. You can see the result of this example in Figure I-9.

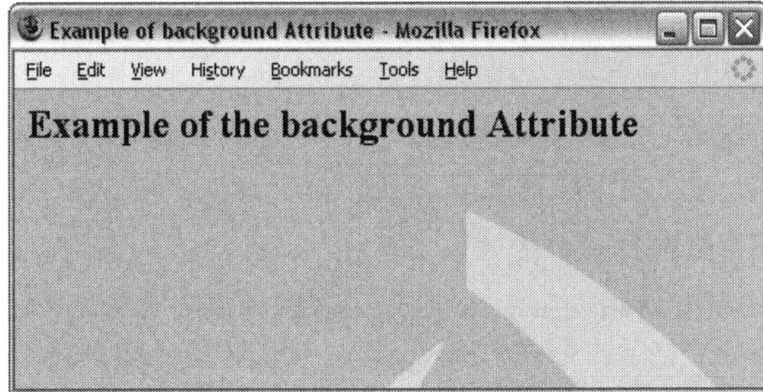

Figure I-9

Formatting

The next set of elements and attributes help you format and position elements and their content on the page.

The <center> Element

The `<center>` element was introduced by Netscape to allow authors to center content on a page. Anything between the opening and closing `<center>` tags will be centered horizontally in the middle of the page or the containing element. It was added to the HTML 3.2 specification and deprecated in HTML 4.

The following is an example of how the `<center>` element was used. The example also contains a table because of the interesting way in which tables are dealt with inside a `<center>` element (`ai_eg10.html`).

```
<body>
  <h2>Example of the &lt;center&gt; Element</h2>
  <center>
    Anything inside a &lt;center&gt; element is centered on the page, or within
    its containing element.<br /><br />
    <table width="600" border="1">
      <tr>
        <td>Cells whose content is written inside a &lt;center&gt; will be
            centered within the cell, like the one to the right.</td>
        <td><center>This cell's content should be centered.</center></td>
      </tr>
      <tr>
        <td><center>This cell's content should be centered.</center></td>
        <td>Cells whose content is written inside a &lt;center&gt; will
            be centered within the cell, like the one to the left.</td>
      </tr>
    </table>
  </center>
</body>
```

In this example (see Figure I-10), you can see how the `<center>` tag (just after the `<h1>` element) centers the content of the rest of the page. Interestingly, it centers any text on the page, and the table itself, but it does not center the text in the cells unless they contain `<center>` elements inside the `<td>` elements. (The table in this example has been given a border using the `border` attribute to illustrate where its edges lie.)

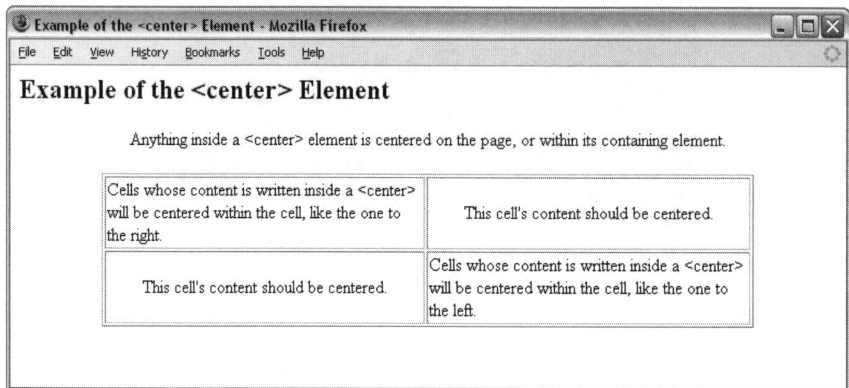

Figure I-10

The preferred method of aligning text content is to use CSS properties such as `text-align`.

The align Attribute

The `align` attribute is used with many elements to indicate positioning of an element within the browser or its containing element. It was deprecated in HTML 4.01.

The possible values for the `align` attribute are shown in the table that follows. Note that the value `justify` works with text only, and that `top`, `middle`, and `bottom` are less supported than `left`, `right`, and `center`.

Value	Purpose
`left`	Aligns element with the left side of the page or containing element
`right`	Aligns element with the right side of the page or containing element
`center`	Centers the element within the page or containing element
`justify`	Justifies words across the page or containing element so that the left and right side of the text touches the container
`top`	Aligns element with the top of the browser window or containing element
`middle`	Vertically aligns element in the middle of the browser window or containing element
`bottom`	Aligns element with the bottom of the browser window or containing element

Here are the elements that could carry the `align` attribute:

```
<caption> <applet> <iframe> <img> <input> <object> <legend> <table> <hr>
<div> <h1> <h2> <h3> <h4> <h5> <h6> <p>
```

The following code contains a few examples of how the `align` attribute can be used (`ai_eg11.html`):

```
<body>
  <h2 align="center">Example of the align Attribute</h2>

    <table width="600" align="center" border="1">
      <tr>
        <td align="left">This cell's content should be left-aligned.</td>
        <td align="right">This cell's content should be right-aligned.</td>
      </tr>
      <tr>
        <td align="center">This cell's content should be centered.</td>
        <td width="300" align="justify">This cell's content should be
        justified, but it needs to spread across more than one line to
        show it working.</td>
      </tr>
    </table>
</body>
```

You can see here that the `<h1>` and `<table>` elements are both centered, and then each cell in the table uses a different kind of alignment.

In order for text to be justified, it needs to wrap onto more than one line (which is why that `<td>` element carries a `width` attribute in this example). The last line of a justified paragraph does not have to stretch to the left and right borders of the browser or its containing element as the other lines do.

Figure I-11 shows what this page looks like.

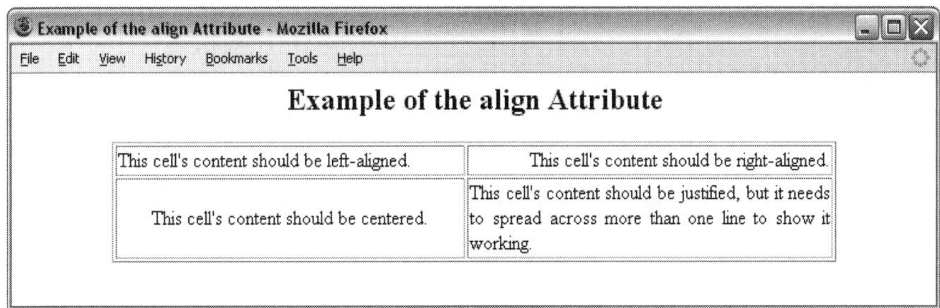

Figure I-11

The preferred method of aligning text and inline elements in CSS is to use the `text-align` and `vertical-align` properties, and for block-level elements, the `float` property.

The width Attribute

The `width` attribute sets the width of an element in pixels. While we still use this attribute on the `<img>` and `<object>` elements, it also used to be seen on many other elements, in particular on tables, and `<div>` elements.

Here you can see an example of the `width` attribute on a table and an `<hr />` element (`ai_eg12.html`):

```
<body>
  <h2>Example of the width Attribute</h2>

    <table width="600" border="1">
      <tr>
        <td width="200">This cell should be 200 pixels wide.</td>
        <td width="400">This cell should be 400 pixels wide.</td>
      </tr>
      <tr>
        <td width="200">This cell should be 200 pixels wide.</td>
        <td width="400">This cell should be 400 pixels wide.</td>
      </tr>
    </table>
   <br /><br />
  <hr width="300" />
</body>
```

Figure I-12 shows what this looks like in a browser.

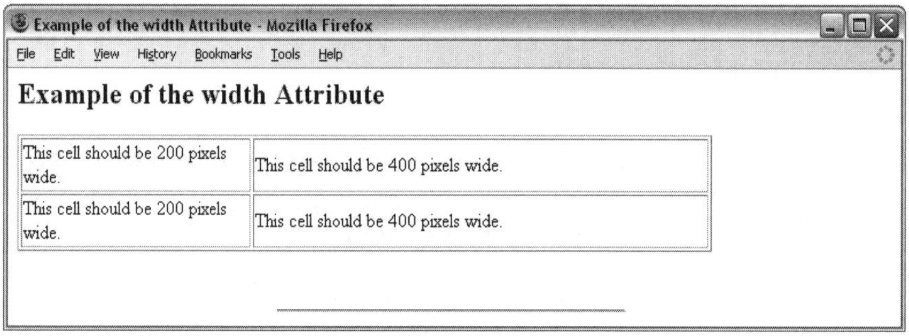

This cell should be 200 pixels wide.	This cell should be 400 pixels wide.
This cell should be 200 pixels wide.	This cell should be 400 pixels wide.

Figure I-12

The preferred method of setting the width for these elements is the `width` property in CSS.

The height Attribute

The `height` attribute sets the height of an element in pixels. While we still use this attribute on the `<img>` and `<object>` elements, it also used to be seen on many other elements, such as the `<th>`, `<td>`, and `<applet>` elements. Here you can see the `height` attribute used on the `<td>` element (`ai_eg13.html`):

```
<body>
  <h2>Example of the height Attribute</h2>

    <table width="600" border="1">
      <tr>
        <td width="300" height="300">This cell should be 300 pixels
        high.</td>
        <td width="300" height="300">This cell should be 300 pixels
        high.</td>
      </tr>
    </table>

</body>
```

As you can see from Figure I-13, these table cells are square.

The preferred method of setting the height for these elements is the `height` property in CSS.

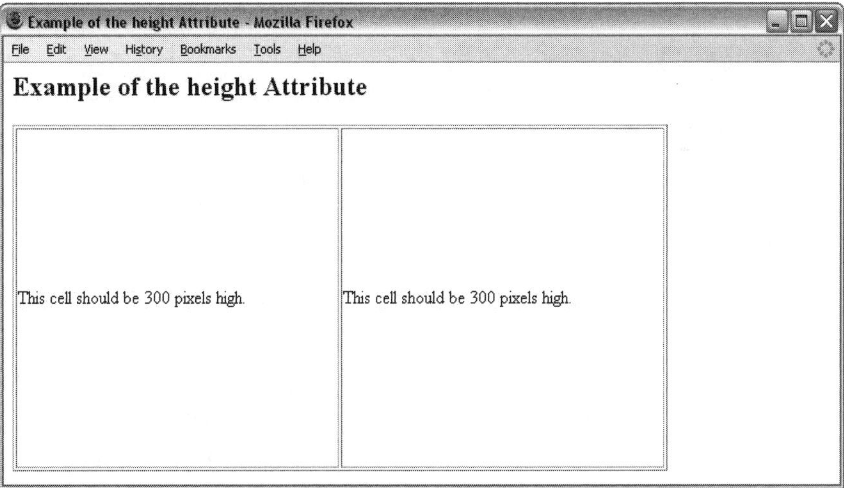

Figure I-13

The vspace Attribute

The `vspace` attribute specifies the amount of white space or padding that should appear above or below an HTML element. Its value is given in pixels.

The following example shows how the vspace attribute on the <img> element makes sure that there are 20 pixels above and beneath the image to separate it from the text (ai_eg14.html):

```
<body>
    <h2>Example of the vspace Attribute</h2>

    <p>Lorem ipsum dolor sit amet, consectetur adipisicing elit, sed
do eiusmod  tempor incididunt ut labore et dolore magna aliqua. Ut enim
ad minim veniam, quis nostrud exercitation ullamco laboris nisi ut
aliquip ex ea commodo consequat. Duis aute irure dolor in reprehenderit
in voluptate velit esse cillum dolore eu fugiat nulla pariatur. Excepteur
sint occaecat cupidatat non proident, sunt in culpa qui officia deserunt
mollit anim id est laborum.
    <img src="images/logo_small.gif" alt="wrox logo" vspace="20" border="1" />
    Lorem ipsum dolor sit amet, consectetur adipisicing elit, sed do
eiusmod tempor incididunt ut labore et dolore magna aliqua. Ut enim ad minim
veniam, quis nostrud exercitation ullamco laboris nisi ut aliquip ex ea
commodo consequat. Duis aute irure dolor in reprehenderit in voluptate velit
esse cillum dolore eu fugiat nulla pariatur. Excepteur sint occaecat
cupidatat non proident, sunt in culpa qui officia deserunt mollit anim id est
laborum.</p>

</body>
```

You can see the result in Figure I-14.

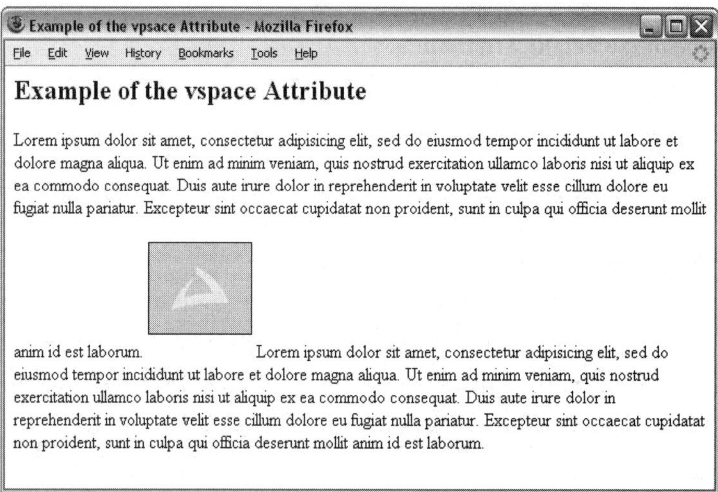

Figure I-14

This has been replaced by the padding and margin properties in the CSS box model, and could also be reproduced with the border property in CSS.

The hspace Attribute

The `hspace` attribute is the horizontal equivalent of the `vspace` attribute and ensures that there is padding or white space to the left and right of an element.

Here you can see that the `hspace` attribute is used to create 40 pixels of padding to the left and right of the image (`ai_eg15.html`):

```
<body>
  <h2>Example of the hspace Attribute</h2>

  <p><img src="images/logo_small.gif" alt="wrox logo" hspace="40" border="1" />
  There should be 40 pixels between the image and the edge of the window, and
  another 40 pixels between the edge of the image and this text.</p>

</body>
```

You can see the result in Figure I-15.

This has been replaced by the `padding` and `margin` properties in the CSS box model.

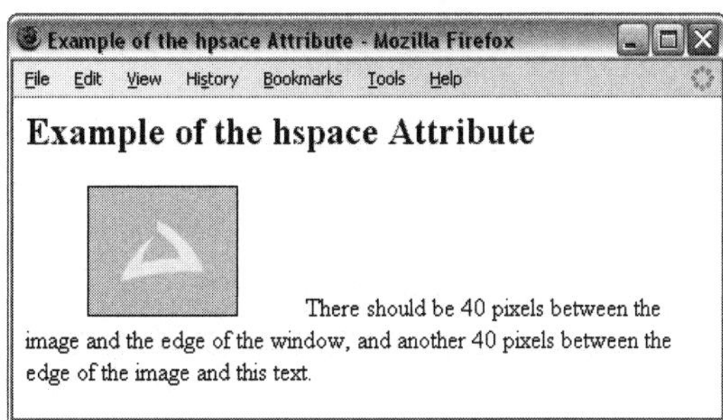

Figure I-15

The clear Attribute (on <br /> element)

The `clear` attribute used on a line break element `<br />` indicates how the browser should display the line after the `<br />` element. The `clear` attribute can take the values `left`, `right`, `all`, and `none`. Its use is best explained by way of an example (`ai_eg16.html`):

```
<body>
       <h2>Example of the clear Attribute</h2>
   <img src="images/logo_small.gif" alt="wrox logo" align="left" border="1"/>
   The text after this image will be displayed next to the image and wrap
   to the next line until you see the line break element.<br clear="left">
   Now it should be on a new line underneath (not next to) the image.
</body>
```

If the `clear` attribute is used on a `<br />` element, then the text or element that follows it will not be displayed until there is nothing next to the border indicated as a value of the `clear` attribute. In this case, because the `<br />` element has a `clear` attribute whose value is `left`, the text after the `<br />` element will not be shown until there is nothing to the left of it (within the containing element or box). In this example, the text does not continue until after the image, which was to the left of this text.

You can see the result in Figure I-16 — and note how the text continues under the image. If it were not for the `clear` attribute, this text would simply appear on the next line.

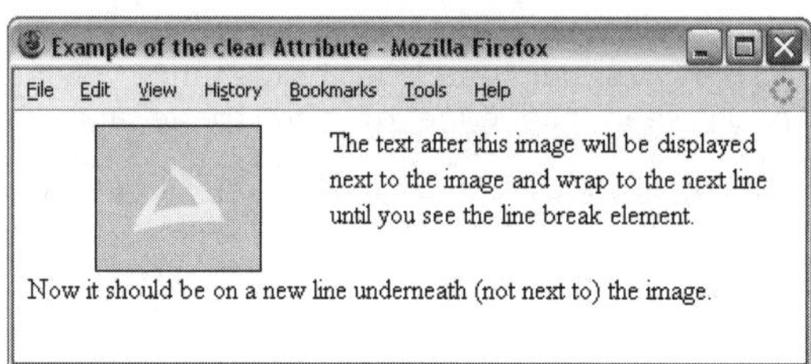

Figure I-16

If the value `all` is given, there must not be anything to the `left` or `right` of the text or element.

CSS has its own `clear` property to replace this attribute.

Links

You may have noticed on some web sites that the colors of links change when you have visited a page or when you click the link. As you can see in the table that follows, there are three attributes that allow you to change the colors of links: `alink`, `link`, and `vlink`. Each should be specified on the `<body>` element.

Attribute	Use	Values
`alink`	Specify the color of an active link or selected link.	A hex code or color name
`link`	Specify the default color of all links in the document.	A hex code or color name
`vlink`	Specify the color of visited links.	A hex code or color name

The following is an example of the how these attributes affect the colors of links (`ai_eg17.html`):

```
<body alink="333399" link="#ccffff" vlink="#669999">
    <h2>Example of the Link Attribute</h2>
    <p>This example contains some links, which you should play with to see
       how they behave:</p>
```

```
    <ul>
      <li>The <a href="http://www.wrox.com/">Wrox Web site</a> tells you
          about existing and forthcoming Wrox books.</li>
      <li>The <a href="http://www.w3.org/">W3C Web site</a> is the home of
          the XHTML and CSS recommendations.</li>
      <li>The <a href="http://www.google.com/">Google Web site</a> is a
          popular search engine.</li>
    </ul>
</body>
```

In this example, there are different shades of blue for links that have not yet been visited and those that the user has already been to. This helps users navigate a site because they can identify links they have already visited (which helps them find a page again).

Usually the colors for links that have and have not been visited are quite similar. This is the case with the links you can see in Figure I-17 (which may be hard to distinguish in the grayscale used in this book). For a better idea of how this example works, try it out for yourself (it is available for download along with the rest of the code for this appendix).

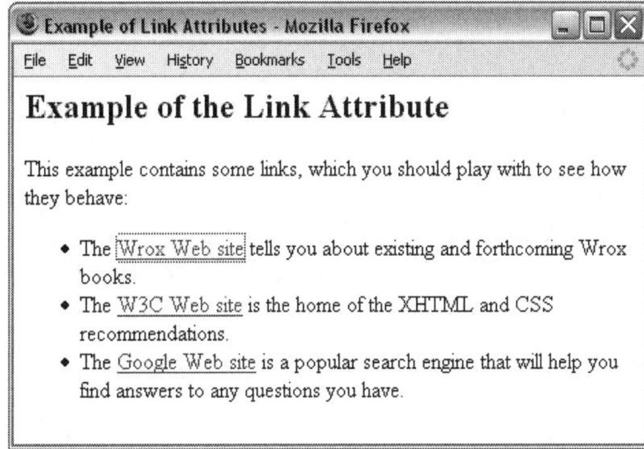

Figure I-17

Lists

Several elements and attributes relating to lists have been deprecated or are no longer permitted, from attributes that helped order and style lists to other elements that created visual effects similar to lists.

The start Attribute

The `start` attribute is used on the `<ol>` element of ordered lists to indicate at what number a browser should start numbering a list. The default is, of course, 1. The following example shows a list starting at number 4 (`ai_eg18.html`):

```
<body>
  <ol start="4">
    <li>This list should start at four</li>
    <li>Therefore this item should be five</li>
    <li>And this item should be six</li>
  </ol>
</body>
```

You can see the result of this in Figure I-18.

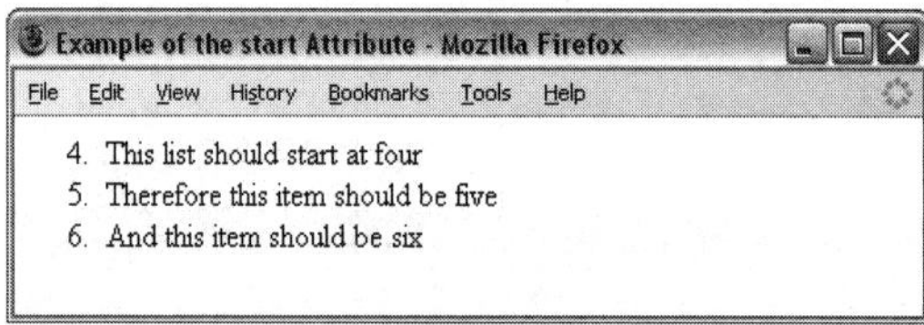

Figure I-18

This has been replaced by CSS counters and the `counter-reset` property. However, browsers were slow to support CSS counters, so you will probably have to use this attribute if you want a list to start with a number other than 1 and to work in a wide range of browsers.

The value Attribute

The `value` attribute was designed to be used on the `<li>` element to indicate what number that line item should be in numbered lists. It therefore allows you to create numbered lists that leave out numbers or are out of sequence. Here you can see an example (`ai_eg19.html`):

```
<body>
  <ol>
    <li value="3">one</li>
    <li value="7">two</li>
    <li value="1">three</li>
    <li value="9">four</li>
    <li value="4">five</li>
  </ol>
</body>
```

You can see the result and how the points are numbered out of sequence in Figure I-19.

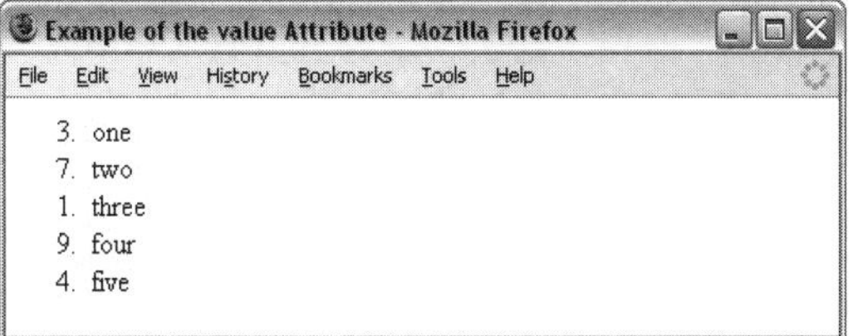

Figure I-19

The type Attribute

The `type` attribute controls the type of bullet point or numbering (also known as the *marker*) that is used on lists. This attribute can be used on the `<li>`, `<ol>`, and `<ul>` elements.

The following table shows different types of markers for bullet points and numbering systems:

Value	Description
disc	A solid circle
square	A solid square
circle	An empty circle
1	Numbers 1, 2, 3, 4
a	Lowercase letters a, b, c, d
A	Uppercase letters A, B, C, D
i	Lowercase Roman numerals i, ii, iii, iv
I	Uppercase Roman numerals I, II, III, IV

The default for unordered lists is the disc, and the default for ordered lists is 1, 2, 3, and so on. Here you can see these values for the `type` attribute in use (`ai_eg20.html`):

```
<body>
  <ul>
    <li type="disc">Disc bullet point</li>
    <li type="square">Square bullet point</li>
    <li type="circle">Circle bullet point</li>
  </ul>

  <ol>
    <li type="1">Numbers</li>
    <li type="a">Lowercase letters</li>
```

```
    <li type="A">Uppercase letters</li>
    <li type="i">Lowercase Roman numerals</li>
    <li type="I">Uppercase Roman numerals</li>
  </ol>

</body>
```

You can see each of these in Figure I-20.

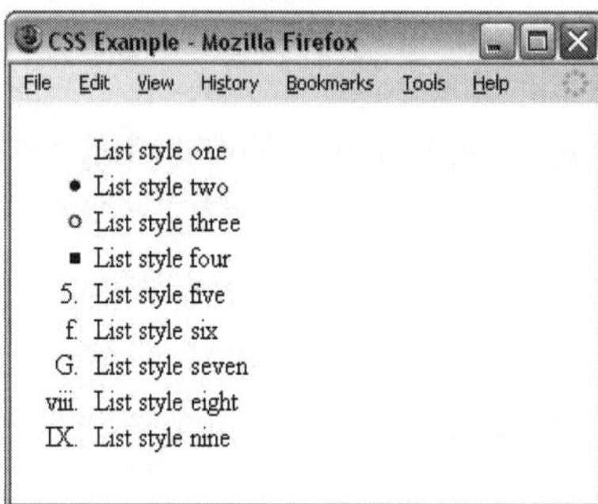

Figure I-20

The <dir> and <menu> Elements

The `<dir>` and `<menu>` elements were added in the HTML 2.0 specification, and are used to create unordered bulleted lists and nested lists. They are almost exactly the same as each other and the `<ul>` element (`ai_eg21.html`).

```
<dir>
  <li>Item 1</li>
  <li>Item 2</li>
  <li>Item 3</li>
  <li>Item 4</li>
  <dir>
    <li>Item 4.1</li>
    <li>Item 4.2</li>
    <li>Item 4.3</li>
    <li>Item 4.4</li>
  </dir>
</dir>

<menu>
  <li>Item 1</li>
  <li>Item 2</li>
```

```
    <li>Item 3</li>
    <li>Item 4</li>
    <menu>
      <li>Item 4.1</li>
      <li>Item 4.2</li>
      <li>Item 4.3</li>
      <li>Item 4.4</li>
    </menu>
  </menu>
```

You can see the result of each of these elements in Figure I-21.

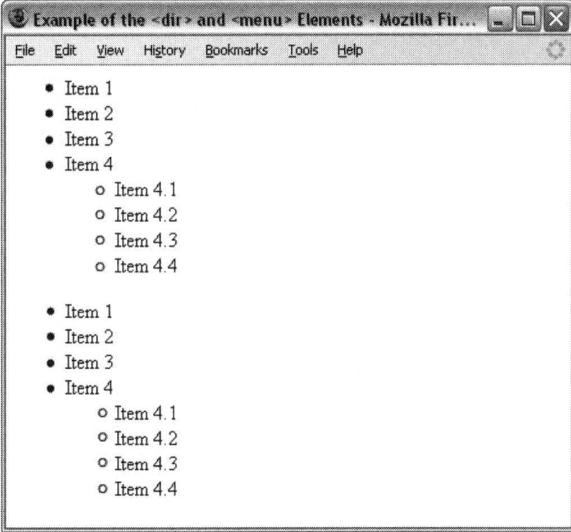

Figure I-21

The `<dir>` element was initially intended to list files in a directory, whereas the `<menu>` element was devised for a menu of links and can therefore be displayed a little bit more compactly in some browsers than the content of `<ul>` and `<dir>` elements. You should simply use the `<ul>` element instead of either of these deprecated elements.

Tables

There are a few attributes that have been deprecated that were previously allowed on the `<table>` element — notably the `align`, `bgcolor`, and `width` attributes, which you have already met, and also the `nowrap` attribute, which is covered next.

The nowrap Attribute

The `nowrap` attribute used to be available on the `<td>` and `<th>` elements, and prevented the text from wrapping within that table cell. For example (`ai_eg22.html`):

```
<table width="200">
  <tr>
    <td nowrap>This text should not wrap even though the table is only
        supposed to be 200 pixels wide.</td>
  </tr>
</table>
```

As you can see in Figure I-22, although the table is supposed to be only 200 pixels wide, it actually stretches for as long as the line — the text does not wrap.

Figure I-22

The replacement for the `nowrap` attribute is the `white-space` property in CSS with the value of `nowrap`.

Miscellaneous Attributes

This section describes a selection of other elements and attributes that have been deprecated but do not easily fit into one of the preceding sections.

The border Attribute

The `border` attribute specifies the thickness of a border around an element in pixels. For example, here is an `<img>` element with a `border` attribute (`ai_eg23.html`):

```
<body>
    <img src="images/logo_small.gif" border="4" alt="wrox logo" />
</body>
```

You can see the result in Figure I-23.

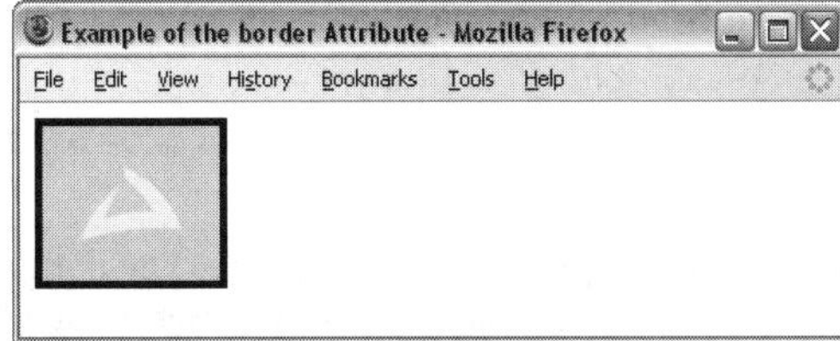

Figure I-23

This attribute has been replaced by the `border-width` property of CSS.

You are most likely to see this attribute used with a value of `0` on images that are links. This is because IE will, by default, draw a single-pixel blue border around any image that is a link. Therefore, by giving the `border` attribute a value of `0` it is possible to remove this extra line. This can also be removed using the `border` property in CSS.

The compact Attribute

The `compact` attribute tells the browser to show text with less height between lines than normal. It does not take a value (although if it were used with Transitional XHTML 1.0, it would require a value of `compact`).

The default value is `false`. This attribute has been replaced by the `line-height` property in CSS.

The language Attribute

The `language` attribute was most commonly used on the `<script>` element to indicate what scripting language is being used. For example:

```
<script language="JavaScript">
```

The `language` attribute has been replaced with the `type` attribute, whose value is a MIME type (for example `type="text/JavaScript"`).

The version Attribute

The `version` attribute specifies which version of the HTML DTD the document is written according to.

This has been dropped because it duplicates information that should be provided by the `DOCTYPE` declaration.

The <applet> Element

The `<applet>` element was used to embed Java applets into an HTML page. The element and its attributes were introduced in HTML 3.2 and have been replaced by the `<object>` element, which was discussed in Chapter 3.

The table that follows shows the attributes that <applet> can carry.

Attribute	Use
code	The filename of the Java applet's compiled code. The path to the applet file specified by the code is relative to the codebase of the applet (not a URL or absolute path).
codebase	Specifies the directory for the Java applet code. If the codebase attribute is not specified, the applet files are assumed to be in the same directory as the HTML file.
object	Specifies the filename of the Java applet's compiled code that stores a serialized representation of an applet's state. The path to the file should be relative only to the codebase of the applet (not a URL or absolute path).
name	Specifies the name of the element so that scripts can communicate with it (only deprecated for use with the <applet> element).
archive	A space-delimited set of URLs with multiple Java classes or other resources that will be loaded into the browser to improve applet performance (only deprecated for use with the <applet> element).
width	The width of the applet in pixels.
height	The height of the applet in pixels.

The <embed> Element

The <embed> element was used before the <object> element was introduced into HTML as a way of including a file that required a special plug-in application. For example, it was used to include Flash animations in pages.

Once the <object> element had been introduced into HTML it was still used as a way of ensuring that plug-ins were implemented across different browsers because the support for the <embed> element was poor in IE; you will still often see it in use today (you can refer to Chapter 3 to see examples of how the <embed> element was used inside the <object> element).

The object to be included would be identified using the src attribute — just like an image. You indicate the type of content to be included using the type attribute, whose value is a MIME type for that resource (or just leave the browser to work it out itself).

The attributes that the <embed> element can take are listed in the table that follows:

Attribute	Use
align	Specifies the alignment of the object within the page or its containing element.
border	Specifies the width of the border for the object (in pixels).
height	Specifies the height of the object (in pixels).

Attribute	Use
hidden	Hides the object from the user (making it 0 pixels wide and 0 pixels high). This is sometimes used for audio.
hspace	Specifies the horizontal space that should be left to the left and right of the object (in pixels).
name	As with the name attribute on other elements, this is used to identify that element.
palette	In IE, the value is a pair of hexadecimal color values separated by a vertical bar. The first is the foreground color and the second is the background color. In Netscape, the palette attribute is either foreground *or* background, indicating which palette of window system colors the plug-in should use.
pluginspage	Specifies the URL of a Web page from which you can download the plug-in required to use the file (Netscape only).
src	The URL of the object you want to embed.
type	Indicates the MIME type of the object to be included in the page (which determines the plug-in used to view the object).
units	Allows you to change the units of measurement that indicate the height and width of the embedded object from the default of pixels to the relative en unit (half of the width of the text's point size).
vspace	Specifies the amount of vertical space that should be left to the top and bottom of the object (in pixels).
width	Specifies the width of the object (in pixels).

The <embed> element can also carry attributes that are specific to the plug-in required to view them. You should refer to the documentation for the particular plug-in you need to use for documentation on these attributes, as there are too many to list here.

If you are using Flash to include graphics in your pages, you will find that some versions of the publishing tool give you the HTML code to include Flash animations in your pages, which not only uses the <object> *element to include the animation in the page, but also provides the* <embed> *element for any browser that is older and does not understand the* <object> *element.*

The <isindex> Element

The <isindex> element was introduced in HTML 2.0 to create a single-line text field without the need for a <form> element (the user's entry would be sent using the HTTP get method back to the same page that contains the <isindex> element). When the user presses the Enter (or Return) key, the form is submitted and spaces are replaced with a + character. (A program or page on the server would then have to respond to, or act upon, the data sent.)

When it is displayed, the textbox will have a horizontal rule above and beneath it.

While you can use several <isindex> tags, only the last one with content will be sent to the server. It can also carry the prompt attribute, which allows you to provide a hint to users as to what they should be entering into the box. For example, here is an <isindex> element used to create a search box (ai_eg24.html):

```
<body>
    <isindex prompt="search">
</body>
```

You can see the result of this with its horizontal lines in Figure I-24, although you could not use it with an HTML page because HTML has no way to process the value the user entered (it would need to go to a page that contained a server-side script or program to interpret the content).

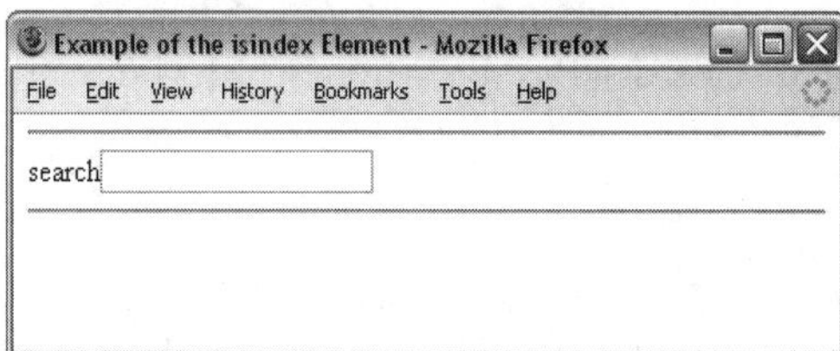

Figure I-24

The <nobr> Element

Firefox, Netscape, and IE all support an extension to the XHTML recommendation that prevents line breaks: the <nobr> element. (This retains the normal style of its containing element and does not result in the text being displayed in a monospaced font like the <pre> element does.) If you choose to use the <nobr> element, it can contain another child element called <wbr> to indicate where a break can occur within a <nobr> element, although this is an extension as well.

IE-Specific Elements

The table that follows lists five elements that IE supports that are not part of the HTML recommendations, but which you might still come across. You should generally avoid these elements unless you are providing different pages for different browsers or you know all your visitors will be using IE.

Element	IE	Purpose
<bgsound>	2	Plays a sound file in the background (replaced by the <object> element)
<marquee>	2	Renders text in a scrolling fashion
<ruby>	5	Provides pronunciation support
<rt>	5	Provides pronunciation support
<xml>	5	Creates an XML data island, embedding an XML recordset into the page

IE-Specific Attributes

The following table lists IE-specific attributes:

Attribute	Purpose
atomicselection	Specifies whether the grouping element (such as <div> and <span>) and its content must be selected as a whole.
balance	The balance of audio between the left and right speakers (used with <bgsound>).
behavior	Specifies how content of a <marquee> element scrolls.
bgproperties	Sets a fixed background image for a page; also known as a watermark.
bordercolordark	When cells in a table are rendered with 3D borders, this attribute specifies the darker of the colors used. Used on the <table> element.
bordercolorlight	When cells in a table are rendered with 3D borders, this attribute specifies the lighter of the colors used. Used on the <table> element.
bottommargin	Specifies the bottom margin for the page in pixels. Used on the <body> element.
contenteditable	Determines whether the content of a grouping element can be edited by a user.
dataformatas	Sets or retrieves whether data contained by the grouping element should be displayed as text or HTML.
datafld	Used in databinding when the browser is connected to a server-side database (see a reference on ASP/ASP.NET for more information).
datasrc	Used in databinding when the browser is connected to a server-side database (see a reference on ASP/ASP.NET for more information).
datapagesize	Used in databinding when the browser is connected to a server-side database (see a reference on ASP/ASP.NET for more information).
direction	Indicates the direction of scrolling text within a <marquee> element.
dynsrc	Used for embedding movies into client-side caches.
framespacing	Specifies the amount of space between frames in a frameset in pixels.
hidefocus	Used to prevent a visible line showing around an element when it is in focus.
leftmargin	Specifies the left margin for the page in pixels. Used on the <body> element.

(continued)

Attribute	Purpose
rightmargin	Specifies the right margin for the page in pixels. Used on the <body> element.
loop	Specifies the number of times the content of a <marquee> element should scroll.
lowsrc	Allows you to specify a low-resolution version of an image on an <img> element that should be loaded first.
scrolldelay	Specifies the time delay in milliseconds between each drawing of the <marquee> element. (The default is that it is redrawn every 60 milliseconds.)
topmargin	Specifies the top margin for the page in pixels. Used on the <body> element.
truespeed	A Boolean attribute indicating whether the scrolldelay value should be used. Default is false; if true, the <marquee> element will use the values that are indicated in the scrollamount and scrolldelay attributes. (Any value under 60 milliseconds is ignored.)
unselectable	Indicates an element cannot be selected.
volume	Indicates the volume at which the content of a <bgsound> element should be played, with values from –10000 to 0 (default is 0, which is full volume).

Of particular note from this table are the topmargin and leftmargin attributes, which you might see used on the <body> element of some pages; this prevents IE from adding a gap between the edge of the browser window and the content.

```
<body topmargin="0" leftmargin="0" border="0">
```

You can safely use the topmargin and leftmargin attributes in Transitional XHTML, as Netscape and other browsers should simply ignore the attributes they do not understand, although they would not be valid as they are not part of the markup. (Validation is discussed in Chapter 13.) It would be preferable to use the margin property in CSS instead of these attributes.

IE-Specific CSS Styles

The table that follows lists some CSS styles that are supported only by IE (and the version they were introduced with). The layout-grid properties are used with Asian languages that often employ page layout for characters in order to format text using a one- or two-dimensional grid.

Property	IE	Purpose
behavior	5	Was used to specify the URL of a behavior file, for a short lived technology called DHTML behaviors.
ime-mode	5	Allows input of Chinese, Japanese, and Korean characters when used with an input method indicator.
layout-grid	5	Shorthand for other layout-grid properties.
layout-grid-char	5	Specifies the size of the character grid for rendering text (similar to `line-height` property).
layout-grid-charspacing	5	Specifies spacing between characters (similar effect to `line-height`).
layout-grid-line	5	Specifies grid line value used to render text (similar to `line-height`).
layout-grid-mode	5	Specifies whether the grid uses one or two dimensions.
layout-grid-type	5	Specifies the type (if any) of page layout grid to be used when rendering an element's content.
line-break	5	Specifies rules for when a line should break in Japanese.
text-autospace	5	Controls the autospacing and narrow space width adjustment behavior of text; of particular use with ideographs used in Asian languages.
text-justify	5	Justifies text in an element.
text-kashida-space	5.5	Controls the ratio of kashida expansion to white-space expansion when justifying text in an element. A kashida is a typographic effect that justifies lines of text by elongating certain characters in specific points; often used in Arabic.
text-underline-position	5.5	Specifies how far an underline should appear beneath the text when the `text-decoration` property is used.
word-break	5	Controls line breaking within words; of particular use with documents containing multiple languages.
word-wrap	5.5	Controls where a long word should break if it is too large for its containing element.
writing-mode	5.5	Controls horizontal and vertical direction of flow of content in object.
zoom	5.5	Specifies magnification scale of an object.

There are also several CSS styles that are particular to the presentation of a scrollbar. It does not hurt to add these properties to any CSS style sheet, as browsers that do not understand these properties will just ignore them. All colors can be specified as a color name, hex code, or RGB value (as with all colors in CSS).

Property	IE	Purpose
`scrollbar-3dlight-color`	5.5	Color of top and left edges of scroll box and scroll arrows on the scrollbar
`scrollbar-arrow-color`	5.5	Color of the arrows on a scroll arrow
`scrollbar-base-color`	5.5	Color of main elements of a scrollbar, which includes the scroll box, track, and scroll arrows
`scrollbar-darkshadow-color`	5.5	Color of the gutter of a scrollbar
`scrollbar-face-color`	5.5	Color of the scroll box and scroll arrows of a scrollbar
`scrollbar-highlight-color`	5.5	Color of the top and left edges of the scroll box and scroll arrows of a scrollbar
`scrollbar-shadow-color`	5.5	Color of the bottom and right edges of the scroll box and scroll arrows of a scrollbar

Index

C

E

M

N

O

P

U

X

Y

Z